501 MOVIE DIRECTORS

VIRTUTIS GLORIA MERCES

REID

EX-LIBRIS

D1439600

CASSELL
ILLUSTRATED

A Quint**essence** Book

First published in Great Britain in 2007 by Cassell Illustrated
a division of Octopus Publishing Group Limited
2–4 Heron Quays, London E14 4JP
An Hachette Livre UK company

A CIP catalogue record for this book is available from the British Library.

ISBN-13: 978-1-84403-573-1
QSS.FAZ

This book was designed and produced by
Quint**essence**
226 City Road
London EC1V 2TT

Project Editor	Victoria Wiggins
Editors	Rebecca Gee, Lucinda Hawksley,
	Carol King, Irene Lyford, Fiona Plowman
Editorial Assistant	Jenny Evans
Designer	Rod Teasdale
Editorial Director	Jane Laing
Publisher	Tristan de Lancey

Manufactured in Singapore by Pica Digital Pte Ltd.
Printed in China by SNP Leefung Printers Ltd.

CONTENTS

CONTENTS

CONTENTS

PREFACE

By Aubrey Day, Editor-in-Chief, *Total Film* and *Sky Movies*

"But, of course, what I really want to do is *direct* . . . ." It's the timeless declaration of actors, writers, producers, and sundry other players from Hollywood and beyond. And why not? There are surely few more thrilling (or glamorous-sounding) vocations than being a movie director. Being the boss, in effect, of a crew of A-list heroes, stunning heroines, world-class cinematographers, cameramen, carpenters, caterers, etc., etc. (or, in the case of *Blair Witch*, half a dozen mates and a sandwich maker . . .).

As Quentin Tarantino once put it: "I get to live the life of an artist, and in the most expensive art form in the world."

Like films themselves, film directors come in all shapes and sizes. Portly and pervy and disinclined to put a foot on set, having done all the thinking in pre-production (step forward, Alfred Hitchcock) to kinetic, chattering, totally "hands-on" auteurs who dabble in everything from the script to the soundtrack (enter jack-of-all-trades, Robert Rodriguez). But, be it dyed-in-the-wool studio men like John Ford or rule rewriters like John Cassavetes, you'll find every type of helmer over the following pages, alongside details of their bodies of work and insights into the themes and issues that color their creations.

Working on film magazines, my colleagues and I sometimes get to see today's crop of moviemakers first-hand and, while budgets have rocketed, expectations increased, and risk-taking perhaps diminished, some things never seem to change. Everyone still yells "action" to kick-start proceedings (well, apart from Clint Eastwood, who tends to mumble "okay" to get the ball rolling). Most still want "just one more take" to be on the safe side (apart from David Fincher, whose "last take" tends to be followed by several dozen more). And, should you find yourself in a dingy bar at the end of a day's shoot with the prettiest girl you've ever seen, sadly, telling her "I'm a film journalist" *still* won't persuade her to give you the time of day.

Tell her you're a film director, however, and it's a whole different ball game . . . .

Aubrey

London, England
April 2007

INTRODUCTION

By Steven Jay Schneider, General Editor

It is hard to imagine an art form more collaborative by its very nature than filmmaking. There may well be movies conceived, developed, financed, produced, written, directed, shot, edited, mixed, lit, and acted in by just one person—home movies aside—but even the idea of such a solipsistic pursuit seems diametrically opposed to the cinematic spirit, according to which a group of individuals with skills in highly specific areas (by no means limited to those listed above) are brought together—often kicking and screaming—in an effort at achieving onscreen a united creative and/or commercial vision. No small feat!

Nevertheless, and even acknowledging the death of auteur theory in contemporary film studies, we can say with confidence that movies do indeed have authors—and that there is no better candidate for the title of author of any particular cinematic text than its director. This is certainly the case if only in the weak sense that audiences find it helpful and comforting, perhaps essential, to impose a signature on what they see. And it is arguably the case in the stronger sense that, despite input and constraints coming literally from all sides, it is the director who is usually responsible for making more of the decisions—and the more important decisions—over the course of any specific production.

With this in mind, the book you are now holding celebrates 501 of the most dynamic, original, influential, and gifted directors in history, across the entire cinematic terrain: geographic, stylistic, cultural, popular, artistic, and so on. Whether those filmmakers included herein have made many movies, some movies, or only a few, what they all share is a commitment to craft, a distinctive vision that manifests across both undeniable masterpieces and ostensible "failures," and an uncanny ability—sometimes and in some ways a curse—to reveal aspects of themselves through(out) their work.

It is hard to understate, and almost impossible to underestimate, the importance of movies in the modern world. This book is a love letter to those men and women who have changed our lives as a result of their celluloid dreams.

Steven J. Schneider

Los Angeles, U.S.
April 2007

GEORGES MÉLIÈS

Born: Marie-Georges-Jean Méliès, December 8, 1861 (Paris, France); died 1938 (Paris, France).

Directing style: Innovator of special effects; discoverer of the stop trick; used multiple exposures, time-lapse photography, dissolves, hand-painted color.

Top Takes...

Cabby's Nightmare 1914

Cendrillon ou La pantoufle mystérieuse 1912
  (*Cinderella or The Glass Slipper*)

Les aventures de baron de Munchhausen 1911
  (*Baron Munchausen's Dream*)

Hydrothérapie fantastique 1910
  (*The Doctor's Secret*)

Fortune Favors the Brave 1909

Le fakir de Singapoure 1908
  (*The Indian Sorcerer*)

20,000 lieues sous les mers 1907
  (*20,000 Leagues Under the Sea*)

Le voyage à travers l'impossible 1904
  (*The Impossible Voyage*)

Le voyage dans la lune 1902
  (*Voyage to the Moon*)

Le manoir du diable 1896 (*Manor of the Devil*)

"We sat with our mouths open, without speaking, filled with amazement."

Marie-Georges-Jean Méliès invented movies.

What about Thomas Edison, the Lumière brothers? The cinema pioneered by those guys was a technological curio with a short shelf life. Georges Méliès hijacked the train and sent it toward what we know today as the movies—fiction films as spectacle and entertainment.

In 1896, the Lumières invited Méliès to the unveiling of their invention. He was one of the small audience of thirty-three that first went to the movies. What he saw entranced him—Méliès was a commercial magician whose theater depended on magic lantern shows. But the Lumières wouldn't sell him their contraption—so he made his own.

Méliès's films were not records of prosaic, real events, but told of events that never happened, from a world that cannot exist. The camera had scarcely been invented and here was a man who realized not only that the camera can lie, but that at the heart of film technology was a magic trick. It took a magician to understand that movies are, by definition, magic.

The legend goes that one day, while filming traffic, the celluloid jammed in the camera. Minutes were wasted jostling the box and, when it started again, the traffic had moved on. When the film was projected later, a hearse was seen crossing the screen . . . suddenly transposing into a bus. Méliès created special effects on screen he could never accomplish live on stage. As time went on, the grandeur of Méliès's effects ballooned. His most famous work was *Le voyage dans la lune* (1902) (*Voyage to the Moon*). His increasingly ambitious creations spiraled his company into bankruptcy, however. By 1914 it had come to an end and Méliès had sunk into ruin and obscurity. **DK**

AUGUST BLOM

Born: August Blom, December 26, 1869 (Copenhagen, Denmark); died 1947 (Copenhagen, Denmark).

Directing style: Maker of melodramas of the silent era; innovative use of low-key lighting; emphasis on realism; large productions of literary adaptations.

August Blom's influence on silent film was not limited to his native Denmark: his esteem rose when he became the artistic director for the Nordisk Films Company, at that time the leading European production company. Blom entered the industry as an actor in the mystery genre projects that Nordisk produced, but took a turn behind the camera, most notably with *Den Skæbnesvangre Opfindelse* (1910) (*Dr. Jekyll and Mr. Hyde*). He also made *Hamlet* (1910), a short based on the Shakespeare play. Shot at Kronborg Castle, near Elsinore, the film is regarded as an early example of cinéma vérité.

Blom continued to find success with other black and white silent films such as *For Åbent Tæppe* (1912) (*Desdemona*), based on William Shakespeare's *Othello*. The relationship between Shakespeare's title character and Desdemona parallels that of a couple in Blom's film. *Guvernørens Datter* (1912) brought success in the form of a melodramatic love triangle of an arranged marriage. His most notable film, *Atlantis* (1913), brought prestige and recognition to Nordisk and is considered a crowning achievement of silent cinema for its sophistication and naturalistic acting. The movie was criticized for its subject matter, however, despite the fact that it was not based on the 1912 *Titanic* tragedy. To the surprise of many, the inspiration for *Atlantis* was a voyage to the United States by the German novelist Gerhart Hauptmann. The film also saw Blom mentoring future Hollywood director Michael Curtiz, who worked as his assistant on the movie. Other notable movies directed by August Blom include *Verdens Undergang* (1916) (*The End of the World*). After retiring from directing in 1924, Blom ran a movie theater in Copenhagen until his death in 1947. **ES**

Top Takes...

Det store hjerte 1925
Præsten i Vejlby 1920 (*The Vicar of Vejlby*)
Grevindens ære 1919 (*The Countess' Honour*)
Den mystiske selskabsdame 1917
   (*The Mysterious Lady*)
Verdens Undergang 1916
   (*The End of the World*)
Af elskovs naade 1914
Atlantis 1913
Historien om en moder 1912
   (*The Story of a Mother*)
For Åbent Tæppe 1912 (*Desdemona*)
Guvernørens Datter 1912
Ved Fængslets Port 1911
Hamlet 1910
Den Skæbnesvangre Opfindelse 1910
   (*Dr. Jekyll and Mr. Hyde*)

"... he proved that he was the best and most tasteful director of his time."—Harald Engberg

EDWIN S. PORTER

Born: Edwin Stratton Porter, April 21, 1870 (Connellsville, Pennsylvania, U.S.); died 1941 (New York City, New York, U.S.).

Directing style: The father of movie editing, who used continuity shots to build the narrative and made innovative use of multiple viewpoints to suggest action.

Top Takes...

"Jump-cuts or cross-cuts were a new, sophisticated editing technique . . . ."—Tim Dirks

RIGHT: Porter films *A Country Girl's Seminary Life and Experiences*, at Edison Studio.

The directorial career of Edwin S. Porter, one of the earliest movie moguls, spanned only a few years, with films no longer than ten minutes; yet the man was a true filmmaking pioneer.

This was the very dawn of movies, when technique was primitive: see Porter's uninspired staging of *Uncle Tom's Cabin* (1903), as an example of the camera being used simply as a spectator at a play. Eventually, movies really did move, with action shattered into fragments, individual shots, and moments collaged together into a cinematic whole.

The fiery climax of Porter's action thriller *Life of an American Fireman* (1903) seemed to employ the earliest known example of crosscutting, shuffling together two differing viewpoints. Film historians fell over themselves to anoint Porter the father of movie editing—until an unaltered original print of *Life of an American Fireman* turned up and revealed that Porter had subsequently re-edited the film to prove he had been first. Ironically, Porter didn't need tampered evidence to stake his claim: in early landmarks such as *The Great Train Robbery* (1903), the first screen Western and the earliest primitive movie to have any genuine suspense, he had already shown a precocious understanding of screen space. Starting as a lowly projectionist at Thomas Edison's film production company, The Edison Manufacturing Company, Porter was promoted quickly to cameraman, director, and eventually head of all production. Thanks to this success, he launched his own production company in 1909, but sold it a few years later to become an even bigger mogul, joining Adolph Zukor as one of the backers of the new Famous Players studio. Porter eventually left the movie business and returned to his engineering roots, founding the Precision Motor Company. **DK**

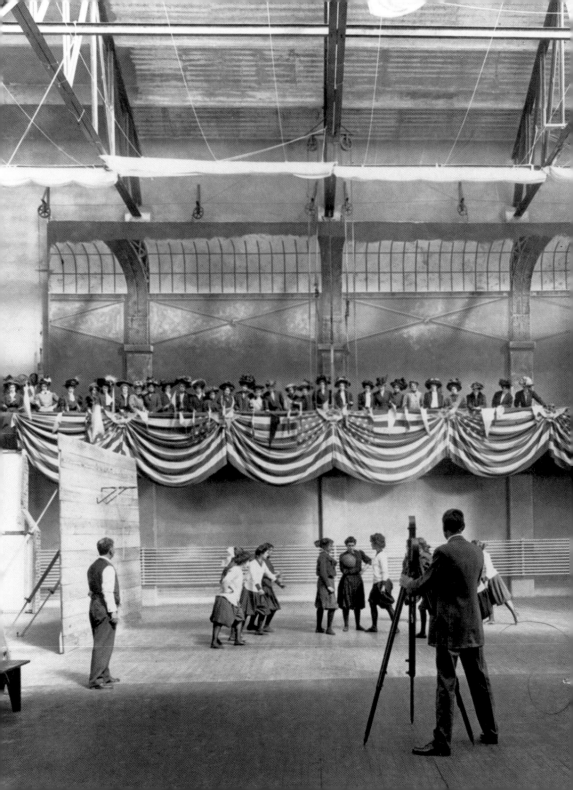

LOUIS FEUILLADE

Born: Louis Jean Feuillade, February 19, 1873 (Lunel, Hérault, Languedoc-Roussillon, France); died 1925 (Nice, Alpes-Maritimes, Provence-Alpes-Côte d'Azur, France).

Directing style: Inventor of comic-book suspense thriller; simple camerawork; photographic naturalism; innovative use of location and the cinematic frame.

Top Takes…

Pierrot, Pierrete 1924
L'Orphelin de Paris 1924
La Fille bien gardée 1924
Le Stigmate 1924
Le Gamin de Paris 1923 (Paris Urchin)
La Gosseline 1923
Vindicta 1923
Le Fils du flibustier 1922
Parisette 1921
Judex 1916
Les vampires 1915 (The Vampires)
Le mort qui tue 1913
   (The Dead Man Who Killed)
Fantômas—À L'ombre de la guillotine 1913
Judith et Holopherne 1909
   (Judith and Holofernes)

During his brief but prolific career, Louis Feuillade generated more than 700 motion pictures for France's Gaumont Studios, helping to establish Gaumont as one of the country's leading studios. His *métier* was cliff-hanger serials: *Fantômas—À L'ombre de la guillotine* (1913), *Les vampires* (1915) (*The Vampires*), and *Judex* (1916) chief among them. He was the inventor of the comic-book suspense thriller. Any self-respecting movie buff needs to know and venerate Feuillade's name, for he is the Big Bang that set into orbit Fritz Lang, Alfred Hitchcock, and almost everyone else of consequence.

Objectively speaking, Feuillade's technique is literally primitive. The D. W. Griffiths and Thomas Inces, the Fritz Langs and F. W. Murnaus, the Sergei Eisensteins and Lev Kuleshovs had yet to develop the cinematic language known today. That Feuillade's films—manufactured at the very dawn of the medium—enthrall and enrapture modern audiences speaks of something else in their construction. Feuillade's simple, unadorned camerawork and blandly realistic production design give way to dreamscapes, irrationality, and illogicality that intrude casually into the frame. The world is not as it seems—horror can break through the surface of reality without notice. The movies were postmodern masterpieces. Feuillade understood the inherent menace of new technology, the pervasiveness of evil, and the untrustworthiness of appearances. But it is the not the case that his films were ahead of their time: watching many films of that era gives the impression of looking through a window into the past, a vision of a simpler and more innocent age. Feuillade's movies offer a window into an alternate dreamlike dimension, to a time and place that never existed. **DK**

> "Give up your search, otherwise bad luck awaits you!"
>
> —The Vampires, *The Vampires*

ROBERT WIENE

Born: Robert Wiene, April 24, 1873 (Breslau, Silesia, Germany); died 1938 (Paris, France).

Directing style: Leading figure of German Expressionist film movement; used surreal settings and distorted angles to represent the psyche in early horror movies.

Robert Wiene was a versatile German writer and director, best known for his influential German Expressionist horror classic *Das Cabinet des Dr. Caligari* (1920) (*The Cabinet of Dr. Caligari*).

The son of Carl Wiene, a noted stage actor, Wiene grew up surrounded by the theater. After studying law at the University of Vienna, where he enrolled in 1895, he practiced law in Weimar and worked in various administrative positions in the theater before entering the film industry. He made his screenwriting and directing debut with *Die Waffen der Jugend* (1913); then, over the next seven years, made another 16 films, codirecting some with his actor brother, Conrad Wiene.

In September 1919, Wiene began filming the low-budget *The Cabinet of Dr. Caligari*, working with designers to utilize the Expressionist style, a turn of the century artistic movement seen in German painting, literature, and theater. Featuring surreal landscapes with distorted angles to convey the fractured psyche of the film's protagonist, the film was an international success, and is considered one of the leading examples of the German Expressionist period of 1919 to 1926.

Wiene went on to work as a director in various genres for studios in Berlin and Vienna. He also remained highly prolific with his production companies, Lionardo Film and Camera Film Productions. He teamed up once more with Conradt Veidt—*The Cabinet of Dr. Caligari* lead—for another influential horror film, *Orlacs Hände* (1924) (*The Hands of Orlac*). In the 1930s, Wiene easily made the transition to sound films. Understanding the importance of this new medium, he tried, unsuccessfully, to find funding for a sound remake of *The Cabinet of Dr. Caligari*. Exiled from Germany under Nazi rule, Robert Wiene died in Paris in 1938. **WW**

Top Takes...

Ultimatum 1938
Eine Nacht in Venedig 1934 (*A Night in Venice*)
Polizeiakte 909 1933
Panik in Chicago 1931 (*Panic in Chicago*)
Der liebesexpress 1931
   (*Eight Days of Happiness*)
Der Andere 1930 (*The Other*)
Le Procureur Hallers 1930 (*L'Autre*)
Die Frau auf der Folter 1928 (*Scandal in Paris*)
Orlacs Hände 1924 (*The Hands of Orlac*)
Raskolnikow 1923 (*Crime and Punishment*)
Das Cabinet des Dr. Caligari 1920
   (*The Cabinet of Dr. Caligari*)
Arme Eva 1914 (*Dear Eva*)
Die Waffen der Jugend 1913

"I must penetrate the heart of his secret! I must become Caligari!"—Dr. Caligari

ALICE GUY

Born: Alice Guy, July 1, 1873 (Paris, France); died 1968 (Mahwah, New Jersey, U.S.).

Directing style: First female director; pioneer of narrative filmmaking and use of color; swift and prolific output; innovator of special effects such as double-exposure masking techniques.

Top Takes...

Vampire 1920
The Great Adventure 1918
House of Cards 1917
My Madonna 1915
Shadows of the Moulin Rouge 1913
A House Divided 1913
The Pit and the Pendulum 1913
A Fool and His Money 1912
Phantom Paradise 1912
Fanfan la Tulipe 1907
La fée Printemps 1906 *(The Spring Fairy)*
La vie du Christ 1906
   (The Birth, the Life and the Death of Christ)
Esmeralda 1905
Danse fleur de lotus 1897
La fée aux choux 1896

Alice Guy was born in Paris and spent her childhood in France, Switzerland, and Chile. In 1894 she began work as secretary to Léon Gaumont, later of the Gaumont Studios, and from 1896 to 1906 directed dozens of shorts for the studio, including one of the earliest fiction movies, *La fée aux choux* (1896). With her speedy output and commercial viability, she rose to become supervisor to Gaumont's other directors and head of production, before directing *La vie du Christ* (1906) (*The Birth, the Life and the Death of Christ*), one of the earliest full-length films helmed by a woman, which even uses some color.

After marrying Herbert Blaché, an Englishman who ran the company's British and German offices, in 1907, the newlyweds moved to the United States where they administered offices for Gaumont before forming their own New Jersey-based studio, The Solax Company, in 1910. Early successes such as *Shadows of the Moulin Rouge* (1913) and *Vampire* (1920) made Solax profitable. With the film industry's move to California, however, and divorced from Blaché in 1922, Guy lacked support to continue making films. She returned to France and sank into obscurity for decades before returning to the United States in 1964, where she remained until her death. In recent years, Guy's reputation has grown, especially in feminist circles where her status as a cinema pioneer has been championed, and particularly because her career marks the turn from Continental European to U.S. movie dominance. Aside from her remarkable filmography, comprising hundreds of titles, Guy was also known for having an experimental style and for being technically innovative, which no doubt made her popular but ultimately out of step with the male-dominated industry she left in midlife. **GCQ**

> "My youth, my lack of experience, my sex all conspired against me."

FRED NIBLO

Born: Frederick Liedtke, January 6, 1874 (York, Nebraska, U.S.); died 1948 (New Orleans, Louisiana, U.S.).

Directing style: Founding father of the Academy of Motion Picture Arts and Sciences; director of silent-era action movies and Hollywood blockbusters.

Fred Niblo was born in Nebraska in 1874 to a U.S. Civil War veteran. Using the stage name Niblo, he traveled the world for many years as a successful performer on the vaudeville and dramatic stage. In Australia he wrote, directed, and starred in his debut movie *Get-Rich-Quick Wallingford* (1916).

Eventually, Niblo moved to Hollywood and was established as a director with such titles as *Sex* (1920), and the Douglas Fairbanks vehicle *The Mark of Zorro* (1920). He directed Fairbanks again in *The Three Musketeers* (1921), and then capitalized on Rudolph Valentino in *Blood and Sand* (1922). His career hit its capstone with *Ben-Hur: A Tale of the Christ* (1925), one of the most commercially successful silent films in history.

Niblo retired in 1933, but leading up to this final curtain were gems such as *The Temptress* (1926) and *The Mysterious Lady* (1928) with Greta Garbo, and his first talking picture, *Redemption* (1930) with John Gilbert and Renée Adorée. His final years were filled with programmatic movies such as *Way Out West* (1930) and *Diamond Cut Diamond* (1932).

But perhaps Niblo's greatest achievement was being one of the founders of the Academy of Motion Picture Arts and Sciences. The seeds were sown during a dinner in 1927 at the home of MGM studio head Louis B. Mayer, attended by Niblo and producer Fred Beetson. They agreed that there should be an organized group to benefit the entire industry, help solve technological problems, aid in arbitrating labor disputes, and assist in policing screen content. They arranged another dinner for the following week, inviting representatives from all the creative branches of the motion-picture industry whom they hoped would support such an organization. They did, and the Oscars were born. **GCQ**

Top Takes...

Diamond Cut Diamond 1932
Two White Arms 1932
Way Out West 1930
Redemption 1930
The Mysterious Lady 1928
Camille 1926
The Temptress 1926
Ben-Hur: A Tale of the Christ 1925
The Red Lily 1924
Blood and Sand 1922
The Woman He Married 1922
The Three Musketeers 1921
The Mark of Zorro 1920
The Woman in the Suitcase 1920
Get-Rich-Quick Wallingford 1916

"[Ben Hur] is an excellent piece of camera work . . . ."
—New York Times

D. W. GRIFFITH

Born: David Llewellyn Wark Griffith, January 22, 1875 (La Grange, Kentucky, U.S.); died 1948 (Hollywood, California, U.S.).

Directing style: The father of film technique; innovative narrative filmmaking; maker of epics that sometimes contained racist content; pioneer of crosscut.

Top Takes…

The Struggle 1931

Abraham Lincoln 1930

Lady of the Pavements 1929

The Battle of the Sexes 1928

The Sorrows of Satan 1926

America 1924

Orphans of the Storm 1921

Way Down East 1920

The Mother and the Law 1919

Broken Blossoms 1919

Intolerance: Love's Struggle Throughout the Ages 1916

The Birth of a Nation 1915

The Battle of the Sexes 1914

Judith of Bethulia 1914

The Perfidy of Mary 1913

The Musketeers of Pig Alley 1912

The Girl and Her Trust 1912

A Woman Scorned 1911

The Impalement 1910

In Old California 1910

A Corner in Wheat 1909

The Lonely Villa 1909

The Greaser's Gauntlet 1908

Movies began as both an artisanal tinkering into the nature of portrait art and a scientific study of motion. Neither approach suggested the story-making potential of the medium.

Yet early on, the artisans managed to harness scientific tools to better render reality, which meant there was a need to develop a cinematic language whereby individual shots might relate to one another, as well as more stylish techniques. Early filmmakers had to establish a method for telling stories, and audiences had to learn how to interpret the stories and drive the commercial engine making it all possible. The movies required a champion—and D. W. Griffith was to fulfill this role.

Griffith began life as the son of a confederate army Civil War hero, far from the U.S. cultural centers of New York and Los Angeles. He grew up in the Old South during its lengthy economic struggle to confront an urban world, helping him form a very conservative, and Christian, world view. Smitten with the actor's bug, he set out in 1897 to be a performer and writer for the stage but, having enjoyed only limited success, he began acting in motion pictures for Edwin S. Porter at the Edison Company. Not greatly enamored of the short

RIGHT: (*left to right*) **Douglas Fairbanks Sr., Mary Pickford, Charlie Chaplin, D. W. Griffith.**

performances possible in single-reel movies of the day, Griffith turned to filmmaking with American Mutoscope & Biograph Co., where he directed hundreds of shorts between 1908 and 1915. It was during this stage of extraordinary output and experimentation that Griffith began establishing a sure hand with the basic syntax of movies, enabling him to transform this screen language into a series of popular, and still surviving, short films. Three Griffith gems from this period— *The Lonely Villa* (1909), *A Corner in Wheat* (1909), and *The Musketeers of Pig Alley* (1912)—helped promote the use of flashbacks, iris shots, and crosscuts as a means of expressing simultaneous activities with clearly defined heroes and villains.

ABOVE: Henry Walthall as Colonel Ben Cameron in Griffith's *The Birth of a Nation*.

"Actors should never be important. Only directors should have power and place."

In 1910 Griffith discovered a little village in California in which to shoot many of the Biograph films, including *In Old California*

Uniting Artists

D. W. Griffith, together with Charles Chaplin, Douglas Fairbanks, and Mary Pickford, founded United Artists in 1919. The company struggled with the coming of sound and had virtually ceased to exist as a producer or distributer by the late 1940s. The latest twist in its fortunes is the 2006 acquisition of a stake in the studio by Tom Cruise and Paula Wagner.

- 1919: United Artists (U.A.) founded by Griffith, Chaplin, Fairbanks, and Pickford.
- 1924: Joseph Schenck hired as president.
- 1933: Schenck resigns; replaced by Al Lichtman, who resigns a few months later.
- 1951: U.A. taken over by Arthur Krim and Robert Benjamin.
- 1951/1952: two major hits for U.A.— *The African Queen* and *Moulin Rouge*.
- 1955: Mary Pickford leaves U.A.
- 1956: U.A. goes public.
- 1967: Control of U.A. sold to insurance giant Transamerica Corp.
- 1973: U.A. takes over the sales and distribution of MGM films.
- 1975: U.A. buys 50 percent stake in Danjaq LLC, holding company for Bond movies. U.A. remains silent partner.
- 1990: MGA/U.A. bought by promoter Giancarlo Parretti, but bank forecloses.
- 2006: Tom Cruise and Paula Wagner resurrect United Artists.

(1910). The weather was good and there was room for expansion. The village was known as Hollywood. He and the pioneers at Biograph turned Hollywood from a small farming town into the movie and entertainment capital of the world.

A dichotomous legacy

Griffith directed *The Birth of a Nation* (1915), his technically masterful Civil War and Reconstruction era epic, sketching the plight of a white Southern family as it endures the tragedy of losing a war and finding subsequent peace before re-emerging through the Ku Klux Klan. The next year saw *Intolerance: Love's Struggle Throughout the Ages* (1916), a test of both cinematic storytelling technique and audiences' ability to follow along.

Griffith's reputation often rests on these two films, but there were later works, too, including *The Mother and the Law* (1919), *Way Down East* (1920), *The Sorrows of Satan* (1926), and *Abraham Lincoln* (1930). Along the way, in 1920, he helped establish United Artists with Charles Chaplin, Douglas Fairbanks, and Mary Pickford. Although his career largely predated the modern movie machine, Griffith was awarded an honorary Academy Award in 1936, and an honorary lifetime membership in the relatively new Directors Guild of America.

Griffith died in 1948, having retired in the early 1930s. He is remembered today largely as the filmmaker of some of the earliest and, in retrospect, most racist, screen epics. **GCQ**

RIGHT: Elmer Clifton and Constance Talmadge in the historical drama *Intolerence*.

VICTOR SJÖSTRÖM

Born: Victor David Sjöström, September 20, 1879 (Silbodal, Värmlands län, Sweden); died 1960 (Stockholm, Stockholms län, Sweden).

Directing style: Pioneer of Nordic cinema; landscape used as integral part of a film's beauty and to provide dramatic context for characters' actions.

Victor Sjöström entered the Swedish film industry first as an actor and then as a director. With Mauritz Stiller, he was a crucial figure in the early creative blooming of Nordic cinema. In *Berg-Ejvind och Hans Hustru* (1918) (*You and I*), Sjöström established one of the most important features of his poetic vision, the discovery of nature: landscape was introduced not only as an integral part of the film's pictorial beauty, but to provide an illuminating dramatic context for the characters' actions. With *Klostret i Sendomir* (1920) (*Monastery of Sendomir*), Sjöström turned his attention to close space as a means of exposing Lutheran preoccupations with turmoil and suffering.

In 1924 Sjöström went to the United States and directed *He Who Gets Slapped* (1924), a brilliant combination of tenderness and cruelty, emotional sincerity, and grotesque pathos and irony in the story of a clown. Two of the most significant Sjöström films were made with Lillian Gish: *The Scarlet Letter* (1926) and *The Wind* (1928). Reducing Nathaniel Hawthorne's ethical and puritanical doubts to pure melodramatic components, Sjöström treats *The Scarlet Letter* in such a way that the narrative's strong emotional core compensates for his omission of the moral and religious insights that are of central importance in the novel. *The Wind* represents the culmination of Sjöström's melodramatic imagination: wild nature is a reflection and embodiment of the characters' inner lives. Ultimately, the power of *The Wind* lies in the director's elemental mise-en-scène. *Under the Red Robe* (1937) was Sjöström's last movie as director, but he continued with his acting career, most touchingly as an aging professor in Ingmar Bergman's *Smultronstället* (1957) (*Wild Strawberries*). **AB**

Top Takes...

Under the Red Robe 1937
Markurells i Wadköping 1931 (*Father and Son*)
Väter und Söhne 1930
The Wind 1928
The Scarlet Letter 1926
Confessions of a Queen 1925
He Who Gets Slapped 1924
Eld ombord 1923 (*Fire on Board*)
Körkarlen 1921 (*The Phantom Carriage*)
Klostret i Sedomir 1920
  (*Monastery of Sendomir*)
Berg-Ejvind och Hans Hustru 1918 (*You and I*)
Terje Vigen 1917 (*A Man There Was*)
Skomakare, bliv vid din läst 1915
  (*Stick to Your Last, Shoemaker*)
Ett Hemligt giftermål 1912 (*A Ruined Life*)

"No one would deny that *The Wind* is a work of art . . . ."

—*Guardian Unlimited*

BENJAMIN CHRISTENSEN

Born: Benjamin Christensen, September 28, 1879 (Viborg, Denmark); died 1959 (Copenhagen, Denmark).

Directing style: Danish master of early horror movies; used complex lighting set-ups with silhouettes and transitional effects to create malevolent atmosphere.

Top Takes...

Extreme stage fright kept Danish-born Benjamin Christensen from pursuing a career as an opera singer. Instead, he turned his feelings of unease and discomfort toward film. His first, *Det Hemmelighedsfulde X* (1914) (*The Mysterious X*), is an impressive melodrama, employing complex lighting set-ups and compositions to create a sustained atmosphere of desperation and foreboding. Christensen received equal acclaim with the thriller *Hævnens Nat* (1916) (*Night of Revenge*), and then disappeared from view for six years.

Christensen resurfaced with *Häxan* (1922) (*The Witches*). Part documentary about superstitious beliefs in witchcraft and its repression through the Inquisition, part fictional retelling of folktales, *The Witches* contains meticulous descriptions of torture instruments, eerie reenactings of local legends, and an orgiastic witches' Sabbath lorded over by a most wicked Satan, played by Christensen himself. Again, his use of lighting, close-ups, and superimposed images added to the atmosphere.

The Witches' controversial reputation allowed Christensen to move to Hollywood, where he made a series of highly regarded horror movies—of which only *Seven Footprints to Satan* (1929) seems to have survived—and secured his place in the pantheon of horrormeisters. After the advent of sound, Christensen returned to Denmark where he directed several remarkable films, including the sensitive *Skilsmissens Børn* (1939) (*Children of Divorce*), which Christensen insisted be screened for adults only. Such feelings confirm the unity of his oeuvre as being among the first, and most accomplished, to establish uncomfortable connections between outright depictions of malevolence and stylized suggestions that evil is just another point of view. **EM**

> "*[The Witches]* hold[s] the onlooker in a sort of medieval spell."—*New York Times*

MACK SENNETT

Born: Michael Sinnott, January 17, 1880 (Richmond, Québec, Canada); died 1960 (Los Angeles, California, U.S.).

Directing style: Introduced slapstick to U.S. audiences; anarchic plots; wild improvisations; chase scenes; knockabout characters in absurd clothing.

Mack Sennett was a poor kid whose showbiz ambitions led him to Biograph Studios where he worked with D. W. Griffith. Griffith made portentous, serious movies, and Sennett cranked out the wildest and silliest films his joke-addled imagination could fathom. Some ideas he borrowed from French comedians; mostly he invented something new, U.S. slapstick.

In 1912, Sennett launched Keystone Studios as a vehicle for movies showcasing his lover Mabel Normand. Always searching for new talent, Sennett launched the careers of Charlie Chaplin, Roscoe "Fatty" Arbuckle, Harry Langdon, and W. C. Fields, and created the Keystone Kops. Most of his comedians quit to pursue greener fields (Sennett's purse strings were notoriously tight), but he had a keen eye for talent, not to mention an innate understanding of U.S. jazz-age audiences. The formula was raw knockabout: grotesque figures in absurd clothing flinging themselves violently across the screen. Plots were rudimentary, the attitude anarchic and irreverent. Every screen comedy of the silent age either followed Sennett's pattern or self-consciously resisted it; no one could ignore him.

In 1915, Sennett joined with Griffith to found the Triangle Pictures Corporation, a super-sized studio with megalomaniacal ambitions. Triangle's attempted monopoly was undermined when Chaplin decamped. Without the superstar, Triangle lacked the power to drive its competition to ruin, and instead the studio ran aground in 1917.

Sennett survived the Triangle collapse and continued to discover legendary comedians until the advent of sound, a marvel that redirected screen comedy away from his brand of lunatic chaos. He was honored with a special Academy Award in 1937 "for his lasting contribution to the comedy technique of the screen." **DK**

Top Takes…

The Timid Young Man 1935
Hypnotized 1932
I Surrender Dear 1931
Jazz Mamas 1929
The Good-Bye Kiss 1928
Oh, Mabel Behave 1922
A Small Town Idol 1921
A Clever Dummy 1917
Safety First Ambrose 1916
The Cannon Ball 1915
Tillie's Punctured Romance 1914
Mabel's New Hero 1913
The Water Nymph 1912
A Victim of Circumstances 1911

"We have no scenario— [the] chase … is the essence of our comedy."

YAKOV PROTAZANOV

Born: Yakov Aleksandrovich Protazanov, February 4, 1881 (Moscow, Russia); died 1945 (Moscow, Russia).

Directing style: Founding father of Russian cinema; early, dark, costume melodramas; purveyor of realistic, popular entertainment; slow pace; static, long takes.

Top Takes...

Nasreddin v Bukhare 1943
  (*Adventures in Bokhara*)
Salavat Yulayev 1941 (*The Eagle of the Steppe*)
Tommi 1931 (*Tommy*)
Yego prizyv 1925 (*His Call*)
Zakroyshchik iz Torzhka 1925
  (*The Tailor from Torzhok*)
Aelita 1924 (*Aelita: Queen of Mars*)
Otets Sergei 1917 (*Father Sergius*)
Pikovaya dama 1916 (*The Queen of Spades*)
Klyuch schastiya 1913 (*The Keys to Happiness*)
Ukhod velikovo startza 1912
  (*Departure of a Grand Old Man*)

One of the outstanding figures at the dawn of Russian cinema, the prolific Yakov Protazanov was the first to develop an original voice, and the only major director to return from exile after the 1917 February Revolution.

Early notoriety came with *Ukhod velikovo startza* (1912) (*Departure of a Grand Old Man*), a controversial dramatization of the last days of Leo Tolstoy that outraged the great novelist's widow, and was banned in Russia. Undaunted, Protazanov went on to direct dozens of short films, most of which are now lost, and quickly established himself as a name director specializing in dark, costume melodramas. *Klyuch schastiya* (1913) (*The Keys to Happiness*) was the most successful Russian film of the Tsarist era, and his adaptations of Alexander Pushkin's *Pikovaya dama* (1916) (*The Queen of Spades*) and Tolstoy's *Otets Sergei* (1917) (*Father Sergius*), starring the great screen idol Ivan Mozzhukhin, are regarded as his finest work.

After October 1917, Protazanov, along with most of the Russian film industry, fled nationalization and civil war. Continuing to direct in Paris and Berlin, in 1923, as a consequence of Vladimir Lenin's New Economic Policy, he was invited back to join the new Mezhrabpom-Russ studio in Moscow. His first Soviet production, *Aelita* (1924) (*Aelita: Queen of Mars*) is the film for which he is best known today. A big-budget, feature-length drama designed to show that Soviet cinema could compete with the best of Western output, it had a plot and striking science-fiction sequences (with Constructivist costumes and set designs) that influenced Fritz Lang's *Metropolis* (1927). Despite subsequent criticism, Protazanov proved to be far more than just a journeyman director. Today his legacy is ripe for re-evaluation. **RB**

"[Protazanov] was always ... striving for something new and more interesting."—Aleksei Fajko

CECIL B. DeMILLE

Born: Cecil Blount DeMille, August 12, 1881 (Ashfield, Massachusetts, U.S.); died 1959 (Hollywood, California, U.S.).

Directing style: Made Hollywood the center of the motion-picture map; master of the majestic epic; use of multiple cameras to capture action sequences.

Much more than just the director of *Samson and Delilah* (1949) or *The Ten Commandments* (1956), Cecil B. DeMille needs rescuing from his own reputation.

Legend insists that DeMille invented Hollywood when he decided to shoot *The Squaw Man* (1914) there because it was raining at his original choice of location, Flagstaff, Arizona. Director of the first Hollywood movie; one of the few whose name alone could sell a picture; and still making award-winning box-office smashes in the 1950s: this is achievement enough. But it is a pity that his status as an impersonal assembler of epic spectacles and as the quintessential Hollywood autocrat impedes true acknowledgment of his versatility and the range of his achievements.

He was a pioneer of Westerns; he made a star of Gloria Swanson in silent examinations of Art Deco sexual mores; and he was a master of pre-Code society dramas—those brittle, surprisingly erotic chamber pieces that were so characteristic of the early sound era. *Dynamite* (1929) and *Madam Satan* (1930) are true lost masterpieces of the form, as are the politically charged *This Day and Age* (1933) and *Four Frightened People* (1934), a sexual satire with Claudette Colbert, on how the smart set conduct themselves in the wilderness.

And yes, there are those epics. But they, too, reflect their times, from the silent *The Ten Commandments* (1923), set partially in the 1920s, through Claudette Colbert's jazz-baby *Cleopatra* (1934), up to and concluding with the *Ten Commandments* remake in 1956 that vindicated Cinemascope, the last technical innovation DeMille lived long enough to make his own. These majestic films are no longer respected, but future students will surely wonder why. **MC**

Top Takes...

The Ten Commandments 1956
***The Greatest Show on Earth* 1952** ☆
Samson and Delilah 1949
Reap the Wild Wind 1942
North West Mounted Police 1940
Union Pacific 1939
Cleopatra 1934
Four Frightened People 1934
This Day and Age 1933
The Sign of the Cross 1932
Madam Satan 1930
Dynamite 1929
The King of Kings 1927
The Volga Boatman 1926
The Ten Commandments 1923
The Squaw Man 1914

"Give me any two pages of the Bible and I'll give you a picture."

TOD BROWNING

Born: Charles Albert Browning, July 12, 1882 (Louisville, Kentucky, U.S.); died 1962 (Hollywood, California, U.S.).

Directing style: Daring maker of melodramas and classic horror movies; meticulous set design; macabre fantastical atmospheres.

At age sixteen, Tod Browning fell in love with the circus and ran away from his middle-class family to work as a clown in circuses, carnivals, and sideshows. This fascination with the fantastical would later influence his directorial style in the horror movies he created. He then found work as director of a variety theater, where he met D. W. Griffith, and began working as an actor in silent films. From 1913 to 1919, he acted in more than 50 films, and made his directorial debut with *By the Sun's Rays* (1914).

Although often dismissed today, Tod Browning is the indisputable architect of the modern horror film. His version of *Dracula* (1931) with Béla Lugosi became the template for nearly all subsequent horror filmmaking. Although the film has some dull patches and structural problems, such as the abrupt ending that seems to occur to satisfy time constraints, it is the granddaddy of the genre—the first horror film with all the trappings. And it is still a singularly weird movie, with a nightmarish, otherworldly feel, thanks to Lugosi's stylized performance and Browning's atmosphere-driven direction. Much of the groundwork for the film lay in the macabre silent melodramas Browning had previously crafted. Few of these

Top Takes...

The Devil-Doll 1936
Mark of the Vampire 1935
Fast Workers 1933
Freaks 1932
Iron Man 1931
Dracula 1931
Outside the Law 1930
The Thirteenth Chair 1929
West of Zanzibar 1928
London After Midnight 1927
The Unknown 1927
The Show 1927
The Road to Mandalay 1926
The Blackbird 1926
The Unholy Three 1925
Silk Stocking Sal 1924
The Day of Faith 1923
The Wicked Darling 1919
Revenge 1918
The Eyes of Mystery 1918
The Jury of Fate 1917
Jim Bludso 1917
Everybody's Doing It 1916
The Spell of the Poppy 1915
By the Sun's Rays 1914

RIGHT: A scene from *Freaks*, Tod Browning's 1932 masterpiece, which is set in a circus.

ABOVE: Browning's take on *Dracula* set new standards of horror filmmaking.

films can be called horror pictures, although many contain elements of the genre, such as the pet gorilla in *The Unholy Three* (1925) and the poisonous iguana in *The Show* (1927). Similarly, there's a tendency to play up physical deformities and an almost sadistic fascination with pain.

But above all, there is Browning's ability to create an almost tangibly unwholesome atmosphere. It is this amazing talent that imbues *Dracula* with greatness. Individually, Browning's touches such as scuttling bugs, inexplicable mists, and extended silences seem almost silly. Taken as a whole, however, they are unsettling in a way that is still unique today.

A similar feel pervades *Freaks* (1932), the film often cited as Browning's masterpiece, and his unfairly dismissed remake of his lost silent, *London After Midnight*—retitled *Mark of the Vampire* (1935). Browning may be more style than substance, but it is a style that still fascinates and disturbs. **KH**

Classic Collaborations

Many of Tod Browning's movies starred Lon Chaney, who went on to become one of cinema's great character actors, known as "The Man of a Thousand Faces." Their classic collaborations include *The Unholy Three* (1925), *The Unknown* (1927), *London After Midnight* (1927), and *West of Zanzibar* (1928). Chaney, the son of deaf-mute parents, learned as a child to rely on nonverbal communication skills. This, coupled with his expertise in applying elaborate stage makeup, helped propel him to stardom. He is remembered particularly for his part as Quasimodo in *The Hunchback of Notre Dame* (1923).

THOMAS H. INCE

Born: Thomas Harper Ince, November 6, 1882 (Newport, Rhode Island, U.S.); died 1924 (Los Angeles, California, U.S.).

Directing style: Innovator of movie-production process and Hollywood studio system; maker of Westerns and U.S. Civil War action movies; no-frills narratives.

Top Takes...

Anna Christie 1923
The Dividend 1916
Civilization 1916
The Stepping Stone 1916
The Alien 1915
The Devil 1915
The Power of the Angelus 1914
A Relic of Old Japan 1914
Star of the North 1914
In Love and War 1913
The Battle of Gettysburg 1913
The Civilian 1912
The Indian Massacre 1912
Sweet Memories 1911
Little Nell's Tobacco 1910

Born into a family of actors, Ince began working for Biograph Studios and the Independent Motion Pictures Company in 1910. A year later he joined the New York Motion Picture Company (NYMP), where he made his debut with *Little Nell's Tobacco* (1910), starring Mary Pickford. Ince set up shop in the Santa Ynez Canyon in California, and by 1913 had made "Inceville" a thriving studio.

After he made *The Battle of Gettysburg* (1913), Ince started moving away from directing pictures to refining their overall production, and he is perhaps best remembered for bringing industrialization to the nascent movie industry, including the use of a shooting script, the application of a rational budgeting system, the specialization of crew positions, especially among writers, directors, and editors, and systemized attention to the assembly line of production.

In 1915, Ince partnered with D. W. Griffith and Mack Sennett to create the Triangle Film Corporation, only to sell out in 1918 to build Culver City Studios, later the home of MGM. In this venue Ince produced the comedy *23½ Hours' Leave* (1919), but marketplace exigencies were restrictive, and only the adaptation of a Eugene O'Neill play, *Anna Christie* (1923), was notable. Ince died in 1924 under famously suspicious circumstances—possibly shot, possibly having heart failure, or possibly having acute indigestion—while a guest aboard newspaper magnate William Randolph Hearst's yacht. The cause of his death is still unclear, and has led to speculation that Ince took a shot intended for Charlie Chaplin, whom Hearst suspected was dallying with his mistress, the actress Marion Davies. His passing has become a cautionary tale about crossing paths with the powerful. **GCQ**

"The man who virtually invented the Hollywood studio system . . . ."—New York Times

GERMAINE DULAC

Born: Charlotte Elisabeth Germaine Saisset-Schneider, November 17, 1882 (Amiens, France); died 1942 (Paris, France).

Directing style: Leading figure of the Impressionist movement in French films; constructed films on the principles of musical phrasing, lyrical evocation of mood.

One of France's first female directors, Germaine Dulac began her career as a journalist, becoming the editor of the feminist journal *La Française*, and an important figure in the women's suffrage movement. She became increasingly focused on cinema and, in the early 1920s, established herself as a director with features such as *La Fête Espagnole* (1920) (*Spanish Fiesta*).

Dulac was a key personality in what came to be known as the "second avant-garde" or "Impressionist" school of filmmaking, which included such theorists and directors as Jean Epstein and Abel Gance. With theoretical roots in nineteenth-century Symbolism, the Impressionists sought a pure cinema, untainted by other media such as theater or the novel, and based more on the principles of musical phrasing or construction, as is evident in the title of Dulac's film, *Thèmes et variations* (1928) (*Themes and Variations*).

In contrast to the aggressive dissociation of the Surrealists, Dulac and her fellow Impressionists strove for an emotional cinema of suggestiveness, evocation, and association. Dulac's *L'Invitation au voyage* (1927) (*Invitation to a Journey*) is a lyrical evocation that uses associative images of clouds, sails, and waves as subjective representations of feelings or moods. Despite their obvious antipathies, Dulac collaborated with notorious Surrealist Antonin Artaud on what many consider to be one of the first Surrealist movies, the experimental *La coquille et le clergyman* (1928) (*The Seashell and the Clergyman*).

Dulac's cinematic experiments came to an end with the advent of sound, which proved largely unsuitable for the visual musicality of her imagery. However, she continued working in film as head of newsreel production at both Pathé and Gaumont studios until her retirement. **GC**

Top Takes...

Je n'ai plus rien 1934

Étude cinégraphique sur une arabesque 1929

La coquille et le clergyman 1928
  (*The Seashell and the Clergyman*)

Thèmes et variations 1928
  (*Themes and Variations*)

Princesse Mandane 1928 (*L'Oublié*)

L'invitation au voyage 1927
  (*Invitation to a Journey*)

Antoinette Sabrier 1927

La folie des vaillants 1926
  (*The Madness of the Valiants*)

Ame d'artiste 1924

La souriante Madame Beudet 1922
  (*The Smiling Madame Beudet*)

La Belle dame sans merci 1920

La Fête espagnole 1920 (*Spanish Fiesta*)

"I believe that cinematographic work must come out of a shock of sensibility . . . ."—*Mon Ciné*

SAM WOOD

Born: Samuel Grosvenor Wood, July 10, 1883 (Philadelphia, Pennsylvania, U.S.); died 1949 (Hollywood, California, U.S.).

Directing style: Master of a range of genres, from comedies to dramas; no-nonsense approach produced Oscar-winning performances from a string of actors.

Top Takes...

Command Decision 1948

Ivy 1947

Guest Wife 1945

Casanova Brown 1944

For Whom the Bell Tolls 1943

The Pride of the Yankees 1942

Kings Row 1942 ☆

The Devil and Miss Jones 1941

**Kitty Foyle: The Natural History
   of a Woman 1940** ☆

Our Town 1940

Goodbye, Mr. Chips 1939 ☆

A Day at the Races 1937

A Night at the Opera 1935

Hold Your Man 1933

Paid 1930

By all accounts Sam Wood, who directed *A Night at the Opera* (1935) and *A Day at the Races* (1937), did not hit it off with the Marx Brothers. He found them undignified, while the Brothers resented Wood's humorlessness and penchant for retakes. The story goes that after several takes of a scene in *A Day at the Races*, Wood said dismissively of Groucho, "You can't make an actor out of clay;" whereupon Groucho rapidly fired back, "Nor a director out of Wood."

History has, for the most part, sided with Groucho, concluding that Wood's many fondly remembered hit films, such as *Goodbye, Mr. Chips* (1939), *Our Town*, (1940), and *For Whom the Bell Tolls* (1943), were foolproof commercial movies that several of his contemporaries could have brought in equally well, and almost certainly with more personality. But good professional craftsmanship is hardly undeserving of praise, and—not to mention the fact that he directed 11 actors in Oscar-nominated performances—there are a number of neglected gems in Wood's filmography. *Paid* (1930) and *Hold Your Man* (1933) are sleazy delights from MGM's pre-Code days, with Joan Crawford running her customary emotional gamut in the former, and Clark Gable and Jean Harlow sparking nicely in the latter. Jean Arthur was never better than in *The Devil and Miss Jones* (1941); the same can be said of Joan Fontaine in *Ivy* (1947), a fine slab of barnstorming melodrama; ditto Don Ameche in *Guest Wife* (1945), a screwball comedy with Claudette Colbert giving the kind of relaxed, funny performance she usually reserved for Frank Capra or Preston Sturges. Nothing reveals an unsuitable director as cruelly as farce, and, loath as one is to argue with Groucho Marx, Wood did fine here. **MC**

> "Either he's dead or my watch has stopped . . . ."
>
> —Dr. Hackenbush, *A Day at the Races*

MAURITZ STILLER

Born: Moshe Stiller, July 17, 1883 (Helsinki, Finland); died 1928 (Stockholm, Stockholms län, Sweden).

Directing style: "The founding father of Swedish cinema"; director of silent films across a range of genres; themes on the outsider in society.

The brief life of silent-era director Mauritz Stiller is marked by a series of unfortunate events, beginning perhaps with the suicide of his mother in 1887, and culminating in the assigning of his star on the Hollywood Walk of Fame to "Maurice Diller," an egregious error that was left uncorrected for almost 50 years. Born to Russian-Jewish parents in 1883, Stiller was raised by family friends in Finland, and later fled to Sweden rather than fight in the Russian army of Czar Nicholas II. It was there that he made his first forays into film, and by 1912 he was scriptwriting and acting in short productions. However, it was not until 1918 that Stiller made his feature-length directorial debut, *Thomas Graals bästa barn* (1918) (*Thomas Graal's First Child*), a movie that won him critical acclaim.

By 1920, Stiller had risen to the forefront of Swedish cinema with more than 30 films under his belt. But it was not until he discovered a certain Greta Gustafsson—the young actress who would later become screen siren Greta Garbo—that overseas critics took note of his talent. Following Garbo's startling performance in *Gösta Berlings saga* (1924), MGM boss Louis B. Mayer invited the director to work for him in Hollywood. However, the strictures of the studio system rapidly proved too rigid for Stiller, and he became embroiled in frequent arguments with colleagues, resulting in his replacement on the set of *The Temptress* (1926) by U.S. director Fred Niblo. Thankfully, Famous Players-Lasky quickly enlisted Stiller's directorial expertise for a series of World War I dramas, including *Hotel Imperial* (1927). Unfortunately, the quarrels continued and Stiller finally returned to Sweden, where he died of pleurisy a year later, aged only forty-five. Garbo is said to have been devastated. **LC**

Top Takes...

Hotel Imperial 1927
The Temptress 1926
Gösta Berlings saga 1924
Gunnar Hedes saga 1923 (*The Blizzard*)
Erotikon 1920 (*Bonds That Chafe*)
Herr Arnes pengar 1919 (*Sir Arne's Treasure*)
Thomas Graals bästa barn 1918
  (*Thomas Graal's First Child*)
Thomas Graals bästa film 1917
  (*Thomas Graal's Best Film*)
Vingarne 1916 (*The Wings*)

"I have all my life wondered where I belong . . . ."
—On his frustration with Hollywood

OSCAR MICHEAUX

Born: Oscar Micheaux, January 2, 1884 (Metropolis, Illinois. U.S.); died 1951 (Charlotte, North Carolina, U.S.).

Directing style: Daring African-American pioneer of independent filmmaking; used film to educate audiences about contemporary racial issues.

Top Takes...

The Betrayal 1948
Birthright 1939
Lying Lips 1939
Swing! 1938
Temptation 1935
Black Magic 1932
The Exile 1931
Darktown Revue 1931
Easy Street 1930
Wages of Sin 1929
Millionaire 1927
Body and Soul 1925
A Son of Satan 1924
Deceit 1923
The Symbol of the Unconquered 1920
Within Our Gates 1920

"...the most famous producer of race films."
—*Who's Who in Colored America*

As one of U.S. cinema's first African-American directors, Oscar Micheaux occupies an important place in film history, but his career has only recently begun to receive the attention it deserves. Close inspection of his oeuvre reveals a dedicated artist willing to engage in controversial themes.

The son of former slaves, Micheaux penned seven novels. The first of these, *The Conquest: The Story of a Negro Pioneer* (1913) anticipates a recurring theme in his films—the struggle against prejudices from both within and outside of the African-American community. But it was cinema as an art form and as a medium for educating people that most interested him.

As an independent filmmaker, Micheaux struggled to obtain financial backing for his productions. His actors frequently improvised their scenes while he filmed them in single takes; he often had to distribute his movies without the support of an established company; and, at times, he traveled across the United States with a projector, screening his features whenever and wherever possible.

Micheaux rarely missed the opportunity to imbue conventional forms and familiar genres with provocative themes, such as the personal and cultural ramifications of miscegenation and the activities of hate groups such as the Ku Klux Klan. Several of his films, for instance *Body and Soul* (1925), stand out as among the most important "race films" of the early silent and sound years. But it is *Within Our Gates* (1920) for which he is best remembered. Crafted as a response to D. W. Griffith's *The Birth of a Nation* (1915), it is a powder keg of incendiary motifs, from depictions of overt and institutional racism to graphic scenes of rape, lynching, and immolation. **JM**

ROBERT FLAHERTY

Born: Robert Joseph Flaherty, February 16, 1884 (Iron Mountain, Michigan, U.S.); died 1951 (Brattleboro, Vermont, U.S.).

Directing style: One of the founding fathers of documentary filmmaking; made films in collaboration with the local communities; pioneer of cinéma vérité.

A pioneer of film documentary in the 1920s, Robert Flaherty set out to document and depict the lives of the people participating in his filmmaking projects. His most famous film, *Nanook of the North* (1922), concerns itself with the lives of an Eskimo, or Inuit, family. Flaherty aimed for a cinéma vérité style and approach, and established himself through his early film work as a major presence and force behind this burgeoning genre. His films are sometimes described as "ethnographic" (from *ethnos* meaning "people" and *graphein* meaning "writing") and they work just as this label suggests, representing the people on whom they are focused.

However, Flaherty's claims to be merely documenting Inuit life in the early twentieth century were later challenged, and it was suggested that he had set up certain sequences in his 1922 film. Regardless of this controversy and of the creative hand that Flaherty may have had in his documentary making, *Nanook of the North* remains a cinematic masterpiece, as much for its intent and purpose as for its realization.

Flaherty brought his ethnographic research to bear on a range of other subjects, including working with F. W. Murnau on the tale of Polynesian life depicted in *Tabu: A Story of the South Seas* (1931). He turned his camera on U.S. life in a number of productions, among them *The Land* (1942), telling of U.S. agriculture and cotton production. Once again, Flaherty showed the struggle of communities, this time in facing the advances of modernity rather than fighting nature's elements. Without Flaherty's daring and his commitment to capturing societies, realities, and ordinary lives on film, the history of cinema—and the history of documentary filmmaking specifically—would be much the poorer. **MH**

Top Takes...

The Titan: Story of Michelangelo 1950
Louisiana Story 1948
The Land 1942
Elephant Boy 1937
Man of Aran 1934
Art of the English Craftsman 1933
The English Potter 1933
Industrial Britain 1933
White Shadows in the South Seas 1928
The Twenty-Four Dollar Island 1927
Moana 1926
The Potterymaker 1925
Nanook of the North 1922

"... *The Land* divines its own raison d'être from the material it has to organize."—Deane Williams

SACHA GUITRY

Born: Alexandre Georges-Pierre Guitry, February 21, 1885 (St. Petersburg, Russia); died 1957 (Paris, France).

Directing style: Innovative French director of romantic comedies and historical extravaganzas; precursor to the French New Wave; cameo roles in his films; witty.

Top Takes…

Napoléon 1955

Si Versailles m'était conté 1954
  (*Royal Affairs in Versailles*)

Le Comédien 1948 (*The Private Life of an Actor*)

Ils étaient neuf célibataires 1939
  (*Nine Bachelors*)

Quadrille 1938

Les perles de la couronne 1937
  (*Pearls of the Crown*)

Le Roman d'un tricheur 1936
  (*The Story of a Cheat*)

Mon père avait raison 1936

Bonne chance! 1935 (*Good Luck*)

Ceux de chez nous 1915 (*Those of Our Land*)

"Sacha" was the nickname of Alexandre Georges-Pierre Guitry, the son of a Parisian stage actor who was himself a much loved polymath of stage and screen. Prodigiously gifted, Guitry wrote his first play at seventeen and made his first short film at thirty. Finding that silent film little suited his gift for witty dialogue and word play, he waited until the talkies were firmly established before making *Bonne chance!* (1935) (*Good Luck*), a romantic comedy costarring his third wife, Jacqueline Delubac.

It was the start of an incredibly fertile period and from 1936 to 1937 he released seven films, among them two of his best: *Le Roman d'un tricheur* (1936) (*The Story of a Cheat*) and *Les perles de la couronne* (1937) (*Pearls of the Crown*). The former, framed as the memoirs of a charming scoundrel, was a direct influence on the Ealing classic *Kind Hearts and Coronets* (1949); the latter employed an audacious trilingual narration to recount a series of colorful historical vignettes.

Essentially a stage performer and raconteur, Guitry playfully acknowledges in his films the artificiality of the medium. For this reason, despite being considered an anachronism by the *Cahiers du cinéma* group, his innovations have since been recognized as anticipating those of the New Wave. After the liberation of Paris from the Nazi occupation, Guitry was wrongfully imprisoned for collaboration, and later exonerated. After marrying his fifth and final wife, Lana Marconi, Guitry's last decade produced comic historical extravaganzas that lacked the sprightliness of his prewar films but demonstrated that his wit remained sharp. Of these, *Si Versailles m'était conté* (1954) (*Royal Affairs in Versailles*) and *Napoléon* (1955) are the best known, both featuring cameos by Orson Welles, to whom Guitry is often compared. **RB**

> "You can pretend to be serious; you can't pretend to be witty."

PAUL LENI

Born: Paul Josef Levi, July 8, 1885 (Stuttgart, Baden-Württemberg, Germany); died 1929 (Los Angeles, California, U.S.).

Directing style: German Expressionist and virtuoso of silent horror genre; spooky set designs; manic camera movements; stylish use of close-ups; overlapping images.

Of all the German Expressionist filmmakers imported to Hollywood, Paul Leni made the most successful transition. A stylist with an interest in experiment, and a populist whose films appealed to wide audiences, Leni worked as a production designer, and even a costume designer, in his native Germany.

He first directed on *Das Tagebuch des Dr. Hart* (1916) then progressed to *Prima Vera* (1917) (*Camille*), an adaptation of the well-known story *La Dame aux Camélias*, and the Conrad Veidt vehicles *Das Rätsel von Bangalor* (1918) and *Prinz Kuckuck—Die Höllenfahrt eines Wollüstlings* (1919). Leni's most important German films are *Hintertreppe* (1921) (*Backstairs*), a sentimental slum drama, and *Das Wachsfigurenkabinett* (1924) (*The Three Wax Works*), a slightly camp Gothic horror movie with stories spun off from the wax figures of three villains, Haroun al Raschid, Ivan the Terrible, and Jack the Ripper.

Universal Studios imported Leni for *The Cat and the Canary* (1927), a comedy horror that established many of the conventions James Whale would revive for his talkie Gothics. Leni made two more mystery thrillers, *The Chinese Parrot* (1927), an early outing for Charlie Chan, and the haunted theater drama *The Last Warning* (1929). But his most elaborate U.S. movie was *The Man Who Laughs* (1928), based on the Victor Hugo novel, with Conrad Veidt offering Lon Chaney serious competition as an eternally grinning avenger in a rich period setting.

Leni died prematurely before he could make a full talkie, though *The Last Warning* has some sound sequences. There is little doubt that, had he lived, he would have been on the short list to direct *Dracula* (1931) and/or *Frankenstein* (1931), films that owe a great deal to his silent work at Universal Studios. **KN**

Top Takes...

The Last Warning 1929
The Man Who Laughs 1928
The Chinese Parrot 1927
The Cat and the Canary 1927
Das Wachsfigurenkabinett 1924
  (*The Three Wax Works*)
Hintertreppe 1921 (*Backstairs*)
Die Verschwörung zu Genua 1982
Patience 1920 (*Die Karten des Todes*)
Prinz Kuckuck—Die Höllenfahrt eines
  Wollüstlings 1919
Die Platonische Ehe 1919
Das Rätsel von Bangalor 1918
Dornröschen 1917
Prima Vera 1917 (*Camille*)
Das Tagebuch des Dr. Hart 1916

" . . . a master at creating nightmarish suspense . . . ."
——*New York Times*

GEORG WILHELM PABST

Born: Georg Wilhelm Pabst, August 25, 1885 (Raudnitz, Bohemia, Austria-Hungary); died 1967 (Vienna, Austria).

Directing style: Austrian director of silent era; rapport with actresses; themes covering role of women in society; fluid mastery of narrative style.

Top Takes…

Der Letzte Akt 1955 (*Hitler: The Last Ten Days*)
Westfront 1918 1930 (*Comrades of 1918*)
Kameradschaft 1931 (*Comradeship*)
Die 3groschenoper 1931
  (*The Threepenny Opera*)
Tagebuch einer Verlorenen 1929
  (*Diary of a Lost Girl*)
Die Büchse der Pandora 1929 (*Pandora's Box*)
Die Liebe der Jeanne Ney 1927
  (*The Love of Jeanne Ney*)
Geheimnisse einer Seele 1926 (*Secrets of a Soul*)
Die Freudlose Gasse 1925 (*The Joyless Street*)

During the 1920s, the heyday of German silent cinema, Georg Wilhelm Pabst was considered one of its foremost directors, ranked alongside Fritz Lang and F. W. Murnau. His reputation suffered in the 1930s, when he turned out a series of indifferent films, and was destroyed during the war when, for reasons that still remain unclear, he made films for the Third Reich.

Pabst first came to international attention with the socialrealist *Die Freudlose Gasse* (1925) (*The Joyless Street*), which teamed Asta Nielsen and the young Greta Garbo; and *Geheimnisse einer Seele* (1926) (*Secrets of a Soul*), one of the earliest cinematic explorations of Freudian ideas. In *Die Liebe der Jeanne Ney* (1927) (*The Love of Jeanne Ney*), Pabst, always a fine director of actresses, drew a subtle performance from Édith Jéhanne in the title role. His best work, however, was the two films he made with Louise Brooks, *Die Büchse der Pandora* (1929) (*Pandora's Box*) and *Tagebuch einer Verlorenen* (1929) (*Diary of a Lost Girl*). Perceiving in Brooks an unabashed, oddly innocent sensuality that no other director had yet brought out, and lavishing on her all his fluid mastery of narrative style, he turned her into one of cinema's great icons. Moving into the 1930s, *Die 3groschenoper* (1931) (*The Threepenny Opera*) was a decent realization of Bertolt Brecht and Kurt Weill's scathing music satire, although Brecht loathed it. *Kameradschaft* (1931) (*Comradeship*), a leftish plea for universal brotherhood much praised at the time, now looks simplistic and naive, as does *Westfront 1918* (1930) (*Comrades of 1918*), the German counterpart to *All Quiet on the Western Front* (1930). From here on, it was a steady, sad decline to his wartime disgrace. Rehabilitated after the war, Pabst continued making films until 1956, but few of them attracted much notice. **PK**

> "Pabst arranges real-life material with veracity as his sole object."—Siegfried Kracauer

ERICH VON STROHEIM

Born: Erich Oswald Stroheim, September 22, 1885 (Vienna, Austria); died 1957 (Yvelines, Île-de-France, France).

Directing style: Obsessive attention to detail; opulent set design; themes of sexual corruption and spoilt innocence; well-drawn characters created by subtle touches.

Perhaps Erich von Stroheim's greatest creation was himself. He was born into a middle-class Viennese Jewish family and deserted from the Austrian army after only a few weeks' undistinguished service, but by the time he hit Hollywood he had acquired the aristocratic "von," and become "the son of a German baroness and an Austrian count" and a decorated war veteran. From then on, the stiff Prussian bearing, the monocle, and the autocratic temperament conspired to bolster von Stroheim's image, and ruin his directorial career.

Von Stroheim acted in several films, cultivating the persona of "The Man You Love To Hate" by playing the European seducer bent on subverting the morals of an innocent all-American girl. This was the plot of his debut feature, *Blind Husbands* (1919).

Yet he was already acquiring the reputation of a perfectionist with a disregard for schedules and budgets. Irving Thalberg, studio boss at Universal Studios, took *Foolish Wives* (1922) away from the director, recut it from 30 reels down to ten, and ordered him off his next movie, *Merry-Go-Round* (1923). Despite these clashes, von Stroheim was unmistakably one of the finest directors of the silent period, with an eye for composition, décor, and lighting and a sharp sense of psychological subtleties.

Quitting Universal for Goldwyn Pictures, von Stroheim embarked on his opus, *Greed* (1924), his cut running to nine hours and 42 reels. But Goldwyn was taken over by Metro Pictures Corporation, which became MGM, with Thalberg in charge of production. Despite von Stroheim's protests, *Greed* was released at 10½ reels. Even so, the power and intensity of his vision shocked audiences and the film was widely denounced. A year later he scored a box-office hit with *The Merry Widow*, but abandoned directing in 1934 to return to acting. **PK**

Top Takes…

Fugitive Road 1934
Hello Sister 1933
The Great Gabbo 1929
Queen Kelly 1929
The Wedding March 1928
The Honeymoon 1928
The Merry Widow 1925
Greed 1924
Merry-Go-Round 1923
Foolish Wives 1922
Blind Husbands 1919

"The man who cut my picture has nothing on his head but a hat!"—On the cutting of *Greed*

HENRY KING

Born: Henry King, January 24, 1886 (Christiansburg, Virginia, U.S.); died 1982 (Toluca Lake, California, U.S.).

Directing style: Instinctive feel for portraying Americana; created historical dramas on an epic scale; economical camerawork; master of action sequences.

Top Takes…

Tender is the Night 1962
Beloved Infidel 1959
The Bravados 1958
The Sun Also Rises 1957
Carousel 1956
Love is a Many-Splendored Thing 1955
David and Bathsheba 1951
Wilson 1944 ☆
The Song of Bernadette 1943 ☆
Jesse James 1939
Alexander's Ragtime Band 1938
Seventh Heaven 1937
In Old Chicago 1937
Lloyd's of London 1936
The Winning of Barbara Worth 1926
Tol'able David 1921

Henry King worked across a range of genres, from dramas to Westerns and action movies. He started out as an actor in repertory theater, then entered the movie industry as an actor in 1912. By 1915, King had moved behind the camera to sit in the director's chair. He continued his long and accomplished career until the 1960s, directing more than 100 films.

An early success was the silent movie *Tol'able David* (1921), a landmark slice of rural Americana with Richard Barthelmess as a young boy out to prove his worth as a man against the bad guys. King was established as a name, and moved on to bigger budget productions such as *The Winning of Barbara Worth* (1926), one of the last silent Westerns.

He continued to work at a prolific rate and made the transition to talkies easily. He worked frequently with one of Twentieth Century Fox's brightest stars of the era, Tyrone Power, on the musical *Alexander's Ragtime Band* (1938) and on the Western *Jesse James* (1939). But King wasn't just a director of action movies and swashbucklers. Although too sentimental for some tastes, King's *The Song of Bernadette* (1943) earned Jennifer Jones a Best Actress Academy Award for her lead performance in a film about the religious visions of a French peasant girl. In the 1950s, King continued to vary his output, mixing Biblical epics such as *David and Bathsheba* (1951) with musicals like *Carousel* (1956) and Westerns such as *The Bravados* (1958). Although always totally professional, Henry King never had a readily identifiable style or theme as a director; his films, however, were consistently well made and entertaining. He was one of the 36 founders of the Academy of Motion Picture Arts and Sciences that awards the annual Oscars. **EB**

> "Wake up! Now! . . . You are playing with fire, Bernadette."
>
> —Peyramale, *The Song of Bernadette*

FRANK LLOYD

Born: Frank Lloyd, February 2, 1886 (Glasgow, Scotland); died 1960 (Santa Monica, California, U.S.).

Directing style: Prolific craftsman of the silents and talkies who worked across a range of genres; deft editing to enhance storytelling pace.

Frank Lloyd was one of the founders of the Academy of Motion Picture Arts and Sciences, the organization responsible for bestowing Academy Awards, and served as the group's president from 1934 to 1935. In this administrative role, he helped mainstream and legitimize motion pictures. He also earned a capstone of peer recognition during the period of 1929 to 1935, when he earned three Oscar nominations for *Weary River* (1929), *Drag* (1929), and *Mutiny on the Bounty* (1935), and two Academy Award wins for *The Divine Lady* (1929) and *Cavalcade* (1933). Sadly, because Lloyd was more of a professional craftsman than a filmmaker with an auteur stamp, his early influence on the medium has often been overlooked.

Born in Scotland, Lloyd started out as a stage actor, following in the footsteps of his father, a musical comedy actor, before emigrating to the United States. He began his film career in the silent era, acting in, writing, and directing such shorts as *The Law of His Kind* (1914). He then started to make feature films with literary adaptations such as *A Tale of Two Cities* (1917), often writing his own scripts and producing or coproducing his films. His productivity continued unabated for the next 11 years with dozens of titles, including the Zane Grey Western *Riders of the Purple Sage* (1918), and *Oliver Twist* (1922), which saw Lloyd's judicious editing adapt Charles Dickens's novel to the fast pace of the silver screen.

The dawn of sound films swelled budgets to match the greater technical demands, and Lloyd adapted well to the studio system. His first sound movie with a synchronized musical soundtrack was *Adoration* (1928). Lloyd worked steadily throughout the rest of his career, making such distinctive features as *The Howards of Virginia* (1940). **GCQ**

Top Takes...

The Last Command 1955
Blood on the Sun 1945
Forever and a Day 1943
The Howards of Virginia 1940
Under Two Flags 1936
Mutiny on the Bounty 1935 ☆
Cavalcade 1933 ★
Drag 1929 ☆
The Divine Lady 1929 ★
Weary River 1929 ☆
Oliver Twist 1922
Riders of the Purple Sage 1918
A Tale of Two Cities 1917
The Law of His Kind 1914

"Mutiny on the Bounty . . . is superlatively thrilling."
—*New York Times*

MICHAEL CURTIZ

Born: Mihály Kertész Kaminer, December 24, 1886 (Budapest, Hungary); died 1962 (Hollywood, California, U.S.).

Directing style: Perfectionist taskmaster; maker of classic movies; created action and spectacle using complex compositions and high-contrast lighting.

Top Takes…

The Comancheros 1961

The Adventures of Huckleberry Finn 1960

The Man in the Net 1959

White Christmas 1954

Mildred Pierce 1945

Mission to Moscow 1943

Casablanca 1942 ★

Yankee Doodle Dandy 1942 ☆

The Sea Hawk 1940

The Private Lives of Elizabeth and Essex 1939

Angels with Dirty Faces 1938 ☆

Four Daughters 1938 ☆

The Adventures of Robin Hood 1938

The Charge of the Light Brigade 1936

Captain Blood 1935 ☆

20,000 Years in Sing Sing 1933

"Play it, Sam. For old times' sake … Play 'As Time Goes By'"

—Ilsa, *Casablanca*

Workhorse directors, who were reliable, professional, and ready to take on whatever assignment was thrown at them, formed the solid foundation of the classic Hollywood studio system. And foremost among them was Michael Curtiz. Thrillers, weepies, war movies, comedies, horror, film noir—the Hungarian-born Curtiz tackled them all. Yet his forte was action movies and swashbucklers, in particular, to which he brought an infectious brio. *The Adventures of Robin Hood* (1938) still stands as one of the finest action movies ever made.

Prolific from the first, he directed nearly 50 films under his birth name of Mihály Kertész in his native Hungary before moving to Austria in 1919, where he made biblical spectaculars in the Cecil B. DeMille style. He headed to the United States in 1926. Renamed, Curtiz soon became Warner Brothers's top in-house director, entrusted with its A-list stars and productions. Over the next 28 years he directed over 80 Warner Brothers films, among them *20,000 Years in Sing Sing* (1933), *Captain Blood* (1935), *The Charge of the Light Brigade* (1936), *Angels with Dirty Faces* (1938), *The Private Lives of Elizabeth and Essex* (1939), *The Sea Hawk* (1940), *Yankee Doodle Dandy* (1942), *Mission to Moscow* (1943), *Mildred Pierce* (1945) and, most famously of all, *Casablanca* (1942), which won him his only Best Director Academy Award. Even after quitting Warner Brothers in 1954, offended at being asked to take a pay cut, Curtiz continued to turn out a couple of movies a year on a freelance basis. One of these, the saccharine musical *White Christmas* (1954), gave him the biggest commercial hit of his career. Indefatigably productive to the last, Curtiz continued directing films until a few months before his death at the age of seventy-five. **PK**

RAOUL WALSH

Born: Albert Edward Walsh, March 11, 1887 (New York City, New York, U.S.); died 1980 (Simi Valley, California, U.S.).

Directing style: Maker of Westerns and adventure films; exciting action sequences; classic storytelling of the lone, offbeat hero winning against all odds.

Raoul Walsh had a colorful career. He left home at age fifteen, after his mother died, and wandered through Texas, Montana, Cuba, and Mexico working as a cowboy. But his youthful adventures meant that he could ride a horse, which led to a job working with director D. W. Griffith. He later directed his first film *Life of Villa* (1912) under Griffith's supervision. For the biopic of the Mexican revolutionary Pancho Villa, Walsh shot some documentary footage; at the same time, he played Villa as a young man. He also appeared in Griffith's epic *The Birth of a Nation* (1915). Many of Walsh's silent features are sadly lost, but his picture about World War I, *What Price Glory* (1926), stands as a landmark. Walsh lost an eye while filming *In Old Arizona* (1928), and thereafter sported his trademark eye patch.

Westerns became something of a specialty for the director, and *The Big Trail* (1930) gave John Wayne his first starring role. Walsh's career in the 1930s marked time as he moved among a variety of genres, but he produced popular favorites *The Roaring Twenties* (1939) and *High Sierra* (1941), which offered meaty parts to James Cagney and Humphrey Bogart in tough crime melodramas. Established as a top-flight director, especially of action films, Walsh directed Errol Flynn as General Custer in *They Died with Their Boots On* (1941) and in the war film *Northern Pursuit* (1943). His later Westerns, including *Pursued* (1947), *Colorado Territory* (1949), and *The Tall Men* (1955), are among the best in the genre, marked by exciting action sequences and moments of psychological insight into character. He continued to work in the gangster genre, and *White Heat* (1949), with Cagney as a psychotic criminal, is a major achievement. Fittingly, Walsh's last film, *A Distant Trumpet* (1964), was a cavalry Western. **EB**

Top Takes...

A Distant Trumpet 1964
The Tall Men 1955
Colorado Territory 1949
White Heat 1949
Pursued 1947
Northern Pursuit 1943
They Died with Their Boots On 1941
The Roaring Twenties 1939
The Bowery 1933
The Big Trail 1930
In Old Arizona 1928
What Price Glory 1926
The Thief of Bagdad 1924
Regeneration 1915
Life of Villa 1912

"Oh, stuffy, huh? I'll give ya a litte air."

—Cody Jarrett, *White Heat*

F. W. MURNAU

Born: Friedrich Wilhelm Plumpe, December 28, 1888 (Bielefeld, North-Rhine-Westphalia, Germany); died 1931 (Santa Barbara, California, U.S.).

Directing style: Master of horror movies; pioneer of handheld camera; eerie stop-motion animation tricks; canted angles; innovative makeup effects and set design.

Top Takes…

Tabu: A Story of the South Seas 1931

City Girl 1930

4 Devils 1928

Sunrise: A Song of Two Humans 1927

Faust 1926

Herr Tartüff 1926 (*Tartuffe*)

Der Letzte Mann 1924 (*The Last Laugh*)

Die Finanzen des Grossherzogs 1924
    (*Finances of the Grand Duke*)

Die Austreibung 1923 (*The Expulsion*)

Phantom 1922

Nosferatu, eine Symphonie des Grauens 1922
    (*Nosferatu, the Vampire*)

Der Brennende Acker 1922 (*Burning Soil*)

Schloss Vogeloed 1921 (*The Haunted Castle*)

Sehnsucht 1921 (*Desire*)

Der Gang in die Nacht 1921
    (*Journey Into the Night*)

Abend—Nacht—Morgen 1920

Der Januskopf 1920 (*Dr. Jekyll and Mr. Hyde*)

Der Bucklige und die Tänzerin 1920
    (*The Hunchback and The Dancer*)

Satanas 1920 (*Satan*)

Der Knabe in Blau 1919 (*Emerald of Death*)

One of the top three German film directors of the twentieth century, alongside Fritz Lang and Ernst Lubitsch, Friedrich Wilhelm Plumpe was born in 1888. He studied art at the University of Heidelberg, then became a fighter pilot in World War I. He later changed his surname to "Murnau."

Murnau made his directorial debut with *Der Knabe in Blau* (1919) (*Emerald of Death*), and honed his art during the period of German Expressionism. Indeed Murnau was at the forefront of this movement, directing films such as *Schloss Vogeloed* (1921) (*The Haunted Castle*), before his first recognized masterpiece, *Nosferatu, eine Symphonie des Grauens* (1922) (*Nosferatu, the Vampire*). A retelling of vampire myth, the film is awash with eerie stop-motion animation tricks, canted angles, and a plot devoted to a plague-like vampire infestation. His second masterpiece, *Der Letzte Mann* (1924) (*The Last Laugh*), is often credited as being among the first films to use a handheld camera to provide a subjective point of view.

Two years later Murnau directed *Faust* (1926), whose success allowed him to emigrate from Germany to Hollywood. There, he contracted to Fox Film Corporation, and made *Sunrise:*

RIGHT: George O'Brien and Janet Gaynor
star in *Sunrise: A Song of Two Humans*.

A Song of Two Humans (1927), one of the last great silent movies. Exceedingly beautiful, innovative for its use of moving camera, and revolutionary for exposing how a moving camera affects character, *Sunrise* won several Academy Awards and remains a fitting example of visual storytelling.

With the arrival of sound, however, Murnau foundered and his next two movies, *4 Devils* (1928) and *City Girl* (1930), were largely ignored by critics and audiences. His last film *Tabu: A Story of the South Seas* (1931), a romance about forbidden love, was made first in collaboration with documentary maker Robert Flaherty; Murnau took over the project. Sadly, he didn't live to see *Tabu*'s premiere—he died in a car accident in 1931.

Murnau was a closet homosexual, and the dominant themes running through his work are now typically reinterpreted through the lens of his sexuality. Even so, his films remain as memorable examples of a true master's craft. **GCQ**

ABOVE: The eerie shadow of Graf Orlok (played by Max Schreck) in *Nosferatu*.

Stepping Back in Time

With more than a century of learning about the nature of screen storytelling having passed, it can be difficult today to step back in time and imagine that earlier era when narrative conventions were not so well established. But a journey into the past is often paved with surprises and rare glimpses of timeless beauty. If one were somehow taken back to the early 1900s, when movies were entering their adolescence, but before the revolution of sound, one might uncover some of the earliest filmmakers, such as Murnau, Lang, and Lubitsch, plying their craft in works that still resonate today, decades later.

1880s

CARL DREYER

Born: Carl Theodor Dreyer, February 3, 1888 (Copenhagen, Denmark); died 1968 (Copenhagen, Denmark).

Directing style: Early master of melodramas and horror movies; themes covering angst of characters in crisis; careful compositions; long takes; stark lighting.

Top Takes…

Gertrud 1964 (*Gertrud*)

Ordet 1955 (*The Word*)

Et slot i et slot 1955
  (*The Castle Within the Castle*)

Storstrømsbroen 1950 (*The Storstrom Bridge*)

Thorvaldsen 1949

De nåede færgen 1948 (*They Caught the Ferry*)

Landsbykirken 1947
  (*The Danish Village Church*)

Kampen mod kræften 1947
  (*The Struggle Against Cancer*)

Vredens Dag 1943 (*Day of Wrath*)

Vampyr—Der Traum des Allan Grey 1932
  (*The Strange Adventure of David Gray*)

La Passion de Jeanne d'Arc 1928
  (*The Passion of Joan of Arc*)

Glomdalsbruden 1926 (*The Bride of Glomdal*)

Du Skal ære din Hustru 1925
  (*Master of the House*)

Mikaël 1924 (*Chained*)

Der var engang 1922 (*Once Upon a Time*)

Die Gezeicheneten 1922 (*Love One Another*)

Prästänkan 1920 (*The Witch Woman*)

Præsidenten 1919 (*The President*)

Carl Dreyer is often seen as the melancholy Dane of world cinema, a purveyor of metaphysical gloom and anguish. This reading, however, overlooks the warm, humanistic aspect of his work, the side that celebrates love and sensuality.

Dreyer's career falls into two halves. In the dozen years that began with his directorial debut, *Præsidenten* (1919) (*The President*), he directed ten films in five different countries. But the costly flop of his most ambitious film, *La Passion de Jeanne d'Arc* (1928) (*The Passion of Joan of Arc*), blighted his reputation. For more than ten years Dreyer found it impossible to realize any of his projects, and even when he resumed directing in 1943, funding remained perpetually elusive.

Dreyer's early work presents a wide variety of moods that belie his reputation as a monolithic filmmaker. *Du Skal ære din Hustru* (1925) (*Master of the House*) is a sly domestic comedy, whereas *Glomdalsbruden* (1926) (*The Bride of Glomdal*), a lyrical love story, makes poetic use of the sweeping Norwegian landscape. In contrast, *Mikaël* (1924) (*Chained*), the drama of a triangular relationship, plays out in the heated, claustrophobic setting of an artist's studio.

RIGHT: Maria Falconetti as the martyred Jeanne in *The Passion of Joan of Arc*.

Dreyer once wrote, "Nothing in the world can be compared to the human face. It is a land one can never tire of exploring." His intense use of facial close-ups reached its apogee in *The Passion of Joan of Arc*, where his camera tirelessly explores Joan's anguish and the malevolence of her accusers. *Joan of Arc* has achieved iconic status, but *Vredens Dag* (1943) (*Day of Wrath*) is perhaps his most perfectly realized film, presenting, in its visual texture, the supreme example of his use of light and darkness to express moral and emotional concerns.

Dreyer's last two films—*Ordet* (1955) (*The Word*) and *Gertrud* (1964)—form the culmination of the process of simplification and increasing austerity in his shooting style. On its release, *Gertrud* was received with incomprehension and hostility, but it now seems the logical end point of Dreyer's highly individual creative journey: the final, serene testament of a filmmaker who always carved out his own path. **PK**

ABOVE: Lisbeth Movin plays Absalon's second wife in the horror film *Day of Wrath*.

Joan of Arc on Trial

Dreyer based his portrayal of Joan of Arc on documentation from her 1431 trial. Joan began claiming to have visions at the age of twelve. In 1428, as the English prepared to attack the city of Orleans, she obeyed the orders of her personal saints to lead an army against the English and Burgundians. Her leadership led to a reversal of French fortunes in the Hundred Years' War but, after her failure to recapture Paris, she was handed over to the English who tried her and burned her as a heretic in 1431. Dreyer's film focuses on Joan's anguish and the malevolence of her accusers during the trial.

VICTOR FLEMING

Born: Victor Fleming, February 23, 1889 (La Cañada, California, U.S.); died 1949 (Cottonwood, Arizona, U.S.).

Directing style: Master of action movies during the silent era; maker of elegantly crafted and entertaining Hollywood classics in its Golden Age.

Top Takes…

Joan of Arc 1948
Adventure 1945
A Guy Named Joe 1943
Tortilla Flat 1942
Dr. Jekyll and Mr. Hyde 1941
Gone with the Wind 1939 ★
The Wizard of Oz 1939
Test Pilot 1938
Captains Courageous 1937
Treasure Island 1934
Around the World in 80 Minutes
  with Douglas Fairbanks 1931
Renegades 1930
The Virginian 1929
Lord Jim 1925
When the Clouds Roll By 1919

> "With enough courage, you can do without a reputation."
>
> —Rhett Butler, Gone with the Wind

Victor Fleming was the sole credited director on *The Wizard of Oz* (1939) and *Gone with the Wind* (1939)—the latter for which he took the Best Director Oscar. Both stand as lasting achievements of Hollywood's Golden Age. However, he was a hired hand, replacing other directors such as Richard Thorpe and George Cukor in mid production, and he himself was replaced by uncredited filmmakers King Vidor and Sam Wood for crucial sequences. So although his reputation is secured by these credits alone, he still remains an unsung hero to many.

Fleming began his film career as a stuntman in 1910. A former mechanic and professional race-car driver, he specialized in stunt driving. He soon became interested in working on the other side of the camera, and got a job as a cameraman on many of Douglas Fairbanks's films. He moved on to directing with pleasant, manly Fairbanks comic vehicles, such as *When the Clouds Roll By* (1919), and a few prestige efforts such as *Lord Jim* (1925). When talkies came in, he stayed on the A-list, directing Gary Cooper in his first big hit, *The Virginian* (1929). His studio was MGM, where he had a reputation as a dependable fix-it man. He was known as a tough guy who could stand up to the studios and get on with actors, which led to his many uncredited tidy-up shoots, such as on *Red Dust* (1932). After his Oscar win, Fleming worked less often, on self-consciously big, awards-bid films suffused with a kind of pretentiousness not found in his breezier work. He made an entertaining but murky *Dr. Jekyll and Mr. Hyde* (1941) with Spencer Tracy, the John Steinbeck adaptation *Tortilla Flat* (1942), and the wartime fantasy *A Guy Named Joe* (1943). His last film was the turgid but expensive Ingrid Bergman version of *Joan of Arc* (1948). **KN**

W. S. VAN DYKE

Born: Woodbridge Strong Van Dyke II, March 21, 1889 (San Diego, California, U.S.); died 1943 (Brentwood, California, U.S.).

Directing style: Consummate studio craftsman who worked across genres; visual stylist; improvisation; elicited relaxed, natural performances from his cast.

Woodbridge Strong Van Dyke never knew his father, but spent his childhood on the road with his mother, who appeared in a variety of roles in vaudeville and traveling stock companies. Through a chance meeting, Van Dyke got a job as an assistant to D. W. Griffith on the director's *Intolerance: Love's Struggle Throughout the Ages* (1916). By the following year Van Dyke had graduated to the director's chair, with a series of Westerns including *The Land of Long Shadows* (1917), and continued cranking out low-budget Westerns for a decade, until MGM asked him to replace documentary maker Robert Flaherty on the film *White Shadows in the South Seas* (1928), which Van Dyke did with his customary speed and facility.

A no-nonsense taskmaster, Van Dyke was legendarily hard on casts and crews, pushing them to their limits to get his films in on time and under budget, much to the delight of his bosses. With *White Shadows* salvaged, MGM handed Van Dyke the task of directing *Trader Horn* (1931), the first sync-sound film ever shot in Africa. A rousing adventure tale, it was a box-office hit.

Returning from Africa after a bruising expedition, the prolific Van Dyke directed a number of genre classics, including *Tarzan the Ape Man* (1932), before making a lasting name for himself with *The Thin Man* (1934). Based on a crime novel by Dashiell Hammett, *The Thin Man* was shot in just 12 days. The film was an enormous hit, and Van Dyke's fortune was assured. He remained popular with his bosses at MGM and continued working feverishly until his death in 1943. W. S. Van Dyke was the consummate studio craftsman, willing to take on any project, utterly lacking in personal vanity, and always conscious of the bottom line. He was also a remarkable stylist. **WWD**

Top Takes...

Journey for Margaret 1942
Cairo 1942
I Married An Angel 1942
Bitter Sweet 1940
Sweethearts 1938
Marie Antoinette 1938
San Francisco 1936 ☆
Rose-Marie 1936
Naughty Marietta 1935
The Thin Man 1934 ☆
Manhattan Melodrama 1934
Eskimo 1933
Tarzan the Ape Man 1932
Trader Horn 1931
White Shadows in the South Seas 1928
The Land of Long Shadows 1917

"Oh, Nicky, I love you because you know such lovely people."

—Nora Charles, *The Thin Man*

Top Takes...

CHARLES CHAPLIN

Born: Charles Spencer Chaplin, April 16, 1889 (Walworth, London, England); died 1977 (Vevey, Switzerland).

Directing style: Slapstick comedy, inventive set-ups; choreographed gags; subtle and seductive moves; hilariously funny, hopelessly romantic; clumsy yet graceful.

Besides being the most celebrated silent slapstick comedy director, Sir Charles Chaplin was also a composer, early cinema's top star, and cofounder in 1919 of United Artists, a major studio.

Having learned the craft of entertainment in vaudeville and traveling shows, Chaplin was initiated into film through Keystone Studios comedies. He soon began directing and during his two years at Essanay he directed 26 two-reel films. *The Tramp* (1915), *The Vagabond* (1916), and *Easy Street* (1917) show steady improvement in kick-and-run slapstick routines combined with pathos, making his films at once funny and touching, rebellious and caring.

Chaplin gradually attuned his films to the ethos of the times, broaching sensitive issues. Though these did not go down well with conservative commentators, audiences loved them and Chaplin became a hero, the symbol of an emerging immigrant nation. He consolidated his popularity through masterpieces such as *A Dog's Life* (1918).

Chaplin lowered his work rhythm to one film every few years, and his carefully choreographed gags, emotional tactfulness, and awareness for detail guaranteed brilliance.

RIGHT: Chaplin with fellow cofounders of United Artists, which was formed in 1919.

Modern Times (1936) and *The Great Dictator* (1940) are timeless classics. Their comedic timing, originality of gags, evocation of emotions through the tiniest of movements and cinematographic skill (especially in toying with the edges of the camera frame) push the boundaries of comedy to the limits, while their social concern for class consciousness and tolerance gave them a pressing topical relevance. Thus, as Chaplin's popularity waned in the 1940s, his prestige grew.

Sadly, the rest of the world did not listen to the satirical and energetic antifascist warnings in *The Great Dictator*. Smearing campaigns forced Chaplin out of the United States, and the few films he made afterward, such as *Limelight* (1952), were of a reflective, acquiescent tone. Thankfully, Chaplin's legacy as one of the original geniuses of cinema and the spirit of the twentieth century's most immediately recognizable popular icon, The Tramp, is still celebrated everywhere. **EM**

ABOVE: The Tramp and his dog Scraps sit forlornly on a doorstep in *A Dog's Life*.

In a Class of His Own

Charles Chaplin's awards testify to the breadth and brilliance of his talent.

- 1927/1928: Special Award "for acting, writing, directing, and producing *The Circus.*" The Academy's letter to Chaplin noted, "The collective accomplishments thus displayed place you in a class by yourself."
- 1971: Honorary Award "for the incalculable effect he has had in making motion pictures the art form of this century."
- 1972: Oscar for Music, Original Dramatic Score, for *Limelight.*

JEAN COCTEAU

Born: Jean Maurice Eugène Clément Cocteau, July 5, 1889 (Maisons-Lafitte, Yvelines, Île-de-France, France); died 1963 (Milly-la-Forêt, Essonne, Île-de-France, France).

Directing style: Icon of French avant-garde cinema; master of surrealism; created a personal mythology onscreen; reverse-filming techniques; fantastical set design.

Painter, poet, playwright, novelist, set designer, and director, Jean Cocteau perfected the art of the surrealist special effect. He is perhaps most famous for his masterwork, the Orphic trilogy: *Le sang d'un poète* (1930) (*The Blood of a Poet*), *Orphée* (1950) (*Orpheus*), and *Le testament d'Orphée, ou ne me demandez pas pourquoi!* (1960) (*The Testament of Orpheus*).

In *The Blood of a Poet* the viewer is taken on an odyssey into the mind of the artist, replete with talking statues, attempts to fly, and suicide. In *Orpheus*, poetic transmissions on a car radio lure Orphée into his deepest desires and the underworld. Orphée was played by Cocteau's long-time homosexual lover, Jean Marais. He communes with the princess of death by walking through a mirror into Cocteau's underworld. Characters return from the dead by reverse imagery, the film running backward so they can spring back into the living world. When Beauty enters the hall of the Beast, enchantment bursts forth via a procession of disembodied arms reaching out of the walls, torches in hand, to light her way.

The Testament of Orpheus stars Cocteau as the poet, and features appearances by artist Pablo Picasso and novelist Françoise Sagan. The poet looks back on a long career of artistic achievement, and comes to realize the existence of immortality through his artworks. Cocteau created a self-contained world that is truly unique, one in which leather-clad bikers are escorts into the underworld, and a battle among warring factions of artists at the poets' café is believably the most important issue of day-to-day existence. *La belle et la bête* (1946) (*Beauty and the Beast*) is a visually splendid screen telling of the fairy tale that must be seen for Marais's portrayal of the exceedingly charming beast. **HB**

Top Takes...

Le testament d'Orphée, ou ne me demandez pas pourquoi! 1960 (*The Testament of Orpheus*)

8 x 8: A Chess Sonata in 8 Movements 1957

La Villa Santo-Sospir 1952

Orphée 1950 (*Orpheus*)

Coriolan 1950

Les parents terribles 1948 (*The Storm Within*)

L'aigle à deux têtes 1948 (*The Eagle has Two Heads*)

La belle et la bête 1946 (*Beauty and the Beast*)

Le sang d'un poète 1930 (*The Blood of a Poet*)

Jean Coceau fait du cinéma 1925

> "I love cats because I enjoy my home; and little by little they become its visible soul."

RIGHT: Jean Marais, Jean Cocteau, and Josette Day on the set of *Beauty and the Beast*.

JAMES WHALE

Born: James Whale, July 22, 1889 (Dudley, Worcestershire, England); died 1957 (Hollywood, California, U.S.).

Directing style: Innovative director of horror movies; fluid camerawork; sharp angles; formalized framing; high-contrast lighting.

James Whale was a theater director before debuting as a filmmaker with *Journey's End* (1930), based on the celebrated antiwar play. He never intended to be a horror director until a project abandoned by Robert Florey was dropped into his lap. History is sometimes made upon such accidents, and it was certainly made with Whale's adaptation of *Frankenstein* (1931).

Whale created a style inspired by German Expressionism, depicting a personal world of oppression and insecurity. His fluid camera painted a convincing three-dimensional space, while his penchant for close-ups, together with a talent for inspired casting, brought out the best from his performers.

With *Frankenstein* he provided the shape and look to a mode that became a fully-fledged genre at Universal Studios. Through a layered, ambivalent approach and sympathy for "The Monster," it questioned the established notions of right and wrong, beautiful and bestial. The sophisticated Whale brought subtlety, wit, and compassion to the genre, creating in *Frankenstein* one of the twentieth century's lasting icons.

The full potentials of this Faustian tale and its Promethean director were showcased in the superior sequel, *Bride of*

Top Takes...

Hello Out There 1949

They Dare Not Love 1941

Green Hell 1940

The Man in the Iron Mask 1939

Port of Seven Seas 1938

Wives Under Suspicion 1938

Sinners in Paradise 1938

The Great Garrick 1937

Show Boat 1936

Remember Last Night? 1935

Bride of Frankenstein 1935

One More River 1934

By Candlelight 1933

The Invisible Man 1933

The Kiss Before the Mirror 1933

The Old Dark House 1932

Impatient Maiden 1932

Frankenstein 1931

Waterloo Bridge 1931

Hell's Angels 1930

Journey's End 1930

RIGHT: Lobby card for *Show Boat* with Irene Dunne, Allan Jones, and Paul Robeson.

Frankenstein (1935). As Universal's moneymaker, Whale could sneak in more subversion and imagery laced with macabre humor and sensitive pathos. Oozing with camp and odium for the normal, *Bride of Frankenstein* embraced the outcasts and celebrated a new world of gods and monsters. *Bride* remains his timeless masterpiece, and a first-rate cinema classic.

Eccentrics rule the night in *The Old Dark House* (1932), with the formula of people stranded in a spooky house on a stormy night turned into a black comedy of characters. Even better is *The Invisible Man* (1933), its burlesque humor combined with amazement and horror, leading to a heartfelt ending.

Whale's films outside the horror genre were not so successful, excepting the musical *Show Boat* (1936), his personal favorite. Falling from grace with the new management at Universal, he retired from directing and went back to painting, until his life ended with an apparent suicide. **DO**

Creating a Monster

The film *Frankenstein* was based on the novel by Mary Shelley, who was the daughter of the feminist writer Mary Wollstonecraft (who died giving birth to her) and wife of the poet Percy Bysshe Shelley. Inspiration for the novel apparently came from a dream Mary had of her own stillborn child being brought to life by the warmth of a fire. The Monster in Whale's film does not physically resemble Mary Shelley's character. Makeup artist Jack P. Pierce came up with innovations such as the flat head, the bolts through the neck, the droopy eyelids, and the ill-fitting suit.

ABEL GANCE

Born: Abel Gance, October 25, 1889 (Paris, France); died 1981 (Paris, France).

Directing style: Visionary innovator of special effects; one of the most technically skilled directors of the silent era; handheld camerawork to heighten drama; pioneering use of widescreen; rapid cutting technique.

Top Takes...

> "... he understands the spiritual power of the cinema."
>
> ——New York Times

One of the most accomplished directors of the silent era, Abel Gance spent most of his early career pushing forward the supposed limits of the form in terms of storytelling, special effects, and even the technology of film production itself—until ironically the latter, in particular, the advent of sound, hindered his output as he struggled to adapt.

Born in Paris, Gance started work as an actor, but by 1911 was working steadily as a director. The pioneering short *La Folie du docteur Tube* (1915) is one of the few surviving examples of his early work, although already his ambition was clear when it came to visual effects and storytelling devices. During World War I, Gance entered the army and fought on the front line. His experiences led, upon his return, to the antiwar *J'Accuse!* (1919) (*I Accuse*), a film whose popularity bolstered Gance's increasingly bold bids for creative independence.

La Roue (1923) (*The Wheel*) proved epic in scope and expense, though Gance ultimately abandoned the movie, directing the short digression *Au secours!* (1924) (*Help!*), before beginning his masterpiece, the audacious and epic *Napoléon* (1927). The film played with varying aspect ratios and nascent visual effects, such as widescreen, its achievements monumental compared to many contemporaneous films—and, in some cases, even to some of the films that have followed. Yet subsequent experiments floundered, with Gance failing to find a place in the world of talkies. Over the following decades, he gradually faded from prominence until the interest of supporters, such as director Francis Ford Coppola, prompted the restoration of *Napoléon*. This in turn restored Gance's reputation as one of cinema's most important visionaries. **JK**

LLOYD BACON

Born: Lloyd Francis Bacon, December 4, 1889 (San Jose, California, U.S.); died 1955 (Burbank, California, U.S.).

Directing style: Versatile no-frills director across a range of genres; notable for slick, fast-paced musicals; frequent use of close-up shots; often naval themes.

Born into a theatrical family, Lloyd Bacon began his career as an actor in stock companies and touring shows, before entering films as a bit-part player at Essanay. Fellow Essanay player Charlie Chaplin employed Bacon as an actor and production assistant when they moved to other studios. He appeared in numerous Chaplin comedies before beginning to direct comedy shorts for producer Mack Sennett. Bacon's role in film history was secured when he directed the first film to have recorded dialogue throughout—*The Singing Fool* (1928).

In the 1930s Bacon was a contract director at Warner Brothers, working in a variety of genres; but he is principally known today for his musicals, including *42nd Street* (1933), *Footlight Parade* (1933), *In Caliente* (1935), and *Gold Diggers of 1937* (1936). These films combined slick, fast-paced comedy with elaborate dance numbers directed by choreographer Busby Berkeley. Bacon was also adept at the crime melodramas, equally favored by Warner Brothers. *Marked Woman* (1937) is a good example of Bacon's work: no frills, good acting, and an entertaining, well-focused narrative.

Bacon could turn his hand to most kinds of moviemaking. *The Oklahoma Kid* (1939) is a Western, starring, somewhat improbably, James Cagney and Humphrey Bogart; *Brother Orchid* (1940) is a comedy gangster film with Edward G. Robinson; and *Knute Rockne All American* (1940) is the inspirational biopic of a football player.

In 1944 Bacon moved to Twentieth Century Fox, where he continued to prove a competent and adaptable director of modest projects with Fox's second-rank stars, many of them musicals such as *I Wonder Who's Kissing Her Now* (1947), *You Were Meant for Me* (1948), and *Give My Regards to Broadway* (1948). **EB**

Top Takes...

She Couldn't Say No 1954
The Great Sioux Uprising 1953
Call Me Mister 1951
Give My Regards to Broadway 1948
You Were Meant for Me 1948
I Wonder Who's Kissing Her Now 1947
Knute Rockne All American 1940
Brother Orchid 1940
The Oklahoma Kid 1939
A Slight Case of Murder 1938
Gold Diggers of 1937 1936
Marked Woman 1937
In Caliente 1935
Footlight Parade 1933
42nd Street 1933
The Singing Fool 1928

"Now go out there and be so swell you'll make me hate you!"
—Dorothy Brock, *42nd Street*

CLARENCE BROWN

Born: Clarence Leon Brown, May 1, 1890 (Clinton, Massachusetts, U.S.); died 1987 (Santa Monica, California, U.S.).

Directing style: Master pictorialist; visual stylist who could capture the beauty of leading stars onscreen; historical and literary adaptations with emotional depth.

Top Takes...

Plymouth Adventure 1952
It's a Big Country 1951
Angels in the Outfield 1951
Intruder in the Dust 1949
The Yearling 1946 ☆
National Velvet 1944 ☆
The White Cliffs of Dover 1944
The Human Comedy 1943 ☆
The Rains Came 1939
Of Human Hearts 1938
Anna Karenina 1935
Anna Christie 1930 ☆
A Free Soul 1930 ☆
Romance 1930 ☆
Flesh and the Devil 1926
The Last of the Mohicans 1920

Clarence Brown was an old studio hand of enormous talent who learned his craft at the side of French director Maurice Tourneur. Their collaboration culminated in the most beautifully realized of all the screen adaptations of James Fenimore Cooper's *The Last of the Mohicans* (1920).

Brown spent most of his career at MGM where, perhaps because he was an exquisite visual stylist talented at rendering the human body at its most glamorous, he was often assigned projects featuring the studio's impressive bevy of beautiful actresses, especially Joan Crawford and Greta Garbo. *Anna Christie* (1930), *Flesh and the Devil* (1926), and *Anna Karenina* (1935) display the complexities of Garbo's enigmatic screen persona to their best advantage, with a static, highly detailed style creating an atmosphere of contemplation and depth.

Brown also showed considerable talent with projects dependent upon multilayered melodramatic effects, and produced some of the classic era's most memorable bits of Americana. For example: *The Human Comedy* (1943), with its nostalgia for small-town life, its loving embrace of multi-ethnicity, and its humanistic optimism; *The Yearling* (1946), which movingly stages a difficult conflict between parents and child; and *Intruder in the Dust* (1949), with its sensitive handling of William Faulkner's interracial conflict, and its marshaling of small-town Mississippi settings and extras to lend political weight and reinforce the writer's message that the South can manage its own racial problems.

Clarence Brown's films could descend into high-class soap opera—as witness the bathos of *National Velvet* (1944); but even that predictable tearjerker shows the sure touch of a master pictorialist. **BP**

> "Oh, I didn't bother him . . .
> I just arranged it with God."
>
> —Velvet Brown, *National Velvet*

FRITZ LANG

Born: Friedrich Christian Anton Lang, December 5, 1890 (Vienna, Austria); died 1976 (Los Angeles, California, U.S.).

Directing style: Legendary autocratic director of a variety of genres; themes place the individual against bureaucracy and explore the abuse of power.

Nobody's oeuvre better embodies the ambitions and anxieties, successes and suspicions of the twentieth century, than that of Vienna-born Fritz Lang. The German-speaking world's most legendary filmmaker, he is also one of Hollywood's most underrated directors.

At surface level, Lang is best known for his masterful contributions to German Expressionism but, ironically enough, Lang had to decline directing the first overtly Expressionist film, *Das Cabinet des Dr. Caligari* (1920) (*The Cabinet of Dr. Caligari*) because he was contracted to direct a sequel to *Die Spinnen, 1. Teil—Der Goldene See* (1919) (*The Spiders, Part 1: The Golden Lake*), an action adventure film that had brought him success. Fortunately, the producer of *The Spiders* financed Lang's Expressionist ballad *Der Müde Tod* (1921) (*Between Two Worlds*), which brought him huge acclaim throughout Europe.

In 1921, Lang and his second wife, screenwriter Thea Von Harbou, initiated a series of films around the character of Doctor Mabuse. *Dr. Mabuse, der Spieler—Ein Bild der Zeit* (1922) (*Dr. Mabuse, King of Crime*) and its sequels were complex,

Top Takes...

Die 1000 Augen des Dr. Mabuse 1960 (*The Shadow vs. the Thousand Eyes of Dr. Mabuse*)

Der Tiger von Eschnapur 1959 (*The Tiger of Eschnapur*)

Beyond a Reasonable Doubt 1956

The Big Heat 1953

Clash by Night 1952

House by the River 1950

Secret Beyond the Door 1948

Scarlet Street 1945

Ministry of Fear 1944

Hangmen Also Die! 1943

Man Hunt 1941

You Only Live Once 1937

Fury 1936

M 1931

Frau im Mond 1929 (*By Rocket to the Moon*)

Spione 1928 (*Spies*)

Metropolis 1927

Die Nibelungen: Kriemhilds Rache 1924 (*Kriemhild's Revenge*)

Die Nibelungen: Siegfried 1924 (*Siegfried*)

Dr. Mabuse, der Spieler—Ein Bild der Zeit 1922 (*Dr. Mabuse, King of Crime*)

Der Müde Tod 1921 (*Between Two Worlds*)

Die Spinnen, 1. Teil—Der Goldene See 1919 (*The Spiders, Part 1: The Golden Lake*)

LEFT: Peter Lorre as the sinister serial killer Hans Beckert in the groundbreaking film *M*.

Making *Metropolis*

Like Lang's previous two films, *Metropolis* was a hugely ambitious, expensive project, which brought the Universum Film AG studio—at the time the biggest European production company—near bankruptcy:

- The cast included more than 37,000 extras, including 25,000 men, 11,000 women, 1,100 bald men, 750 children, 100 dark-skinned people, and 25 Asians.
- *Metropolis* took two years to shoot.
- The multiple-exposed sequences were created during filming by repeatedly rewinding the film in the camera and exposing it again.
- The film was one of the most expensive movies of the time, costing around five million Deutsche Marks.
- Around one quarter of the original film has been lost. Of the original film, only an incomplete original negative and copies of shortened and re-edited release prints survive.
- The image quality of the 2001 digitally restored version is considered to be the best since the original film.
- While working on *Metropolis*, German cinematographer Eugen Schüfftan developed a special movie effect, now known as the Schüfftan process. A specially prepared mirror was used to create the illusion of actors interacting with huge realistic-looking sets (in fact, miniatures of skyscrapers.)

action-packed films filled with spies, betrayal, chases, and gadgets, predating James Bond movies by decades. The success allowed Lang and Von Harbou to initiate an Expressionist adaptation of the mythological *Nibelungen* saga in two parts, *Die Nibelungen: Siegfried* (1924) (*Siegfried*) and *Die Nibelungen: Kriemhilds Rache* (1924) (*Kriemhild's Revenge*), and eventually led to their most ambitious project, *Metropolis* (1927). In production for two years, and with a cast of thousands, *Metropolis* was too ambitious to achieve success, and its politics of class collaboration through semimessianic intervention were too muddled to be fully appreciated. But its imagery of a futurist city filled with skyscrapers, Moloch-like factories, and a sexy female robot called Maria, painted such a powerful dystopian picture of society that it was imprinted into the collective consciousness, and has been a model for science-fiction cinema ever since.

Life after *Metropolis*

The inevitable financial failure of *Metropolis* led Lang to abandon Expressionism in favor of smaller projects, such as *Frau im Mond* (1929) (*By Rocket to the Moon*), a more modest science-fiction film, and *Spione* (1928) (*Spies*), an action movie with a foreshadowing of Cold War fear. Fear was also at the heart of *M* (1931), a chilling story of a child murderer put on trial by the local organized crime consortium. One of the first ever serial killer movies, *M* metaphorically exposed the German people's fear of the future and is an almost prophetic description of the Nazis' rise to power.

That rise had personal consequences for Lang. After Hitler's takeover, he was forced to flee Germany, leaving his wife, a dedicated Nazi party member, behind. Lang arrived in Hollywood, where his first U.S. film, *Fury* (1936), is a fitting elaboration on *M*; this time the accused is innocent and the mob rule is portrayed as viciously wrong.

Lang's Hollywood career was mostly confined to genre films, often from Poverty Row, but he still established a remarkable oeuvre. The early film noir *You Only Live Once*

ABOVE: A scene from Fritz Lang's most ambitious project, the futuristic *Metropolis*.

(1937), the war thrillers *Man Hunt* (1941) and *Hangmen Also Die!* (1943), and the dark espionage mystery *Ministry of Fear* (1944), illustrated how motives such as suspicion, accusation, and paranoia now received full exposure. Following the end of World War II, Lang shifted to psychologically more complex thrillers, such as *Scarlet Street* (1945) and *Beyond a Reasonable Doubt* (1956). He then returned to Germany where, before retiring, he directed *Die 1000 Augen des Dr. Mabuse* (1960) (*The Shadow vs. the Thousand Eyes of Dr. Mabuse*), which predicted the onset of a surveillance society.

"I can't help what I do! I can't help it, I can't . . . ."
—Hans Beckert, *M*

As tempting as it is to equate German film history with Fritz Lang's cinema, it reduces his significance. Beyond one nation's scope, Lang's continuous investigations into abuse of power are pertinent for everyone. **EM**

1890s

EDMUND GOULDING

Born: Edmund Goulding, March 20, 1891 (Feltham, Middlesex, England); died 1959 (Los Angeles, California, U.S.).

Directing style: Dark, brooding dramas; well-crafted storytelling; compelling characters; often directed glamorous leading ladies; mentor of aspiring actors.

Top Takes...

Mister 880 1950
Nightmare Alley 1947
The Razor's Edge 1946
Of Human Bondage 1946
The Constant Nymph 1943
The Great Lie 1941
The Old Maid 1939
Dark Victory 1939
The Dawn Patrol 1938
White Banners 1938
Grand Hotel 1932 ★
Hell's Angels 1930
The Trespasser 1929
Love 1927
Sally, Irene and Mary 1925

The multiskilled director of the award-winning *Grand Hotel* (1932) became just as well known for his talents as a bisexual host of Hollywood orgies. Born in England, Edmund Goulding began his career as a relatively successful actor, playwright, and director on the London stage. During World War I, he was wounded in battle, then invalided out of the service. He subsequently headed to the United States, where he made his stage bow as a singer. However, it was as a writer that he first found fame, scoring a hit as cowriter of Henry King's silent masterpiece *Tol'able David* (1921).

After scripting the film version of his own novel *Fury* (1923), Goulding was signed up by MGM and developed a reputation as a woman's director, turning out tasteful dramas and drawing-room comedies. He directed Joan Crawford in *Sally, Irene and Mary* (1925), her first notable role, and Greta Garbo in the hit *Love* (1927), as well as penning the script for the first film musical, *The Broadway Melody* (1929). Goulding also directed Gloria Swanson in her first talkie, *The Trespasser* (1929). He had his greatest triumph with the star-studded *Grand Hotel* (1932), which landed a Best Picture Oscar. Moving to Warner Brothers in 1937, Goulding's successes included *The Dawn Patrol* (1938) and a string of weepies with Bette Davis that became critical hits. However, one of his best known films, which captures the essence of his style, is *Nightmare Alley* (1947), a brooding film noir of corruption in high and low society that brought out the best in Tyrone Power. Goulding's subsequent output failed to capture former glories. His suicide in Los Angeles in 1959 has been attributed to his hi-octane private life and his penchant for voyeurism and Hollywood sex parties. **TE**

> "I want to be alone . . . I have never been so tired in my life."
>
> —Grusinskaya, *Grand Hotel*

AUGUSTO GENINA

Born: Augusto Genina, January 28, 1892 (Rome, Italy); died 1957 (Rome, Italy).

Directing style: Versatile and prolific Italian filmmaker and storyteller of war dramas during Italy's fascist regime; also directed many French and German movies; rapport with female stars.

Augusto Genina began his career as a screenwriter, and today his name is attached to more than 150 films. He switched to directing, making his debut with the silent short *Beatrice d'Este* (1912). Gaining momentum, he directed the first of his more popular films, *Squadrone bianco* (1936) (*White Squadron*), about an army lieutenant who gets transferred to a new location following a failed romance. *L'assedio dell'Alcazar* (1940) (*The Siege of the Alcazar*) tells of a 1936 military coup d'état that triggered a national uprising in Spain.

Throughout the 1930s and 1940s, Genina continued to produce, write, and direct military genre movies, such as *Bengasi* (1942), which won the Best Italian Film award at the Venice Film Festival—although this was during the premiership of the fascist Benito Mussolini, and at that time the award was known as the Mussolini Cup.

Moving away from military themes, *Tre storie proibite* (1951) (*Three Forbidden Stories*) recreates a contemporary real-life tragedy that occurred when a stairway collapsed in an office building. Two hundred young women were visiting the offices at the time, attending interviews for a secretarial position, and the film's stories refer to the lives of three of the young women. *Maddelena* (1955) tells the story of a woman, played by Märta Torén, who uses her sexuality against the oppressive forces of man and God; whereas *Prix de beauté (Miss Europe)* (1930) (*Beauty Prize*) is an early French talkie that stands out as Louise Brooks's last starring role and her only film made in France. Other notable movies by Genina include *Cirano di Bergerac* (1925) (*Cyrano de Bergerac*), *Naples au baiser de feu* (1938) (*The Kiss of Fire*), *Cielo sulla palude* (1949) (*Heaven Over the Marshes*), and *Frou-Frou* (1955) (*The Toy Wife*). **ES**

Top Takes...

Frou-Frou 1955 (*The Toy Wife*)

Maddelena 1955

Tre storie proibite 1951
  (*Three Forbidden Stories*)

Cielo sulla palude 1949
  (*Heaven Over the Marshes*)

Bengasi 1942

L'assedio dell'Alcazar 1940
  (*The Siege of the Alcazar*)

Naples au baiser de feu 1938 (*The Kiss of Fire*)

Squadrone bianco 1936 (*White Squadron*)

Vergiss mein nicht 1935 (*Forget Me Not*)

Nous ne sommes plus des enfants 1934
  (*We Are Not Children*)

Prix de beauté (Miss Europe) 1930 (*Beauty Prize*)

Cirano di Bergerac 1925 (*Cyrano de Bergerac*)

Beatrice d'Este 1912

"[*White Squadron* is] always entertaining, and at times gripping . . . ."—*New York Times*

ERNST LUBITSCH

Born: Ernst Lubitsch, January 28, 1892 (Berlin, Germany); died 1947 (Hollywood, California, U.S.).

Directing style: Sophisticated visual stylist; graceful, witty, fast-paced, romantic comedies; subtle sexual innuendo; poignant plot surprises; flawless screenplays.

A German émigré who initially made a name for himself in silent films, Ernst Lubitsch brought a touch of Old World romanticism to his Hollywood comedies, but leavened it with a decidedly clear-eyed European sophistication. So while Nicole de Loiselle, played by Claudette Colbert in *Bluebeard's Eighth Wife* (1938), might eventually be swept off her feet by Michael Brandon, played by Gary Cooper, those feet lead him first on a chase of double entendres, cons, and the wicked laugh of a worldly woman who knows exactly what she wants.

A Lubitsch character always enters a romance fully aware of any relationship's risks, and of its fleetingness. The epitome of such urbane passion is *Trouble in Paradise* (1932), the tale of a liaison in Europe between two U.S. thieves and the French heiress who enters their sexual intrigue. The romantic stakes are firmly established in an early scene of seduction between Lily, played by Miriam Hopkins, and Gaston Monescu, played by Herbert Marshall—she posing as a countess, he as a baron. At the end of the evening they realize they've spent most of the night picking each other's pockets, thus affirming their rightness for one another: both are swindlers on the make.

Top Takes…

That Lady in Ermine 1948
Cluny Brown 1946
A Royal Scandal 1945
Heaven Can Wait 1943 ☆
To Be or Not to Be 1942
That Uncertain Feeling 1941
The Shop Around the Corner 1940
Ninotchka 1939
Bluebeard's Eighth Wife 1938
Angel 1937
The Merry Widow 1934
La veuve joyeuse 1934
Design for Living 1933
If I Had a Million 1932
Trouble in Paradise 1932
Une heure près de toi 1932 (*One Hour with You*)
Broken Lullaby 1932
The Smiling Lieutenant 1931
Monte Carlo 1930
Paramount on Parade 1930
The Love Parade 1929 ☆
Eternal Love 1929
The Patriot 1928 ☆
The Student Prince in Old Heidelberg 1927
The Marriage Circle 1924
Rosita 1923

RIGHT: David Niven, Gary Cooper, and Claudette Colbert in *Bluebeard's Eighth Wife*.

1890s

Lubitsch's films are characterized by a seemingly seamless, elegant visual style. Despite this, he manages to balance the soignée with the absurd. Take, for instance, the deliriously refined romantic dinner in *Ninotchka* (1939), complete with champagne and a luminous heroine, played by Greta Garbo; but be sure to note that this heroine is a communist emissary sent from Russia to sell confiscated jewels for the good of the government, and that her date is a playboy out to break her will on the rack of Parisian sumptuousness. Lubitsch risks sentimentality but earns it, and ultimately has his audience begging for it. Who can deny the heart-wrenching import of that silly little hat Ninotchka longs for, and not only the transformation of her face but surely her heart's palpitations once she puts it on? And a copy of *Anna Karenina* with a red carnation in it will forever stand as a symbol of the stalwart, plucky individual begging to be unmasked as a romantic. **HB**

ABOVE: Margaret Sullavan and James Stewart in *The Shop Around the Corner*.

The Lubitsch Touch

People speak of the "Lubitsch Touch," which has been variously defined as a certain refinement of mise-en-scène, a complex continental wit, and a romantic humor threaded through with a knowledge of life's bitter truths. It is easier identified than defined. Just one example: the imperious Mr. Matuschek in *The Shop Around the Corner*, seemingly getting to have his Christmas goose and eat it—but with Rudy the errand boy intercepting Matuschek's attempted suicide after learning of his wife's infidelities. Matuschek's cynicism is both honed and humbled by that Lubitsch wit.

GREGORY LA CAVA

Born: George Gregory La Cava, March 10, 1892 (Towanda, Pennsylvania, U.S.); died 1952 (Malibu, California, U.S.).

Directing style: Classic comedies with raucously complex comedic interchanges; scenes built up from improvisational rehearsals; unobtrusive editing style.

Gregory La Cava has been unjustly relegated to the level of a competent, reliable hireling, providing solid enough pictures but without stylistic flair or individuality. However, he was a sophisticated talent and an early pioneer of the invisible editing style so admired in more widely recognized directors such as Howard Hawks. La Cava deployed the same unobtrusive editing style across various genres, and he was as light on his directorial feet as Ernst Lubitsch.

La Cava began his career as a cartoonist and animator on such classics as the *The Katzenjammer Kids* series. Throughout the 1910s and 1920s, he honed his directorial and comedic skills on shorts, most notably with his friend W. C. Fields. He emerged in the 1930s as a top feature director, crafting such classics as *The Half Naked Truth* (1932), *My Man Godfrey* (1936), and *Stage Door* (1937). In *My Man Godfrey*, the narrative in which Carole Lombard's impulsive childlike rich girl meets William Powell's irrepressible straight man predated Hawks's similar set-up in *Bringing Up Baby* (1938). Both films share a natural, improvisational quality and sense of camaraderie among the actors. This quality forms the core of the more dramatic *Stage Door*, an ensemble piece in which La Cava proves himself as adept at directing women as George Cukor. Indeed, with this film La Cava helped revive the career of Katharine Hepburn, arguably Cukor's favorite leading lady. Sadly, despite the success of his early work, La Cava's heavy drinking and his producers' frustration over his unconventional working habits—he often worked without a script—caused his career to flounder in the 1940s. However, he still managed to finish three more movies before his death in 1952. **GC**

Top Takes...

One Touch of Venus 1948
Living in a Big Way 1947
Unfinished Business 1941
Stage Door 1937 ☆
My Man Godfrey 1936 ☆
Private Worlds 1935
Gabriel Over the White House 1933
Bed of Roses 1933
The Half Naked Truth 1932
The Age of Consent 1932
Feel My Pulse 1928
Running Wild 1927
So's Your Old Man 1926
Restless Wives 1924
In Oil 1920
Der Captain's Magic Act 1916

"We started off on the wrong foot. Let's stay that way."

—Jean Maidland, *Stage Door*

FRANK BORZAGE

Born: Frank Borzage, April 23, 1893 (Salt Lake City, Utah, U.S.); died 1962 (Hollywood, California, U.S.).

Directing style: Emotionally intense, beautiful romances; use of soft focus and lighting to emphasize the emotional life of characters; graceful camerawork.

Beginning as an actor, often as a heavy, Frank Borzage became a director in 1913. His early movies were often Westerns or thrillers and only in the 1920s did he establish the style and themes that were to make him one of Hollywood's most successful directors and the maestro of the romance, complete with voluptuous imagery verging on the sentimental.

Seventh Heaven (1927), for which Borzage won the first ever Academy Award for Best Director, is entirely typical of his oeuvre. It is a lyrical love story in which Jane Gaynor and Charles Farrell overcome seemingly impossible odds, set against the backdrop of World War I. The heightened romanticism of Borzage's subject matter is enhanced by his love of soft focus and graceful camerawork. Gaynor and Farrell worked together for Borzage on two further occasions, starring in the tender love stories *Street Angel* (1928) and *Lucky Star* (1929). *A Farewell to Arms* (1932) was based on Ernest Hemingway's tragic love story set in Italy during World War I, and starred Gary Cooper and Helen Hayes; *Man's Castle* (1933), a tale of love blighted by the despair of the Depression, starring Spencer Tracy and Loretta Young, is equally affecting.

In *Desire* (1936), Borzage showed he could direct with a lighter touch; the film is a poignant romantic comedy with Marlene Dietrich as a glamorous jewel thief pitted against Cooper. *History Is Made at Night* (1937)— an archetypal Borzage title—conjures some irresistible romance from a story about a divorcée pursued by her jealous ex-husband. *The Mortal Storm* (1940), starring Margaret Sullavan and James Stewart, proved Borzage's ability to deal with sterner stuff, in a movie about the effect on an ordinary German family of the Nazi ascent to power. **EB**

Top Takes…

L'Atlantide 1961 (*Journey Beneath the Desert*)
The Big Fisherman 1959
China Doll 1958
Moonrise 1948
That's My Man 1947
Magnificent Doll 1946
The Spanish Main 1945
The Mortal Storm 1940
History Is Made at Night 1937
Desire 1936
Man's Castle 1933
A Farewell to Arms 1932
Bad Girl 1931 ★
Lucky Star 1929
Street Angel 1928
Seventh Heaven 1927 ★

"Make the audience sentimental instead of the player. Make the audience act."

ALEXANDER KORDA

Born: Sándor László Kellner, September 16, 1893 (Pusztatúrpásztó, Hungary); died 1956 (London, England).

Directing style: Legendary founder of the British film industry; inspirational producer; director of entertaining, patriotic, imperial epics and historical films.

Top Takes...

An Ideal Husband 1947
Perfect Strangers 1945
That Hamilton Woman 1941
The Thief of Baghdad 1940
Rembrandt 1936
The Private Life of Don Juan 1934
The Girl from Maxim's 1933
The Private Life of Henry VIII 1933
Wedding Rehearsal 1932
Service for Ladies 1932
Lilies of the Field 1930
The Private Life of Helen of Troy 1927
The Stolen Bride 1927
Az Aranyember 1918 (*Man of Gold*)
Orhaz a Karpatokban 1914

Sir Alexander Korda was a journalist and critic before beginning his career in the movies directing *Orhaz a Karpatokban* (1914). He went on to become the premier director in his native Hungary before political instability forced him to flee via Germany, France, and Austria to the United States. There, in the late 1920s, he became closely associated with United Artists. Although his earliest films date to the mid-1910s in his native Hungary, his first Hollywood movie, *The Stolen Bride* (1927), is generally considered his career's foundation. More than a dozen films followed including *The Private Life of Helen of Troy* (1927) and *Lilies of the Field* (1930), before *Service for Ladies* (1932) marked a new point in Korda's career.

Along with a group of young Hungarians, including his younger brothers, Zoltán Korda, a film director, and Vincent Korda, an art director, Korda relocated to London where he founded the influential studio London Films, which eventually became a part of the Rank Organisation. There he earned an Academy Award nomination for Best Picture for *The Private Life of Henry VIII* (1933), and helped put the British film industry on the U.S. map. Increasingly a businessman, Korda's work as director tapered off, aside from highlights such as *The Private Life of Don Juan* (1934). Yet over the last twenty years of his life he produced dozens of pictures that have continued to shape the British film industry, including *The Thief of Bagdad* (1940), *Anna Karenina* (1948), and *The Third Man* (1949). In 1942 Korda was knighted by King George VI, the first film producer to be so honored. He died in London in 1956, and the British Academy of Film and Television Arts thereafter named its Outstanding British Film of the Year award "The Alexander Korda Award." **GCQ**

> "It's not enough to be Hungarian; you must have talent too."

JOHN FORD

Born: John Martin Feeney, February 1, 1894 (Cape Elizabeth, Maine, U.S.); died 1973 (Palm Desert, California, U.S.).

Directing style: Titan maker of Westerns and nostalgic historical dramas; simple shots; heroic characters; cinematic painter of the U.S. landscape; poetic realism.

John Ford was a consummate professional, largely indifferent to the critical acclaim he began to receive late in his career. Critics have celebrated Ford for his intense pictorialism—not just of the beautiful landscapes his films made characteristic through evocative reuse (notably Arizona's Monument Valley)—but also of grouped human figures, especially posed statically and iconically. Also much praised has been Ford's ability to communicate through images rather than relying on the script, which he insisted be reduced to a bare minimum.

Working within a system where he sometimes had little choice about projects, Ford was usually able to make something interesting out of bad scripts and poorly chosen casts. Relatively weak films, such as *Mary of Scotland* (1936), do not manifest the personality prized by auteurist critics, but they are competently mounted entertainment.

At his best, Ford made some of the most memorable films Hollywood ever released. *Young Mr. Lincoln* (1939) shows Ford's sense of visual beauty at its most impressive, transforming a somewhat pedestrian script into a memorable hagiography.

Top Takes...

Cheyenne Autumn 1964
The Man Who Shot Liberty Valance 1962
Two Rode Together 1961
Sergeant Rutledge 1960
The Horse Soldiers 1959
The Searchers 1956
Mister Roberts 1955
The Quiet Man 1952 ★
Rio Grande 1950
She Wore a Yellow Ribbon 1949
Fort Apache 1948
The Fugitive 1947
My Darling Clementine 1946
They Were Expendable 1945
The Battle of Midway 1942
How Green Was My Valley 1941 ★
The Long Voyage Home 1940
The Grapes of Wrath 1940 ★
Young Mr. Lincoln 1939
Stagecoach 1939 ☆
Wee Willie Winkie 1937
Mary of Scotland 1936
The Informer 1935 ★
The Lost Patrol 1934
The Tornado 1917

LEFT: James Stewart, Ford, and John Wayne on the set of *Liberty Valance*.

Filming a Classic

The Grapes of Wrath, the classic novel by John Steinbeck, is set in the United States during the Great Depression, and focuses on the members of a poor family forced by drought and destitution to leave their home. The Dust Bowl was the result of a series of dust storms in the central United States and Canada from 1931 to 1939, brought about by the mechanization of agriculture.

- The film was based on the novel by John Steinbeck, published in 1939 and awarded the Nobel Prize for Literature in 1962.
- Darryl F. Zanuck paid $100,000 for the rights to the novel (a huge amount of money at the time). Steinbeck insisted that the material be shown reverence and the project treated responsibly.
- The budget for the movie was $750,000.
- Henry Fonda agreed reluctantly to a seven-year, eight-picture contract with Twentieth Century Fox studios when the part of Tom Joad in *The Grapes of Wrath* was offered to him.
- *The Grapes of Wrath* was shot in just seven weeks.
- Darryl F. Zanuck was allowed by John Ford to supervise the editing of the film.
- Makeup and perfume were banned from the set of *The Grapes of Wrath* as they were considered inappropriate to the theme of the movie.

Stagecoach (1939) resurrected the Western from B-programmer status. The movie provided a memorable gallery of stereotypes and transformed John Wayne's good/bad guy into a national myth that Ford exploited in a series of other Westerns, such as *Rio Grande* (1950), before deconstructing the myth in both *The Searchers* (1956) and *The Man Who Shot Liberty Valance* (1962), both of which expose the shallowness and, perhaps, the pathology of the loner who refuses civilized life.

Before the genre revisionists of the post-studio era, Ford had already explored the Western's ideological blind spots and exclusions. *Sergeant Rutledge* (1960) treats racism, whereas *Cheyenne Autumn* (1964) takes the viewpoint of Native Americans pushed to desperation by the threat of extinction. Ford's work in the genre, however, tends to lack the moral subtlety of the 1950s adult Western at its best.

Ford's Westerns generally derive their force and vigor from the exploitation of stereotypes. *Liberty Valance* deconstructs the myth of the good/bad guy by both endorsing it and following its tragic logic to conclusion. But by never showing the physical pain outlaw violence causes others to endure, Ford fails to question its legitimacy.

Patriotism, Poverty, and Tradition

An unquestioning patriotism, espoused by men with stiff upper lips, characterizes his war films as well, productions whose convincing realism owes something to Ford's own experiences as a combat filmmaker. *They Were Expendable* (1945) traces the fates of Patrol Torpedo boat crews asked to slow the tide of Japanese advance in the Philippines without hope of reinforcement or rescue. It is an unforgettable hymn to bravery, its understated performances indirectly evocative of deep emotion. Set in the U.S. Civil War, *The Horse Soldiers* (1959) opposes gung-ho cavalry commander Wayne, whose loyalty is to the mission, to his regimental surgeon, who sorrows over the grisly cost of war, but the philosophical debate is scarcely pursued beyond a rough and ready clash of sensibilities, to be resolved, in true Fordian fashion, by a fistfight.

ABOVE: Lobby card for *The Grapes of Wrath*, which won an Oscar for John Ford in 1940.

Ford also had no little success as an adaptor of prestige literary properties, for which carefully designed visuals provided the proper atmosphere. In Ford's screening of John Steinbeck's *The Grapes of Wrath*, the poverty and ruin of the Dust Bowl era is evoked with a canny mixture of real location shooting and carefully dressed sound stages. This exteriorizing technique, with a concomitant de-emphasizing of dialogue, is less successful in *The Fugitive* (1947), based on Graham Greene's *The Power and the Glory*, a novel about the inner spiritual life and the inextricability of good with evil. Best loved of Ford's films, however, were those on Celtic themes, most notably *The Quiet Man* (1952) and *How Green Was My Valley* (1941), both of which effectively evoke family and tradition, village life, and a distrust of modern ways. **BP**

"It is easier to get an actor to be a cowboy than to get a cowboy to be an actor."

KING VIDOR

Born: King Wallis Vidor, February 8, 1894 (Galveston, Texas, U.S.); died 1982 (Paso Robles, California, U.S.).

Directing style: Masterful director of silent dramas and later epic features; superb editing; themes tackling racism and the plight of the poor.

1890s

Top Takes...

Solomon and Sheba 1959
War and Peace 1955 ☆
Lightning Strikes Twice 1951
Beyond the Forest 1949
The Fountainhead 1949
Duel in the Sun 1946
The Citadel 1938 ☆
Stella Dallas 1937
Our Daily Bread 1934
The Champ 1931 ☆
Hallelujah! 1929 ☆
Show People 1928
The Crowd 1928 ☆
The Big Parade 1925
Hurricane in Galveston 1913

The relative obscurity into which King Vidor's name has fallen is as inexplicable as it is undeserved. His career was as long and successful as Cecil B. DeMille's, he was as pioneering as D. W. Griffith, as innovative as Rouben Mamoulian, and like all three he had a sure sense of what went over big at the box office: he made *Hallelujah!* (1929), *The Champ* (1931), *Stella Dallas* (1937), *Duel in the Sun* (1946), and *Solomon and Sheba* (1959).

He started out as a newsreel cameraman and cinema projectionist, before making his debut with *Hurricane in Galveston* (1913). His best films reflect his preoccupation with depicting the experiences of ordinary people in extraordinary situations. *The Big Parade* (1925), the highest grossing movie of the silent era, ambitiously humanized the story of World War I by conveying it subjectively through the eyes of one soldier. This notion was extended in *The Crowd* (1928), a dramatization of a few days in the life of a downtrodden city office worker. Time and again Vidor was advised that the public wanted escapism, not reminders of reality. He was forced to finance *Our Daily Bread* (1934) himself, ironically mirroring the fate of its characters: victims of the Depression who pull together to manage an abandoned farm. It ends with an amazing sequence of choreographed toil: the workers divert a stream through a hastily constructed ditch to irrigate the crops. Through superb editing and composition, Vidor turns the stuff of documentary realism into compelling, magnificent, poetic cinema.

"In Hollywood, the cameraman lights the star. In Europe, he lights the set."

In the 1950s, only the epic genre was big enough for his reputation. So unfashionable are such films today, it is almost heretical to concede that *War and Peace* (1955) is majestic filmmaking, and as engaging in its quiet verses as it is vivid in its action choruses. But it is. **MC**

JOSEF von STERNBERG

Born: Jonas Sternberg, May 29, 1894 (Vienna, Austria); died 1969 (Hollywood, California, U.S.).

Directing style: Sumptuous, psychosexual dramas; legendary collaboration with actress Marlene Dietrich; striking use of light and shadow; long takes.

Not long ago, any serious list of the greatest filmmakers would have included Josef von Sternberg. In recent years, however, his ornate style has fallen out of favor. More is the pity, because von Sternberg was a true original, a visual stylist without peer, and one of cinema's great obsessives. He made his name with the independently produced *The Salvation Hunters* (1925), and his fortune with the first true gangster film *Underworld* (1927). None of his surviving silents are without interest—*The Last Command* (1928) is brilliant—and his first talkie, *Thunderbolt* (1929), shows an immediate grasp of how to use sound. But it was with *Der Blaue Engel* (1930) (*The Blue Angel*) that von Sternberg came into his own, not least because of meeting legendary screen siren Marlene Dietrich.

He made six more films with Dietrich, obsessing over his star and their relationship. Those six films—*Morocco* (1930), *Dishonored* (1931), *Shanghai Express* (1932), *Blonde Venus* (1932), *The Scarlet Empress* (1934), and *The Devil Is a Woman* (1935)—are among the most remarkable ever made. The best of them, *Shanghai Express*, is a stunning foray into pure design and stylized writing that transcends its form to become a moving drama of love and faith without losing its cynical psychosexual edge. Nearly as good is the baroque *The Scarlet Empress*, probably the most style-driven movie of the 1930s.

Von Sternberg's post-Dietrich work was often interesting, and *The Shanghai Gesture* (1941) was especially striking visually, with its glamorous casino and spinning roulette wheels, as von Sternberg showed the dangers of gambling addiction. But nothing else ever scaled the heights of his richest and most obsessive period, and his name will remain ever linked with that of Dietrich. **KH**

Top Takes...

Macao 1952
The Shanghai Gesture 1941
Sergeant Madden 1939
The Devil Is a Woman 1935
The Scarlet Empress 1934
Blonde Venus 1932
Shanghai Express 1932 ☆
Dishonored 1931
Morocco 1930 ☆
Der Blaue Engel 1930 (*The Blue Angel*)
Thunderbolt 1929
The Docks of New York 1928
The Last Command 1928
Underworld 1927
A Woman of the Sea 1926
The Salvation Hunters 1925

"You'd better go now. I'm … beginning to like you."
—Amy Jolly, *Morocco*

ABRAM ROOM

Born: Abram Room, June 28, 1894 (Vilnius, Lithuania); died 1976 (Moscow, Russia).

Directing style: Daring Russian director of romantic melodramas; innovative visuals; roving camerawork; sexual frankness; critiques of totalitarian society; satirical humor; naturalistic acting.

Top Takes…

Tsvety zapozdalye 1969 (*Belated Flowers*)
Granatovyy braslet 1964 (*The Garnet Bracelet*)
Shkola zloslovya 1952 (*The School of Scandal*)
Nashestviye 1945 (*The Invasion*)
Strogiy yunosha 1934 (*A Severe Young Man*)
Plan velikikh rabot 1930 (*Plan for Great Works*)
Tretya meshchanskaya 1927 (*Bed and Sofa*)
Bukhta smerti 1926 (*The Bay of Death*)
Predatel 1926 (*The Traitor*)

Abram Room's career path to becoming a film director was a scattered one that saw him take in dentistry, journalism, and amateur dramatics. After studying under director Lev Kuleshov at film school he finally made his debut with the silent drama *Predatel* (1926) (*The Traitor*), and various documentaries.

It was a few years before he directed the movie that made him notorious, the psychological drama *Tretya meshchanskaya* (1927) (*Bed and Sofa*). The tale of a construction worker, Kolia, who invites his unemployed friend Volodia to stay with him and his wife Liuda at his cramped apartment during a Moscow housing shortage, soon develops into a complicated romance as Volodia finds himself in Liuda's bed. Surprisingly the husband accepts this, and the two men then share Liuda's sexual favors.

Risqué for its time in its depiction of a *ménage à trois*, *Bed and Sofa* was refused a public screening in Britain. The film won massive popularity among Russian audiences for its humor, naturalistic handling of the bleak situation that leads to the trio's bed-hopping, and innovative roving camerawork, but it was Room's sensitive portrayal of his female character which made the movie a hit, as she opts for a new life liberated from her lovers and with her unborn child. Room went on to make the Soviet Union's first sound film, *Plan velikikh rabot* (1930) (*Plan for Great Works*), but fell into trouble with *Strogiy yunosha* (1934) (*A Severe Young Man*). Banned by the Soviet authorities because it tackled themes of equality, Room's subsequent output was sporadic, although he had a renaissance of sorts with his adaptation of an Anton Chekov novel, *Tsvety zapozdalye* (1969) (*Belated Flowers*), which again deals with forbidden love. But he will best be remembered for his early frank portrayal of the sexual revolution. **CK**

"The conservativism of *Belated Flowers* has the effect of being spectacular today."—*New York Times*

1890s

ALEKSANDR DOVZHENKO

Born: Aleksandr Petrovich Dovzhenko, September 11, 1894 (Sosnitsa, Chernihiv, Ukraine); died 1956 (Moscow, Russia).

Directing style: Realist director of poetic, meditative dramas; use of montage; visually stunning landscapes used as metaphor; often Ukranian folk culture themes.

Unquestionably one of the giants of early Soviet cinema, Aleksandr Dovzhenko was not associated with the theoretical school of Lev Kuleshov and Sergei Eisenstein, and his films, while no less radical or political, were appreciably more personal.

In 1926, aged thirty-two, he abandoned his former life as a cartoonist and struggling painter to seek work at the VUFKU film studios in Odessa. A forceful, charismatic personality and restless creativity ensured that within a few months he was writing and directing his own features.

With his second film, *Zvenigora* (1928), Dovzhenko dazzled and bewildered his peers, and was immediately recognized as a major new talent. *Zvenigora* was a complex, lyrical picture drawing upon 1,000 years of folklore to tell its revolutionary parable; it was followed by *Arsenal* (1928), a more overtly political work whose radical techniques prefigure those of the French New Wave. Two years later, he made *Zemlya* (1930) (*Earth*); perhaps his finest achievement, the film is now regarded as an all-time classic of world cinema. Beautifully shot by Daniil Demutsky, the plot, concerning the impact of collectivization on a small farming community, is incidental to Dovzhenko's poetic meditation on the Ukrainian landscape and its natural cycles of fertility and decay.

A committed communist, Dovzhenko's determinedly naturalistic approach was nevertheless at odds with the official aesthetic of socialist realism in the 1930s. After the troubled production of *Shchors* (1939) (*Shors*), undertaken at Josef Stalin's "suggestion," he completed only one more feature film. After Dovzhenko's death in 1956, many of his unfinished projects were completed by his wife, Yuliya Solntseva, eponymous star of *Aelita* (1924), and a distinguished director in her own right. **RB**

Top Takes...

Shchors 1939 (*Shors*)
Ivan 1932
Zemlya 1930 (*Earth*)
Arsenal 1928
Zvenigora 1928

"[*Zvenigora* was] in 2,000 meters of film, a whole millennium."

JEAN RENOIR

Born: Jean Renoir, September 15, 1894 (Paris, France); died 1979 (Los Angeles, California, U.S.).

Directing style: Exploration of class conflict, and the relationship between man and nature; intricate characterization; elegant realism; painterly use of vivid color.

Top Takes...

Le petit théâtre de Jean Renoir 1970
Le caporal épinglé 1962 (The Elusive Corporal)
Elena et les hommes 1956 (Elena and Her Men)
French Cancan 1954
Le carosse d'or 1953 (The Golden Coach)
The Woman on the Beach 1947
The Diary of a Chambermaid 1946
The Southerner 1945 ☆
Swamp Water 1941
La règle du jeu 1939 (The Rules of the Game)
La grande illusion 1937 (The Grand Illusion)
La vie est à nous 1936 (The People of France)
Le crime de Monsieur Lange 1936
   (The Crime of Monsieur Lange)
Partie de campagne 1936
   (A Day in the Country)
Toni 1935
Madame Bovary 1933
Boudu, sauvé des eaux 1932
   (Boudu Saved from Drowning)
La chienne 1931 (Isn't Life a Bitch?)
On purge bébé 1931
Nana 1926
La fille de l'eau 1925 (Whirlpool of Fate)
Une vie sans joie 1924 (Backbiters)

RIGHT: Werner Krauss, Catherine Hessling,
Jean Angelo, and Renoir on the set of Nana.

The son of Impressionist master Pierre-Auguste Renoir, Jean Renoir had big shoes to fill. His father's positive, poetic realism became a point of reference for Renoir, who also inherited his father's sympathetic attitude toward the commoner.

Renoir's debut, Une vie sans joie (1924) (Backbiters), displayed the core themes of his oeuvre: a struggle between masters and servants, and a clear contempt for the hypocrisy of the leisure class. His early career served the ambitions of his wife, Catherine Hessling, whom he directed in several silent films, such as La fille de l'eau (1925) (Whirlpool of Fate) and Nana (1926).

In the early 1930s, Renoir and Hessling divorced, and the separation seemed to liberate Renoir from his father's legacy. He crafted a raw realism, replacing studio interiors with outdoor locations, unpolished but undeniably optimistic. With films such as Boudu, sauvé des eaux (1932) (Boudu Saved from Drowning), he found his mature voice, displaying a radical novelty particularly visible in the anarchist attitude of Boudu, whose vagabond's rebellion against society's petty rules upsets even the household of the poor antiquarian who rescued him from drowning. Madame Bovary (1933) and Toni (1935) further

highlighted Renoir's sympathy for outcasts and the working class, and his denunciation of the bourgeoisie.

In the mid-1930s, with crucial elections ahead, Renoir put his talents to the service of the left-wing Popular Front of France with intelligent, committed films such as *Le crime de Monsieur Lange* (1936) (*The Crime of Monsieur Lange*) and *La vie est à nous* (1936) (*The People of France*). Still, Renoir was better when let off the leash, as in the largely improvised countryside romance *Partie de campagne* (1936) (*A Day in the Country*), a sweet, innocent, miniature masterpiece, and the film closest in spirit to his father's paintings. Renoir reached his zenith with the humanist antiwar epic *La grande illusion* (1937) (*The Grand Illusion*), which set the standard for all prison camp escape films; and *La règle du jeu* (1939) (*The Rules of the Game*), a

ABOVE: Renoir adjusts the camera over Françoise Arnoul on the set of *French Cancan*.

"The Western is always the same, which gives the director tremendous freedom."

Renoir in Hollywood

Jean Renoir, with his second wife Dido, fled to the United States in May 1940, following the German occupation of France. He became a naturalized U.S. citizen in 1946 and remained there until 1951, when he traveled to India to make *The River*, his first movie in color. Renoir also revisited his native France to make *The Golden Coach* in 1952. Here are some of his Hollywood highlights:

- *Swamp Water* (1941): a tale of injustice and vengeance, set in America's Deep South and starring Walter Brennan, Walter Huston, Anne Baxter, and Dana Andrews.
- *This Land is Mine* (1943): an anti-Nazi film set in German-occupied France, starring Maureen O'Hara and Charles Laughton. Regarded as one of the best films ever produced by RKO Pictures.
- *The Southerner* (1945): a film about a poor cotton-picking Texas family. Often regarded as Renoir's best work in the United States, for which he was nominated for an Academy Award. Starring Zachary Scott and Betty Field.
- *The Diary of a Chambermaid* (1946): an adaptation of a novel by the French novelist Octave Mirbeau, *Le Journal d'une Femme de Chambre*, starring Paulette Goddard and Burgess Meredith.
- *The Woman on the Beach* (1947): Joan Bennett, Robert Ryan, and Charles Bickford star in a brooding love triangle.

metaphor about class conflict during a weekend hunting party at a stately mansion. The latter, his most personal film, is also his most complex. Regularly voted among the best films ever made, its depiction of amoral, uncaring nobility was packed with subtle, venomous humor and cruelty. As a whole, Renoir's films of the 1930s are a model for all realist cinema, influencing contemporaries such as William Wyler and Orson Welles, as well as Italy's postwar neorealists such as Luchino Visconti.

Bringing realism to Hollywood

At the outbreak of war, Renoir fled to Hollywood, where he enjoyed a mixed reception. His U.S. movies *Swamp Water* (1941) and *The Southerner* (1945) were unique in transferring Renoir's realism and attitude to the warm, moist environments of the Deep South—the United States's most class-stifled region. But it took years for critics to appreciate this, and by then Renoir had returned to France, where, embracing color cinema, his odd but compelling *La carosse d'or* (1953) (*The Golden Coach*) and the popular *French Cancan* (1954) quickly reinstated him to the French canon.

By the 1960s, Renoir had withdrawn from filming. Instead, he enjoyed the absolute adoration of a new wave of French directors, and settled into his role as film history's living legend—a well-deserved retirement for a man the French had come to know as "Le Patron." **EM**

RIGHT: A portly Renoir directs Ingrid Bergman on the set of *Elena and Her Men*.

MARIO CAMERINI

Born: Mario Camerini, February 6, 1895 (Rome, Italy); died 1981 (Gardone Riviera, Trentino-Alto Adige, Italy).

Directing style: Fast-paced comedies of manners and mistaken identity; lighthearted sentimental themes; impeccable screenplays; naturalistic characterizations.

After studying law and serving in World War I as a light infantry officer, Mario Camerini entered the film industry in 1920 working for his cousin, director Augusto Genina, before later directing his own projects at Rome's Cines studios. His effect on Italian cinema was profound, and by the 1930s Camerini was considered one of Italy's most important directors.

In a career straddling both the silent and the sound eras, notable success came with films such as *Gli uomini, che mascalzoni!* (1932) (*What Scoundrels Men Are!*), a commercial triumph that initiated a more naturalistic form of Italian cinema. Then came what has become known as the "*Telefoni Bianchi*" or "White Telephones" period of Italian cinema, which lasted from the late 1930s to the early 1940s, and saw a euphoric fascist Italy celebrating its imperial power. The making of lighthearted comedies was encouraged; intellectual films with a political slant were not. Camerini's frequent casting of future director Vittorio De Sica was typified in *Darò un milione* (1936) (*I'll Give a Million*) and *Il Signor Max* (1937) (*Mister Max*), both of which paired the growing matinée idol with Camerini's wife Assia Noris. The two films exemplified Camerini's oeuvre: comedies of manners and mistaken identity, often pivoting on interclass relations that seemed to indicate a deeper social critique.

But the tide was against him: after the war his style was seen as too lightweight, an escapist fantasy at a time when the stark realities of just how grim life could be were in vogue with neorealism. As with many of his contemporaries, Camerini was never able to shake off the dust that settled on his shoulders after working during the fascist period, and he never again achieved the public acclaim of his heyday. **RH**

Top Takes…

Don Camillo e i giovani d'oggi 1972
Delitto quasi perfetto 1966
 (*The Imperfect Murder*)
Crimen 1961 (*. . . And Suddenly It's Murder!*)
La bella mugnaia 1955 (*The Miller's Wife*)
Molti sogni per le strade 1948
 (*The Street Has Many Dreams*)
Una storia d'amore 1942 (*Love Story*)
I grandi magazzini 1939 (*Department Store*)
Il Signor Max 1937 (*Mister Max*)
Darò un milione 1936 (*I'll give a Million*)
Come le foglie 1934 (*Like the Leaves*)
Gli uomini, che mascalzoni! 1932
 (*What Scoundrels Men Are!*)
La casa dei pulcini 1924 (*The House of Pulcini*)
Walli 1923

"Italian comedy is seldom subtle, but it can be amusing."
—*New York Times*

MARCEL PAGNOL

Born: Marcel Pagnol, February 28, 1895 (Aubagne, Bouches-du-Rhône, Provence-Alpes-Côte d'Azur, France); died 1974 (Paris, France).

Directing style: Innovative French maker of nostalgic, poetic dramas and romances; strong dialogue; naturalistic settings; themes of everyday life.

Top Takes…

Les lettres de mon moulin 1954
  (*Letters from My Windmill*)
Manon des Sources 1953 (*Manon of the Spring*)
Topaze 1951
La belle meunière 1948 (*The Pretty Miller Girl*)
La prière aux étoiles 1941
La fille du puisatier 1940
  (*The Well-Digger's Daughter*)
La femme du boulanger 1938 (*The Baker's Wife*)
Le Schpountz 1938 (*Heartbeat*)
Regain 1937
César 1936
Cigalon 1935
Merlusse 1935
Angèle 1934
Marius 1931

Marcel Pagnol was born in the southern region of France near Marseille in 1895. The son of a schoolteacher and a seamstress, he displayed a keen intelligence at a very young age. When most children were playing with toys, Pagnol was learning how to read, much to the amazement of his parents. At the age of fifteen, Pagnol wrote his first play. Following in his father's professional footsteps, he went on to become a secondary school English teacher. However, he ended this profession upon his move to Paris, and instead devoted his life to the art of playwriting. This led to the completion of his first play, *Les merchands de gloire* (1924) (*Merchants of Glory*). He later wrote *Marius* (1929) for the stage, a play that would also be turned into Pagnol's first film in 1931. Pagnol was quick to see the potential of the medium of film. He set up his own studio to make talkies and released his films through Gaumont.

Marius tells the story of César Olivier, a Marseille bar owner whose son grapples with conflicting desires involving his longtime love and untamed goals. Due to the huge success of the film, his "Marseille Trilogy" developed, with *Fanny* (1932), which he wrote, and *César* (1936), which he also directed. These became his best-known films and were later adapted into the musical, *Fanny* (1955). Pagnol continued to write plays, novels, and screenplays throughout his career. He adapted his two-part novel of Provençal life into a film, *Manon des Sources* (1953) (*Manon of the Spring*), which was later remade by director Claude Berri into two movies, *Jean de Florette* (1986) and *Manon des Sources* (1986) (*Manon of the Spring*). In 1947 Pagnol became the first filmmaker to be accepted into the renowned Académie Française. He became the president of the jury at the Cannes Film Festival in 1955. **ES**

"You know, Marius, a woman's honor is like a match. You can only use it once."—César, *Fanny*

LEWIS MILESTONE

Born: Lev Milstein, September 30, 1895 (Chisinau, Moldova); died 1980
(Los Angeles, California, U.S.).

Directing style: Classic output across a variety of genres; master of epic battle
sequences; fast lateral tracking shots; use of close-ups to add emotional appeal.

Lewis Milestone could be considered exceptionally lucky—or
unusually unlucky. Early in his career he directed *All Quiet on
the Western Front* (1930), which was instantly hailed as a classic,
and is still highly regarded. On the strength of that film, one
might argue, he rarely lacked work, despite a not particularly
distinguished output. A more sympathetic view might be that
he peaked too soon and spent the rest of his career dogged by
expectations of repeating his early triumph.

The battle scenes in *All Quiet on the Western Front* gave
Milestone ample scope for the fast lateral tracking shots that
became his stock in trade. He put them to equally effective use
in *The Front Page* (1931), the first version of Ben Hecht and
Charles MacArthur's often filmed newsroom comedy drama,
proving that new-fangled sound technology did not have to
shackle the camera. Of his other 1930s movies, only *The General
Died at Dawn* (1936) and the John Steinbeck adaptation *Of
Mice and Men* (1939) stand out from the surrounding dross.

With the outbreak of war, Milestone could return to the
genre that made his name. *The North Star* (1943) had energy to
spare, but its pro-Soviet sentiments would later become an
embarrassment to all concerned. Yet *A Walk in the Sun* (1945)
stands beside *All Quiet on the Western
Front* for its compassion for the ordinary
soldier and absence of patriotic bombast,
unlike his next war film, the gung ho *Halls
of Montezuma* (1950)—although Milestone
was under pressure at this time from the
communist-haters in both Washington
and Hollywood. Milestone's final assignment was *Mutiny on the
Bounty* (1962), on which he capitulated in the face of Marlon
Brando's towering ego. It was a dispiriting end to a career that
had shown such early promise. **PK**

Top Takes...

Mutiny on the Bounty 1962
Ocean's Eleven 1960
Les Misérables 1952
Halls of Montezuma 1950
The Red Pony 1949
A Walk in the Sun 1945
The Purple Heart 1944
The North Star 1943
Edge of Darkness 1943
Of Mice and Men 1939
The General Died at Dawn 1936
Anything Goes 1936
Paris in Spring 1935
The Front Page 1931 ☆
All Quiet on the Western Front 1930 ★
Two Arabian Knights 1927 ★

"We try not to be killed, but
sometimes we are. That's all."

—Paul Bäumer, *All Quiet on the Western Front*

BUSTER KEATON

Born: Joseph Francis Keaton Jr., October 4, 1895 (Piqua, Kansas, U.S.); died 1966 (Los Angeles, California, U.S.).

Directing style: Innovative comedian; sophisticated humor; creative use of stunts and gadgets for comedic effect; superb writing; roughhouse spontaneity.

Top Takes…

RIGHT: Buster Keaton, Sybil Sealy, and Roscoe "Fatty" Arbuckle.

Born Joseph Keaton Jr., at age three he fell headfirst down a flight of stairs and emerged happy and unscathed. Illusionist Harry Houdini, a Keaton family friend, wowed, "What a buster your kid took!"—and a legend was born. Buster Keaton was a naturally gifted comedian, an acrobat with the mind of an inventor—or was he an engineer with the body of a gymnast? At the dawn of movies, when special effects were in their infancy, he created effects that even now startle audiences jaded by computer-generated imagery.

At the age of twenty-one, Keaton turned down the chance of lucrative Broadway stardom to join instead the rowdy world of movie comedy. Roscoe "Fatty" Arbuckle, one of Hollywood's most gifted comedians, took Buster under his wing and taught him the mechanics of filmmaking. Alongside Arbuckle, Keaton rocketed to fame, before breaking solo for his own comedies, most of them artworks beyond compare.

Keaton brought a cynical, unromantic sensibility, a surrealist's eye for potent imagery and a small boy's fascination with gadgets to bear on the business of making people laugh. From two-reel classics such as *One Week* (1920) to grandiose

cinematic masterpieces such as *The General* (1927), Keaton made films that were as awe-inspiring as they were funny.

The coming of sound was disastrous for Keaton. He lost control of his work, and was demoted to a mere actor in the machinery of MGM's bloated studio factory. Personal problems collided with professional frustration, and sent him to the bottle. Although this period is largely written off, some of his talkie films are underrated gems in their own right. His alcoholism cost him a place in Hollywood's top echelons, but he continued to churn out gags in low-budget shorts through the late 1930s and early 1940s, a trouper to the last.

In the 1950s, Keaton's genius was rediscovered by a new generation of fans, his greatest accomplishments from the silent era spilling once again on to the screen. In 1959 he earned an Honorary Academy Award for his lifetime's contribution to movie culture. **DK**

ABOVE: Keaton, Kathryn McGuire, and a fetching tiger skin rug in *The Navigator*.

Adrift on *The Navigator*

Directed by Donald Crisp and Buster Keaton, *The Navigator* (1924) was inspired by Buster Keaton's purchase of a large passenger ship, *The Burford*, which was about to be scrapped.

- *The Burford* had been used in the early part of the century to deport suspected Bolsheviks from the United States.

- The underwater scenes of Keaton carrying out repairs to the ship were filmed in Lake Tahoe.

- Codirector Donald Crisp played a cameo role as the face of the captain at the porthole.

BEN SHARPSTEEN

Born: Ben Sharpsteen, November 4, 1895 (Tacoma, Washington, U.S.); died 1980 (Sonoma County, California, U.S.).

Directing style: Groundbreaking feature-length musical animated films, and live action children's movies; touching and amusing content.

Top Takes...

Mickey Mouse Disco 1980
Mysteries of the Deep 1959
Lapland 1957
Out of the Frying Pan Into the Firing Line 1942
Dumbo 1941
Fantasia 1940
Pinocchio 1940
Mickey's Trailer 1938
Hawaiian Holiday 1937
Moose Hunters 1937
Donald and Pluto 1936
Mickey's Circus 1936
Moving Day 1936
Orphan's Picnic 1936
Two-Gun Mickey 1934
The Village Blacksmith 1920

"Now, remember, Pinocchio, be a good boy."

—The Blue Fairy, *Pinocchio*

Walt Disney described Ben Sharpsteen as having "played a very important part" in the development of the Disney organization. Indeed, Sharpsteen made significant contributions to many of the company's animated shorts and to several of its most venerated and well-loved feature-length classics.

Born in Tacoma, Washington, Sharpsteen studied agriculture at the University of California, and served with the U.S. Marines in World War I. A talented artist, soon after the war he became involved in animation, working on early animated series such as *Happy Hooligan* at the Hearst International Film Service. Recommended by a mutual friend, he joined the Walt Disney Studios in 1929. Sharpsteen animated on 97 Mickey Mouse cartoons, as well as the *Silly Symphonies* series, and worked closely with Walt Disney himself on many levels of production.

In the 1930s, Sharpsteen began directing animated shorts for the studio, such as *Two-Gun Mickey* (1934), *Moving Day* (1936), which contains a famous and acclaimed sequence where Goofy wrestles with a piano, and *Donald and Pluto* (1936). He was sequence director on Disney's landmark first full-length feature, *Snow White and the Seven Dwarfs* (1937), and supervising codirector on *Pinocchio* (1940). He went on to codirect the esteemed and highly innovative *Fantasia* (1940) and the touching and amusing *Dumbo* (1941), which, as well as being critically acclaimed, was a huge commercial success, taking in more at the box office on original release than the original grosses of *Pinocchio* and *Fantasia* combined. In later years Sharpsteen concentrated on production, and produced almost all of Disney's live-action *True-Life Adventures* films, eight of which received Oscars. He retired in 1962, after 33 years with the company. **KM**

BUSBY BERKELEY

Born: William Berkeley Enos, November 29, 1895 (Los Angeles, California, U.S.);
died 1976 (Palm Springs, California, U.S.).

Directing style: Innovative choreographer of mesmerizing chorus girl routines;
masterful use of dizzying overhead shots; geometric, kaleidoscope imagery.

A legendary choreographer and director of Hollywood's Golden Age, Busby Berkeley redefined the musical sequence, deploying masses of long-stemmed, identically dressed chorines to create intricate geometric patterns. He turned beautiful girls into abstract swirls, subverted scale and perspective with the cheeky facility of a born surrealist, and imagined uniquely cinematic dance numbers whose fearful symmetry could only be appreciated in dizzying overhead shots. Berkeley lacked formal dance training, but his production numbers are so flamboyantly mesmerizing that hardly anyone notices the dearth of actual dancing, excepting solos for bona fide hoofers such as Ruby Keeler, the steel buttercup whose kewpie-doll mugging apparently bewitched moviegoers into ignoring her stumpy legs.

Born in Los Angeles but raised in New York, Berkeley came from a theatrical family. His father died when Berkeley was eight years old, and his mother sent him to boarding school so she could tour. He attended military school and dabbled in acting before enlisting in 1918. In an "isn't it ironic" twist

Top Takes...

Annie Get Your Gun 1950
The Gang's All Here 1943
Girl Crazy 1943
Three Cheers for the Girls 1943
For Me and My Gal 1942
Calling All Girls 1942
Babes on Broadway 1941
Blonde Inspiration 1941
Strike Up the Band 1940
Forty Little Mothers 1940
Babes in Arms 1939
Fast and Furious 1939
They Made Me a Criminal 1939
Comet Over Broadway 1938
Garden of the Moon 1938
Men Are Such Fools 1938
Hollywood Hotel 1937
The Go Getter 1937
Gold Diggers of 1937 1936
Stage Struck 1936
Bright Lights 1935
Gold Diggers of 1935 1935
Dames 1934
She Had to Say Yes 1933

LEFT: Nothing is out of place in this rousing chorus from Berkeley's *Babes in Arms*.

Busby's Best Bits

Busby Berkeley's choreography skills in early U.S. musicals were legendary. In his own words: "In an era of breadlines, depression and wars, I tried to help people get away from all the misery . . . to turn their minds to something else. I wanted to make people happy, if only for an hour."

- Berkeley knew how to use props to good advantage: is there a more famous still from early movie musicals than the double row of chorus girls clinging to man-sized bananas in "The Lady in the Tutti-Fruitti Hat" number from *The Gang's All Here* (1943)?

- He indulged cheerful lewdness in the song "Pettin' in the Park," from *Gold Diggers of 1933* (1933), a lengthy fantasy on a theme of outdoor recreation that includes a bevy of beauties stripping out of their rain-soaked frocks behind a backlit scrim, and donning boyfriend-proof metal swimsuits.

- He tapped the rhythm in everyday movement for *42nd Street*'s (1933) title number, which weaves B-girls, barbers, drunken louts, commuters, and even a living cigar-store Indian into a vigorous street ballet; and for *Footlight Parade*'s "Honeymoon Hotel," synchronizing the activities of staff and guests.

- Berkeley directed Gene Kelly in his first picture, *For Me and My Gal* (1942). Kelly, who choreographed his own numbers, learned a lot from the director.

straight from an old movie, the army taught him to direct. Berkeley staged parades, drill routines, and troop theatricals, and upon returning to civilian life, he renamed himself "Busby" (after stage actress Amy Busby), and threw himself into theater. Directing, producing, and staging dance numbers became his specialty, and a short-lived musical called *Holka Polka* (1925) established him on Broadway and introduced him to veteran showman Florenz Ziegfeld. The movie version of Ziegfeld's *Whoopee!* (1930), in which Berkeley pioneered the geometric, kaleidoscope imagery that became his trademark, introduced Berkeley to Hollywood.

Signature production numbers

The *New York Times* once called Berkeley "the master of scenic prestidigitation," a fit term for the man who made gleaming white grand pianos appear to dance, used mirrors to multiply dozens of girls into hundreds, and grafted lovely ladies on to pieces of scenery. Berkeley exploited the power of numbers: four tapping tootsies is a dance school recital, but 60 bottle-blondes doing the same basic heel-toe, side shuffles and kicks with drill team precision is a show. Especially if they are dressed in gold-coin covered scanties as in "We're in the Money" in *Gold Diggers of 1933* (1933); mincing in pussycat suits as in "Sitting on a Backyard Fence" in *Footlight Parade* (1933); or floating in a pool, smoothly lacing and unlacing their legs like the teeth of a zipper as in "By a Waterfall" in *Footlight Parade*. Berkeley recognized the hypnotic allure of girls arranged in concentric circles, swaying and dipping like underwater plants; or doing the same twist-and-tuck motion in opposite directions, like interlocking cogs in an infernal machine. And he excelled at telling self-contained stories in musical sequences, of which the greatest may be "Lullaby of Broadway" from *Gold Diggers of 1935* (1935), an elegantly chilling, flapper-age cautionary tale that ends with an incautious Broadway baby crowded off a balcony to her death by a predatory pack of Art Deco harpies.

In all, Berkeley contributed dance numbers to at least 40 movie musicals, some of which he also directed. His nonmusical

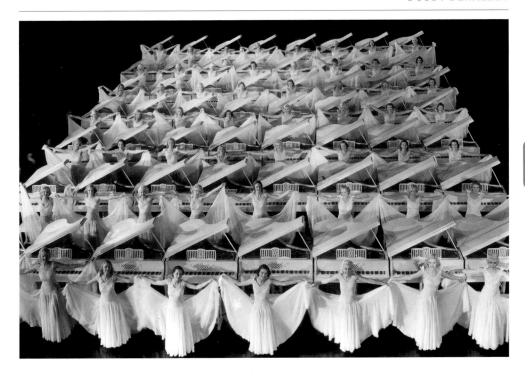

credits included *She Had to Say Yes* (1933), a tough little melodrama about sexual harassment in the workplace, and the John Garfield crime drama *They Made Me a Criminal* (1939). Berkeley's career survived scandal—an alienation of affections suit filed by a Hollywood actress's husband, second-degree murder charges stemming from a drunken car crash in 1935—but not changing public taste; by the early 1960s, lavish Hollywood musicals were passé and Berkeley was largely forgotten. The rise of camp granted him a brief resurgence, and five years before he died, Berkeley directed a Broadway rival of *No, No, Nanette* (1971). Although modern filmmakers occasionally try to parody or pay homage to his signature pieces, none can match Berkeley's ability to whip a gaggle of unruly chorus girls into a conquering army of tapping feet. **MM**

ABOVE: Rows of girls are interspersed with bright white pianos in *Gold Diggers of 1935*.

"Well, we've got all these beautiful girls in the picture, why not let the public see them?"

DZIGA VERTOV

Born: Denis Abramovich Kaufman, January 2, 1896 (Bialystok, Poland); died 1954 (Moscow, Russia).

Directing style: Avant-garde documentaries during the Soviet era; fast-paced editing; multiple exposures; split-screen effects; themes of the Soviet worker.

Top Takes...

Dziga Vertov is now best remembered for *Chelovek s kino-apparatom* (1929) (*Living Russia, or The Man with a Movie Camera*), not so much a documentary as a visual poem that embodies the pulsating excitement unleashed by the Russian Revolution. Made just before the dead weight of Stalinist orthodoxy crushed down on the movement, it represents Soviet cinema's avant-garde in its last, most brilliant phase.

When the revolution broke out, Vertov joined the cinema committee and began working on newsreels. Multitalented, tirelessly enthusiastic, and energetic, he gradually began to introduce more inventive editing techniques, dramatic montage, and specially shot scenes. With his wife and his younger brother Mikhail Kaufman, he formed a group called "Kino-Otis" ("Cinema-Eyes"). They produced 23 issues of *Kino-Pravda* (1922–1925), in which Vertov pushed his techniques of manipulated documentary ever closer to Expressionism.

Enjoying the support of Vladimir Lenin and traveling all over the Soviet Union in specially equipped "agit-trains," Vertov and his team filmed and exhibited as they went. He proceeded to develop his technique in longer films, including *Kinoglaz* (1924) (*Kino-Eye—Life Caught Unawares*), *Shagay, sovet!* (1926) (*Forward, Soviet!*), and *Living Russia, or The Man with a Camera*. With the coming of sound he made audacious use of the new technology in *Entuziazm: Simfoniya Donbassa* (1931) (*Enthusiasm*) and *Tri Pesni o Lenine* (1934) (*Three Songs of Lenin*). But he now found himself subjected to accusations of formalism and his freedom of creation was drastically curtailed. This meant that Vertov's later years were spent editing together Soviet newsreels in accordance with official policy. **PK**

> "[*Tri Pesni o Lenine* is] a work of unusual beauty and emotional exaltation."—*New York Times*

WILLIAM A. WELLMAN

Born: William Augustus Wellman, February 29, 1896 (Brookline, Massachusetts, U.S.); died 1975 (Los Angeles, California, U.S.).

Directing style: Daredevil maestro of flying sequences; master of comedies and macho action movies; innovative use of musical soundtrack.

1890s

William A. Wellman started out as a professional ice hockey player, but in 1917 he left the United States to join the French Foreign Legion where he learned to fly. When the United States entered World War I, Wellman signed up as a fighter pilot and was given the nickname "Wild Bill." It was a sobriquet that persisted through his movie career, given his reputation as a colorful character and ladies' man with a reputation for drinking and brawling. After the war he became a stunt pilot and an actor, before becoming a director in 1920, making Westerns. His big break came when he directed the romantic war drama *Wings* (1927), with its stunning aerial sequences.

In the 1930s, Wellman cemented his reputation with some spectacularly successful films in a variety of genres. *The Public Enemy* (1931) made James Cagney's reputation, with his portrait of a gangster. *Wild Boys of the Road* (1933) was a socially conscious film about the Depression. In contrast, *A Star Is Born* (1937) starred Janet Gaynor and Fredric March in a glossy tale about an actress's rise to fame in Hollywood. *Nothing Sacred* (1937) again starred March, this time teamed with Carole Lombard in a fast-paced comedy. *Beau Geste* (1939), with Gary Cooper, was to become a classic tale of derring-do in the French Foreign Legion. *Roxie Hart* (1942), a smart and cynical comedy starring Ginger Rogers later became the basis for the stage and screen musical *Chicago*.

Wellman turned his hand to anything, but specialized in action films, particularly Westerns such as the antilynching *The Ox-Bow Incident* (1943). He also directed some notably gritty war movies, such as *Story of G.I. Joe* (1945). His last film, *Lafayette Escadrille* (1958), was Wellman's return to the world of World War I fliers, a formative influence on his life. **EB**

Top Takes...

Lafayette Escadrille 1958 (*Hell Bent for Glory*)
Darby's Rangers 1958
Good-bye, My Lady 1956
Blood Alley 1955
The High and the Mighty 1954 ☆
Battleground 1949 ☆
Yellow Sky 1948
Story of G.I. Joe 1945
The Ox-Bow Incident 1943
Roxie Hart 1942
Beau Geste 1939
Nothing Sacred 1937
A Star Is Born 1937 ☆
Wild Boys of the Road 1933
The Public Enemy 1931
Wings 1927

"His work is beginning to interfere with his drinking."

——Casey Burke, *A Star is Born*

HOWARD HAWKS

Born: Howard Winchester Hawks, May 30, 1896 (Goshen, Indiana, U.S.); died 1977 (Palm Springs, California, U.S.).

Directing style: Craftsman of Hollywood classics in a variety of genres; fast-paced dialogue; energetic aviation and motor-racing scenes; an eye for acting talent.

Top Takes...

Rio Lobo 1970

El Dorado 1966

Red Line 7000 1965

Man's Favorite Sport? 1964

Rio Bravo 1959

Land of the Pharoahs 1955

Gentlemen Prefer Blondes 1953

O. Henry's Full House 1952

Monkey Business 1952

The Big Sky 1952

I Was a Male War Bride 1949

A Song is Born 1948

Red River 1948

The Big Sleep 1946

To Have and Have Not 1944

The Outlaw 1943

Sergeant York 1941 ☆

His Girl Friday 1940

Only Angels Have Wings 1939

Bringing Up Baby 1938

Twentieth Century 1934

The Crowd Roars 1932

Scarface 1932

The Dawn Patrol 1930

The Road to Glory 1926

RIGHT: Paul Muni stars as the gangster Tony in Howard Hawks's classic *Scarface*.

Howard Hawks spent his early years racing cars professionally, and flew planes in the Army Air Corps in World War I. Both of these interests surfaced in his films. He made his directorial debut with *The Road to Glory* (1926) then drew on his flying experience during the war for *The Dawn Patrol* (1930). *The Crowd Roars* (1932) has James Cagney as a racing-car driver in a movie that benefits greatly from Hawks's personal knowledge of this milieu. In *Scarface* (1932), a gangster film that has become a classic, Paul Muni gives a masterly performance as a thinly disguised Al Capone. *Twentieth Century* (1934) is a dazzlingly energetic screwball comedy.

Hawks had his failures, too. *Viva Villa!* (1934) was an ill-fated biopic of the Mexican revolutionary Pancho Villa, and Hawks was replaced as director by Jack Conway. But in the space of a few years at the end of the 1930s Hawks directed a series of enduring masterpieces. *Bringing Up Baby* (1938) is unsurpassed among Hollywood comedies; *Only Angels Have Wings* (1939) is the best of Hawks's flying pictures; and *Sergeant York* (1941) stars Gary Cooper as a World War I hero, a performance that won him an Academy Award for Best Actor.

1890s

ABOVE: Katharine Hepburn, Cary Grant, and "Baby" (the leopard) in *Bringing Up Baby*.

Through the 1940s Hawks explored new genres with equal success. He teamed a young Lauren Bacall with Humphrey Bogart in a romantic thriller based on an Ernest Hemingway novel, *To Have and Have Not* (1944). So successful was the partnership that Hawks teamed them again in the *The Big Sleep* (1946). Two years later Hawks ventured into the Western genre with *Red River* (1948). He returned to comedy with *I Was a Male War Bride* (1949), starring Cary Grant in drag.

Hawks's films present, for the most part, a masculine world in which an elite band of heroes unite in the achievement of a goal. Women can be admitted to this circle, but only if they can keep up with the pace and maintain the necessary sangfroid. His films are simply and efficiently made, all the focus being on the presentation of story and character. Suave in appearance and

"I'm such a coward that unless I get a good writer, I don't want to make a picture."

The Real Sergeant York

Howard Hawks's 1941 film was based on the diary of Corporal Alvin C. York, who single-handedly killed more than 20 German soldiers and captured 132 others during an infantry attack on a German position in France during World War I.

- Alvin C. York was born in Pall Mall, Tennessee, on December 13, 1887.
- He learned to shoot as a boy, and was an expert with both pistol and rifle.
- After becoming a born-again Christian, York gave up drinking, smoking, gambling, and bare-knuckle fighting.
- When drafted into the U.S. army during World War I, he sought exemption as a conscientious objector; this was refused.
- On October 8, 1918, York's company in France was sent to attack a heavily guarded hill. They were discovered and ten Americans were killed within minutes.
- York made his way to a position where he was able to kill the heavily armed German soldiers, using a rifle and pistol.
- Demoralized, the remaining Germans surrendered; York led the prisoners and the remaining members of his squad to regimental headquarters.
- York was promoted to sergeant and awarded the Congressional Medal of Honor.
- York used the proceeds from his written life story and the movie to establish schools for poor mountain children.

something of a ladies' man, Hawks gave little away in his public persona, preferring to let his films speak for themselves. But in the 1950s his work was championed by an influential group of critics writing for the French journal *Cahiers du cinéma*, who included Jean-Luc Godard and François Truffaut, and eventually the quality of his films was recognized.

Rio Bravo and beyond

In the 1950s, Hawks explored yet more genres, including the musical in *Gentlemen Prefer Blondes* (1953) and *Land of the Pharaohs* (1955), a biblical epic that was one of the director's rare flops. It was followed by what is perhaps his masterpiece, *Rio Bravo* (1959), starring John Wayne and Angie Dickinson. The relationship between Wayne and the gallant band of misfits is uncovered with tact and delicacy, and the romance between Wayne and Dickinson is surprisingly tender.

In the 1960s, Hawks's powers declined, though *Man's Favorite Sport?* (1964) is an amusing comedy. *El Dorado* (1966), another Western, united Wayne and Robert Mitchum in what is virtually a remake of *Rio Bravo*. By then, Hawks was finding finance difficult to come by, and consequently could not attract the same quality of stars, forcing him to make *Red Line 7000* (1965), a return to the racing car milieu of his youth, with a cast of unknowns. But Wayne, loyal as ever, returned to the fold for Hawks's last movie, *Rio Lobo* (1970). **EB**

RIGHT: John Wayne and Walter Brennan in a scene from the Western *Rio Bravo*.

WILLIAM CAMERON MENZIES

Born: William Cameron Menzies, July 29, 1896 (New Haven, Connecticut, U.S.); died 1957 (Los Angeles, California, U.S.).

Directing style: Pioneering production designer and gifted visual designer; outstanding use of color to enhance dramatic mood; dreamlike montage sequences.

William Cameron Menzies is far better remembered as one of cinema's foremost production designers than as a director. Possibly with good reason, according to the art director Lyle Wheeler, who worked with Menzies at Fox Film Corporation: "He was no damn good as a director . . . . He wanted to photograph ceilings and didn't give a damn what the actors were saying." And H. G. Wells, the writer of *Things to Come* (1936), dismissed him as "a sort of Cecil B. DeMille without his imagination; his mind ran on loud machinery and crowd effects."

Menzies came to fame as a designer in the 1920s, his success crowned with a Best Art Direction Oscar at the first ever Academy Awards ceremony in 1928 for *The Dove* (1927) and *Tempest* (1928). He took up directing in 1931, and was credited as codirector on a handful of negligible films. His first solo directing commission was *Things to Come*; it looked superb, but Menzies was inexperienced with actors, and struggled to help his cast work with Wells's rigid dialogue. He directed one more film in Britain, *The Green Cockatoo* (1937), from a story by Graham Greene, but the producers called in another U.S. expatriate, William K. Howard, to reshoot most of the dialogue scenes. Back in the United States, after winning a Special Award Oscar for his art direction on *Gone with the Wind* (1939), Menzies directed five more movies, the best of which was the Cold War science-fiction allegory *Invaders from Mars* (1953). But *The Whip Hand* (1951) also has points of interest, despite atrocious dialogue and acting. A paranoid thriller in which a man on a fishing trip stumbles across a nest of communists in rural Minnesota, it originally had Nazis as the baddies until studio boss Howard Hughes stepped in and forced the change. **PK**

Top Takes...

The Maze 1953
Invaders from Mars 1953
The Whip Hand 1951
Drums in the Deep South 1951
Duel in the Sun 1946
Address Unknown 1944
The Thief of Bagdad 1940
The Green Cockatoo 1937
Things to Come 1936
Wharf Angel 1934
Chandu the Magician 1932
Almost Married 1932
Always Goodbye 1931

"Well, ah, David says something landed in the field out back."
—George MacLean, *Invaders from Mars*

JULIEN DUVIVIER

Born: Julien Duvivier, October 3, 1896 (Lille, Nord, Nord-Pas-de-Calais, France); died 1967 (Paris, France).

Directing style: Icon of French avant-garde cinema; poetic realism; scripted many of his films; multistoried films; postwar pessimist depiction of French society.

Top Takes…

Diaboliquement vôtre 1967 (Diabolically Yours)

Chair de poule 1963 (Highway Pick-Up)

Le diable et les dix commandements 1962
(The Devil and the Ten Commandments)

La chambre ardente 1962 (The Burning Court)

La femme et le pantin 1959 (The Female)

Anna Karenina 1948

The Imposter 1944

Flesh and Fantasy 1943

Tales of Manhattan 1942

Lydia 1941

The Great Waltz 1938

Un carnet de bal 1937 (Dance Program)

Pépé le Moko 1937

La Bandera 1935 (Escape from Yesterday)

Maria Chapdelaine 1934

The career of Julien Duvivier, and the manner in which it was shaped and diverted by Hollywood, is still relevant as a case study today. Duvivier started out in 1916 as an actor on the Paris stage, before becoming a director in his native France in 1919. He came to international prominence in the late 1930s with *Pépé le Moko* (1937), one of several of his films to star Jean Gabin. A romantic thriller with exotic locations and a film noir feel, it was remade in Hollywood as *Algiers* (1938), with Charles Boyer and Hedy Lamarr. *Un carnet de bal* (1937) (*Dance Program*), a poignant psychological drama that looks ahead to Ingmar Bergman in its themes and style, also caught something of the international mood. As a result, both Duvivier and Gabin were offered Hollywood contracts—Duvivier's to direct *The Great Waltz* (1938) for MGM.

Duvivier spent the war years in Hollywood drifting from studio to studio, lending a touch of European sophistication to some rather obvious projects. *Lydia* (1941) remakes *Dance Program*, while the multiple-story films *Tales of Manhattan* (1942) and *Flesh and Fantasy* (1943) ape its narrative structure. *The Impostor* (1944) reunited Duvivier with Gabin. The second episode of *Flesh and Fantasy*, an adaptation of an Oscar Wilde story of a man driven to murder by the predictions of a fortune-teller, is probably the director's best U.S. work. Apart from a trip to Britain to take up Alexander Korda's offer of directing Vivien Leigh as *Anna Karenina* (1948), Duvivier's remaining movies were all made in France, but he never quite regained his prewar form or popularity. He was killed in a car crash in 1967, shortly after completing his final film, the amnesia drama *Diaboliquement vôtre* (1967) (*Diabolically Yours*). **MC**

> *"Tales of Manhattan . . . achieves an impressive effect."*
> —New York Times

DOROTHY ARZNER

Born: Dorothy Arzner, January 3, 1897 (San Francisco, California, U.S.); died 1979 (La Quinta, California, U.S.).

Directing style: Trailblazing female director of romantic melodramas; savvy editing; coded lesbian themes; use of dance; exploration of women's role in society.

The only woman directing in Hollywood in the 1930s, Dorothy Arzner was born in San Francisco. Working as a waitress in a small Hollywood restaurant owned by her father, she rubbed elbows with a number of working actors, directors, and writers on a daily basis. After serving in the Ambulance Corps during World War I, Arzner broke into the film business as a secretary in the script department of Famous Players-Lasky, working under director William C. de Mille, brother of Cecil B. DeMille. Advancing rapidly because of her skill and intelligence, Arzner became successively a script clerk, and then a negative cutter, and finally a film editor, where she made her first real mark editing the bullfighting sequences of *Blood and Sand* (1922).

Director James Cruze then offered Arzner the chance to cut his Western epic *The Covered Wagon* (1923), which she did with finesse. Having proved herself accordingly, Paramount Pictures gave her a modest feature film to direct, *Fashions for Women* (1927). The movie was a commercial and critical hit, and Arzner built on this success with two other jazz-age features, *Ten Modern Commandments* (1927) and *Get Your Man* (1927).

Her reputation as a conscientious craftsperson only increased with her subsequent films, especially *The Wild Party* (1929) and the early Katharine Hepburn drama *Christopher Strong* (1933). *Craig's Wife* (1936) was perhaps her biggest hit, but feminist scholars remember her most strongly for the acidulous *Dance, Girl, Dance* (1940), an exposé of the grimy nature of burlesque starring Lucille Ball.

Although she never considered herself a feminist, Arzner's example has inspired countless other women to enter the industry, and her best films remain an interesting alternative to the male-dominated cinema of classical Hollywood. **WWD**

Top Takes…

First Comes Courage 1943
Dance, Girl, Dance 1940
The Bride Wore Red 1937
Craig's Wife 1936
Nana 1934
Christopher Strong 1933
Merrily We Go to Hell 1932
Working Girls 1931
Honor Among Lovers 1931
Anybody's Woman 1930
Paramount on Parade 1930
The Wild Party 1929
Get Your Man 1927
Ten Modern Commandments 1927
Fashions for Women 1927
Blood and Sand 1922

"I threatened to quit each time I didn't get my way, but no one ever let me walk out."

1890s

DOUGLAS SIRK

Born: Hans Detlef Sierck, April 26, 1897 (Hamburg, Germany); died 1987 (Lugano, Ticino, Switzerland).

Directing style: Auteur of ironic melodramas; themes explore 1950s U.S. society, and the moral choices individuals make within it; fluid camerawork.

Top Takes…

Bourbon Street Blues 1979
Imitation of Life 1959
A Time to Love and a Time to Die 1958
The Tarnished Angels 1958
Interlude 1957
Written on the Wind 1956
All That Heaven Allows 1955
Magnificent Obsession 1954
Taza, Son of Cochise 1954
All I Desire 1953
Take Me to Town 1953
Has Anybody Seen My Gal? 1952
No Room for the Groom 1952
Slightly French 1949
Shockproof 1949
Sleep, My Love 1948
A Scandal in Paris 1946
Summer Storm 1944
Hitler's Madman 1943
La Habanera 1937
Schlussakkord 1936 (Final Accord)
April, April! 1935
Das Mädchen vom Moorhof, 1935
  (The Girl of the Moors)
Zwei Genies 1934

RIGHT: Al Shean and John Carradine in the war docudrama, *Hitler's Madman*.

Born in Germany to Danish parents, Douglas Sirk started out as a theater director. He directed his first German film, *Zwei Genies* (1934), and for a time did well in the Nazi movie industry. But his second wife was Jewish and the couple left Germany, eventually making their way to Hollywood. Renaming himself "Douglas Sirk," the director's first U.S. film was *Hitler's Madman* (1943), a drama about the assassination of Reinhard Heydrich, the Nazi ruler of Czechoslovakia.

Most of Sirk's early Hollywood films are lightweight genre pieces: film noirs such as *Shockproof* (1949); comedies such as *Slightly French* (1949); and Westerns such as *Take Me to Town* (1953). A hint of what was to come can be detected in *All I Desire* (1953), a melodrama in which Barbara Stanwyck makes waves by returning to the small town she left ten years earlier. Sirk finally hit his stride with *Magnificent Obsession* (1954). This was a glossy adventure in which spoiled playboy Rock Hudson's thoughtless behavior causes the death of a better man than he. Appalled by his life, he seeks salvation in good works, while falling in love with the dead man's widow, played by Jane Wyman. This star pairing was repeated in *All That Heaven Allows*

1890s

(1955), in which Wyman plays a widow who, in the teeth of opposition from her bourgeois friends and conformist children, embarks on an affair with a young gardener.

Sirk's masterpiece is *Written on the Wind* (1956), in which the neurotic children of a wealthy oilman ensnare their childhood friend, played by Hudson, in their emotional turmoil. His final Hollywood movie, *Imitation of Life* (1959), was both a major commercial success and a triumphal demonstration of his ability to turn soap-opera material into subtly crafted filmmaking. In the film, Lana Turner befriends an African-American woman and her daughter, giving them work as servants. But when the daughter begins to pass as white, tragedy ensues.

Sirk's films were taken up by the young, iconoclastic French critics of *Cahiers du cinéma*, and his work became increasingly important; for example, his influences can be seen in the work of German director Rainer Werner Fassbinder. **EB**

Master of Irony

Historically dismisssed as colorful and banal melodramas in the 1950s, Sirk's films were re-evaluated in the 1970s and 1980s and became regarded as masterpieces of irony. His mature films all belong to the critically despised genre of the "domestic or women's picture," but the subtlety of his direction manages to impart a critique of the conventional, Middle America milieu in which they are set. The visual aspects of his work, often inspired by his interest in painting, are laced with symbolism and Sirk's mise-en-scène, with its luscious décor, conspicuous style, and fluid camerawork, evokes a life of empty excess.

FRANK CAPRA

Born: Frank Rosario Capra, May 18, 1897 (Bisacquino, Sicily, Italy); died 1991 (La Quinta, California, U.S.).

Directing style: Themes reflect contemporary social conditions; often optimistic in tone; innovator of overlapping dialogue; fast-paced acting; dynamic rhythm.

1890s

Top Takes...

Pocketful of Miracles 1961
A Hole in the Head 1959
Here Comes the Groom 1951
Riding High 1950
State of the Union 1948
It's a Wonderful Life 1946 ☆
Arsenic and Old Lace 1944
The Battle of Britain 1943
Meet John Doe 1941
Mr. Smith Goes to Washington 1939 ☆
You Can't Take It With You 1938 ★
Lost Horizon 1937
Mr. Deeds Goes to Town 1936
Broadway Bill 1934
It Happened One Night 1934 ★
Lady for a Day 1933 ☆
The Bitter Tea of General Yen 1933
American Madness 1932
Platinum Blonde 1931
The Miracle Woman 1931
Ladies of Leisure 1930
For the Love of Mike 1927
Long Pants 1927
The Strong Man 1926

At a time when Hollywood hardly looked outside its studios, Frank Capra crafted a unique combination of social commentary and slapstick caprioles. Populist and humanist, uplifting, fast, and funny, Capra's creations are among Hollywood's most memorable movies and are nostalgically treasured and ritually reviewed as true cult classics.

Between 1915 and 1926, Capra worked his way up the ranks from extra to directing movies *The Strong Man* (1926), *Long Pants* (1927), and *For the Love of Mike* (1927) landing him a contract with Columbia Pictures. Capra made a flawless transition to talkies with *Ladies of Leisure* (1930) and *The Miracle Woman* (1931) and Columbia gradually gave him more freedom, which Capra used to cut the entrances and exits of actors, and let actions jump from scene to scene without dissolves—all signs of a maturing, experienced director.

American Madness (1932) introduced Capra's favorite theme, the struggle of a plain individual versus a rigid corporation, with nothing less than the "American Dream" itself at stake. The next decade saw Capra bring this theme to perfection in a string of masterpieces. The fast pace of *It Happened One Night*

RIGHT: Clark Gable and Claudette Colbert in a scene from *It Happened One Night*.

ABOVE: James Stewart (second from left) as George Bailey in *It's a Wonderful Life.*

(1934) initiated the screwball-comedy genre but also highlighted problems of the Depression. This combination of crazy comedy and concern for social problems was Capra's first Oscar success, with wins for Best Picture and Best Director. In *Mr. Deeds Goes to Town* (1936), Capra used a "what if?" plot device to explore similar themes, winning him his second Oscar. His approach prompted critics to call him "the gee whiz" director, known for unbridled optimism in overcoming opposition. Displaying this approach at its best are two films with Jean Arthur and James Stewart: the cute and heartfelt *You Can't Take It With You* (1938), which won Academy Awards for Best Picture and Best Director again; and *Mr. Smith Goes to Washington* (1939).

Meet John Doe (1941) is perhaps Capra's most direct political comment, exposing the fabrications and cynicism of the

"There are no rules in filmmaking. Only sins. And the cardinal sin is dullness."

Being Frank

Despair befell Frank Capra on the evening of March 16, 1934, when he attended the Oscars ceremony as one of the Best Director nominees, for *Lady for a Day*. Capra had caught Oscar fever and, in his own words, "In the interim between the nominations and the final voting . . . my mind was on those Oscars."

- When Oscar host Will Rogers opened the envelope for Best Director, he commented, "Well, well, well. What do you know. I've watched this young man for a long time, saw him come up from the bottom, and I mean the bottom. It couldn't have happened to a nicer guy. Come on up and get it, Frank!"

- Capra got up and, squeezing his way past tables, made his way to the dance floor to accept his Oscar. "The spotlight searched around trying to find me. 'Over here!' I waved. Then it suddenly swept away from me, and picked up a flustered man standing on the other side of the dance floor—Frank Lloyd!"

- Frank Lloyd went up to accept his statuette, while a voice behind Capra yelled, "Down in front!"

- Capra's walk back to his table turned into the "longest, saddest, most shattering walk in my life. I wished I could have crawled under the rug like a miserable worm. When I slumped in my chair I felt like one. All of my friends at the table were crying."

corporate press before joint community action exposes its evil. During World War II, Capra headed a propaganda unit and directed *The Battle of Britain* (1943), part of the seven-volume *Why We Fight* series, each part an invaluable historical document. Having left Columbia, Capra's next film, *Arsenic and Old Lace* (1944), was an uncharacteristic piece: a zany, macabre, and satirical screwball comedy. It was nevertheless a big success.

A wonderful life

As if to atone for the vitriol of *Arsenic and Old Lace*, and in a softening of his trademark idealism, *It's a Wonderful Life* (1946) was a heartwarming parable of community commitment and social recognition, dedicated to the true cornerstones of the American dream: family, friendship, and caring. It soon became— and remains to this day—the United States's favorite Christmas movie. For Capra, it was also his last major effort. The romantic comedy *State of the Union* (1948) is a nice reprise from the themes of innocence and politics, and his two Bing Crosby films, *Riding High* (1950) and *Here Comes the Groom* (1951), are fun, but lack the sting and relevance of his earlier works.

After *A Hole in the Head* (1959) and *Pocketful of Miracles* (1961), Capra retired. It is easy to say that his optimism was naive and his characters gullible, but at a time when the Great Depression and then World War II made reality grim enough, his films provided belief and relief—wishful gee whiz, but why not? **EM**

RIGHT: Cary Grant entertains the ladies with his usual charm in *Arsenic and Old Lace*.

1890s

ROUBEN MAMOULIAN

Born: Rouben Mamoulian, October 8, 1897 (Tbilisi, Georgia); died 1987 (Los Angeles, California, U.S.).

Directing style: Innovator of moving the camera for panning shots; economic editing; striking images; believer in realism and naturalism; often made musicals.

Of all the stage directors summoned by the movies at the dawn of sound, Rouben Mamoulian most completely embraced the medium of film. From the initial frames of his first film, *Applause* (1929), it was obvious that Mamoulian had no interest in canned theater, although he frequently enlarged on effects he had used onstage (echoes of his stage production of *Porgy* (1927) appear in several films.) His camera moved with surprising fluidity; his editing brisk, and his use of techniques such as dissolves and optical wipes assured and unique.

By the time of his second film, the unfortunately obscure gangster picture *City Streets* (1931), Mamoulian was in complete control of his filmmaking technique. His *Dr. Jekyll and Mr. Hyde* (1931), made by Paramount Pictures to cash in on the successful horror cycle at Universal Studios, was little short of a masterpiece—his nonstop invention only occasionally thwarted by the slightly purple prose of the screenplay.

Mamoulian undertook the Maurice Chevalier and Jeanette MacDonald vehicle *Love Me Tonight* (1932) as a favor to the studio, only to turn around and create his masterpiece. From beginning to end, the film is as close to perfection as anything ever made: an explosion of cinematic creativity where everything works, nothing is left to chance, all seems effortless. The film defines Mamoulian's cinematic vocabulary; one need only compare its ending to that of his Leo Tolstoy adaptation, *We Live Again* (1934), to see the similarity of approach. Mamoulian's great period ends with *Becky Sharp* (1935), but much of interest remains, especially his final film, the musical comedy starring Fred Astaire, *Silk Stockings* (1957), which is nearly on a par with his stylistic experiments of the early sound era. **KH**

Top Takes...

Silk Stockings 1957
The Wild Heart 1952
Summer Holiday 1948
Laura 1944
Rings on Her Fingers 1942
Blood and Sand 1941
The Mark of Zorro 1940
Golden Boy 1939
High, Wide, and Handsome 1937
The Gay Desperado 1936
Becky Sharp 1935
We Live Again 1934
Love Me Tonight 1932
Dr. Jekyll and Mr. Hyde 1931
City Streets 1931
Applause 1929

"I visualize a whole film before I come to the set and then I try to match it."

Top Takes...

**RIGHT: Ivan mockingly crowns Vladimir
in a scene from Ivan the Terrible, Part II.**

SERGEI M. EISENSTEIN

Born: Sergei Mikhailovich Eizenshtein, January 23, 1898 (Riga, Latvia); died 1948 (Moscow, Russia).

Directing style: Spectacular epics; richness of mise-en-scène; character-driven narrative; starkly beautiful visuals; closet critiques of Stalinist tyranny.

An intellectual who pursued a bewildering variety of interests, artistic and cultural, Sergei M. Eisenstein has left an indelible mark on the history and practice of film.

Eisenstein made four films for the fledgling Soviet government in the early 1920s, intended to help those who found themselves in an unfamiliar political structure understand the nature of the revolution. *Stachka* (1925) (*Strike*) and *Oktyabr* (1928) (*Ten Days That Shook the World*) are strident attempts to provide an emerging socialist society with a history and scheme of values, whereas *Bronenosets Potyomkin* (1925) (*Battleship Potemkin*) dramatizes the conversion from loyalty to the old regime to participation in the new. These films studiously avoid those features that had made Hollywood film into a world standard—an emphasis on character-driven narrative; the reinforcement of consensus values and the fulfillment of unsatisfiable desires; and the deployment of glamorous, star-quality performers. Instead, they argue for the abandonment of individuality in the face of group solidarity.

By the end of the 1920s, Eisenstein had become disillusioned with the opportunities for truly creative work and relocated to

Hollywood, where he embarked on a history of the Mexican revolution entitled *¡Que Viva Mexico!* (1932). Despite the support of novelist Upton Sinclair and the shooting of more than 100,000 feet of film, however, Eisenstein was unable to pull the project together and returned to Russia.

The films he then made are celebrated, and justly so, emphasizing a richness of mise-en-scène, an emphasis on a pleasing visual style, and a focus on two-dimensional main characters. *Aleksandr Nevskiy* (1938) (*Alexander Nevsky*) is a spectacular epic, displacing the then-current Russo-German conflict back into the Middle Ages and providing Soviet culture with a nationalistic look back to its ethnic roots. The *Ivan Groznyy* (1944, 1958) (*Ivan the Terrible*) films are cold, starkly beautiful pictures, difficult to watch, gloomy, and compelling at the same time. Perhaps they offer a closet critique of Stalinist tyranny, and the cult of personality. **BP**

ABOVE: Cossacks slaughter citizens of Odessa in *Battleship Potemkin*.

The *Potemkin* Uprising

Battleship Potemkin was based on a real event that occurred in 1905. The film is structured around five episodes:

- Men and Maggots: the sailors refuse to eat soup made from rotten meat.
- Drama at the Harbor: the crew mutiny and their leader Vakulinchuk is killed.
- A Dead Man Calls for Justice: the leader's body is brought ashore, sparking unrest.
- The Odessa Staircase: citizens of Odessa slaughtered on the harbor steps.
- Meeting the Squadron: Russian fleet brought in to subdue the ship.

HENRY HATHAWAY

Born: Marquis Henri Leonard de Fiennes, March 13, 1898 (Sacramento, California, U.S.); died 1985 (Hollywood, California, U.S.).

Directing style: Tough director of Westerns and film noirs; semidocumentary style; sizzling action sequences; flair for shooting on location; memorable visual effects.

Of Belgian aristocratic descent, Henry Hathaway was born Marquis Henri Leonard de Fiennes. The son of actors Jean and Rhody Hathaway, he was accustomed to Hollywood life from an early age, working as a child actor in the Westerns of Allan Dwan. World War I took Hathaway away from the silver screen and into combat, but upon his return, he assisted filmmaking legends such as Frank Lloyd, Paul Bern, Josef von Sternberg, and also Fred Niblo on *Ben-Hur: A Tale of the Christ* (1925).

He made his directorial debut with the Western *Heritage of the Desert* (1932), an adaptation of a Zane Grey novel starring future star Randolph Scott, and achieved critical recognition soon after with *The Lives of a Bengal Lancer* (1935). The movie told the story of the 41st Bengal Lancer regiment, stationed on the Northwest Frontier of a then-British India. It was nominated for seven Academy Awards, including one for Best Director.

Having made his name, Hathaway moved into the film noir genre with pictures such as *The House on 92nd Street* (1945). The film tells the story of the Federal Bureau of Investigation's (FBI) counterespionage activities against the Nazis. It was notable for its semidocumentary style (a technique Hathaway would use frequently), using real-life FBI agents for some scenes. His thriller *Niagara* (1953) starred Marilyn Monroe, whose image as the prototypical blonde bombshell followed the release of Hathaway's film. He returned to Westerns to direct John Wayne in many pictures, including Wayne's Best Actor Oscar-winning role in *True Grit* (1969). He also directed Steve McQueen in the Western *Nevada Smith* (1966). Hathaway is best remembered as a tough director of action movies who had a flair for shooting on location, leading to some memorable visual effects. **ES**

"To be a good director you've got to be a bastard. I'm a bastard and I know it."

1890s

KENJI MIZOGUCHI

Born: Kenji Mizoguchi, May 16, 1898 (Asakusa, Tokyo, Japan); died 1956 (Kyoto, Japan).

Directing style: Legendary for his depiction of the role of women in Japanese society; use of static camera for slow, reflective pace and observation.

Whatever regrets there are at the loss of Kenji Mizoguchi's silent films, what has survived (several 1930s films, including the magnificent *Zangiku Monogatari* (1939) (*The Story of the Late Chrysanthemums*), and his postwar films) is one of the most vital and impressive bodies of work in the history of cinema.

It is perhaps a truism to vaunt the director's representation of women, but it needs repeating: only Max Ophüls's *Letter from an Unknown Woman* (1948) and Alfred Hitchcock's *Vertigo* (1958) can challenge Mizoguchi's preeminence in this field, in particular the rigor with which he sets about representing and deconstructing the prejudice, hypocrisy, and arrogance by which society transforms women into goods and chattels.

Unlike Hitchcock and Ophüls, Mizoguchi eschews psychoanalysis—although a Lacanian reading of male desire in relation to the coveted female body is crucial in understanding *Utamaro o meguru gonin no onna* (1946) (*Five Women Around Utamaru*)—and prefers a more consciously Marxist approach, something he shares with Luis Buñuel. The ways in which money, power, male privilege, and ambition are articulated in his three great masterpieces—*Saikaku ichidai onna* (1952) (*The Life of Oharu*), *Ugetsu monogatari* (1953) (*Tales of Ugetsu*), and *Chikamatsu monogatari* (1954) (*A Story from Chikamatsu*)—cannot be dissociated from the representation of the couple or the family, and the use of sexual and class domination within the cinematic frame: *The Life of Oharu* is exemplary here. At a time when frenzied editing fragments space and compromises the spectator's reflexive gaze, the cinema of Mizoguchi, with its often static camera and its movement of characters within the frame, has become a necessary antidote to the influence of advertising spots. **ReH**

Top Takes...

Akasen chitai 1956 (*Street of Shame*)

Shin heike monogatari 1955 (*Legend of the Taira Clan*)

Chikamatsu monogatari 1954 (*A Story from Chikamatsu*)

Uwasa no onna 1954 (*The Crucified Woman*)

Sanshô dayû 1954 (*Legend of Bailiff Sansho*)

Gion bayasha 1953 (*A Geisha*)

Ugetsu monogatari 1953 (*Tales of Ugetsu*)

Saikaku ichidai onna 1952 (*Diary of Oharu*)

Utamaro o meguru gonin no onna 1946 (*Five Woman Around Utamaru*)

Meito bijomaru 1945 (*The Famous Sword*)

Genroku chushingura 1941 (*47 Samurai*)

Zangiku monogatari 1939 (*The Story of the Last Chrysanthemums*)

Naniwa erejî 1936 (*Naniwa Elegy*)

"I was able finally to learn to show life as I see it."
—On *Naniwa Elegy*

PRESTON STURGES

Born: Edmund Preston Biden, August 29, 1898 (Chicago, Illinois, U.S.); died 1959 (New York City, New York, U.S.).

Directing style: One of the first writers of screenplays to become a director; maker of sophisticated screwball comedies; witty dialogue; long takes.

Preston Sturges has such an immense reputation that it's easy to forget that he was hot for only a few scant years as the wonder man of Paramount Pictures, during which time he turned out greats such as *The Great McGinty* (1940), *Christmas in July* (1940), *The Lady Eve* (1941), *Sullivan's Travels* (1941), *The Palm Beach Story* (1942), *The Miracle of Morgan's Creek* (1944), *Hail the Conquering Hero* (1944), and *The Great Moment* (1944). And that was after ten years of screenwriting.

Selling *The Great McGinty* to Paramount for next to nothing so he could sit in the director's chair, Sturges became one of the first great writer/directors. His Paramount movies were not always big moneymakers, but he was the studio's prestige filmmaker and the darling of the critics. His approach combined sophisticated comedy with slapstick, and his hard-edged cynicism, combined with a streak of morbidity, was often undercut by surprising evidences of sentimentality.

Sturges tended to favor long takes, often achieved with a moving camera, to integrate characters into their surroundings. His most personal movie and probably his best work, *Sullivan's Travels*, combined his typical comedy and brilliant comedic dialogue with more serious themes, all the while lampooning his own desire for those themes. When Paramount let him go, Sturges teamed with Howard Hughes in an ill-fated attempt to revive Harold Lloyd's career with *The Sin of Harold Diddlebock* (1947), but returned to form with the exceptional black comedy *Unfaithfully Yours* (1948) at Twentieth Century Fox. Its commercial failure, however, largely ended his career, and only two negligible films followed. He died of a heart attack, living on the hotel's tab, at the Algonquin Hotel in New York City in 1959. **KH**

Top Takes…

Les carnets du Major Thompson 1955
(*The Diary of Major Thompson*)
The Beautiful Blonde from Bashful Bend 1949
Unfaithfully Yours 1948
The Sin of Harold Diddlebock 1947
The Great Moment 1944
Hail the Conquering Hero 1944
The Miracle of Morgan's Creek 1944
The Palm Beach Story 1942
Sullivan's Travels 1941
The Lady Eve 1941
Christmas in July 1940
The Great McGinty 1940

"The most incredible thing about my career is that I had one."

NORMAN Z. McLEOD

Born: Norman Zenos McLeod, September 20, 1898 (Grayling, Michigan, U.S.); died 1964 (Hollywood, California, U.S.).

Directing style: Maker of offbeat 1930s comedies and later musicals; witty dialogue; ability to indulge a visual gag; sense of the absurd.

In *The Hound of the Baskervilles* (1902) Sherlock Holmes tells Doctor Watson: "Some people, without possessing genius, have a remarkable power of stimulating." For a comedian's director such as Norman Z. McLeod, this would be a flattering appraisal. After all, there is something innately ludicrous about the notion of anybody actually directing the Marx Brothers or W. C. Fields. But both acts could—and did—make bad movies when not properly handled. Meanwhile, *Monkey Business* (1931), *Horse Feathers* (1932), and *It's a Gift* (1933)—all with McLeod at the helm—have no business outside of anybody's list of the 20 greatest comedies ever made.

What did McLeod have that other directors lacked? He didn't try to impose his personality to the detriment of theirs; he also obviously understood all the jokes. His films tapped perfectly into the commercial mood of their times, which is why they were popular then, are often forgotten today, and frequently have incredibly evocative titles such as *Redheads on Parade* (1935) and *Swing Shift Maisie* (1943).

McLeod began as an animator, the best training for 1930s comedy, and learned his trade at the Christie Film Company, which specialized in comedy shorts. After World War I military service, he was brought in as assistant to director William A. Wellman on *Wings* (1927), and made his directorial debut with the Western *Taking a Chance* (1928).

Although McLeod's best work was at Paramount Pictures in the early 1930s, his move to Hal Roach Studios toward the end of the decade also brought him success. His career was crowned by the charming supernatural comedy *Topper* (1937); *The Secret Life of Walter Mitty* (1947); and five Bob Hope vehicles including *Road to Rio* (1947) and *The Paleface* (1948). **MC**

Top Takes...

Alias Jesse James 1959
Public Pigeon No. One 1957
Casanova's Big Night 1954
The Paleface 1948
Isn't It Romantic? 1948
Road to Rio 1947
The Secret Life of Walter Mitty 1947
The Kid from Brooklyn 1946
Swing Shift Maisie 1943
The Powers Girl 1943
Topper 1937
Redheads on Parade 1935
It's a Gift 1933
Horse Feathers 1932
Monkey Business 1931
Taking a Chance 1928

"The clock didn't strike.
I definitely heard it not strike."

——Mrs. Mitty, *The Secret Life of Walter Mitty*

LEO McCAREY

Born: Thomas Leo McCarey, October 3, 1898 (Los Angeles, California, U.S.); died 1969 (Santa Monica, California, U.S.).

Directing style: Maker of witty, sentimental comedies; responsible for teaming the legendary comic duo of Stan Laurel and Oliver Hardy.

Leo McCarey started his career working for Hal Roach Studios, turning out two-reel comedies and hitting on the idea of teaming Stan Laurel and Oliver Hardy. McCarey's early sound features were relatively indifferent, but he hit his stride with the Eddie Cantor musical comedy *The Kid from Spain* (1932).

McCarey's output for the next five years was remarkable. *Duck Soup* (1933) is not only the best Marx Brothers film but striking filmmaking in its own right. His Mae West vehicle, *Belle of the Nineties* (1934), is her best film, and offers a glimpse into the more serious side of the director. *Ruggles of Red Gap* (1935), however, suggested the humanist depths that would find full expression in McCarey's arguable masterpiece, *Make Way for Tomorrow* (1937). He then tapped into the full potential of Cary Grant with the romantic comedy *The Awful Truth* (1937), for which he won an Oscar for Best Director. The film also cleaned up with Oscars for Best Picture and Best Writing (Original Story), and McCarey became the first director to win three major categories at the Academy Awards.

Love Affair (1939) signaled McCarey's increasing desire to make serious films—a desire that hampered his subsequent work. There was still much good in his next few films, *Once Upon a Honeymoon* (1942) and *Going My Way* (1944), but by 1948 McCarey was burned out. Somewhat embarrassing is the McCarthy-era propaganda of *My Son John* (1952), the tone of which also marked his equally hysteria-driven final movie, *Satan Never Sleeps* (1962), which was a weird blend of anti-Mao rant and disturbing variations on *Going My Way*. His best late film is *An Affair to Remember* (1957), a remake of *Love Affair* that shows some of the old skill, along with his later propensity for saccharine sentiment. **KH**

Top Takes…

Satan Never Sleeps 1962
An Affair to Remember 1957
You Can Change the World 1951
Good Sam 1948
The Bells of St. Mary's 1945 ☆
Going My Way 1944 ★
Once Upon a Honeymoon 1942
Love Affair 1939
The Awful Truth 1937 ★
Make Way for Tomorrow 1937
The Milky Way 1936
Ruggles of Red Gap 1935
Belle of the Nineties 1934
Duck Soup 1933
The Kid from Spain 1932

> "I'll show 'em they can't fiddle around with old firefly!"
>
> —Rufus T. Firefly, *Duck Soup*

1890s

RENÉ CLAIR

Born: René-Lucien Chomette, November 11, 1898 (Paris, France); died 1981 (Neuilly-sur-Seine, Hauts-de-Seine, Île-de-France, France).

Directing style: Maker of silent-era farces and later frivolous, witty talkies; lighthearted, frothy social satires; comic chases; elegant imagery of Paris.

1890s

During the 1930s, René Clair ranked with Renoir and Carné as one of the foremost French directors. His reputation has since declined and comparison with Renoir may suggest why. Clair's work, though witty, stylish, and accomplished, seems to lack a dimension; there's a fastidious turning away from the messier, more complex aspects of life. Yet at their best, Clair's films have the sparkle and exhilaration of champagne and it seems churlish to expect nourishment as well.

In the silent era, Clair directed one of cinema's finest silent farces, *Un chapeau de paille d'Italie* (1928) (*An Italian Straw Hat*), full of visual gags and a mocking disdain for bourgeois conventions. Initially skeptical about the coming of sound, Clair soon grasped its creative possibilities in four lighthearted films that brought him international fame: *Sous les toits de Paris* (1930) (*Under the Roofs of Paris*), *Le million* (1931) (*The Million*), *À nous la liberté* (1931) (*Liberty for Us*), and *Quatorze Juillet* (1933) (*July 14*). But charges of frivolity spurred him into making a film with more significance. *Le dernier milliardaire* (1934) (*The Last Millionaire*) flopped, sending Clair into creative exile. His six English-language films, two made in Britain, four in the United States, feel uneasy; the fantasy is strained and unconvincing.

By the time Clair returned to France in 1946, he and the world had changed. In place of the lighthearted gaiety of his earlier films, his postwar work displayed a new-found maturity and emotional depth, suffused with an autumnal melancholy that at times verges on tragedy. But Clair's films, for all their wit and sophistication, had fallen out of fashion, and he came under attack from the young rebels of the French New Wave. His last two films were critically dismissed, and his reputation has yet to recover. **PK**

Top Takes...

Les grandes manoeuvres 1955
 (*The Grand Manoeuver*)
And Then There Were None 1945
It Happened Tomorrow 1944
Forever and a Day 1943
I Married a Witch 1942
The Flame of New Orleans 1941
The Ghost Goes West 1935
Le dernier milliardaire 1934
 (*The Last Millionaire*)
Quatorze Juillet 1933 (*July 14*)
À nous la liberté 1931 (*Liberty for Us*)
Le million 1931 (*The Million*)
Sous les toits de Paris 1930
 (*Under the Roofs of Paris*)
Un chapeau de paille d'Italie 1928
 (*An Italian Straw Hat*)

> "[*Liberty for Us*] bristles with strange originality."
> —*New York Times*

JORIS IVENS

Born: George Henri Anton Ivens, November 18, 1898 (Nijmegen, Gelderland, Netherlands); died 1989 (Paris, France).

Directing style: Dutch maker of hard-hitting documentaries and antifascist propaganda; themes of the effects of war and capitalism on the working class.

1890s

Top Takes...

Une histoire de vent 1989 (*A Tale of the Wind*)

Comment Yukong déplaca les montagnes 1976
(*How Yukong Moved the Mountains*)

Le peuple et ses fusils 1970
(*The People and Their Guns*)

Le 17e parallèle: La guerre du peuple 1968
(*17th Parallel: Vietnam in War*)

Le Mistral 1965

La Seine a rencontré Paris 1957
(*The Seine Meets Paris*)

Know Your Enemy: Japan 1945

Our Russian Front 1942

The 400 Million 1939

The Spanish Earth 1937

Nieuwe gronden 1934 (*New Earth*)

Regen 1929 (*Rain*)

De Brug 1928 (*The Bridge*)

"Ivens was an eyewitness on many battlefields, his camera always ready . . . ."—André Stufkens

Born the son of a photography expert and equipment dealer, Joris Ivens was to later demonstrate an extensive repertoire of photographic knowledge and technique in his movies. After serving in the Dutch army during World War I, Ivens cofounded Film Liga in 1927, and began his cinematic career.

Two of his silent films, *De Brug* (1928) (*The Bridge*) and *Regen* (1929) (*Rain*), garnered international acclaim for Ivens's innovative technical prowess. A devout communist, he made socially controversial pictures during the Great Depression. *Borinage* (1933) was about life in a coal-mining region in the middle of militaristic activity, whereas the docudrama *Nieuwe gronden* (1934) (*New Earth*) followed the damaging effect of stock market speculation on the ordinary worker.

In 1936 Ivens relocated to the United States, where he continued to make antifascist films: *The Spanish Earth* (1937)—about the problems faced by the Spanish government in the Spanish Civil War—was narrated by John Dos Passos and Ernest Hemingway; and *The 400 Million* (1939) was about Chinese resistance to the Japanese invasion. He then joined forces with the United States and Canada to produce propaganda films during World War II, including *Our Russian Front* (1942) and *Know Your Enemy: Japan* (1945). With the rise of McCarthyism, Ivens left the United States but continued his visual political campaigns, throwing himself into works such as *Le 17e parallèle: La guerre du peuple* (1968) (*17th Parallel: Vietnam in War*) and *Le peuple et ses fusils* (1970) (*The People and Their Guns*), which denounced the U.S. war efforts. In tribute to these worthy efforts, Ivens was awarded the World Peace Prize in 1955, and was honored with a Knighthood in the Order of the Dutch Lion in 1989. **ES**

LEV KULESHOV

Born: Lev Vladimirovich Kuleshov, January 1, 1899 (Tambov, Russia); died 1970 (Moscow, Russia).

Directing style: Stood against Soviet authorities and refused to make propaganda movies, preferring to entertain; inventor of "the Kuleshov effect."

Lev Kuleshov, an early Russian film theorist and director, is regarded as one of the most instrumental figures in the field of editing during early Soviet cinema. The son of an artist and schoolteacher, he moved to Moscow with his widowed mother in 1910. After studying painting at the Moscow School of Painting, Architecture and Sculpture, he entered the film industry in 1916 as a set designer. When the revolution broke out in 1917, he joined the Bolshevik army and covered the war on the Eastern front with a documentary crew. He delivered his feature debut, *Proekt inzhenera Prayta* (1918) (*Engineer Prite's Project*), at the age of nineteen and was employed a year later as an instructor at the State Film School in Moscow.

During this period, Kuleshov introduced several ideas to Soviet cinema. He developed a style of acting explicitly for the screen that required the actor to use the entire body to express emotions, rather than just the face. He is best known, however, for his advances in film editing, most notably for "the Kuleshov effect." This emerged from experiments where Kuleshov would juxtapose shots in order to create a sensation in viewers—for instance, a shot of a forlorn man would be followed by a shot of a bowl of soup, subconsciously inducing hunger.

Kuleshov's most recognized film, the political satire *Neobychainye priklyucheniya mistera Vesta v strane bolshevikov* (1924) (*The Extraordinary Adventures of Mr. West in the Land of the Bolsheviks*) emulated the movies of U.S. silent film stars such as Buster Keaton and Harold Lloyd. Kuleshov was a great proponent of films coming from Hollywood and what he deemed "Americanism" in cinema. Consequently, he suffered severe criticism for his beliefs in entertainment over Soviet ideology. **WW**

Top Takes...

Boyevoy kinosbornik 13 1943
Klyatva Timura 1942 (*Timour's Oath*)
Sluchay v vulkane 1941 (*Descent in a Volcano*)
Sibiryaki 1940 (*Siberians*)
Dokhunda 1934
Velikiy uteshitel 1933 (*The Great Consoler*)
Gorizont 1932 (*Horizon*)
Sorokserdets 1931 (*Forty Hearts*)
Dva-Buldi-dva 1929 (*Two-Buildi-Two*)
Po zakonu 1926 (*By the Law*)
Neobychainye priklyucheniya mistera Vesta v strane bolshevikov 1924
    (*The Extraordinary Adventures of Mr. West in the Land of the Bolsheviks*)
Proekt inshenera Prayta 1918
    (*Engineer Prite's Project*)

"Kuleshov refused to remain silent about the reality he saw around him . . . ."—Andrew J. Horton

LOTTE REINIGER

Born: Lotte Reiniger, June 2, 1899 (Berlin, Germany); died 1981 (Dettenhausen, Germany).

Directing style: Pioneer and maker of silhouette animated films; classic fairy tales complete with elegant shadow puppets and imagery meticulously made by hand.

Top Takes...

In the specialized and highly demanding field of silhouette animation, the name of Lotte Reiniger stands supreme. In a career lasting 60 years, no one came near her for the wit, delicacy, ingenuity, and sheer brio of her work. Jean Renoir compared her to composer Wolfgang Amadeus Mozart—and the comparison holds good: like Mozart, Reiniger can make the most sophisticated technique seem lucidly simple.

Reiniger came to fame with her first and only feature-length animated film, *Die Abenteuer des Prinzen Achmed* (1926) (*The Adventures of Prince Achmed*). Like most of her work, it was based on a fairy tale, an Arabian Nights-style fantasy. Reiniger had studied at Max Reinhardt's acting studio and, though she rarely acted in person, she acted instead through her silhouettes, endowing her characters with expressive gestures and balletic grace. For *The Adventures of Prince Achmed*, as throughout her career, she cut out all the figures herself and devised her own animation. Unsurprisingly, the film took three years to make.

Reiniger's only other feature, *Die Jagd nach dem Glück* (1930) (*Running After Luck*), was part live action and part animation—an ill-fated mixture. That apart, for the rest of her career she stuck to shorts or inserts in other people's films, such as the shadow-play in Renoir's *La Marseillaise* (1938) (*The Marseillaise*). In the mid-1930s, Reiniger and her husband, the art historian Carl Koch, who acted as her producer and camera operator, quit Germany for Britain; she later took British citizenship. After Koch's death in 1963, Reiniger retired but was coaxed back in the 1970s to make two films for the National Film Board of Canada, *Aucassin and Nicolette* (1975) and *The Rose and the Ring* (1979), both of which showed that her fingers had lost none of their dexterity. **PK**

> "Lotte endowed every tale with enchanting touches . . . ."
>
> —William Moritz

GEORGE CUKOR

Born: George Dewey Cukor, July 7, 1899 (New York City, New York, U.S.); died 1983 (Los Angeles, California, U.S.).

Directing style: Actor's director who elicited dazzling performances from a cast; notable for skills working with female stars; perfect dialogue; elegant dramas.

1890s

It may seem a backhanded kind of compliment to say of any director that what one remembers most in his films are the performances—but George Cukor was happy to be known as the consummate actor's director, especially noted for his skill in getting the best from often temperamental actresses.

Cukor was also one of Hollywood's subtlest and most literate directors, with a gift for perfectly pitched dialogue scenes and for preserving the essence of plays and novels. His *The Personal History, Adventures, Experience, and Observation of David Copperfield, the Younger* (1935) remains the best Hollywood ever did by Charles Dickens; and while he was not quite able to turn Leslie Howard and Norma Shearer with their combined age of eighty-two years into *Romeo and Juliet* (1936), it is hard to imagine any other director capable even of trying.

Cukor's confidence in juggling large star casts was first evidenced in *Dinner at Eight* (1933), a sublime attempt to recreate the all-star success of Edmund Goulding's *Grand Hotel* (1932), distinguished by a superb comic performance from Jean Harlow. This rare talent for keeping fragile egos happy

Top Takes...

Rich and Famous 1981
The Blue Bird 1976
My Fair Lady 1964 ★
Something's Got to Give 1962
Let's Make Love 1960
The Marrying Kind 1952
Born Yesterday 1950 ☆
Adam's Rib 1949
A Double Life 1947 ☆
Gaslight 1944
The Philadelphia Story 1940 ☆
Gone with the Wind 1939
The Women 1939
Holiday 1938
Camille 1936
Romeo and Juliet 1936
Sylvia Scarlett 1935
*The Personal History, Adventures, Experience,
    and Observation of David Copperfield,
    the Younger* 1935
Little Women 1933 ☆
Dinner at Eight 1933
One Hour With You 1932
The Royal Family of Broadway 1930

LEFT: The all-star cast of Cukor's romantic comedy *The Philadelphia Story* in action.

Something's Got to Give

George Cukor was director of what turned out to be Marilyn Monroe's final movie, *Something's Got to Give*. Cukor hated the project and Monroe had to face his resentment every day. She was anxious to leave Fox and find better movie deals. Her new hairdo, however—a bouffant, sideswept style that made her look even younger than her 1950s image—was a huge success, and she enjoyed working with Dean Martin and Cyd Charisse.

- The film was an intended remake of *My Favorite Wife* (1940) with Irene Dunne and Cary Grant.
- For one sequence, Monroe was to wear a flesh-colored bathing suit, so as to appear to be swimming nude. When the scene was being shot, she removed the suit and was actually filmed nude. The resulting publicity photos guaranteed the film worldwide media coverage.
- When Monroe died unexpectedly in August 1962, the movie was abandoned, Dean Martin refusing to finish filming with anyone else.
- The TV documentary *Marilyn Monroe: The Final Days* (2001) includes a 37-minute segment from unused footage that had been shot for *Something's Got to Give*.
- This material eventually became *Move Over, Darling* (1963) with Doris Day and James Garner replacing Monroe and Martin. Many of the sets constructed for the original film were reused.

without disrupting the fabric of ensemble narratives made him the ideal choice for *The Women* (1939), which manages quite miraculously to show Norma Shearer, Rosalind Russell, Joan Crawford, Paulette Goddard, and Joan Fontaine all at, or near, their best. By the same token, there is no doubt that the vivid spectacle so ably handled by Victor Fleming in *Gone with the Wind* (1939) would have carried far less emotional weight if Cukor had not been there first to coax and encourage so complete a performance from Vivien Leigh.

A rewarding association

Cukor directed Greta Garbo twice and Crawford four times, but the actress with whom he was most fruitfully associated was Katharine Hepburn. Her brittle, prickly style only occasionally translated into box-office success, but Cukor, more than any other director, was able to bring out her more vulnerable, human side without ever compromising her authority. He also underlined her versatility by casting her in a literary adaptation, *Little Women* (1932); a sophisticated comedy, *Holiday* (1938); and oddities such as *Sylvia Scarlett* (1935), through much of which she is disguised as a boy.

Adam's Rib (1949) is the best of Hepburn's costarring vehicles with Spencer Tracy and arguably Cukor's last masterpiece, but their finest collaboration of all is *The Philadelphia Story* (1940), with Hepburn's Tracy Lord an unforgettable mix of ice and fragility, and Cary Grant and James Stewart responding to Cukor's touch with new-found nuances and subtleties. With Cukor, even such seasoned supporting players as Roland Young and John Halliday, who couldn't give a bad performance if they tried, managed to raise their game a notch.

Cukor's best work is additionally characterized by an unfussy precision in all technical details. Camera placement, set dressing, lighting, and composition were always as unobtrusive as they were perfectly judged. For Cukor, good direction was invisible. For instance, *Gaslight* (1944), essentially a barnstorming melodrama, became in his hands a thing of sheer elegance, sumptuously detailed, and magnetically

ABOVE: Audrey Hepburn as Eliza Doolittle in the musical adaptation of *My Fair Lady*.

performed by Ingrid Bergman and Charles Boyer. And all without ever compromising its narrative purpose. It is still a rattling good thriller.

The collapse of the studio system left Cukor with little option other than safe, expensive prestige movies. Glossy handling, big budgets, and attractive stars were not enough to turn *My Fair Lady* (1964) or *The Blue Bird* (1976) into projects worthy of his gifts, although his instinctive rapport with actresses did coax some nice work from Marilyn Monroe in *Let's Make Love* (1960). Under the circumstances it hardly mattered that *Rich and Famous* (1981) was a basically unsuccessful update of Vincent Sherman's *Old Acquaintance* (1943): the point is that it was made at all, and that the eighty-two-year-old Cukor was still around to make it. **MC**

"Give me a good script and I'll be a hundred times better as a director."

ALFRED HITCHCOCK

Born: Alfred Joseph Hitchcock, August 13, 1899 (Leytonstone, London, England); died 1980 (Los Angeles, California, U.S.).

Directing style: Venerated master of thriller genre; genius of suspense; trademark cameos in his own films; fluid camera takes; detailed social observation.

Top Takes…

Frenzy 1972
Topaz 1969
Marnie 1964
The Birds 1963
Psycho 1960 ☆
North by Northwest 1959
Vertigo 1958
The Man Who Knew Too Much 1956
To Catch a Thief 1955
Rear Window 1954 ☆
Strangers on a Train 1951
Rope 1948
The Paradine Case 1947
Notorious 1946
Spellbound 1945 ☆
Lifeboat 1944 ☆
Shadow of a Doubt 1943
Saboteur 1942
Suspicion 1941
Rebecca 1940 ☆
The Lady Vanishes 1938
Sabotage 1936
The 39 Steps 1935
Blackmail 1929
The Lodger 1927

RIGHT: Joan Fontaine is wide-eyed as the second Mrs. de Winter in the eerie *Rebecca*.

When he died in 1980, Sir Alfred "Hitch" Hitchcock had completed 57 feature films without ever winning an Academy Award. For some, Hitchcock is among the greatest of all filmmakers; he was indisputably the master of suspense. From early in his career he was eager to dispel the notion that suspense and surprise are similar. With surprise, the audience discovers something it does not know. With suspense, the audience knows something the character does not know, and watches to see what will happen as the character learns it.

Hitchcock grew up in Leytonstone, in London's East End, and received a Jesuit education. He wrote macabre short fiction, became terrified of jails and the police, was deeply bonded to his mother, and was intrigued by railway timetables, especially for far-off places. After drafting advertisements for an electrical firm, he made title cards for Famous Players-Lasky in the 1920s, and then assisted on set, where he met Alma Reville. They were married in 1926, a harmonious union, with Alma loyally assisting Hitchcock on scripting and editing. She also served up formidable cooking, her husband's appreciation

1890s

for which helped shape his world-renowned figure. Hitchcock was generally sober and businesslike at work, chummy to his confederates, yet so demanding that more than one writer was dismissed following long sessions of collaboration when, on a vital matter, he did not see eye to eye with the moviemaker.

ABOVE: Hitchcock directs the action from above on the set on the thriller *Rear Window*.

Filmmaking was principally an optical matter for Hitchcock. He would envision shots and sequences, and frequently worked from detailed sketches. After a sour experience working with the testy producer David O. Selznick on *Rebecca* (1940), his first film in the United States (he was naturalized in 1956), he devised a shooting system that made it impossible to edit in any but the way he wanted. His British films, including *The Lodger* (1927) about serial murder; the first British sound feature *Blackmail* (1929); the espionage thrillers *The 39 Steps*

"The length of a film should be directly related to the endurance of the human bladder."

In the Background

Alfred Hitchcock's highly acclaimed 1960 suspense/horror film *Psycho* was based on the novel of the same name by Robert Bloch, which was in turn inspired by the real-life crimes of a Wisconsin serial killer. Janet Leigh starred as Marion Crane, the secretary on the run, and Anthony Perkins as the lonely psychopath Norman Bates.

- Hitchcock bought the rights to the novel from Robert Bloch for $9,000.

- The film was shot in black and white as Hitchcock wanted to keep the cost down. It cost only $800,000 to make and has earned more than $40 million. It is also said that Hitchcock thought the film would be too gory if shot in color.

- Bosco Chocolate Syrup was used as fake blood in the shower scene. The syrup is still on sale throughout the United States and Europe.

- Janet Leigh had to cover her private parts with a moleskin suit while filming the shower scene to avoid "obscenity."

- When the shower scene was being filmed, Anthony Perkins was actually in New York, preparing for a play.

- Alfred Hitchcock's traditional cameo role occurs about four minutes in, when he appears outside Marion's office, wearing a cowboy hat.

- *Psycho* was Hitchcock's last movie for Paramount, although much of the film was shot at his new offices at Universal.

RIGHT: Lobby card for Alfred Hitchcock's highly praised horror movie *Psycho*.

(1935) and *The Lady Vanishes* (1938); and *Sabotage* (1936) brought him a huge reputation. In the United States of the 1940s, he made a number of stylish black and white films: *Suspicion* (1941); *Saboteur* (1942) with its compelling finale on the Statue of Liberty; *Shadow of a Doubt* (1943) about a troubled family in a California town; *Spellbound* (1945) about psychoanalysis; *Notorious* (1946) about a Nazi cadre in South America; and *The Paradine Case* (1947) about a beautiful woman accused of murdering her husband.

By the late 1940s Hitchcock was producing his own work. *Rope* (1948) is shot with 11-minute masters, and carefully edited so as to seem a single fluid camera take. Given the cumbersome Technicolor camera of the time and the intense lighting it required, the production required moving sets and strategically choreographed movements, as well as performances of the highest quality, since each actual take was very long and difficult to repeat.

The work of a movie master

Beyond technical experimentation, Hitchcock's true mastery lay in his melding of dense philosophical reflection on themes of universal significance to brilliant, often scathing, detailed social observation. Viewers can gain a deep appreciation for Hitchcock's work by noting its profoundly visual nature: meticulous camera placement and movement, use of insert shots to detail objects and views, and a profound sense of color and form. On top of this, Hitchcock's dialogue is not only witty and apt, but refined and often stunning.

To see that Hitchcock enriched the cinema, one need only recall the photographer paralyzed in a cast in *Rear Window* (1954); the U.S. tourist screaming during a concert in the remake of *The Man Who Knew Too Much* (1956); the deeply disorienting dolly/zoom combination in the tower of *Vertigo* (1958); Grant diving into a cornfield to escape an attacking crop-duster in *North by Northwest* (1959); Leigh blithely showering in *Psycho* (1960); Hedren being attacked by gulls in the finale of *The Birds* (1963); or thieving in *Marnie* (1964). **MP**

THE BIG NEWS IS THAT "PSYCHO" IS HITCHCOCK'S GREATEST CHILLER!

LUIS BUÑUEL

Born: Luis Buñuel Portolés, February 22, 1900 (Calanda, Teruel, Aragón, Spain); died 1983 (Mexico City, Mexico).

Directing style: Audacious and inventive father of cinematic surrealism; often used shocking imagery; insightful and outrageous themes.

Top Takes…

Cet obscur objet du désir 1977
  (That Obscure Object of Desire)
Le fantôme de la liberté 1974
  (The Phantom of Liberty)
Le charme discret de la bourgeoisie 1972
  (The Discreet Charm of the Bourgeosie)
Tristana 1970
La voie lactée 1969 (The Milky Way)
Belle de jour 1967
Simón del desierto 1965 (Simon of the Desert)
Le journal d'une femme de chambre 1964
  (Diary of a Chambermaid)
El ángel exterminador 1962
  (The Exterminating Angel)
Viridiana 1961
The Young One 1960
La fièvre monte à El Pao 1959
Nazarín 1959
La mort en ce jardin 1956
Ensayo de un crimen 1955
Una mujer sin amor 1952
Los olvidados 1950
  (The Young and the Damned)
Las Hurdes 1933 (Land Without Bread)
L'âge d'or 1930 (The Golden Age)
Un chien andalou 1929 (An Andalusian Dog)

RIGHT: Simone Mareuil and someone
"itching to kill" in An Andalusian Dog.

In Luis Buñuel's oeuvre, nothing is true and everything is permitted. Spanish-bred Buñuel burst on to the Paris scene with Un chien andalou (1929) (An Andalusian Dog), created with compatriot Salvador Dalí. The opening, a thin cloud covering a full moon, intercut with a razor slitting an eyeball, is one of the most spine-cringing ever to be put on film—catch the clever metaphor of destroying visual trust in truth? Causing outrage and awe, the film remains the definitive surrealist statement. He followed it with L'âge d'or (1930) (The Golden Age); it was more apostolic, chiefly in its attack on the Roman Catholic church.

Returning to Spain, Buñuel made Las Hurdes (1933) (Land Without Bread), a documentary about peasant life in remote rural areas. The Spanish Civil War exiled him to Mexico where he contented himself with underrated Mexican melodramas in which the surrealism is surpassed by the cruelty of life itself.

With Viridiana (1961), Buñuel drew the wider public's eye, causing a furor for the film's perceived blasphemous content. Its earthy style became a model for the autumn of Buñuel's career when he refocused on the absurdity of life's ceremonies and the bourgeoisie's forlorn attempts to remain dignified.

1900s

The dark, austere *Le journal d'une femme de chambre* (1964) (*Diary of a Chambermaid*) was followed by *Belle de jour* (1967), his most kinky film. Here, Buñuel is the perfect Freudian, linking sexual desire with capitalism. In *Le charme discret de la bourgeoisie* (1972) (*The Discreet Charm of the Bourgeoisie*), he satirized the robustness of routines, petty lies, and deceits common to polite intercourse. Even while the revolution starts, the dinner guests prefer sophisticated conversation to inconvenient reality.

Buñuel's last two films, *Le fantôme de la liberté* (1974) (*The Phantom of Liberty*) and *Cet obscur objet du désir* (1977) (*That Obscure Object of Desire*), are perhaps his most wicked. The first showcased the banality of violence, the second explicated surrealists' fascination with fetishism. Buñuel has often been accused of deception, even in his autobiography, but his sense of humor allows his lack of honesty to be forgiven. After all, the shrink's own phantasm is so much better than the truth. **EM**

ABOVE: Catherine Deneuve as Séverine Serizy in the surrealist *Belle de jour*.

An Atheist, Thank God!

Despite, or because of, his strict Jesuit education, Buñuel was a lifelong atheist.

- He famously declared, "I am still, thank God, an atheist"—though he later appeared to modify this statement, saying, "I'm not a Christian, but I'm not an atheist either."

- *The Golden Age* was interpreted as an attack on Catholicism and banned by the French police. In the film, a bishop is shown being thrown out of a window.

- Buñuel's former friend and collaborator Salvador Dalí denounced him as a communist and atheist.

ALESSANDRO BLASETTI

Born: Alessandro Blasetti, July 3, 1900 (Rome, Lazio, Italy); died 1987 (Rome, Lazio, Italy).

Directing style: One of the fathers of Italian neorealism; leading director of fascist regime; grandiose and formal; creator of episodic film genre.

1900s

Top Takes...

Simón Bolívar 1969

Liolà 1964 (*A Very Handy Man*)

Europa di notte 1959 (*European Nights*)

Peccato che sia una canaglia 1954 (*Too Bad She's Bad*)

Nessuno torna indietro 1945 (*Responsibility Comes Back*)

Quattro passi fra le nuvole 1942 (*Four Steps in the Clouds*)

La cena delle beffe 1942

La corona di ferro 1941 (*The Iron Crown*)

Un'avventura di Salvator Rosa 1939 (*An Adventure of Salvator Rosa*)

Vecchia guardia 1934 (*The Old Guard*)

1860 1934

Palio 1932

Terra madre 1931

Along with Mario Camerini, Alessandro Blasetti was the key director in 1930s Italy, doing much to shape the future of Italian cinema. His influence was not so much in what he directed, as in what he proved was possible. Having trained as a lawyer, he soon switched careers, acting as the film critic for *L'Impero*, and later editing both *Lo Spettacolo d'Italia* and *Cinematografo*, in whose pages he campaigned for a new, specifically Italian style of filmmaking. Over a 50-year career his output was eclectic, taking in the historical epic *1860* (1934), and the literary *La cena delle beffe* (1942), among others.

Critical opinion on Blasetti's body of work has always been mixed. Some see films such as *Terra madre* (1931), *Palio* (1932), and *Vecchia guardia* (1934) (*The Old Guard*) as expressing a kind of fascistic nationalist spirit, to which his grandiose formal style was said to act as a kind of supporting pillar. Others look toward films such as *La corona di ferro* (1941) (*The Iron Crown*) as a veiled critique of the authoritarian regime within which he was bound to work. Of the latter, Nazi Germany's Propaganda Minister Joseph Goebbels is reported to have said, "If a German director made this film today, in Germany, he would face the firing squad." In the postwar period, Blasetti produced some commercially successful films, but his star was on the wane. Despite doing much to promote Sophia Loren's cause in the comedy *Peccato che sia una canaglia* (1954) (*Too Bad She's Bad*), films such as *Europa di notte* (1959) (*European Nights*) only demonstrated the rather haphazard nature of his later output. As with Camerini, despite having a relatively successful postwar career—more so than any other prewar director—the stains of working during the fascist period could never quite be washed away. **RH**

"[*Too Bad She's Bad*] has so [much] to recommend it that it hurts to have it get away."—*New York Times*

ROBERT SIODMAK

Born: Robert Siodmak, August 8, 1900 (Dresden, Saxony, Germany); died 1993 (Locarno, Ticino, Switzerland).

Directing style: Auteur director of classic film noir; Expressionistic lighting; use of flashback and mise-en-scène; imaginative décor.

German-born Robert Siodmak worked as a stage director and banker before moving into films with the aid of his producer cousin. His directorial debut, the silent *Menschen am Sonntag* (1930) (*People on Sunday*), saw him collaborate with other future big names—Billy Wilder and Fred Zinnemann. Being Jewish, Siodmak's career in Germany was cut short when the Nazis came to power and, after working in France, he moved to Hollywood in 1940. In order to obtain a visa to enter the United States, he claimed to have been born in Memphis, Tennessee, when his parents were on vacation there. His early films were low-budget thrillers and horror movies, but he made his name with a series of strikingly directed film noirs in the later 1940s.

The *Spiral Staircase* (1946) is a period drama about a serial killer preying on vulnerable women. Siodmak made masterly use of his main set, a creepy Victorian house. In *The Killers* (1946), Ava Gardner played a beautiful femme fatale who seals Burt Lancaster's fate. The director's use of light and shadow was exemplary. In *The Dark Mirror* (1946), Olivia de Havilland played identical twins, one of whom is suspected of murder, while *Cry of the City* (1948) has Victor Mature as a cop pitted against killer Richard Conte, whom he has known since childhood. In *Criss Cross* (1949), Lancaster is once again overcome by a femme fatale, this time played by Yvonne De Carlo.

All these films are distinguished by imaginative décor, atmospheric camerawork, and Siodmak's keen eye for quirky, even grotesque, minor characters. He returned to his native Germany, where he made several more features, with a solitary excursion back into English-language cinema for the big-budget Western, *Custer of the West* (1967), shot in widescreen. **EB**

1900s

Top Takes...

Custer of the West 1967
Escape from East Berlin 1962
Katia 1959
Le grand jeu 1954 (*Card of Fate*)
The Crimson Pirate 1952
The File on Thelma Jordan 1950
Criss Cross 1949
Cry of the City 1948
The Dark Mirror 1946
The Killers 1946 ☆
The Spiral Staircase 1946
Christmas Holiday 1944
Cobra Woman 1944
Phantom Lady 1944
Menschen am Sonntag 1930
   (*People on Sunday*)

"He's dead now, except for he's breathing."

——Jail ward doctor, *The Killers*

MERVYN LeROY

Born: Mervyn LeRoy, October 15, 1900 (San Francisco, California, U.S.); died 1987 (Los Angeles, California, U.S.).

Directing style: Highly adept at spotting and capitalizing on current social themes and trends; prolific director of dramas in the early 1930s.

Top Takes...

No Time for Sergeants 1958

The Bad Seed 1956

Mister Roberts 1955

Million Dollar Mermaid 1952

Quo Vadis 1951

The House I Live In 1945

Thirty Seconds Over Tokyo 1944

Madame Curie 1943

Random Harvest 1942 ☆

Johnny Eager 1942

They Won't Forget 1937

Tugboat Annie 1933

Gold Diggers of 1933 1933

I Am a Fugitive From a Chain Gang 1932

Five Star Final 1931

Little Caesar 1931

Mervyn LeRoy's childhood was often difficult. Having dropped out of school by the age of twelve, he drifted into acting in vaudeville and, in 1919, decided to try his luck in Hollywood. Urged on by his cousin, he soon found employment in the wardrobe and costume department of Famous Players-Lasky.

After appearing before the camera in bit parts in lightweight films, LeRoy turned his talents to gag writing, and worked on a string of popular comedies and melodramas. He made his breakthrough as a director at Warner Brothers in 1930 with the hard-boiled crime drama *Little Caesar* (1931), which propelled actor Edward G. Robinson to stardom and launched the early 1930s cycle of gangster pictures. By 1931, LeRoy had become one of Warners' top directors, specializing in brutal Depression-era realism in films such as *Five Star Final* (1931), and perhaps his finest film as a director, *I Am a Fugitive From a Chain Gang* (1932), which offered a scathing indictment of prison conditions in the U.S. South. He directed the dramatic sections of *Gold Diggers of 1933* (1933), and proved an adept farceur with the raucous comedy *Tugboat Annie* (1933).

Leaving Warners in 1938, LeRoy found a new home at MGM, where he shifted more toward the producer's chair, but he returned to directing with the crime drama *Johnny Eager* (1942), the historical biography *Madame Curie* (1943), and the patriotic war film *Thirty Seconds Over Tokyo* (1944). In the 1950s, he moved into larger productions, such as *Quo Vadis* (1951). LeRoy never lost sight of what the public wanted in its movie entertainment. If his late films seem somewhat slack, he more than made up for it with his early social dramas, which remain some of the most riveting examples of early Hollywood sound cinema. **WWD**

"He'd accept me. He'd pity me. And he'd resent me."

——Paula, *Random Harvest*

RIGHT: Edward G. Robinson and Boris Karloff in the crime drama *Five Star Final*.

ROBERT BRESSON

Born: Robert Bresson, September 25, 1901 (Bromont-Lamothe, Puy-de-Dôme, Auvergne, France); died 1999 (Paris, France).

Directing style: Minimalist auteur; flat characterization; pared-down mise-en-scène; "actor-model" directing method; preoccupation with redemption and salvation.

Top Takes...

L'Argent 1983 (Money)

Le diable probablement 1977
  (The Devil Probably)

Lancelot du Lac 1974 (Lancelot of the Lake)

Quatre nuits d'un rêveur 1971
  (Four Nights of a Dreamer)

Une femme douce 1969 (A Gentle Creature)

Mouchette 1967

Au hasard Balthazar 1966 (Balthazar)

Procès de Jeanne d'Arc 1962
  (Trial of Joan of Arc)

Pickpocket 1959

Un condamné à mort s'est échappé
  ou Le vent souffle où il veut 1956
  (A Man Escaped)

Journal d'un curé de campagne 1951
  (Diary of a Country Priest)

Les dames du Bois de Boulogne 1945
  (Ladies of the Park)

Les anges du péché 1943 (Angels of the Streets)

Les affaires publiques 1934 (Public Affairs)

Seemingly influenced by no one, his idiosyncratic approach to filmmaking the result of some mysterious process of self-fashioning, Robert Bresson paradoxically became one of the most influential directors of his generation. Like Sergei M. Eisenstein and Jean-Luc Godard, Bresson's aura derives in large measure because of the often dense, mandarin intellectuality of his meditations on the cinema. And his films, like theirs, pose fascinating problems of structure and meaning. Spare in mise-en-scène, their dramatic moments often uncontextualized, the characters reduced to enigmatic physical presences, Bresson's films deconstruct almost completely the spectator's expectations for cinematic meaning.

Yet they are among the richest spiritual films the cinema has ever produced. His characters are unexpectedly offered opportunities to transcend their fate that they are unable to refuse. Emptied almost entirely of that which signifies the everyday, Bresson's films suggest from the outset a life lived in response only to the essential realities of existence, whose nature defies description and that can only be registered by the absence of what would otherwise mask their presence.

RIGHT: In *A Man Escaped* a prisoner escapes but finds spiritual salvation in the process.

Journal d'un curé de campagne (1951) (*Diary of a Country Priest*), an adaptation from Georges Bernanos, is a touching, if very abstract, treatment of spiritual growth. *Pickpocket* (1959), borrowing the theme of crime and punishment from Fyodor Doestoevsky, traces the discovery by the eponymous hero of his profession, his arrest for theft, but then his liberation by an unmerited profession of love from a woman he has abused.

Later in his career, and working in color, Bresson offered two of world cinema's most affecting meditations on human fallibility. *Lancelot du Lac* (1974) (*Lancelot of the Lake*) pierces to the core of the medieval legend, exploring the bond of honor that affords mutual respect, whereas *L'Argent* (1983) (*Money*), like a medieval exemplum, dissects the destructiveness of greed. Every film Bresson produced offers a commentary on the medium itself, and on its potential to uncover the mysteries of human experience. **BP**

ABOVE: *Lancelot of the Lake* was Bresson's haunting take on the Arthurian legend.

Natural Performers

Robert Bresson did not think of his performers as actors, but rather as "models." He instructed them to empty their faces of emotion and speak their lines without expression, often providing them with no information about the dramatic content of a shot. After *Les dames du Bois de Boulogne* (1945) (*Ladies of the Park*), he virtually stopped working with professional actors. Bresson's performers are encouraged simply to be—he thus invests them with a meaning that is never artificially confected. This "actor-model" method contributed to Bresson's uniquely spare and intensely personal style.

WALT DISNEY

Born: Walter Elias Disney, December 5, 1901 (Chicago, Illinois, U.S.); died 1966 (Los Angeles, California, U.S.).

Directing style: King of animation; founder of global studio; inventor of Mickey Mouse; innovator who created first cartoon to use synchronized sound.

Top Takes...

Health for the Americas: Cleanliness Brings Health 1945

The Winged Scourge 1943

The Golden Touch 1935

Just Mickey 1930

The Barnyard Concert 1930

The Jazz Fool 1929

When the Cat's Away 1929

The Opry House 1929

Jungle Rhythm 1929

Steamboat Willie 1928

Sleigh Bells 1928

Alice's Wonderland 1923

Cinderella 1922

Jack and the Beanstalk 1922

Little Red Riding Hood 1922

"We keep moving forward, opening up new doors and doing new things . . . ."

Walt Disney was more a producer and entrepreneur than a director, though he was given director credit for many of his early animated shorts, including *Steamboat Willie* (1928), which featured his iconic creation, Mickey Mouse, as well as his groundbreaking *Snow White and the Seven Dwarfs* (1937).

Disney was raised in rural Missouri, where he developed both his affinity for animals and his ability to draw. His talents included a strong sense of narrative drive and an everyman feel for what would entertain the public. He was also gifted at maximizing the talents of others, including his older brother, Roy Disney, who directed the financial side of Walt Disney Studios through often lean times.

Disney combined serious storytelling with classic cartoon slapstick, exemplified by the different styles used in *Snow White*. The romantic leads are given realistic features and movement, whereas the seven dwarfs exhibit the stretchy, bouncy qualities of comic animation. Disney was a technical innovator as well, utilizing sound and the Technicolor process in his animated shorts almost as soon as they were available. Use of the multiplane camera gave his productions a lifelike depth and texture previously unknown in animation. Disney Studios later moved into live-action TV and film, anchoring the fledgling ABC-TV network with its *Disneyland* (1954–1990), and producing another cultural icon with the fantasy musical *Mary Poppins* (1964). It also integrated live and animated actors in films such as *Song of the South* (1946).

Disney's final creative legacy was his world-famous theme parks: Disneyland Park, which opened in California in 1955, and Walt Disney World Resort, which opened in Florida a few years after his death in late 1966. **WSW**

MAX OPHÜLS

Born: Max Oppenheimer Ophüls, May 6, 1902 (Saarbrücken, Saarland, Germany); died 1957 (Hamburg, Germany).

Directing style: Use of long takes that weave intricate, gliding patterns around sets and actors; romantically themed dramas, often set in Vienna, Austria.

Though he lived there for only a year in his early twenties, Vienna—specifically pre-World War I Hapsburg Vienna—was Max Ophüls's spiritual home, and in his movies he returned there again and again.

Hapsburg Vienna was the setting for the best of Ophüls's early films, *Liebelei* (1933) (*Flirtation*), which tells of a shy young girl who falls for a dashing officer. Evident in *Flirtation* is Ophüls's foremost stylistic trait, his love for the moving camera. Whenever possible, he liked to tell his story with long sinuous takes lasting several minutes. But this constant movement isn't merely decorative or showing off. Décor, in Ophüls's film, is all important, and in restlessly exploring his sets, he is demonstrating how his characters are defined, and often constrained, by their surroundings.

Ophüls spent most of the 1940s in Hollywood. Though unhappy there, he directed some of his finest work at this time. Trapped women feature in *Caught* (1949) and *The Reckless Moment* (1949), but his masterpiece of these years is *Letter from an Unknown Woman* (1948), a moving study of unrequited love that is based in Vienna and has distinctly Viennese themes.

Returning to France, his adopted country, Ophüls directed his best-known film, *La Ronde* (1950) (*Roundabout*), an elegant expression of the ceaseless pursuit of love. He made only three more films before his death. *Le Plaisir* (1952) (*House of Pleasure*); *Madame de . . .* (1953) (*The Earrings of Madame de . . .*), where the erotic carousel is symbolized by a pair of earrings that pass from hand to hand; and *Lola Montès* (1955), a biopic of the nineteenth-century courtesan. This, his only color film, was mutilated by its producers; a restored version, long thought lost, has only recently surfaced. **PK**

Top Takes...

Les amants de Montparnasse (*Montarnasse 19*) 1958 (*Modigliani of Montparnasse*)

Lola Montès 1955

Madame de . . . 1953 (*The Earrings of Madame de . . .*)

Le Plaisir 1952 (*House of Pleasure*)

Vendetta 1950

La Ronde 1950 (*Roundabout*)

The Reckless Moment 1949

Caught 1949

Letter from an Unknown Woman 1948

The Exile 1947

L'école des femmes 1940

La tendre ennemie 1936 (*The Tender Enemy*)

Liebelei 1933 (*Flirtation*)

Die verliebte Firma 1931 (*The Company in Love*)

"You don't know how a family can surround you at times."

—Lucia Harper, *The Reckless Moment*

ANATOLE LITVAK

Born: Mikhail Anatole Litvak, May 10, 1902 (Kiev, Ukraine); died 1974 (Neuilly-sur-Seine, Hauts-de-Seine, Île-de-France, France).

Directing style: Maker of groundbreaking crime thrillers and romantic dramas, often with a European flavor; notable rapport with actors; frequent takes.

Russian-born Anatole Litvak was an assistant director on Abel Gance's *Napoléon* (1927). In the first half of the 1930s, Litvak directed in Germany on films such as *Dolly macht Karriere* (1930) (*Dolly Gets Ahead*); in France on films such as *Mayerling* (1936); and in Britain on *Sleeping Car* (1933).

He then went to Hollywood to direct the French-themed World War I drama *The Woman I Love* (1937). He later fetched up at Warner Brothers, and picked up a U.S. edge to turn out *The Amazing Dr. Clitterhouse* (1938), an Edward G. Robinson and Humphrey Bogart crime comedy; *Castle on the Hudson* (1940), a John Garfield prison movie; and *City for Conquest* (1940), a boxing picture starring James Cagney. *Confessions of a Nazi Spy* (1939), a fact-based account of the activities of pro-Hitler groups within the United States, proved controversial with U.S. isolationists of the time. He also worked with Warner Brothers's female stars, directing Bette Davis in *The Sisters* (1938) and *All This, and Heaven Too* (1940).

When World War II arrived, he served with the U.S. army and worked with director Frank Capra to make *Why We Fight* shorts. Because of his ability to speak Russian, German, and French, he played a significant role as the head of the army's photography division. Following the war he resumed his career with a couple of outstanding film noir women's pictures, eliciting great hysteria from Barbara Stanwyck as a menaced invalid in *Sorry, Wrong Number* (1948), and Olivia de Havilland as a psychiatric patient in the Oscar-nominated *The Snake Pit* (1948). As he grew older, Litvak worked infrequently, both in Europe and the United States, although it was on high-profile movies such as the Oscar-nominated *Decision Before Dawn* (1951). **KN**

> "I just don't know where it's all gonna end!"
>
> —Celia Sommerville, *The Snake Pit*

BORIS BARNET

Born: Boris Vasilyevich Barnet, June 18, 1902 (Moscow, Russia); died 1965 (Riga, Latvia).

Directing style: Father of Russian comedy; master of charming, Chaplinesque tragicomic satires; poignant romantic humor combined with absurdist slapstick.

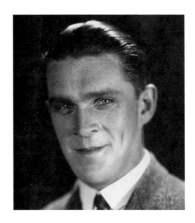

Boris Barnet found that his tragicomic satirical skills as an actor and director were a double-edged sword when faced with an intractable Soviet state bureaucracy. However, he made two acknowledged masterpieces, *Okraina* (1933) (*The Patriots*) and *U samogo sinyego morya* (1936) (*By the Bluest of Seas*), during a turbulent career that ended in suicide.

His paternal grandfather, an English printer, settled in Moscow where Barnet was born in 1902. He studied painting before serving as a medic and physical fitness instructor in the Red Army. He became a professional boxer after the Russian Civil War. Director Lev Kuleshov saw one of Barnet's bouts and invited him to work as a handyman in his movie workshop.

Soaking up directing skills, Barnet's first solo effort was *Devushka s korobkoy* (1927) (*When Moscow Laughs*), whose Chaplinesque blend of tragedy and comedy gently poked fun at the government. A subsequent film, *Dom na Trubnoy* (1928) (*The House on Trubnaya*), suggesting how the Russian Revolution divided a small community, did not endear him to the regime. His next offering, the almost Chekhovian *The Patriots*, continued the theme but was lambasted for portraying the masses in a negative light. *By The Bluest of Seas* received an even more hostile reception for perceived allegorical references at a time when the Soviet Union was unusually sensitive.

Toeing the line, *Noch v sentyabre* (1939) (*A Night in September*) portrayed the secret police as heroes fighting state sabotage. World War II dominated his subsequent output and he was awarded the Stalin Prize in 1948. Nonetheless, during a career spanning four decades, Barnet proved to be a subversive artist dressed as a mainstream director. He took his own life while filming in Riga, Latvia in 1965. **TE**

Top Takes…

Alyonka 1961
Lyana 1955
Kontsert masterov ukrainskogo iskusstva 1952
   (*Concert of the Masters of Ukrainian Art*)
Shchedroye leto 1950
Podvig razvedchika 1947 (*The Secret Agent*)
Noch v sentyabre 1939 (*A Night in September*)
U samogo sinyego morya 1936
   (*By the Bluest of Seas*)
Okraina 1933 (*The Patriots*)
Ledolom 1931 (*The Thaw*)
Privideniya 1931 (*The Ghost*)
Zhivye dela 1930 (*Living Things*)
Dom na Trubnoy 1928 (*The House on Trubnaya*)
Moskva v oktyabre 1927 (*Moscow in October*)
Devushka s korobkoy 1927
   (*When Moscow Laughs*)

> "His films displayed a mastery of visual technique . . . ."
> —Richard Taylor

WILLIAM WYLER

Born: Wilhelm Weiller, July 1, 1902 (Mulhouse, Haut-Rhin, France); died 1981 (Los Angeles, California, U.S.).

Directing style: Pioneer of deep-focus cinematography to create illusion of depth and heighten naturalism and drama: maker of monumental epics.

Top Takes…

Funny Girl 1968
How to Steal a Million 1966
The Collector 1965
Ben-Hur 1959
The Big Country 1958
Friendly Persuasion 1956
Roman Holiday 1953 ☆
Carrie 1952
Detective Story 1951 ☆
The Heiress 1949 ☆
The Best Years of Our Lives 1946 ★
Memphis Belle: A Story of a Flying Fortress 1944
Mrs. Miniver 1942 ★
The Little Foxes 1941 ☆
The Letter 1940 ☆
Wuthering Heights 1939 ☆
Jezebel 1938
Dead End 1937
Come and Get It 1936
Dodsworth 1936 ☆
These Three 1936
The Good Fairy 1935
Tom Brown of Culver 1932
The Storm 1930
Hell's Heroes 1930

RIGHT: Teresa Wright and Greer Garson in Wyler's Oscar-winning *Mrs. Miniver*.

There was a time when William Wyler was hailed as one of the finest of all directors, praised for his use of deep-focus cinematography and long, unbroken takes. Today his reputation has declined—a filmmaker dethroned by critical fashion, damned for those very qualities for which he was once lauded. His restraint has come to be seen as impersonality, his good taste as complacency, his seriousness as pomposity, his technical skill and lucidity as bland.

Wyler learned his craft making silent Westerns for Universal Studios. His finest period began when he teamed with Sam Goldwyn in 1935. The two shared a commitment to high-quality films often adapted from classic literature; Wyler's version of *Wuthering Heights* (1939) still stands up well; two Lillian Hellman plays, *These Three* (1936) and *The Little Foxes* (1941), allowed Wyler to develop his technique of expressing the psychological relationship between characters through framing, composition, and camera angles.

Famous for his tireless perfectionism—his nickname was "90-Take Wyler"—Wyler was loved and loathed by his actors, who went through hell on his sets, but often reaped their

ABOVE: The famous chariot race in *Ben-Hur* was directed by stuntman Yakima Canutt.

1900s

compensation in awards. Wyler himself won a Best Director Academy Award for *Mrs. Miniver* (1942), a propaganda piece supporting Britain's war effort. It may look sentimental now, but it was hugely successful at the time. A more honest treatment of the war came in Wyler's bomber documentary *Memphis Belle: A Story of a Flying Fortress* (1944), followed by *The Best Years of Our Lives* (1946).

Wyler's postwar films often seemed overcome by grandiosity; not just the biblical epic *Ben-Hur* (1959), but the Western *The Big Country* (1958), which told a simple story in monumental style. Better were the more intimate chamber works such as *The Heiress* (1949); the comedy *Roman Holiday* (1953) that brought stardom to Audrey Hepburn; and *The Collector* (1965), from John Fowles's novel of creepy obsession. Whatever the genre or the scale, Wyler never brought to any of his films less than impeccable craftsmanship. **PK**

Joining the War Effort

William Wyler made *Mrs. Miniver* as an encouragement to the United States to join the war against Nazism. Winston Churchill and President Franklin D. Roosevelt were among the film's admirers.

- The vicar's rousing speech (delivered by actor Henry Wilcoxon) was subsequently broadcast on Voice of America and printed on propaganda leaflets dropped over Europe.
- William Wyler joined the U.S. Army Signal Corps after completing the film.
- Wyler was on overseas service the night he received his Oscar for the film.

VITTORIO DE SICA

Born: Vittorio De Sica, July 7, 1902 (Sora, Lazio, Italy); died 1974 (Neuilly-sur-Seine, Hauts-de-Seine, Île-de-France, France).

Directing style: Maker of comedies in his early career; later career made intense neorealist dramas that highlighted contemporary social issues; poignant themes.

1900s

Top Takes...

Il Viaggio 1974 (The Journey)

Una breve vacanza 1973 (A Brief Vacation)

Il Giardino dei Finzi-Contini 1970
(The Garden of the Finzi-Continis)

Caccia alla volpe 1966 (After the Fox)

Matrimonio all'Italiana 1964
(Marriage, Italian-Style)

La Ciociara 1960 (Two Women)

Stazione Termini 1953
(Indiscretion of an American Wife)

Umberto D. 1952

Miracolo a Milano 1951 (Miracle in Milan)

Ladri di biciclette 1948 (The Bicycle Thief)

Sciuscià 1946 (Shoe-Shine)

I bambini ci guardano 1944
(The Children Are Watching Us)

Rose scarlatte 1940 (Red Roses)

Vittorio De Sica spent his childhood in Naples. Drawn to acting, he became a matinee idol of Italian theater in his twenties and began his directorial career in film with *Rose scarlatte* (1940) (*Red Roses*). When he encountered the writer Cesare Zavattini, his life was changed. Collaborating with Zavattini, he made *I bambini ci guardano* (1944) (*The Children Are Watching Us*), *Sciuscià* (1946) (*Shoe-Shine*), and the classic *Ladri di biciclette* (1948) (*The Bicycle Thief*), all films that touchingly pose the vulnerabilities of childhood and poverty in relation to one another, and heralded the advent of neorealism.

Miracolo a Milano (1951) (*Miracle in Milan*) is a scathing portrait of class difference in Italy, with its cadre of homeless folk encamped outside the city, dispossessed of their cardboard shacks and hovels by a heartless magnate who wants his land. In the finale they ascend to heaven. *Umberto D.* (1952) recounts the life of a lonely old man rejected by society and community; in the heartbreaking finale, he attempts to leap in front of a train, holding his pet dog. The dog runs off. Now he must follow it into a park, the dog at first distrustful but soon regaining his affection for the frail old man. *Stazione Termini* (1953) (*Indiscretion of an American Wife*) stars Jennifer Jones and Montgomery Clift in a tale of indecisive love. *Matrimonio all'Italiana* (1964) (*Marriage, Italian-Style*) joins a prostitute and an arrogant businessman, played by Sophia Loren and Marcello Mastroianni respectively, in a remake of Edouardo de Filippo's 1951 movie. *Il Giardino dei Finzi-Contini* (1970) (*The Garden of the Finzi-Continis*) is set in Benito Mussolini's Italy, and shows the blithe unawareness with which it is possible to live a bourgeois life under desperate political circumstances. **MP**

"Children are always prisoners of grownups."

—Micol, *The Garden of the Finzi-Continis*

LENI RIEFENSTAHL

Born: Helene Bertha Amalie Riefenstahl, August 22, 1902 (Wedding, Berlin, Germany); died 2003 (Poecking, Germany).

Directing style: Maker of documentary propaganda films for the German Nazi Party; smooth cinematography; glorification of concept of Aryan physical beauty.

Leni Riefenstahl was the Third Reich's key visual ideologue. As such her films are known as pure propaganda, treaties of Nazi policy. Her involvement with Adolf Hitler and Joseph Goebbels ties her to the horror of Nazi atrocities, and her films cannot be viewed in isolation of that awareness: they share the blame.

Pre-Nazi Riefenstahl was an instinctive filmmaker with a sharp eye for human bodies in action, eroticized in full performance. After starring in several Arnold Fanck adventure films, she made her directorial debut with *Das blaue Licht* (1932) (*The Blue Light*), a film whose celebration of *Körperkultur* (meaning, in this case, an admiration for the Aryan physique) struck a chord with Nazi Party leaders. After the uninspiring *Der Sieg des Glaubens* (1933) (*Victory of the Faith*), Riefenstahl demanded full access and collaboration and managed to capture, and perhaps help create, the mass-hypnotic spirit of the Party Days celebrations in Nuremberg in 1934. The careful choreography, smooth cinematography, and painstakingly precise editing turned *Triumph des Willens* (1935) (*Triumph of the Will*) into a groundbreaking documentary, a milestone in propaganda, and a global advertisement for Hitler. Riefenstahl's next film, *Olympia 1. Teil—Fest der Völker* (1938) (*Olympia Part One: Festival of the Nations*), the first of a two-volume report on the 1936 Berlin Olympics, revolutionized sports coverage, establishing techniques still in use today.

Ostracized after the war, Riefenstahl made only one more feature, *Tiefland* (1954) (*Lowlands*), and, in 2002, the documentary *Impressionen unter Wasser* (*Underwater Impressions*), a final example of her creative genius. She remained, until her death, a troubled veteran, unrepentant and irritated by insistent interrogation, but also visibly haunted by her past. **EM**

Top Takes...

Impressionen unter Wasser 2002
  (*Underwater Impressions*)

Tiefland 1954 (*Lowlands*)

Olympia 1. Teil—Fest der Völker 1938
  (*Olympia Part One: Festival of the Nations*)

Olympia 2. Teil—Fest der Schönheit 1938
  (*Olympia Part Two: Festival of Beauty*)

Fesliches Nürnberg 1937

Triumph des Willens 1935
  (*Triumph of the Will*)

Tag Der Freiheit-Unsere Wehrmacht 1935

Das blaue Licht 1932
  (*The Blue Light*)

"[*Olympia* is] a lavish hymn to sporting prowess and physical beauty and strength."—*Guardian*

POWELL AND PRESSBURGER

Pressburger: Born Imre József Emmerich Pressburger, December 5, 1902 (Miskolc, Hungary); died 1988 (Saxstead, Suffolk, England).

Powell: Born Michael Latham Powell, September 30, 1905 (Bekesbourne, Kent, England); died 1990 (Avening, Gloucestershire, England).

Directing style: Duo notable for stiff-upper-lip war films; unexpected thematic and stylistic idiosyncrasies, such as the use of Expressionist lighting and framings.

Top Takes...

Ill Met by Moonlight 1957

The Battle of the River Plate 1956

Oh . . . Rosalinda!! 1955

The Wild Heart 1952

The Tales of Hoffmann 1951

Gone to Earth 1950

The Elusive Pimpernel 1950

The Small Back Room 1949

The Red Shoes 1948

Black Narcissus 1947

A Matter of Life and Death 1946

I Know where I'm Going! 1945

A Canterbury Tale 1944

The Volunteer 1943

The Life and Death of Colonel Blimp 1943

One of Our Aircraft is Missing 1942

The most notable writer and director team in world cinema history, Michael Powell and Emeric Pressburger exemplify the characteristic virtues of the British cinema as well as its imaginative limitations. Although the duo proved skilled at the drama of manners with broadly social themes, developed from a middle-class perspective (*The Life and Death of Colonel Blimp* (1943) is perhaps the most notable British film in that genre ever made), they could also handle realist projects with documentary styling and social themes, such as *One of Our Aircraft is Missing* (1942) and *The Battle of the River Plate* (1956). Both movies have become established classics in one of the British industry's most profitable and critically successful war era and postwar genres—the stiff-upper-lip war film.

Powell began his career as the 1927 Cinematograph Act revitalized a hitherto moribund national film industry, learning the craft of directing with the steady employment afforded by these often forgettable (and now mostly lost) films. Teamed with Pressburger as World War II began, Powell revealed a penchant for romanticism, alongside more conventionally

RIGHT: Anna Massey and Karlheinz Böhm
starred in the terrifying *Peeping Tom*.

realist projects in a series of fantasy films unlike any others in the national cinema: *The Red Shoes* (1948) and, most miraculous of all, *Black Narcissus* (1947), a lushly photographed meditation on the erotic life of the religious vowed to chastity.

These films proved immensely popular, making celebrities of the pair. Perhaps their turn toward the fantastic and the romantic was the result of their youthful experience in the industry. As a young man, Powell had worked for Rex Ingram, assisting on films with supernatural themes, such as *The Garden of Allah* (1927). Pressburger, a Hungarian Jew, worked in Paris and Berlin before finding sanctuary in London.

In the postwar era, Powell and Pressburger scored successes with more British productions. *I Know Where I'm Going!* (1945) traces the romantic odyssey of a young English woman, while *Ill Met by Moonlight* (1957) benefits from an interesting performance by Dirk Bogarde and film-noirish Cretan settings. **BP**

ABOVE: A scene from the duo's Best Picture Oscar-nominated romance, *The Red Shoes*.

Peeping Tom

"When they got me on my own [the critics] gleefully sawed off the limbs and jumped up and down on the corpse." Such was Michael Powell's fate after his notorious solo effort, *Peeping Tom* (1960). The story of a murderer who records the terror of his victims on camera as they die, this groundbreaking horror was reviled for its deeply disturbing and violent content. Shunned by the film industry, Powell did not return to the public eye until the late 1960s, when he was "rediscovered" by admirers Francis Ford Coppola and Martin Scorsese. Powell has since been cited as a key influence in both directors' work.

VINCENTE MINNELLI

Born: Lester Anthony Minnelli, February 28, 1903 (Chicago, Illinois, U.S.); died 1986 (Beverly Hills, California, U.S.).

Directing style: Father of the Hollywood musical; lavishly constructed sets; enchanting, romantic themes; magical dream sequences; stylish use of vivid color.

Vincente Minnelli had early experience as a child performer before becoming a set and costume designer, and then a director on Broadway. He was taken to Hollywood by the celebrated producer of musicals, Arthur Freed. After directing musical numbers in some Busby Berkeley films, Minnelli's first feature as director was *Cabin in the Sky* (1943).

His talent both as a creator of stylish spectacle and as a director of actors became evident in *Meet Me in St. Louis* (1944) with Judy Garland. He married Garland, the first of his four wives, in 1945 and their daughter, singer and actress Liza Minnelli, was born in 1946. More musicals followed, including *The Pirate* (1948), also starring Garland, and the sumptuous and innovative *An American in Paris* (1951). The latter saw Leslie Caron make her film debut and starred Gene Kelly at the pinnacle of his powers. Minnelli even managed to create a passable version of Paris in Hollywood studios, on the back lot. His work became distinguished for its visual beauty: in his words, "The search in films, what you try to create, is a little magic."

Although Minnelli continued to direct further magical musicals such as *The Band Wagon* (1953) with Fred Astaire, and *Gigi* (1958) with Caron and Maurice Chevalier, he was turning his hand to comedy with films such as *Father of the Bride* (1950), and to melodramas such as *The Bad and the Beautiful* (1952), with Kirk Douglas as a megalomaniac Hollywood producer. Minnelli's dramas from this period are equally memorable, and equally stylishly mounted with fluid camerawork and elegant design. They include *The Cobweb* (1955), a medical drama with a stellar cast; *Lust for Life* (1956) with Douglas as van Gogh; and *Home from the Hill* (1960) starring Robert Mitchum. **EB**

> "Play the game. Be gay, extravagant, outrageous!"
> —Honore Lachaille, *Gigi*

1900s

YASUJIRO OZU

Born: Yasujiro Ozu, December 12, 1903 (Tokyo, Japan); died 1963 (Tokyo, Japan).

Directing style: Socially aware Japanese director whose films explore themes of family life in contemporary society; use of static camera only a few feet above ground; innovative and perfectionist.

Of the great Japanese directors, Yasujiro Ozu is often cited as the most authentically Japanese, his work a byword for cool austerity. Scorning such vulgar devices as fades, dissolves, tracking shots, or pans, he shoots with a largely unmoving camera, almost always from about three feet above the ground—roughly the eye line, it has often been noted, of someone sitting cross-legged on a *tatami* mat. His painfully buttoned-up characters converse mostly in courteous banalities, yet, beneath this polite surface, emotions are churning and now and then break out to devastating effect. A slap in the face, in an Ozu film, is more shocking than any lavish bloodletting from Quentin Tarantino or John Woo.

This ascetic style applies predominantly to his postwar work from *Banshun* (1949) (*Late Spring*) onward—the films that first brought him to international notice. Ozu's early work includes college comedies and gangster movies, and even toward the end of his career he was happy to incorporate playfully vulgar jokes into his films. In *Otona no miru ehon—umarete wa mita keredo* (1932) (*I Was Born, But . . . .*) there is a running gag

Top Takes...

Sanma no aji 1962 (*An Autumn Afternoon*)
Kohayagawa-ke no aki 1961
  (*The End of Summer*)
Akibiyori 1960 (*Late Autumn*)
Ukigusa 1959 (*Floating Weeds*)
Ohayô 1959 (*Good Morning*)
Tokyo boshoku 1957 (*Tokyo Twilight*)
Soshun 1956 (*Early Spring*)
Tokyo monogatari 1953 (*Tokyo Story*)
Ochazuke no aji 1952
  (*Flavor of Green Tea Over Rice*)
Bakushû 1951 (*Early Summer*)
Munekata kyoudai 1950 (*The Munekata Sisters*)
Banshun 1949 (*Late Spring*)
Kaze no naka no mendori 1948
  (*A Hen in the Wind*)
Nagaya shinshiroku 1947
  (*The Record of a Tenement Gentleman*)
Todake no kyodai 1941
  (*The Brothes and Sisters of the Toda Family*)
Chichi ariki 1942 (*There Was a Father*)
Ukikusa monogatari 1934
  (*A Story of Floating Weeds*)
Otona no miru ehon—umarete wa mita keredo
  1932 (*I Was Born, But . . . .*)
Kabocha 1928 (*Pumpkin*)

LEFT: Chishu Ruy and Chieko Higashiyama as the elderly couple in *Tokyo Story*.

Putting Ozu in Context

Japanese cinema began in June 1899 with the short documentary *Geisha no teodori*. Yasujiro Ozu was born into the silent era of Japanese cinema, which continued until the 1930s, a decade later than in the United States. Few films survive from this period, largely because of the 1923 earthquake and Allied bombing of Tokyo during World War II.

- Seven genres can be identified in Japanese cinema: anime (animated films); jidaigeki (period pieces featuring samurai); horror; cult horror; kaiji (monster films); pink films (soft porn); yakusa films (about mobsters).

- Matsunosuke Onoe, a kabuki actor, was the first star of Japanese films.

- Tokuko Nagai Takagi, a dancer and actress, was the first woman to appear in a Japanese film.

- Akira Kurosawa made his debut with *Sugata Sanshiro* in 1943.

- Three Japanese films from the 1950s were included in *Sight and Sound*'s 2002 Critics and Directors Poll of the best films of all times: Akira Kurosawa's *Rashômon* (1950) and *Shichinin no samurai* (1954) (*Seven Samurai*); and Ozu's *Tokyo monogatari* (1953) (*Tokyo Story*).

- *Rashômon* won an Academy Award for Best Foreign Film.

- *Seven Samurai* was remade in the West as *The Magnificent Seven* (1960).

involving three young boys having farting contests. It was a silent film, but Ozu remade it with sound and color as *Ohayô* (1959). And his last film, *Sanma no aji* (1962), derives sly humor from an elderly husband struggling to meet the sexual demands of his young wife.

Apart from his directorial debut, the costume drama *Zange no yaiba* (1927) (*Sword of Penitence*), which he disowned when he saw the final cut, all Ozu's films were set in contemporary Japan. Many of them explore the tension between generations, the clash when the individualism of the young comes up against the devotion of their elders to traditional values. Ozu's sympathies extend to all his characters, even those whose behavior seems rigid or selfish. In the famous *Tokyo monogatari* (1953) (*Tokyo Story*), an old couple from the country visit their married children in Tokyo and are made to feel very unwelcome. But Ozu lets the audience understand why, for the offspring, these two unworldly old people have become an irrelevance, without condoning the younger family members' behavior.

Exploring family life in postwar Japan

Ozu mapped out his relatively narrow chosen territory early in his career, but then explored it in great depth and with acute, generous insight. The same actors often reappear in his films, almost constituting an informal Ozu repertory company. Even his titles, often season-based such as *Late Spring*, indicate his deliberately restricted compass. Certain situations recur, viewed from different angles. In *Kohayagawa-ke no aki* (1961) (*The End of Summer*), a family disintegrates due to the philandering of its elderly patriarch. In *Tokyo boshoku* (1957), Ozu's last film in black and white and one of his darkest, two daughters who thought their mother was dead discover she is still alive but living with another man; the younger daughter, already unstable after an abortion, commits suicide. An elderly father cared for by his unmarried daughter in *Late Spring*, worried that she will be left alone when he dies, tricks her into thinking that he plans to remarry so that she will find herself a husband. Ozu's characters, emotionally repressed, frequently

ABOVE: *The End of Summer*, Yasujiro's penultimate film, and one of his best.

conceal their own feelings or misread those of others, often with the best of intentions but disastrous results.

Ozu's supposed aesthetic conservatism did not extend into all facets of his life. He supported the great actress Kinuyo Tanaka in her bid to become Japan's first female director when she was furiously opposed by her own lover, the director Kenji Mizoguchi. He shunned the jingoistic patriotism of the prewar and wartime period, and contrived to avoid directing any militaristic films. Sent to Singapore in 1943 to make propaganda films, he came back without having produced any. As for his reputation outside Japan as the most rigorously Oriental of filmmakers, he once remarked with gentle irony, "Whenever Westerners don't understand something, they simply think it is Zen." **PK**

"For me there was no such thing as a teacher. I have relied entirely on my own strength."

TERENCE FISHER

Born: Terence Fisher, February 23, 1904 (London, England); died 1980 (Twickenham, Middlesex, England).

Directing style: Introduced realistic characterizations into horror genre; made stars of Christopher Lee and Peter Cushing; transformed British horror-movie industry.

Top Takes…

Frankenstein and the Monster from Hell 1974
Frankenstein Must Be Destroyed 1969
The Devil Rides Out 1968
Frankenstein Created Woman 1967
Night of the Big Heat 1967
Dracula: Prince of Darkness 1966
The Earth Dies Screaming 1965
The Gorgon 1964
The Curse of the Werewolf 1961
The Two Faces of Dr. Jekyll 1960
The Brides of Dracula 1960
The Mummy 1959
The Hound of the Baskervilles 1959
The Revenge of Frankenstein 1958
Dracula 1958
The Curse of Frankenstein 1957

Terence Fisher became famous overnight at the age of fifty-three for directing *The Curse of Frankenstein* (1957). He followed this—the first of Hammer Film Productions's remakes of the celebrated Universal Studios's films of the 1930s—with remakes of *Dracula* (1958) and *The Mummy* (1959), the fascinating *The Two Faces of Dr. Jekyll* (1960)—a revisionist version of the Rouben Mamoulian film with Mr. Edward Hyde as a handsome young womanizer—as well as *The Curse of the Werewolf* (1961), which barely resembled either *Werewolf of London* (1935) or *The Hound of the Baskervilles* (1959). He then tackled a myth not yet brought to the screen, *The Gorgon* (1964), and the theme of satanism with *The Devil Rides Out* (1968), an effective film that is more conventional but less interesting than Jacques Tourneur's excursion into that territory, *Night of the Demon* (1957).

Fisher was to make two more vampire films: *The Brides of Dracula* (1960) and *Dracula: Prince of Darkness* (1966). As with *Dracula*, Fisher chose to highlight the sexual nature of the vampiric encounter, particularly the way repressed young women in Victorian England showed appetites as much for sex as for blood when bitten by a vampire. Unfortunately, this was treated in a reactionary fashion in *Dracula: Prince of Darkness*, whereas the films devoted to Frankenstein are more critical of society. If James Whale's *Frankenstein* was well meaning, Fisher's was as ruthless and single-minded as any mad doctor of the 1930s. The one partial exception is Fisher's finest achievement, *Frankenstein Created Woman* (1967). Here the doctor is more humble and humane in a context where womankind is not only chattel, but a victim of wealthy drones who meet their comeuppance at the hands of the victimized girl and her working-class boyfriend. **ReH**

> "I've harmed nobody, just robbed a few graves!"
>
> —Frankenstein, *The Curse of Frankenstein*

EDGAR G. ULMER

Born: Edgar George Ulmer, September 17, 1904 (Olomouc, Czech Republic); died 1972 (Los Angeles, California, U.S.).

Directing style: Cult director of low-budget movies who sought creative independence from the studio system; maker of Yiddish movies of the 1930s.

Edgar Ulmer, "King of the B-movies," was born in the Czech Republic, not in Vienna as legend would have it. And, according to Ulmer himself, he almost single-handedly gave birth to German Expressionist cinema.

In the 1920 and 1930s, Ulmer worked for Universal Studios where he made a series of quick, cheap, but brilliant ethnic films, many in Yiddish, plus a film with an all-black amateur cast. These were commissioned works, but in the first half of the 1940s Ulmer sought his creative freedom. As a director with the U.S. based Producers' Releasing Corporation, he made some of his best films, including the horror movie *Bluebeard* (1944), starring John Carradine as a portrait painter and murderer; and one of the greatest B-movies ever made, the film noir classic *Detour* (1945), starring Tom Neal as a nightclub pianist down on his luck. Both characters almost seemed to reflect Ulmer's own artistic struggles and disenchantment.

From the mid-1940s to the early 1960s, Ulmer was desperate for projects and commuted between the United States and Europe. He was known as a director who could make something out of nothing, which is a valuable skill, but he had a reputation that led to his consistently being offered mostly cheap scripts and monumental costume dramas. His last film, the war drama *Sette contro la morte* (1964) (*The Cavern*), was made under the cloud of terrible financial and health problems, and he died from a stroke in 1972.

Ulmer's films were rediscovered in the 1990s. He was, and still is, the nonconformist, unclassifiable filmmaker par excellence. As an émigré director, he represents an alternative history of cinema; not the history of powerful and canonized successes, but the counter history of a minor and extremely flexible cinema. **BH**

Top Takes...

Sette contro la morte 1964 (*The Cavern*)
L'Atlantide 1961
  (*Atlantis, City Beneath the Desert*)
The Amazing Transparent Man 1960
Annibale 1959 (*Hannibal*)
Daughter of Dr. Jekyll 1957
The Man From Planet X 1951
Ruthless 1948
The Strange Woman 1946
Detour 1945
Strange Illusion 1945
Bluebeard 1944
Green Fields 1937
The Black Cat 1934
Menschen am Sonntag 1930
  (*People on Sunday*)

"I really am looking for absolution for all the things I had to do for money's sake."

JACQUES TOURNEUR

Born: Jacques Tourneur, November 12, 1904 (Paris, France); died 1977 (Bergerac, Dordogne, Aquitaine, France).

Directing style: Leading director of horror genre and film noir; elaborate lighting; tracking shots to create three-dimensional space; music used to create mood.

Top Takes...

RIGHT: Simone Simon as the beautiful, mysterious Irena Dubrovna in *Cat People*.

French-born Jacques Tourneur made his debut in the U.S. film industry as a script clerk for his father, director Maurice Tourneur, when the pair went to Hollywood in 1913. In 1930, he returned to France, where he worked as an assistant director and editor before he was finally able to direct feature films such as *Les filles de la concierge* (1934).

Back in the United States in 1934, Tourneur did some second-unit director work, including some for producer David O. Selznick on *A Tale of Two Cities* (1935), and became part of MGM's short-subjects team. There, he managed to polish his subtly elliptical poetic style. After a few uneven B-pictures, Tourneur finally met commercial success with *Cat People* (1942), a film that offered a new direction for the horror genre, characterized by suggestion rather than special effects or makeup to frighten the audience. His technical mastery and light touch made the bland appear spine-chilling. This RKO Pictures production spearheaded by Val Lewton was quickly followed by two other films in the same vein.

Tourneur used to say that he never turned down a script, and he thus tackled a wide variety of genres, from film noir's

quintessential and beautifully composed *Out of the Past* (1947) to the stunning color photography of the Western *Canyon Passage* (1946), to dramas, war films, and sword-and-scandal epics. In almost every case, he managed to put his mark on the production both aesthetically and thematically, often using architecture or machinery to convey the psychological state of his characters.

Tourneur returned to the horror genre in 1957 with his British-produced *Night of the Demon*, in which a monstrous creature was shown onscreen against the director's will because the producers meddled with his conception. Yet it became a cult classic over the years and is still the subject of an ongoing aesthetic discussion. Tourneur shot his last images for TV, a medium that he repeatedly worked in from the mid-1950s, directing shows such as *Bonanza* (1960) and *The Twilight Zone* (1964). He eventually retired in France. **FL**

ABOVE: Virginia Huston and Robert Mitchum in a scene from Tourneur's *Out of the Past*.

Slaying Demons

Cult-classic *Night of the Demon* (1957) saw Tourneur's return to the horror genre after a decade of working in other genres. Based on the story *Casting the Runes* by M. R. James, the film was released under the title *Curse of the Demon*, and has since inspired references in two songs:

- *The Hounds of Love* by Kate Bush has the sampled line from the film: "It's in the trees! It's coming!"
- The opening song in *The Rocky Horror Picture Show* has the line: "Dana Andrews said prunes gave him the runes, but passing them used lots of skill."

GEORGE STEVENS

Born: George Stevens, December 18, 1904 (Oakland, California, U.S.); died 1975 (Lancaster, California, U.S.).

Directing style: A legendary sharp eye for detail that enhanced visual storytelling; rapport with actors produced memorable performances from Hollywood's greats.

Top Takes...

D-Day: The Color Footage 1999
The Only Game in Town 1970
The Greatest Story Ever Told 1965
The Diary of Anne Frank 1959 ☆
Giant 1956 ★
Shane 1953 ☆
Something to Live For 1952
A Place in the Sun 1951 ★
I Remember Mama 1948
On Our Merry Way 1948
The Nazi Plan 1945
Nazi Concentration Camps 1945
The More the Merrier 1943 ☆
The Talk of the Town 1942
Woman of the Year 1942
Vigil in the Night 1940
Gunga Din 1939
Vivacious Lady 1938
A Damsel in Distress 1937
Quality Street 1937
Swing Time 1936
Alice Adams 1935
Kentucky Kernels 1934
The Cohens and Kellys in Trouble 1933
A Divorce Courtship 1933

RIGHT: Brandon de Wilde and Alan Ladd in a scene from Stevens's classic Shane.

George Stevens is notable as a creator of classic U.S. cinema. He was nominated five times for an Academy Award as Best Director, winning twice, and six of the movies he produced and directed were nominated for Best Picture Oscars.

Each of Stevens's films has his unique stamp. He was a craftsman with an eye for detail and the ability to create a credible world onscreen for his characters to inhabit. *Shane* (1953), an undisputed classic, has Alan Ladd playing the charismatic hero who leads a group of small-scale farmers against a despotic rancher. With its epic use of landscape and excellent performances all around, it remains one of the most popular of all Westerns. Another of Stevens's talents was his ability to get the best from his cast, eliciting compelling performances from some of Hollywood's greatest actors.

Perhaps Stevens developed such flair during his early apprenticeship: he was a child actor before entering films as a cameraman, and began directing comedy shorts in the early 1930s. His first significant feature was *Alice Adams* (1935), a comedy based on Booth Tarkington's novel about the social pretensions of small-town Americans.

Later, working with established stars, Stevens showed what he could do with a witty script and excellent performers. *Swing Time* (1936) starred Astaire and Rogers at the height of their fame. In rapid succession he directed *Quality Street* (1937), *A Damsel in Distress* (1937), and *Vivacious Lady* (1938).

During World War II Stevens joined the Army Signal Corps and filmed dramatic war footage such as the liberation of the Dachau concentration camp. His war experiences, however, left him in a more serious mood. *A Place in the Sun* (1951) starred Elizabeth Taylor and Montgomery Clift in a version of Theodore Dreiser's somber novel of social realism. He followed this with *Giant* (1956), starring James Dean, which won Stevens a Best Director Oscar. Stevens's meticulous working methods meant that he made fewer films. *The Greatest Story Ever Told* (1965), his epic version of the Gospels, was slow-moving and overly reverential, and his reputation went into decline. **EB**

ABOVE: George Stevens gives instructions to actor James Dean on the set of *Giant*.

Birth of a Legend

James Dean—from whom George Stevens wrought a striking performance in his Oscar-winning *Giant* (1956)—played major roles in only three movies before his untimely death in 1955 during the filming of *Giant*. The first was his role as Caleb in Elia Kazan's 1955 production of the John Steinbeck novel, *East of Eden*. His second, which fixed forever his image in American culture, was as the rebellious teenager Jim Stark in Nicholas Ray's *Rebel Without a Cause* (1955). In *Giant*, he plays nonconformist, cowhand Jett Rink, based upon the true story of Irish immigrant made good, Glenn McCarthy.

GRIGORI KOZINTSEV

Born: Grigori Mikhailovich Kozintsov, March 22, 1905 (Kiev, Ukraine); died 1973 (St. Petersburg, Russia).

Directing style: Eclectic Expressionist-influenced agit-prop comedies, and faithful literary adaptations; artistic collaboration with composer Dimitri Shostakovich.

Top Takes...

Korol Lir 1969 (*King Lear*)

Gamlet 1964 (*Hamlet*)

Don Kikhot 1957 (*Don Quixote*)

Belinskiy 1951

Pirogov 1947

Prostyye lyudi 1946 (*Plain People*)

Nashi devushki 1943

Odnazhdy nochyu 1941 (*Dark Is the Night*)

Vyborgskaya storona 1939 (*The Vyborg Side*)

Vozvrashcheniye Maksima 1937 (*The Return of Maxim*)

Yunost Maksima 1935 (*The Youth of Maxim*)

Novyy Vavilon 1929 (*The New Babylon*)

Shinel 1926 (*The Overcoat*)

Pokhozhdeniya Oktyabriny 1924 (*The Adventures of an Octoberite*)

With his codirecting partner Leonid Trauberg, Grigori Kozintsev was a pioneer of early Soviet cinema who produced his most celebrated work in the post-Stalinist era. He cofounded the avant-garde artist's collective the Factory of Eccentric Actors (FEKS) and the group's productions were taken up by SevZapKino studios, where their German Expressionist-influenced agit-prop comedies were transferred to the screen. Their early burlesque style matured via Nikolai Gogol-derived satire into *Novyy Vavilon* (1929) (*The New Babylon*). One of the great Soviet silent films, it was enhanced by the debut score of fellow FEKS veteran, composer Dimitri Shostakovich.

Adapting to the new demands of sound and increasingly draconian government interference, the duo produced their most popular work, the Maxim trilogy: *Yunost Maksima* (1935) (*The Youth of Maxim*), *Vozvrashcheniye Maksima* (1937) (*The Return of Maxim*), and *Vyborgskaya storona* (1939) (*The Vyborg Side*). The films employed a free-flowing, episodic structure to follow the progress of an archetypal Bolshevik, played by Boris Chirkov. Despite this success, they ran into official trouble with their first postwar film, *Prostyye lyudi* (1946) (*Plain People*), which was suppressed for ten years before a revised version was later released. Chastened by the experience, the pair split and Kozintsev concentrated on theater and teaching. After Josef Stalin's death, Kozintsev refocused on film and helmed adaptations of *Don Kikhot* (1957) (*Don Quixote*), *Gamlet* (1964) (*Hamlet*), and *Korol Lir* (1969) (*King Lear*). Powerful performances, brooding cinematography, and rich scores (once more by Shostakovich) brought these latter films international acclaim and recognition for Kozintsev as one of world cinema's great directors. **RB**

> "...every one of us...in the course of his whole life, shoots a single film of *his own*."

JEAN VIGO

Born: Jean Bonaventure de Vigo Almereyda, April 26, 1905 (Paris, France); died 1934 (Paris, France).

Directing style: Antiestablishment French director; inventive use of camera angles for surreal sequences and nonlinear storytelling; poetic realism; witty and absurd.

From birth, Jean Vigo seemed to have all the odds stacked against him: he suffered chronic illness; grew up in France during World War I; and his father died in mysterious circumstances when he was twelve. His father was renowned anarchist Eugène Bonaventure de Vigo, known as Miguel Almareyda, who was arrested by the French police and later found dead in his cell, strangled with his own shoelaces. With so much anguish, it is all the more remarkable that Vigo's films are poetic, spirited and, above all, wickedly funny and absurd in their celebration of the odd opportunities that life offers.

Vigo directed only four films. His first, *À propos de Nice* (1930), is an intelligent short documentary, a combination of clash-montage and nonlinear storytelling, mocking bourgeois society. *Taris, roi de L'eau* (1931) (*Jean Taris, Swimming Champion*) is a mesmeric water ballet. His last two films, *Zéro de conduite: Jeunes diables au collège* (1933) (*Zero for Conduct*) and *L'Atalante* (1934), are masterpieces of surreal realism. Both were set in confined, restricted regimes (a boarding school and a canal barge respectively), within which Vigo introduced anarchistic elements. The conflict between order and chaos, repression and liberty, so central to Vigo's life, is resolved through humor and surreal dream sequences, captured in powerful rooftop and underwater shots. Both films injected French film culture with a realist élan that would continue throughout the decade. Vigo did not live to see his work recognized, dying of tuberculosis at a young age. Declared "anti-French" by contemporary political institutions, *Zero for Conduct* was banned and *L'Atalante* was released only posthumously. But the anarchist spirit of Vigo's films survived him, and has left a lasting imprint on cinema history. **EM**

Top Takes...

L'Atalante 1934

Zéro de conduite: Jeunes diables au collège 1933 (*Zero for Conduct*)

Taris, roi de l'eau 1931 (*Jean Taris, Swimming Champion*)

À propos de Nice 1930

"[*Zero for Conduct* has] moments of comedy, satire and tender romance . . . ."—*New York Times*

HENRY KOSTER

Born: Herman Kosterlitz, May 1, 1905 (Berlin, Germany); died 1988 (Camarillo, California, U.S.).

Directing style: Prolific director of lighthearted musicals, epic costume dramas, and family comedies; notable artistic collaborations with actor James Stewart.

Top Takes...

The Singing Nun 1966
Flower Drum Song 1961
The Naked Maja 1958
The Virgin Queen 1955
Desirée 1954
The Robe 1953
My Cousin Rachel 1952
Harvey 1950
Come to the Stable 1949
The Bishop's Wife 1947 ☆
The Unfinished Dance 1947
Three Smart Girls Grow Up 1939
One Hundred Men and a Girl 1937
Three Smart Girls 1936
Das Abenteuer der Thea Roland 1932
  (*The Adventure of Thea Roland*)

"The only people who grow old were born old to begin with."—Dudley, *The Bishop's Wife*

RIGHT: Elwood P. Dowd with Harvey, the rabbit, his invisible friend in the film.

The world of movies entered Henry Koster's life after the opening of a theater by an uncle in 1910, when such venues were rare. He assisted director Curtis Bernhardt, until one day Koster filled in for Bernhardt on the set, and helmed the rest of the project. This marked the beginning of Koster's career, and he proceeded to direct for Germany's Universum Film AG.

Being Jewish, Koster fled Nazi persecution and eventually arrived in Budapest. There he met producer Joe Pasternak, who represented Universal Studios's presence in Europe. This 1934 meeting resulted in the production of films in Hungary, and Koster's fostering of relations with a major movie studio. The pair moved to the United States in 1936, where they made *Three Smart Girls* (1936), a lighthearted tale of three sisters who travel to New York to prevent the impending union between their divorced father and a scheming social figure. *Three Smart Girls* featured the up-and-coming actress Deanna Durbin, and the massive success of the film took Universal Studios out of an impending bankruptcy. Koster's second film with the studio, *One Hundred Men and a Girl* (1937), brought the director, along with his protégé Pasternak, into the limelight. Koster continued to direct musicals and family-oriented movies, including *Spring Parade* (1940) and *Music for Millions* (1944). After moving to MGM, he discovered Bud Abbott and Lou Costello and convinced Universal Studios to hire them. In 1947, he received an Academy Award Best Director nod for *The Bishop's Wife* (1947). Riding on this acclaim, his picture *Harvey* (1950), starring James Stewart, became his most successful. He went on to direct a clutch of major films including Richard Burton's first U.S. film, *My Cousin Rachel* (1952) and the Cinemascope epic *The Robe* (1953). **ES**

MIKIO NARUSE

Born: Mikio Naruse, August 20, 1905 (Yotsuya, Tokyo, Japan); died 1969 (Tokyo, Japan).

Directing style: Maker of realistic, often melancholy, melodramas; strong female protagonists; themes of the problems faced in everyday life by the working class; slow pace; psychological subtlety of characterization.

Top Takes…

Midaregumo 1967 (*Scattered Clouds*)
Onna ga kaidan wo agaru toki 1960
  (*When a Woman Ascends the Stairs*)
Ukigumo 1955 (*Floating Clouds*)
Okaasan 1952 (*Mother*)
Meshi 1951 (*Repast*)
Tsuma yo bara no yo ni 1935 (*Kimiko*)
Yogoto no yume 1933 (*Every Night Dreams*)
Kimi to wakarete 1933 (*After Our Separation*)
Koshiben gambare 1931 (*Flunky, Work Hard!*)
Ai wa chikara da 1930 (*Love Is Strength*)
Oshikiri shinkonki 1930
  (*A Record of Shameless Newlyweds*)

Mikio Naruse's work bridged the cinematic gap between the silent film era, the advent of talkies, and the introduction of color films. His output was prolific, and he became one of the most prominent Japanese filmmakers of his time.

Naruse started out at Shochiku Studio as a property manager and assistant director. It was not until *Oshikiri shinkonki* (1930) (*A Record of Shameless Newlyweds*) that he was able to work independently on a project. One of his earliest features is *Koshiben gambare* (1931) (*Flunky, Work Hard!*), which combined the qualities of a melodrama and slapstick picture in an attempt to meet the demands of the studio.

He quit Shochiku Studio and went on to experience great commercial success in the 1930s making working-class melodramas with strong female protagonists, culminating in his first major film, *Tsuma yo bara no yo ni* (1935) (*Kimiko*). It was the first Japanese picture to receive a theatrical release in the United States, and tells the story of a young woman whose father deserts his family for a geisha.

Naruse adopted the same themes throughout the rest of his career, with an increasingly melancholy output. His films were marked by a slow pace that allowed his characters to reveal their psychological depth, with subtle gestures revealing their acceptance of the problems of everyday life. In the wake of a drawn-out divorce from his wife, Sachiko Chiba, who starred in some of his films, Naruse entered a creative slump. As a result, the postwar period saw him involved in film collaborations, and adopting an increased focus on the act of directing, leaving the storylines to be written by others. *Midaregumo* (1967) (*Scattered Clouds*) was Naruse's last film, and is regarded as one of his greatest. **ES**

> "[Naruse's] characters battle to satisfy basic physical, social, and economic needs."—Freda Freiberg

HIROSHI INAGAKI

Born: Hiroshi Inagaki, December 30, 1905 (Tokyo, Japan); died 1980 (Tokyo, Japan).

Directing style: Japanese director of large-scale period dramas, and quintessential samurai movies; carefully crafted battle sequences; notable creative partnership with actor Toshirô Mifune.

Hiroshi Inagaki was one of the great Toho studio directors, and a key player in the *jidaigeki* (period drama) genre.

After the international success of *Rashômon* (1950) (*Rasho-Mon*), Inagaki forged a partnership with Akira Kurosawa's favorite leading man, Toshirô Mifune, and they made a trilogy chronicling the adventures of Miyamoto Musashi, the legendary sixteenth-century samurai. Remakes of Inagaki's 1940s originals, when retitled *Samurai I* to *III* and released in the West, they proved tremendously popular, and the first won the Oscar for Best Foreign Language Film in 1955.

Further series followed, but *Muhomatsu no issho* (1958) (*The Rickshaw Man*) was a notable departure. Eschewing the customary swordplay and high adventure, Inagaki cast Mifune against type as a humble rickshaw driver who becomes a father figure to a wealthy widow's son. A classic romantic weepy, it also cleverly explored class divisions, and the upheaval of Japan's rapid modernization.

Returning to historical epics, Inagaki helmed perhaps the greatest of them all. *Chushingura—Hana no maki yuki no maki* (1962) (*47 Samurai*) was a retelling of one of Japan's favorite myths. Previously filmed by Kenji Mizoguchi in 1941, this was a Toho Studios thirtieth anniversary widescreen extravaganza, exquisitely photographed, and almost four hours long.

Several more distinguished films followed, notably *Furin kazan* (1969) (*Under the Banner of Samurai*), but, in the recession-hit 1970s, expensive period dramas became passé and Inagaki was sidelined. At his peak he was writing and directing three movies a year; now, unable to find work, he succumbed to alcoholism and, unlike Kurosawa, did not live to enjoy a revival late in his career. **RB**

Top Takes…

Furin kazan 1969 (*Under the Banner of Samurai*)

Chushingura—Hana no maki yuki no maki 1962 (*47 Samurai*)

Muhomatsu no issho 1958 (*The Rickshaw Man*)

Miyamoto Musashi kanketsuhen: kettô Ganryûjima 1956 (*Samurai III*)

Zoku Miyamoto Musashi: Ichijôji no kettô 1955 (*Samurai Part II*)

Miyamoto Musashi 1954 (*Samurai*)

Muhomatsu no issho 1943 (*The Life of Matsu the Untamed*)

Miyamoto Musashi—Dai-ichi-bu: Kusawake no hitobito—Dai-ni-bu: Eitatsu no mon 1940 (*Samurai*)

Mazô 1938

Hôrô zanmai 1928 (*The Wandering Gambler*)

"Of all the dozens of films I made, only a handful had I actually wanted to make."

ROBERTO ROSSELLINI

Born: Roberto Rossellini, May 8, 1906 (Rome, Italy); died 1977 (Rome, Italy).

Directing style: One of the influential founding fathers of Italian neorealism; depictions of the world in crisis; artistic collaboration (and romantic involvement) with actress Ingrid Bergman.

Top Takes...

Il Messia 1976 (*The Messiah*)

Anno uno 1974 (*Year One*)

Anima nera 1962

Vanina Vanini 1961 (*The Betrayer*)

Viva l'Italia! 1961

Il Generale della Rovere 1959

India: Matri Bhumi 1959

Giovanna d'Arco al rogo 1954
　(*Joan at the Stake*)

La Paura 1954 (*Fear*)

Viaggio in Italia 1954 (*Journey to Italy*)

Europa '51 1952 (*The Greatest Love*)

Francesco, giullare di Dio 1950
　(*Francis, God's Jester*)

Stromboli 1950

Germania anno zero 1948 (*Germany Year Zero*)

Paisà 1946 (*Paisan*)

Roma, città aperta 1945 (*Open City*)

L'uomo dalla croce 1943
　(*Man with a Cross*)

La nave bianca 1942 (*The White Ship*)

Un pilota ritorna 1942 (*A Pilot Returns*)

Il Ruscello di Ripasottile 1941

Dafne 1936

Roberto Rossellini was one of cinema's most influential and controversial directors. Although often considered one of the key figures in the Italian neorealist movement, his career really began under the auspices of dictator Benito Mussolini. During World War II, he directed three highly propagandistic films, *La nave bianca* (1942) (*The White Ship*), *Un pilota ritorna* (1942) (*A Pilot Returns*), and *L'uomo dalla croce* (1943) (*Man with a Cross*).

Rossellini rose to international prominence with his acclaimed war trilogy, a series of films tracing the progression of Allied forces from Rome to Berlin and chronicling the impact of the devastation of World War II on both civilian and military populations. The first, the masterpiece *Roma, città aperta* (1945) (*Open City*) was shot primarily on location, frequently using available light and varying film stocks. These material conditions, coupled with naturalistic acting and the use of colloquial expressions, gave the film a profoundly documentary feel. Although the second two films in the trilogy, *Paisà* (1946) (*Paisan*) and *Germania anno zero* (1948) (*Germany Year Zero*), were more in keeping with the neorealist aesthetics of his contemporaries, Marxist theorists and other champions of

RIGHT: A scene from *Open City*, a war drama set in Nazi-occupied Rome.

neorealist critics began to distance themselves from Rossellini, beginning with *Stromboli* (1950), the director's first artistic collaboration with his eventual second wife, Ingrid Bergman.

Despite the controversy and contentious reviews that surrounded his work, Rossellini remained a prolific and influential director. Films such as *Europa '51* (1952) (*The Greatest Love*) and *Viaggio in Italia* (1954) (*Journey to Italy*) exerted a profound influence upon French New Wave critics and filmmakers such as Jean-Luc Godard, as well as other major directors, from Federico Fellini to Martin Scorsese. During a period of artistic and personal difficulties capped by his divorce from Bergman, Rossellini went to India to shoot material for a TV documentary series. He continued to make feature films and documentaries, but became increasingly involved in TV productions. By the time of his death in 1977, he had directed more than 50 pictures. **JM**

ABOVE: Ingrid Bergman in *The Greatest Love*, part of the so-called "Ingrid trilogy."

A Love Story

In 1948, Ingrid Bergman—already a well-known actress—introduced herself to Roberto Rossellini as a Swedish actress, who spoke fluent English and German, but whose only words in Italian were "*ti amo.*" Rossellini was clearly intrigued and so the romantic and working relationship between the two began. Both were married at the time, and the affair caused scandal, especially when they decided to have children together (the actress Isabella Rossellini is one of them). The best known of the six films they made together are *Stromboli*, *The Greatest Love*, and *Journey to Italy*.

BILLY WILDER

Born: Samuel Wilder, June 22, 1906 (Sucha Beskidzka, Poland); died 2002 (West Los Angeles, California, U.S.).

Directing style: Versatile creator of Hollywood golden age film noirs and satirical farces; cynical humor; witty dialogue; fruitful rapport with actor Jack Lemmon.

Top Takes...

Buddy Buddy 1981

Fedora 1978

The Front Page 1974

Avanti! 1972

The Fortune Cookie 1966

Kiss Me, Stupid 1964

Irma la Douce 1963

One, Two, Three 1961

The Apartment 1960 ★

Some Like It Hot 1959 ☆

Witness for the Prosecution 1957 ☆

Love in the Afternoon 1957

The Spirit of St. Louis 1957

The Seven Year Itch 1955

Sabrina 1954 ☆

Stalag 17 1953 ☆

Ace in the Hole 1951

Sunset Blvd. 1950 ☆

A Foreign Affair 1948

The Emperor Waltz 1948

The Lost Weekend 1945 ★

Double Indemnity 1944 ☆

Five Graves to Cairo 1943

The Major and the Minor 1942

Mauvaise graine 1934 (*Bad Seed*)

RIGHT: Shirley MacLaine and Jack Lemmon are an unforgettable duo in *The Apartment.*

One of the greatest writer/directors Hollywood ever produced, Billy Wilder once summed up his career in a towering example of understatement: "I just made pictures I would've liked to see." Yet Wilder is behind some of the most memorable images and lines in movie history, whether it be Marilyn Monroe standing over a subway grate in that famously billowing white dress, Jack Lemmon and Tony Curtis as crossdressing musicians in *Some Like It Hot* (1959), or Fred MacMurray's convincing portrayal of the insurance salesman-turned-killer in *Double Indemnity* (1944). He was even responsible for making Greta Garbo laugh in her first comedy (*Ninotchka*, 1939).

Wilder created one of the most brilliant and eclectic canons of work in U.S. cinema, his films characterized by their tight plots, smart characters, and clever dialogue. Unusally, perhaps, for a director so associated with comedy, Wilder consistently pushed the limits of U.S. censorship of the day with his provocative choice of subject matter that included adultery (*Double Indemnity*, 1944), alcoholism (*The Lost Weekend*, 1945), and the younger, kept man (*Sunset Blvd.*, 1950).

MARILYN MONROE *and her bosom companions* TONY CURTIS JACK LEMMON

HOT

in a BILLY WILDER Production "SOME LIKE IT HOT"

Born in 1906 in a part of Austria-Hungary later absorbed into Poland, Wilder's mother nicknamed him "Billy" out of her fascination with U.S. culture. After ending up in Berlin working as a newspaper stringer, the young Wilder discovered an interest in films. He became a screenwriter in the German film industry, but in the wake of Adolf Hitler's rise to power he moved to Paris, where he made his directorial debut with *Mauvaise graine* (1934) (*Bad Seed*). When he later arrived in Hollywood speaking no English, he was quick to study both the language and form of the movies there, becoming a notable screenwriter with such titles as Joe May's *Music in the Air* (1934) and A. Edward Sullivan's *Champagne Waltz* (1937).

Perhaps out of not being a native English speaker, Wilder always liked to write with a partner. With Charles Brackett, he

ABOVE: Wilder introduced crossdressing to Hollywood with *Some Like It Hot*.

"A director needs to be a policeman, a midwife, a psychoanalyst … and a bastard."

1900s

Working with Spielberg

Billy Wilder once quipped "The Austrians are brilliant people. They made the world believe that Hitler was a German and Mozart an Austrian." The director's caustic wit and acerbic view of life can be traced back to his Austrian-Jewish background. He spent his early life constantly on the move from place to place around Europe, an experience that inevitably marked him out as the foreigner and the outsider.

Little did Wilder know, when he moved to Berlin in the late 1920s, that this would be the last he'd see of his family. After World War II, Wilder searched for his missing family in the concentration camps of Europe, later discovering that his mother, grandmother, and stepfather had all perished in Auschwitz. He refused to ever speak about the experience.

Yet, in a project that was starkly different to the rest of his cinematic output, Wilder later collaborated closely with Steven Spielberg on the script of *Schindler's List* (1993). Spielberg had trouble finding a director—Roman Polanski and Martin Scorsese had walked away from the film. Wilder felt that he was too old to direct it and that it would bring him too close to his own harrowing history. In the end Wilder suggested that Spielberg should direct it himself. It went on to become Spielberg's most important movie, winning Academy Awards for Best Director and Best Picture.

penned a string of classic comedies including *Ninotchka* (1939) and *Ball of Fire* (1941). He was then promoted to writer and director for a script he had written with Brackett, *The Major and the Minor* (1942). Teaming up with crime writer Raymond Chandler to adapt James M. Cain's novella gave Wilder his first classic, the film noir *Double Indemnity* (1944). This landmark film established such noirish conventions as the use of atmospheric "venetian blind" lighting and voice-over narration. For the rest of the 1940s, Wilder rode a streak of hits and acclaim, including *The Lost Weekend* (1945) and the much celebrated *Sunset Blvd.* (1950), which marked his final collaboration with Brackett.

Latterly, Wilder's comedy became more cynical, his dramatic interludes more intense, and his artistic confidence heightened with the ability to write, produce, and direct titles of his own creation. Out of the gates in this new chapter was a tragedy that missed an audience *Ace in the Hole* (1951), the beloved *Sabrina* (1954), *The Seven Year Itch* (1955), and his first writing collaboration with the other important partner of his career, I. A. L. Diamond (*Love in the Afternoon*, 1957).

Wilder's heyday

With the exception of *Witness for the Prosecution* (1957), Diamond and Wilder cowrote all the remaining projects of their careers. At the height of their powers, they created the sublime comedies *Some Like It Hot* (1959) and *The Apartment* (1960). With the latter, Wilder gained entry to an elite group of directors who have won Oscars for Best Director, Best Picture, and Best Screenplay for the same film. As the film brats took over Hollywood in the 1970s, veteran talents such as Wilder were often overlooked, but out of this waning period still came *Avanti!* (1972) and *The Front Page* (1974).

During his career, Wilder won two Oscars for directing and three Oscars (out of nine nominations) for screenwriting (*The Lost Weekend*; *Sunset Blvd.*; *The Apartment*), a record only surpassed in 1997, fittingly, by that other great writer/director Woody Allen for *Deconstructing Harry*. **GCQ**

RIGHT: Monroe enjoys the "delicious" subway breeze in *The Seven Year Itch*.

ANTHONY MANN

Born: Emil Anton Bundesmann, June 30, 1906 (San Diego, California, U.S.); died 1967 (Berlin, Germany).

Directing style: Famous for early film noirs followed by Westerns and later epics; masterful use of cinematography of the U.S. Western landscape.

Anthony Mann is considered one of the greatest directors of Westerns, but he is also greatly admired as a director of 1940s film noir and of 1960s historical epics such as *El Cid* (1961).

Mann was born in San Diego, California, but a decade later his family relocated to New York City, where he attended Central High School with future RKO Pictures production chief, and future head of MGM, Dore Schary. From 1924 to 1926, Mann was a member of the Neighborhood Playhouse Acting Company in Manhattan's Lower East Side. He spent the next few years as an actor, including a year in the New York Repertory Company. His theatrical debut as a director came in 1933, and he continued as a theater director through 1940.

Mann moved to Hollywood in 1941. After his inauspicious motion picture debut *Dr. Broadway* (1942), he directed low-budget melodramas and musicals for various studios. Although his film noir thriller *Desperate* (1947) was a success, his subsequent films were more so, coinciding with his propitious collaboration with cinematographer John Alton. *T-Men* (1947), *Raw Deal* (1948), *Reign of Terror* (1949), and *Border Incident* (1949) are all highly esteemed film noirs.

Top Takes...

The Heroes of Telemark 1965
The Fall of the Roman Empire 1964
El Cid 1961
Cimarron 1960
Man of the West 1958
God's Little Acre 1958
The Tin Star 1957
Serenade 1956
The Man From Laramie 1955
Strategic Air Command 1955
The Far Country 1954
The Glenn Miller Story 1953
The Naked Spur 1953
Bend of the River 1952
The Furies 1950
Winchester '73 1950
Side Street 1950
Devil's Doorway 1950
Border Incident 1949
Reign of Terror 1949
Follow Me Quietly 1949
Raw Deal 1948
T-Men 1947
Desperate 1947
Dr. Broadway 1942

RIGHT: Gary Cooper and Julie London starred in the excellent *Man of the West*.

Mann's first Western was *Devil's Doorway* (1950), a tragedy about racism and bigotry. After seeing the film, James Stewart asked Mann to direct *Winchester '73* (1950). They made a further seven films together, including *Bend of the River* (1952), *The Naked Spur* (1953), *The Far Country* (1954), and *The Man From Laramie* (1955). Mann's last Western (without Stewart) was the masterful *Man of the West* (1958), starring Gary Cooper.

After that triumph, Mann became less prolific. In 1959, after clashing with star/producer Kirk Douglas, Mann asked to be removed from *Spartacus* (1960). He began the Western *Cimarron* (1960), but again left because of creative differences with the producer, although his name was retained as director. His final triumph was *El Cid* (1961), a grand epic about Spain's famous cultural hero. His next film was also an epic, *The Fall of the Roman Empire* (1964). Mann's last completed film was the World War II thriller, *The Heroes of Telemark* (1965). **SU**

ABOVE: Charlton Heston as the legendary Spanish hero El Cid in Mann's 1961 epic.

Dramatic Landscapes

Mann's films are known for their scenes of violence, and the director used hostile landscapes to add dramatic effect. His characters suffer at the hands of nature: no mountain is left unscaled—witness the hero's grimace as he toils in the endeavor—and gun battles are enacted among barren rocks where there is a real danger of death by ricochet. Mann also structured his narratives as journeys, in which each stage is marked by new surroundings: from fertile valley to snowcapped peak, the landscape becomes increasingly inhospitable as the film goes on, symbolic of the hero's descent into barbarism.

JOHN HUSTON

Born: John Marcellus Huston, August 5, 1906 (Nevada, Missouri, U.S.); died 1987 (Middletown, Rhode Island, U.S.).

Directing style: Legendary rebellious director also known for his acting and writing skills; fearless maker of timeless classic dramas and adventure movies.

Top Takes...

The Dead 1987
Prizzi's Honor 1985 ☆
Wise Blood 1979
The Man Who Would Be King 1975
The Life and Times of Judge Roy Bean 1972
Fat City 1972
The Kremlin Letter 1970
Reflections in a Golden Eye 1967
The Unforgiven 1960
Moulin Rouge 1952 ☆
The African Queen 1951 ☆
The Asphalt Jungle 1950 ☆
Key Largo 1948
The Treasure of the Sierra Madre 1948 ★
The Maltese Falcon 1941

> "Nature . . . is what we are put in this world to rise above."
>
> —Rose Sayer, *The African Queen*

John Huston was one of the most bewilderingly uneven of U.S. directors. Throughout his career, his finest movies appeared cheek-by-jowl with his worst: no decade of his work was without its masterpieces or its turkeys. Huston himself affected an insouciant attitude to his variable oeuvre, interspersing committed films with shrugged-off assignments.

After an eventful childhood and a picaresque youth that took in boxing, journalism, and a spell with the Mexican cavalry, Huston settled to steady work in 1937 as a scriptwriter at Warner Brothers. He made his directorial debut with *The Maltese Falcon* (1941), which was hailed as an instant classic, and gave Humphrey Bogart one of his most iconic roles.

After directing three powerful wartime documentaries, Huston returned to features with a major commercial and critical hit, *The Treasure of the Sierra Madre* (1948), which mapped out one of his favorite themes: a quest obsessively pursued to the point of disaster. Huston went on to explore this scenario in several of his finest movies, including *The Asphalt Jungle* (1950) and *The African Queen* (1951).

During the 1960s, Huston's critical standing slumped. But his reputation later revived thanks to the seemingly effortless mastery shown in *Fat City* (1972), a compassionate look at the world of small-time professional boxers; his epic *The Man Who Would Be King* (1975); and *Wise Blood* (1979), a dark, comic parable of sin and salvation. His final film, *The Dead* (1987), shot with Huston linked up to an iron lung in the final stages of emphysema, was the most perfect of his many literary adaptations, treating James Joyce's short story with love, joy, and an aching sense of regret—a poignant valediction, glowing with the beauty and transience of life. **PK**

JACQUES BECKER

Born: Jacques Becker, September 15, 1906 (Paris, France); died 1960 (Paris, France).

Directing style: Influential French director of atmospheric movies across a wide range of genres; small but impressive output; elegant imagery; fluid narrative; sensitive attention to milieu.

One of the generation of French filmmakers who flourished in the years between the Golden Age of the 1930s and the rise of the New Wave in the late 1950s, Jacques Becker is a champion of understatement among directors, with no interest in flashy technical devices or show-off camera moves. His dexterity, the unstressed elegance of his images, and the wit and fluency of his narrative style have led some critics to write him off as a lightweight filmmaker, lacking in seriousness. Becker also loved to explore fresh territory and different genres—which is no way to build a reputation as a respected auteur.

After serving his cinematic apprenticeship through the 1930s as Jean Renoir's assistant, Becker struck out on his own with *Dernier atout* (1942), a lighthearted pastiche of a Hollywood thriller. After that he completed just a dozen more films during his all-too-brief directorial career. But that dozen took in the rustic melodrama *Goupi mains rouges* (1943) (*It Happened at the Inn*), the social comedy *Édouard et Caroline* (1951) (*Edward and Caroline*), the costume drama *Casque d'or* (1952) (*Golden Helmet*), the biopic *Les amants de Montparnasse* (*Montparnasse 19*) (1958) (*Modigliani of Montparnasse*), and in *Touchez pas au grisbi* (1954) (*Grisbi*), one of the finest and most influential of French gangster movies.

By constantly roving among different types of material, Becker was able to bring a fresh eye to everything he undertook. His attention to milieu was unfailingly sensitive, and as a director he was famous for his insight in handling his actors. His last film, the taut *Le trou* (1960) (*The Night Watch*), was completed only days before his death at the age of fifty-four. It showed that, despite illness, Becker was still working at the height of his powers and tirelessly exploring new territory. **PK**

Top Takes…

Le trou 1960 (*The Night Watch*)

Les amants de Montparnasse (Montparnasse 19) 1958 (*Modigliani of Montparnasse*)

Les Aventures d'Arsène Lupin 1957 (*The Adventures of Arsène Lupin*)

Ali Baba et les quarante voleurs 1954 (*Ali Baba and the Forty Thieves*)

Touchez pas au grisbi 1954 (*Grisbi*)

Rue de l'estrapade 1953 (*Françoise Steps Out*)

Casque d'or 1952 (*Golden Helmet*)

Édouard et Caroline 1951 (*Edward and Caroline*)

Rendez-vous de juillet 1949

Antoine et Antoinette 1947

Goupi mains rouges 1943 (*It Happened at the Inn*)

Dernier atout 1942

"[*The Night Watch* is] handled with genuine tension and even some originality."—*New York Times*

LUCHINO VISCONTI

Born: Luchino Visconti di Modrone, November 2, 1906 (Milan, Lombardy, Italy); died 1976 (Rome, Italy).

Directing style: Vanguard director of Italian neorealism; moved between sublime melodramas and earthy subject matter; Marxist influenced; family life themes.

Top Takes...

L'innocente 1976 (The Innocent)

Gruppo de famiglia in un interno 1974 (Conversation Piece)

Ludwig 1972

Morte a Venezia 1971 (Death in Venice)

La caduta degli dei 1969 (The Damned)

Lo Straniero 1967 (The Stranger)

Vaghe stelle dell'Orsa 1965 (Sandra of a Thousand Delights)

Il Gattopardo 1963 (The Leopard)

Rocco e i suoi fratelli 1960 (Rocco and His Brothers)

Le notti bianche 1957 (White Nights)

Senso 1954 (Livia)

La terra trema: Episodio del mare 1948 (The Earth Trembles)

Ossessione 1943

"The creation of beauty and purity is a spiritual act."

—Gustav, Death in Venice

A respected film and theater director, Luchino Visconti di Modrone was born into one of Northern Italy's richest families, one of the Duke of Modrone's seven children. He was a truly enigmatic figure, closely linked to the Italian Communist Party his whole life; but hailing from a premier aristocratic family, Visconti's films often display the struggle between his leftist politics and his own heritage.

Many have seen Visconti's adaptation of James M. Cain's novel The Postman Always Rings Twice—Ossessione (1943)—as kickstarting the neorealist film movement in its presaging of exterior shooting and deployment of a rougher, more naturalistic performance style. Thematically, the film's burning undercurrent of steamy sexuality was to infuse much of Visconti's later work. The film La terra trema: Episodio del mare (1948) (The Earth Trembles), however, came much closer to visiting neorealism's heartland, with its earthy subject matter and the casting of nonprofessional actors, many of whom were local fishermen.

Unlike other directors associated with the movement, Visconti continued to work long after the nails had been hammered into neorealism's coffin. For a period he seemed interested in exploring Italian history with films that were often elaborated with his own kind of grandiose, operatic aplomb, such as Il Gattopardo (1963) (The Leopard). Rocco e i suoi fratelli (1960) (Rocco and His Brothers) saw a return to the social commentary presaged in his earlier films although it also underlined his interest in both splintered family life and the effects of a wider societal decadence. Late Visconti films were often dark and sometimes obsessive, as with Morte a Venezia (1971) (Death in Venice), and the somnambulant mood that ran through his oeuvre was ever present. **RH**

OTTO PREMINGER

Born: Otto Ludwig Preminger, December 5, 1906 (Vienna, Austria); died 1986 (New York City, New York, U.S.).

Directing style: Maker of classic film noirs and star-studded blockbusters; often tackled controversial topics; characters typified by conflicting points of view.

Austrian-born Otto Preminger emigrated to the United States in order to fulfill his dream of becoming a movie director. From his early film noir *Laura* (1944) to his thriller *Bunny Lake Is Missing* (1965), he showed a remarkable ability to be independent, intelligent, demanding, and successful. If his later work is perhaps best forgotten, one must not ignore what he contributed to classical Hollywood.

Two words come to mind when discussing a Preminger movie—"objectivity" and "ambiguity." These are central to his mise-en-scène, but did not prevent him from taking sides. In his finest achievements, Preminger leaves his audience in no doubt as to where he stands, thanks to an acute sense of what details matter and a rigorous use of the camera. His awareness of the complexities of human psychology—that famous "ambiguity"—is why his characters are seldom cut and dried. His films demand that the spectator must constantly review his or her point of view.

One example is the way Preminger films the detective's interrogation of Waldo Lydecker in the opening sequence of *Laura*. The former's insistence on details comes as the latter, who dismisses them, is paying great attention to his clothes—the only way Preminger had to hint at his character's feminine side and therefore his homosexuality. In *Angel Face* (1952), Robert Mitchum's fascination with the young heroine soon becomes a morbid mixture of voyeurism and masochism, and is revealed via a complex play of looks and editing that involves the spectator in the deadly game the two will play. In *Anatomy of a Murder* (1959), it is a case of representing the need for the law to give the benefit of the doubt even when everything appears to be clear. **ReH**

Top Takes...

The Human Factor 1979
Skidoo 1968
Bunny Lake Is Missing 1965
The Cardinal 1963 ☆
Exodus 1960
Anatomy of a Murder 1959 ☆
Porgy and Bess 1959
Bonjour tristesse 1958
Saint Joan 1957
The Man with the Golden Arm 1956
Carmen Jones 1954
Die Jungfrau auf dem Dach 1953
Angel Face 1952
The 13th Letter 1951
Where the Sidewalk Ends 1950
Laura 1944 ☆

> "God, don't let my brother die at the end of a British rope."
>
> —Barak Ben Canaan, *Exodus*

CAROL REED

Born: Carol Reed, December 30, 1906 (Putney, London, England); died 1976 (Chelsea, London, England).

Directing style: Most notable for his subtle treatment of suspenseful thrillers; flair for casting; fruitful collaborations with writer Graham Greene.

Top Takes...

Oliver! 1968 ★
The Agony and the Ecstasy 1965
The Running Man 1963
Mutiny on the Bounty 1962
Our Man in Havana 1959
Trapeze 1956
The Man Between 1953
Outcast of the Islands 1952
The Third Man 1949 ☆
The Fallen Idol 1948 ☆
Odd Man Out 1947
The True Glory 1945
The Way Ahead 1944
The Stars Look Down 1940
Climbing High 1938
Bank Holiday 1938

Sir Carol Reed's early movies are a mixed bag, ranging from social dramas, such as *Bank Holiday* (1938), to screwball comedies such as *Climbing High* (1938). His first major film, *The Stars Look Down* (1940), charted the rise of an idealistic miner's son to a seat in government, and brought a grim authenticity to its pithead scenes. Reed then directed one of the finest British wartime propaganda films, *The Way Ahead* (1944).

After the war, Reed hit his stride with a trio of films that for the first time seemed personal to him, revealing something deeper and darker in his nature—a fatalism and sense of tragic irony. *Odd Man Out* (1947) follows the last hours of an Irish nationalist on the run in Belfast. In *The Fallen Idol* (1948), a diplomat's son believes he has seen the one man he cares about commit murder. In *The Third Man* (1949), set in the divided city of Vienna, a naive American is forced to realize that his oldest friend is a foul exploiter and killer. The last two films were scripted by Graham Greene, and *The Third Man* was immediately hailed as a classic. In this film, Reed's strongest qualities—his feel for location and his flair for casting and direction of actors—reached their peak, and he was widely regarded as the best living British director. But, as if this moment of self-revelation had upset his equilibrium, Reed then seemed to lose his way. *Outcast of the Islands* (1952) proved a disappointment, and *The Man Between* (1953) felt like a tired retread of *The Third Man*. Only twice was there something of a return to form. *Our Man in Havana* (1959) reunited him with Greene in a stylish, sardonic, spy comedy. And a stack of Academy Awards, including Reed's only Oscar as Best Director, greeted *Oliver!* (1968), his lively film version of Lionel Bart's Dickensian musical. **PK**

> "Some living. Lord help me, some living!"
> —Nancy, *Oliver!*

FRED ZINNEMANN

Born: Fred Zinnemann, April 29, 1907 (Vienna, Austria); died 1997 (London, England).

Directing style: Supreme craftsman; passionate believer in the importance of the script; gift for casting; famed for attention to detail and realism.

Fred Zinnemann initially wanted to become a musician, but then studied law at the University of Vienna. Interested in cinema, he became a cameraman and worked in Germany with a number of talented filmmakers, including Billy Wilder and Robert Siodmak, before emigrating to the United States. Zinnemann found work directing shorts for MGM and won an Academy Award for Best Short Subject with his one-reeler biopic *That Mothers Might Live* (1938).

Zinnemann's first feature was *Redes* (1936) (*The Wave*), which was shot in Mexico with a cast of local, nonprofessional actors—his penchant for realism and authenticity already evident. His first hit was *The Seventh Cross* (1944), set in Nazi Germany, which followed the fortunes of concentration camp escapees. Once again the director was noted for his realism, this time the vivid portrayal of the harshness of the camp.

In the 1950s, Zinnemann directed two major successes. *High Noon* (1952) was an innovatively structured Western, starring Gary Cooper as a sheriff left alone to defend his town against a gang of killers. *From Here to Eternity* (1953) had a star-studded cast in a powerful romantic drama set on a U.S. army base during World War II. The movie became famous for its steamy sex scenes and Zinnemann's psychological insight into his characters.

Zinnemann's reputation as a safe pair of hands meant he was given big-budget projects such as the musical Western *Oklahoma!* (1955) and the lavish costume drama *A Man for All Seasons* (1966), which won six Academy Awards, including Best Director. He continued with a string of successes such as *The Day of the Jackal* (1973), but his crowning later achievement was *Julia* (1977), which was based on the life of playwright Lillian Hellman. **EB**

Top Takes...

Julia 1977 ☆
The Day of the Jackal 1973
***A Man for All Seasons* 1966 ★**
***The Sundowners* 1960 ☆**
***The Nun's Story* 1959 ☆**
The Old Man and the Sea 1958
A Hatful of Rain 1957
Oklahoma! 1955
***From Here to Eternity* 1953 ★**
***High Noon* 1952 ☆**
Benjy 1951
The Men 1950
***The Search* 1948 ☆**
The Seventh Cross 1944
That Mothers Might Live 1938
Redes 1936 (*The Wave*)

"The three most important things about a film are the script, the script, the script."

HUMPHREY JENNINGS

Born: Humphrey Jennings, August 19, 1907 (Walberswick, England); died 1950 (Poros, Greece).

Directing style: Member of the 1930s British documentary film movement; morale-boosting propaganda films in World War II; notable use of montage.

Top Takes…

The Changing Face of Europe 1951
Family Portrait 1950
The Dim Little Island 1949
A Defeated People 1946
A Diary for Timothy 1945
Myra Hess 1945
The Eighty Days 1944
V.1 1944
The Silent Village 1943
Fires Were Started 1943
The True Story of Lilli Marlene 1943
Listen to Britain 1942
London Can Take It! 1940
Welfare of the Workers 1940
Design for Spring 1938
The Story of the Wheel 1934

"[Fires Were Started] achieves its heart-breaking impact by the simplest means."—New York Times

In the documentary tradition, and especially in that documentary tradition that considers the intersection of observation recording and story construction, Humphrey Jennings stands like a colossus. During World War II, he applied his considerable gifts to the crisis of British identity, motivating patriotic action through sentimental appeals. As such, his work is always politically motivated and nationalistic but eminently watchable. Certain titles, such as *Listen to Britain* (1942) and *A Diary for Timothy* (1945), have become staples among educators because they so clearly demonstrate excellent film technique in his deployment of montage and manipulation of sequencing, along with the instructive value of documentary films. But these titles also shed light on the constructed nature of documentary, and how this can be used to enhance the entertainment value of socially useful movies, along with advancing a particular ideological program.

Trained as a writer, theatrical craftsman, and editor, Jennings fell in with the pioneering documentary filmmaker John Grierson's General Post Office Film Unit during the 1930s. In 1937 he cofounded the Mass Observation movement with Charles Madge and Tom Harrisson. Mass Observation pioneered a method that involved making meticulous observations of what people did during their daily life. During the war, Jennings continued making well-regarded, propagandistic shorts before his untimely death in 1950 while scouting locations on the Greek island of Poros.

Aside from such standout shorts as *The Story of the Wheel* (1934), *Design for Spring* (1938), *A Defeated People* (1946), and *Family Portrait* (1950), Jennings's one feature film is *Fires Were Started* (1943), describing the efforts of firefighters. **GCQ**

HENRI STORCK

Born: Henri Storck, September 5, 1907 (Oostende, West Flanders, Belgium); died 1999 (Brussels, Belgium).

Directing style: Father of Belgian film culture; political activist and maker of documentaries; pioneering films of the lives of famous Belgian artists.

If Belgians are seen as among the world's most discerning cinephiles, they have Henri Storck to thank for it. He started the country's first *cinéclubs*, protected the nation's film heritage fiercely (he cofounded the highly reputed Royal Film Archive), was instrumental in political and documentary film movements across Europe, and heavily influenced Belgium's film policy.

Storck's first shorts, the city symphony *Images d'Ostende* (1929) and the pacifist collage *Histoire du soldat inconnu* (1932), received wide praise for their poetic tone and dynamism. In the 1930s, his career took a political turn and he achieved worldwide notoriety with *Borinage* (1933), a clandestine film he codirected with Joris Ivens, meticulously chronicling the oppression of striking coal miners in Belgium. *Borinage* was banned in several countries, but it became a landmark for activist filmmaking.

After World War II, Storck refined his editing techniques to shoot pedagogic art documentaries such as *Rubens* (1949) and *Permeke* (1985), both in a genre he helped to popularize, and the occasional fiction film such as *Le banquet des fraudeurs* (1952) (*The Smugglers' Banquet*). Storck's significance for cinema is best encapsulated by two cameo roles. He appeared as a priest in Jean Vigo's *Zéro de conduite: Jeunes diables au collège* (1933) (*Zero for Conduct*); and in Chantal Akerman's breakthrough film *Jeanne Dielman: 23 Quai du Commerce, 1080 Bruxelles* (1976), Storck was the first patron to enter Dielman's house, a nod to his importance as the father of Belgian film culture. Both appearances are endorsements of filmmakers beginning their careers, exercises in understanding the politics of everyday reality, and testimony of that typically Belgian finesse in film appreciation. **EM**

Top Takes...

Permeke 1985
Le chant du peintre 1978
Les fêtes de Belgique 1973
Le bonheur d'être aimé 1962
Le banquet des fraudeurs 1952
  (*The Smugglers' Banquet*)
Rubens 1949
Boerensymfonie 1944 (*Peasant Symphony*)
Borinage 1933
Histoire du soldat inconnu 1932
Sur les bords de la caméra 1932
Idylle à la plage 1931
La mort de Vénus 1930
Suzanne au bain 1930 (*Suzanne's Bad*)
Trains de plaisir 1930
Images d'Ostende 1929

"There emerges forcefully the personality of a cineaste . . . ."
—Jacqueline Aubenas, of Henri Storck

HENRI-GEORGES CLOUZOT

Born: Henri-Georges Clouzot, November 20, 1907 (Niort, Deux-Sèvres, Poitou-Charentes, France); died 1977 (Paris, France).

Directing style: Master of suspense thrillers; created tension within the ordinary; black humor; plots with twist endings; dark psychological overtones.

Top Takes...

La Prisonnière 1968 (Female Prisoner)

Messa da Requiem von Giuseppe Verdi 1967
  (Giuseppe Verdi: Requiem)

L'enfer 1964

La vérité 1960 (The Truth)

Les espions 1957 (The Spies)

Le mystère Picasso 1956
  (The Mystery of Picasso)

Les diaboliques 1955

Le salaire de la peur 1953 (The Wages of Fear)

Miquette et sa mère 1950 (Miquette)

Le voyage en Brésil 1950

Retour à la vie 1949

Manon 1949

Quai des orfèvres 1947 (Jenny Lamour)

Le corbeau 1943 (The Raven)

L'assassin habite ... au 21 1942
  (The Murderer Lives at Number 21)

Tout pour l'amour 1933

Caprice de princesse 1933

La terreur des batignolles 1931

Along with the likes of Alfred Hitchcock and Claude Chabrol, Henri-Georges Clouzot can rightly be credited as a pioneer and leading creator of classic movie thrillers. After starting out as a journalist, he worked as supervisor for a film company in Berlin in the 1920s, at a time when Germany was at the hub of innovative camerawork. Returning to France, Clouzot turned his writing skills to film scripts, then made his directorial debut with the short *La terreur des batignolles* (1931). His feature debut was the detective thriller *L'assassin habite ... au 21* (1942) (*The Murderer Lives at Number 21*). Rich in characterization and black humor, and visually elegant, the film set the tone for the work that was yet to come.

Among Clouzot's finest and most gripping works is *Le salaire de la peur* (1953) (*The Wages of Fear*). Portraying truck drivers who transport loads of unstable nitroglycerine across dangerous territory, the film is a study in the precariousness of existence, with characters finding themselves tested to the extreme.

By contrast, Clouzot's other memorable masterpiece, *Les diaboliques* (1955), has a far less exotic and extraordinary setting, concerning a small-town boarding school where the

RIGHT: Romy Schneider with Henri-Georges Clouzot and Alfred Hitchcock.

wife and mistress of the school's sadistic headmaster plot his murder. Creating incredible tension within the locales of everyday life, and demonstrating that the most thrilling films don't need outlandish set-ups, or even Technicolor and extravagant special effects, *Les diaboliques* is required viewing for anyone wanting to appreciate or produce emotionally powerful movies. (The film was based on a novel by Pierre Boileau and Thomas Nercejac, whose work Hitchcock later adapted in his 1958 masterpiece *Vertigo*.)

Les diaboliques was remade as the U.S. film *Diabolique* (1996), although the earlier movie stands out in its superior realization. And Claude Chabrol directed *L'enfer* (1994) as an act of homage to Clouzot's 1964 script and production of the same name. Although Hitchcock's work has attracted more critical attention, Clouzot, as "The French Hitchcock," has just as much claim to the title of greatest ever thriller director. **MH**

ABOVE: Simone Signoret and Clouzot's wife, Véra, on the set of *Les diaboliques*.

Partners in Suspense

Clouzot's wife Véra starred alongside Simone Signoret in *Les diaboliques*, playing the wife of the murdered school headmaster.

- Véra Gibson-Amado was born in Rio de Janeiro, Brazil, in 1913. She settled in France after World War II.

- Véra appeared only in films directed by her husband; her first film was the 1953 thriller *The Wages of Fear*.

- She cowrote the screenplay for Clouzot's *La vérité* (1960) (*The Truth*).

- Véra died suddenly, of an apparent heart attack, in 1960, at the age of forty-seven.

TEX AVERY

Born: Frederick Bean Avery, February 26, 1908 (Taylor, Texas, U.S.); died 1980 (Burbank, California, U.S.).

Directing style: Genius innovative cartoonist; creator of characters such as Daffy Duck; wildly creative animations that changed the face of U.S. animation industry.

Top Takes...

Crazy Mixed Up Pup 1954
Magical Maestro 1952
Droopy's Good Deed 1951
King-Size Canary 1947
The Shooting of Dan McGoo 1945
Screwball Squirrel 1944
Red Hot Riding Hood 1943
Blitz Wolf 1942
All This and Rabbit Stew 1941
A Wild Hare 1940
Thugs with Dirty Mugs 1939
Daffy Duck & Egghead 1937
Little Red Walking Hood 1937
Ain't We Got Fun 1937
Porky's Duck Hunt 1937
Don't Look Now 1936

Fred "Tex" Avery was the King of Cartoons: a free-wheeling anarchist whose distinctive sense of humor changed the face of U.S. animation forever. Generations later, his films can still reduce audiences to hysterics and inspire other cartoonists.

Avery started drawing comic strips in high school, before spending a summer studying art at the Chicago Art Institute. He moved to California and began work in 1929 as a grunt animator at Walter Lantz Studios. In 1936, Avery joined the Warner Brothers lot, where animation chief Leon Schlesinger put Avery in charge of his most unruly bunch. Cartoonists such as Chuck Jones and Bob Clampett hunkered down with Avery in a bug-infested shack called "Termite Terrace" and proceeded to invent a new breed of U.S. cartoon.

Avery steered Warner Brothers' cartoons away from mild Disney mimicry into gag-addled joke fests with an addiction to speed. He refined Porky Pig, created Daffy Duck, dreamed up a nemesis for Daffy that would evolve into Elmer Fudd, and gave Bugs Bunny his trademark quip, "What's up, Doc?"

Having all but invented the Looney Tunes as known today, Avery jumped ship to join rival outfit MGM in 1942. Here he would truly blossom, letting loose a demented imagination like no other. Characters would chase one another off the edge of the screen, outside the bounds of Technicolor, into the audience itself, with no regard for logic or the laws of physics. In 1954, Avery returned to Walter Lantz Studios, where he had cut his teeth 20 years earlier. He brought his MGM-esque insanity with him, invigorating the moribund studio and earning it Academy Award nods in the process. He left over a salary dispute after helming only four shorts, and went into advertising. **DK**

> "Avery poured his heart and soul into his work."
>
> —Hal Erickson

ROBERT ROSSEN

Born: Robert Rosen, March 16, 1908 (New York City, New York, U.S.); died 1966 (Hollywood, California, U.S.).

Directing style: Creator of tough, crime melodramas with a social conscience; movies often contain socialist political themes; close attention to script.

Born into a poor Russian-Jewish immigrant family in 1908 on the lower east side of New York, Robert Rossen worked as a writer on Broadway, then went in 1936 to Warner Brothers, where he wrote tough, socially minded crime melodramas such as *Marked Woman* (1937) and *The Roaring Twenties* (1939). He also wrote the screenplay for Lewis Milestone's excellent war film, *A Walk in the Sun* (1945), before becoming a director.

Body and Soul (1947), which Rossen directed from Abraham Polonsky's script, was a tough boxing film with a radical social conscience. His next film, *All the King's Men* (1949), based on Robert Penn Warren's novel about the career of Louisiana governor Huey Long, won an Academy Award for Best Picture.

In 1951 Rossen was identified as a communist to the House Un-American Activities Committee and was blacklisted after refusing to name other communists. Two years later, however, he recanted and named 57 colleagues. Permitted to work again, Rossen preferred not to return to Hollywood, filming in Europe on such productions as *Mambo* (1954) and *Alexander the Great* (1956). *They Came to Cordura* (1959) was an action movie set in Mexico during the revolutionary period, but Rossen's best picture is undoubtedly *The Hustler* (1961), in which he returned to U.S. material with a story set in the shady world of pool halls and gambling joints. Paul Newman was charismatic as the hustler of the title, with terrific support from Jackie Gleason and George C. Scott. *The Hustler* garnered Rossen a second Oscar nomination. His last film, *Lilith* (1964), stars Jean Seberg as a young woman in a psychiatric hospital who has an affair with her doctor. Although the film failed to find an audience, it was a highly creditable failure. Rossen died soon after, in 1966. **EB**

Top Takes...

Lilith 1964
The Hustler 1961 ☆
They Came to Cordura 1959
Island in the Sun 1957
Alexander the Great 1956
Mambo 1954
The Brave Bulls 1951
All the King's Men 1949 ☆
Body and Soul 1947
Johnny O'Clock 1947

> "I'm going to stay in this race
> ... and I'm out for blood."
> —Willie Stark, *All the King's Men*

DAVID LEAN

Born: David Lean, March 25, 1908 (Croydon, Surrey, England); died 1991 (London, England).

Directing style: Maker of epic historical and literary adaptations, often operatic in nature; impressive pictorialism; detailed mise-en-scène.

Top Takes...

A giant of the British cinema, Sir David Lean demonstrated how to make big pictures that would turn a sizable profit on the international market. Lean's five huge projects, spanning three decades, earned him worldwide renown.

The Bridge on the River Kwai (1957) turned novelist Pierre Boulle's enigmatic meditation on national character and honor into an epic war film. At the film's dramatic center is the struggle for control between an English officer and a Japanese commandant. *Lawrence of Arabia* (1962) demonstrated that Lean could handle an even more demanding production. The film offers an engaging, if simplistic, portrait of one of the twentieth century's most puzzling English colonialists. Lean then turned to a subject of even greater cultural and intellectual complexity, the Russian revolution, with Boris Pasternak's *Doctor Zhivago* (1965). Choosing to feature the novel's romance, Lean leaves barely explored the political and cultural upheavals it described. Oddly stagebound, the film fails to evoke the diverse vastness of Russia, providing a disappointing contrast to Lean's masterful marriage of wide-screen cinematography and striking locations in *Lawrence of Arabia*.

RIGHT: Alec Guinness and Sessue Hayakawa working together in the River Kwai.

ABOVE: Omar Sharif and Julie Christie in the Russian revolution saga *Doctor Zhivago*.

Lean's inability to think beyond cultural clichés is even more evident in *A Passage to India* (1984), whose impressive pictorialism does little to hide the limited performances given by a star-studded cast. If the novel critiques what is now called "Orientalism," Lean's film furthered these stereotypes with unselfconscious energy. In a further disappointment, *Ryan's Daughter* (1970) fails to integrate a failed romance between young Rosy Ryan Shaughnessy and a young English officer with a half hearted evocation of the Irish troubles.

The international Lean was preceded by a less ambitious self; his detailed mise-en-scène and skillful camerawork made instant classics of *Great Expectations* (1946) and *Oliver Twist* (1948), while the self-limiting restraint that figures as the quintessential element of bourgeois morality was never more poignantly evoked than in *Brief Encounter* (1945), one of the finest achievements of the British realist fiction film. **BP**

Desert Hero

David Lean's *Lawrence of Arabia* (1962), with Peter O'Toole in the title role, was based on the writings of T. E. Lawrence.

- Albert Finney was offered the role of T. E. Lawrence, but turned it down. Marlon Brando was also considered for the part.
- Most of the Arab soldiers in the film are played by members of the Arab Legion, courtesy of King Hussein of Jordan.
- King Hussein met his second wife, Antoinette, on the set of the film.
- A 482mm Panavision lens (known as the "David Lean lens" was used to film Omar Sharif's entrance through a mirage.

EDWARD DMYTRYK

Born: Edward Dmytryk, September 4, 1908 (Grand Forks, British Columbia, Canada); died 1999 (Encino, California, U.S.).

Directing style: Controversial figure for his actions during the McCarthy era; early work in film noir and films of left-wing political content.

The life of Edward Dmytryk is a testament to the redemptive power of the movies. Born in Canada to abusive Ukranian immigrant parents, his hardscrabble youth was as Dickensian as they come. Instead of ending in juvenile hall, however, it ended in the employment office of a movie studio.

By the 1940s, Dmytryk was a fast-rising star as a director, specializing in tough dramas—*Murder, My Sweet* (1944), *Cornered* (1945), and *Crossfire* (1947) chief among them. And then came the House Un-American Activities Committee (HUAC), keen to root out all subversive elements from Hollywood. Dmytryk, like many other honorable Americans, had joined the Communist Party in the years leading up to World War II as the only organized force in the United States then opposing Adolf Hitler's evil. That same moral sense led Dmytryk to resist HUAC's unconstitutional questioning of his political beliefs.

Such bullying had a name, the "blacklist," a mechanism by which Hollywood appeared to purge itself of leftist influences. Dmytryk railed against the blacklist, helming a daring production in England—*Give Us This Day* (1949)—with other blacklisted actors and craftspeople working proudly under their own names. It backfired: *Give Us This Day* won accolades across Europe but was essentially banned in the United States and Dmytryk was imprisoned. Months in jail changed his mind and Dmytryk opted to name names. It won him his freedom and a place in Hollywood once again, but it left a lasting stigma that haunted him to the grave. In the second period of his career, Dmytryk lacked the brash energy of his youth and in 1976 he left filmmaking to teach and write about the craft. He died in 1999, a controversial figure to the end. **DK**

"My lifelong ambition has been to spend my money as soon as I can get it."

RIGHT: Dick Powell starred as Laurence Gerard on a postwar mission in *Cornered*.

MANOEL DE OLIVEIRA

Born: Manoel Candido Pinto de Oliveira, December 11, 1908 (Oporto, Portugal).

Directing style: Portuguese director of theatrical satirical dramas; static shots; long takes; dense dialogue; themes exploring cultural myths and Roman Catholicism; minimalist performances.

1900s

Top Takes...

Espelho Mágico 2005

A Talking Picture 2003

La Lettre 1999 (*The Letter*)

Party 1996

O Convento 1995 (*The Convent*)

O dia do desespero 1992 (*The Day of Despair*)

Le soulier de satin 1985 (*The Satin Slipper*)

Francisca 1981

O passado e o presente 1972 (*Past and Present*)

Acto de primavera 1963 (*Rite of Spring*)

The Artist and the City 1956

Aniki Bóbó 1942

Famalicão 1941

Douro, Faina Fluvial 1931
   (*Labor on the Douro River*)

Manoel de Oliveira is perhaps best known for the astounding fact that, as he approaches his centenary, he continues to direct at least one film per year.

Early in his life, he pursued many interests, but he settled into directing after seeing a Walter Ruttmann documentary in 1927. This resulted in Oliveira's first film, the silent documentary *Douro, Faina Fluvial* (1931) (*Labor on the Douro River*). His interest in neorealism extended into his first feature film, *Aniki Bóbó* (1942), but then economic circumstances prevented Oliveira from directing, and he did not return in force until the stunning *Acto de primavera* (1963) (*Rite of Spring*).

Although several of Oliveira's films have received substantial critical acclaim, it was not until *Francisca* (1981) that he became an internationally renowned artist. Starting with *Le soulier de satin* (1985) (*The Satin Slipper*), Oliveira began creating films at an astonishing rate, developing a signature style comprised of static shots, long takes, and flat, unaffected acting.

His style is often compared to that of Luis Buñuel or Robert Bresson. Oliveira encourages minimalist performances that recall Bresson's conceptualization of actors as models and, like Buñuel, Oliveira routinely satirizes the bourgeoisie. However, Oliveira's work is complicated by his sympathy for the elite class he pokes fun at. Consequently, his use of verbal and visual irony is less overt, and more circumspect. Other recurring motifs include an interest in literature and a rigorous engagement with the underlying theological tenets of his Roman Catholic faith, as evidenced by *Espelho Mágico* (2005). However, the extraordinary clarity and passionate force of *The Satin Slipper* will likely stand as his definitive take on the issue. **ND**

> "I make movies for the sheer pleasure of doing it, regardless of critical reaction."

JOSEPH LOSEY

Born: Joseph Walton Losey, January 14, 1909 (La Crosse, Wisconsin, U.S.); died 1984 (London, England).

Directing style: Early career dominated by masterful film noirs; fast camera movement; Marxist themes and perceptive critiques of British class system.

Joseph Losey's Hollywood career ended in 1951 after five films. He was named as a communist in 1951, and moved to England, where he worked for the rest of his life. Not until 1956, with his film *Time Without Pity* (1957), was he able to use his real name; the arm of the blacklist was long.

With the exception of *The Boy with Green Hair* (1948), Losey's U.S. films were all examples of film noir, the domain where the Hollywood left-wing excelled in its critique of an alienated and alienating society, where fate was economic and not mere bad luck. Losey's greatest Hollywood movie was *The Prowler* (1951), with its cynical and self-indulgent cop perfectly representing the inability of socially inept characters to recognize the context in which they had foundered, interpreting life in individual and not collective terms. The extraordinary ending in the ghost town with its slagheap symbolizes both a return to repression in the United States and an annihilation of hope for an improved social conscience.

Losey collaborated with fellow blacklistees, Ben Barzman and Millard Lampell, on his most remarkable British film, *Blind Date* (1959), which shows that a U.S. Marxist understood more about the British class system than the indigenous British Left. His next film, *The Criminal* (1960), was sufficiently Hollywood and unBritish to elicit total hostility and incomprehension: it remains the most systematic reflection on the links between crime and capitalism Anglo-American cinema has given the world. Sadly, from 1962 on, Losey's work became self-conscious and self-indulgent but delighted those who had understood nothing of his earlier movies. Only the exemplary *King & Country* (1964) and *The Go-Between* (1970) reach the level of his finest film noirs. **ReH**

Top Takes...

Steaming 1985
Don Giovanni 1979
Monsieur Klein 1976
The Romantic Englishwoman 1975
A Doll's House 1973
The Go-Between 1970
Accident 1967
Modesty Blaise 1966
King & Country 1964
The Servant 1963
Eva 1962
The Criminal 1960
Blind Date 1959
Time Without Pity 1957
The Prowler 1951
The Boy with Green Hair 1948

"Film is a dog: the head is commerce, the tail is art ... rarely does the tail wag the dog."

1900s

JOSEPH L. MANKIEWICZ

Born: Joseph Leo Mankiewicz, February 11, 1909 (Wilkes-Barre, Pennsylvania, U.S.); died 1993 (Bedford, New York, U.S.).

Directing style: Use of snappy dialogue to create witty, meditative, and engaging comedies of manners; masterful employment of flashback; rapport with actors.

Before getting a chance to direct, Joseph L. Mankiewicz worked for more than 15 years as a writer and producer in Hollywood, scripting a number of the 1930s' most notable films and producing for a number of important directors such as George Cukor on *The Philadelphia Story* (1940). His first directorial effort, *Dragonwyck* (1946), is an overly stagy Gothic, hampered by bad casting and indifferent performances.

Mankiewicz's breakthrough film was *A Letter to Three Wives* (1949), which he developed from a women's magazine story about an unmarried femme fatale who steals the husband of one of her three best friends, then leaves the group in a state of confusion about which of their husbands she has run away with. The film rises above its material, sparkling with perceptive observations about social class and regional distinctions. Its finely detailed characters come to life with snappy dialogue and Mankiewicz's expert direction. It also offers interesting meditations on the development of mass culture, the dislocations caused by the war, consumer culture, and feminism.

The remainder of his oeuvre is remarkably varied, a series of films that are uniformly literate and engaging, if not visually

RIGHT: Ann Sothern and Kirk Douglas in the Oscar-winning *A Letter to Three Wives.*

striking. He achieved notoriety for overseeing the final stages of one of Hollywood's most notable disasters, *Cleopatra* (1963), proving that he was no master of the large-scale spectacle.

Mankiewicz's métier was the witty comedy of manners, and no American has proven more able at the genre. *A Letter to Three Wives* is an undoubted masterpiece, but *All About Eve* (1950) has no peers. This backstage drama offers a dark and pessimistic meditation on fame and celebrity, and the ways, often less than honest, in which they can be achieved. Although it deals with Broadway rather than Hollywood, the film seems a slightly wicked comment on the industry with which Mankiewicz, an Ivy League-educated intellectual, was associated. It takes a jaundiced view, perhaps, of commercial filmmaking and its obsession with star performers, writers, and directors, of which group Mankiewicz himself was one of the most celebrated for more than a decade. **BP**

ABOVE: Gary Merrill, Anne Baxter, and Bette Davis in Mankiewicz's acclaimed *All About Eve*.

A Peerless Movie

With 14 nominations, *All About Eve* (1950) ranks first in the list of most Academy Award nominated films.

- Mankiewicz based his screenplay on a story by Mary Orr that first appeared in *Cosmopolitan* magazine in 1946.
- Twentieth Century Fox paid Mary Orr $3,500 for the rights to *The Wisdom of Eve*.
- Bette Davis took over the role of Margo Channing when Claudette Colbert suffered a back injury. Marlene Dietrich, Anne Baxter, Tallulah Bankhead, and Susan Hayward were all also considered for the part.

RICCARDO FREDA

Born: Riccardo Freda, February 24, 1909 (Alexandria, Egypt); died 1999 (Rome, Italy).

Directing style: Leading Italian director of popular historical action movies and thrillers; resisted the neorealism dominant in postwar Italy; master of cult horror films who revived the genre in his country.

Top Takes...

Murder Obsession 1981
L'iguana dalla lingua di fuoco 1971
  (*The Iguana with the Tongue of Fire*)
La salamandra del deserto 1970
Lo Spettro 1963 (*The Ghost*)
L'orribile segreto del Dr. Hichcock 1962
  (*The Horrible Dr. Hichcock*)
Maciste all'inferno 1962 (*The Witch's Curse*)
I giganti della Tessaglia 1961
  (*The Giants of Thessaly*)
Caltiki—il mostro immortale 1959
  (*Caltiki, The Undying Monster*)
I vampiri 1956 (*The Vampires*)
Aquila nera 1946 (*Return of the Black Eagle*)
Don Cesare di Bazan 1942

Born in Egypt of Italian parents, Riccardo Freda was educated in Milan. He started out as a sculptor, then became a newspaper art critic. He began his movie career in 1937 and toiled in the Italian film industry in many capacities, eventually rising through the ranks to become a director on the sword-and-sandals film *Don Cesare di Bazan* (1942).

In the aftermath of World War II, with neorealism dominating Italian cinema, Freda specialized in critically unfashionable but always popular historical action adventure, directing films such as the stylish adaptation of an Alexander Pushkin story, *Aquila nera* (1946) (*Return of the Black Eagle*). Freda branched into more fantastical genres with the first major Italian horror film, the delicate and witty *I vampiri* (1956) (*The Vampires*), and the science-fictional alien-blob picture *Caltiki—il mostro immortale* (1959) (*Caltiki, The Undying Monster*). On *The Vampires*, Freda encountered difficulties with the investors and quit the production before it was complete. Cinematographer Mario Bava was entrusted with directing the final two days of filming, thus initiating the career of another giant of Italian cinema.

In the 1960s, Freda made more personal Gothic horror films, notably two movies with Barbara Steele, *L'orribile segreto del Dr. Hichcock* (1962) (*The Horrible Dr. Hichcock*) and *Lo Spettro* (1963) (*The Ghost*). In *Maciste all'inferno* (1962) (*The Witch's Curse*), the heroic muscleman tackles witchcraft in seventeenth-century Scotland, and then goes to hell. Always adaptable, he also made spy films, Westerns, and perverse violent *gialli*, or thrillers, such as *L'iguana dalla lingua di fuoco* (1971) (*The Iguana with the Tongue of Fire*). Freda was set to return to his old style with *La fille de d'Artagnan* (1994) (*D'Artagnan's Daughter*), but was fired and replaced by Bertrand Tavernier. **KN**

> "Horror . . . sharp as a razor's edge!"
> —Tagline for *Lo Spettro*

MARCEL CARNÉ

Born: Marcel Carné, August 18, 1909 (Paris, France); died 1996 (Clamart, Hauts-de-Seine, Île-de-France, France).

Directing style: Stylistic poetic realism of French cinema; melodramatic and poignant; fruitful collaboration with surrealist poet/screenwriter Jacques Prévert.

On the face of it, Marcel Carné and Jacques Prévert had little in common. Prévert was gregarious, highly political, a great lover of women, and one of the most popular French poets of the twentieth century. Carné was cool, apolitical, ultracontrolled, and fastidiously gay. Yet together they created seven films that include three of the towering masterpieces of French cinema.

Jenny (1936), Carné's feature debut and his first with Prévert, already showed his skill as a director of actors, though its crime melodrama plot links it more to Jacques Feyder, who originally planned to direct it. *Drôle de Drame ou L'étrange aventure de Docteur Molyneux* (1937) (*Bizarre, Bizarre*) was more Prévert than Carné—a delirious farce set in a wildly improbable London. But then came *Le quai des brumes* (1938) (*Port of Shadows*), the pair's first masterpiece of poetic realism, with a tailor-made role for Jean Gabin as an army deserter on the run. There followed *Hôtel du Nord* (1938) in the same vein, though minus Prévert, and then the two reunited for *Le jour se lève* (1939) (*Daybreak*), with Gabin holed up and the cops closing in; the metaphor for France on the brink of catastrophe was explicit.

After the medieval allegory *Les visiteurs du soir* (1942) (*The Devil's Envoys*) came the most ambitious French film ever made, and the climax of the Carné–Prévert partnership. *Les enfants du paradis* (1945) (*Children of Paradise*) represented a huge, multifaceted, defiant expression of French culture, set in the rich gamey world of mid-nineteenth-century Parisian theater.

Carné and Prévert's last film together, *Les portes de la nuit* (1946) (*Gates of the Night*), flopped woefully; the national mood had changed, and their partnership was dissolved. Carné continued making films until the 1970s, but they are scarcely remembered compared with his early output. **PK**

Top Takes...

Le merveilleuse visite 1974
  (*The Marvellous Visit*)
Les assassins de l'ordre 1971 (*Law Breakers*)
Les jeunes loups 1968 (*Young Wolves*)
Trois chambres à Manhattan 1965
  (*Three Rooms in Manhattan*)
Terraine vague 1960 (*Wasteland*)
Les portes de la nuit 1946 (*Gates of the Night*)
Les enfants du paradis 1945
  (*Children of Paradise*)
Les visiteurs du soir 1942 (*The Devil's Envoys*)
Le jour se lève 1939 (*Daybreak*)
Hôtel du Nord 1938
Le quai des brumes 1938 (*Port of Shadows*)
*Drôle de Drame ou L'étrange aventure de
  Docteur Molyneux* 1937 (*Bizarre, Bizarre*)
Jenny 1936

"Funny how blood stains clothes but washes off hands."
—Zabel, *Port of Shadows*

ELIA KAZAN

Born: Elias Kazanjoglou, September 7, 1909 (Istanbul, Turkey); died 2003 (New York City, New York, U.S.).

Directing style: Hollywood masterpieces that often explored controversial themes such as anti-Semitism; proponent of Method acting; literary adaptations.

Top Takes...

The Last Tycoon 1976
The Visitors 1972
The Arrangement 1969
America America 1963 ☆
Splendor in the Grass 1961
Wild River 1960
A Face in the Crowd 1957
Baby Doll 1956
East of Eden 1955 ☆
On the Waterfront 1954 ★
Man on a Tightrope 1953
Viva Zapata! 1952
A Streetcar Named Desire 1951 ☆
Panic in the Streets 1950
Pinky 1949
Gentleman's Agreement 1947 ★
Boomerang! 1947
The Sea of Grass 1947
Watchtower Over Tomorrow 1945
A Tree Grows in Brooklyn 1945
The People of the Cumberland 1937

If the postwar Broadway stage, with its breakthrough representations of the psychosexual life, exerted a powerful influence on Hollywood filmmaking, Elia Kazan must be given much of the credit. His adaptation of Tennessee Williams's *A Streetcar Named Desire* (1951) inaugurated the tradition of small-scale, black and white adult drama that served the industry so well in its era of postwar financial recession.

The small adult film was a genre that Kazan worked in with much critical success for the remainder of the decade. *A Face in the Crowd* (1957) addresses a time-honored U.S. theme—a Southern populism, based on a cult of authentic personality and its sexual allure that might threaten hegemony of the northeastern white Anglo-Saxon Protestant establishment. *Baby Doll* (1956) marries a cynical, comic look at sexual pieties with the neorealist stylizations of European realism.

Splendor in the Grass (1961) effectively recreates for the cinema playwright William Inge's poignant meditations of Midwestern sexual malaise, and in particular the stultifying effects for women of the so-called "double standard." The film anticipated by nearly a decade the inception of a U.S. art film

RIGHT: Marlon Brando and Vivien Leigh in Kazan's *A Streetcar Named Desire*.

1900s

tradition during the Hollywood renaissance, and the creation of a different kind of woman's picture.

Kazan, of course, was no stranger to controversy of another kind, occasioned by his forthcoming testimony before the House Un-American Activities Committee confirming the identification of fellow communists in the industry. Hollywood never completely forgave that indiscretion.

Kazan's other films mine something of a European social realist and art theater vein: *Pinky* (1949), in which a white actor plays a black character; *Viva Zapata!* (1952) with its Mexican revolutionary politics; *East of Eden* (1955) and *Wild River* (1960), which charted the inevitable discontents of social progress and generational change. Even Kazan's more conventional projects display a craftsmanship and intellectual sophistication that elevates them above mere entertainment. Hollywood has seen few directors of such breadth of talent and artistic vision. **BP**

ABOVE: James Dean and Julie Harris in *East of Eden*, based on the John Steinbeck novel.

Streetcar Revisited

Tennessee Williams's Pulitzer Prize-winning play *A Streetcar Named Desire* has been subject to various reinterpretations:

- Elia Kazan's 1951 film of the play won several awards, including an Oscar for Vivien Leigh as Best Actress.

- The play was made into an opera in 1995, with music by André Previn and libretto by Philip Littell. It premiered at the San Francisco Opera in 1998.

- A ballet production of the play was performed in Montreal, Canada, in 1952.

- The Simpsons parodied the play in *A Streetcar Named Marge* in 1992.

JACQUES TATI

Born: Jacques Tatischeff, October 9, 1909 (Yvelines, Île-de-France, France); died 1982 (Paris, France).

Directing style: Witty comedies of social observation; creator of the bumbling Monsieur Hulot character; sparse dialogue; visual gags; innovative sound effects.

Top Takes...

Forza Bastia 2002
Parade 1974
Trafic 1971 (Traffic)
Play Time 1967
Mon oncle 1958 (My Uncle)
Les Vacances de monsieur Hulot 1953
   (Mr. Hulot's Holiday)
Jour de fête 1949 (Holiday)
L'école des facteurs 1947 (School for Postmen)
Gai dimanche 1935

Born Jacques Tatischeff in France in 1909, Jacques Tati moved from mime to filmmaking in the early 1930s. He is responsible for only 15 films, of which *Jour de fête* (1949) (*Holiday*), and a quartet involving his character Monsieur Hulot with his trademark raincoat, umbrella, and pipe, remain especially significant. The Hulot films are an idiosyncratic and brilliant contribution to the understanding of social arrangements, notwithstanding their arch and irregularly modulated wit.

Les Vacances de monsieur Hulot (1953) (*Mr. Hulot's Holiday*), *Mon oncle* (1958) (*My Uncle*), and *Trafic* (1971) (*Traffic*) follow the speechless, umbrella-carrying bumbler through an insane social maze. Tati produced films that are little universes, where all the parts are geared together but where relief, value, and truth seem entirely beyond reach. *My Uncle* centers on Hulot's visit to relatives who own a vast plastics plant and live in a modern architect's nightmare. *Traffic* is a road caper, with Hulot in a specially designed camper on a vacation when everything goes wrong. *Mr. Hulot's Holiday* brings the generally stunned Hulot to a beachside hotel, where every relationship is overflowing with misunderstanding. Tati's masterpiece is *Play Time* (1967), a study of modernity in the city, shot in 70mm with play-toy color, and some of the most intensively choreographed and complex sequences ever filmed. Hulot is among U.S. tourists in a bureaucratic jungle with walls of glass, mirrors, circular roadways, gawking pedestrians, officious bureaucrats, and transportation havoc everywhere. The nightclub scene is a tour de force of cinema. This film bankrupted Tati, who had constructed a city with massive building façades on railway tracks in order to film it. He died of pneumonia in 1982. **MP**

> "... most of [*Mr. Hulot's Holiday*] is good, fast, wholesome fun."
>
> —*New York Times*

AKIRA KUROSAWA

Born: Akira Kurosawa, March 23, 1910 (Omori, Tokyo, Japan); died 1998 (Setagaya, Tokyo, Japan).

Directing style: Legendary Japanese maker of comedies and epics that bridged the gap between Asian and Hollywood cinema; use of wipe effect; intense on set.

Akira Kurosawa's filmmaking journey begins with images and sounds: of samurai swords, of rainstorms, of arrows impaling a man, and of a dog carrying a severed hand down the streets of a poor village. The director's own experiences support these memories: from dorm room to art house to living room. Then he slowly adds a sense of context: of world wars, Westernization, and non-Hollywood film traditions infiltrating the world through the most popular mass medium of the twentieth century. With time, new images and sounds keep pace with the old and thus the context in Kurosawa's work gains depth with each passing year; we see references to movies from the 1920s and 1930s, notice symbolism, and witness vibrant experiments with color that revealed the director's impending sense of mortality.

Born in 1910, Akira Kurosawa grew to maturity under Japanese imperial might. He transmuted his interests in painting to enter his native film industry in the mid-1930s, making his directorial debut with *Uma* (1941) (*Horse*), and after World War II became a cultural export. Early works were generally nationalistic, such as *Ichiban utsukushiku* (1944) (*The*

Top Takes...

Madadayo 1993 (*Not Yet*)
Hachi-gatsu no kyôshikyoku 1991
   (*Rhapsody in August*)
Yume 1990 (*Akira Kurosawa's Dreams*)
***Ran* 1985** ☆
Kagemusha 1980
   (*Kagemusha the Shadow Warrior*)
Dersu Uzala 1975
Dô desu ka den 1970 (*Clickety-Clack*)
Akahige 1965 (*Red Beard*)
Tengoku to jigoku 1963 (*High and Low*)
Tsubaki Sanjûrô 1962 (*Sanjuro*)
Yojimbo 1961 (*Yojimbo the Bodyguard*)
Warui yatsu hodo yoku nemuru 1960
   (*The Bad Sleep Well*)
Kakushi-toride no san-akunin 1958
   (*The Hidden Fortress*)
Kumonosu jô 1957 (*Throne of Blood*)
Ikimono no kiroku 1955 (*I Live in Fear*)
Shichinin no samurai 1954 (*The Seven Samurai*)
Ikiru 1952 (*Doomed*)
Rashômon 1950 (*In the Woods*)
Nora inu 1949 (*Stray Dog*)
Waga seishun ni kuinashi 1946
   (*No Regrets for My Youth*)
Zoku Sugata Sanshiro 1945 (*Judo Saga II*)

1910s

LEFT: Kurosawa with U.S. fans, the directors Francis Ford Coppola and George Lucas.

Western Hero

Akira Kurosawa has always been more popular with Western audiences than with those in his native Japan. Critics in his own country were often suspicious of his familiarity with the Western literary tradition on which he drew creatively in his films. In turn, Kurosawa proved to be a great inspiration for filmmakers in Europe and the United States.

- He liked to reset Shakespeare's plays in Japanese feudal settings—*Ran* is based on *King Lear* and *Kumonosu jô* (*Throne of Blood*) on *Macbeth*.

- *Ikiru* (*Doomed*) was an adaptation of Russian author Leo Tolstoy's *The Death of Ivan Ilyich* and *Tengoku to jigoku* (*High and Low*) was based on *King's Ransom* by U.S. crime writer Ed McBain.

- Kurosawa's movies were often copied and remade by other filmmakers. Sergio Leone's *Per un pugno di dollari* (1964) (*A Fistful of Dollars*) was based on *Yojimbo* (*The Bodyguard*). *Kakushi toride no san akunin* (*Hidden Fortress*) was an acknowledged influence on the *Star Wars* movies. Kurosawa's use of the "wipe effect"—where one scene fades to another—was a technique George Lucas adapted for use in *Star Wars*.

- Kurosawa was a huge fan of John Ford. Like the famous director of U.S. Westerns, Kurosawa often worked with the same cast and crew repeatedly.

Most Beautiful) and *Zoku sugata sanshiro* (1945) (*Judo Saga II*), and now interesting only because of what they would point to later on. Yet after the war, his focus turned a critical eye on contemporary Japan, as in *Waga seishun ni kuinashi* (1946) (*No Regrets for My Youth*) and *Nora inu* (1949) (*Stray Dog*).

Postwar popularity in the West

Enter *Rashômon* (1950) (*In the Woods*), the story of five competing points of view about a single event, but also a period drama set in Japan's feudal past. It won the Golden Lion at the Venice Film Festival and introduced Kurosawa to a global audience. The film was especially influential in Europe and the United States, where Kurosawa gradually became synonymous with reworked Western genres in the Far East. The association was meaningful because Japan was a hated and fallen foe after World War II. Kurosawa's popularity was partly due to his familiarity with silent film conventions such as histrionic acting, composition in depth, and transitional devices including wipes; and partly to his familiarity with the Western literary tradition, including Shakespeare and Dostoyevsky. Kurosawa was familiar to Western moviegoers, both technically and thematically, and this made him easier to accept abroad despite the general xenophobia of the period. Important work followed in a parade of cinematographic showcases, carefully executed action sequences, and attention to details of the natural world at the edge of civilization in works such as *Shichinin no samurai* (1954) (*The Seven Samurai*) and *Yojimbo* (1961) (*Yojimbo the Bodyguard*). Kurosawa became a commercial draw, and was labeled an auteur. Western studios poached his ideas for other films and his actors began appearing in non-Japanese movies.

Then his rank as lone colossus astride the crossroads of East and West exploded in an industry debate about his value to his native Japan and his crossover appeal elsewhere. Kurosawa's old-man status excited new Japanese filmmakers wishing to depart from his example just as certain Westerners, such as directors George Lucas and Francis Ford Coppola, considered him an idol, and a cause worthy of support.

A difficult period for the director stretched from the early 1960s to the early 1970s, when Kurosawa produced rich works such as *Tsubaki Sanjûrô* (1962) (*Sanjuro*) and *Akahige* (1965) (*Red Beard*) but was unsuccessful in the marketplace. He even attempted suicide at one especially low point. But, eventually he earned Russian financing for another masterwork, *Dersu Uzala* (1975). He went on to make a number of epic works, including *Kagemusha* (1980) (*Kagemusha the Shadow Warrior*), *Ran* (1985), which earned him an Oscar nomination, and *Hachi-gatsu no kyôshikyoku* (1991) (*Rhapsody in August*).

From viewing the body of Akira Kurosawa's oeuvre, indelible images and sounds linger: those of allegory, sudden violence, and the magic of falling in love. These are what have outlived the master. **GCQ**

ABOVE: Kurosawa's *The Seven Samurai* was the template for *The Magnificent Seven.*

"In all my films, there's three or maybe four minutes of real cinema."

CHARLES CRICHTON

Born: Charles Ainslie Crichton, August 6, 1910 (Wallasey, Cheshire, England); died 1999 (South Kensington, London, England).

Directing style: British director of dramas and Ealing comedies; black humor with an absurdist twist; everyday settings; skilled editor producing fast-paced timing.

Top Takes...

A Fish Called Wanda **1988** ☆
He Who Rides a Tiger 1965
The Third Secret 1964
The Boy Who Stole a Million 1960
The Battle of the Sexes 1959
Floods of Fear 1959
Law and Disorder 1958
The Man in the Sky 1957
The Divided Heart 1954
The Titfield Thunderbolt 1953
Hunted 1952
The Lavender Hill Mob 1951
Dance Hall 1950
Against the Wind 1948
Hue and Cry 1947

Despite the fact Charles Crichton made as many dramas as comedies, it is as a comedy director that he is best remembered, and specifically for the comedies he made at Ealing Studios. *Hue and Cry* (1947) set the template for the Ealing Studios's comedy style: realistic, everyday settings for events pushed just over the edge of absurdity, and a tone of mildly populist insubordination. Crichton's best, and best-loved, Ealing Studios film is *The Lavender Hill Mob* (1951), a crime comedy that gave Sir Alec Guinness, as the Bank of England clerk who sets out to steal from his employers, one of his classic roles. Crichton, who trained as an editor, keeps the rhythm crisp and alert while relishing the wealth of quirky detail.

By the time Crichton came to direct *The Titfield Thunderbolt* (1953), the studio's comic impulse was declining into coziness. Charming though it is, the film lacks the sharp social insights of the earlier films. Of Crichton's other work at Ealing Studios, the most interesting is *Against the Wind* (1948), an unconventional World War II movie that took a downbeat, disenchanted view of Allied undercover work in Nazi-occupied Belgium.

After Ealing folded, Crichton had trouble keeping his career on the rails. *The Battle of the Sexes* (1959) should have offered ideal black-comedy material, but it was soft and sentimentalized. In the 1960s he retreated into TV work, and then into directing corporate videos—for John Cleese's Video Arts Training Films. At Cleese's invitation Crichton made his return to the cinema after 23 years, with the heist comedy *A Fish Called Wanda* (1988). He directed and cowrote the screenplay, receiving Oscar nominations in both categories. Well-paced, crisply edited, and mining a vein of ruthless black humor, the film was a major international hit. **PK**

> "The central message of Buddhism is not 'every man for himself.'"—*A Fish Called Wanda*

KAREL ZEMAN

Born: Karel Zeman, November 3, 1910 (Ostromer u Nové Paky, Bohemia, Austria-Hungary); died 1989 (Prague, Czech Republic).

Directing style: Cofounder of the Czech animated film industry; maker of science fiction and fantasy features with a wit appealing to adults and children.

Karel Zeman is seen as the cofounder of Czech animated film thanks to his groundbreaking combination of live action, animation, and special effects. The most successful products of this method were the stunning *Cesta do praveku* (1955) (*Journey to Prehistory*), that has since been compared to Steven Spielberg's *Jurassic Park* (1993), and *Vynález zkázy* (1958) (*The Fabulous World of Jules Verne*). Like Spielberg, his movies appealed to children yet retained a wit and visual style that also entranced adults.

Unconvincing on a realistic level, Zeman's special effects evoke a poetry missing from today's orgies of computer-generated graphics. Born in 1910, his early occupations included window dressing and poster painting, before he moved into advertising in Marseilles. His first animation experience was a soup advertisement, and then he landed a place at the Zlín animation studio in 1943. With animator Hermína Týrlová, he created the movie *Vánocní sen* (1946) (*The Christmas Dream*), which gained the Best Animation award at Cannes.

Zeman's first solo project was a series of films featuring the accident-prone Mr. Prokouk. After his success with *The Fabulous World of Jules Verne*, he embarked on adaptations of other Verne books, as well as classic stories such as *Baron Prásil* (1961) (*The Fabulous Baron Munchausen*). His method was to use sets painted in a Victorian style, and then have live actors stroll through the animated settings. Away from these sci-fi and fantasy features, his most intriguing success was the short *Inspirace* (1949) (*Inspiration*), where he used glass figurines to produce a silkily smooth style. *Pohádka o Honzíkovi a Marence* (1980) (*The Tale of John and Marie*) saw Zeman returning to classical forms of animation. **TE**

Top Takes…

Pohádka o Honzíkovi a Marence 1980
 (*The Tale of John and Marie*)
Carodejuv ucen 1977
Pohádky tisíce a jedné noci 1974
 (*A Thousand and One Nights*)
Zkrocený démon 1974
Dobrodruství námorník a Sindinbáda 1971
Na komete 1970 (*Hector Servadac's Ark*)
Ukradená vzducholod 1967 (*The Stolen Airship*)
Bláznova kronika 1964 (*The Jester's Tale*)
Baron Prásil 1961
 (*The Fabulous Baron Munchausen*)
Vynález zkázy 1958
 (*The Fabulous World of Jules Verne*)
Cesta do praveku 1955 (*Journey to Prehistory*)
Inspirace 1949 (*Inspiration*)
Vánocní sen 1946 (*The Christmas Dream*)

1910s

"Zeman's work created astonishing visions of ancient and modern worlds."—Karl Cohen

JOHN STURGES

Born: John Eliot Sturges, January 3, 1911 (Oak Park, Illinois, U.S.); died 1992 (San Luis Obispo, California, U.S.).

Directing style: The dean of action-adventure movies and Westerns; flawless and innovative action sequences; male-dominated films; compelling storytelling.

Top Takes...

The Eagle Has Landed 1976
McQ 1974
Marooned 1969
Ice Station Zebra 1968
Hour of the Gun 1967
The Hallelujah Trail 1965
The Satan Bug 1965
The Great Escape 1963
The Magnificent Seven 1960
Never So Few 1959
Last Train from Gun Hill 1959
The Old Man and the Sea 1958
The Law and Jake Wade 1958
Gunfight at the O.K. Corral 1957
Bad Day at Black Rock 1955 ☆
The Man Who Dared 1946

John Sturges began his career in the backroom of RKO Pictures, working as an editor and production assistant. Service in the U.S. Army Air Corps in World War II gave him the opportunity to direct documentaries, and upon returning to Hollywood he got his first chance to make a feature with the thriller *The Man Who Dared* (1946). Over the next ten years Sturges directed a series of modest little films, often action films or dramas. In the powerful thriller *Bad Day at Black Rock* (1955), Sturges showed what he could do with a good script and a major star in the shape of Spencer Tracy as a one-armed war veteran. *Gunfight at the O.K. Corral* (1957), starring Burt Lancaster and Kirk Douglas, was a big success and established Sturges as one of Hollywood's specialists in the Western, revealing his talent for the tightly controlled, unpretentious genre film.

Two more excellent Westerns followed, *The Law and Jake Wade* (1958) and *Last Train from Gun Hill* (1959), before he made the epic Western *The Magnificent Seven* (1960). Based on Japanese director Akira Kurosawa's *Shichinin no samurai* (1954) (*The Seven Samurai*), Sturges transposed the action to Mexico, and the film was a huge international hit that generated many remakes. *The Great Escape* (1963), a World War II prison-camp drama, made Steve McQueen a superstar and was another great success. It became the classic prison escape movie, noted for its epiphanic and exuberant motorbike sequence. Sturges's direction of these films is never less than efficient, and the action sequences are flawlessly staged. *Hour of the Gun* (1967), a sequel to *Gunfight at the O.K. Corral*, with James Garner as Wyatt Earp, is an even better movie, but Sturges's later Westerns, such as *Joe Kidd* (1972), with Clint Eastwood, were disappointing. **EB**

> "We have in effect put all our rotten eggs in one basket."
>
> —Von Luger, *The Great Escape*

ROBERT HAMER

Born: Robert Hamer, March 31, 1911 (Kidderminster, West Midlands, England); died 1963 (London, England).

Directing style: Maker of 1940s Ealing Studios black comedies; fruitful working relationship with actor Sir Alec Guinness; ironic wit and charm; outsider themes.

Sadly, Robert Hamer drank himself to death, destroying one of the most potentially impressive careers in British cinema. He directed one undisputed masterpiece, *Kind Hearts and Coronets* (1949), one of the wittiest black comedies ever made. Throughout his work there is a sardonic melancholia, a love of language, a self-lacerating intelligence, a fascination with the shadowy side of life.

He began his film career as a cutting room assistant for the British studio Gaumont in 1934, later joining the General Post Office Film Unit before World War II. But his best work came out of London's Ealing Studios. Hamer's films evoke a dark, dangerous world lurking below the calm surface of everyday life. The son in *Pink String and Sealing Wax* (1946) escapes his stifling Victorian family for a glittering nocturnal world of drink, lust, and murder. A married woman's convict ex-lover returns to disrupt her drab domesticity in *It Always Rains on Sunday* (1947), and the serial killings of *Kind Hearts and Coronets* are subversively played out amid stiff Edwardian formality.

As his career hit the skids Hamer's films became increasingly personal, often centering around isolated, unattached individuals. These disaffected characters must confront their own malevolent alter egos, as with the police detective and the criminal of *The Spider and the Fly* (1949); the ex-con and the man who framed him in *The Long Memory* (1952); and Father Brown and Flambeau in *Father Brown* (1954). This process reaches its logical conclusion in *The Scapegoat* (1959), a murder mystery in which a man must outwit his doppelganger. It is as if Hamer is playing out onscreen the battle between his own creative and destructive sides, as can be seen in the abortive projects of his final decade. **PK**

Top Takes…

School for Scoundrels or How to Win Without Actually Cheating! 1960
The Scapegoat 1959
To Paris with Love 1955
Father Brown 1954 (*The Detective*)
His Excellency 1952
The Long Memory 1952
Kind Hearts and Coronets 1949
The Spider and the Fly 1949
It Always Rains on Sunday 1947
Pink String and Sealing Wax 1946
Dead of Night 1945

"*[Kind Hearts and Coronets]* has become a sort of yardstick for everything else I've done."

NICHOLAS RAY

Born: Raymond Nicholas Kienzle, August 7, 1911 (Galesville, Wisconsin, U.S.); died 1979 (New York City, New York, U.S.).

Directing style: Highly influential on a generation of filmmakers; dramatic use of architecture; themes portraying the young and the outsiders of society.

Top Takes...

Lightning Over Water 1980
Marco 1978
We Can't Go Home Again 1976
55 Days at Peking 1963
King of Kings 1961
The Savage Innocents 1960
Party Girl 1958
Bitter Victory 1957
Bigger Than Life 1956
Hot Blood 1956
Rebel Without a Cause 1955
Johnny Guitar 1954
On Dangerous Ground 1952
Flying Leathernecks 1951
In a Lonely Place 1950
They Live by Night 1948

"I don't know what to do anymore. Except maybe die."

—Jim Stark, *Rebel Without a Cause*

RIGHT: Ray on set with James Dean, who plays Jim Stark in *Rebel Without a Cause*.

After writing and producing radio programs in his teens, Nicholas Ray studied architecture with Frank Lloyd Wright, from whom he learned the value of the horizontal line that would become a feature in his work for the big screen. He began filmmaking with *They Live by Night* (1948). He went on to direct more than 20 pictures, including *Knock on Any Door* (1949), *Born to Be Bad* (1950), *The Lusty Men* (1952), *Wind Across the Everglades* (1958), and *55 Days at Peking* (1963). On the set of *55 Days at Peking* he suffered a heart attack, causing a hiatus in his career and he did not return to the director's chair again until the mid-1970s. He taught acting at the State University of New York at Binghamton, becoming a beloved figure to his students, and to actors. Influential upon directors Wim Wenders and Jim Jarmusch, he was a hero of the French New Wave critics.

Five films by Ray are recognized as masterpieces. *In a Lonely Place* (1950), one of the most poetic and haunting film noirs ever shot, has Humphrey Bogart as an angry screenwriter and Gloria Grahame (Ray's third wife) as the girl who loves, and then confounds him. *Johnny Guitar* (1954) stars Sterling Hayden as the most peaceable cowboy ever filmed, with Joan Crawford and Mercedes McCambridge shooting it out in the finale. *Bigger Than Life* (1956) centers on drug problems in middle-class life. *Bitter Victory* (1957) is a war story of conflict and hope in the African desert. And *Rebel Without a Cause* (1955), with James Dean, treated juvenile delinquency. Ray's direction of actors was legendary, centering on his belief that a character's line of feeling and expression should guide the structure of the shot. His death from cancer in 1979 is depicted in his moving swan song, the docudrama *Lightning Over Water* (1980), that Wenders codirected and completed. **MP**

JULES DASSIN

Born: Julius Dassin, December 18, 1911 (Middletown, Connecticut, U.S.).

Directing style: Influential creator of classic film noirs, sparkling comedies, dramas, and documentaries; successful collaborations with Greek actress Melina Mercouri; fast pace.

Jules Dassin was born the son of a Russian-Jewish barber, and after early work in the Yiddish Proletarian Theater company in New York, he began directing shorts in Hollywood. His early features were unremarkable, but *Brute Force* (1947) was a tough, at times savage, prison drama with Burt Lancaster as a prisoner pitted against Hume Cronyn, the sadistic chief of the guards. Shot in a semidocumentary style on location in New York City, *The Naked City* (1948) was an innovative crime melodrama. *Thieves' Highway* (1949) was a gritty film noir with forceful performances by Richard Conte and Lee J. Cobb.

Dassin's promising career in Hollywood was then wrecked when he was named as a communist to the House Un-American Activities Committee by director Edward Dmytryk in 1952. Relocating to England, Dassin made another impressive film noir, *Night and the City* (1950), starring Richard Widmark. He then moved to France for his next production, perhaps the one for which he is best known. *Du rififi chez les hommes* (1955) (*Rififi*) is a tense heist movie about a daring jewel robbery, in which Dassin himself plays a substantial role. Filmed in a wintry Paris, the lengthy sequence in which the safe is robbed is a tour de force of wordless suspense. Dassin's career underwent another radical shift when he directed his second wife, the Greek actress Melina Mercouri, in *Pote tin Kyriaki* (1960) (*Never on Sunday*). She played Ilya, a life-affirming prostitute who lifts the spirits of all those who meet her. The movie was a huge success. Mercouri also starred in *Phaedra* (1962), Dassin's version of the play by Euripides. Dassin's next film, *Topkapi* (1964), a comedy thriller starring Mercouri and Peter Ustinov, was a box-office success, but his later films struggled to find an audience. **EB**

> "Louis B. Mayer's arm around your shoulder meant his hand was closer to your throat."

GEORGES FRANJU

Born: Georges Franju, April 12, 1912 (Fougères, Ille-et-Vilaine, Bretagne, France); died 1987 (Paris, France).

Directing style: Maker of stark documentaries and features; poetic and surrealist dreamscapes; literary adaptations; social commentary; sometimes brutal content.

Georges Franju was too complex and fiercely individual a filmmaker to fit into any particular school, which may explain the current neglect of his work. His films, an edgy mixture of savagery and tenderness strongly imbued with the disquieting poetry of surrealism, present unsettlingly offbeat images that transform their seemingly mundane surroundings into outlandish dreamscapes. Underlying all his work is a simmering anger at the narrowness and cruelty of human institutions.

With Henri Langlois, Franju founded the Cinémathèque Française in 1937, and protected its riches under the Nazi occupation, preserving it as an invaluable archive and the spiritual home of the New Wave. Several of the documentaries he directed after the war explore the dark underside of civilized society. *Le sang des bêtes* (1949) (*The Blood of the Beasts*) looks unflinchingly at the work of a Paris abattoir, while *Hôtel des Invalides* (1952) denounces the glorification of war. But *Le Grand Méliès* (1952) is an affectionate portrait of the cinematic pioneer whose sense of fantasy Franju shared.

Not until he was forty-six years old did Franju start directing features. His best known, *Les yeux sans visage* (1960) (*Eyes Without a Face*), brought an austere, melancholy lyricism to its horror movie plot. *Thomas l'imposteur* (1964) (*Thomas the Impostor*), adapted from Jean Cocteau's novel, treats images of war and destruction with an ambiguous beauty, whereas *Thérèse Desqueyroux* (1962) (*Therese*) contrives to be faithful both to the stern Catholicism of the author of the original novel, Claude Mauriac, and to Franju's atheism. By contrast, *La faute de l'abbé Mouret* (1970) (*The Demise of Abbé Mouret*), adapted from Émile Zola's novel, gives vent to the director's anticlericalism. **PK**

Top Takes...

La faute de l'abbé Mouret 1970
   (*The Demise of Father Mouret*)
Marcel Allain 1966
Thomas l'imposteur 1964
   (*Thomas the Impostor*)
Judex 1963
Thérèse Desqueyroux 1962 (*Therese*)
Pleins feux sur l'assassin 1961
   (*Spotlight on a Murderer*)
Les yeux sans visage 1960 (*Eyes Without a Face*)
La tête contre les murs 1959
   (*Head Against the Wall*)
La première nuit 1958
Notre Dame—cathédrale de Paris 1957
Monsieur et Madame Curie 1956
Le Grand Méliès 1952
Le sang des bêtes 1949 (*Blood of the Beasts*)

"Perhaps the most elegant horror movie ever made."
—Pauline Kael on *Eyes Without a Face*

MARCEL CAMUS

Born: Marcel Camus, April 21, 1912 (Chappes, France); died 1982 (Paris, France).

Directing style: French director of dramas and comedies; innovative use of music; lyrical, otherworldly feel; lack of formal structure; sentimental celebration of the poor.

Top Takes...

Os Pastores da Noite 1975 (*Bahia*)
Le mur de l'Atlantique 1970 (*Atlantic Wall*)
Un été sauvage 1970 (*A Savage Summer*)
L'homme de New York 1967
Vivre la nuit 1967 (*Love in the Night*)
Le chant du monde 1965 (*Song of the World*)
L'oiseau de paradis 1962 (*Dragon Sky*)
Os Bandeirantes 1960 (*The Pioneers*)
Orfeu Negro 1959 (*Black Orpheus*)
Mort en fraude 1957 (*Fugitive in Saigon*)
Interdit de séjour 1955

Orfeu Negro (1959) (*Black Orpheus*), the legend of Orpheus and Eurydice transferred to the *favelas* of Rio de Janeiro, became the first movie with an all-black cast to win both the Palme d'Or and an Academy Award for Best Foreign Language Film. A milestone in black cinema, its unlikely auteur was a forty-seven-year-old white Frenchman, Marcel Camus, who was directing, on a shoestring, only his second feature film.

Camus (brother of writer Albert) was, however, not short of experience, and had worked as an assistant director with the likes of Alexandre Astruc, Jacques Becker, and Luis Buñuel since entering the French film industry in the 1940s. With memorable performances from an amateur cast, *Black Orpheus*'s vibrant cinematography and dance sequences immersed the audience in the spectacle of the Rio carnival, and the film's score introduced the world to *bossa nova*, the jazz–samba hybrid that would soon become a global craze.

Perhaps inevitably, Camus would never enjoy such dizzying success again. By the time of *Le chant du monde* (1965) (*Song of the World*), a Romeo and Juliet-style tale set in rural Provence, he was starting to be seen as a one-hit wonder, and *Un été sauvage* (1970) (*A Savage Summer*), a youth film set in Saint Tropez, was dismissed as inauthentic. However, *Le mur de l'Atlantique* (1970) (*Atlantic Wall*), a gentle nostalgic comedy starring Léon Duchemin, was more successful, and it set the tone for the TV productions that Camus focused on thereafter. Although much of his work has been criticized, with some justification, for its lack of formal structure, its romantic view of ethnic peoples, and its sentimental celebration of the noble poor, Camus's cinematic achievements, especially with *Black Orpheus*, should not be overlooked. **RB**

> "Dated in its sentimentality but timeless in splendor."
>
> —Donald Levit on *Black Orpheus*

KANETO SHINDÔ

Born: Kaneto Shindô, April 28, 1912 (Hiroshima, Japan).

Directing style: Japanese maker of contemplative dramas and horror movies; use of long silences and ambient sound; fantastic imagery; minimalist black and white camerawork.

Vital and prolific Japanese director Kaneto Shindô was born in 1912 in Hiroshima—the inspiration for *Gembaku no ko* (1952) (*Children of Hiroshima*), a personal, contemplative account of his city's nuclear devastation. In his best films, Shindô deals with the human condition stripped to its essentials, as in *Hadaka no shima* (1960) (*The Island*), a stark, dialogue-free, minimalist portrayal of survival in the harshest circumstances. His use of long silences and ambient sound was even more stylized in his most memorable film, *Onibaba* (1964) (*Devil Woman*), about two feral women trying to survive by means of murder. Shindô's stunning, high-contrast, black and white photography portrays them with a mixture of sympathy and detachment. The reeds constantly blown by the wind provide a suitable metaphor for societal tumult, but also of the wild nature and passions emerging from beneath layers of civilization.

In *Yabu no naka no kuroneko* (1968) (*Black Cat from the Grove*), a young woman and her mother-in-law are raped and killed by marauding samurai. They return as ghosts bent on seducing and killing the hateful warriors. Beautiful, poetic, but quite gory as well, this is a horror film with an intelligent subtext and a strong moral core. It condemns both the samurai and their contemptible rulers, while showing revenge to be spiritually dubious. Strong eroticism permeates Shindô's later films, too: *Hokusai manga* (1981) (*Edo Porn*) is a layered biopic of artist and printmaker Katsushika Hokusai, and *Bokuto kidan* (1992) (*The Strange Tale of Oyuki*) is an erotic drama about a man who searches for his feminine ideal among prostitutes. In all his films, Shindô observes, understands, and sympathizes with his characters, while delineating the forces that enthrall them. **DO**

Top Takes...

Fukuro 2003 (*Owl*)
Ikitai 1999 (*Will to Live*)
Gogo no Yuigon-jo 1995 (*A Last Note*)
Bokuto kidan 1992 (*The Strange Tale of Oyuki*)
Sakura-tai Chiru 1988
Raku-yo-ju 1986 (*Tree Without Leaves*)
Chihei-sen 1984 (*The Horizon*)
Hokusai manga 1981 (*Edo Porn*)
Kôsatsu 1979 (*The Strangling*)
Chikuzan hitori tabi 1977 (*The Life of Chikuzan*)
Sanka 1972
Yabu no naka no kuroneko 1968
   (*Black Cat from the Grove*)
Onibaba 1964 (*Devil Woman*)
Hadaka no shima 1960 (*The Island*)
Gembaku no ko 1952 (*Children of Hiroshima*)

1910s

"Spare, searing . . . . An extraordinary picture."
—Glenn Kenny, on *Onibaba*

RICHARD BROOKS

Born: Ruben Sax, May 18, 1912 (Philadelphia, Pennsylvania, U.S.); died 1992 (Los Angeles, California, U.S.).

Directing style: Maker of edgy films with moral themes; often tackled literary adaptations; penchant for creating male camaraderie onscreen.

Top Takes…

Fever Pitch 1985
Looking for Mr. Goodbar 1977
Bite the Bullet 1975
$ 1971
The Happy Ending 1969
In Cold Blood 1967 ☆
The Professionals 1966 ☆
Lord Jim 1965
Sweet Bird of Youth 1962
Elmer Gantry 1960
Cat on a Hot Tin Roof 1958 ☆
The Brothers Karamazov 1958
The Last Hunt 1956
Blackboard Jungle 1955
The Last Time I Saw Paris 1954
Take the High Ground! 1953

"Love is the morning and the evening star."

—Elmer Gantry, *Elmer Gantry*

Richard Brooks sustained a varied career. A screenwriter turned director, he won his only Academy Award for writing the screenplay for *Elmer Gantry* (1960), but was nominated several times as both a director and a writer.

He turned his own experience as a U.S. marine during World War II to good use in a series of well-paced action films whose trademark is a sensitive feel for male camaraderie: the war films *Battle Circus* (1953) and *Take the High Ground!* (1953), and the revisionist Western *The Last Hunt* (1956) are all great examples of the action genre. *The Professionals* (1966), a Western caper film, improves on its model, John Sturges's *The Magnificent Seven* (1960), and manifests Brooks's considerable skill in handling different male types in the forms of Lee Marvin, Burt Lancaster, Jack Palance, and Robert Ryan.

Brooks did less well with straighter dramatic fare, including his directorial debut *Crisis* (1950), based on his own script; *The Last Time I Saw Paris* (1954), a Fitzgeraldesque treatment of a Lost Generation marital crisis, lacks the emotional intensity that would make its melodrama come alive. Brooks had his best success with two Tennessee Williams adaptations, *Cat on a Hot Tin Roof* (1958) and *Sweet Bird of Youth* (1962), perhaps because they highlighted the kind of male life crisis he could understand. The more ambitious *Lord Jim* (1965) offered Peter O'Toole a chance to reprise the enigmatic moralism of his famed impersonation of T. E. Lawrence, and Brooks gave this interior drama a proper epic setting.

In Cold Blood (1967) is a brutal true-life crime drama, based on the novel by Truman Capote, while *Looking for Mr. Goodbar* (1977) makes memorable use of difficult, but riveting, material for a modern audience. **BP**

DORIS WISHMAN

Born: Doris Wishman, June 1, 1912 (New York City, New York, U.S.); died 2002 (Miami, Florida, U.S.).

Directing style: Trailblazing female maker of cult sexploitation movies; early nudist films; protofeminist themes.

Doris Wishman was a brave pioneer of territory that was strictly the male domain: sexploitation. Her prolific output testifies to the fact that she followed the rules of vulgar commercialism, but with a difference in terms of directorial sensibility, and the use of idiosyncratic stylistic devices, ranging from innovative shot-counter shot dialogue composition where those who speak are usually out of frame, to obsessional and fetishistic inserts of actors' feet without narrative justification.

In *Diary of a Nudist* (1961), Wishman lasciviously presents the naked truth about one emerging movement for a healthy and natural life, but in *Bad Girls Go to Hell* (1965) she turns her attention to the darker side of modern life: violence against women. However, at the peak of Wishman's work are two films, *Deadly Weapons* (1974) and *Double Agent 73* (1974), made with her muse, Polish-born Chesty Morgan. In the director's mise-en-scène, Morgan was objectified and unable to produce even a basic human emotion. What remained was an unpleasant image of the female body, a body reduced only to itself, an empty mechanical portrayal of nudity.

Perhaps *Deadly Weapons* and *Double Agent 73* were conceived as spectacles of carnal sensuality: in fact, they represent a kind of erotic *reductio ad absurdum*, not because of their overblown voluptuous iconography, but because of the apathy of everything else. Was the result a poignant, maybe even feminist inspired, subversion of standard erotic codes and male fascination with big breasts, or just painfully obvious technical and stylistic incompetence on behalf of the director and her star? These are the wonders and dilemmas of genuine exploitation cinema: Wishman is wish fulfillment for every fan of trash extravaganzas. **AB**

Top Takes...

Dildo Heaven 2002
Each Time I Kill 2002
Satan Was a Lady 2001
A Night to Dismember 1983
Let Me Die a Woman 1978
The Immoral Three 1975
Deadly Weapons 1974
Double Agent 73 1974
Keyholes Are for Peeping 1972
My Brother's Wife 1966
Bad Girls Go to Hell 1965
Behind the Nudist Curtain 1964
Playgirls International 1963
Blaze Starr Goes Back to Nature 1962
Gentlemen Prefer Nature Girls 1962
Diary of a Nudist 1961

1910s

"Her trump card was that impudent, dirty-minded little girl imagination. . . ."—Beau Gillespie

SAMUEL FULLER

Born: Samuel Michael Fuller, August 12, 1912 (Worcester, Massachusetts, U.S.); died 1997 (Hollywood, California, U.S.).

Directing style: Cult director of low-budget films tackling controversial themes like racism; energetic visual storytelling; provocative and unusual characterizations.

Top Takes...

Samuel Fuller was long a victim of the politically correct, his anticommunism seen as a sign of right-wing extremism. That he was a politically incorrect director is obvious. Who but Fuller would launch a career by making a movie *I Shot Jesse James* (1949) where the hero is the man who shot the outlaw?

Westerns, war films, thrillers, and dramas make up the battleground that, for Fuller, was cinema. He was constantly waging his own war for or against certain values, but a close look shows that the definition of those values is not simple. *Pickup on South Street* (1953) is an anticommunist movie, but Fuller's rejection of FBI style patriotism comes from his sympathy for the underdog. The fact that the FBI agents tailing a suspect in the subway could feasibly be gangsters, and that the gangsters of *Underworld U.S.A.* (1961) are impeccably dressed businessmen, puts things in perspective: Fuller was closer to the Hollywood left than to the Republican right.

Racism was a favorite target, and Fuller often took an unusual stance. In *Run of the Arrow* (1957), it is a Northern soldier who dies to save an Indian boy from quicksand, and the Confederate soldier who goes to live with the Indians is a deluded reactionary. In *The Crimson Kimono* (1959), U.S. prejudices concerning Japanese-Americans lead to hostility. *China Gate*, however, (1957) is the most revealing of his films. What is an audience to make of the fact that the U.S. soldier rejects the half-breed child of the Angie Dickinson character, whereas the communist North Vietnamese officer is happy to accept both mother and child? Fuller enjoyed bullying audiences into admitting that the values looked upon as "American" were in reality "un-American" in their smugness and intolerance. **ReH**

> "I hate violence. That has never prevented me from using it in my films."

ALEXANDER MACKENDRICK

Born: Alexander Mackendrick, September 8, 1912 (Boston, Massachusetts, U.S.); died 1993 (Los Angeles, California, U.S.).

Directing style: Key director of madcap Ealing comedies; charming social satires with a dark edge; incisive double-edged humor; master of visual storytelling.

The most consistently talented of the Ealing Studios mavericks, Alexander Mackendrick slipped his skeptical world view and mordant Scottish humor into the snug world of Ealing Studios comedy like a razor blade into a tea cake.

In his debut movie *Whisky Galore!* (1949), the sole honest man on a Hebridean island is gulled and destroyed by the ruthlessly pragmatic locals. Similarly, an idealistic young scientist in *The Man in the White Suit* (1951) finds himself hunted down by a lynch mob of bosses and workers, their differences forgotten in the pursuit of violence. In another Scottish comedy, *The Maggie* (1954), a U.S. businessman is exploited and assaulted by the crew of an old boat he is misled into hiring. A gang of criminals in *The Ladykillers* (1955) are driven to murder each other in the face of unbending Victorian morality embodied by one little old lady.

Mackendrick's only drama at Ealing Studios was *Mandy* (1952), where the plight of a child born deaf, handled with a refreshing lack of sentimentality, is used to explore a society paralyzed by convention and preconceived ideas. But all his Ealing Studios films can be read as subversive comments on the condition of Britain: born in the United States and raised in Scotland, Mackendrick always retained the cool, watchful eye of the instinctive outsider. Alone of the Ealing Studios directors Mackendrick produced a post-Ealing masterpiece (his first Hollywood film): *Sweet Smell of Success* (1957), a gleamingly rancid study of Manhattan journalism that captures, like no other filmmaker before Martin Scorsese, New York City's pungent mix of visual and emotional aggression. He quit directing in 1969 to become an outstanding teacher of film at the California Institute of the Arts. **PK**

Top Takes...

Don't Make Waves 1967
A High Wind in Jamaica 1965
Sammy Going South 1963
Sweet Smell of Success 1957
The Ladykillers 1955
The Maggie 1954
Mandy 1952
The Man in the White Suit 1951
Whisky Galore! 1949

1910s

"There's a moment toward the end of certain kinds of comedy when they ought to get nasty."

CHUCK JONES

Born: Charles Martin Jones, September 21, 1912 (Spokane, Washington, U.S.); died 2002 (Corona Del Mar, California, U.S.).

Directing style: Prolific and innovative master of animation; blend of classical music and cartoon; ingenious visual gags; parody and pastiche; credible characters.

Top Takes…

Another Froggy Evening 1995
Chariots of Fur 1994
The Phantom Tollbooth 1970
Cannery Rodent 1967
Of Feline Bondage 1965
Adventures of the Road-Runner 1962
Ready, Woolen and Able 1960
What's Opera, Doc? 1957
One Froggy Evening 1955
Duck Amuck 1953
Little Beau Pepé 1952
Rabbit of Seville 1950
Rabbit Hood 1949
Hair-Raising Hare 1946
Elmer's Candid Camera 1940
Daffy Duck and the Dinosaur 1939

Bugs Bunny, Chuck Jones noted, is who everyone would like to be, and Daffy Duck is who everyone mostly is. The cool, confident rabbit, and the cowardly, "dethpicable" duck define the parameters of Jones's animated universe. Although he cannot be credited with having created either character, he molded both of them, and their hapless hunter Elmer Fudd, into their quintessential form and nature. Whereas Bugs Bunny and Daffy Duck were born out of the collaborative creative ferment of the Warner Brothers animation studios of the 1940s, Jones stands as sole begetter of that other symbiotic animated pair, Wile E. Coyote and the Road Runner. Also of Pepé Le Pew, the French-accented skunk, who was never discouraged despite countless amorous rebuffs.

In Jones's hands, these characters take on a life of their own. Bugs Bunny, Daffy Duck, and his other animated stars invariably act in character, and were never distorted to fit the gag. Wile E. Coyote and Road Runner perform infinite, ingenious variations of the same joke, heightened by the fact that the audience's sympathy lies with the ever-frustrated Wile E. Coyote.

Jones's range of cultural reference was wide and enriched his work, in horror movies such as *Hare-Raising Hare* (1946); to swashbucklers like *Rabbit Hood* (1949); to the use of classical music such as Gioachino Antonio Rossini in *Rabbit of Seville* (1950). In *Duck Amuck* (1953) he deconstructs the whole animation process, subjecting the luckless Daffy Duck to existential angst at the hands of the animator who is revealed to be Bugs Bunny himself. Sadness often shades the laughter: *One Froggy Evening* (1955) must be one of the most poignant cartoons ever made. As Jones liked to point out, "Animation isn't the illusion of life; it is life." **PK**

"If you start with character, you probably will end up with good drawings."

MICHELANGELO ANTONIONI

Born: Michelangelo Antonioni, September 29, 1912 (Ferrara, Emilia-Romagna, Italy).

Directing style: Influential Italian director; dreamy, painterly visuals; examinations of Italian bourgeois society, sexual desire, greed, reality, and illusion; long takes; collaborations with actress Monica Vitti.

After more than a dozen features made between the early 1940s and the late 1950s, Michelangelo Antonioni's international reputation was established with *L'Avventura* (1960) (*The Adventure*), the first of three films engaging consciousness, alienation, modernity, and middle-class privilege in Italian society. Antonioni studied at the University of Bologna and the Centro Sperimentale di Cinematografia, Rome, and worked with Roberto Rossellini. In all of his films, but emphatically after 1960, the Antonionian camera operates to structure the narrative with special precision, and exquisite compositional taste.

La Notte (1961) (*The Night*) and *L'Eclisse* (1962) (*Eclipse*) are both paeans to isolation, emptiness, existential repose, hopelessness, and the sociological developments of modernity. The first begins with a stunning credit shot in which the camera appears to descend outside a glassed apartment building but not to approach the ground. The film shows a couple settled silently and routinely into a marriage prison, ending with an extraordinary and very lengthy soiree sequence at a bourgeois

Top Takes...

Eros 2004

Lo Sguardo di Michelangelo 2004 (*Michelangelo Eye to Eye*)

Al di là delle nuvole 1995 (*Beyond the Clouds*)

Noto, Mandorli, Vulcano, Stromboli, Carnevale 1993

12 registi per 12 città 1989

Kumbha Mela 1989

Identificazione di una donna 1982 (*Identification of a Woman*)

Il Mistero di Oberwald 1981 (*The Mystery of Oberwald*)

Professione: reporter 1975 (*The Passenger*)

Chung Kuo–Cina 1972 (*China*)

Zabriskie Point 1970

Blowup 1966

Il Deserto rosso 1964 (*The Red Desert*)

L'Eclisse 1962 (*Eclipse*)

La Notte 1961 (*The Night*)

L'Avventura 1960 (*The Adventure*)

Il Grido 1957 (*The Cry*)

Le Amiche 1955 (*The Girlfriends*)

L'Amore in città 1953 (*Love in the City*)

I Vinti 1953 (*The Vanquished*)

LEFT: Lea Massari and Monica Vitti search for their missing friend in *The Adventure*.

Blowup

As well as being critically acclaimed, *Blowup* was Michelangelo Antonioni's biggest commercial success. It was also his first English-language movie. David Hemmings plays the photographer in swinging sixties London caught up in a murder case, and the movie also features Vanessa Redgrave, Sarah Miles, and Jane Birkin. The film received Academy Award nominations for Best Director and Best Screenplay, and Antonioni won the Palme d'Or at the Cannes Film Festival. More than 30 years after its release, Antonioni's ambiguous masterpiece continues to enthrall the world.

- The film was based on a short story, "Las Babas del Diablo," by the Argentinian writer Julio Cortázar.

- Controversial for its sexually explicit scenes and full frontal female nudity, the film's release was initially blocked under the MPAA Production Code. MGM got around it by creating a subsidiary company, unaffiliated to the Code, to release the film. The Code subsequently collapsed.

- David Hemmings's character is said to be loosely based on real-life fashion photographers David Bailey and Terence Donovan.

- It influenced Brian De Palma's *Blow Out* (1981) in which John Travolta plays a soundman who inadvertently records a conspiracy.

palace. In this scene, the man, played by Marcello Mastroianni, wanders off from his wife, played by Jeanne Moreau, is picked up by a bored girl, played by Monica Vitti, but finally finds his wife again as they amble through an empty golf course at dawn. *Eclipse* centers on the impossible relationship between a young woman, played by Vitti, and a stockbroker lothario, played by Alain Delon, and contains a lengthy silent sequence in which the camera travels across the empty city.

Antonioni's first color film, *Il Deserto rosso* (1964) (*The Red Desert*) is set in Ravenna, against a background of pollution and social decay. Hiding a mental illness from her husband, Giuliana, played by Vitti, befriends and sexually dallies with a foreign industrialist, played by Richard Harris, but is constrained by the needs of her paralyzed child. The color compositions—the rust of the quarantine ship against the morning mist and the billowing yellow smoke against the blue sky—often recall the composition of Piet Mondrian and the palette of Mark Rothko.

Trio of seminal works

Working on a three-picture deal with producer Carlo Ponti in English-language movies, Antonioni made a group of groundbreaking films that have continued to amaze audiences and influence filmmakers around the world. *Blowup* (1966), shot in London, follows a hip and narcissistic photographer, played by David Hemmings, as he produces pictures of a woman with her lover in the park; only later to realize that the man was being set up for an assassination. Playing with the ambiguity of perception, the meaning of imagery, the tenuousness of relationships, and the nature of objective reality, Antonioni weaves his tale with arch commentary on the fashion world, music by the Yardbirds and Herbie Hancock, a display of almost magical color, and cool, modern behavior. Less well-received, the Los Angeles-set *Zabriskie Point* (1970) features two young people protesting against adulthood, U.S. warmongering, capitalism, and reality. *Professione: reporter* (1975) (*The Passenger*) stars Jack Nicholson as a bored and depressed reporter who assumes the identity of a dead British

arms merchant. The movie's finale sequence is one of the justly celebrated technical achievements in cinema, an 11-minute continuous shot in which a camera performs a 360-degree circuit out of a hotel room, into the surrounding courtyard and back again, only to discover that a man who was dozing at the start of the shot has now been murdered.

ABOVE: David Hemmings on a photo shoot with the model Veruschka in *Blowup*.

Il Mistero di Oberwald (1981) (*The Mystery of the Oberwald*) and *Identificazione di una donna* (1982) (*Identification of a Woman*) continue Antonioni's fascinations with the allure of women, the alienation of wealth, and the desiccation of modern experience. A stroke in 1985 rendered him speechless but did not end his career. Nor did it really affect the quality of his filmmaking, since his dialogue was always notable for its sparseness, and his direction has been charged by the demands of the eye. **MP**

> "Actors are like cows. You have to lead them through a fence."

DON SIEGEL

Born: Donald Siegel, October 26, 1912 (Chicago, Illinois, U.S.); died 1991 (Nipoma, California, U.S.).

Directing style: Inspiring director across a range of genres; skilled use of montage; collaborator and mentor of actor and director Clint Eastwood.

Top Takes...

Born in Chicago, Don Siegel went to Hollywood in the mid-1930s. He started out as a film librarian at Warner Brothers, and advanced through the editing department. He gained invaluable experience in the montage department, where he learned how to create dynamic action sequences, and was noted for his skill. His feature debut came with the thriller *The Verdict* (1946), after which Siegel worked in several genres. *Riot in Cell Block 11* (1954) is a taut prison movie; *Invasion of the Body Snatchers* (1956) is an innovative science-fiction film; and *Baby Face Nelson* (1957) a film noir set in 1930s Chicago.

Having served his time doing B-movies, Siegel started to move on up to the A-list, and the turn of the decade saw him direct singer Elvis Presley in the Western *Flaming Star* (1960), which is generally considered the star's best movie. Steve McQueen starred in Siegel's next picture, a tense war drama entitled *Hell Is for Heroes* (1962). Siegel returned to the crime genre in *The Killers* (1964); with Ronald Reagan playing a memorable villain and Lee Marvin as a heartless hit man, Siegel created an atmosphere of fear and paranoia.

Siegel's most important professional partnership began with *Coogan's Bluff* (1968), which starred Clint Eastwood as a sheriff from Arizona who goes to New York to collect a prisoner. Further collaborations with Eastwood soon followed: a Western, *Two Mules for Sister Sara* (1970), and a U.S. Civil War drama, *The Beguiled* (1971). The duo followed this up with *Dirty Harry* (1971) in which Eastwood played a rogue detective. The movie was a huge success and has become a classic. Siegel's last picture with Eastwood was *Escape from Alcatraz* (1979). Siegel died in 1991, and Eastwood dedicated his Western *Unforgiven* (1992) to him. **EB**

> "If you shake a movie, ten minutes will fall out."
> —On editing

GORDON PARKS

Born: Gordon Alexander Parks, November 30, 1912 (Fort Scott, Kansas, U.S.); died 2006 (New York City, New York, U.S.).

Directing style: Trailblazing African-American director of documentaries and hip blaxploitation movies; challenger of bigotry, racism, and discrimination.

Even as the U.S. civil rights movement opened up opportunities and possibilities for millions of citizens long denied the freedoms enjoyed by the majority, the motion-picture industry remained disappointingly slow to open its doors to filmmakers of color. In some sense those very restrictions set the stage for someone such as Gordon Parks to independently devise his own alternatives to Hollywood's strict rule book.

Born to a large family in Kansas, Parks left home after his mother's death and moved to Minnesota, where he found work as a piano player and as a waiter. Inspired by a series of photographs of migrant workers, Parks bought a cheap camera and entered the photographic trade himself, moving to Chicago and taking vivid portraits of the blue-collar workers and families (as well as, after relocating to New York, the occasional fashion spread) in a country still very divided by race and class. A 1948 photo essay on a Harlem gang leader earned him a job as a photo-journalist for *Life* magazine.

Parks wrote the autobiographical *The Learning Tree* (1969), about life as an African-American man growing up in Kansas. The next year he adapted it for the screen, directed it, and even scored it. His next cinematic bow would hardly be so sentimental. *Shaft* (1971) closely followed director Melvin Van Peebles's *Sweet Sweetback's Baadasssss Song* (1971) as one of the first major Hollywood films helmed by an African-American director, its hard-boiled, streetwise detective story an iconic product of the so-called "blaxploitation" movement. Alas, Parks ended up painting himself into a corner with that genre, and later attempts to capitalize on the success of *Shaft* met with little success. He thereafter devoted his energies to writing, composing, and photography. **JK**

Top Takes...

Leadbelly 1976

The Super Cops 1974

Shaft's Big Score! 1972

Shaft 1971

The Learning Tree 1969

The World of Piri Thomas 1968

Flavio 1964

1910s

"The subject matter is so much more important than the photographer."

FRANK TASHLIN

Born: Francis Frederick von Taschlein, February 19, 1913 (Weehawken, New Jersey, U.S.); died 1972 (Hollywood, California, U.S.).

Directing style: Innovative animator; introduced cinematic techniques to cartoons, such as fast-paced editing and montage; cartoonlike live action films.

Top Takes...

Frank Tashlin started out drawing comic strips for his high-school newspaper. He then worked as a gag writer for comic Charley Chase at the Hal Roach Studio in the mid-1930s, before writing and directing cartoons for Leon Schlesinger's famous Warner Brothers cartoon unit. There he worked creating Porky Pig and Daffy Duck on fun-filled, anarchic seven-minute epics such as *The Case of the Stuttering Pig* (1937) and *Plane Daffy* (1944). He also directed propagandist Private Snafu black and white cartoon shorts during World War II. The Private Snafu character was created by director Frank Capra, chairman of the U.S. Army Air Force First Motion Picture Unit.

Tashlin moved into live action by taking over uncredited from Sidney Lanfield on the Bob Hope vehicle *The Lemon Drop Kid* (1951), before making his official debut with the comedy, *The First Time* (1952). He soon established himself as a major comedy director, bringing his animator's view of the world to bear on his live-action movies, giving them a fast pace and many visual gags. He went on to work with Hope on *Son of Paleface* (1952), and comedian Jerry Lewis on films such as *Rock-a-Bye Baby* (1958). His masterpiece was *The Girl Can't Help It* (1956), in which hustler Tom Ewell has to launch zaftig no-talent Jayne Mansfield as a star to please her gangster boyfriend Edmond O'Brien. In screen-filling Cinemascope, with cartoon gags, and a dozen or so rock 'n' roll greats, *The Girl Can't Help It* was followed by the similar, excellent Mansfield vehicle *Will Success Spoil Rock Hunter?* (1957). Tashlin's 1960s films, such as the Hercule Poirot mystery *The Alphabet Murders* (1965) and the Doris Day spy romp *Caprice* (1967), are mostly likable, but fail to reach the heights of his earlier work. **KN**

> "I got into a fight with Walt Disney: I always pick the wrong people to fight with."

JIRÍ WEISS

Born: Jirí Weiss, March 29, 1913 (Prague, Czech Republic); died 2004 (Santa Monica, California, U.S.).

Directing style: Major Czech filmmaker who often explored themes regarding the Nazi occupation of his country; use of overhead camera angles.

The grim experience of Czechoslovakia under the Nazi jackboot provided the raw material for the movies of Jirí Weiss. *The Rape of Czechoslovakia* (1939) and *Before the Raid* (1943) powerfully documented his country's suffering under occupation. His subsequent fictional works also dealt with World War II's darker days, particularly the dramas *Zbabelec* (1961) (*The Coward*), and his last film, *Martha et moi* (1991) (*Martha and I*).

The Jewish Weiss first studied law, and then worked as a journalist. He began making documentaries, and his directorial debut *Lidé na slunci* (1935) (*People In the Sun*) won an award at the Venice Film Festival. When the Nazis invaded in 1938, Weiss fled Prague. He headed first for Paris, and then to London, where he began working on his war-themed factual accounts. *Before The Raid* told the story of a Norwegian fishing village occupied by the Nazis. After the war, Weiss returned to Czechoslovakia and, despite the repression of Stalinist rule following the 1948 coup d'etat, was able to work in the difficult era of political uncertainty up to 1968's Prague Spring. Weiss's output included the acclaimed *Vlcí jáma* (1957) (*The Wolf Trap*), his first fiction feature and a gritty study of middle-class frustration. Returning to the themes of his war work, *Romeo, Julia a tma* (1960) (*Romeo, Juliet, and Darkness*) and *The Coward* both dealt with life under the shadow of a fascist regime.

With the arrival of the Czech New Wave and filmmakers like Milos Forman, Weiss began to satirize contemporary life. However, the black comedy *Vrazda po cesku* (1967) (*Murder Czech Style*) was his last picture for 24 years. Fleeing the Soviet invasion, Weiss settled in the United States in 1968 and taught film. In 1989 he made his comeback with *Martha and I*, again dealing with the Czech occupation. **TE**

Top Takes...

Martha et moi 1991 (*Martha and I*)
Vrazda po cesku 1967 (*Murder Czech Style*)
Ninety Degrees in the Shade 1965
Zbabelec 1961 (*The Coward*)
Romeo, Julia a tma 1960
  (*Romeo, Juliet, and Darkness*)
Takova laska 1959 (*That Kind of Love*)
Vlcí jáma 1957 (*The Wolf Trap*)
Hra o zivot 1956 (*A Life at Stake*)
Muj prítel Fabián 1955 (*My Friend the Gypsy*)
Radostné dny 1951 (*Days of Joy*)
Poslední výstrel 1950 (*The Last Shot*)
Night and Day 1945
Before the Raid 1943
Eternal Prague 1940
The Rape of Czechoslovakia 1939

"Before the Raid is an absorbing and dramatically effective film." —*New York Times*

1910s

BOB CLAMPETT

Born: Robert Emerson Clampett, May 8, 1913 (San Diego, California, U.S.); died 1984 (Detroit, Michigan, U.S.).

Directing style: Innovative animator and puppeteer; creator of Tweety Bird character; hilarious, irreverent, outrageous, and bizarre cartoons.

Top Takes...

Warner Brothers's vast stable of Looney Tunes characters and creators did justice to the cartoon series' colorful name, but among them director Bob Clampett stood out for his particularly oddball and, inspired by Salvador Dalí, often very surreal brand of lunacy, which pushed his shorts into parts unknown and unexpected.

Clampett worked briefly for Walt Disney designing toys, including Mickey Mouse dolls, before moving on to the animation department of Hugh Harman and Rudolf Ising at Warner Brothers in 1931, where he worked on the Looney Tunes and Merrie Melodies series. After creative partnerships with directors Friz Freleng and Tex Avery in the studio's famous "Termite Terrace," Clampett himself switched to directing in 1937, quickly using the platform to shape some of the most classic and memorable Looney Tunes moments. Among them were *Porky in Wackyland* (1938), with its bizarre scenario of Porky Pig in search of the Do-Do Bird in Africa, its abstract surreal landscape and bendy characters that defy the laws of physics; and *A Tale of Two Kitties* (1942), which introduced the deceptively malicious character of Tweety Bird, whom Clampett reportedly based on pictures of himself as a baby.

Clampett directed several politically-themed shorts such as the Adolf Hitler-baiting *Russian Rhapsody* (1944) setting Russian gremlins against the Nazi leader, and *Draftee Daffy* (1945) featuring Daffy Duck attempting to shirk his wartime duties. After *The Big Snooze* (1946), for which he did not receive credit, Clampett left Warner Brothers for TV, where he made the puppet-show series *Time for Beany* (1949). His name is still remembered alongside other Looney Tunes legends such as Freleng, Avery, and Chuck Jones. **JK**

> "A masterpiece of preposterous fantasy."
>
> —*L.A. Herald*, on *Porky in Wackyland*

GERARDO DE LEÓN

Born: Manong de León, September 12, 1913 (Manila, Philippines); died 1981 (Manila, Philippines).

Directing style: Lauded Filipino director of energetic low-budget horror and schlock movies; often violent and grotesque content; literary adaptations.

Filipino director Gerardo de León got into the movies as an actor making his debut in *Ang Dangal* (1934). He moved behind the camera in the late 1930s and directed dozens of movies in almost every genre over the next 30 years. Among them are the musical *Bahay-Kubo* (1939); adaptations of Filipino anticolonialist writer Jose Rizal's novels *Noli me tangere* (1961) (*Touch Me Not*) and *El Filibusterismo* (1962); political potboiler *Moises Padilla Story* (1961); and some anti-U.S. propaganda films produced for the occupying Japanese forces during World War II.

Yet widespread international acclaim never materialized, because of a frustrating lack of available material from his most productive period as a director. However, a series of low-budget, independently produced, and mostly U.S.-funded films he directed in the 1950s and 1960s remain abundantly available, and for all their reliance on schlock they provide a rewarding glimpse into his talent. Among the best are the war movie *Intramuros* (1964) (*The Walls of Hell*), and *Kulay dugo ang gabi* (1966) (*The Blood Drinkers*), a vampire film that reveals de León's trademark lack of narrative and use of deep-focus setups. *Terror Is a Man* (1959), his over-the-top take on H. G. Wells's *The Island of Dr. Moreau* (1896), and its increasingly formulaic follow-ups, *Mad Doctor of Blood Island* (1968) and *Brides of Blood* (1968), are beautiful to look at if somewhat trashy B-movie fare. He returned to making Filipino productions in the early 1970s, but his next few films were not released internationally. De León switched between making award-winning movies at some points in his career, to creating disposable offerings at others, yet even in the latter his talent is evident. **MH**

Top Takes...

Women in Cages 1971
Lilet 1971
Brides of Blood 1968
Mad Doctor of Blood Island 1968
Kulay dugo ang gabi 1966 (*The Blood Drinkers*)
Daigdig ng mga api, Ang 1965
Intramuros 1964 (*The Walls of Hell*)
Ako ang katarungan 1962 (*I Am Justice*)
El Filibusterismo 1962
Moises Padilla Story 1961
Noli me tangere 1961 (*Touch Me Not*)
Huwag mo akong limutin 1960
Terror Is a Man 1959
Ifugao 1954
Pedro Penduko 1954

1910s

"He creates dynamic tension at the very source of each action."
—Charles Tesson

STANLEY KRAMER

Born: Stanley Earl Kramer, September 29, 1913 (New York City, New York, U.S.); died 2001 (Los Angeles, California, U.S.).

Directing style: Independent producer/director who bucked the tide of the studio system to produce films he believed in; sentimental liberal of the U.S. screen.

Top Takes...

The Runner Stumbles 1979
The Domino Principle 1977
Oklahoma Crude 1973
Bless the Beasts & Children 1971
R.P.M. 1970
The Secret of Santa Vittoria 1969
Guess Who's Coming to Dinner 1967 ☆
Ship of Fools 1965
It's a Mad Mad Mad Mad World 1963
Judgment at Nuremberg 1961 ☆
Inherit the Wind 1960
On the Beach 1959
The Defiant Ones 1958 ☆
The Pride and the Passion 1957
Not as a Stranger 1955

"I'm always pursuing the next dream, hunting for the next truth."

Producer and director Stanley Kramer specialized in message pictures that often failed to live up to their initial promise. He began his cinema career in the 1930s, working in a variety of capacities, including editor, writer, and researcher, before achieving the status of associate producer by the 1940s. After military service in World War II, Kramer began his own company, Screen Plays, before joining Columbia Pictures in 1951 to gain greater distribution and economic backing for his projects. As a director, he was probably better off as a producer, as seen by such classics as Fred Zinnemann's politically-conscious Western *High Noon* (1952), and László Benedek's motorcycle drama *The Wild One* (1953), which propelled the young Marlon Brando to overnight stardom. But when directing his own movies, Kramer too often fell into the trap of transparent moralizing.

And yet in his finest films, such as the racial drama *The Defiant Ones* (1958), in which two escaped convicts, played by Tony Curtis and Sidney Poitier, run for their lives in the segregated U.S. South, or *It's A Mad Mad Mad Mad World* (1963), surely the most spectacular and vicious comedy ever filmed, Kramer displays a deft hand at unmasking the greed and prejudice underlying U.S. society. His most famous movie is probably *Judgment at Nuremberg* (1961), and features a memorable and shattering performance by Montgomery Clift as a survivor of Nazi brutality. Kramer's movies all share a desire for engagement with the major political and social issues of their era, and although with his later movies he seemed more out of touch with what those issues were, he was a genuine original: he made movies that he believed in, and straddled the fence between art and commerce for more than 30 years in the industry. **WWD**

MARGUERITE DURAS

Born: Marguerite Donnadieu, April 4, 1914 (Gia Dinh, Vietnam); died 1996 (Paris, France).

Directing style: Experimental feminist French filmmaker and writer; use of voice-over and autobiographical material; themes of love, death, and memory.

French novelist and director Marguerite Duras is best known as the Oscar-nominated screenwriter of the disturbing drama *Hiroshima mon amour* (1959) (*Hiroshima, My Love*). Directed by Alan Resnais, the film recounted the experience of a young woman in occupied France, and her brief affair with a Japanese architect, who survives the atomic bombing of the city.

Born in what was then colonial French Indochina in 1914, Duras lost both parents young and went to Paris to study law. While working as an archivist in the French Colonial Office, World War II broke out, and she joined a Resistance group led by future French President François Mitterand (he memorably rescued Duras's husband from Dachau). After the war, she dedicated herself to writing novels, particularly in the minimalist style of the *nouveau roman* literary movement. By the late 1950s, her canon expanded to include plays and film scripts, including *Hiroshima, My Love*, and by the 1970s she devoted herself almost exclusively to cinema.

Experimental in form, Duras's movies featured characters that might have also appeared in her plays or novels and also utilized a voice-over that alluded to rather than told a story. Notable works included the fantasy drama *India Song* (1975) and the skewed romance *Le Camion* (1977) (*The Truck*), in which Duras starred alongside Gérard Depardieu. She published her critically-acclaimed, loosely autobiographical novel *L'Amant* (*The Lover*) in 1984, which told the story of a French girl living in Vietnam who has an affair with a rich Chinese man; the novel was adapted for cinema in 1992. In 1984, Duras wrote and codirected her final film, the comedy *Les Enfants* (1984) (*The Children*). Her writing later provided raw material for several more movies. **TE**

Top Takes...

Les Enfants 1984 (*The Children*)
Il Dialogo di Roma 1982
L'homme atlantique 1981
Agatha et les lectures illimitées 1981
Le Navire Night 1979
Aurelia Steiner (Melbourne) 1979
Aurélia Steiner (Vancouver) 1979
Cesarée 1978
Les mains négatives 1978
Baxter, Vera Baxter 1977
Le Camion 1977 (*The Truck*)
Son nom de Venise dans Calcutta désert 1976
Des journées entières dans les arbres 1976
  (*Entire Days in the Trees*)
India Song 1975
Nathalie Granger 1972

1910s

"Men like women who write. Even though they don't say so. A writer is a foreign country."

MARIO BAVA

Born: Mario Bava, July 31, 1914 (San Remo, Liguria, Italy); died 1980 (Rome, Italy).

Directing style: Influential Italian maestro of horror, slasher, science fiction, comic-book adaptations, and murder mystery movies; genius of special effects; painterly use of vivid color.

Top Takes...

RIGHT: Wide-eyed actress Barbara Steele becomes a horror star in *Black Sunday*.

The son of silent film cinematographer and special-effects artist Eugenio Bava, Mario Bava studied painting and retained an artist's sensibility when he followed his father into film. Bava worked steadily as a cinematographer for some 20 years from the late 1930s shooting for such luminaries as Roberto Rossellini and Raoul Walsh. Bava shared his father's love for optical-effects work, and devised ingenious strategies to give inexpensive films a high-gloss look that belied their budgets.

He began his transition to feature directing by completing two troubled productions, *I vampiri* (1956) (*Lust of the Vampire*) and *Caltiki—il mostro immortale* (1959) (*Caltiki, the Immortal Monster*), for director Riccardo Freda and a third, *La Battaglia di Maratona* (1959) (*Giant of Marathon*), for Jacques Tourneur. When given the opportunity to make his own film, Bava delivered a moody symphony in light and shadow called *La maschera del demonio* (1960) (*Black Sunday*), which transformed unknown English starlet Barbara Steele into a cult icon.

Lust of the Vampire is widely credited with kicking off the golden age of Italian Gothic horror films and Bava defined the *giallo*—Italy's particular twist on the mystery genre, dominated

by elaborate, show-stopping murder sequences and an overwhelming air of perversity—with *La ragazza che sapeva troppo* (1963) (*The Evil Eye*) and *Sei donne per l'assassino* (1964) (*Blood and Black Lace*). His production *Reazione a catena* (1971) (*A Bay of Blood*) was the template for *Friday the 13th* (1980) and all later slasher films. Equally at home with misty black and white and lurid color, Bava worked in a variety of genres. His diverse credits include the sexadelic comedy *Quante volte . . . quella notte* (1972) (*Four Times That Night*), a bizarre variation on the Japanese *Rashômon* (1950) (*In the Woods*), the super-stylish caper spoof *Diabolik* (1968) (*Danger: Diabolik*)—whose swinging 1960s décor and fantastic gadgetry are lovingly recreated in Roman Coppola's *CQ* (2001)—and the atmospheric science fiction outing *Terrore nello spazio* (1965) (*Planet of the Vampires*), to which *Alien* (1979) owes a deep and unacknowledged debt. **MM**

ABOVE: Vampire Boris Karloff holds a decapitated head in *Black Sabbath*.

The Bava Effect

- Bava's many admirers include Quentin Tarantino, Tim Burton, John Carpenter, Martin Scorsese and, of course, *giallo* director Dario Argento. Ozzy Osborne's rock group Black Sabbath was named after Bava's *I tre volti della paura* (1963) (*Black Sabbath*).

- His vision of the devil as an angelic little girl with a red ball in *Operazione paura* (1966) (*Kill, Baby . . . Kill!*) has been quoted in films as varied as Federico Fellini's "Toby Dammit" segment of the omnibus film *Histoires extraordinaires* (1968) (*Spirits of the Dead*) and William Malone's shabby *FeardotCom* (2002).

ROBERT WISE

Born: Robert Earl Wise, September 10, 1914 (Winchester, Indiana, U.S.); died 2005 (Los Angeles, California, U.S.).

Directing style: Versatility of genres including musicals; groundbreaking director of psycho horror; use of carefully composed images; tight editing; fast pace.

Top Takes...

RIGHT: Wise fought to shoot *West Side Story* on location in New York City's gritty streets.

Robert Wise began as a film editor, working with distinction on Orson Welles's *Citizen Kane* (1941) and *The Magnificent Ambersons* (1942), then reediting and partially reshooting the latter after Welles fell from favor at RKO Pictures. Somehow guilty by association, Wise was demoted to RKO Pictures' B-film unit, where he ironically found himself working for producer Val Lewton, then at work on his great cycle of subtle psychological horror films. Wise was hired to direct *The Curse of the Cat People* (1944), a sequel to Lewton's hit *Cat People* (1942), but despite its title it's a gentle fantasy rather than a horror film. Wise made two more movies for Lewton, including the masterpiece *The Body Snatcher* (1945) starring Boris Karloff.

Wise's career rapidly ascended out of B-movies. Over the next 60 years or so he produced a prolific body of work that embraced a remarkably diverse range of genres: noir (*Born to Kill*, 1947; *The Set-Up*, 1949); science fiction (*The Day the Earth Stood Still*, 1951); war (*Run Silent Run Deep*, 1958; *The Sand Pebbles*, 1966); Westerns (*Tribute to a Bad Man*, 1956); and melodrama (*So Big*, 1953; *I Want to Live!*, 1958). He's best known as the creative force behind two of the most successful

1910s

musicals in the history of cinema: *West Side Story* (1961) and *The Sound of Music* (1965). Both films picked up a host of Academy Awards, including Best Director for Wise and Best Picture. *West Side Story*, which Wise codirected with Jerome Robbins, was a massive hit with both critics and the public. Superbly choreographed, it broke the mold of musical theater by moving into darker themes of ethnic and social tension.

Wise made movies until he was well into his eighties. Films such as *The Day the Earth Stood Still* (1951) and *Star Trek* (1979) point back to his early experiments with special effects during the 1940s. Some have criticized him for rigidly adhering to genre rather than evolving his own discernible directorial style. A tall order, perhaps, considering his range. Nonetheless, Wise's films were all stamped with the same degree of professionalism. And they were undeniably successful, winning awards as well as pleasing the moviegoing hordes. **MC**

ABOVE: The original film poster for Rodgers and Hammerstein's *The Sound of Music*.

Welles the Maverick

Director, producer, and editor Robert Wise stumbled into the film business. When he was nineteen he got an odd job at RKO Pictures studios. He had already established himself as a film editor by the time he met the twenty-five-year-old Orson Welles, fresh from his trailblazing radio and stage work in New York. Welles picked Wise to edit *Citizen Kane* and they went on to work together on *The Magnificent Ambersons*. On Welles's premature fall from grace, Wise once said: "He simply never fulfilled himself after that magnificent start. His own fault—lack of self discipline."

ORSON WELLES

Born: George Orson Welles, May 6, 1915 (Kenosha, Wisconsin, U.S.); died 1985 (Hollywood, California, U.S.).

Directing style: Controversial Hollywood wunderkind; auteur actor, writer, director, and producer; innovative and unorthodox casting; themes of power and madness.

Top Takes...

Moby Dick 1999

It's All True 1993

Don Quijote de Orson Welles 1992
  (Don Quixote)

The Spirit of Charles Lindbergh 1984

Vérités et mensonges 1974 *(F for Fake)*

The Other Side of the Wind 1972

London 1971

The Golden Honeymoon 1970

The Deep 1970

The Immortal Story 1968

Vienna 1968

Campanadas a medianoche 1965
  (Chimes at Midnight)

Le Procès 1962 *(The Trial)*

Touch of Evil 1958

Mr. Arkadin 1955

*The Tragedy of Othello: The Moor
  of Venice* 1952

Macbeth 1948

The Lady from Shanghai 1947

The Stranger 1946

The Magnificent Ambersons 1942

Citizen Kane 1941 ☆

Too Much Johnson 1938

RIGHT: In *F for Fake* Welles continues to explore the illusionary nature of his art.

Ego is simultaneously a blunt weapon and a shield from the world. In the case of Orson Welles, ego is the key for interpreting a career of such uneven result that, were it not for strength of ego, he never would have succeeded at all. But because of that same ego, he upset many, lost great fortunes, and was always searching for work. The other key for interpreting Welles is performance; not just of actors standing before cameras, but the more existential theme of how identity is connected with wearing a mask, playing to crowds, and reacting to circumstances. This issue of performance is central to Welles, since most of his films are concerned with madness and control, and power and weakness: attitudes adopted both in his movies and by the characters in them.

Welles was born a brilliant and beautiful child, interested in music, magic, and painting. His mother died when he was nine years old, his father when he was fifteen, and he spent the rest of his childhood as the ward of a doctor. He tried becoming an actor, first in Ireland, then in England, and finally in New York. Quickly established on radio for possessing one of the world's

most distinctive voices, he embarked on a fruitful collaboration with actor John Houseman, forming the Mercury Theater in 1937. The next year the pair produced the famous Halloween broadcast of H. G. Wells's 1898 novel, *The War of the Worlds*, and garnered great attention for their staging of classic plays in unusual ways, for instance in the so-called "voodoo" version of *The Tragedy of Macbeth*, which featured an all-black cast.

ABOVE: Welles both directed and starred in, with Rita Hayworth, *The Lady from Shanghai*.

Having developed a reputation for being a polymath and a big personality given to wine, women, food, and song, Welles received an unparalleled carte-blanche opportunity at RKO Pictures to make any film he wished. He chose to embellish the life of newspaper tycoon William Randolph Hearst with certain autobiographical touches of his own and produced *Citizen Kane* (1941).

"Everybody denies that I am a genius—but nobody ever called me one."

Battle over *Citizen Kane*

From its famous opening scene when a dying tycoon mysteriously utters the word "Rosebud," as the camera moves from the "No Trespassing" sign outside the Xanadu mansion, then to the inside of a snowglobe, *Citizen Kane* dramatically broke with movie tradition. The story then unfolds mainly in flashback. *Kane* is the only film over which Orson Welles had complete artistic control and is a living testament to his cinematic innovation.

Welles's idea for the story was conceived with screenwriter Herman Mankiewicz, who knew and despised the media mogul William Randolph Hearst. Welles wisely guided Mankiewicz away from a direct portrayal of Hearst, and he incorporated aspects from other figures, including director Howard Hughes. Kane's character thus became a far broader depiction of power than the narrow one Mankiewicz originally intended.

When Hearst got wind of the film he tried to have it boycotted, threatening to withdraw advertising for any movie theater that screened it and to expose 15 years of suppressed Hollywood scandal. The movie's release was delayed and it was poorly distributed, all adding to its financial loss. While critically praised, cinemagoers of the time did not warm to the movie's unconventional style. Across time, the film has acquired classic status although it continues to divide audiences.

1910s

RIGHT: Welles as the media magnate John Foster Kane in his masterwork *Citizen Kane*.

Despite artistic innovations in narrative, camera technique, set design, performance, and use of symbolism, *Citizen Kane* was a commercial failure, although it did garner Welles an Oscar for Best Original Screenplay. RKO Pictures again gave him great liberties on *The Magnificent Ambersons* (1942), although the studio recut this movie and released it to even greater commercial disappointment and critical indifference. Disgusted by the experience, and by now seen as a poor risk, Welles was only entrusted with three more Hollywood movies: *The Stranger* (1946), *The Lady from Shanghai* (1947), and *Touch of Evil* (1958). From the late 1940s onward he spent his life in Europe, working on other people's films so that he could finance his personal projects, beginning with *Macbeth* (1948).

The outsider within

Although Welles became an industry outsider, his charms onscreen were still in demand as an actor and narrator. He produced memorable works such as *The Tragedy of Othello: The Moor of Venice* (1952), *Mr. Arkadin* (1955), and *Le Procès* (1962) (*The Trial*), as well as two masterpieces, both notable for being produced in penury and for being extraordinarily effective— *Campanadas a medianoche* (1965) (*Chimes at Midnight*) and *Vérités et mensonges* (1974) (*F for Fake*).

Welles also used his considerable charm to promote himself on TV shows where his hulking body was seen to grow ever larger with each year. His obesity, like his artistic temperament and the subjects he chose for screen projects, tended to illuminate a profound confidence in his abilities, juxtaposed with disgust at his physical person. His size was often hyperbolized with makeup, costume, lighting, and camera angles. That this ego would choose to manipulate so grotesque a body through onscreen performance is a naked exposure of sacrificing self for the sake of creativity.

In 1975, the American Film Institute gave him a Lifetime Achievement Award. His work was reconsidered and he was promoted as a misunderstood artist. Welles's abilities and *Citizen Kane* are now held up as paragons of cinema. **GCQ**

TERENCE YOUNG

Born: Stewart Terence Herbert Young, June 20, 1915 (Shanghai, China); died 1994 (Cannes, Alpes-Maritimes, Provence-Alpes-Côte d'Azur, France).

Directing style: British director of dramas and gentlemanly tough-guy movies; maker of early James Bond films; helped create the sophisticated Bond image.

Top Takes...

Terence Young is perhaps most famous for directing three of the first four James Bond movies—*Dr. No* (1962), *From Russia with Love* (1963), and *Thunderball* (1965). He has also been credited with grooming Sean Connery for the part of the über-spy, giving him a patina of sophistication.

Young started out codirecting *Theirs Is the Glory* (1946), a documentary about the World War II Battle of Arnhem, in which he himself had participated as a paratrooper for the British army. He became a competent director of gentlemanly but tough British films, such as *Valley of Eagles* (1951), *The Red Beret* (1953), and *No Time to Die* (1958). *Serious Charge* (1959) stands out particularly from this period as a gloomy modern drama about a vicar, played by Anthony Quayle, accused of molesting a teenage boy.

After his 007 movies, Young stayed with international intrigue in the World War II spy film *Triple Cross* (1966) and the bizarre antidrug tract *Poppies Are Also Flowers* (1966). He did well by Audrey Hepburn in the suspense picture *Wait Until Dark* (1967). Interestingly, the sixteen-year-old Hepburn, a volunteer nurse, had cared for him 20 years earlier after he was wounded in the Battle of Arnhem. In the 1970s he made a run of coproductions with Charles Bronson, most memorably *The Valachi Papers* (1972), as well as riotous kitsch such as *The Klansman* (1974) and Sidney Sheldon's *Bloodline* (1979). His later career is mostly notable for collaborations with the sort of dubious tyrants whose underground lairs Bond would have blown up: *Al-Ayyam al-Tawila* (1980) (*Long Days*) is based on Saddam Hussein's ghostwritten self-serving autobiography and the Korean War film *Inchon* (1982) was sponsored by cult leader the Reverend Sun Myung Moon. **KN**

> "Bond was how Fleming saw himself; the sardonic . . . mouth, the hard, tight skinned face."

KON ICHIKAWA

Born: Uji Yamada, November 20, 1915 (Mie, Japan).

Directing style: Offbeat and versatile Japanese director across a range of genres; wry, quirky humor; cartoonlike visual sophistication; frequent collaborator with his screenwriter wife Natto Wada; use of widescreen.

Erratic, eclectic, uneven: adjectives such as these are often mentioned with Kon Ichikawa's name. Prolific even by Japanese standards over his 60-year-long career, Ichikawa has tackled a bewilderingly wide range of genres and succeeded in sneaking elements of wry humor and visual sophistication into even the most routine projects. His best-known film *Yukinojo henge* (1963) (*An Actor's Revenge*) was imposed on him as a punishment by studio Daiei after his previous two movies had lost money. Faced with a remake of an old *kabuki* melodrama, with seriously overage lead actors cast in twin swashbuckling roles, Ichikawa gleefully plays up everything absurd and theatrical about the story, unpredictably switching tone and idiom, drawing on his cartoon background to throw in thought bubbles, fake sets, anomalous music, and distorted visuals.

Ichikawa's quirky humor—he names Jean Renoir, Charles Chaplin, and Walt Disney among his prime influences—comes out strongly in the cartoonish *Pu-san* (1953) (*Mr. Pu*); in *Watashi wa nisai* (1962) (*Being Two Isn't Easy*), narrated by a two-year-old; and in *Wagahai wa neko de aru* (1975) (*I Am a Cat*), narrated by the eponymous feline. But even his lighter films have their darker side and in *Biruma no tategoto* (1956) (*The Burmese Harp*) and *Nobi* (1959) (*Fires on the Plain*), he created two of the most agonizing war films ever made. His approach to genre is typically offbeat: *Matatabi* (1973) (*The Wanderers*), his take on the samurai movie, features three young peasants, would-be samurais, constantly stymied by their own ineptitude. *Tokyo orimpikku* (1965) (*Tokyo Olympiad*) outraged the Olympic authorities because Ichikawa shunned nationalist triumphalism to tell the story of individual winners, losers, and spectators involved. **PK**

Top Takes...

Shijushichinin no shikaku 1994 (*47 Ronin*)
Gokumon-to 1977 (*Guillotine Island*)
Wagahai wa neko de aru 1975 (*I Am a Cat*)
Matatabi 1973 (*The Wanderers*)
Genji monogatari 1966 (*The Tale of Genji*)
Tokyo orimpikku 1965 (*Tokyo Olympiad*)
Yukinojo henge 1963 (*An Actor's Revenge*)
Watashi wa nisai 1962 (*Being Two Isn't Easy*)
Kuroi junin no onna 1961 (*Ten Dark Women*)
Jokyo 1960 (*A Woman's Testament*)
Nobi 1959 (*Fires on the Plain*)
Enjo 1958 (*Conflagration*)
Biruma no tategoto 1956 (*The Burmese Harp*)
Pu-san 1953 (*Mr. Pu*)
Koibito 1951 (*The Lover*)
Ningen moyo 1949 (*Human Patterns*)

1910s

"I don't have any unifying theme. I just make pictures I like . . . ."

MASAKI KOBAYASHI

Born: Masaki Kobayashi, February 14, 1916 (Hokkaido, Japan); died 1996 (Tokyo, Japan).

Directing style: Left-wing director whose films often carry a contemporary social message; elegantly stylized visual compositions; use of vivid color.

Top Takes...

The dilemma of the dissentient—the principled individual who finds himself inescapably at odds with society—underlies all Masaki Kobayashi's work, stemming directly from his own personal experience. In 1942, only a few months into his cinematic career, he was forcibly drafted into the Imperial Japanese Army. A pacifist, he refused all promotion above the rank of private, and was beaten repeatedly for defying orders.

That formative experience was directly distilled into his towering, nine-hour epic trilogy, *Ningen no joken* (1959–1961) (*The Human Condition*), in which Kobayashi's surrogate, the pacifist Kaji, played by his favorite actor Tatsuya Nakadai struggles against the brutality of a militarized society. His two most powerful period films, *Seppuku* (1962) (*Harakiri*) and *Jôi-uchi: Hairyô tsuma shimatsu* (1967) (*Rebellion*), located the same theme in Japanese history. In each, a lone samurai warrior dares to stand against the cruelty of the inflexible feudal system only to die a heroic but ultimately futile death.

Kobayashi tackled specific contemporary issues: war criminals in *Kabe atsuki heya* (1953) (*The Thick-Walled Room*), which was suppressed until 1956; corruption in sport in *Anata kaimasu* (1956) (*I'll Buy You*); and organized crime in *Kuroi kawa* (1957) (*Black River*). But the social concerns of his films never precluded aesthetic awareness. Both *Harakiri* and *Rebellion* are marked by an austere formal beauty while *Kaidan* (1964) (*Ghost Stories*), adapted from four of Lafcadio Hearn's ghost stories, for once carried no social message, but developed a strikingly original use of color. From the late 1960s onward Kobayashi's left-wing principles made it increasingly difficult for him to find backing; as a consequence, his later work reflects a sense of disillusion. **PK**

> "The suspicious mind conjures its own demons."
>
> —Hanshiro Tsugumo, *Harakiri*

BUDD BOETTICHER

Born: Oscar Boetticher Jr., July 29, 1916 (Chicago, Illinois, U.S.); died 2001 (Ramona, California, U.S.).

Directing style: Maverick director of bullfighting and action movies; cult B-Westerns; notable artistic collaborations with Randolph Scott; bare shooting style.

Born in Chicago in 1916, Budd Boetticher became a college athlete, and then went to Mexico to study bullfighting. This led to his becoming technical adviser to Rouben Mamoulian's romance of the bullring, *Blood and Sand* (1941). Boetticher became a director of routine action films before completing his first personal project, *Bullfighter and the Lady* (1951), for which he was nominated for an Oscar for Best Writing, Motion Picture Story, despite his belief that the film had been ruined in the editing process. Further competent action films followed, many of them Westerns, but it was not until the late 1950s that Boetticher made the pictures that secured his reputation.

Working with Randolph Scott, Boetticher directed *Seven Men from Now* (1956), from a script by Burt Kennedy. A spare, tightly constructed and elegantly shot film, it was followed by *The Tall T* (1957), again with Scott in the lead, another script by Kennedy, and this time produced by Scott's business partner Harry Joe Brown. The partnership with Scott and Brown continued over several more films, the best of them, such as *Ride Lonesome* (1959) and *Comanche Station* (1960), also scripted by Kennedy. Striking in their visual appeal, mostly shot in the Lone Pine area in California, they are also marked by a singular conception of the Western hero as stoical, self-contained, and indomitable; injections of humor are provided by a series of charming villains.

He directed an excellent gangster film, *The Rise and Fall of Legs Diamond* (1960), before going to Mexico to make a documentary, *Arruza* (1972), about his friend, the matador Carlos Arruza. The project took seven years to complete. Boetticher made one final Western in Hollywood, *A Time for Dying* (1969), which starred Audie Murphy as Jesse James. **EB**

Top Takes...

Arruza 1972
A Time for Dying 1969
Comanche Station 1960
The Rise and Fall of Legs Diamond 1960
Ride Lonesome 1959
Buchanan Rides Alone 1958
The Tall T 1957
Seven Men from Now 1956
The Killer Is Loose 1956
The Magnificent Matador 1955
The Cimarron Kid 1952
Bullfighter and the Lady 1951
Black Midnight 1949
Assigned to Danger 1948
The Fleet That Came to Stay 1945
One Mysterious Night 1944

1910s

"I got a great script and I shot it and I added to it. That's what a director is supposed to do."

GEORGE SIDNEY

Born: George Sidney, October 4, 1916 (Long Island City, New York, U.S.); died 2002 (Las Vegas, Nevada, U.S.).

Directing style: Maker of optimistic romantic musicals; integration of song and dance with narrative; innovative pairing of live actors with animated characters.

Top Takes…

Half a Sixpence 1967
Viva Las Vegas 1964
Bye Bye Birdie 1963
Pal Joey 1957
Kiss Me Kate 1953
Scaramouche 1952
Show Boat 1951
Annie Get Your Gun 1950
The Three Musketeers 1948
The Harvey Girls 1946
Anchors Aweigh 1945
Pilot #5 1943
Pacific Rendezvous 1942
Quicker'n a Wink 1940
Dog Daze 1939
Party Fever 1938

1910s

George Sidney was born into show business. His father was a successful Broadway producer and his mother and uncle were stage performers. As a child Sidney appeared in vaudeville before starting his film career at MGM as a messenger; he went on to spend much of his career at the studios. He began making promotional shorts such as *Pacific Paradise* (1937) and *Billy Rose's Casa Mañana Revue* (1938), before being assigned to the *Our Gang* series of shorts, beginning with *Party Fever* (1938) and ending with *Dog Daze* (1939). He then went back to making promotional shorts, often about developing film technologies such as *Quicker'n a Wink* (1940). After his feature debut *Pacific Rendezvous* (1942), he very quickly established himself both as a director of stars and musicals with *Anchors Aweigh* (1945), starring Frank Sinatra and Gene Kelly, and *The Harvey Girls* (1946) headlined by Judy Garland.

During the same period, he helped William Hanna and Joseph Barbera finance their production company. Sidney's *Anchors Aweigh* features Hanna-Barbera's animated mouse, Jerry. He thereafter made mostly musicals, including the Elvis Presley vehicle *Viva Las Vegas* (1964) and his final film *Half a Sixpence* (1967), along with such classics as *Annie Get Your Gun* (1950), *Show Boat* (1951), *Kiss Me Kate* (1953), *Pal Joey* (1957), and *Bye Bye Birdie* (1963). He also sampled other genres, such as the swashbuckler *The Three Musketeers* (1948), starring Gene Kelly and Van Heflin. Sidney's musicals were the most successful films of a valued but often forgotten career. Optimism runs throughout his work, as if a smile and catchy tune can overcome all obstacles. His musicals remain entertaining for his light directorial touch and the polished integration of song and dance with story. **GCQ**

"I was in silent movies, I was in radio, I was in burlesque . . . . I'm all show business!"

DINO RISI

Born: Dino Risi, December 23, 1916 (Milan, Lombardy, Italy).

Directing style: Italian director who frequently uses biting humor to comment on social conditions in contemporary society, particularly those of the poor; belongs to a family of filmmakers; writer.

It is a curious twist of fate that Dino Risi became a film director at all. After graduating in psychiatric medicine and originally practicing as a psychiatrist, Risi fell into moviemaking almost by chance. Perhaps it took a psychiatrist to probe the psyche of Italian film culture in the way Risi ultimately did. By the end of the director's film adventures he had worked in all the key postwar Italian genres, absorbing and recrafting neorealism, social neorealism, pink neorealism and, later, giving a hard filmic center to Italy's *commedia all'italiana* tradition. After a brief stint as a film critic, he made several documentaries such as *Buio in sala* (1948), and his initial forays into the world of feature films were as assistant director to Mario Soldati and Alberto Lattuada. After moving to Rome from his native Milan, he began to carve out a career as a witty and socially critical filmmaker. Risi was always caustic, satirical, and erudite.

His most famous work dealt with poverty in postwar Italy but was always handled with a sharp comedic touch, moving away from the more serious treatment of such subject matter by neorealism in movies like *Pane, amore e . . . .* (1955) (*Scandal in Sorrento*) and *Poveri ma belli* (1957) (*Poor But Beautiful*). A Risi film represented poverty with a defiant wink to the camera. However, some were critical of this rose-tinted neorealism, rooted as it was in the ebullience and hope of Italy's apparent economic revival. But by the 1960s Risi was using biting humor combined with an unforgiving focus on the difficulty of daily life to probe his country's failure to deliver the fruits of this revival to the public. As his various takes on realism morphed once again, and despite a later darker period, it was his mastery of this form of *commedia all'italiana* that was to cement Risi's place in the history of Italian cinema. **RH**

Top Takes...

I nuovi mostri 1978 (*The New Monsters*)
Profumo di donna 1974 (*Scent of a Woman*)
Sessomatto 1973 (*How Funny Can Sex Be?*)
Mordi e fuggi 1973 (*Dirty Weekend*)
Il profeta 1968 (*The Prophet*)
Il tigre 1967 (*The Tiger and the Pussycat*)
Operazione San Gennaro 1966
  (*The Treasure of San Gennaro*)
L'Ombrellone 1966 (*Weekend Wives*)
Le bambole 1965 (*The Dolls*)
Il sorpasso 1962 (*The Easy Life*)
Una vita difficile 1961 (*A Difficult Life*)
Il mattatore 1960 (*Love and Larceny*)
Belle ma povere 1957 (*Poor Girl, Pretty Girl*)
Poveri ma belli 1957 (*Poor But Beautiful*)
Pane, amore e . . . . 1955 (*Scandal in Sorrento*)

"The truths [Risi] underlines give his uncluttered film meaning."
—On *The Easy Life, New York Times*

GIUSEPPE DE SANTIS

Born: Giuseppe de Santis, February 11, 1917 (Fondi, Latium, Italy); died 1997 (Rome, Italy).

Directing style: Italian director memorable for postwar period of neorealist films; maker of social commentaries and sensational melodramas on the harsh side of life.

Top Takes…

Oggi è un altro giorno 1995
  (Today and Another Day)
*Un apprezzato professionista di sicuro
  avvenire* 1971
Italiani brava gente 1965 *(Attack and Retreat)*
La garçonnière 1960
La strada lunga un anno 1958
  (The Year Long Road)
Uomini e lupi 1956 *(Men and Wolves)*
Giorni d'amore 1954 *(Days of Love)*
Un marito per Anna Zaccheo 1953
  (A Husband for Anna)
Roma ore 11 1952 *(Rome 11:00)*
Non c'è pace tra gli ulivi 1950
  (Under the Olive Tree)
Riso amaro 1949 *(Bitter Rice)*
Caccia tragica 1947 *(The Tragic Hunt)*

"A great poet of working men and farmers."—On *Bitter Rice*, Gilles Jacob, Cannes Film Festival

In many ways the career of Giuseppe de Santis reads like a checklist of things to do to become a postwar Italian film director. Having studied literature and philosophy at the University of Rome, he became a short-story writer and then a critic for *Cinema* magazine, where he passionately set about critiquing film practice in the late 1930s and early 1940s, advocating a style that was later to become neorealism.

After a stint at the Centro Sperimentale di Cinematografia in Rome, he acted as assistant director to Luchino Visconti on *Ossessione* (1943). He also began to write screenplays. It was his self-penned *Riso amaro* (1949) (*Bitter Rice*), a film tracing the harsh lives of paddy field workers in the Po valley, for which he was to become most known. *Bitter Rice*'s mix of social commentary (and daring flashes of actress Silvana Mangano replete with devilishly short hot pants) garnered it an Academy Award nomination for Best Writing, Motion Picture Story. His debut film, *Caccia tragica* (1947) (*The Tragic Hunt*), as with the later *Roma ore 11* (1952) (*Rome 11:00*), was typical of de Santis's work overall, depicting as it did the harsh lives of Italy's rural and urban working classes. His work was often seen as an impassioned call for social justice, although he was also criticized for a muddled ideological stance and a tendency toward sensationalism. After trying to adapt his films to the 1950s trend toward more intimate dramas, the gradual passing of neorealism in Italy affected de Santis greatly. Although *Un marito per Anna Zaccheo* (1953) (*A Husband for Anna*) was touching and *Italiani brava gente* (1965) (*Attack and Retreat*) an interesting critique of Italy's disastrous military campaign in the Soviet Union, he was never again to reach the peaks of his earlier neorealist period. **RH**

MAYA DEREN

Born: Eleanora Derenkowsky, April 29, 1917 (Kiev, Ukraine, Russia); died 1961 (New York City, New York, U.S.).

Directing style: Experimental short and documentary filmmaker; themes of time, magic, science, and religion; use of montage, choreography, and slow motion.

Born in Russia, Maya Deren fled to the United States with her family to avoid the pogroms against Russian Jews. She is hailed as one of the pioneers in U.S. experimental short film. Her masterpiece *Meshes of the Afternoon* (1943), a collaboration with her first husband, the avant-garde photographer Alexander Hammid, stars Deren as a lady who enters her house and falls asleep. After this she is faced with her two other selves from different periods of time, along with a hooded, mirror-faced figure. Demonstrating Deren's fascination with the concept of time, the film follows the logic of memories, in which all things exist simultaneously. Deren takes the audience inside her lead character's mind to witness the emotional state of a frail tormented woman in her last moments.

Her subsequent films, such as *At Land* (1944) and *Ritual in Transfigured Time* (1946), would further utilize montage, inserting several different locations within a single scene, thus enabling a causality that fluently served her purposes. Other recurring elements in Deren's work were choreography and slow motion. Between 1947 and 1951 she made multiple trips to Haiti during which she documented Haitian dance and the rituals of voodoo. The resulting footage was posthumously compiled into *Divine Horsemen: The Living Gods of Haiti* (1985). Deren's final movie *The Very Eye of the Night* (1958) differs considerably from her previous work. A collaboration with the Metropolitan Opera's School of Ballet, the film was presented in reversed colors and features dancers posing as celestial figures wandering through space.

Deren worked tirelessly to promote independent film; she distributed and financed her own work. In 1946 she was awarded the first Guggenheim Fellowship for filmmaking. **LL**

Top Takes…

Divine Horsemen: The Living Gods of Haiti 1985
The Very Eye of Night 1958
Meditation on Violence 1948
Ritual in Transfigured Time 1946
A Study in Choreography for Camera 1945
At Land 1944
Witch's Cradle 1944
Meshes of the Afternoon 1943

1910s

"She is the mother of us all."
—Stan Brakhage, pioneering avant-garde film director

JEAN ROUCH

Born: Jean Rouch, May 31, 1917 (Paris, France); died 2004 (Birni N'Konni, Niger).

Directing style: French anthropologist and documentary filmmaker; innovator of cinéma vérité; exploration of colonialism and racism, often with African subjects; adventurous reportage; ethnofiction.

1910s

> "I am violently opposed to film crews … the filmmaker must be the cameraman."

Jean Rouch was a French filmmaker and anthropologist, known for his provocative documentaries. In the early 1940s he worked as a civil engineer in Niger, fueling a long-term fascination with that country, which was interrupted by his participation in the French Resistance during World War II. After the war, he returned to Niger, where he is now buried after having died in a car crash in 2004.

By the late 1950s he had become known for his style of reportage and "ethnofiction," in which painstakingly researched ethnographic work is portrayed in a fictitious way, through such films as *Les maîtres fous* (1955) (*The Mad Masters*), *Jaguar* (1967), and *Moi un noir* (1958) (*I, a Negro*). However, it was *Chronique d'un été* (1961) (*Chronicle of a Summer*) that proved his lasting impact on world cinema. Having coined the term "cinéma vérité," Rouch's innovation was to include the process of documentary production in the finished film, including his active participation and that of his main collaborator, Edgar Morin. Along with employing a theme—in this case asking Parisians "Are you happy?" and filming the results—Rouch capitalized on new, lighter-weight cameras and synchronized sound-recording equipment to take his investigation into the streets. Debuting at the beginning of the French New Wave, this self-conscious style of documentary sent ripples across the world, most significantly in helping organize Direct Cinema in the United States and requiring the social sciences to include image-making. Later, he made such notable movies as *La chasse au lion à l'arc* (1965) (*The Lion Hunters*) and *Ciné-portrait de Margaret Mead* (1977) (*Margaret Mead: A Portrait by a Friend*), as well as running the Cinémathèque Française in Paris. **GCQ**

JEAN-PIERRE MELVILLE

Born: Jean-Pierre Grumbach, October 20, 1917 (Paris, France); died 1973 (Paris, France).

Directing style: French director notable for stylish, dark, gangster movies; themes of honor, loyalty, and camaraderie; austere narrative style; use of real locations.

Jean-Pierre Melville harbored a passion for all things American, especially classic Hollywood gangster movies. But Melville's *policiers*, or cops, are no slavish imitations. Although reveling in the iconography of the genre—the snap-brim hats, the belted trench coats, the huge finned cars, and the smoky nightclub dives—he turned its conventions to his own purposes. His crime films take place in a mythic, highly stylized world, allowing for atmospheric, downbeat meditations on Melville's favorite themes of loyalty, friendship, honor, and treachery.

Born Jean-Pierre Grumbach, of Alsatian Jewish stock, Melville adopted his surname from the U.S. novelist Herman Melville. During World War II he joined the French Resistance and the Nazi occupation provided the subject of his debut feature film. *Le silence de la mer* (1949) already displayed his characteristic mix of intensity and austerity. He returned to the same period with the Bressonian *Léon Morin, prêtre* (1961) (*The Forgiven Sinner*), which featured the moral torments of a priest in provincial occupied France.

But it is for his gangster films that Melville is best known. Lighter in tone than his later work, *Bob le flambeur* (1955) (*Fever Heat*) with its freewheeling narrative, location shooting, and reliance on available light, made him an unofficial godfather to the filmmakers of the French New Wave. He described *Le Doulos* (1962) (*Doulos: The Finger Man*) as his "first real *policier*." Its fatalistic, laconic tone initiated the great run of crime movies of his maturity—*L'aîné des ferchaux* (1963) (*Magnet of Doom*), *Le deuxième souffle* (1966) (*Second Breath*), and the film generally considered to be his masterpiece, *Le Samouraï* (1967) (*The Godson*), which gave Alain Delon the finest role of his career. **PK**

Top Takes...

Un flic 1972 (*Dirty Money*)
Le cercle rouge 1970 (*The Red Circle*)
L'armée des ombres 1969
  (*Army in the Shadows*)
Le Samouraï 1967 (*The Godson*)
Le deuxième souffle 1966 (*Second Breath*)
L'aîné des ferchaux 1963 (*Magnet of Doom*)
Le Doulos 1962 (*Doulos: The Finger Man*)
Léon Morin, prêtre 1961 (*The Forgiven Sinner*)
Deux hommes dans Manhattan 1959
  (*Two Men in Manhattan*)
Bob le flambeur 1955 (*Fever Heat*)
Quand tu liras cette lettre 1953
  (*When You Read This Letter*)
Les enfants terribles 1950 (*The Strange Ones*)
Le silence de la mer 1949

1910s

"All men are guilty. They're born innocent, but it doesn't last."—Chief of Police, *The Red Circle*

IDA LUPINO

Born: Ida Lupino, February 4, 1918 (Camberwell, London, England); died 1995 (Los Angeles, California, U.S.).

Directing style: Actress turned pioneering female director; protofeminist themes of women trapped by social conventions; melodramas and film noirs.

Top Takes…

During the early 1950s Ida Lupino was virtually the only female director working in mainstream Hollywood. Although her output was small—seven films in all—her matter-of-fact professionalism served as an inspiration for other women, not least the great Japanese actress Kinuyo Tanaka, who pursued her own directing career after meeting Lupino.

Lupino started acting in films at the age of thirteen, but never achieved the success her talents deserved. Hailed on her debut as "The English Jean Harlow," she later found herself pigeonholed by Hollywood as, in her own rueful words, "a poor man's Bette Davis." Dissatisfied, she turned to scriptwriting and established her own production company. For her first film, *Not Wanted* (1949), she hired a veteran B-movie director, Elmer Clifton. Three days into shooting Clifton succumbed to a heart attack and Lupino took over behind the camera.

Not Wanted, credited to Clifton, concerns a small-town girl who has an illegitimate baby. It was the first of Lupino's studies of women trapped by social mores. As with most of her films, its low-budget documentary texture and gritty sense of place are lightened by compassion for her characters. The heroine of her first film as credited director, *Never Fear* (1949), is a dancer crippled by polio, whereas *Outrage* (1950) is a frank treatment of rape. In *The Bigamist* (1953) a weak, well-meaning salesman winds up married to two women in different cities. Lupino, who played one of the wives, lets the audience feel sorry for him without playing down the damage caused by his deceptions. Her finest feature film was *The Hitch-Hiker* (1953), a taut thriller about two men on vacation who unwittingly pick up an escaped convict. Lupino also enjoyed a long career directing for TV. **PK**

> "Any woman who wishes to smash into the world of men isn't very feminine."

GABRIEL AXEL

Born: Gabriel Axel Mørch, April 18, 1918 (Århus, Denmark).

Directing style: Danish actor turned director of comedy dramas and farces with a surreal twist; often literary adaptations; simple, sparse dialogue; well-drawn characterizations.

A prolific writer, actor, and producer, as well as director, Gabriel Axel was born in Århus, Denmark, but most of his childhood was spent in France. He has subsequently lived and worked in both countries. Axel trained as an actor at the Royal Danish Theater in Copenhagen and worked in Paris for several years, including with the Louis Jouvet theater ensemble. He returned to Denmark in the early 1950s, branching out from the theater to include TV and film work, such as the movie *Guld og grønne skove* (1958) (*The Girls Are Willing*), and the TV miniseries *Regnvejr Og Ingen Penge* (1965). His most notable work from the 1960s was his Viking romance feature *Den røde kappe* (1967) (*Hagbard and Signe*), which was awarded the Grand Prix de la Technique at the Cannes Film Festival.

Returning to France, Axel went on to direct several acclaimed projects for television. He remains best known for *Babettes gæstebud* (1987) (*Babette's Feast*). Adapted from a Karen Blixen short story of the same name, it won the 1988 Academy Award for Best Foreign Language Film. Through its meticulous attention to detail and character development, this affecting comedy drama has one of the most successful realizations of the food-as-love metaphor in cinema. In the story, a French woman, Babette Harsant, is in exile in Denmark, where she finds work as a maid and cook for two elderly spinsters in an austere, religious community. When she is later allowed to return to her homeland, Babette's "feast" is both a memorable farewell and valuable life lesson.

Axel also directed *Prince of Jutland* (1994), a retelling of *Hamlet* that bypasses William Shakespeare and uses the original Danish source material, and which starred Gabriel Byrne, Dame Helen Mirren, and Christian Bale. **KM**

Top Takes...

Leïla 2001

Prince of Jutland 1994

Christian 1989

Babettes gæstebud 1987 (*Babette's Feast*)

Alt på et bræt 1977 (*Going for Broke*)

Familien Gyldenkål 1975
  (*The Goldcabbage Family*)

Med kærlig hilsen 1971 (*Love Me Darling*)

Amour 1970

Det kære legetøj 1968

Den røde kappe 1967 (*Hagbard and Signe*)

Paradis retur 1964 (*Paradise and Back*)

Vi har det jo dejligt 1963

Oskar 1962

Guld og grønne skove 1958
  (*The Girls Are Willing*)

> "I know how exacting it is to be on the other side of the camera."
>
> —On his acting experience

INGMAR BERGMAN

Born: Ernst Ingmar Bergman, July 14, 1918 (Uppsala, Uppsala län, Sweden).

Directing style: Titan modernist auteur director of Scandinavian cinema; powerful imagery and symbolism; acting improvisation; themes exploring women's lives, religion, and psychology.

Top Takes...

Fanny och Alexander 1982 ☆
  (Fanny and Alexander)

Höstsonaten 1978 (Autumn Sonata)

The Serpent's Egg 1977

Ansikte mot ansikte 1976 ☆
  (Face to Face)

Scener ur ett äktenskap 1973
  (Scenes from a Marriage)

Viskningar och rop 1972 ☆
  (Cries and Whispers)

Skammen 1968 (Shame)

Vargtimmen 1968 (Hour of the Wolf)

Persona 1966

För att inte tala om alla dessa kvinnor 1964
  (All These Women)

Nattvardsgästerna 1962 (Winter Light)

Såsom i en spegel 1961
  (Through a Glass Darkly)

Djävulens öga 1960 (The Devil's Eye)

Jungfrukällan 1960 (The Virgin Spring)

Smultronstället 1957 (Wild Strawberries)

Det sjunde inseglet 1957 (The Seventh Seal)

Sommaren med Monika 1953
  (Monika, the Story of a Bad Girl)

Törst 1949 (Thirst)

Fängelse 1949 (The Devil's Wanton)

RIGHT: Bergman's *Wild Strawberries* was a landmark film in his cinematic career.

Ernst Ingmar Bergman, who would become an exemplary figure of modernist cinema and a champion of auteurist critics, was born in Uppsala, Sweden. His father, a Lutheran minister, was a strict, possibly abusive disciplinarian whose style of child rearing left its mark on his son's art. From a young age, Bergman fell in love with the theater. While studying at the University of Stockholm, he became involved in the theater as both an actor and director. In 1939 he obtained a post as a production assistant at Stockholm's Royal Dramatic Theater.

While employed at Svensk Filmindustri, where he started work in 1943, Bergman was given the chance to write a script. This became his first film, *Hets* (1944) (*Torment*). Directed by Alf Sjöberg, it centered on a young man tormented by his sadistic Latin teacher. The film's success gave him the chance to both write and direct. The first film revealing his future artistic direction was *Fängelse* (1949) (*The Devil's Wanton*), a philosophical work exploring the themes of pain, psychological suffering, and death. His growing interest in psychology was shown in his next film, *Törst* (1949) (*Thirst*). The sexual life of

a young woman was daringly explored in *Sommaren med Monika* (1953) (*Monika, the Story of a Bad Girl*), which focused on a destructive femme fatale unrestrained by Victorian inhibitions. The movie's taboo-breaking subject matter preceded Roger Vadim's *Et Dieu . . . créa la femme* (1956) (*. . . And God Created Woman*) by three years, and received great praise from the then-critic, and later director, Jean-Luc Godard.

ABOVE: Bengt Ekerot, unforgettable as the Grim Reaper, Death, in *The Seventh Seal*.

Yet it was *Det sjunde inseglet* (1957) (*The Seventh Seal*) that established Bergman's international reputation. Starring Max von Sydow as a knight returning from the Crusades, it was also an allegory about the search for meaning at a moment in history when human extinction through nuclear war was considered probable. The film's powerful imagery further upheld Bergman as a visual stylist, but his

"No form of art goes beyond ordinary consciousness as film does."

The Actor's Auteur

French director François Truffaut once commented that "Bergman's preeminent strength is the direction he gives his actors." During his career Ingmar Bergman has created his own personal company of Swedish actors whom he repeatedly cast in his films.

- This elite group of actors includes Max von Sydow, Bibi Andersson, Erland Josephson, Ingrid Thulin, and Gunnar Björnstrand. Such consistent casting works because Bergman never typecasts his performers. As Truffaut observed, "They are completely different from one film to the next, often playing diametrically opposite roles."

- Norwegian actress Liv Ullmann became Bergman's muse for a number of years. She also became romantically involved with Bergman and had a daughter with him, the writer Linn Ullmann.

- Bergman has always viewed his actors as collaborators and increasingly allowed them to improvise their dialogue. He believes that actors are in a vulnerable position in the film process and need a supportive director in order to produce their best work. Bergman usually writes his own scripts, and in his later films he often simply put down the ideas behind the dialogue rather than the dialogue itself. As the director himself puts it, "I write scripts to serve as skeletons awaiting the flesh and sinew of images."

RIGHT: *Fanny and Alexander* won Bergman Oscar nominations for directing and writing.

directorial talents were matched by the abilities of gifted cinematographers, in this instance by Gunnar Fischer.

The 1950s was Bergman's decade. *The Seventh Seal* was followed by the more personal *Smultronstället* (1957) (*Wild Strawberries*), starring Victor Sjöström, a towering figure in Scandinavian cinema, who played an old man journeying toward death. Bergmanesque in its melancholy, the film was laden with symbolism: the wild strawberries were an objective correlative for, among other things, his idyllic youth as well as lost love. Bergman used the journey to structure the plot.

Jungfrukällan (1960) (*The Virgin Spring*), again set in the Middle Ages, also employed the journey, but examined the uneasy hold of Christian belief on former pagans. Despite its violence, it was yet another triumph and was his first collaboration with cinematographer Sven Nykvist. The films that followed, among them *Nattvardsgästerna* (1962) (*Winter Light*), also studied the problem of religious belief in the modern world. But critics began to find Bergman's films redundant and he temporarily fell from favor. *Persona* (1966), starring Liv Ullman and Bibi Andersson, marked Bergman's return to his analysis of women's lives and psychology.

Bergman in exile

In 1976 Bergman was arrested for tax fraud. Although the charges were later dropped, he had a nervous breakdown and moved to Germany. *The Serpent's Egg* (1977), the first film he made after this debacle and his first in the English language, portrayed events in Germany leading to the rise of Adolf Hitler. Next came *Höstsonaten* (1978) (*Autumn Sonata*), a film depicting the difficult relationship between a mother and daughter, and starring Ingrid Bergman in her last role.

Returning to Sweden in 1978, Bergman was fêted as a national artistic treasure. In 1982 he directed what he said would be his final feature film, the autobiographical *Fanny och Alexander* (1982) (*Fanny and Alexander*). Unfortunately for his moviegoing fans, most of his energies since then have been devoted to his work for theater and television. **SU**

ROBERT ALDRICH

Born: Robert Aldrich, August 9, 1918 (Cranston, Rhode Island, U.S.); died 1983 (Los Angeles, California, U.S.).

Directing style: Maverick director; films often portray an antihero challenging conventional notions of good and bad; master of melodramas and war movies.

Top Takes...

RIGHT: Gaby Rodgers is a little more than startled in the thriller *Kiss Me Deadly*.

Despite his stature among critics, Robert Aldrich, who is perhaps most famous for his hugely successful film *The Dirty Dozen* (1967), never won a major film award in Hollywood.

Eager to become a director, Aldrich moved to New York in 1952 where he directed several episodes of the NBC TV series *The Doctor* (1952). His first feature, for MGM, was *Big Leaguer* (1953), starring Edward G. Robinson, about amateur baseball players striving for a chance in the big leagues. With his second feature, *World for Ransom* (1954), about a kidnapped nuclear scientist for sale to the highest bidder, Aldrich's characteristic themes and motifs began to emerge: the protagonist is a cynical antihero, who acts only according to his personal moral code in an incalculably strange and impenetrable world. *World for Ransom* was poorly received by the critics, but garnered the attention of producers Harold Hecht and Burt Lancaster, who offered him his first major production, *Apache* (1954). Aldrich subsequently directed Lancaster in the Western adventure *Vera Cruz* (1954), costarring Gary Cooper.

It was his next feature, the remarkably stylish film noir *Kiss Me Deadly* (1955), that revealed both the artistic ambition and

1910s

audacity of Aldrich, and established his critical reputation. The movie's story, about a thuggish private detective searching for a mysterious black box, is at times absurd, grotesque, and a seeming apocalyptic allegory. He went on to direct Joan Crawford in the melodrama *Autumn Leaves* (1956), for which he won the Best Director award at the Berlin International Film Festival. The film's success enabled him to persuade Crawford to work alongside archrival Bette Davis in the critically and commercially successful Gothic melodrama *What Ever Happened to Baby Jane?* (1962).

Subsequent films, including *Hush . . . Hush, Sweet Charlotte* (1964), *The Flight of the Phoenix* (1965), and the World War II action film *The Dirty Dozen*, saw Aldrich at the height of success. Among his best final films are the brutal Western *Ulzana's Raid* (1972), *Emperor of the North Pole* (1973), and his last commercial success *The Longest Yard* (1974). **SU**

ABOVE: An all-star cast in *The Dirty Dozen,* one of the greatest war adventure dramas.

Working His Way Up

Aldrich entered the film industry in 1941, and began working his way through the ranks. His first job was as a production clerk at RKO Pictures. During World War II he worked as a second assistant director for Edward Dmytryk and Leslie Goodwins. By 1944, he was working as first assistant director; among the noted directors with whom he apprenticed over the next few years were Jean Renoir for *The Southerner,* (1945); Lewis Milestone, who Aldrich greatly admired; Albert Lewin; William Wellman; Abraham Polonsky, who became a close friend; Joseph Losey; and Sir Charles Chaplin for *Limelight* (1952).

GÉRARD OURY

Born: Max-Gérard Tannenbaum, April 29, 1919 (Paris, France); died 2006 (Saint-Tropez, Var, Provence-Alpes-Côte d'Azur, France).

Directing style: Director of French comedy classics; themes often tackle issues of racism and xenophobia; artistic collaborations with actor Louis de Funès.

Top Takes…

Le Schpountz 1999

Fantôme avec chauffeur 1996 (Ghost with Driver)

La soif de l'or 1993 (The Thirst for Gold)

Lévy et Goliath 1987 (Levy and Goliath)

Le coup du parapluie 1980 (Umbrella Coup)

La carapate 1978 (Out of It)

Les aventures de Rabbi Jacob 1973 (The Mad Adventures of "Rabbi" Jacob)

La folie des grandeurs 1971 (Delusions of Grandeur)

La grande vadrouille 1966 (Don't Look Now—We're Being Shot At)

Le corniaud 1965 (The Sucker)

Le crime ne paie pas 1962 (Crime Does Not Pay)

La menace 1960 (The Menace)

Actor and director Gérard Oury studied at the Conservatoire National Supérieur d'Art Dramatique in France. He was accepted into the Comédie-Française just before the start of World War II, but because he was Jewish he fled to Switzerland.

Oury returned to France after the war, and successfully revived his budding acting career. He made his directorial debut with the film noir La menace (1960) (The Menace), but his first real success came with the drama Le crime ne paie pas (1962) (Crime Does Not Pay). Oury then changed tack and cast Bourvil and Louis de Funès in the farce Le corniaud (1965) (The Sucker), which went on to become a comedy classic. A gangster parody, it tells the story of a shopkeeper on his way to holiday in Italy who suffers a car crash. He compensates for his ruined trip by driving a U.S. friend's car from Naples to Bordeaux, but it happens to be filled with stolen money, jewelry, and drugs.

Oury teamed up again with Bourvil and de Funès for La grande vadrouille (1966) (Don't Look Now—We're Being Shot At). It tells the story of an Allied bomber plane shot down over Paris by the Nazis. With the help of French civilians, the surviving crewman, played by Terry Thomas, attempts to escape to safety in Nazi-unoccupied southern France. The film became the most attended movie in France until the release of Titanic (1997). Oury went on to make a string of popular films, often using comedy to tackle themes such as xenophobia and racism. Les aventures de Rabbi Jacob (1973) (The Mad Adventures of "Rabbi" Jacob) saw de Funès play an anti-Semitic businessman who disguises himself as a rabbi to shake off potential assassins. However, the movie came out at the time of the Yom Kippur War and proved controversial, with Oury receiving death threats as a result. **ES**

"It was a risk to deal with religion, racism, and xenophobia through comedy."

SHIRLEY CLARKE

Born: Shirley Brimberg, October 2, 1919 (New York City, New York, U.S.); died 1997 (Boston, Massachusetts, U.S.).

Directing style: Independent filmmaker of features and documentaries; merging of documentary footage with fiction; integration of color, music, and choreography.

One-time dancer and wannabe choreographer Shirley Clarke gave up on her dream profession to become a film director at the suggestion of a psychiatrist. Clarke, the daughter of a wealthy Polish manufacturer, began her career in New York's avant-garde dance scene but—after a lack of success—decided to explore her interest in film. Her first picture, *Dance in the Sun* (1953), met with immediate success, and led to her membership of a circle of independent filmmakers in Greenwich Village.

Utilizing her knowledge of dance, she made the short semidocumentaries *Bridges-Go-Round* (1958), notable for its Abstract Expressionism, and *Skyscraper* (1960), which won her an Oscar nomination for Best Short Subject, Live Action Subjects. She then challenged the industry's strict censorship rules with the feature *The Connection* (1962), based on Jack Gelber's play about heroin-addicted jazz musicians. In the same year she cofounded The Film-Makers' Cooperative in New York, and won an Oscar for Best Documentary, Features, for *Robert Frost: A Lover's Quarrel with the World* (1963). Sidestepping Hollywood cliché, she unsensationally focused on African-American Harlem street gangs in the drama *The Cool World* (1964). Three years later, *Portrait of Jason* (1967), a *cinéma vérité* interview with an African-American male prostitute edited down from 12 hours of footage, began to get her noticed in Europe following indifference in the United States.

The late 1960s saw her wooed by the big studios to no avail, and her output suffered with the closure of the Film-Makers' Distribution Center, which she also cofounded, because of a lack of funds in 1970. She spent the latter days of her career making movies on video for her loyal following, and lecturing in film at the University of California, Los Angeles. **TE**

Top Takes...

Ornette: Made in America 1985
Ornette Coleman: A Jazz Video Game 1984
The Box 1983
Performance 1982
Savage/Love 1981
A Visual Diary 1980
Portrait of Jason 1967
The Cool World 1964
Robert Frost: A Lover's Quarrel with the World 1963
The Connection 1962
Skyscraper 1960
Bridges-Go-Round 1958
Brussels Loops 1957
Moment in Love 1956
Dance in the Sun 1953

1910s

"The [film] industry's been rotten. The history of women in all the arts has been rotten."

KI-YOUNG KIM

Born: Ki-young Kim, October 10, 1919 (Seoul, South Korea); died 1998 (Seoul, South Korea).

Directing style: "The Master of Madness"; cult experimental Korean filmmaker of B-movie psychosexual melodramas; themes exploring the role of women in society.

Top Takes…

Jukeodo joheun gyeongheom 1995
   (*An Experience Worth Dying for*)
Cheonsayeo aknyeoga doila 1990
   (*Be a Wicked Woman*)
Babo sanyang 1984 (*Hunting of Fools*)
Jayucheonyeo 1982 (*Free Woman*)
Hwanyeo '82 1982 (*The Woman of Fire '82*)
Ban Geum-ryeon 1982
Salinnabileul ggotneun yeoja 1978
   (*Killer Butterfly*)
Iodo 1977 (*Io Island*)
Hyeolyukae 1976 (*Love of Blood Relations*)
Chungyo 1972 (*The Insect Woman*)
Asphalt 1964
Hanyo 1960 (*The Housemaid*)
Yangsan do 1955 (*Yangsan Island*)
Jukeomiui sangja 1955 (*Box of Death*)

"He was truly an independent filmmaker."
—Bong Joon Ho

Korean director Ki-young Kim has been called "The Master of Madness;" he has been compared to both Alfred Hitchcock and Roger Corman; he specialized in oversexed melodramas that leaned heavily on the tawdriest tricks of 1970s art theater fare; and he is one of the most important and influential figures of South Korean cinema.

Although contemporary South Korean cinema is arguably the best and most vibrant in the world today, back in the 1970s, when Kim was at the top of his game, the rest of Korean cinema was underfunded and primitive, crushed under the heel of repressive censorship by a military dictatorship. And that is exactly the point. At a time when South Korea could barely force its own citizens to sit through homegrown fare, here was a fellow who could make delirious genre pictures that made profits, drew crowds, expressed a unique personal vision, and inspired future generations of filmmakers.

Kim worked in a poverty-stricken ghetto of commercial genre flicks, but stretched their limits, imprinting a distinctive and wacky personal vision. From his first feature in 1955 to his last in 1995, Kim blended rape fantasies, horrific imagery, and idiosyncratic and unpredictable approaches to filmmaking. Kim's film *Hanyo* (1960) (*The Housemaid*), about a married man who has an affair with his housemaid, is looked on as a classic that provides a peephole into contemporary Korean society. In 1997, a retrospective of Kim's work brought him newfound attention and renewed respect. At the age of seventy-eight, he started to plan a new movie. Sadly, it was never to be made. Shortly before he was to be celebrated at the 1998 Berlin International Film Festival, he died in a house fire. **DK**

FEDERICO FELLINI

Born: Federico Fellini, January 20, 1920 (Rimini, Emilia-Romagna, Italy); died 1993 (Rome, Italy).

Directing style: Maestro of Italian cinema; wild color and fantastical costumes; dreamlike imagery in ordinary situations; collaboration with Giulietta Masina.

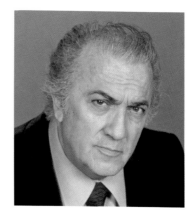

Federico Fellini's critical reputation has fluctuated over the years: acknowledged internationally in the 1960s as one of the great masters, his work has more recently come under attack for being oversentimental, insufficiently critical, too whimsical, lacking in political engagement, too pretty visually, and, one strongly suspects, more entertaining than the work of a serious artist has any business being. The qualities in Fellini's work that once seemed daring and new—the celebration of misfits and outcasts, the lurches from realism into fantasy and back again, and the presentation of decadence and criminality without condemnation—tend now to be overshadowed by those that once seemed reassuringly traditional: the commitment to narrative and characterization, the communication of emotion, the underlying optimism, and the love of showbiz and artifice.

Fellini entered the film industry in the early 1940s as a writer and occasional actor. His early films as director gave notice of his preoccupations, but what now seems the instantly identifiable Fellini style was perfected in three consecutive masterpieces, *La strada* (1954) (*The Road*), the lesser known *Il*

Top Takes...

La tivù de Fellini 2003
La voca della luna 1990 (*The Voice of the Moon*)
Intervista 1987
Ginger and Fred 1986
E la vave va 1983 (*And the Ship Sails On*)
La città delle donne 1980 (*City of Woman*)
Prova d'orchestra 1978 (*Orchestra Rehearsal*)
Il Casanova di Federico Fellini 1976
  (*Fellini's Casanova*)
Amarcord 1973 ☆
Roma 1972
I Clowns 1971 (*The Clowns*)
Fellini—Satyricon 1969 ☆
Giulietta degli spiriti 1965 (*Juliet of the Spirits*)
8½ 1963 ☆
Boccaccio '70 1962
La dolce vita 1960 ☆
Le notti di Cabiria 1957 (*Nights of Cabiria*)
Il bidone 1955
La strada 1954 (*The Road*)
L'amore in città 1953 (*Love in the City*)
I Vitelloni 1953
Lo sceicco bianco 1952 (*The White Sheik*)
Luci del varietà 1950 (*Variety Lights*)

LEFT: Fellini's wife, Giulietta Masina,
stars in his masterpiece *Nights of Cabiria*.

1920s

Maestro and Muse

Federico Fellini's wife Giulietta Masina starred in three of his masterpieces—*The Road* (1954), *Il bidone* (1955), and *Nights of Cabiria* (1957).

- Giulia Anna (Giulietta) Masina was born on February 22, 1921. Her father was a violinist and her mother a schoolteacher.
- Masina and Federico Fellini married in October 1943.
- A few months after the marriage, Masina suffered a miscarriage after falling down some stairs. This loss was followed in 1945 by the death of their baby son Pierfederico when he was just one month old.
- These tragedies, along with his dreams and other life experiences, formed the raw material of Fellini's films.
- Another influence on Fellini's work was his discovery of the work of Carl Jung, whose ideas about the collective unconscious and archetypes Fellini explored in later films, such as *Giulietta degli spiriti* (1965) (*Juliet of the Spirits*). In this film, the protagonist (played by Giulietta Masina) explores her subconscious as well as the odd lifestyle of her neighbor.
- In 1957 Masina won the Best Actress Award at the Cannes Film Festival for her role in *Nights of Cabiria*.
- Masina died in 1994, just months after her husband's death.

bidone (1955), and *Le notti di Cabiria* (1957) (*Nights of Cabiria*), perhaps his best film of all. All three feature his wife, actress Giulietta Masina, who was half Doris Day, half Harpo Marx. Strange yet completely accessible, these films are visually imaginative and richly textured, combining uncompromising eccentricity with an engaging simplicity and generosity of spirit.

Finding international recognition

The scenarios are depressing. The first has Masina as a simple-minded young girl sold by her mother to a traveling strongman played by Anthony Quinn; he mistreats and rejects her, realizing her true worth only when she dies. The second is the picaresque story of a band of traveling con men, disguised as priests, who rob the poor. Masina was wasted in a subsidiary housewife role. The third returns Masina triumphantly to center stage as a naive prostitute, whose dreams of love and happiness are constantly met with sorrow and bad luck.

Fellini's handling elevates these films from mundane realism almost to the level of fairy tale, aided in every case by beautiful use of locations, stylized composition, a rich, often grotesque, gallery of supporting players, Nino Rota's hauntingly distinctive scores, and Masina's amazing performances. Their dramatic climaxes—Quinn's enigmatic moment of anguished realization on a darkened beach in *The Road*; Masina stoically walking in step with a band of strolling musicians after yet another crushing betrayal in *Nights of Cabiria*—transcend their immediate pessimism to become deeply moving, cathartic experiences for the audience, more epiphany than tragedy.

La dolce vita (1960), which both confirmed and consolidated Fellini's international reputation, is glossy, stylish, and still relevant in its skepticism toward a society proudly cutting itself loose from its core values. Its pose of total objectivity remains its most striking feature, along with its now iconic visual highlights such as the massive Christ being airlifted over Brazil. But there is a brazen self-assurance that was new for the director, a kind of methodological shorthand that seems to suggest Fellini knew he was now established and could afford

ABOVE: Anita Ekberg is memorable in *La dolce vita*, arguably Fellini's best-known film.

to play the maestro, showier and less rigorous. With *8½* (1963), his gaze turned inward and, despite the usual mastery of style, there is a sense of self-indulgence in its attempt to turn director's block into existential crisis. Both are important works, full of good things, but they lack the emotional resonance of Fellini's less autobiographical movies.

It could be argued that Fellini's keen sense of himself as auteur got the better of him after 1963: *Fellini—Satyricon* (1969) and *Il Casanova di Federico Fellini* (1976) (*Fellini's Casanova*) are certainly as hubristic as they sound. His later pictures are all worth watching, but only *Amarcord* (1973) is really essential viewing. Fellini wears his heart on his sleeve and is never afraid to be deemed naive, but he was never better than in the three works made immediately prior to *La dolce vita*. **MC**

"All art is autobiographical. The pearl is the oyster's autobiography."

1920s

ERIC ROHMER

Born: Jean-Marie Maurice Schérer, April 4, 1920 (Nancy, Meurthe-et-Moselle, Lorraine, France).

Directing style: French art theater director; themes of sensitive characters dealing with everyday life; innovator of film-cycle concept; long shots; slow pace.

Top Takes...

> "I'm not very operational in life."
>
> —Delphine, *Summer*

Former editor of the influential French film magazine *Cahiers du cinéma,* prolific film director, and still active in his eighties, Eric Rohmer is best known for his breakthrough feature *Ma nuit chez Maud* (1969) (*My Night at Maud's*), and most loved for *Le rayon vert* (1986) (*Summer*). His movies produce enamored fans and irritated detractors, but nothing in between.

Rohmer's films are often criticized as being "uncinematic," meaning they are more akin to filmed stage plays, the action confined to very few locations and occurring in a short period of time when nothing much seems to happen. The average shot length in Rohmer's films is significantly longer than those of contemporary Hollywood. This doesn't make Rohmer's movies uncinematic, however. When directing, Rohmer maintains a talking distance from his actors that lends his scenes an intimacy not achievable in conventional stage productions. His long takes keep key episodes in the story world synchronized with the actual time it would take for them to occur. The problems driving his narratives forward are typically the most mundane kinds of issues that people encounter in their daily lives. With deep sympathy for his exceptionally sensitive characters, his films allow the audience to view the maturation of the protagonist, and the unfolding of a person's fundamental nature. Most of Rohmer's best films fall within one of three thematically grouped series of four to six pictures forming cycles: *Six contes moraux* (*Six Moral Tales*), *Comédies et proverbes* (*Comedies and Proverbs*), and *Contes des quatre saisons* (*Tales of Four Seasons*). In addition to *My Night at Maud's* and *Summer*, no one interested in Rohmer's work should miss *Les nuits de la pleine lune* (1984) (*Full Moon in Paris*) or *Conte d'automne* (1998) (*Autumn Tale*). **AS**

FRANKLIN J. SCHAFFNER

Born: Franklin James Schaffner, May 30, 1920 (Tokyo, Japan); died 1989 (Santa Monica, California, U.S.).

Directing style: Innovative director of U.S. network live TV and movies; dynamic camerawork; moves between intimate dramas and epic-scale blockbusters.

Born the son of U.S. missionaries, Franklin J. Schaffner grew up in Japan. He first made his name in live TV, directing *Twelve Angry Men* (1954), *The Great Gatsby* (1958), and *The Legend of Lylah Clare* (1963). He also directed *Cry Vengeance!* (1961), one of the first TV movies, and the highly rated special *Tour of the White House* (1962). *The Stripper* (1963) and *The Best Man* (1964), his first features, were theatrical adaptations, intensely acted but not far removed from his TV work.

Schaffner established himself as a man of the cinema in partnership with Charlton Heston—whom he had directed as Macbeth on *Studio One*—bringing physicality and a sense of landscape to the revisionist medieval picture *The War Lord* (1965) and the science-fiction satire *Planet of the Apes* (1968). Both have a great deal of convincing action, but are as full of ideas and personal conflict as any live TV drama of the 1950s. Along with the Yul Brynner spy picture *The Double Man* (1967), these films established Schaffner as an A-lister, and he helmed three mammoth Oscar-bid productions in succession: *Patton* (1970), *Nicholas and Alexandra* (1971), and *Papillon* (1973).

Thereafter, Schaffner seemed to falter with an undercooked adaptation of an Ernest Hemingway story, *Islands in the Stream* (1977), which reunited him with *Patton* star George C. Scott, followed by the entertaining, wicked, and stylish *The Boys From Brazil* (1978). But then came three disastrous flops: *Sphinx* (1981), *Yes, Giorgio* (1982), and *Lionheart* (1987). *Welcome Home* (1989), Schaffner's last movie, was a return to his roots, a TV-style small-scale drama about a U.S. soldier, played by Kris Kristofferson, who was thought to have been killed in the Vietnam War but who then shows up alive nearly two decades later. **KN**

Top Takes...

Welcome Home 1989
The Boys From Brazil 1978
Islands in the Stream 1977
Papillon 1973
Nicholas and Alexandra 1971
***Patton* 1970 ★**
Planet of the Apes 1968
The Double Man 1967
The War Lord 1965
The Best Man 1964
The Stripper 1963

1920s

"... no bastard ever won a war by dying for his country."
—General George S. Patton, *Patton*

JACK CLAYTON

Born: Jack Clayton, March 1, 1921 (Brighton, East Sussex, England); died 1995 (Slough, Berkshire, England).

Directing style: British maker of early kitchen-sink dramas dealing with class differences; later lavish literary adaptations; attention to visual detail.

Jack Clayton's 1959 adaptation of John Braine's popular novel *Room at the Top* ushered in a new age of British filmmaking, dramatizing for the first time the issues of social class, personal authenticity, and upward mobility. The film reflects a restricted middlebrow sensibility that tends to reduce those of the upper and lower orders to one-dimensional types: the submissive, heart-of-gold proles, and the self-concerned and heedlessly patronizing former Royal Air Force pilot. And yet Clayton otherwise fills the screen with interestingly realized and realistically portrayed relationships, particularly the doomed romance between the young man on his way to the top and the older married woman who, in true D. H. Lawrence fashion, introduces him to sexual joy, yet must be brutally discarded so that he can make the right marriage.

The Pumpkin Eater (1964), likewise, focuses on sexual dissatisfaction and gender politics but avoids the unconvincing stereotypes of the earlier production—Harold Pinter wrote the screenplay in a fruitful collaboration with the director. Perhaps Britain's finest contribution to the international art theater cinema of the era, the film features finely tuned, complex performances from Anne Bancroft, James Mason, Peter Finch, and Maggie Smith. Apart from these two noteworthy films, Clayton's career proved a distinct disappointment. An adaptation of *The Turn of the Screw* ghost story, *The Innocents* (1961), is a beautifully mounted but strangely unengaging bit of Jamesiana. Clayton's big-budget version of *The Great Gatsby* (1974) surprisingly struggles in its attempt to portray the gender politics and class divisions so brilliantly anatomized in F. Scott Fitzgerald's novel, running afoul of its glamorous sets, costumes, and star-vehicle status. **BP**

> "... a superb job in directing an excitingly effective cast."
>
> —On *Room at the Top, New York Times*

SATYAJIT RAY

Born: Satyajit Ray, May 2, 1921 (Calcutta, West Bengal, India); died 1992 (Calcutta, West Bengal, India).

Directing style: Prolific filmmaker of features, documentaries, and short stories; themes exploring struggle between traditional and modern values in Indian life.

In 1956, the Cannes Film Festival screening of Satyajit Ray's debut film, *Pather Panchali* (1955) (*Song of the Road*), created a sensation similar to that of Kurosawa's *Rashômon* (1950) (*In the Woods*) in Venice five years earlier. Once again the eyes of the world were opened to a national cinema that had previously been ignored or dismissed, and once again an unknown director found himself acclaimed. Ironic, as Ray had struggled to make the film without support and that the Indian government had been reluctant to have it shown abroad, lest it give an adverse impression of modern India. Yet with *Song of the Road's* release, for the first time, Indian cinema was taken seriously.

Born into a cultured Bengali family, Ray set out to make films utterly unlike the sprawling, formulaic productions of what would become known as "Bollywood." His inspiration was predominantly European, but he brought to his work qualities that were wholly his own. Trained as an artist and self-taught as a composer, his artist's eye and his composer's sense of rhythm lend grace to his films, while his warm, watchful compassion embraces all his characters, good or bad.

Top Takes...

Agantuk 1991 (*The Visitor*)
Shakha Proshakha 1990
  (*The Branches of the Tree*)
Ganashatru 1989 (*An Enemy of the People*)
Sukumar Ray 1987
Ghare-Baire 1984 (*The Home and the World*)
Heerak Rajar Deshe 1980
  (*The Kingdom of Diamonds*)
Joi Baba Felunath 1978 (*The Elephant God*)
Shatranj Ke Khilari 1977 (*The Chess Players*)
Jana Aranya 1976 (*The Masses' Music*)
Bala 1976
Sonar Kella 1974 (*The Golden Fortress*)
Ashani Sanket 1973 (*Distant Thunder*)
Pratidwandi 1972 (*Siddharta and the City*)
Aranyer Din Ratri 1970
  (*Days and Nights in the Forest*)
Goopy Gyne Bagha Byne 1968
  (*The Adventures of Goopy and Bagha*)
Charulata 1964 (*The Lonely Wife*)
Mahanagar 1963 (*The Big City*)
Kanchanjungha 1962
Apur Sansar 1959 (*The World of Apu*)
Jalsaghar 1958 (*The Music Room*)
Aparajito 1956 (*The Unvanquished*)
Pather Panchali 1955 (*Song of the Road*)

LEFT: A scene from *Song of the Road*, part of Satyajit Ray's "Apu Trilogy."

1920s

An Indelible Influence

Satyajit Ray is regarded as one of the most important movie directors of the twentieth century. In 1991 he was given an Honorary Academy Award "in recognition of his rare mastery of the art of motion pictures, and of his profound humanitarian outlook, which has had an indelible influence on filmmakers and audiences throughout the world."

- Ray's first film, *Song of the Road* (1955), won an award at the Cannes Film Festival for Best Human Document, and a Bodil award for Best Non-European Film. The film was also nominated for a BAFTA Best Film award, and for a Golden Palm award at Cannes.
- *Song of the Road*, together with *The Unvanquished* and *The World of Apu*, form Ray's renowned "Apu trilogy."
- Ray's father, Sukumar Ray, was an important poet and writer on the history of Bengali literature.
- Ray studied science and economics at college. He became interested in filmmaking after meeting the French filmmaker Jean Renoir, and seeing the Italian neorealist film *Bicycle Thieves* (1948), directed by Vittorio De Sica.
- Ray directed 37 films, including features, shorts, and documentaries.
- As well as directing movies, Ray was involved in scripting, scoring, casting, and designing publicity material.

1920s

With *Song of the Road*, Ray captured Bengali village life in lyrical detail, demonstrating a poetic sense of the rhythms and happenings of nature. The film traces the childhood of Apu, the son of a poor Brahmin; the successive films *Aparajito* (1956) (*The Unvanquished*) and *Apur Sansar* (1959) (*The World of Apu*) follow Apu through to manhood. This trio remains among Ray's best-known and best-loved works.

Ray would return again to village life in the much tougher, more political *Ashani Sanket* (1973) (*Distant Thunder*). But most of his films are set in his native city of Calcutta, whose teeming chaos he regards with a mixture of dismay and rueful humor. His view of the city steadily darkened. In *Mahanagar* (1963) (*The Big City*), a married woman discovers, to her surprise and delight, that she can hold down a responsible job. By the 1970s the hero of *Pratidwandi* (1972) (*Siddharta and the City*) can get no job at all, and in *Jana Aranya* (1976) (*The Masses' Music*), a richly Dickensian satire, an eager-to-please young man imperceptibly slips from cheating, to bribery, to pimping.

A lighter touch

At other times the humor of Ray's films is light, subtle, and often playful. In *Aranyer Din Ratri* (1970) (*Days and Nights in the Forest*), four young urban men take a vacation in the forests of Bihar; Ray observes the resulting culture clash with an ironic eye. *Charulata* (1964) (*The Lonely Wife*), adapted from a novel by Ray's teacher, Rabindranath Tagore, and his own favorite film, brings humor and a delicate sensuality to bear on the tale of a neglected married woman who finds herself drawn to her cousin.

Like his father and grandfather, Ray delighted in writing and illustrating for children. He revived the children's magazine they published, *Sandesh*, and directed a number of children's films, including *Goopy Gyne Bagha Byne* (1968) (*The Adventures of Goopy and Bagha*) and *Sonar Kella* (1974) (*The Golden Fortress*).

Ray's films were generally more highly regarded abroad than in his native country, where they received only limited distribution. This was partly because he shunned the crowd-pleasing conventions of Bollywood, but also because he filmed

in the minority language of Bengali, and refused to have his films dubbed into Hindi or other Indian languages. His only Hindi-language film was *Shatranj Ke Khilari* (1977) (*The Chess Players*). It did poorly at the box office, thanks partly to spoiling tactics by the powerful Bombay studios. But if any mainstream filmmaker can claim to be a true auteur, it is Satyajit Ray. He scripted, cast, directed, and produced all his movies, as well as designing the publicity posters and, from *Kanchanjungha* (1962) onward, composing his own scores. And beginning with *The Big City*, he took to operating his own camera.

ABOVE: *The Chess Players* was the director's only Hindi-language film.

"Whatever God does is for the best."

—Harihar Ray, *Song of the Road*

The sizable body of his work—nearly 40 movies—bears his unmistakably personal stamp. At their best they move to their own inner rhythm, individual and satisfying, full of warmth, humor, and a constant sense of intrigued discovery. **PK**

1920s

LUIS GARCÍA BERLANGA

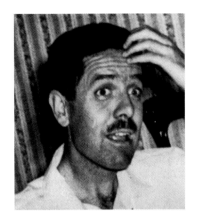

Born: Luis García Berlanga Martí, June 12, 1921 (Valencia, Spain).

Directing style: Courageous Spanish director; often chooses political themes that humorously attack the State; sophisticated visual style; use of long takes and sequence shots.

Top Takes...

Paris Tombuctú 1999 (*Paris Timbuktu*)

Nacional III 1982

Patrimonio nacional 1981 (*National Heritage*)

La ecopeta nacional 1978
(*The National Shotgun*)

Grandeur nature 1974 (*Life Size*)

¡Vivan los novios! 1970
(*Long Live the Bride and Groom*)

El verdugo 1963 (*Not on Your Life*)

Plácido 1961

Los jueves, milagro 1957 (*Miracles of Thursday*)

Calabuch 1956

Novio a la vista 1954 (*Boyfriend in Sight*)

Esa pareja feliz 1953 (*That Happy Couple*)

Bienvenido Mister Marshall 1953
(*Welcome Mr. Marshall*)

Luis García Berlanga has been widely acclaimed as one of the masters of Spanish cinema. Born in 1921, he came to international prominence with the release of his first solo directorial effort, *Bienvenido Mister Marshall* (1953) (*Welcome Mr. Marshall*). A satirical take on the mores of Franco's Spain, and in particular the attempts to take that nation back into the international arena, the film won the International Prize and a Special Mention at the Cannes Film Festival, and was nominated for the Grand Prize of the Festival. At about the same time, Berlanga worked with another important Spanish director of the period, Juan Antonio Bardem, codirecting the light comedy *Esa pareja feliz* (1953) (*That Happy Couple*).

Although he might still be best known outside Spain for *Welcome Mr. Marshall*, Berlanga's best films were made in the early 1960s, when he forged the most significant creative partnership of his career with the screenwriter Rafael Azcona. Together they collaborated on *Plácido* (1961) and *El verdugo* (1963) (*Not on Your Life*), a pair of darkly humorous films that attacked the corrupt morality of the Spanish state. The latter film was to prove especially troublesome for the Spanish authorities, and for the next four years Berlanga found it difficult to get any projects off the ground. Once the Franco era ended in 1975 Berlanga was able to work freely once again. He made a series of farces that attacked the old-style authority figures who remained in power during, and indeed after, the transition to democracy.

Following the release of *Paris Tombuctú* (1999) (*Paris Timbuktu*), Berlanga announced his retirement from filmmaking, bringing down the curtain on one of the most unique and undervalued filmographies in postwar European cinema. **AW**

> "[Berlanga] never lost his acerbic eye for the ridiculous aspects of power."—Steven Marsh, *Senses of Cinema*

CHRIS MARKER

Born: Christian François Bouche-Villeneuve, July 29, 1921 (Neuilly-sur-Seine, Hauts-de-Seine, Île-de-France, France).

Directing style: Elusive avant-garde filmmaker; stunning use of still photography; mix of montage and documentary footage; innovator of the cinematic essay.

French avant-garde filmmaker, multimedia manipulator, and cinematic essayist, Chris Marker can best be described as an enigma, flickering between fact and fiction. Shunning the cult of the celebrity moviemaker, he has tended, on the whole, to stay out of the limelight, allowing his phenomenal work as a director to speak for itself. Marker has worked on a huge variety of projects in different media, from his first film *Olympia 52* (1952) to *Chat perchés* (2004) (*The Case of the Grinning Cat*), which combines politics with bizarre feline images.

His short *La Jetée* (1962) (*The Pier*), has become a cause célèbre among cinephiles, and it can be noted as Marker's most infamous contribution to the history books and annals of film. Inspiring generations of moviemakers, not to mention Terry Gilliam's big-budget fantasy *12 Monkeys* (1995), *The Pier* does something so bold, so simple, and yet so powerful that it rightly deserves its classic status. A science-fiction parable, it is told through a succession of still images rather than moving pictures, with the exception of one moment where what is assumed to be another still flutters eerily to life.

The magic of cinema, with its creation of lifelike movements from projected film cells, is usually taken for granted by audiences. Yet Marker restores a sense of wonder along with a visceral and intellectual impact to the slightest of onscreen movements. This is film reduced to its barest essence, and the director's role boiled down to a fundamental choice—just how should moving pictures move?

Marker's achievements as a filmmaker are many and varied, but thanks to the fascinating brilliance of *The Pier*, his work will never lie completely frozen in the past, but continue to live on as cinematic inspiration. **MH**

Top Takes...

Chat perchés 2004
   (*The Case of the Grinning Cat*)
Le souvenir d'un avenir 2001
   (*Remembrance of Things to Come*)
Level Five 1997
Le tombeau d'Alexandre 1992
   (*The Last Bolshevik*)
Sans soleil 1983
Le fond de l'air est rouge 1977
   (*Grin Without a Cat*)
Vive le baleine 1972
Le train en marche 1971 (*The Train Rolls On*)
Loin du Vietnam 1967 (*Far from Vietnam*)
La Jetée 1962 (*The Pier*)
Lettre de Sibéria 1957 (*Letter from Siberia*)
Olympia 52 1952

"The Pier is one of the strangest movies ever conceived ...."
—Jaime N. Christley, *Senses of Cinema*

1920s

MIKLÓS JANCSÓ

Born: Miklós Jancsó, September 29, 1921 (Vac, Hungary).

Directing style: Hungarian modernist director; master of the long take; use of widescreen and lateral tracking shots to create geometrical arrangements; often political and historical themes.

Top Takes…

" . . . a harrowing portrait of spiritual desolation . . . ."

—Strictly Film School, on The Round-Up

In contrast to other masters of the long take, Hungary's greatest modernist director, Miklós Jancsó, is not so much interested in the mimetic potential of this stylistic device as concerned with the possibilities of artificially constructed scenes, which means that naturalism is replaced in favor of ideology as in *Még kér a nép* (1972) (*Red Psalm*), politics as in *Fényes szelek* (1969) (*The Confrontation*), and mythology as in *Szerelmem, Elektra* (1974) (*Electra, My Love*). In Jancsó's mise-en-scène, narrative progress is primarily realized through spatial organization, and time is experienced not as flow, but as duration. He tends to put people and things in geometrical arrangements, with specific placement of lines and columns in order to achieve abstract systematization and an understanding of the aftermath of crucial historic periods. For Jancsó, man is some kind of sculpture in a landscape of chaotic circumstances. The audience can sense the personal tragedy of the characters, but what is more important for Jancsó is the contemplative depiction of mechanisms of history and power.

From the humanistic *Így jöttem* (1965) (*My Way Home*) to the highly ritualized *Electra, My Love*, Jancsó investigates different methods of repression and oppression. Jancsó treats this major theme most coherently in his most famous work, *Szegénylegények* (1966) (*The Round-Up*). In the gloomy ambience of a prison for participants of the failed 1848 revolution, he builds up a harrowing account of the oppression destroying man's body and soul. However, Jancsó's most aberrant film, *Vizi privati, pubbliche virtù* (1975) (*Private Vices, Public Pleasures*), shows with lascivious humor the flip side of the same coin: this time oppression is transformed into emancipation, a movement that turns politics into pornography. **AB**

1920s

ANDRZEJ MUNK

Born: Andrzej Munk, October 16, 1921 (Kraków, Poland); died 1961 (Łódź, Poland).

Directing style: Nonconformist Polish director of dark tragicomedies and dramas—often with political and historical themes; visual gags; use of flashback narrative.

When Andrzej Munk died in a car crash while returning from filming at the site of the Auschwitz concentration camp in Poland, he left a small but stunning cinematic legacy. The movie he was making, *Pasazerka* (1963) (*Passenger*) was reconstructed from the footage he had shot and became a fitting epitaph to one of Poland's most influential directors.

Munk was born in Kraków in 1921. He moved to Warsaw during the Nazi occupation, where his Jewish heritage forced him undercover. Using a false name, he worked as a construction worker, and took part in the Warsaw Uprising in 1944. One of the few to survive, he resumed studies after the war, first in architecture and then at law school, where he became general secretary of the student socialist organization, before attending the Łódź Film School. He made several shorts before being drummed out of the Polish Communist Party in 1952 for "blameworthy behavior."

Munk's nonconformist skepticism would inform his four features, beginning with the milestone *Czlowiek na torze* (1957) (*Man on the Tracks*), a bleak mystery told in reverse and one of the first films of the so-called "Polish Film School." *Eroica* (1958) (*Heroism*) featured two wartime stories dealing with concepts of duty and courage, whereas the tragicomedy *Zezowate szczescie* (1960) (*Bad Luck*) followed the mixed fortunes of a Polish everyman cursed by fate. In 1961, Munk, aged thirty-nine, was killed in a car accident near Łódź. His final, uncompleted film, in which the central character recounts two versions of her past, was finally put together in 1963. It provides a compelling if fragmentary illustration of the reason Munk was such an influence on his cinematic heirs, including Roman Polanski and Jerzy Skolimowski. **TE**

Top Takes…

Pasazerka 1963 (*Passenger*)
Zezowate szczescie 1960 (*Bad Luck*)
Polska kronika filmowa nr 52 A-B 1959
Eroica 1958 (*Heroism*)
Spacerek staromiejski 1958
   (*A Walk in the Old City of Warsaw*)
Czlowiek na torze 1957 (*Man on the Tracks*)
Blekitny krzyz 1955 (*Men of Blue Cross*)
Niedzielny poranek 1955 (*Sunday Morning*)
Gwiazdy musza plonac 1954
Kolejarskie slowo 1953 (*A Railwayman's World*)
Parnietniki chlopów 1952
Poermat symfoniczny Banka St. Moniuski 1952
Nauka blizej zycia 1951
Kierunek—Howa Huta 1951
Zaczelo sie w Hiszpanii 1950 (*It Began in Spain*)

"… remarkable for its grimness and its ambivalence."
—Chris Fujiwara, on *Man on the Tracks*

1920s

GEORGE ROY HILL

Born: George Roy Hill, December 20, 1921 (Minneapolis, Minnesota, U.S.); died 2002 (New York City, New York, U.S.).

Directing style: Maker of entertaining, feel-good Hollywood dramas with a comic touch; successful teamings with actors Robert Redford and Paul Newman.

Top Takes...

Funny Farm 1988
The Little Drummer Girl 1984
The World According to Garp 1982
A Little Romance 1979
Slap Shot 1977
The Great Waldo Pepper 1975
The Sting 1973 ★
Slaughterhouse-Five 1972
Butch Cassidy and the Sundance Kid 1969 ☆
Thoroughly Modern Millie 1967
Hawaii 1966
The World of Henry Orient 1964
Toys in the Attic 1963
Period of Adjustment 1962

Hill is one of the directors who emerged in the 1950s from the medium of TV drama. He directed for prestigious anthology series, such as *Kraft Television Theatre* (1956), then made his big-screen debut with *Period of Adjustment* (1962), an uncharacteristically lightweight Tennessee Williams project. He continued in the same quirky yet literary, serious but comic vein with Lillian Hellman's *Toys in the Attic* (1963) and the Peter Sellers vehicle *The World of Henry Orient* (1964), before he stepped up to the big-budget productions *Hawaii* (1966) and *Thoroughly Modern Millie* (1967).

Hill's first major success came with *Butch Cassidy and the Sundance Kid* (1969). This misty-eyed Western applies the look of a hairspray commercial to the subject matter of a Sam Peckinpah movie, presenting handsome pinups Robert Redford and Paul Newman as epitomes of the doomed outlaw life. The clout Hill acquired with this international hit, renewed in an even cannier teaming of the stars on the entertaining caper *The Sting* (1973), enabled him to command large budgets for more offbeat projects: Kurt Vonnegut's *Slaughterhouse-Five* (1972); the Redford-starring barnstorming aviation drama *The Great Waldo Pepper* (1975); the Newman-starring hockey picture *Slap Shot* (1977); the simple love story *A Little Romance* (1979) from his own script; and an adaptation of John Irving's *The World According to Garp* (1982). Hill could moderate his soft-focus style to produce grit, but there was always a sense he was straining hard with material that would have come easier for Michael Ritchie, Robert Altman, or the early Steven Spielberg. Before retirement, he managed a John le Carré adaptation, *The Little Drummer Girl* (1984), and a Chevy Chase vehicle, *Funny Farm* (1988). **KN**

> "Think ya used enough dynamite there, Butch?"
>
> —*Butch Cassidy and the Sundance Kid*

PIER PAOLO PASOLINI

Born: Pier Paolo Pasolini, March 5, 1922 (Bologna, Emilia-Romagna, Italy); died 1975 (Ostia, Latium, Italy).

Directing style: Italian director whose work embodies and exemplifies the contest between good and evil in the modern world; disturbing and provocative.

The tragic figure of Pier Paolo Pasolini continues to inspire a new generation of filmmakers, even though his violent death prevented his career from reaching its full zenith. His first film, *Accatone* (1961), caused a sensation for its frank depiction of the seamy underside of Roman society. *Mamma Roma* (1962) starred Anna Magnani as a woman who dreams of rising out of the squalor of prostitution to create a better life for herself. His real breakthrough, however, was with *Il vangelo secondo Matteo* (1964) (*The Gospel According to St. Matthew*), one of the most unconventional religious films ever made—a documentary black and white vision of the life of Christ that was all the more remarkable because of Pasolini's atheism and Marxist beliefs.

Later films, such as *Il Decameron* (1971) (*The Decameron*) and *I racconti di Canterbury* (1972) (*The Canterbury Tales*), are relatively lavish historical pageants, but Pasolini retained his desire to shock and disturb his audiences with socialist parables such as *Teorema* (1968) (*Theorem*), a study of the disintegration of a bourgeois Italian household. That Pasolini was moving away from the optimism of *The Gospel According to St. Matthew* became readily apparent with the production of what was to be his final film, *Salò o le 120 giornate di Sodoma* (1975) (*Salo, or the 120 Days of Sodom*), based on the novel by the Marquis de Sade. It presents a catalog of cruelty and sadism, both deeply disturbing and resolutely lacking in hope.

In 1975, Pasolini was murdered in suspicious circumstances that may have been related to his homosexuality. He had never denied his sexual orientation, nor shied away from depicting the darker side of life in his films; but viewed as a whole, one can see the journey of a man who sought to encompass the whole of human experience in his films. **WWD**

Top Takes…

Salò o le 120 giornate de Sodoma 1975
Il fiore delle mille e una notte 1974
  (*Arabian Nights*)
I racconti di Canterbury 1972
  (*The Canterbury Tales*)
Il Decameron 1971 (*The Decameron*)
Medea 1970 (*Medea*)
Porcile 1969 (*Pigpen*)
Amore e rabbia 1969
Teorema 1968 (*Theorem*)
Capriccio all'italiana 1968
Edipo re 1967 (*Oedipus Rex*)
Le streghe 1967 (*The Witches*)
Il vangelo secondo Matteo 1964
  (*The Gospel According to St. Matthew*)
Mamma Roma 1962
Accatone 1961

"I may be an unbeliever, but I am an unbeliever who has a nostalgia for a belief."

RUSS MEYER

Born: Russell Albion Meyer, March 21, 1922 (Oakland, California, U.S.); died 2004 (Hollywood Hills, California, U.S.).

Directing style: "King Leer"; X-rated soft-core pornography; large-breasted women; camp comedy; exploitative violence; voice-over narration; montage sequences.

Top Takes…

During World War II, Russ Meyer worked for the U.S. army as a combat cameraman in Europe where he developed a penchant for unusual photographic framing. Upon returning to the United States, he was able to combine this passion with a lifelong obsession with enormous breasts, gaining work as a *Playboy* magazine photographer. He kick-started his filmmaking career with *The Immoral Mr. Teas* (1959), a nudie-cutie film responsible for many Americans' first-ever glimpse of a naked woman onscreen. The financial success of this charming movie enabled Meyer to self-finance his next projects, including *Lorna* (1964), *Mudhoney* (1965), *Faster, Pussycat! Kill! Kill!* (1965), and *Motor Psycho* (1965). These four films, shot in black and white, established Meyer's surreal style, which blends camp comedy with exploitative violence, and where action is often propelled by Amazonian, highly sexualized female characters.

As a director, Meyer was technically innovative. His use of nondiegetic inserts, montage sequences, and voice-over narration are stylistic tropes that can be traced from his debut through his entire body of work. Self-financed and profiting from almost all of his pictures, the director retained a high level of control over each project. Meyer's films oscillated between exploitation and Hollywood modes of production, and this middle ground became spectacularly confused when Twentieth Century Fox produced and released *Beyond the Valley of the Dolls* (1970), a rock 'n' roll horror movie that remains his most well-known work. Meyer continued to produce his own brand of soft-core pornography well into the 1970s, but he was increasingly disillusioned with the hard-core direction the genre had taken. **AK**

> "I guess liquor's considered pretty square."
>
> —Susan, *Beyond the Valley of the Dolls*

JUAN ANTONIO BARDEM

Born: Juan Antonio Bardem Muñoz, June 2, 1922 (Madrid, Spain); died 2002 (Madrid, Spain).

Directing style: Antifascist Spanish director; work frequently censored; stylish critiques of contemporary Spanish society; Italian neorealism influence; fast pace.

Juan Antonio Bardem began his career as coscriptwriter on the landmark film *Bienvenido Mister Marshall* (1952) (*Welcome Mr. Marshall*). He was then credited as a codirector, with Luis García Berlanga, on the light comedy *Esa pareja feliz* (1953) (*That Happy Couple*). But despite these comic origins, the films that made his reputation were more renowned for their translation of neorealist aesthetics into Spanish cinema. *Muerte de un ciclista* (1955) (*Age of Infidelity*) and *Calle Mayor* (1956) (*The Lovemaker*) established Bardem as one of the most prominent Spanish directors of the 1950s. However, his membership in the banned Communist Party during this period led to a number of arrests and, as the 1960s progressed and the "New Spanish Cinema" of Carlos Saura and others emerged, his position within Spanish film culture became more marginalized. By the mid-1960s Bardem had turned to more commercial, international projects such as *Los pianos mecánicos* (1965) (*The Uninhibited*), which starred Hardy Krüger and James Mason.

The early 1970s saw Bardem shift increasingly to genre pieces such as the war movie *El último día de la guerra* (1970) (*The Last Day of the War*) and the fantasy *La isla misteriosa y el capitán Nemo* (1973) (*The Mysterious Island*). Although each of these contained allegorical moments that alluded to the political oppression in Spain, none of them were convincingly the work of a politically motivated artist.

With the death of Franco in 1975, Bardem was once again able to turn toward more politically charged subjects. This new freedom allowed him to complete such works as *Siete días de enero* (1979) (*Seven Days in January*), about the 1977 Massacre of Atocha, and *Die Mahnung* (1982) (*The Warning*), concerning the Bulgarian revolutionary Georgi Dimitrov. **AW**

Top Takes...

Die Mahnung 1982 (*The Warning*)
Siete días de enero 1979
   (*Seven Days in January*)
El Puente 1977 (*Foul Play*)
La corrupción de Chris Miller 1973
   (*The Corruption of Chris Miller*)
La isla misteriosa y el capitán Nemo 1973
   (*The Mysterious Island*)
Variétes 1971 (*Varieties*)
El último día de la guerra 1970
   (*The Last Day of the War*)
Los pianos mecánicos 1965 (*The Uninhibited*)
Los Innocentes 1963 (*The Innocents*)
Nunca pasa nada 1963 (*Nothing Ever Happens*)
Calle Mayor 1956 (*The Lovemaker*)
Muerte de un ciclista 1955 (*Age of Infidelity*)
Esa pareja feliz 1953 (*That Happy Couple*)

"Spanish cinema is politically futile, socially false, intellectually worthless . . . ."

ALAIN RESNAIS

Born: Alain Resnais, June 3, 1922 (Vannes, Morbihan, Bretagne, France).

Directing style: Founding figure of French New Wave; innovative use of flashback technique to explore memory and time; ambiguous viewpoints and narratives.

Top Takes...

Coeurs 2006 (Private Fears in Public Places)
On connaît la chanson 1997
Smoking/No Smoking 1993
L'amour à mort 1984
La vie est un roman 1983 (Life is a Bed of Roses)
Mon oncle d'Amérique 1980
Providence 1977
Stavisky 1974
La guerre est finie 1966 (The War is Over)
L'année dernière à Marienbad 1961
   (Last Year at Marienbad)
Hiroshima mon amour 1959
   (Hiroshima, My Love)
Nuit et brouillard 1955 (Night and Fog)
Gaugin 1950
Guernica 1950

Alain Resnais was a founding figure of the French New Wave, though he was a full decade older than François Truffaut and already making a name for himself in the late 1940s and early 1950s with unusual documentaries. The best of these is the striking *Nuit et brouillard* (1955) (*Night and Fog*). Some were made in partnership with Chris Marker, another New Wave figure, whose formal experimentation, much of it clearly pre-postmodern, seems to have greatly influenced Resnais.

Resnais's breakthrough film was *Hiroshima mon amour* (1959) (*Hiroshima, My Love*). Its profound meditations on time, memory, culture, and history contrast strongly with the cultural and autobiographical elements in early Jean-Luc Godard and Truffaut. This was an interest he sustained throughout his career, as seen in little-known films, such as *Providence* (1977), which traces the interplay between memory and fantasy in the mind of a dying novelist contemplating both his demise and his next venture. Resnais's intellectuality is also apparent in the strong interest he took in experimental writing, particularly the "new novel," which was all the rage in bohemian Paris at the height of his career. Jean Cayrol, Jorge Semprún, and, especially, Marguerite Duras, who wrote *Hiroshima, My Love*, all influenced him greatly. Resnais's collaboration with Alain Robbe-Grillet in *L'année dernière à Marienbad* (1961) (*Last Year at Marienbad*) produced one of international art theater cinema's most notoriously difficult films. His fascination with formal experimentation and impenetrable structure has endured into the twilight of his career. *Smoking/No Smoking* (1993) is a set of two films that can be viewed in either order—the story has 12 possible conclusions, yet only one obvious and universal ending; each of the finales plays out in a graveyard. **BP**

> "*[Last Year at Marienbad]* is, in short, an experience, full of beauty and mood."—*New York Times*

RIGHT: Delphine Seyrig in a scene from Resnais's ambitious *Last Year at Marienbad*.

BLAKE EDWARDS

Born: William Blake Crump, July 26, 1922 (Tulsa, Oklahoma, U.S.).

Directing style: Maker of comedies combining slapstick, sophisticated wit, melancholia, and social criticism; homages to the silent cinema; creator of *The Pink Panther* series.

Top Takes...

1920s

"Make 'em redecorate your office. That's primary, to let them know where you stand."

For a film career spanning nearly five decades, nearly four as writer and director, Blake Edwards deserves three hearty cheers for longevity, adaptability, and intelligence. Only with his very last movies has he faltered, his comic sense seeming more forced, but even so, one of his major achievements is *Sunset* (1988). This film is part comedy, part Western, and part satire, but in its wit and subtlety far more than a sum of its parts.

Edwards is essentially a director of comedies, one of the greatest since Howard Hawks and Ernst Lubitsch. But to say so is already to risk missing out on his true greatness—an ability to render tributes to others without becoming self-conscious or smug; an extraordinary sensitivity to the possibilities and traps inherent in mood switches; a respect both for characters' weaknesses and for his audiences' readiness to approach comedy seriously. In no other director can one find slapstick, sophisticated wit, melancholia, social criticism, and moments of drama coexisting in an equilibrium that is sometimes uneasy, but more often amazingly successful.

The celebrity of *Breakfast at Tiffany's* (1961) has led to the neglect of more interesting and successful movies, notably *The Great Race* (1965) and *Darling Lili* (1970). However uneven, *The Great Race* often shows Edwards's talents at their best: his articulation of adventure, slapstick, homages to the silent cinema and Stan Laurel and Oliver Hardy, and genuine pathos. The same goes for the more somber *That's Life!* (1986). The best moments of *The Pink Panther* series, such as the opening of *A Shot in the Dark* (1964) and the encounters between Inspector Jacques Clouseau and his servant Cato Fong in *The Pink Panther Strikes Again* (1976), show Edwards's skill as a narrator and his sense of comic timing. **ReH**

ARTHUR PENN

Born: Arthur Penn, September 27, 1922 (Philadelphia, Pennsylvania, U.S.).

Directing style: Early focus on the outcasts of society; themes that observe and subvert the ideology and mythology of contemporary U.S. society; focus on the impulse to violence in U.S. society.

From the mid-1960s to the mid-1970s, Arthur Penn was one of the most exciting, stimulating, and unpredictable directors in U.S. films. Then, for no discernible reason, he lost it, and since then his films have been sporadic and unremarkable.

Penn's talent was evident in his debut film *The Left-Handed Gun* (1958), where he drew from Paul Newman, playing Billy the Kid, a performance of intense, immediate physicality. He hit his stride with *Bonnie and Clyde* (1967), which survived initial critical disdain to become one of the most influential U.S. films of the decade. A box-office success internationally, the film captured the troubled mood and disenchantment of contemporary youth. Penn chose to explore his fascination with outsider figures again in the hippies of *Alice's Restaurant* (1969) and the Cheyenne American-Indians of *Little Big Man* (1970), a film that cast a side-glance at the Vietnam War while subverting the heroic mythology of the Western.

Though strongly influenced by European filmmakers in terms of style, Penn has always concentrated on U.S. subjects, and in particular on the impulse to violence that he discerns at the root of U.S. society. The gloom and paranoia of the post-Watergate years were reflected in the most pessimistic of his films, *Night Moves* (1975), a thriller in the convoluted film-noir tradition of writers Dashiell Hammett and Raymond Chandler, but further soured by disillusion. *The Missouri Breaks* (1976), a highly eccentric Western, took further sideswipes at frontier mythology while featuring a performance of shameless high camp from Marlon Brando. Six years passed until Penn's next movie, *Four Friends* (1981), in which a loss of intensity was evident, and his subsequent films have continued that trend. **PK**

Top Takes...

Inside 1996
The Portrait 1993
Penn & Teller Get Killed 1989
Dead of Winter 1987
The Missouri Breaks 1976
Night Moves 1975
Visions of Eight 1973
Little Big Man 1970
Alice's Restaurant 1969 ☆
Flesh and Blood 1968
Bonnie and Clyde 1967 ☆
The Chase 1966
Mickey One 1965
The Miracle Worker 1962 ☆
The Left-Handed Gun 1958

> "This here's Miss Bonnie Parker. I'm Clyde Barrow. We rob banks."
> —Clyde Barrow, *Bonnie and Clyde*

FRANCESCO ROSI

Born: Francesco Rosi, November 15, 1922 (Naples, Campania, Italy).

Directing style: Courageous Italian filmmaker of feature films, including literary adaptations and incisive, investigative semidocumentaries; explores themes of the corruption of power.

Top Takes…

Francesco Rosi's career before entering the film business was diverse in the extreme. After his days as a law student, he took turns as an illustrator, actor, writer, and director for Radio Naples, before following that well-trodden path into the Italian film industry: working as an assistant director to Luchino Visconti. His directorial debut came with *La sfida* (1958) (*The Challenge*), a Special Jury Prize award winner at the Venice Film Festival in 1958. It was the start of a probing form of political cinema that was to typify Rosi's early work, such as *Salvatore Giuliano* (1962), *Le mani sulla città* (1963) (*Hands Over the City*), *Il caso Mattei* (1972) (*The Mattei Affair*), and *Lucky Luciano* (1973), much of which explored the corruption of power in a very Italian context, highlighting the jumbled connections between the state, big business, and organized crime.

Later, Rosi's career moved briefly away from political cinema, taking on a more literary bent in the late 1970s and early 1980s. Some of his works in this period were adventurous diversions such as *Carmen* (1984) and *Cronaca di una morte annunciata* (1987) (*Chronicle of a Death Foretold*), while *Cadaveri eccellenti* (1976) (*Illustrious Corpses*) and his brilliant adaptation of Carlo Levi's *Cristo si è fermato a Eboli* (1979) (*Christ Stopped at Eboli*) were closer to home, addressing old themes: corruption and Italy's perennial issues with its southern reaches. A master of the political exposé, Rosi's work reflected much wider sociopolitical neuroses. To understand him, then, is to understand Italy during the political and social upheaval of "the years of lead," when terrorism was rife and sides were hard to take. He was scratching a very Italian kind of itch. Rosi is a rare creature indeed—an award-winning filmmaker little known outside his own shores. **RH**

> "When there is war, two things to remember: shoes, then food."
> —Il Greco, *The Truce*

JONAS MEKAS

Born: Jonas Mekas, December 24, 1922 (Semeniskiai, Lithuania).

Directing style: Lithuanian-born director of experimental avant-garde cinema; maker of quasi-documentaries and lyrical autobiographical diaries of everyday life; use of personal commentary.

The high priest of U.S. avant-garde cinema, Lithuanian-born Jonas Mekas spent much of World War II as a displaced person, confined in German labor camps. He left Germany and emigrated to the United States in 1949. New York City in the late 1950s and early 1960s was a hotbed of cinematic creativity and Mekas soon gained prominence as a writer and critic for *The Village Voice*. He also spearheaded the creation of the Filmmakers' Cinematheque and The Film-Makers' Cooperative, which screened and distributed experimental or underground films. Andy Warhol, Marie Menken, and Bruce Conner were key members of the movement, which favored personal filmmaking on a shoestring budget, to create films that were daring, individual, and often broke taboos.

In addition to his work as a publicist, critic, and impresario, Mekas produced a number of influential films, such as *The Brig* (1964), which documented one grueling day in a Marine Corps lockup. It won Best Documentary at the 1964 Venice Film Festival, though it was an entirely fictional construct.

During this period, Mekas was also working on diaries of his life and work, which eventually emerged as the epic film *Diaries Notes and Sketches* (1969), and continued with *Reminiscences of a Journey to Lithuania* (1972), and *Lost, Lost, Lost* (1976). He also became a champion of the structuralist school of cinema, and was instrumental in the creation of an archival museum of essential works of the cinema. Mekas's contribution to experimental cinema is immense, and his timeless work as an advocate for independent cinema, coupled with his own lyrical, often autobiographical, cinema diaries, assures him a place in the pantheon of modern U.S. avant-garde cinema. **WWD**

Top Takes...

Elvis 2001

Wien & Mozart 2001

As I Was Moving Ahead Occasionally I Saw Brief Glimpses of Beauty 2000

Birth of a Nation 1997

Happy Birthday to John 1996

Self Portrait 1990

He Stands in a Desert Counting the Seconds of his Life 1986

Paradise Not Yet Lost, or Oona's Third Year 1980

Lost, Lost, Lost 1976

Reminiscences of a Journey to Lithuania 1972

Diaries Notes and Sketches 1969

Cassis 1966

The Brig 1964

Guns of the Trees 1964

"It's the ultimate Dogma movie, before the birth of Dogma."
—Mekas, of *As I Was Moving Ahead . . .*

1920s

OUSMANE SEMBÈNE

Born: Ousmane Sembène, January 1, 1923 (Ziguenchor, Casamance, Senegal).

Directing style: Known as "The Father of African film"; Senegalese Marxist director; themes tackle social, political, and religious issues in postcolonial Africa; humor and vitality.

Top Takes...

Still active in his eighties, the Senegalese-born Ousmane Sembène ranks as the doyen of African filmmakers. Apart from his debut feature, *La Noire de . . . .* (1966) (*Black Girl*), all his movies have been located and shot in sub-Saharan West Africa, valiantly overcoming the vagaries of African production and distribution and, often enough, the disapproval of the same national authorities from whom he has been obliged to seek funding. Although varying in scale from the domestic *Mandabi* (1968) (*The Money Order*) to the epic *Ceddo* (1977) (*Outsiders*) and *Camp de Thiaroye* (1987) (*The Camp at Thiaroye*), Sembène's films never neglect the social and political dimension of their stories. Nor does he shy away from tackling major themes, whether endemic political corruption as in *Xala* (1975) (*Impotence*), religious oppression as in *Outsiders*, or the practice of female genital mutilation as in *Moolaadé* (2004). Yet his films never descend into solemn polemic. Even at their most serious, they are full of humor, vitality, and the color of African life.

Equally, Sembène's Marxist background does not mislead him into taking a simplistic attitude to the problems he explores. Subtle and ambivalent, his films acknowledge the value of traditions and regret their erosion, but they also expose the system of oppression and injustice these traditions often upheld. In *Guelwaar* (1992), the eponymous late political activist is celebrated as a hero and possibly a martyr in his people's cause—but Sembène makes clear that his love of freedom and respect for human rights never extended to his own family. And in *Moolaadé* he shows that one irrational custom, stringing a thin crimson thread across a doorway to create an impregnable sanctuary, can also be used to combat another—the mutilation of young girls. **PK**

> "At a moral level, I don't think we have any lesson to learn from Europe."

CHEH CHANG

Born: Cheh Chang, February 10, 1923 (Qingtian, Zhejiang Province, China); died 2002 (Hong Kong, China).

Directing style: "The Godfather of Hong Kong cinema"; prolific director of 1970s martial arts movies; revolutionary maker of violent period sword-fighting films.

One of the most prolific directors in the history of Hong Kong cinema, Cheh Chang was also one of the most distinguished makers of martial arts films.

Chang came to prominence in the mid-1960s with a series of *wuxia pian* (period swordplay) movies, including *Bian cheng san xia* (1966) (*Heroic Three*), *Dubei dao* (1967) (*One-Armed Swordsman*), and *Du bei dao wang* (1969) (*Return of the One-Armed Swordsman*), where he put the male hero to the forefront in bloody fight scenes, and the focus on loyalty, honor, and camaraderie. Many of these were made for the Shaw Brothers Studio—sometimes referred to as Hong Kong's "Hollywood of the East"—and they often starred one of the biggest names in martial arts cinema of the period, Yu Wang.

As the popularity of the swordplay film began to wane in the 1970s, Chang's skills were employed to produce works that centered more on hand-to-hand combat—the kung fu film. He continued to be adept at making these action movies, whether that was kung fu action or kung fu comedy, and his ability to work quickly and within budget meant that he was able to average around five films a year in the period between 1972 and 1983. Chang's prolific output did not always mean, however, that the quality of his movies suffered. Working within the tight constraints of the Hong Kong studio structure, he was able to continue to produce impressive works that increasingly showcased authentic martial arts skills. Fans of the genre still celebrate this aspect of his work in films such as *Hong quan yu yong chun* (1974) (*Shaolin Martial Arts*) and *Wu du* (1978) (*Five Deadly Venoms*).

Chang died in 2002 having created some of the finest displays of Chinese martial arts ever seen onscreen. **AW**

Top Takes...

Gong wu kei bing 1993 (*Hidden Hero*)

Wu dun ren shu 1982 (*Chinese Super Ninjas*)

Nan Shao Lin yu bei Shao Lin 1978

Wu du 1978 (*Five Deadly Venoms*)

Can que 1978 (*Mortal Combat*)

Hong quan yu yong chun 1974
  (*Shaolin Martial Arts*)

Ci Ma 1973 (*Dynasty of Blood*)

Shui hu zhuan 1972
  (*Seven Blows of the Dragon*)

Ying wang 1971

Da jue dou 1971 (*Duel of the Iron Fist*)

Du bei dao Wang 1969
  (*Return of the One-Armed Swordsman*)

Dubei dao 1967 (*One-Armed Swordsman*)

Bian cheng san xia 1966 (*Heroic Three*)

1920s

"Cheh's films are the perfect blending of art and commerce."
—Ethan de Seife, *Senses of Cinema*

FRANCO ZEFFIRELLI

Born: Gianfranco Corsi, February 12, 1923 (Florence, Tuscany, Italy).

Directing style: Italian maker of lavish operatic, literary, and Shakespearean adaptations; often inspired by religion and highbrow culture; careful attention to detail.

Top Takes...

"Americans just simply don't understand picnics!"

—Lady Hester, *Tea with Mussolini*

Franco Zeffirelli is inextricably linked to the classics of music and literature. After being educated in architecture at the University of Florence, and finding employment as an actor in several of Luchino Visconti's stage productions, he was quickly promoted to assistant director on many of Visconti's most celebrated works—*La Terra trema: Episodio del mare* (1948) (*The Earth Trembles*), *Bellissima* (1951), and *Senso* (1954) (*Livia*)— while simultaneously using his talents as a set and costume designer for numerous opera and stage productions.

Extravagant, colorful, and ambitious, Zeffirelli's work on both stage and screen has always tended toward the spectacular, his vast productions oozing with extravagant attention to detail. His fluency in English (he was a partisan translator for the British army during World War II) and interest in William Shakespeare led to his directing many of the bard's plays in both Italy and England. Entering film in the late 1960s, his trademark colorful opulence was immediately apparent, with *Romeo and Juliet* (1968) breaking box-office records for Paramount Pictures and propelling him on to the world stage. His film work has to a large extent been an extension of his first love, the stage, with his work alternating among operatic adaptations such as *La Traviata* (1983); the Shakespearean such as *Hamlet* (1990); and the literary or classical such as *Jane Eyre* (1996). Zeffirelli's campishly exuberant if waspish charm has always ensured his cult status, though it was his semi-autobiographical *Tea With Mussolini* (1999) that brought him briefly back to the public's attention. For someone who is alleged to have been a one-time lover of Visconti, Zeffirelli's later Catholic conservativism and career in Italian politics is a curious footnote to a rich career. **RH**

LINDSAY ANDERSON

Born: Lindsay Gordon Anderson, April 17, 1923 (Bangalore, Karnataka, India); died 1994 (Angoulême, Charente, Poitou-Charentes, France).

Directing style: Film and documentary director; pioneer of the Free Cinema Movement that helped put Britain's working classes on the big screen.

Lindsay Anderson was a rebel who used cinema to provoke change, and in many ways he succeeded. Sadly, the distribution of his best work is dismal and though he was responsible for some of the best cinema ever produced, few now realize it.

Anderson spent most of his early career directing documentary shorts, commercials, working in the theater, and writing film critiques. He was particularly interested in shifting the middle-class focus of 1950s British cinema toward a working-class dedication. With directors Karel Reisz and Tony Richardson, he developed the Free Cinema Movement, whose films shared not only common themes but were often produced on a low budget, using handheld 16mm cameras. His first feature was *This Sporting Life* (1963), but it was in *The White Bus* (1967) that he displayed the unique surrealist style and condemnation of British society that would later be indicative of his best work.

His breakthrough film was *If . . .* (1968), a story of rebellion in a British boys' school, starring newcomer Malcolm McDowell. It incorporated a sly mix of realist and surrealist scenes that often startled audiences. This unusual style, coupled with its shockingly violent, anarchistic ending, made it an international hit with young people in the late 1960s.

A sequel of sorts, *O Lucky Man!* (1973) was inspired by McDowell's own experiences as a coffee salesman. The film followed an ambitious young capitalist who finally finds salvation in art. Again, the film deliberately confuses perceptions of reality, fantasy, life, and art in a form that is endlessly enchanting. Anderson supplemented his remaining years much as he did his early career, but *If . . .* and *O Lucky Man!* arguably remain his masterworks. **DW**

Top Takes...

Is That All There Is? 1993
Glory! Glory! 1989
The Whales of August 1987
Wish You Were There 1985
Wham! in China: Foreign Skies 1984
Britannia Hospital 1982
Look Back in Anger 1980
In Celebration 1975
O Lucky Man! 1973
If . . . 1968
The White Bus 1967
The Singing Lesson 1967
This Sporting Life 1963
Every Day Except Christmas 1957
Thursday's Children 1954
O Dreamland 1953

> "Violence and revolution are the only pure acts."
> —Mick Travis, *If . . .*

1920s

MRINAL SEN

Born: Mrinal Sen, May 14, 1923 (Faridpur, Bangladesh).

Directing style: Bengali director of politically conscious dramas and comedies that focus on the poor and marginalized; influenced by neorealism; experimental narrative structure.

Top Takes...

Aamaar Bhuvan 2002 (*My Land*)

Antareen 1994 (*The Confined*)

Mahaprithivi 1992 (*World Within, World Without*)

City Life 1990

Ek Din Achanak 1989 (*Suddenly, One Day*)

Genesis 1986

Khandar 1984 (*The Ruins*)

Kharij 1982 (*The Case Is Closed*)

Ek Din Pratidin 1979 (*One Day Like Another*)

Oka Oori Katha 1977 (*The Outsiders*)

Chorus 1974

Padatik 1973 (*The Guerilla Fighter*)

Calcutta 71 1971

Interview 1971

Matira Manisha 1966 (*Two Brothers*)

Raat Bhore 1956 (*The Dawn*)

Born in Bangladesh, Mrinal Sen is one of the best-known directors associated with what has become known as India's "parallel cinema" of the 1970s. After studying physics at college, Sen worked as a journalist, salesman, and then as a sound technician in a film studio. He became interested in film and in Marxist politics after joining the Indian People's Theatre's Association, which had links with the Communist Party.

One of the most stridently political filmmakers to come to prominence in the 1970s, Sen addressed the plight of India's poor and downtrodden in his early movies, such as *Interview* (1971) and *Calcutta 71* (1971). Continuing his left-wing critique, he produced *Chorus* (1974); this time the film was an attack on multinational companies, and their exploitation of India, its people, and its resources.

A number of Sen's later films also focus on the poor and the marginalized in society. Typical of these are perhaps his best-known film, *Oka Oori Katha* (1977) (*The Outsiders*), and *Genesis* (1986). Films such as *Kharij* (1982) (*The Case Is Closed*) and *Ek Din Achanak* (1989) (*Suddenly, One Day*), investigate the impact that small events can have on ordinary people, and the way in which these occurrences do, or do not, set off a series of events.

Throughout his career, Mrinal Sen has produced films that are not easy viewing. He has linked his work to that of the European modernists of the 1960s, such as Michelangelo Antonioni, and his political perspective and antifascist stance have meant that others have seen strong affinities with anticolonial movements such as "Third Cinema" in his work. However one chooses to look at Sen's films, one thing is certain—they are some of the most striking examples of noncommercial cinema ever produced in India. **AW**

"What we wanted to do in *Calcutta 71* was to define history, put it in its right perspective."

SEIJUN SUZUKI

Born: Seitaro Suzuki, May 24, 1923 (Tokyo, Japan).

Directing style: Prolific, innovative Japanese master of the *yakuza* genre, and B-movies; hip, Pop Art feel; the plot is secondary to the movie's entertainment value; irreverent humor.

At the age of eighty-two, Seijun Suzuki released the musical *Operetta tanuki goten* (2005) (*Princess Raccoon*). Since his debut with *Hozuna wa utau: Umi no junjo* (1956) (*Pure Emotions of the Sea*), Suzuki has turned his hands to many of Japanese cinema's popular genres. However, for most of those who have come across his strikingly individual films, he is most closely associated with the *yakuza* film, a type of Japanese gangster movie. *Yakuza* films became very popular in the 1960s and Suzuki produced a number of his best-known works during this period for the Nikkatsu Studios. Essentially B-pictures, films such as *Yaju no seishun* (1963) (*The Brute*) and the historically set *Irezumi ichidai* (1965) (*Tattooed Life*) marked the director out as a Japanese Sam Fuller—someone who works within popular genres but still manages to bring his vast imagination to bear on projects, often taking them in unexpected directions.

It was Suzuki's willingness to stretch the limits of genre filmmaking that ultimately brought him into conflict with his studio bosses. *Tôkyô nagaremono* (1966) (*Tokyo Drifter*) stretched the patience of those in charge, but unwilling to rein in his artistic aspirations he produced *Koroshi no rakuin* (1967) (*Branded to Kill*), an even more absurd tale. This proved to be the last straw and he was fired, with the head of Nikkatsu complaining that the film was wholly incomprehensible. Although Suzuki continued to work, it was only in the 1990s that a new generation of young Japanese critics and directors began to be influenced by his pop art sensibilities. The turn of the century saw him deliver a belated return to the world of the *yakuza* with *Pisutoru opera* (2001) (*Pistol Opera*), but by then Japanese audiences were more used to the extreme version of the genre being offered up. **AW**

Top Takes...

Operetta tanuki goten 2005 (*Princess Raccoon*)
Pisutoru opera 2001 (*Pistol Opera*)
Yumeji 1991
Rupan sansei: Babiron no Ogon densetsu 1985
   (*Rupan III: Legend of the Gold of Babylon*)
Tsigoineruwaizen 1980
Koroshi no rakuin 1967 (*Branded to Kill*)
Kenka erejii 1966 (*The Born Fighter*)
Tôkyô nagaremono 1966 (*Tokyo Drifter*)
Shunpu den 1965 (*Story of a Prostitute*)
Irezumi ichidai 1965 (*Tattooed Life*)
Kanto mushuku 1963 (*Kanto Wanderer*)
Yaju no seishun 1963 (*The Brute*)
Ankokugai no bijo 1958 (*Underworld Beauty*)
Hozuna wa utau: Umi no junjo 1956
   (*Pure Emotions of the Sea*)

> "I think it's okay to live my life as a pistol."
>
> —Myuki Minazuki, *Pistol Opera*

1920s

HARRY SMITH

Born: Harry Everett Smith, May 29, 1923 (Portland, Oregon, U.S.); died 1991 (New York City, New York, U.S.).

Directing style: Visionary abstract animator and experimental filmmaker; mystical themes; multiplane camerawork; black and white images drawn on film.

Top Takes…

Harry Smith was born in Portland, Oregon, and early on in his career acquired a reputation as a filmmaker, experimental film artist, and music archivist (his *Anthology of American Folk Music* is one of the most important collections in the field.)

Smith's experimental animations began in 1939 with *Number 1*, which developed into the *Early Abstractions* series of complex animated abstractions. These incorporate multiplane camerawork, drawing directly on the film and black and white images projected on a wall, then photographed again. Looking at Smith's films, one is struck by the depth of his imagery, the glowing and luminous quality of his traditional cell animations, and the free-spirited anarchy of his direct film drawings. The *Early Abstractions* series was mounted into one 35-minute reel in 1964 by Jonas Mekas, then released with a soundtrack culled from The Beatles's first album; this was withdrawn later and alternate soundtracks added to newer versions.

Smith's other key films include *Number 14: Late Superimpositions* (1965) made between 1963 and 1965, which consists mostly of live-action material manipulated in the camera. It is scored to the soundtrack of *Aufstieg und Fall der Stadt Mahagonny* (1930) (*Rise and Fall of the City of Mahogonny*), an opera by Kurt Weill and Bertolt Brecht. Smith lived for many years at the Hotel Chelsea in New York City, in a single room on the second floor of the hotel. The author of this piece visited him there in the late 1960s and found him still busily working on numerous projects that, because of the director's death in 1991, sadly remained unfinished. Eccentric, sometimes difficult, and entirely original, Smith's animations are some of the most sophisticated works that the medium has to offer. **WWD**

> "I'm glad to say my dreams came true. I saw America changed through music."

RICHARD ATTENBOROUGH

Born: Richard Samuel Attenborough, August 29, 1923 (Cambridge, Cambridgeshire, England).

Directing style: Distinguished British actor turned director; lavish and stylish epic-scale biopics; a close eye for detail; notable rapport with actors.

After a distinguished career as an actor, Lord Richard "Dickie" Attenborough made his directorial debut with the satire *Oh! What a Lovely War* (1969), followed by the Churchill biopic *Young Winston* (1972). He was then given the chance to direct *A Bridge Too Far* (1977), a big-budget World War II epic. Like the historical event on which it was based, the film was a failure, yet Attenborough's well-staged action scenes and rapport with actors made an impression in the industry.

Attenborough's most notable directorial efforts are epic biopics of Mahatma Gandhi and Sir Charles Chaplin. With its memorable set pieces, such as the Amritsar massacre, the salt strikes, scenes of Hindu and Moslem mob violence, and superb impersonation by Ben Kingsley of the enigmatic public school graduate and one-time Empire admirer, *Gandhi* (1982) was a huge success, one of several large productions in the early 1980s that revitalized the British film industry.

With *Chaplin* (1992), Attenborough again attempted to follow in the footsteps of David Lean, modeling the film on that director's *Lawrence of Arabia* (1962), but Chaplin seemed less worthy of a hagiographic treatment, and his leftist desertion of national identity less interesting. A box-office failure, the film nevertheless offers a finely detailed, if understated, critique of the protagonist's megalomania, with an Oscar-nominated star performance from Robert Downey Jr.

Adapting the Broadway musical *A Chorus Line* (1985) was a strange misstep, but since then Attenborough has turned, with some success, to smaller-scale romances such as *In Love and War* (1996), *Shadowlands* (1993), and *Grey Owl* (1999)—another affecting biopic of a border-crosser; in this case, a white man gone native. **BP**

Top Takes...

Grey Owl 1999
In Love and War 1996
Shadowlands 1993
Chaplin 1992
Cry Freedom 1987
A Chorus Line 1985
***Gandhi* 1982 ★**
Magic 1978
A Bridge Too Far 1977
Young Winston 1972
Oh! What a Lovely War 1969

1920s

"An eye for an eye ... ends up making the whole world blind."
—Gandhi, *Gandhi*

SERGEI PARAJANOV

Born: Sarkis Parajanian, January 9, 1924 (Tbilisi, Georgia); died 1990 (Yerevan, Armenia).

Directing style: Russian director of poetic studies of native folk culture; use of fluid camerawork, vivid colors, symbolic imagery, and wild indigenous music.

Top Takes...

Parajanov: The Last Spring 1992

The Confession 1990

Ashug-Karibi 1988 (The Lovelorn Minstrel)

Ambavi Suramis tsikhitsa 1984
  (The Legend of the Suram Fortress)

Return to Life 1980

Sayat Nova 1968 (Color of Pomegranates)

Tini zabutykh predkiv 1964
  (Shadows of Forgotten Ancestors)

Tsvetok na kamne 1962 (Flower on the Stone)

Ukrainskaya rapsodiya 1961
  (Ukrainian Rhapsody)

Natalya Ushvij 1957

Zolotye ruki 1957 (Golden Hands)

Moldovskaya skazka 1951
  (Moldavian Fairy Tale)

Raised in Georgia by Armenian parents, Sergei Parajanov studied directing at Moscow's All-Union State Institute of Cinematography before moving to Kiev, where he made a number of documentaries and narrative films that he later dismissed as "garbage." In 1962, he began an adaptation of an old Ukrainian folk tale; the result was *Tini zabutykh predkiv* (1964) (*Shadows of Forgotten Ancestors*), a work of startling originality and dreamlike beauty. Using fluid camerawork, vivid colors, and wild indigenous music, the film created a sensation, but was viewed with deep suspicion by the Soviet authorities.

Parajanov next explored his own ethnic roots with *Sayat Nova* (1968) (*Color of Pomegranates*), a poetic dramatization of episodes in the life of a famous Armenian troubadour, rich in strange, symbolic imagery. It was banned but, even when released in revised form, it was received ecstatically by international critics and is now regarded as Parajanov's masterpiece.

In 1973, Parajanov was denounced as a nationalist agitator, arrested, and thrown into the Gulag. He was released after four years but prevented from returning to film, and in 1982 was arrested again, to serve a further eleven months. Finally, with the dawn of the Mikhail Gorbachev era, Parajanov was once more allowed to direct. Before his death in 1990, he completed two additional films inspired by the history and folklore of the Caucasus: *Ambavi Suramis tsikhitsa* (1984) (*The Legend of the Suram Fortress*) and *Ashug-Karibi* (1988) (*The Lovelorn Minstrel*). The idiosyncratic brilliance of these two films demonstrated that Parajanov's artistic vision remained undimmed after 16 years away from the camera. His unfinished autobiographical final film, *The Confession* (1990) was incorporated into the moving eulogy *Parajanov: The Last Spring* (1992). **RB**

> "They imprisoned him at the height of his artistic powers."
>
> —M. Vartanov, *Parajanov: The Last Spring*

FRANTIŠEK VLÁČIL

Born: František Vláčil, February 19, 1924 (Cieszyn, Poland); died 1999 (Prague, Czech Republic).

Directing style: Czech director of visually rich dramas with a painterly feel; use of historical settings to highlight contemporary social and political issues.

František Vláčil was a painter and designer as well as a director. He studied art history and aesthetics at Masaryk University in Brno, then went on to produce puppet animations. His first feature as a director was a drama, *Holubice* (1960) (*The White Dove*). Vláčil's painterly sensibilities were evident in the film's visual metaphors, setting the tone for the work that was to follow with its poetic feel and knack for lyrical storytelling.

He turned to historical drama with *Udoli vcel* (1967) (*Valley of the Bees*) and *Dablova past* (1961) (*The Devil's Trap*), each time using the power of nostalgia to deal with contemporary issues. But it is his epic *Marketa Lazarová* (1967) that is widely acknowledged as his masterpiece. Set in medieval times, the movie depicts the conflict between rival clans against the backdrop of the shift from paganism to Christianity, and the doomed love affair between a couple on opposing sides. Its examination of good and evil, the hunters and the hunted, and stunning imagery of wintry landscapes inhabited by wolves and horsemen won favor with Czech film critics.

Adelheid (1969) saw Vláčil examine the state of his country after the 1968 Soviet invasion through the lens of a post-World War II romance. It tells the tale of a Czech soldier who takes over the plush home of a German family and falls in love with the former owner's daughter, now maid, who is hiding her soldier brother. Vláčil's story highlights the pain of a country in defeat, and saw the director banned from making feature films by the communist authorities through much of the 1970s. He went on to make shorts for children before returning to features with *Dým bramborové nat'e* (1976) (*Smoke on the Potato Fields*), in which Vláčil once again used landscape as a tool to reveal his characters' psychological states. **CK**

Top Takes…

Stín kapradiny 1984 (*Shades of Fern*)
Stiny horkeho leta 1977 (*Shadows of a Hot Summer*)
Dým bramborové nat'e 1976 (*Smoke on the Potato Fields*)
Adelheid 1969
Marketa Lazarová 1967
Udoli vcel 1967 (*Valley of the Bees*)
Dablova past 1961 (*The Devil's Trap*)
Holubice 1960 (*The White Dove*)

"People then were much more instinctive in their actions . . . ."
——On medieval times

STANLEY DONEN

Born: Stanley Donen, April 13, 1924 (Columbia, South Carolina, U.S.).

Directing style: Known as the "King of the Hollywood musicals"; innovative choreography; took the musical out of the studio and on location; entertaining collaborations with Gene Kelly.

Top Takes…

RIGHT: Frank Sinatra, Jules Munshin, and Gene Kelly, the carefree sailors in *On the Town*.

Stanley Donen is associated with some of the most innovative Hollywood musicals of the late 1940s and 1950s. A dancer himself, in 1941 he began a long association with Gene Kelly, first on Kelly's stage shows, then in films. Donen is credited with the staging of the musical numbers in *Take Me Out to the Ball Game* (1949), in which Kelly costarred with Frank Sinatra.

Donen's first film as director was *On the Town* (1949), again featuring Sinatra and Kelly, the latter sharing the director's credit with Donen. Together, the two brought a new style of dancing to the screen, less polished and sophisticated than that of Fred Astaire, but more virile and down to earth. *On the Town* also made striking use of exterior locations in New York City. After directing Astaire in *Royal Wedding* (1951), Donen again took codirector's credit with Kelly on *Singin' in the Rain* (1952). Regarded as one of the indisputable masterpieces of the musical, it featured some extraordinary dancing from Kelly, Donald O'Connor, and Debbie Reynolds, not to mention a stunning cameo by Cyd Charisse.

Seven Brides for Seven Brothers (1954) was an energetic musical of the backwoods, with choreography by Michael Kidd. Donen

returned to working with Kelly and Kidd on *It's Always Fair Weather* (1955), in which Kidd played one of the leading roles in a bittersweet story of three soldiers reuniting ten years after the war. The more conventional *Funny Face* (1957) saw Donen once more working with Astaire. On *The Pajama Game* (1957) Donen shared director's credit with George Abbott, who wrote and directed the original theatrical performance of the work.

After a couple of romantic comedies with Cary Grant, *Kiss Them for Me* (1957) and *Indiscreet* (1958), Donen was reunited with Abbott on *Damn Yankees!* (1958), a musical set in the world of baseball. Abandoning the musical for comedy and romance, he worked twice more with Grant, on *The Grass Is Greener* (1960) and *Charade* (1963). *Two for the Road* (1967) was a creditable effort at combining the road movie with romance. But Donen's later films are derivative, lacking the verve and freshness of his earlier work. **EB**

ABOVE: The leggy Cyd Charisse wows Gene Kelly in the musical *Singin' in the Rain*.

Dancing Partners

Stanley Donen and Gene Kelly worked together on many musicals, collaborating on both the choreography and direction.

- The duo met on the Broadway production of *Pal Joey*, in which Kelly starred and sixteen-year-old Donen was in the chorus.
- The pair first worked together on *Take Me Out to the Ball Game* (1949), for which Donen staged the musical numbers.
- Donen and Kelly codirected *On the Town* (1949), *Singin' in the Rain* (1952), and *It's Always Fair Weather* (1955).
- Interestingly, Donen's first wife, Jeanne Coyne, later married Gene Kelly.

KAREL KACHYNA

Born: Karel Kachyna, May 1, 1924 (Vyskov, Czech Republic); died 2004 (Prague, Czech Republic).

Directing style: Czech filmmaker of early documentaries and later tragic dramas; frequently focused on the young; themes of life under totalitarian rule.

Top Takes...

Krava 1994 (*The Cow*)

Smrt krásnych srncu 1986 (*Forbidden Dreams*)

Lásky mezi kapkami deste 1979
(*Love Between Raindrops*)

Robinsonka 1974 (*Robinson Girl*)

Ucho 1970 (*The Ear*)

Uz zase skácu pres kaluze 1970
(*Jumping Over Puddles Again*)

Smesny pan 1969 (*Funny Man*)

Noc nevesty 1967 (*The Holy Night*)

Kocár do Vídne 1966 (*Coach to Vienna*)

At' zije Republika 1965 (*Long Live the Republic*)

Nadeje 1964 (*The Hope*)

Krivé zrcadlo 1956 (*Crooked Mirror*)

Ztracená stopa 1956

Dnes vecer vsechno skonci 1954
(*Everything Ends Tonight*)

"Kachyna's direction is remarkably agile . . . ."

—On *The Ear, New York Times*

Known for his psychologically probing works, Czech filmmaker Karel Kachyna graduated from Prague's Film and TV School of the Academy of Performing Arts (where he later taught). He began working on documentaries in the 1950s with former classmate Vojtech Jasny, and the duo made their fictional debut with *Dnes vecer vsechno skonci* (1954) (*Everything Ends Tonight*).

Having split from Jasny, Kachyna made his first solo projects, *Ztracená stopa* (1956) and *Krivé zrcadlo* (1956) (*Crooked Mirror*). He moved into the global spotlight in the 1960s with films that disparaged communism and tested the boundaries and tolerance of government-controlled regulations. His works typically centered on war, revolution, and extensive psychological analysis, and featured children or teenagers.

It is during this period that Kachyna produced his most famous works. *Nadeje* (1964) (*Hope*), analyzes the plight of a carpenter who has lost faith in the world and seeks solace in alcoholism, only to find hope in the form of a woman with a less-than-perfect past. *At' zije Republika* (1965) (*Long Live the Republic*) illustrates the sorrow of a young boy traveling across a land devastated by war, while tapping into the psychological and behavioral effects of his environment. *Kocár do Vídne* (1966) (*Coach to Vienna*) and *Noc nevesty* (1967) (*The Holy Night*) follow similar themes. *Smesny pan* (1969) (*Funny Man*) and *Ucho* (1970) (*The Ear*) were both banned in the wake of Russia's invasion of Czechoslovakia. *The Ear*, a volatile and biting political satire about government surveillance, was banned in the country for 20 years. Following the 1989 Velvet Revolution, Kachyna moved into TV because of the difficulty of finding film funding. He then worked sporadically for the big screen until his death in 2004. **ES**

SIDNEY LUMET

Born: Sidney Lumet, June 25, 1924 (Philadelphia, Pennsylvania, U.S.).

Directing style: Maker of socially aware dramas that tackle important cultural questions; subtle use of technical skills; often set in confined spaces; noted for drawing award-winning performances from cast.

The most notable of the so-called "New York School" directors, Sidney Lumet has had a career marked, like that of Stanley Kramer, by an impressive series of vaguely leftist social dramas. Chief among them are a paean to liberal democracy, *12 Angry Men* (1957); an indictment of irresponsible militarism, *Fail-Safe* (1964); an affecting meditation on survivor guilt and personal responsibility, *The Pawnbroker* (1964); a critique of dehumanizing institutions, *The Hill* (1965); and a defense of the civil-trial lawyer, *The Verdict* (1982). But Lumet has also proved skilled at adapting Broadway dramas such as Tennessee Williams's *The Fugitive Kind* (1959), Eugene O'Neill's *Long Day's Journey Into Night* (1962), and Ira Levin's *Deathtrap* (1982).

Lumet's social dramas have sometimes been marred by inadequate scripts, although he showed himself an able collaborator on *Dog Day Afternoon* (1975) with Frank Pierson, and with Paddy Chayefsky on *Network* (1976). These two films reveal Lumet's interest in unconventional subject matter and extreme forms of behavior that can be glimpsed in his other productions, including the quirky *The Anderson Tapes* (1971) and *Equus* (1977), which treats the morality of horse murder.

Much feted in Hollywood, Lumet is even more noted for drawing excellent performances from his actors, who have garnered an amazing 18 Academy Award nominations for appearances in his films. The various strands of Lumet's career come together in the movie *Daniel* (1983). An expert adaptation of a literary property, the novel by E. L. Doctorow, the film treats an important cultural question—the execution of Ethel and Julius Rosenberg for espionage in 1953—and draws on excellent performances from Timothy Hutton, Lindsay Crouse, and Ed Asner. **BP**

Top Takes...

The Morning After 1986
Daniel 1983
The Verdict 1982 ☆
Deathtrap 1982
Prince of the City 1981
Equus 1977
Network 1976 ☆
Dog Day Afternoon 1975 ☆
Murder on the Orient Express 1974
The Anderson Tapes 1971
The Hill 1965
Fail-Safe 1964
The Pawnbroker 1964
Long Day's Journey Into Night 1962
The Fugitive Kind 1959
12 Angry Men 1957 ☆

"[Making a movie] is like making a mosaic. Each setup is like a tiny tile."

1920s

ROBERT ALTMAN

Born: Robert Bernard Altman, February 20, 1925 (Kansas City, Missouri, U.S.); died 2006 (Los Angeles, California, U.S.).

Directing style: Innovative director of classic dramas; visionary epics of the contemporary United States; improvised dialogue; tapestries of overlapping lives.

Top Takes...

A Prairie Home Companion 2006
Gosford Park 2001 ☆
Dr. T & The Women 2000
The Gingerbread Man 1998
Prêt-à-Porter 1994
Short Cuts 1993 ☆
The Player 1992 ☆
Vincent & Theo 1990
O.C. and Stiggs 1987
Secret Honor 1984
Streamers 1983
Come Back to the Five and Dime, Jimmy Dean, Jimmy Dean 1982
HealtH 1980
Buffalo Bill and the Indians, or Sitting Bull's History Lesson 1976
Nashville 1975 ☆
California Split 1974
The Long Goodbye 1973
McCabe & Mrs. Miller 1971
Brewster McCloud 1970
M*A*S*H 1970 ☆
That Cold Day in the Park 1969
The Delinquents 1957

After serving in the U.S. Army Air Forces during World War II, Robert Altman moved to Hollywood, hoping to develop a career in movies. After trying acting, composing, and screenwriting without making much of a mark, he gave up and returned to his hometown, Kansas City. And it was there, in Missouri, that he began an earnest career in movies, learning the basics of screen storytelling by making documentaries, industrials, educational films, and advertisements. After a few years, Altman directed his first feature, *The Delinquents* (1957), which caught the eye of Hollywood.

Altman was soon in regular employment as a TV director, with numerous credits that established his reputation. His career hit a rough patch in the mid-1960s, until *That Cold Day in the Park* (1969) earned him the chance to direct *M*A*S*H* (1970). The film—an allegory about the Vietnam War set during the Korean War—was a hit and helped establish Altman as an artist and social critic at the age of forty-five. He earned Oscar and Golden Globe nominations for his efforts, and became a peer to the film school brats, such as Martin Scorsese, Francis

RIGHT: "Hawkeye," "Trapper John," and staff in a scene from Altman's *M*A*S*H*.

Ford Coppola, George Lucas, and Steven Spielberg, who were then gaining prominence in the industry.

The next ten years saw Altman direct a steady stream of important, studio-financed films such as *Brewster McCloud* (1970), *McCabe & Mrs. Miller* (1971), *The Long Goodbye* (1973), *California Split* (1974), and *Nashville* (1975). But it was the commercial flop of *Popeye* (1980) that largely spoiled Altman's welcome.

To keep his career alive, Altman turned to independent financing, where smaller stakes allowed for greater creative flexibility and some interesting work, including *Come Back to the Five and Dime, Jimmy Dean, Jimmy Dean* (1982), *Streamers* (1983), and *O.C. and Stiggs* (1987), although it was his political TV comedy series *Tanner '88* (1988) that earned Altman an Emmy Award and began his return to the fold.

ABOVE: Tim Robbins stars in Altman's Hollywood morality play, *The Player*.

"I feel that [the actors] do the work and I get to watch. And nothing is better than that."

Making M*A*S*H

M*A*S*H established Robert Altman as an artist and social critic, earning several BAFTA Awards, an Oscar for Best Writing, and several Oscar nominations.

- Although the studio insisted on identifying the location of the plot as Korea, the film was interpreted as an antiwar statement about the war in Vietnam, which lasted from 1950 to 1975.
- The lyric to the movie's theme song was written by Altman's fourteen-year-old son, Mike.
- M*A*S*H was released the same year as Mike Nichols's Catch-22, which also satirized war.
- Much of the dialogue was improvised, including the scene where Father Mulcahy blesses the Jeep.
- M.A.S.H. stands for Mobile Army Surgical Hospital.
- During filming, Elliott Gould and Donald Sutherland requested Altman's removal from the film. The studio refused their request.
- In some of the loudspeaker shots, the moon is visible. They were shot in July 1969 while astronauts from the first manned mission to land on the moon (Apollo 11) were actually there.
- The film was based on the novel M*A*S*H by Richard Hooker. The screenplay was by Ring Lardner Jr., who won an Oscar for and was nominated for a Golden Globe.

RIGHT: Jennifer Jason Leigh is less than charming as Lois Kaiser in Short Cuts.

The transition film was Vincent & Theo (1990), a biographical study of Vincent van Gogh and his brother, which was well-received by critics. Then there appeared The Player (1992), a knowing, smarmy, insightful, and brilliantly amoral insider's look at the Hollywood machine from the standpoint of an ambitious studio executive caught up in a murder investigation. Altman again earned Academy Award and Golden Globe nominations, and "the player" entered pop culture as a term of both endearment and derision.

With new attention came new opportunities at an age (his seventies) when most of his peers were entering retirement or dying. There were masterpieces such as the ensemble melodrama Short Cuts (1993), and the period whodunnit Gosford Park (2001), both Academy Award nominated works, alongside misfires such as Prêt-à-Porter (1994) and the experimental thriller The Gingerbread Man (1998).

A controversial character

Altman was a curmudgeon, often politically insensitive to studio personalities and the social pressures operating around him. He was known for his "anti-Hollywood" approach and, away from the industry, was easily lampooned for disparaging remarks he made about President George W. Bush. In part, this sense of honesty and integrity may account for the dry spells in his career—times when he was forced to concentrate on TV or the stage, despite a track record of making respected films.

Yet the undeniable brilliance of Altman's cinema is most closely tied to a simple point made in each of his greatest works: the tapestry of overlapping lives is richer than overproduced spectacle. Witness Nashville, The Player, Short Cuts, or Gosford Park: each film lets characters complicate events by their unique personality traits rather than showcases special-effects technicians and pyrotechnics.

Such is the distinction of Altman in Hollywood, forever reminding people that a movie can be character driven, well written, and cast for the ensemble, and that such attributes lend easily to sharp observations about society in general. **GCQ**

SAM PECKINPAH

Born: David Samuel Peckinpah, February 21, 1925 (Fresno, California, U.S.); died 1984 (Inglewood, California, U.S.).

Directing style: Macho Westerns and dramas; mesmerizing performances; violent and controversial bloody content; balletically choreographed action sequences.

Top Takes...

Over the course of his life, Sam Peckinpah proved iconoclastic, helping to define a kind of out-of-control creative experience, whereby directors harangue, terrorize, and otherwise influence actors to give electric performances.

Peckinpah started in showbiz as an unconnected nobody and worked his way up from the bottom. He directed his first feature, the Western *The Deadly Companions* (1961), before getting his chance to put his unique stamp on the genre with *Ride the High Country* (1962). Telling the story of aging cowboys, Peckinpah began developing his vision of the frontier, where modern, civilizing influences such as woman and the rule of law, come in conflict with instinctual manhood.

He then helmed *Major Dundee* (1965), starring Charlton Heston. Peckinpah was abrasive and difficult, and the studio stepped in and reedited the picture, which was released to small box-office returns. Recovering from this public drubbing was difficult. After several years, Peckinpah's resurrection picture was *The Wild Bunch* (1969), featuring a group of obsolete gunslingers in a face-off against a Mexican army in one of cinema's bloodiest, most balletic scenes of cathartic

RIGHT: The aging outlaws, led by William Holden, mean business in *The Wild Bunch*.

violence ever. Remarkable still, *The Wild Bunch* codified the Peckinpah thematic of men as animals, brought together by loyalty and sundered through civilization. The film proved popular, and put Peckinpah on firm ground for the 1970s. In 1971 *Straw Dogs* was released, the story of a bookish man who returns with his wife to her native village. Critical to the film's reception was its overt sexism, and rape as justice for the meanderings of a manipulative woman. Next was *Junior Bonner* (1972), followed by a pair of classics, the Ali MacGraw and Steve McQueen romantic action film *The Getaway* (1972) and the elegiac *Pat Garrett & Billy the Kid* (1973).

The remaining years of his career were relatively slight. Some argue for *Cross of Iron* (1977) or for sequences in *The Killer Elite* (1975) and *Convoy* (1978). Peckinpah's life ended in 1984 with a fatal stroke; his career, despite several gems, could have amounted to more. **GCQ**

ABOVE: Kris Kristofferson and Bob Dylan in Pekinpah's *Pat Garrett & Billy the Kid.*

Sam's Final Shot

Pat Garrett & Billy the Kid was a classic, not least in the pyrotechnics between MGM president James Aubrey and Peckinpah during production. As Paul D. Zimmerman noted in his review, "This new film is a casualty of a prolonged shoot-out . . . ." After Peckinpah delivered two versions of his director's cut, Aubrey seized control, had the film re-edited, and released—to scathing reviews. Peckinpah, however, arranged for his original cut to be stolen and stored in his personal vault. After his death, this version, which includes a scene where Pat Garrett shoots at his own mirror image, was released to the public.

WOJCIECH HAS

Born: Wojciech Jerzy Has, April 1, 1925 (Kraków, Poland); died 2000 (Łódź, Poland).

Directing style: Polish-born surrealist, poetical, psychological dramas, and literary adaptations; political and outsider overtones; visual nature of narratives; journey motifs.

Top Takes...

Niezwykla podróz Baltazara Kobera 1988

Osobisty pamietnik grzesnika . . . przez niego samego spisany 1986

Pismak 1985

Nieciekawa historia 1983

Sanatorium pod klepsydra 1973
(The Hour-Glass Sanatorium)

Lalka 1968 (The Doll)

Szyfry 1966 (The Codes)

Rekopis znaleziony w Saragossie 1965
(The Saragossa Manuscript)

Jak byc kochana 1963

Zloto 1962

Rozstanie 1961

Wspólny pokój 1960

Petla 1958 (The Noose)

"Time is the domain of . . . film. Playing with time activates the imagination of film viewers."

Polish director Wojciech Has is best known to international viewers as the director of elegantly surreal mind-benders such as *Rekopis znaleziony w Saragossie* (1965) (*The Saragossa Manuscript*), adapted from Jan Potocki's deliriously self-referential 1813 novel, and a favorite of Grateful Dead front man Jerry Garcia who, along with Martin Scorsese, helped finance its restoration in the 1990s; and *Sanatorium pod klepsydra* (1973) (*The Hour-Glass Sanatorium*), based on stories by Bruno Schulz. Has was born in Kraków and died in Łódź, home of the prestigious Leon Schiller's National Higher School of Film, Television and Theater with which he had been associated since the 1970s. He began his career producing documentary and educational films in the mid-1940s. His first commercially released fiction feature was *Petla* (1958) (*The Noose*), a pitiless portrait of an alcoholic on the verge of suicide.

Has worked steadily throughout the 1960s, making films whose visionary, hypnotic beauty offsets their grim subject matter and captivate filmgoers looking for an alternative to earthbound realism. He made his most important films during the 1950s and 1960s heyday of the Polish School, but he maintained a unique identity separate from any movement. Career highlights include *Szyfry* (1966) (*The Codes*), a post-World War II psychological drama starring the Polish James Dean, Zbigniew Cybulski, and scored by noted Polish composer Krzysztof Penderecki; and *Lalka* (1968) (*The Doll*), which was based on the 1899 Boleslaw Prus novel often described as the Polish equivalent of *Madame Bovary*. Although Has made only a handful of films after *The Hour-Glass Sanatorium*, he exerted a powerful influence on a generation of Eastern European filmmakers. **MM**

ROBERT MULLIGAN

Born: Robert Mulligan, August 23, 1925 (New York City, New York, U.S.).

Directing style: Dramas; poignant, period-set, coming-of-age movies and literary adaptations; slow-paced storytelling; strong characterizations; close-up and slow motion shots.

After starting out training to be a priest, Robert Mulligan switched to studying radio communications at Fordham University, then served with the U.S. Marine Corps during World War II. After the war, he worked in the editorial department of the *New York Times*, before leaving to try his luck in TV. He made his name in live TV drama in the 1950s, directing Basil Rathbone in his final screen performance as Sherlock Holmes in *Suspense* (1953), and helming episodes of *The Philco Television Playhouse* and *Playhouse 90*.

Mulligan made a noteworthy debut, signaling the direction of his career, with *Fear Strikes Out* (1957), in which Anthony Perkins plays a baseball player who overcomes mental illness and a domineering father. He also made interesting, low-key films with Tony Curtis, such as *The Rat Race* (1960), and Rock Hudson, such as *Come September* (1961).

In 1962, Mulligan had his great success with a faithful adaptation of Harper Lee's classic, *To Kill a Mockingbird*. Set in the Deep South, the film saw Gregory Peck play a lawyer who defends an African-American against an unfounded rape charge and his own children against racial prejudice. Mulligan was nominated for a Best Director Oscar, and also revealed his skill at getting superior work from movie actors—Peck won an Oscar for Best Actor.

Never a showy filmmaker, Mulligan went on to make a specialty of sensitive, period-set, coming-of-age pictures such as *Summer of '42* (1971), and literary adaptations such as *Same Time, Next Year* (1978). Even when he made a Western or a gangster picture, he took a slow-burning, nuanced approach, letting suspense arise from situations made understandable in character terms rather than from genre gimmickry. **KN**

Top Takes...

The Man in the Moon 1991
Kiss Me Goodbye 1982
Same Time, Next Year 1978
Bloodbrothers 1978
The Nickel Ride 1974
The Other 1972
Summer of '42 1971
The Pursuit of Happiness 1971
The Stalking Moon 1968
Up the Down Staircase 1967
Inside Daisy Clover 1965
Baby the Rain Must Fall 1965
***To Kill a Mockingbird* 1962** ☆
Come September 1961
The Rat Race 1960
Fear Strikes Out 1957

1920s

"She did something that in our society is unspeakable."

—Atticus Finch, *To Kill a Mockingbird*

RITWIK GHATAK

Born: Ritwik Kumar Ghatak, November 4, 1925 (Dhaka, Bangladesh); died 1976 (Calcutta, West Bengal).

Directing style: Bangladeshi director whose films explore themes of social injustice, and the treatment of women and refugees; imaginative use of sound.

Top Takes…

About the same time that Satyajit Ray was setting out to transform the face of Indian cinema with *Pather Panchali* (1955) (*Song of the Road*), his fellow Bengali Ritwik Ghatak was embarking on his own equally revolutionary first feature, *Nagarik* (1952) (*The Citizen*). But *The Citizen* was not released until 30 years later, well after Ghatak's death, and its fortunes foreshadowed Ghatak's own sporadic, ill-starred career.

Ghatak was born in Dacca in Eastern Bengal, and the forced partition of his country that made him for many years an exile from his home caused a psychological wound that never healed. This trauma echoes through several of his films, notably *Subarnarekha* (1962, released 1965) (*The Golden Thread*) and his finest and richest work, *Meghe Dhaka Tara* (1960) (*Hidden Star*). Many scenes seem to quiver with anger in *Hidden Star*, and it brings together several of Ghatak's key preoccupations: social injustice, the treatment of women in a male-oriented society, and the plight of refugees. It is also enriched by his imaginative and often Expressionist use of sound.

A lighter side of Ghatak's work appears in *Ajantrik* (1958) (*Pathetic Fallacy*), his first film to gain release, about a taxi driver irrationally attached to his decrepit old vehicle, although even here elements of humiliation and loss are never far away. Personal problems, not least his heavy drinking, prevented Ghatak from completing any features for ten years after *The Golden Thread*. Invited back to Bangladesh after the country achieved independence, he made *Titash Ekti Nadir Naam* (1973) (*A River Called Titash*), but the splintering intensity of his earlier work was deteriorating into incoherence. He completed only one more feature, *Jukti, Takko Aar Gappo* (1974) (*Reason, Debate and a Story*), before his death at age fifty. **PK**

"Raw meat is not exactly 'Moghlai kebab.' A cook comes somewhere in between."

YOUSSEF CHAHINE

Born: Gabriel Youssef Chahine, January 25, 1926 (Alexandria, Egypt).

Directing style: Independent and often controversial filmmaker, whose work often deals with social conventions and political issues, particularly of his native country, Egypt, and birthplace, Alexandria.

Youssef Chahine is the undisputed father of Egyptian cinema. After studying at the University of Alexandria, he went to the United States, where he studied film and dramatic arts at California's Pasadena Playhouse. After two years he returned to Egypt, where he worked with Gianni Vernuccio. He then made his directorial debut with *Baba Amin* (1950) (*Father Amine*).

Chahine has a fascination with golden age Hollywood musicals: his characters often slide out of their narrative condition and into choreographed musical numbers. He is also obsessed with the cultural and political history of his country, especially Alexandria, which has led to some controversy: *Bab el hadid* (1958) (*The Iron Gate*), a story about a lame man, played by Chahine himself, advocated workers' rights in Egypt and was banned there for 12 years. The director again revealed his political colors in *Al-Asfour* (1972) (*The Sparrow*), which metaphorically portrays Egypt as a country desperate for change and examines its defeat in the Six-Day War with Israel in 1967.

Chahine's most personal work is his autobiographical quartet: *Iskanderija . . . lih?* (1978) (*Alexandria . . . Why?*), *Hadduta misrija* (1982) (*An Egyptian Story*), *Iskanderija, kaman oue kaman* (1990) (*Alexandria Again and Forever*), and *Alexandrie . . . New York* (2004) (*Alexandria . . . New York*). The films spin a tale of Yehia, a dreamy youth confronting war and poverty. Age has not withered Chahine's taste for courting controversy. *Al-Mohager* (1994) (*The Emigrant*) became subject to a *fatwa* in Egypt, and copies of the film were seized because it offended the Islamic authorities. With Amos Gitai, he collaborated to direct *11'9"01—September 11* (2002), in which 11 directors from different countries made 11-minute shorts addressing the World Trade Center attack. **MP**

Top Takes...

Alexandrie . . . New York 2004
  (*Alexandria . . . New York*)
11'9"01—September 11 2002
Skoot hanswwar 2001 (*Silence . . . We're Rolling*)
L'autre 1999 (*The Other*)
Al-Massir 1997 (*Destiny*)
Al-Mohager 1994 (*The Emigrant*)
Cairo As Seen by Chahine 1991
Iskanderija, kaman oue kaman 1990
Al-yawm al-Sadis 1986 (*The Sixth Day*)
Hadduta misrija 1982 (*An Egyptian Story*)
Iskanderija . . . lih? 1978 (*Alexandria . . . Why?*)
Al-Asfour 1972 (*The Sparrow*)
Bab el hadid 1958 (*The Iron Gate*)
Baba Amin 1950 (*Father Amine*)

"The historical film . . . allows the filmmaker the greatest margin of freedom."

JOHN SCHLESINGER

Born: John Richard Schlesinger, February 16, 1926 (London, England); died 2003 (Palm Springs, California, U.S.).

Directing style: Astute British director of early gritty kitchen-sink dramas, realistic literary adaptations, and gripping thrillers; black humor; portraits of British life.

John Schlesinger always stood slightly apart from the other directors of the British New Wave, and rarely enjoyed the same critical acclaim as Royal Court intellectuals Lindsay Anderson, Tony Richardson, and Karel Reisz. But he was the most commercially successful filmmaker of the group, and outlasted them creatively. Not until the late 1970s, after the success of *Marathon Man* (1976), did his career go off the rails; and as late as 1992 he was still capable of such perceptive work as the Alan Bennett-scripted *A Question of Attribution* (1992), even if he had to retreat back to his first home, BBC TV, to make it.

He made his first short *Black Legend* (1948) while still a student at Oxford University studying English literature. After graduating he went into TV and by the late 1950s he was making documentaries for the BBC.

In his earlier films Schlesinger was well attuned to the zeitgeist. *A Kind of Loving* (1962) and *Billy Liar* (1963) tapped into the Northern social realism school, adding an element of sly humor. *Darling* (1965) nailed the hollowness at the heart of swinging London, and *Far from the Madding Crowd* (1967) still looks like the best production yet made of Thomas Hardy's work. Schlesinger's first U.S. picture, *Midnight Cowboy* (1969), brilliantly captured the bleak disillusion at the end of the 1960s. Back in Britain, *Sunday Bloody Sunday* (1971), with its homosexual theme, rates as his most personal and deeply felt movie. But after the intelligent paranoid thriller *Marathon Man*, things started to go wrong. *Yanks* (1979) indulged to easy nostalgia, and *Honky Tonk Freeway* (1981) was a misconceived, elephantine farce. After that none of Schlesinger's films ever seemed to hit the right tone, and only his TV work sustained his reputation. **PK**

> "… what interests me is not the hero but the coward … not the success but the failure."

ANDRZEJ WAJDA

Born: Andrzej Wajda, March 6, 1926 (Suwalki, Poland).

Directing style: Leading member of the Polish Film School; films often contain political content, and portray Polish history during World War II; politically active and served as senator.

Born to a Polish officer who died in World War II, Andrzej Wajda followed his father into the Resistance movement while still a teenager. After the war he studied painting and later film at the Łódź Film School. Working with one of Poland's then-foremost directors, Aleksander Ford, Wajda gravitated to directing himself with his feature debut *Pokolenie* (1955) (*A Generation*), an antiwar film starring Zbigniew Cybulski that also featured a young Roman Polanski. He enlisted Cybulski again for the similarly themed *Kanal* (1957) and *Popiól i diament* (1958) (*Ashes and Diamonds*), and the three films are often considered in a piece, as "The War Trilogy." Following the death of longtime friend Cybulski, Wajda directed *Wszystko na sprzedaz* (1969) (*Everything for Sale*).

In the 1970s, with films such as *Ziemia obiecana* (1975) (*Land of Promise*), Wajda grew increasingly political and made two films explicitly supportive of the Solidarity movement: *Czlowiek z marmuru* (1977) (*Man of Marble*) and *Czlowiek z zelaza* (1981) (*Man of Iron*); the latter featured Lech Walesa and won the Palme d'Or at the Cannes Film Festival. Wajda's continuing conflict with the government led to exile in France but, despite the closure of his production company, he worked regularly.

After the 1989 liberation of Poland, Wajda returned home, resuming his film career but also participating even more directly in politics, serving as senator. Unlike such globetrotters as Polanski and Krzysztof Kieslowski, Wajda rarely strayed from Poland for the setting of his films, although his subject matter proved increasingly diverse. In 1999 he was awarded an Honorary Oscar. He then directed *Zemsta* (2002) (*The Revenge*), which reunited him with Polanski; it was the first time they had worked together in nearly 50 years. **JK**

Top Takes...

Zemsta 2002 (*The Revenge*)
Nastasja 1994
Eine Liebe in Deutschland 1983
  (*A Love in Germany*)
Danton 1983
Czlowiek z zelaza 1981 (*Man of Iron*)
Panny z Wilka 1979 (*The Girl from Wilko*)
Czlowiek z marmuru 1977 (*Man of Marble*)
Ziemia obiecana 1975 (*Land of Promise*)
Wszystko na sprzedaz 1969
  (*Everything for Sale*)
Gates to Paradise 1968
Sibirska Ledi Magbet 1961
  (*Siberian Lady Macbeth*)
Popiól i diament 1958 (*Ashes and Diamonds*)
Kanal 1957
Pokolenie 1955 (*A Generation*)

"We never hoped to live to see the fall of the Soviet Union, to see Poland as a free country."

JERRY LEWIS

Born: Jerome Levitch, March 16, 1926 (Newark, New Jersey, U.S.).

Directing style: Squeaky-voiced, rubbery-faced, goofy comedian; slapstick moments; master of zany improvisation and ad lib; famous pairing with actor Dean Martin; invented the video-assist shooting technique.

Top Takes…

1920s

Jerry Lewis has an international reputation as a comedian and filmmaker, is a member of the Légion d'Honneur, was nominated for the Nobel Peace Prize, is the author of several books, and is a musician and a legendary philanthropist. The son of vaudeville performers, Lewis first appeared onstage at age five. Between July 1946 and July 1956, he paired with Dean Martin as the most successful comedy duo of all time. Martin played the smooth songster tolerating Lewis's manic excess, and the pair became one of the biggest splashes in U.S. entertainment. After 1956 he began to launch his own filmmaking career, working closely with associates at Paramount Pictures to learn the tricks and tools of the trade.

The Bellboy (1960) was shot in less than two weeks on location at Miami's Fontainebleau Hotel. It was written on the go, and is a textbook on improvisational filmmaking. The Ladies Man (1961) celebrates vivid Technicolor and one of the largest sets ever constructed. The Errand Boy (1961) is an artful romp around Paramutual (Paramount) Studios, where an awkward youth played by Lewis is hired to discover why so much money is being lost. For The Family Jewels (1965), Lewis invented the video-assist technique of shooting that makes videotape playback instantly available to the director on set. However, Lewis's acclaimed masterpiece is The Nutty Professor (1963), a retake on the tale of Doctor Jekyll and Mister Hyde, with an absent-minded chemistry professor converted into a slinky lounge lizard. He works carefully as a director to highlight purely cinematic modes of narration with very tight compositions, and employs his knowledge of all aspects of the filmmaking process, a strength that has endeared him to French critics. **MP**

> "I was about as discreet as a bull taking a p** in your living room."

ANDRÉ DELVAUX

Born: André Delvaux, March 21, 1926 (Heverlee, Brabant, Belgium); died 2002 (Valencia, Spain).

Directing style: Founder of Belgian cinema; director of documentaries and films with a magical realism feel; tense thrillers; subtle use of music.

Although sharp documentaries and surreal comedies are the ideological and commercial backbones of Belgian film culture, André Delvaux helped Belgium develop its own distinctive film aesthetic: magic realism, part-Brueghel, part-Rubens, part-Magritte, and part-Hercule Poirot. Delvaux's TV documentaries in the 1960s showed a love for cinema and set up a frame of reference for his own work. His feature debut, *De Man die zijn haar kort liet knippen* (1965) (*The Man Who Had His Hair Cut Short*), is an introverted, dreamy drama and thriller about a teacher obsessed by one of his students: has he killed her, or is it just her image? In its portrayal of the suffering individual, the film heralded the beginning of modernist cinema in Belgium. For Delvaux, it was the start of more ambitious projects.

Un soir, un train (1968) (*One Night . . . a Train*), *Rendez-vous à Bray* (1971) (*Appointment in Bray*), and *Belle* (1973) perfected his unique blend of aporia, chance meetings, mystery thriller, and wondrous wanderings through cold landscapes, which his composer, Frédéric Devreese, punctuated with subtle suites and little waltzes. Although not intended for the commercial market, these movies nevertheless amassed money, as well as awards, and furnished Belgian fiction film with a visibility it had never enjoyed before. When finances dried up, Delvaux resorted to documentaries again, on old Flemish masters with *Met Dieric Bouts* (1975) and newer New York comedians in *To Woody Allen from Europe with Love* (1980). He revived his reveries twice more, with the frescolike *Benvenuta* (1983) and the superbly somber medieval set piece *L'oeuvre au noir* (1988) (*The Abyss*). By the time Delvaux retired, his work had equipped Belgian cinema with a degree of erudition it would find hard to lose. **EM**

Top Takes...

1001 films 1989
L'oeuvre au noir 1988 (*The Abyss*)
Benvenuta 1983
To Woody Allen from Europe with Love 1980
Met Dieric Bouts 1975
Belle 1973
Rendez-vous à Bray 1971 (*Appointment in Bray*)
Un soir, un train 1968 (*One Night . . . a Train*)
De Tolken 1968
De Man die zijn haar kort liet knippen 1965
   (*The Man Who Had His Hair Cut Short*)
Haagschool 1962
Yves boit du lait 1960
Forges 1956
Nous étions treize 1955

"Everyone in Belgian cinema owes something to him. He opened doors."—Philippe Reynaert

1920s

ROGER CORMAN

Born: Roger William Corman, April 5, 1926 (Detroit, Michigan, U.S.).

Directing style: "King of the Bs"; independent auteur; thrifty filmmaker of action-packed, gory, science-fiction movies and literary adaptations; papier-mâché sets and props.

Top Takes...

Frankenstein Unbound 1990

Gas-s-s-s 1971

The Trip 1967

The Wild Angels 1966

The Tomb of Ligeia 1964

The Masque of the Red Death 1964

X 1963

The Raven 1963

Tales of Terror 1962

Pit and the Pendulum 1961

Creature from the Haunted Sea 1961

Last Woman on Earth 1960

The Little Shop of Horrors 1960

House of Usher 1960

The Wasp Woman 1960

A Bucket of Blood 1959

The Undead 1957

Attack of the Crab Monsters 1957

Not of This Earth 1957

It Conquered the World 1956

Day the World Ended 1955

Swamp Women 1955

The original U.S. indie auteur, Roger Corman could make quick and cheap sing like nobody else. An engineer with a love of literature, Corman's intellectual pragmatism gave an immediacy to his work that usually transcended the kiddie-crap story lines dictated by American Releasing Corporation—later American International Pictures (AIP)—bosses. His early science-fiction titles, in particular *Day the World Ended* (1955), *It Conquered the World* (1956), and *Attack of the Crab Monsters* (1957), are snappy, stripped-down pulp gems characterized by resolutely adult relationships and understated dread. They are also a far cry from the big studio giant-bug flicks of the era, and proof positive that Corman's genius was in his ability to combine swiftness with smarts. As such, the no-budget, two-day wonder *The Little Shop of Horrors* (1960) remains his pivotal classic.

Corman's directorial skills waned somewhat with the Edgar Allan Poe adaptations that are, paradoxically, his best reviewed films. Gorgeous, campy fun, these movies are nevertheless pretentious, egregiously padded parlor-room melodramas that evoke Poe largely in spite of themselves. Moreover, Corman visited this well a few times too often before movingon

RIGHT: Vincent Price and Myrna Fahey starred in Corman's *House of Usher*.

on to a new cash cow: the youth exploitation genre. This was a sign that his legendary moneymaking acumen was now a driving force.

Notwithstanding his midcareer distribution of such foreign-canon stalwarts as *Viskningar och Rop* (1972) (*Cries and Whispers*), *Amarcord* (1973), and *Die Blechtrommel* (1979) (*The Tin Drum*), Corman appeared to lose interest in art, too, reflected in his abandonment of directing after the weird and wonderful *Gas-s-s-s* (1971)—his comeback, *Frankenstein Unbound* (1990), was an uninvigorating lark—and the progressive unwatchability of the films he subsequently produced for his companies New World and Concorde.

Despite these shortcomings, Roger Corman deserves his legendary status: there has not been an independent filmmaker since who is half as adept at thinking on his feet, or as steadfast in working outside the profligate Hollywood system. **MH**

ABOVE: *The Little Shop of Horrors* was made in only two days on a very low budget.

On the Cheap

Corman once joked that he could make a film about the Roman Empire with two extras and a bush. His ability to reuse sets, actors, plots, and footage from foreign productions was unique, and there's something awe inspiring about his thriftiness; it is distinctly American and the results are typically engaging. But it also smacks of creative indifference, and paved the way for lesser chop-and-shoot cheapskates who had no interest in art. Today, Corman is also renowned for his development of up-and-coming talent. His protégés include Oscar-winning directors Martin Scorsese and Ron Howard.

MEL BROOKS

Born: Melvin Kaminsky, June 18, 1926 (Brooklyn, New York, U.S.).

Directing style: Politically incorrect auteur and natural ham actor; comic timing; sense of the absurd; slapstick humor; master of cinematic spoof and parody; daring in his use of racial stereotypes and tasteless comedy.

Top Takes…

Spaceballs 1987
History of the World: Part I 1981
High Anxiety 1977
Silent Movie 1976
Young Frankenstein 1974
Blazing Saddles 1974
The Twelve Chairs 1970
The Producers 1968

A genius for making low-class comedy fit for consumption by the upper crust, Mel Brooks is proof that quality potty humor is not necessarily an oxymoron. Brooks broke into comedy on TV's *Your Show Of Shows* (1950), soon teaming with fellow writer and comedian Carl Reiner as a comedy duo. *The Producers* (1968) introduced Brooks as a politically incorrect auteur, his targets broad-reaching and rarely safe.

As a director, Brooks peaked in the mid-1970s with a pair of near-perfect parodies, *Young Frankenstein* (1974) and *Blazing Saddles* (1974). The former took aim at Universal Studios's horror films, specifically the titular scientist and his monstrous creation, and only played for laughs. The latter, also starring frequent foil Gene Wilder, was a gleefully tasteless take on the Western. Both were steeped in ethnic humor and racial stereotypes, but Brooks showed that such taboo subjects were ripe for the taking, mining comic gold from material less daring writer/directors might have deemed anathema.

Alas, Brooks quickly floundered as a filmmaker. His next parody, an Alfred Hitchcock send-up called *High Anxiety* (1977), was a pale imitation of its predecessors, and *History of the World: Part I* (1981) was a scattershot affair. In fact, Brooks concentrated on producing for several years, including several dramas such as David Lynch's *The Elephant Man* (1980) and David Cronenberg's *The Fly* (1986). He returned behind the camera for *Spaceballs* (1987), a better than expected, if belated send-up of the *Star Wars* series. *Life Stinks* (1991), *Robin Hood: Men In Tights* (1993), and *Dracula: Dead and Loving It* (1995) were all stinkers, however. Yet Brooks revitalized himself as a brand with a musical stage adaptation of *The Producers* (2001), which became the toast of Broadway. **JK**

> "I cut my finger. That's tragedy. A man walks into an open sewer and dies. That's comedy."

NORMAN JEWISON

Born: Norman Frederick Jewison, July 21, 1926 (Toronto, Ontario, Canada).

Directing style: Master storyteller of dramas, romantic comedies, and musicals; often uses themes concerned with racial issues, social inequality, and the nature of justice.

Canadian-born Norman Jewison served in the navy during World War II. In the early 1950s he visited the southern United States, where he was shocked by the racism he observed. A master storyteller, Jewison drew on this experience in many of his films, including the racially charged Rod Steiger and Sidney Poitier murder mystery *In the Heat of the Night* (1967).

He worked in TV in the 1950s, typically in light entertainment, before moving to Hollywood. He began his film career with glossy, cosmopolitan, romantic comedies starring actors such as Doris Day, Rock Hudson, James Garner, and Tony Curtis in films such as *40 Pounds of Trouble*, (1962), *The Thrill of It All* (1963), *Send Me No Flowers* (1964), and *The Art of Love* (1965). He changed his tune by stepping in to replace Sam Peckinpah on the Steve McQueen drama *The Cincinatti Kid* (1965).

From the late 1960s, Jewison has handled high-profile zeitgeist-surfing movies, often using satirical comedy or the crime genre to deal with current issues. He did so most notably in the paranoid Carl Reiner and Alan Arkin comedy *The Russians Are Coming the Russians Are Coming* (1966). After the modishly cool Steve McQueen and Faye Dunaway caper *The Thomas Crown Affair* (1968), he handled vastly different adaptations of hit musicals: the traditional *Fiddler on the Roof* (1971) and the free-spirited *Jesus Christ Superstar* (1973). He is most often associated with major studio prestige films: putting James Caan in the dystopian *Rollerball* (1975), Sylvester Stallone in the union drama *F.I.S.T* (1978), Al Pacino in the bitter legal satire *...And Justice for All* (1979), and Bruce Willis in the tale of a Vietnam War veteran *In Country* (1989). He returned to racial issues with Denzel Washington in *A Soldier's Story* (1984) and *The Hurricane* (1999). **KN**

Top Takes...

The Statement 2003
The Hurricane 1999
Other People's Money 1991
Moonstruck 1987 ☆
Agnes of God 1985
A Soldier's Story 1984
...And Justice for All 1979
F.I.S.T 1978
Fiddler on the Roof 1971 ☆
The Thomas Crown Affair 1968
In the Heat of the Night 1967 ☆
The Russians Are Coming the Russians Are Coming 1966
The Cincinnati Kid 1965
The Art of Love 1965
The Thrill of It All 1963

"When I make a film, I never want the film to become a vehicle of social propoganda."

1920s

KAREL REISZ

Born: Karel Reisz, July 21, 1926 (Ostrava, Czechoslovakia); died 2002 (London, England).

Directing style: Pioneer of the Free Cinema Movement that helped put Britain's working classes on the big screen; naturalistic, poetic social realism.

Top Takes...

Everybody Wins 1990
Sweet Dreams 1985
The French Lieutenant's Woman 1981
Who'll Stop the Rain 1978
The Gambler 1974
Isadora 1968
Morgan: A Suitable Case for Treatment 1966
Night Must Fall 1964
Saturday Night and Sunday Morning 1960
We Are the Lambeth Boys 1958
Momma Don't Allow 1955

Karel Reisz was the son of a Jewish lawyer, and fled from Czechoslovakia to Britain to escape the Holocaust. He achieved prominence in British film culture at an early age, and published a handbook on film editing that enjoyed a more than modest reputation among his fellow professionals. Partnering Lindsay Anderson, he founded the Free Cinema Movement, whose poetic documentaries of real life such as *Momma Don't Allow* (1955) and *We Are the Lambeth Boys* (1958) were characterized by a revolutionary combination of modernism and a realism that was more Humphrey Jennings than John Grierson.

Moving into commercial filmmaking as part of the British New Wave, Reisz proved unable to sustain a consistent career, but he did direct several important films. His adaptation of Alan Sillitoe's *Saturday Night and Sunday Morning* (1960) applied the poetically realist approach of Free Cinema toward the life of the working classes and introduced it to an enthusiastic world cinema audience unaccustomed to frank expressions of sexuality, Northern English accents, and bleak urban vistas. *Morgan: A Suitable Case for Treatment* (1966) takes the analysis of a youthful rebel—this time a hallucinating Marxist who thinks he is King Kong—into absurdist comedy, making it a poignant study of the imperative to grow up, and enter into bourgeois society. *Who'll Stop the Rain* (1978), a kind of anti-Vietnam War tract, catches the strength of feeling that animated 1960s protests, whereas the pseudoexistentialism of *The Gambler* (1974) has its nicely detailed moments. Unsurprisingly, Reisz worked best with strong scripts from iconoclastic playwrights, such as Harold Pinter's intricate and innovative dramatization of John Fowles's novel *The French Lieutenant's Woman* (1981). **BP**

> "Style is not a matter of camera angles . . . it is an expression of your particular opinion."

LINA WERTMÜLLER

Born: Arcangela Felice Assunta Job Wertmüller von Elgg Espanol von Brauchich, August 14, 1926 (Rome, Italy).

Directing style: Controversial Italian director of dramas; themes of love, family, war, sexuality, and honor; frequently casts Giancarlo Giannini; use of wide-angle lens.

Lina Wertmüller made her name during an impressive four-year span, from 1972 to 1975, in which she made five Italian films that gained worldwide acclaim, including her masterpiece, *Pasqualino Settebellezze* (1975) (*Seven Beauties*), for which she earned an Oscar nomination for Best Director, the first female director to do so. All were controversial, but her daringly eccentric exploration of big issues such as love, family, war, sexuality, and honor gained her a passionate audience at the time.

Born in Rome to a family of Swiss aristocrats, Wertmüller rebelled by going into the performing arts. After serving an itinerant apprenticeship, she used her friendship with Flora Carabella, wife of Marcello Mastroianni, to land a job as an assistant director for Federico Fellini on his iconic *8½* (1963). Her first film as director was *I Basilischi* (1963) (*The Lizards*), made with Fellini's support. She directed Giancarlo Giannini for the first time in a TV movie, *Rita la Zanzara* (1966) (*Rita the Mosquito*), the start of a long and fruitful actor–director collaboration.

Such bizarre sequences as the slaughterhouse ballet in *Tutto A Posto E Niente In Ordine* (1974) (*All Screwed Up*), and the courtroom scene in *Seven Beauties*, with its gripping musical accompaniment and lack of dialogue, plus her use of the distorting wide-angle lens, caught the fancy of the era, but later viewers objected to the ways she depicted her characters, often making them exaggerated caricatures who were hard to empathize with. *Seven Beauties* remains a masterwork. Wertmüller's use of the searing juxtaposition of carnality, brutality, the horrors of the Nazi ethos, the desperate pursuit of survival, and murder in the service of honor forces its audience to ask serious questions about humanity in a world dominated by shifting, and often debased, standards of morality. **WSW**

Top Takes...

Peperoni ripieni e pesci in faccia 2004 (*Too Much Romance ... It's Time for Stuffed Peppers*)

Lo speriamo che me la cavo 1992 (*Ciao, Professore!*)

Pasqualino Settebellezze 1975 ☆ **(Seven Beauties)**

Travolti da un insolito destino nell'azzurro mare d'agosto 1974 (*Swept Away*)

Tutto a posto e niente in ordine 1974 (*All Screwed Up*)

Film d'amore e d'anarchia, ovvero 'stamattina alle 10 in via dei Fiori nella nota casa di tolleranza ....' 1973 (*Love and Anarchy*)

Mimì metallurgico ferito nell'onore 1972 (*The Seduction of Mimi*)

Rita la zanzara 1966 (*Rita the Mosquito*)

I Basilischi 1963 (*The Lizards*)

> "The ones who keep going, just to see how it will end. Oh yeah."
>
> —Narrator, *Seven Beauties*

SHOHEI IMAMURA

Born: Shohei Imamura, September 15, 1926 (Tokyo, Japan); died 2006 (Tokyo, Japan).

Directing style: Japanese director whose movies often tackle taboo subjects such as incest and superstition; often uses themes of the struggling heroic woman.

Top Takes...

Like many filmmakers, Shohei Imamura frequently cited fellow Japanese directors Akira Kurasawa and Yasujiro Ozu as two of his greatest inspirations. Unlike many filmmakers, however, Imamura's own stature as a filmmaker is such that he is often mentioned in the same breath as those fellow late, great directors. At the least, he is considered one of the leading names of Japan's second wave of cinema. Imamura worked with Ozu as an assistant on *Bakushû* (1951) (*Early Summer*) and *Tokyo monogatari* (1953) (*Tokyo Story*), leaving the Shochiku Studio in 1954 for a stint at Nikkatsu Studios, which hired him to direct his first film *Nusumareta yokujo* (1958) (*Stolen Desire*). He worked steadily through the 1960s, hitting his stride with a series of often controversial depictions of Japanese society, including *Nippon konchuki* (1963) (*The Insect Woman*) and *Jinruigaku nyumon: Erogotshi yori* (1966) (*The Amorists*).

In the 1970s Imamura worked in documentary before returning to narrative film with *Fukushû suruwa wareniari* (1979) (*Vengeance Is Mine*), but his output slowed down in the 1980s after his Palme d'Or win for *Narayama bushiko* (1983) (*The Ballad of Narayama*). He experienced a late career boost with *Unagi* (1997) (*The Eel*), which also won the Palme d'Or, and two well-received subsequent features *Kanzo sensei* (1998) (*Dr. Akagi*) and *Akai hashi no shita no nurui mizu* (2001) (*Warm Water Under a Red Bridge*). Imamura's final film was an entry in the *11'09"01— September 11* (2002) anthology alongside ten other internationally acclaimed directors. Unlike many of the other more literal segments, his segment was an enigmatic antiwar statement about a Japanese World War II soldier and atomic bomb survivor, who is convinced he is a snake. **JK**

> "He takes what society would call vile and makes beautiful meaning out of it."—Salvatore Botti

YORAM GROSS

Born: Yoram Gross, October 18, 1926 (Kraków, Poland).

Directing style: Leading children's animation filmmaker; knack for storytelling; charming, family content; combination of character animation with live action and photographed backgrounds.

Polish producer, writer, and director Yoram Gross counts films such as *Dot and the Kangaroo* (1977), *The Magic Riddle* (1991), and *Blinky Bill* (1992) among his international successes. As Australia's leading children's animation filmmaker, he drew his trademark philosophy of nonviolence and good winning over evil from his early experiences under the Nazis.

Born into a Jewish family, Yoram Gross managed to stay one step ahead of the Nazis (the family were on Schindler's infamous list) by moving hiding places seventy-two times. After the war, he worked for Dutch director Joris Ivens before immigrating to Israel to prosper as a documentary cameraman. Having won numerous awards as an independent producer and director, he moved to Sydney, Australia, and began working on the TV music show *Bandstand* (1968) before establishing the Yoram Gross Film Studios (YGFS).

The fledgling operation gradually expanded from little more than a cottage outfit to Australia's best known and most prolific animation house. The story of a little girl from the Australian bush, *Dot and the Kangaroo* entranced young audiences with its revolutionary use of animation over a live action background. Stars ranging from Mia Farrow to Rolf Harris appeared in Gross's productions, which have been sold to more than 80 countries. The studio diversified into animated series for TV with *The Adventures of Blinky Bill* (1993). In 1995, Gross was awarded the prestigious Order of Australia for his contribution to the Australian film industry. The kangaroo, Skippy, and the world's most famous dolphin, Flipper, have both enjoyed their own animated outings through the studios, while YGFS created its own multimedia divisions with DVD, CD-ROM, and Web offerings. **TE**

Top Takes...

Dot in Space 1994
Blinky Bill 1992
The Magic Riddle 1991
Dot and the Smugglers 1987
Dot Goes to Hollywood 1987
Dot and Keeto 1986
Dot and the Whale 1986
Dot and the Koala 1985
Epic 1985
The Camel Boy 1984
Dot and the Bunny 1984
Around the World with Dot 1981
The Little Convict 1979
Dot and the Kangaroo 1977
Rak Ba'Lira 1963
Ba'al Hahalomot 1962

"If you watch my films carefully, you will see the history of my life."

1920s

ALBERT AND DAVID MAYSLES

Albert: Born November 26, 1926 (Brookline, Massachusetts, U.S.).
David: Born January 10, 1931 (Brookline, Massachusetts, U.S.); died 1987 (New York, U.S.).

Directing style: Sibling duo notable for revolutionary handheld documentary films; 1960s output chronicles pop culture, lives of famous, or notorious figures.

Top Takes...

Muhammad and Larry 1980
Running Fence 1978
Grey Gardens 1975
Christo's Valley Curtain 1974
Gimme Shelter 1970
Salesman 1969
Meet Marlon Brando 1966
A Visit with Truman Capote 1966
Showman 1963

The sibling duo of Albert and David Maysles were maverick documentary makers who defined the genre in the 1960s, working as an effective team from 1957 until David's death in 1987. Albert has since pressed on by himself, and with a variety of other collaborators. After service in the Tank Corps in World War II, Albert taught for several years. He made his first documentary, *Psychiatry in Russia* (1955) while on a motorcycle trip through Eastern Europe. David worked with army intelligence during the war, and then as a producer's assistant on *Bus Stop* (1956) and *The Prince and the Showgirl* (1957) before abandoning Hollywood. The brothers teamed up to make what they termed "direct cinema"—handheld documentary films, shot in synchronized sound, that chronicled the lives of many of the most notorious figures of 1960s pop culture.

After working on the pioneering political documentary *Primary* (1960), Albert joined David to shoot *Showman* (1963), a day in the life of producer Joseph E. Levine; *What's Happening! The Beatles in the U.S.A.* (1964); *A Visit with Truman Capote* (1966); *Meet Marlon Brando* (1966); and *Gimme Shelter* (1970), which chronicled the disastrous concert by The Rolling Stones in California. Many of these projects grew organically, and some were entirely spur of the moment. Other key films by the brothers include *Salesman* (1969), a brutal portrait of door-to-door Bible salesmen selling ornately illustrated Bibles to the poor; and *Grey Gardens* (1975), which documents the reclusive lifestyle of two close relatives of Jacqueline Kennedy Onassis. Albert has continued to work as a documentary maker, switching to digital video, a move that he feels has given him even greater artistic freedom, often in collaboration with the conceptual artist Christo. **WWD**

> "The natural disposition of the camera is to seek out reality."
>
> —Albert Maysles

HIROSHI TESHIGAHARA

Born: Hiroshi Teshigahara, January 28, 1927 (Chiyoda, Tokyo, Japan); died 2001 (Tokyo, Japan).

Directing style: Director of Japanese avant-garde cinema; playful and challenging melding of genres; collaboration with composer Tôru Takemitsu; lush use of color.

Film was just one medium Hiroshi Teshigahara mastered over a fifty-year career in Japanese avant-garde cinema.

Graduating with a degree in painting from Tokyo's University of Fine Arts and Music, it was ten years before he released his first feature film. *Otoshiana* (1962) (*The Pitfall*) was based on an original script by Kôbô Abe with a score by Tôru Takemitsu, Japan's most renowned modernist composer. It earned Teshigahara the NHK New Director Award, and drew comparisons with Michelangelo Antonioni and Alain Resnais.

The trio went on to adapt Abe's most lauded novel, *Suna no onna* (1964) (*Woman of the Dunes*). A hauntingly erotic tale of a scientist trapped in a relationship with a young widow whose house is surrounded by threatening sand dunes, the film won the Jury Special Prize at Cannes, and propelled Teshigahara into the international spotlight. *Tanin no kao* (1966) (*The Face of Another*) and *Moetsukita chizu* (1968) (*The Man Without a Map*) were twisted genre themes mixing horror, science fiction, and thriller into surreal forms, but were less well received, and Teshigahara's relationship with Abe came to an end.

During the next two decades, Teshigahara concentrated on his other aesthetic endeavors and succeeded his father as *Iemoto*, or grand master, of the Sogetsu School of Ikebana in the art of flower arranging for meditative contemplation.

He made a triumphant return to the cinema with *Rikyu* (1989), a dramatization of the conflict between the warlord Hideyoshi Toyotomi and Sen No Rikyu, the founder of the Sansenke schools of tea ceremony. It served to remind the world of the visionary who had previously emerged with *Woman of the Dunes* and, although he made only one more film, he was honored thereafter as a living national treasure. **RB**

Top Takes...

Princess Goh 1992

Rikyu 1989

Antonio Gaudí 1984

Sama soruja 1972 (*Summer Soldiers*)

Moetsukita chizu 1968
  (*The Man Without a Map*)

Bakuso 1967 (*Explosion Course*)

Tanin no kao 1966 (*The Face of Another*)

Suna no onna 1964 ☆
  (Woman of the Dunes)

La fleur de l'âge, ou Les adolescentes 1964
  (*That Tender Age*)

Otoshiana 1962 (*The Pitfall*)

Jose Torres 1959

1920s

"It's useless. The sand can swallow up cities and countries, if it wants to."—*Woman of the Dunes*

KENNETH ANGER

Born: Kenneth Wilbur Anglemyer, February 3, 1927 (Santa Monica, California, U.S.).

Directing style: Notorious and shocking underground, avant-garde, cult filmmaker; often uses occult themes; pioneer of gay cinema; innovative use of pop music and jump cuts.

Top Takes...

"I needed to do something to make money . . . . I told stories to people like François Truffaut."

If there is a devil in the film universe, it must be Kenneth Anger. A prodigious child actor, the impish Anger grew up amid the gossip of Hollywood. Later, he published these seamy stories as *Hollywood Babylon* (1958) a book so scandalous that it alone secured his place in film history. Anger was first noticed with *Fireworks* (1947), an openly homosexual and violent fantasy of sex and domination. Sinful innuendo infused *Rabbit's Moon* (1950) and *Eaux d'artifice* (1953), against a background juxtaposition of finesse and frankness in sound using 1950s pop and Antonio Lucio Vivaldi. The rambunctious *Scorpio Rising* (1964), a rock 'n' roll pseudodocumentary about leather-clad bikers, complete with homosexual inferences and Nazi iconography, was a landmark film that pulled U.S. avant-garde cinema into popular culture, kicking and screaming.

Anger also developed an interest in occultism. This first influenced *Inauguration of the Pleasure Dome* (1954), a wickedly sensual, psychedelic trip. With fad followers The Rolling Stones, he crafted the creepy, droning *Invocation of my Demon Brother* (1969), and the mythological, spitfire-edited, hallucinogenic *Lucifer Rising* (1972), featuring music by Jimmy Page and a member of the Charles Manson family, was a cult film for occult fans. Thirty years of silence ensued, until Anger resurfaced with two shorts, about the notorious British occultist Aleister Crowley's paintings, *The Man We Want to Hang* (2002), and pop-culture icon Mickey Mouse, *Mouse Heaven* (2004). A lot of avant-garde cinema comes down to attitude; Anger publicly announced his own death once. That self-mystification notwithstanding, his oeuvre demonstrates a devilish prowess, and possesses the charm to seduce, the skills to impress, and the power to shock. **EM**

TATSUMI KUMASHIRO

Born: Tatsumi Kumashiro, April 24, 1927 (Saga, Japan); died 1995 (Tokyo, Japan).

Directing style: Director of a style of Japanese soft-core pornographic films; erotic use of female nudity and scenes of simulated sexual activity; strong female characters.

There can be few great directors whose reputation is built on a series of soft-core porn films, but Tatsumi Kumashiro's best work propelled the Japanese *pinku eiga* genre into the art theater.

The emergence of so-called "pink" films in the late 1960s reflected a growing crisis in the Japanese film industry. Traditional genres were waning and competition from TV was driving many studios toward bankruptcy. Even Nikkatsu Studios, Japan's oldest film studio, announced in 1971 it was switching production from action films to the more lucrative soft-core pornography market. Kumashiro, working for Nikkatsu since 1955 and recently graduated from assistant to full-time director, chose to remain rather than seek a career in TV.

His first effort for their new Nikku Roman Porno (Romantic Pornography) line, *Nureta kuchibiru* (1972), was an instant critical and box-office smash. In contrast to most pink films, Kumashiro's female characters were strong and sexually confident, and the censor's restrictions regarding no genitalia or explicit sex acts only spurred his filmic inventiveness. A literate and politically engaged man, his tales were set in the underbelly of Japanese society, depicting hopeless lives made bearable through bawdy humor and uninhibited sex.

Yojohan fusuma no urabari (1973) (*A Man and a Woman Behind the Fusuma Screen*) and *Akai kami no onna* (1979) (*The Woman with Red Hair*) are now among the best Japanese films of the 1970s, earning praise for their feminist stance, superior production values, and their erotic power. The advent of hard-core video porn in the early 1980s spelled the demise of *pinku eiga* but Kumashiro continued to work up until his death. Retrospectives have since ensured that the lost art of his pink films is now finding an international audience. **RB**

Top Takes...

Bo no kanashimi 1994
Kamu onna 1988 (*Love Bites Back*)
Koibumi 1985 (*Love Letter*)
Mika Madoka: yubi o nurasu onna 1984
Modori-gawa 1983
A! Onnatachi: waika 1981
Akai kami no onna 1979
  (*The Woman with Red Hair*)
Dannoura yomakura kassenki 1977
Nureta yokujo: hirake! Tulip 1975
Seishun no satetsu 1974
Yojohan fusuma no urabari 1973 (*A Man and a Woman Behind the Fusuma Screen*)
Nureta yokujo: Tokudashi nijuichi nin 1974
Kagi 1974
Nureta kuchibiru 1972

"If I can shoot what I like, without the pressure of how it will turn out, I am motivated."

HERBERT ROSS

Born: Herbert David Ross, May 13, 1927 (New York City, New York, U.S.); died 2001 (New York City, New York, U.S.).

Directing style: Versatile and innovative choreographer; director of entertaining musicals and dramas; notable artistic collaboration with writer Neil Simon.

Top Takes…

Herbert Ross made his stage debut as Third Witch with a touring company of *Macbeth* (1942). His choreography career began with the American Ballet Theater in 1950. The first movie he choreographed was *Carmen Jones* (1954), but it was working with Barbra Streisand as choreographer and director of musical numbers on *Funny Girl* (1968) that led to his first directorial success, *Goodbye, Mr. Chips* (1969).

There followed *The Owl and the Pussycat* (1970), *T. R. Baskin* (1971), *Play It Again, Sam* (1972), *The Last of Sheila* (1973), and a Streisand reprise, *Funny Lady* (1975). Then he began a fruitful and popular collaboration with Neil Simon through five films, *The Sunshine Boys* (1975), *The Goodbye Girl* (1977), *California Suite* (1978), *I Ought to Be in Pictures* (1982), and *Max Dugan Returns* (1983), while *The Turning Point* (1977) received a wealth of Oscar nominations, including one for Best Director.

The final portion of his career offers one brilliant experiment, *Pennies from Heaven* (1981); a thriller, *The Seven-Per-Cent Solution* (1976); a group of comedies, *Protocol* (1984), *The Secret of My Succe$s* (1987), *My Blue Heaven* (1990), and *Undercover Blues* (1993); and a handful of dramas, *Nijinsky* (1980), *Dancers* (1987), *True Colors* (1991), and *Boys on the Side* (1995). Yet when people remember Ross today, it is primarily because of *Footloose* (1984) and *Steel Magnolias* (1989). Through *Footloose*, he taught teenagers to dance like newcomer Kevin Bacon, and to love soundtrack albums in a way that marked the growing pains of many Generation Xers. In *Steel Magnolias*, Ross made Southern womanhood a subject of bittersweet affection, while affirming Sally Field as a mature screen actress, and helping Julia Roberts on her road to stardom. **GCQ**

> "Laughter through tears is my favorite emotion."
>
> —Truvy, *Steel Magnolias*

LUCIO FULCI

Born: Lucio Fulci, June 17, 1927 (Rome, Italy); died 1996 (Rome, Italy).

Directing style: Italian maker of gory, visceral thrillers and horror movies; controversial anti-Catholic sentiments; flamboyant imagery; trademark cameo appearances in his films.

Lucio Fulci abandoned a career in medicine to study at the Experimental Film School in Rome, and worked in numerous roles for directors such as Luchino Visconti and Federico Fellini, and the writer Steno. He made his directorial debut with *I Ladri* (1959) (*The Thieves*), the first of a number of comedies he both wrote and directed.

Fulci worked in a wide variety of genres before directing his first *giallo*, an Italian twist on the mystery genre, *Una sull'altra* (1969) (*One on Top of the Other*), and went on to make a number of particularly well-crafted examples of the genre, including *Una lucertola con la pelle di donna* (1971) (*Lizard in a Woman's Skin*) and *Non si sevizia un paperino* (1972) (*Don't Torture a Duckling*). Despite the artistic merit of these pictures, their controversial content led to a poor reception, halting Fulci's career. It was not until after a number of TV stints that Fulci achieved international recognition with *Zombi 2* (1979) (*Zombie*), a horror film that was marketed to Europe as a sequel to George A. Romero's *Dawn of the Dead* (1978).

Cementing Fulci's reputation as a gore specialist, the director's early 1980s output included *Paura nella città dei morti viventi* (1980) (*The Gates of Hell*), *E tu vivrai nel terrore—L'aldilà* (1981) (*Seven Doors of Death*), and the notorious video nasty *Lo Squartatore di New York* (1982) (*The New York Ripper*). More master craftsman than auteur, in Fulci's most engaging works it is the director's obsession with the technicality of filmmaking that is revealed; his special effects revel in the physicality of anatomical gore as pure spectacle. With little regard for coherent narrative or character development, the allure of films such as *Seven Doors of Death* lies in the promise of a visceral cinematic experience. **AK**

Top Takes…

Le porte del silenzio 1991 (*Door to Silence*)

Zombi 3 1988

Lo Squartatore di New York 1982
    (*The New York Ripper*)

E tu vivrai nel terrore—L'aldilà 1981
    (*Seven Doors of Death*)

Paura nella città dei morti viventi 1980
    (*The Gates of Hell*)

Zombi 2 1979 (*Zombie*)

I Quattro dell'apocalisse 1975
    (*Four Horsemen of the Apocalypse*)

Non si sevizia un paperino 1972
    (*Don't Torture a Duckling*)

Una lucertola con la pelle di donna 1971
    (*Lizard in a Woman's Skin*)

Una sull'altra 1969 (*One on Top of the Other*)

I Ladri 1959 (*The Thieves*)

"Cinema is everything to me. I live and breathe films —I even eat them."

BOB FOSSE

Born: Robert Louis Fosse, June 23, 1927 (Chicago, Illinois, U.S.); died 1987 (Washington, District of Columbia, U.S.).

Directing style: Maker of musicals and dramas; exciting choreography; skillful editing of action with music; fast cutting; innovator of the serious musical.

Top Takes...

Star 80 1983
All That Jazz 1979 ☆
Lenny 1974 ☆
Cabaret 1972 ★
Sweet Charity 1969

Although the five films Bob Fosse directed were mostly critically acclaimed and commercially successful, his reputation as a film director has not really survived, overshadowed by his credits as a choreographer on *The Pajama Game* (1957), *Damn Yankees!* (1958), *How to Succeed in Business Without Really Trying* (1967) and, on the basis of his original stage production, *Chicago* (2002). Of course, he was identified with musicals; *Sweet Charity* (1969) and *Cabaret* (1972), his first films as director, were adapted from stage shows themselves, and built around lithe, exciting women such as Shirley MacLaine and Liza Minnelli executing the knee-flexes and finger-snaps that were Fosse's trademarks as a choreographer.

In a post-*Sound of Music* (1965) era, when musicals were hyperinflated juggernauts best known for losing huge amounts of money, Fosse's hipper, more politically engaged films connected with audiences, and Oscar voters. However, he branched out with the music-free, black and white *Lenny* (1974), a biopic of comedian Lenny Bruce, played by Dustin Hoffman, that was heavy on revealing performance pieces and had an air of doomed hustling. These elements recurred in Fosse's semiautobiographical *All That Jazz* (1979), a fantasy about his own life and impending death, with Roy Scheider as a directorial stand-in, and deliberately brassy, old-fashioned production numbers. Fosse only managed one more movie, a smaller monument to bad taste, *Star 80* (1983), the luridly sparkly biography of murdered *Playboy* centerfold Dorothy Stratten, played by Mariel Hemingway. There is no doubt that, had Fosse lived, he would have directed a more exciting version of *Chicago* than Rob Marshall; it is even rumored he had pop star Madonna in mind to headline. **KN**

" . . . work like you don't need the money, and dance like nobody's watching."

KEN RUSSELL

Born: Henry Kenneth Alfred Russell, July 3, 1927 (Southampton, Hampshire, England).

Directing style: Daring visionary British filmmaker; moving camera shots; overdramatic, extravagant, and operatic feel; striking, stylish visual imagery; bold use of music.

Legendary and invariably controversial in world cinema, British filmmaker Ken Russell is responsible for some of the most daring movies ever crafted: *Women in Love* (1969), *The Music Lovers* (1970), *The Devils* (1971), *Mahler* (1974), *Tommy* (1975), *Altered States* (1980), and *Crimes of Passion* (1984). Starting at the BBC making simple documentaries, Russell's work quickly gave way to increasingly ambitious biographical dramas, starting with *Monitor: Elgar* (1962). They were marked by the director's striking visuals, brilliant use of music, and strong personal viewpoint. It was not until *Women in Love* that Russell made his mark on world cinema. A breakthrough adaptation of D. H. Lawrence's novel, the film remains a landmark in its frank depiction of sexuality and homosexual themes, which Russell expanded upon in his next picture, *The Music Lovers*.

Working in a distinctly operatic style, but capable of surprising moments of quiet, gentle beauty, Russell has continued to push the boundaries of mainstream film, and what the censors will allow; *The Devils* has never been released without significant cuts. His 1970s work reached its experimental apex with the utterly stylized *Lisztomania* (1975), an influential flop that paved the way for Baz Luhrmann's *Moulin Rouge!* (2001) and Sofia Coppola's *Marie Antoinette* (2006). While no less personal and extravagant, Russell's subsequent work has rarely been as extreme. His films from the 1980s have shown a growing tendency toward a more reflective state of mind, but are less a repudiation of his earlier approach than an outgrowth of it. A strikingly original filmmaker, Russell remains one of the handful of directors to create a wholly personal body of work within the confines of mainstream cinema. **KH**

Top Takes...

Trapped Ashes 2006
Tales of Erotica 1996
The Lair of the White Worm 1988
Salome's Last Dance 1988
Aria 1987
Gothic 1986
Crimes of Passion 1984
Altered States 1980
Tommy 1975
Mahler 1974
The Boy Friend 1971
The Devils 1971
The Music Lovers 1970
Women in Love 1969 ☆
Peepshow 1956

"I want to shock people into awareness. I don't believe there is virtue in understatement."

MARCEL OPHÜLS

Born: Hans Marcel Oppenheimer, November 1, 1927 (Frankfurt am Main, Germany).

Directing style: Hard-hitting German documentary maker; provocative themes covering war, politics, and the nature of patriotism; lengthy movies; famed for bringing twentieth-century atrocities to light.

Top Takes…

Veillées d'armes 1994 (The Troubles We've Seen:
    A History of Journalism in Wartime)

November Days 1991

Hôtel Terminus 1988

The Memory of Justice 1976

A Sense of Loss 1972

Le chagrin et la pitié 1969
    (The Sorrow and the Pity)

Faites vos jeux, mesdames 1965
    (Make Your Bets, Ladies)

Peau de banane 1963 (Banana Peel)

L'amour à vingt ans 1962 (Love at Twenty)

Matisse ou le talent de bonheur 1960

The son of director Max Ophüls, Marcel Ophüls moved with his father to California after the former's exile from Germany. The younger Ophüls attended high school in Hollywood and stayed primarily in state for his subsequent higher education. Ophüls did eventually study at the Sorbonne in Paris, and he remained in France afterward working as an assistant for such directors as Julien Duvivier and John Huston, before dipping his toes into German and French TV.

After directing a handful of unremarkable feature fiction films, Ophüls changed tack to documentary, a decision that would prove quite fruitful with the release of Le chagrin et la pitié (1969) (The Sorrow and the Pity), a 262-minute account of the Nazi occupation of France focusing on the provincial town of Clermont-Ferrand. It revealed the previously seldom chronicled range, nature, and extent of collaboration between the French citizens and their Nazi occupiers. Many consider The Sorrow and the Pity to be Ophüls's crowning achievement, and one of the most important documentaries ever made. Unsurprisingly Ophüls has stuck primarily to documentary ever since, with the occasional digression as actor. His Hôtel Terminus (1988), which documented the life of the notorious Nazi war criminal, Klaus Barbie, who was known for his deeds as the "Butcher of Lyons," won the Best Documentary Academy Award as well as the International Critics Prize at Cannes Film Festival. Ophüls's most recent work, the epic and ambitious Veillées d'armes (1994) (The Troubles We've Seen: A History of Journalism in Wartime) attempted to capture and cover the intricacies and complications of reporting in the midst of armed conflict, focusing on the then-raging war in Sarajevo. **JK**

> "My basic belief is … you must not upset the scene you are filming."—On documentary making

ROGER VADIM

Born: Roger Vladimir Plemiannikov, January 26, 1928 (Paris, France); died 2000 (Paris, France).

Directing style: Daring filmmaker of sexualized melodramas; sensual and erotic content; emblematic shots of beautiful leading ladies; creator of sex-kitten image.

Roger Vadim was one of the founders of the French New Wave, but is seldom remembered for his early accomplishments because he rapidly embraced commercial cinema and entered into a string of relationships that made his personal life more notorious than his films. Born in Paris, Vadim began his career as a writer for *Paris Match*, and a director of live TV. In 1956, he made what would become his signature film, *Et Dieu . . . créa la femme* (. . . *And God Created Woman*), starring his first wife, Brigitte Bardot. Shot in CinemaScope and color, the film looks tame today, but was revolutionary for its time in its unabashed delight in nudity, sexuality, and the fervor of young love.

The movie was an international success, due in large part to its highly sexualized content, but Vadim had shot it so quickly and inexpensively, using a minimal crew, that it soon became an inspiration for young directors Jean-Luc Godard and François Truffaut, who were moved to make films using similar methods, landing the New Wave in France. Alas, Vadim's films settled into a nearly exploitational groove, as he later married Annette Stroyberg and then Jane Fonda, and subsequently created only a few films of lasting value, most notably *Les liaisons dangereuses* (1959) (*Dangerous Love Affairs*), *Et mourir de plaisir* (1960) (*Blood and Roses*) with Stroyberg, and *La Ronde* (1964) (*Circle of Love*), with Fonda, who later starred in the science-fiction spoof *Barbarella* (1968). By the 1970s, Vadim was directing the splatter comedy *Pretty Maids All in a Row* (1971); by the 1980s he arguably hit rock bottom with *And God Created Woman* (1988). He survived on his scandalous reputation, writing a compelling series of tell-all autobiographies and making TV appearances until his death in 2000, a sad ending to a once-promising career. **WWD**

Top Takes...

Surprise Party 1983
The Hot Touch 1982
Night Games 1980
Une femme fidèle 1976 (*Game of Seduction*)
Hellé 1972
Pretty Maids All in a Row 1971
Barbarella 1968
La curée 1966 (*The Game Is Over*)
La Ronde 1964 (*Circle of Love*)
Le vice et la vertu 1963 (*Vice and Virtue*)
Les sept péchés capitaux 1962
  (*The Seven Deadly Sins*)
Et mourir de plaisir 1960 (*Blood and Roses*)
Les liaisons dangereuses 1959
  (*Dangerous Love Affairs*)
Et Dieu . . . créa la femme 1956
  (*And God Created Woman*)

"Make love? But no one's done that for hundreds of centuries!"—Barbarella, *Barbarella*

JACQUES RIVETTE

Born: Pierre Louis Rivette, March 1, 1928 (Rouen, Seine-Maritime, Haute-Normandie, France).

Directing style: Key director of the French New Wave; expansive approach to narrative; challenging intellectual content; complex; use of improvisation.

Top Takes...

Va savoir 2001 (*Va Savoir (Who Knows?)*)

Haut bas fragile 1995 (*Up, Down, Fragile*)

La belle noiseuse 1991
   (*The Beautiful Troublemaker*)

La bande des quatre 1988 (*The Gang of Four*)

Céline et Julie vont en bateau 1974
   (*Celine and Julie Go Boating*)

Out 1 1971

La Religieuse 1966 (*The Nun*)

Paris nous appartient 1960
   (*Paris Belongs to Us*)

Le coup du berger 1956 (*Fool's Mate*)

Le divertissement 1952

Le quadrille 1950

Aux quatre coins 1949

Jacques Rivette is one of the most highly regarded directors of the French New Wave. Throughout his career, he has offered a variety of complex experiences, from the epic *Out 1* (1971) to the delicate *La belle noiseuse* (1991) (*The Beautiful Troublemaker*). Admittedly, such movies require a degree of intellectual commitment from spectators that is at odds with conventional viewing habits. Yet despite, or perhaps because of, the difficult nature of Rivette's work, the rewards are often all the greater.

Rivette began his film career as a critic in the early 1950s, and by 1956 had directed four shorts. By 1958 he had made his first feature, *Paris nous appartient* (1960) (*Paris Belongs to Us*), and the result was an assured yet sprawling examination of human paranoia. While displaying a similar combination of philosophy and immediacy visible in many early French New Wave films, Rivette's distinctive, more expansive approach to narrative, and his texts' greater intellectual scope would come to characterize the remainder of his work.

His subsequent films range from the relatively conventional *La Religieuse* (1966) (*The Nun*) to the formally audacious *Out 1*. *Céline et Julie vont en bateau* (1974) (*Celine and Julie Go Boating*), possibly Rivette's most widely screened picture, is an intricate study of storytelling's consuming power, as two women make visits to a house that seems to be haunted by their own imaginations. Later films, such as *Va savoir* (2001) (*Va Savoir (Who Knows?)*), are experiments in cinematic duration and difficult narrative structures. Despite being overshadowed by the flashy density of Godard's cross-textual references, or Truffaut's more accessible sentimentality, Rivette remains a key figure of the French New Wave, and the creator of some of cinema's most challenging films. **GC**

"Cocteau is someone who has made such a profound impression on me . . . ."

ALAN J. PAKULA

Born: Alan J. Pakula, April 7, 1928 (New York City, New York, U.S.); died 1998 (Long Island, New York, U.S.).

Directing style: Intelligent, stylish dramas and gripping conspiracy thrillers; sophisticated and subtle visuals; socially aware themes; thoughtful characterization.

Although he was far from prolific, Alan J. Pakula's fingerprints can be found on hundreds of films, both directly as producer and director, and indirectly through his continuing influence as a master of conspiracy thrillers. His films were sophisticated and subtle, with carefully drawn character studies. Following his birth in New York in 1928 and his Ivy League education at Yale, Pakula's cinematic career began on a more innocent note as producer of the gentle masterpiece *To Kill a Mockingbird* (1962), which won three Academy Awards.

But it was when the 1960s turned into the 1970s that Pakula tapped into an undercurrent of paranoia and political dissatisfaction for a trio of memorable but unconventional thrillers. *Klute* (1971) starred Jane Fonda as a callgirl mysteriously related to a missing person case, and *The Parallax View* (1974) starred Warren Beatty as a reporter who stumbles upon a nebulous, dangerous, and far-reaching government conspiracy. However, the thoughtful but gripping *All the President's Men* (1976), an adaptation of *Washington Post* reporters Bob Woodward and Carl Bernstein's best-selling book, served as a post-Watergate epigraph and an epilogue to the disaffected and cynical era Pakula's films helped usher in.

Starting Over (1979) and *Sophie's Choice* (1982) showed Pakula still gifted at leading his actors to Oscar nominations, and Meryl Streep won a Best Actress statuette for the latter, but his subsequent work was erratic and rarely as galvanizing as earlier films. A pair of successful adaptations of best sellers, *Presumed Innocent* (1990) and *The Pelican Brief* (1993), were hailed as returns to form, but *The Devil's Own* (1997) proved both a critical and financial disappointment, as well as Pakula's final picture. He died in a car accident in 1998. **JK**

Top Takes...

The Pelican Brief 1993
Consenting Adults 1992
Presumed Innocent 1990
See You in the Morning 1989
Orphans 1987
Dream Lover 1986
Sophie's Choice 1982
Rollover 1981
Starting Over 1979
Comes a Horseman 1978
All the President's Men 1976 ☆
The Parallax View 1974
Love and Pain and the Whole Damn Thing 1973
Klute 1971
The Sterile Cuckoo 1969

1920s

"Inhibitions are always so nice because they're so nice to overcome."—Bree Daniels, *Klute*

AGNÈS VARDA

Born: Agnès Varda, May 30, 1928 (Brussels, Belgium).

Directing style: "Grandmother of the French New Wave"; carefully choreographed and composed shots; combination of documentary material with fictional framing story; independent and single-minded director.

Top Takes…

"[A documentary means] a movement to liberate oneself from egoism."

Agnès Varda is a major force in the French New Wave who happily has remained true to her vision as an independent and uncompromising artist, has readily adapted to technological change in the cinema, and is still active today as a digital filmmaker with a wide audience.

Varda's first feature, *La pointe-courte* (1956), was edited by Alain Resnais, and the resulting mix of documentary material with fictive characters and situations would become a hallmark of her subsequent work. *Cléo de 5 à 7* (1961) (*Cleo from 5 to 7*) demonstrated, in its audacious mixture of color and black and white, a stylistic adventurousness shared by her New Wave colleagues. Her next feature, *Le Bonheur* (1965) (*Happiness*), is a departure for Varda. Shot in a pop art style of colorful excess, reminiscent of the style she found artificial in the films of her husband, Jacques Demy, it tells the tale of a young woman happily married with two children, until her husband takes a mistress. Confronted with her husband's infidelity, she drowns herself. In the film's horrific ending, the mistress replaces the wife in her husband's affections permanently. The children accept her, the husband loves her, and life goes on as before. As the 1960s progressed, Varda made several political films against the Vietnam War, and in support of the Black Panthers, and then in 1985 made a stunning comeback film *Sans toit ni loi* (*Vagabond*). She demonstrated that she had not lost her edge with *Les glaneurs et la glaneuse* (2000) (*The Gleaners & I*), a documentary essay shot entirely on a handheld, digital-video camera. In her late seventies, Varda is as up to date and modern as many of her younger colleagues, and the grandmother of the New Wave continues to inspire a new generation of filmmakers. **WWD**

TONY RICHARDSON

Born: Cecil Antonio Richardson, June 5, 1928 (Shipley, Yorkshire, England); died 1991 (Los Angeles, California, U.S.).

Directing style: British maker of dramas; use of speeded-up motion, burst wipes, and flashbacks; lyrical moments mixed with scenes of brutality.

One of the most influential of the "Angry Young Men" of British cinema, Tony Richardson was forced to attend a regimented secondary school that he hated. There he developed a lifelong fear and distrust of the British class system: a fear that would surface continually in his films as a director, most notably in *The Loneliness of the Long Distance Runner* (1962).

By the early 1950s Richardson was working as a TV and theatrical director. In London, he fell in with Karel Reisz, Lindsay Anderson, and other members of the Free Cinema Movement, and codirected *Momma Don't Allow* (1955) with Reisz.

Richardson's zenith as a director was brief but incandescent. *A Taste of Honey* (1961) documented British working-class life. *The Loneliness of the Long Distance Runner* drew upon his own school experiences to create a vision of earthly hell in a state-run reform school. Richardson stages the film with such dazzling visual brio that it leaps off the screen. His adaptation of Henry Fielding's novel *Tom Jones* (1963) was his most commercial and critical success, but even as this film topped at the box office, Richardson's career was going into reverse. His version of Evelyn Waugh's *The Loved One* (1965) was an intriguing misfire, and subsequent films were even less successful, including *Ned Kelly* (1970) and the John Irving story *The Hotel New Hampshire* (1984).

In 1991, Richardson completed his final and most effective late work, the military drama *Blue Sky* (1994). Tragically, he was diagnosed with AIDS during filming, and died soon after of complications from the disease. Richardson's career is an odd one; but his first pictures are still sharp, aggressive, and beautifully constructed, and his contribution to the cinema, especially the New British Cinema, is both resonant and lasting. **WWD**

Top Takes...

Blue Sky 1994
The Border 1982
A Delicate Balance 1973
Nijinsky: Unfinished Project 1970
Laughter in the Dark 1969
The Charge of the Light Brigade 1968
The Sailor from Gibraltar 1967
Red and Blue 1967
The Loved One 1965
Tom Jones 1963 ★
The Loneliness of the Long Distance Runner 1962
A Taste of Honey 1961
The Entertainer 1960
Look Back in Anger 1958
Momma Don't Allow 1955

"Madam, I despise your politics as much as I do a fart."

—Squire Western, *Tom Jones*

JAMES IVORY

Born: James Francis Ivory, June 7, 1928 (Berkeley, California, U.S.).

Directing style: Developer of the elegant heritage film; lush, romantic adaptations of literary classics; elaborate period reconstructions; attention to detail; well-chosen casts.

Top Takes…

Le Divorce 2003
Surviving Picasso 1996
Jefferson in Paris 1995
The Remains of the Day 1993 ☆
Howards End 1992 ☆
Mr. & Mrs. Bridge 1990
Slaves of New York 1989
Maurice 1987
A Room with a View 1985 ☆
The Bostonians 1984
Heat and Dust 1983
Savages 1972
Shakespeare-Wallah 1965
The Householder 1963
Venice: Themes and Variations 1957

With producer Ismail Merchant and screenwriter Ruth Prawer Jhabvala, James Ivory transformed international art theater cinema by developing and popularizing the heritage film: the reverential mounting of a literary classic, featuring an elaborate period reconstruction, beautifully photographed. The most typical films of this genre are *Howards End* (1992), which resurrects late-Victorian England as a backdrop to E. M. Forster's penetrating analysis of class, and *The Remains of the Day* (1993), which lends an epic sweep to Kazuo Ishiguro's confessional novel about the end of aristocratic country house life in the 1940s. These two international successes emerged from a marriage of high-quality sources, skillful screenwriting, savvy casting, visual beauty, and superb acting, especially from Emma Thompson and Anthony Hopkins, who starred in both.

The trio began their collaboration with a different kind of film, the postcolonial melodrama, and were influenced by the style of director Satyajit Ray. *The Householder* (1963), *Shakespeare-Wallah* (1965), and *Heat and Dust* (1983)—the first two based on Jhabvala's novels—are the best of a number of productions that limn the amusing, bittersweet relations between the English and their colonial, or former colonial, subjects. *The Remains of the Day* recalls these earlier films in its emphasis on romance and sexual and gender politics, themes also to be found in Ivory's more recent work, such as the story of President Thomas Jefferson's youthful relationship with his fifteen-year-old slave girl Sally Hemmings, *Jefferson in Paris* (1995); the story of artist Pablo Picasso from the viewpoint of a mistress, *Surviving Picasso* (1996); and a contemporary tale of sexual malfeasance, based on the novel by Diane Johnson, *Le Divorce* (2003). **BP**

"James Ivory is very, very subtle in his study of human behavior."—Leslie Caron

STANLEY KUBRICK

Born: Stanley Kubrick, July 26, 1928 (New York City, New York, U.S.); died 1999 (Harpenden, Hertfordshire, England).

Directing style: Cult filmmaker; visionary director of literary adaptations; themes of dehumanization; investigations of the dark side of human nature.

As a child Stanley Kubrick learned to play chess, a game of strategy, and then received a camera for his thirteenth birthday. Afterward, his world view was organized around recognizing dynamic relationships among people, and how to represent these struggles through a lens.

He produced the documentary *Flying Padre* (1951), and made two further documentaries, *Day of the Fight* (1951) and *The Seafarers* (1953), before his fictional feature debut, *Fear and Desire* (1953). The film cost Kubrick his first marriage but led to *Killer's Kiss* (1955) and *The Killing* (1956), on the heels of which actor Kirk Douglas invited him to direct the World War I vehicle, *Paths of Glory* (1957).

The Douglas and Kubrick partnership worked well enough through *Spartacus* (1960), although Kubrick would not knuckle under star pressure. Instead, he choreographed thrilling fights along with the straightforward hero's tale, making *Spartacus* a showcase for both himself and Douglas. But studio interference during the film's production so infuriated him that Kubrick left Hollywood, after a second failed marriage. Moving to England,

Top Takes...

Eyes Wide Shut 1999
Full Metal Jacket 1987
The Shining 1980
***Barry Lyndon* 1975** ☆
***A Clockwork Orange* 1971** ☆
***2001: A Space Odyssey* 1968** ☆
***Dr. Strangelove or: How I Learned to Stop Worrying and Love the Bomb* 1964** ☆
Lolita 1962
Spartacus 1960
Paths of Glory 1957
The Killing 1956
Killer's Kiss 1955
The Seafarers 1953
Fear and Desire 1953
Day of the Fight 1951
Flying Padre 1951

LEFT: *Dr. Strangelove* starring Peter Sellers as the archetypal mad German scientist.

Kubrick and Clarke

Stanley Kubrick spent five years developing *2001: A Space Odyssey* (1968). Collaborating with science-fiction writer Sir Arthur C. Clarke, and combining state-of-the-art technology with a study of human nature, the film floored audiences with its monoliths and spaceships choreographed to classical music.

- Clarke and Kubrick cowrote the screenplay for *2001: A Space Odyssey* but had difficulty collaborating on the novel once filming had commenced. The book is credited to Clarke alone and details of the story differ slightly from the movie.

- The film was groundbreaking in terms of special effects (for which Kubrick earned an Academy Award) and was notable for its realistic representation of travel in outer space.

- Theories on the meanings of the film are so numerous that they are perhaps best left to Kubrick himself: "They are the areas I prefer not to discuss, because they are highly subjective and will differ from viewer to viewer. In this sense, the film becomes anything the viewer sees in it. If the film stirs the emotions and penetrates the subconscious of the viewer, if it stimulates, however inchoately, his mythological and religious yearnings and impulses, then it has succeeded."

- After this film Kubrick never experimented as much again.

he spent the rest of his life in relative seclusion, becoming more mysterious, and ever more eccentric.

Next was *Lolita* (1962), an adaptation of Vladimir Nabokov's infamous novel about pedophilia. Then Kubrick responded to Cold War tensions with the black comedy *Dr. Strangelove or: How I Learned to Stop Worrying and Love the Bomb* (1964) that so exactly enlivened the zeitgeist that it became a lasting reference for the antiwar movement. Its success earned him three Oscar nominations for writing, directing, and producing, and led to his becoming firmly established as one of the great directors of his generation, a title affirmed in his upcoming 1968 mind trip, *2001: A Space Odyssey*.

Controversial and creative

An adaptation of Anthony Burgess's novel about an irredeemable ruffian who is worsened through therapy followed: *A Clockwork Orange* (1971). It was, and still is, a deeply controversial film that suffered at the hands of the censors, both for what it explicitly depicts in the form of rape, gang violence, and abject cruelty, along with what it suggests about the state of the world.

With the growing demands of his third marriage combined with the requirements of mounting a period epic, Kubrick's reputation as an exacting director, set-side tyrant, and perfectionist was cemented by his behavior during filming of *Barry Lyndon* (1975). His increasing tendency for artistic control yielded three more Oscar nominations, and lent fuel to the myth of his creative power. That *The Shining* (1980) is a horror film is correct but incomplete. As an adaptation of a novel by Stephen King, it is really a meditation on stardom in the form of star Jack Nicholson, refracted through the effects of isolation on the psyche of a troubled man, which cannot help feeling like an allegory for Kubrick himself in later years.

Kubrick weighed in on the Vietnam War in *Full Metal Jacket* (1987) as both an expression of First World madness practiced on the Third World, and as the right of passage for men transformed into automatons through groupthink and

physical punishment. Critics and audiences liked the film, earning Kubrick another Academy Award nomination for writing. Kubrick's final work, *Eyes Wide Shut* (1999), is a voyage of discovery for a doctor who unravels a world of sexual and moral tension through a night-long adventure. Audiences were cool, critics harsh, its erotica over hyped, and the director approaching death.

ABOVE: A scene from the futuristic thriller *A Clockwork Orange* with Malcolm McDowell.

Altogether, Kubrick's work is frequently tedious, meditative, and lacking in audience identification, which is also what makes him brilliant. For it is with a confident hand that Kubrick left a number of thoughtful questions about the nature of human desire for status and accomplishment. In the end, it bears repeating, but Kubrick was a skillful chess player, an arranger of stratagems, and a masterful framer of pictures. **GCQ**

"The great nations have always acted like gangsters, and the small nations like prostitutes."

ANDY WARHOL

Born: Andrew Varchola, August 6, 1928 (Forest City, Pennsylvania, U.S.); died 1987 (New York City, New York, U.S.).

Directing style: Influential U.S. pop artist and experimental filmmaker; use of static camera; long running times; innovative subversion of narrative conventions.

Top Takes…

L'Amour 1973
Lonesome Cowboys 1969
The Andy Warhol Story 1967
Salvador Dali 1966
Chelsea Girls 1966
My Hustler 1965
Bitch 1965
Poor Little Rich Girl 1965
The Thirteen Most Beautiful Boys 1964
Lips 1964
Empire 1964
Tarzan and Jane Regained . . . Sort of 1964
Sleep 1963
Haircut 1963
Blow Job 1963

The Warhol films, made in huge numbers between 1963 and 1976, were exactly that: films. They were not installations or gallery-exhibited art works, but underground movies for cinema exhibition, albeit made on uncompromising terms. Andy Warhol's art studio, "The Factory," became his film studio, and his casts, drawn from the rich assortment of artists such as Viva, Edie Sedgwick, and, later, Joe Dallesandro who hung out there, were his superstars.

Shot in most cases on an entirely static camera, usually unscripted, with crude jump cuts, and long, sometimes interminable running times, they were intimidating experiments in the dismantling and rearranging of narrative cinema conventions. Mostly shot in silvery black and white, and on film, in the days before high-definition video, they do, however, look beautiful. Among the most famous, or notorious, were *Sleep* (1963) and *Empire* (1964), the first showing actor John Giorno sleeping for almost six hours, and the latter depicting the Empire State Building from one angle for eight hours. His innovation and vision have influenced the video installation work of many contemporary artists, and brought film as a legitimate art form into the artists' arena. Probably Warhol's best, most enduring, and influential work is *Chelsea Girls* (1966), a series of vignettes projected side by side, two at a time, with the projectionist deciding which one the audience hears as well as sees . . . and for how long. From *My Hustler* (1965) onward he gave creative control to Paul Morrissey whose work for Warhol is often misattributed. Many of the most famous Warhol films (*Chelsea Girls*, *Lonesome Cowboys* (1969), and *Flesh* (1968)) are almost entirely Morrissey's work. **MC**

> "My idea of a good picture is one that's in focus and of a famous person."

RIGHT: Movie poster for Warhol's influential masterpiece, *Chelsea Girls*.

Chelsea Girls

NICOLAS ROEG

Born: Nicolas Jack Roeg, August 15, 1928 (London, England).

Directing style: Influential cult British director; use of flashback and cut-up technique that subverts the concept of the linear narrative; themes of journey; beautiful photography.

Top Takes…

1920s

English filmmaker Nicolas Roeg had spent plenty of time behind the camera before he finally got around to directing; he worked as a cinematographer on a number of 1960s nuggets, including Roger Corman's *The Masque of the Red Death* (1964), François Truffaut's *Fahrenheit 451* (1966), and Richard Lester's *Petulia* (1967).

Roeg's directorial debut, *Performance* (1970), codirected with artist Donald Cammell, showed an artful radical had been waiting in the wings to emerge. The movie, starring Mick Jagger, was the very definition of counterculture, with its infamous cut-ups and controversial content about a rock star's descent into decadence. Warner Brothers were perturbed by the film's sex and violence, and delayed its release for two years. *Walkabout* (1971), about a young girl and her brother lost in the Australian outback, followed. Then came the neohorror shocker *Don't Look Now* (1973), which starred Donald Sutherland and Julie Christie as a husband and wife working in Venice and coming to terms with the death of their daughter by an accidental drowning. Both were stunning films whose eerie themes often contrasted with their beautiful look; both were also photographed by Roeg. *The Man Who Fell to Earth* (1976) starred another rock star, David Bowie, as an alien making sense of Earth culture, and trying to save his own planet. After that Roeg's films became even more eccentric. *Bad Timing* (1980), *Insignificance* (1985), and *Eureka* (1984) were cultish in their appeal, but the latter won him some late career notice. By the 1990s, his work had become more erratic and his ability to attract an audience somewhat in doubt. Yet Roeg has kept busy with a number of projects, not just cinematic but for TV as well. **JK**

> "I shoot a lot of stuff. I think that's probably come from not having gone to film school."

CURTIS HARRINGTON

Born: Curtis Harrington, September 17, 1928 (Los Angeles, California, U.S.).

Directing style: Experimental, underground filmmaker turned horror and suspense genre director; decrepit, camp Hollywood B-movie feel; waspish insider jokes.

Curtis Harrington was an amateur filmmaker as a teenager, and made several experimental shorts in 8mm and 16mm from the early 1940s. He went on to become one of the first directors to graduate from the underground film movement to make proper movies within the industry. *Night Tide* (1961), his first feature, is a slice of Venice Beach Gothic that melds the worlds of Val Lewton and Kenneth Anger, with Dennis Hopper as a sailor in love with a perhaps-real mermaid.

Roger Corman gave Harrington fix-up work, letting him shoot lurid inserts for stolid Soviet science-fiction films, and direct the makeshift, but confusing *Voyage to the Prehistoric Planet* (1965) and *Queen of Blood* (1966). *Games* (1967), with James Caan and Katharine Ross, is a modish Los Angeles take on *Les diaboliques* (1955) (*Diabolique*), with waspish insider jokes—Caan and Ross play characters modeled on Hopper and then-wife Brooke Hayward—and a trace of nastiness.

In the 1970s, post-*Psycho* (1960) and *What Ever Happened to Baby Jane?* (1962), Harrington specialized in casting grande dames in Gothic tales. He got shuddery work from Julie Harris and Anthony Perkins in *How Awful About Allan* (1970), Shelley Winters and Debbie Reynolds in *What's the Matter with Helen?* (1971), John Savage in *The Killing Kind* (1973), and Gloria Swanson in *Killer Bees* (1974). All have a distinctive, decrepit Hollywood camp, but connoisseurs also relish his cameo-laden made-for-TV pastiches of 1940s B-style, such as *The Cat Creature* (1973) and *The Dead Don't Die* (1975). Harrington's sole theatrical feature since 1977 is the dreadful Sylvie Kristel version of *Mata Hari* (1985), but he has varied episodic TV credits on a range of popular fluff shows such as *Wonder Woman* (1976). **KN**

Top Takes...

Usher 2002
Ruby 1977
The Killing Kind 1973
What's the Matter with Helen? 1971
Whoever Slew Auntie Roo? 1971
Games 1967
Queen of Blood 1966
Voyage to the Prehistoric Planet 1965
Night Tide 1961
Picnic 1948
Fragment of Seeking 1946

1920s

"I don't storyboard because I don't have many complex action sequences in my films."

NELSON PEREIRA DOS SANTOS

Born: Nelson Pereira dos Santos, October 22, 1928 (São Paulo, Brazil).

Directing style: Groundbreaking Brazilian director; inspiration for Cinema Novo; improvisation and use of nonprofessional actors; exploration of social issues and life of the poor.

Top Takes…

Brasília 18% 2006

Raízes do Brasil—Uma Cinebiografia de Sérgio Buarque de Hollanda 2004

A Terceira Margem do Rio 1994 (The Third Bank of the River)

Memórias do cárcere 1984 (Memories of Prison)

Tenda dos milagres 1977 (Tent of Miracles)

O amuleto de ogum 1974 (The Amulet of Ogum)

Como era gostoso o meu Francês 1971 (How Tasty Was My Little Frenchman)

Boca de Ouro 1963 (The Golden Mouth)

Vidas secas 1963 (Barren Lives)

Rio zona norte 1957 (Rio, Northern Zone)

Rio 40 Graus 1955 (Rio 100 Degrees F.)

Juventude 1949

"…race is a theme that because of my upbringing is incorporated in my existence."

Nelson Pereira dos Santos is one of Brazil's most distinguished directors, who has made close to 20 feature films. In the 1950s he advocated an independent and socially committed Brazilian cinema, and supported the younger generation of filmmakers, who were to become Cinema Novo directors.

Dos Santos's first feature film, *Rio 40 Graus* (1955) (*Rio 100 Degrees F.*), is a magnum opus of Brazilian neorealism, and a precursor of the Cinema Novo movement of the 1960s. The film tells the story of five kids from the *favelas*, or slums, selling peanuts to rich tourists, and depicts the poverty of the *favela* dwellers in Rio de Janeiro. *Rio zona norte* (1957) (*Rio, Northern Zone*) deals with an unrecognized samba composer from the *favela* played by the famous Brazilian black actor Grande Otelo. *Vidas secas* (1963) (*Barren Lives*) is set in the drought-stricken *sertão*, Brazil's poorest region, where a landless family tries to survive. The famous opening shot depicts the harshness of life in the *sertão*: a long static take shows the barren landscape in the glaring sun, accompanied by a grating creak, followed much later by an ox cart—the source of the sound—and the family looking for a place to live. The film is a masterpiece of Cinema Novo, and dos Santos's most acclaimed piece of work.

In the 1970s, he directed various important pictures, such as *Como era gostoso o meu Francês* (1971) (*How Tasty Was My Little Frenchman*), dealing with colonialism and cannibalism in Brazil in the sixteenth century; and *O amuleto de ogum* (1974) (*The Amulet of Ogum*), about Afro-Brazilian religion practiced by the poor in Rio de Janeiro. One of dos Santos's most recent films is *Raízes do Brasil—Uma Cinebiografia de Sérgio Buarque de Hollanda* (2004), a documentary on the Brazilian historian. **PS**

TOMÁS GUTIÉRREZ ALEA

Born: Tomás Gutiérrez Alea, December 11, 1928 (Havana, Cuba); died 1996 (Havana, Cuba).

Directing style: Leading Cuban director; subtle critique of issues in contemporary Cuba; use of cinema as a tool for political and social change.

The most famous Cuban movie ever, *Memorias del subdesarrollo* (1968) (*Memories of Underdevelopment*), combines found footage with portraiture, politically sound observations with melodrama, allowing Tomás Gutiérrez Alea to unveil his first masterpiece as a signpost of Fidel Castro's revolution. Based on a popular novella, the film locates an elite perspective within an everyday problem: a smart guy is overwhelmed by circumstance and is unable to do more than comment on the world changing around him. So, too, for Alea.

After earning a law degree, he spent two years receiving a cinematic education in Rome in the midst of Italian neorealism's full flower. He began making movies before returning to Cuba where he cofounded Instituto Cubano del Arte y la Industria Cinematográphicos (ICAIC). Funded by the state, ICAIC's filmmakers mixed documentary and fiction image-making to incite action and educate the masses. In Alea, at least, there is a tendency to balance the didactic impulse with a reflection on the cinematic tradition, as can be seen in the movies *Esta tierra nuestra* (1959), *Historias de la revolución* (1960) (*Stories of the Revolution*), and *Las doce sillas* (1962) (*The Twelve Chairs*).

Then there was a high point in narrative films, *Memories of Underdevelopment,* after which Alea mixed documentary and fiction and championed younger filmmakers as in *Una pelea Cubana contra los demonios* (1972) (*A Cuban Fight Against Demons*), *La última cena* (1976) (*The Last Supper*), and *Hasta cierto punto* (1983) (*Up to a Certain Point*).

Alea codirected the Oscar-nominated homosexual love story *Strawberry and Chocolate* (1994), and *Guantanamera* (1995); the films stand as a notable finale for a career focused on underdeveloped imagination and human limitation. **GCQ**

Top Takes...

Guantanamera 1995
Fresa y chocolate 1994
  (*Strawberry and Chocolate*)
Hasta cierto punto 1983 (*Up to a Certain Point*)
La última cena 1976 (*The Last Supper*)
Una pelea Cubana contra los demonios 1972
  (*A Cuban Fight Against Demons*)
Memorias del subdesarrollo 1968
  (*Memories of Underdevelopment*)
Las doce sillas 1962 (*The Twelve Chairs*)
Historias de la revolución 1960
  (*Stories of the Revolution*)
Esta tierra nuestra 1959
Una confusión cotidiana 1950
El Faquir 1947

1920s

"Cinema provides an element, which stimulates participation in the revolutionary process."

SERGIO LEONE

Born: Sergio Leone, January 3, 1929 (Rome, Italy); died 1989 (Rome, Italy).

Directing style: Key Italian maker of spaghetti Westerns; artistic collaborations with actor Clint Eastwood and composer Ennio Morricone; visual sense of an Italian Renaissance artist.

Top Takes…

Once Upon a Time in America 1984

Giù la testa 1971 (*A Fistful of Dynamite*)

C'era una volta il West 1968
  (*Once Upon a Time in the West*)

Il buono, il brutto, il cattivo 1966
  (*The Good, the Bad and the Ugly*)

Per qualche dollaro in più 1965
  (*For a Few Dollars More*)

Per un pugno di dollari 1964
  (*A Fistful of Dollars*)

Il Colosso di Rodi 1961 (*The Colossus of Rhodes*)

A legend of Italian cinema, and filmmaking as a whole, Sergio Leone made his name taking one of the most iconic of U.S. film genres, the Western, and refashioning it for a new era.

Leone began as a screenwriter before a director's illness allowed him to step in and complete *Gli ultimi giorni di Pompei* (1959) (*The Last Days of Pompeii*). *Il Colosso di Rodi* (1961) (*The Colossus of Rhodes*) came next, but by then Leone was ready to leave his imprint with something more personal.

Leone got his chance with *Per un pugno di dollari* (1964) (*A Fistful of Dollars*), then regrouped with genius composer Ennio Morricone, who had become an indispensable part of Leone's team, and Clint Eastwood for *Per qualche dollaro in più* (1965) (*For a Few Dollars More*) and *Il buono, il brutto, il cattivo* (1966) (*The Good, the Bad and the Ugly*), the second apotheosis of the spaghetti Western right down to Morricone's twang-filled score, and its three-way duel at the finale. The only way Leone could top such a production was by toning things down, although *C'era una volta il West* (1968) (*Once Upon a Time in the West*), his masterpiece, hardly lacked his trademark style. Dramatically, however, the film was richer; its depiction of the

RIGHT: The man with no name looks pensive in *For a Few Dollars More*.

dying days of the old West at once elegiac and thrilling, and the recasting of Henry Fonda as the sadistic heavy inspired.

Giù la testa (1971) (*A Fistful of Dynamite*) returned Leone to the camp approach of his earlier Westerns and he contributed to several similar films, most conspicuously the hilarious *Il mio nome è Nessuno* (1973) (*My Name is Nobody*). But Leone would not direct another film until *Once Upon a Time in America* (1984), a dream project about the lifelong friendship and rivalry between two Jewish gangsters. The shoot was arduous and costly, and in the end studio meddling robbed Leone's would-be masterwork of much of its strengths, with the film chopped significantly, to the detriment of its narrative and craft.

Leone never directed another film, dying at the age of sixty in 1989. However, upon release on DVD, *Once Upon a Time in America* was belatedly restored to respect Leone's original vision, and hailed accordingly. **JK**

ABOVE: *Once Upon a Time in America* starring Robert de Niro and James Woods.

Spaghetti Style

Per un pugno di dollari (1964) (*A Fistful of Dollars*) jumpstarted the spaghetti Western movement. The film starred a young Clint Eastwood as the iconic man with no name, cynically playing two rival gangs of a town against one another for personal gain. The film made Eastwood an international star, and introduced Leone as a visionary with an uncanny eye for composition, and a sly wit. It also introduced several of Leone's now oft-imitated trademarks, from jarring cuts to long static shots to sudden and striking close-ups, mixed with healthy doses of dark humor.

RADLEY METZGER

Born: Radley Metzger, January 21, 1929 (New York City, New York, U.S.).

Directing style: U.S. pioneer of adult cinema; accomplished auteur; soft-core erotica, porn chic, and XXX fare; elaborate sets; tight narratives; amusing dialogue; visual flair.

Top Takes…

It is easy to discard adult cinema of the 1970s as smut, as U.S. President Richard Nixon famously did. But there is some unexpected sophistication in the genre, especially in the lush labyrinthine phantasms of Radley Metzger. He started out as a distributor, bringing U.S. audiences Scandinavian and Italian skin flicks. The liberalizing of local laws soon allowed him to substitute foreign imports with homegrown produce.

Metzger's first efforts, such as *The Dirty Girls* (1964) and *The Alley Cats* (1966) are now considered tame, but their visual flair, clever structure, use of jazz, high-class settings, and proper dialogue betrayed a filmmaker with talent. Taking his cues from writer Luigi Pirandello and director Pier Paolo Pasolini, Metzger injected his films with more explicit naughtiness, without dropping the classiness. *Carmen, Baby* (1967), *Therese und Isabell* (1968) (*Therese and Isabelle*), and *Camille 2000* (1969) defined the genre of sexploitation, perfectly capturing an era of androgynous glam rock, free love, and amorality. *Score* (1973), Metzger's soft-porn *pièce de résistance*, weaves contemporary issues of feminine liberation and post-Altamont decadence into its core theme of swinging (partner exchange), and was both titillating and critical. As the permissive 1970s progressed, Metzger's movies became proud triple Xs. The satirical, tongue-in-cheek *The Private Afternoons of Pamela Mann* (1975), *The Opening of Misty Beethoven* (1976), *Barbara Broadcast* (1977), and *Maraschino Cherry* (1978) are ultimate porn chic: arousing full-on sex framed within tight narratives and elaborate sets, featuring credible characters with funny dialogue. When the advent of video destroyed theatrical porn, adult cinema's most accomplished auteur retired. **EM**

"Metzger did for sex films what *Playboy* did for magazines."

—*Film Comment*

VERA CHYTILOVÁ

Born: Vera Chytilová, February 2, 1929 (Ostrava, Czech Republic).

Directing style: Committed, feminist experimental filmmaker; surrealist and allegorical content; use of handheld camera for cinéma vérité; visual puns; political themes.

Vera Chytilová is a staunchly feminist Czech filmmaker best known for the experimental movie *Sedmikrasky* (1966) (*Daisies*). Rich with visual puns, this surrealist saga follows the misadventures of a couple of unsympathetic characters both called Marie. Impossible to define, it remains a cinematic enigma to this day.

Born in Ostrava in 1929, Chytilová studied philosophy and architecture. She then took on an assortment of jobs including fashion model, draftswoman, and clapperboard girl, before attending Prague Film School at the relatively late age of twenty-eight. Studying under Otakar Vávra, her initial offering *Strop* (1962) (*Ceiling*) drew on her experiences as a model. Chytilová's first feature, *O necem jinem* (1963) (*Something Different*), focused on a female gymnast and a bored housewife. It led to trouble with the communist authorities for criticizing the role of women in Czech society. Next up, the avant-garde *Daisies* established her reputation abroad, but brought establishment condemnation at home once more.

With the Soviet invasion of 1968, restrictions grew tighter. Yet Chytilová persevered in an atmosphere where films, particularly those with an allegorical content, were routinely shelved. After several barren years she made *Hra o jablko* (1976) (*The Apple Game*), a feminist story about a country midwife, but only after writing what amounted to a begging letter to the Czech president, Gustav Husák. Following the collapse of communism in the late 1980s, Chytilová was finally able to work freely, but the end of censorship also marked a huge cut in state subsidies. Still active in her seventies, her latest offering was the drama *Hezké chvilky bez záruky* (2006) (*Pleasant Moments*). **TE**

Top Takes...

Hezké chvilky bez záruky 2006
  (*Pleasant Moments*)
Pasti, pasti, pasticky 1998
  (*Trap, Trap, Little Trap*)
Dedictví aneb Kurvahosigutntag 1993
  (*The Inheritance or Fuckoffguysgoodday*)
Kopytem sem, kopytem tam 1988
  (*Tainted Horseplay*)
Vlci bouda 1985 (*Wolf's Lair*)
Panelstory 1979
Hra o jablko 1976 (*The Apple Game*)
Ovoce stromu rajskych jime 1969
  (*Fruit of Paradise*)
Perlicky na dne 1966 (*Pearls on the Ground*)
Sedmikrasky 1966 (*Daisies*)
O necem jinem 1963 (*Something Different*)
Strop 1962 (*Ceiling*)

"I'm an enemy of stupidity and simple-mindedness in both men and women."

ALEJANDRO JODOROWSKY

Born: Alejandro Jodorowsky, February 7, 1929 (Tocopilla, Chile).

Directing style: Underground Chilean filmmaker of cult classics; shocking imagery; unorthodox spiritual and metaphysical themes; surreal visual fantasies; mystical Westerns and psychodramas.

Top Takes…

The Rainbow Thief 1990

Santa sangre 1989 (*Holy Blood*)

Tusk 1980

The Holy Mountain 1973

El Topo 1970 (*The Gopher*)

Fando y Lis 1968 (*Fando and Lis*)

Les têtes interverties 1957 (*The Severed Head*)

Born in Chile, Alejandro Jodorowsky spent most of his life in France, but filmed all over the world. A man with no roots and no fixed identity, Jodorowsky is an artist in a constant search for meaning. Filmmaking for him is only one means of exploration: he has also directed avant-garde theater and written plays and books, as well as numerous comic scripts for the French artist Moebius. With merely seven films under his belt, three of which are first-rate cult classics, he has left an indelible mark on world cinema. His restless spirit was nourished equally by circus life—he was a clown and puppeteer—surrealism, and the theater of the absurd, together with the mysticism and occultism of eclectic traditions. Spiritual themes are embodied in often shocking imagery of blood, nudity, skinned and gutted animals, real cripples, and psychiatric patients.

Jodorowsky's first film, *Fando y Lis* (1968) (*Fando and Lis*), is an uneven mystical road movie about the search for utopia in a world out of joint. It merely announced a double whammy to come. *El Topo* (1970) (*The Gopher*) is the quintessential midnight hit with its spaghetti Western iconography, surreal body horrors, and Zen Buddhist influences. A metaphysical quest for spiritual maturity runs through *The Holy Mountain* (1973), a surreal barrage of unforgettable images, raw and dripping with life juices, directed straight at the soul. *Santa sangre* (1989) (*Holy Blood*) is testament to Jodorowsky's "making films with one's balls" approach: with a more coherent and linear structure closest to the horror genre, it is his most accessible, accomplished, and emotionally resonant movie. Jodorowsky's unorthodox style and guerrilla approach to filmmaking has made it difficult for him to find financing for new projects, but he does not give up. **DO**

"Most directors make films with their eyes; I make films with my testicles."

JOSÉ MOJICA MARINS

Born: José Mojica Marins, March 13, 1929 (São Paulo, Brazil).

Directing style: Brazilian director of trash cult movies; hard-core pornography featuring bestiality; trademark appearances as signature character "Coffin Joe"; Grand Guignol gore.

José Mojica Marins may well be the only director taken seriously enough to be in this book who has directed hard-core woman-with-animal pornography, in *24 Horas de Sexo Explicito* (1985) (*24 Hours of Explicit Sex*). Marins writes, produces, directs, and bug-wrangles his vehicles, and is best known for a loose series of auteur works in which he appears in his signature role, "Zé do Caixao," or "Coffin Joe." Initially, Zé was a blasphemous undertaker with distinctive long nails and a top hat, who subjected enemies and lovers to extreme circumstances, often involving venomous creepy-crawlies, as he tried to find a perfect mate, or affront all religious sensibilities. But the character has evolved into an all-purpose bogeyman with a multimedia presence somewhere between Entertaining Comics's Crypt Keeper and DC Comics's Phantom Stranger.

The major Zé films are *À Meia-Noite Levarei Sua Alma* (1964) (*At Midnight I'll Take Your Soul*), *Esta Noite Encarnarei no Teu Cadáver* (1967) (*Tonight I Will Make Your Corpse Turn Red*), *O Estranho Mundo de Zé do Caixão* (1968) (*Strange World of Coffin Joe*), *O Ritual dos Sádicos* (1970) (*Awakening of the Beast*), *Quando os Deuses Adormecem* (1972) (*When the Gods Fall Asleep*), *O Exorcismo Negro* (1974) (*Black Exorcism of Coffin Joe*), *Delírios de um Anormal* (1978) (*Hallucinations of a Deranged Mind*), and *A Encarnaçao do Demônio* (1981). The early films, which seem almost homemade, are considered to be the most interesting, with an ambitious range of effects somewhere between Grand Guignol gore and community religious play. Later, as Marins gravitated toward the more conventional Brazilian film industry, the wildness was muted, and technical competence smoothed away the very real originality of the earlier works. **KN**

Top Takes...

24 Horas de Sexo Explícito 1985
  (*24 Hours of Explicit Sex*)

A Encarnação do Demônio 1981

Delírios de um Anormal 1978
  (*Hallucinations of a Deranged Mind*)

O Exorcismo Negro 1974
  (*Black Exorcism of Coffin Joe*)

Quando os Deuses Adormecem 1972
  (*When the Gods Fall Asleep*)

O Ritual dos Sádicos 1970
  (*Awakening of the Beast*)

O Estranho Mundo de Zé do Caixão 1968
  (*Strange World of Coffin Joe*)

Esta Noite Encarnarei no Teu Cadáver 1967
  (*Tonight I Will Make Your Corpse Turn Red*)

À Meia-Noite Levarei Sua Alma 1964
  (*At Midnight I'll Take Your Soul*)

"My dream is to make a film where I will not need to beg my friends to help me out."

JEAN-PIERRE MOCKY

Born: Jean-Paul Adam Mokiejewski, July 6, 1929 (Nice, Alpes-Maritimes, Provence-Alpes-Côte d'Azur, France).

Directing style: French maker of anarchic comedies and thrillers; bizarre and supernatural elements; use of caricature to tackle failings of contemporary society.

Top Takes…

Le Bénévole 2006
La candide madame Duff 2000
Tout est calme 2000
Vidange 1998
Bonsoir 1994
Mocky story 1991
Agent trouble 1987
Litan 1982
Le Témoin 1978 (The Witness)
Un linceul n'a pas de poches 1974
 (No Pockets in a Shroud)
Solo 1970
La grande frousse 1964 (The Big Scare)
Un drôle de paroissien 1963
 (Light-Fingered George)
Les Dragueurs 1959 (The Chasers)

Officially born in 1929 (1933, according to him), Jean-Pierre Mocky became an actor first in France and then in Italy, where he worked with famous directors such as Michelangelo Antonioni and Luchino Visconti. Back in France, he was able to direct *Les Dragueurs* (1959) (*The Chasers*), a film that is reminiscent of the then-nascent French New Wave. But Mocky has never belonged to any group, and he has since managed to form a coherent body of work, especially through comedies, crime films, and thrillers. He succeeded in enrolling extremely popular actors, and using them against type. In one of his most successful films, *Un drôle de paroissien* (1963) (*Light-Fingered George*), a deeply religious pickpocket in need, interpreted by Bourvil, loots boxes in churches on an ever larger scale.

From *Solo* (1970) and through the 1970s, Mocky himself repeatedly played a cynical but nevertheless romantic character, who is at odds with the world surrounding him and inevitably meets with a tragic end. In all his movies, he uses caricature to tackle the various failings of French society, from sexual and religious behaviors in *Le Témoin* (1978) (*The Witness*), to political corruption in *Un linceul n'a pas de poches* (1974) (*No Pockets in a Shroud*); sometimes even anticipating its evolution with a great clear-sightedness. Even when he does not work within the horror genre, as with the eccentric *La grande frousse* (1964) (*The Big Scare*), supernatural or bizarre elements are almost never absent. Mocky's films have always stood on the fringe of the cinematic institution from an economical, aesthetical, and thematic standpoint, but recently he has gone somewhat underground, working on barely distributed films made with very low budgets. He remains, however, a well-respected name in French cinema. **FL**

> "[*The Chasers*] is a bittersweet, faintly tragic and sardonic romantic drama."—*New York Times*

HAL ASHBY

Born: William Hal Ashby, September 2, 1929 (Ogden, Utah, U.S.); died 1988 (Malibu, California, U.S.).

Directing style: Director of energetic, skillfully acted dramas and witty comedies dealing with socially aware themes; spirit of counterculture; anarchic black humor.

The 1960s produced an important generation of directors, who turned a harsher and more penetrating lens on U.S. culture, and Hal Ashby, despite his propensity for maudlin melodrama, must be counted a central member of the group.

As did Arthur Penn, Ashby grew up within the industry, learning his craft as an assistant editor with such social satirists as Tony Richardson and Norman Jewison. A project given to him by Jewison, *The Landlord* (1970), proved that Ashby could prosper in that then-popular genre of socially conscious comedy. With the help of writer Colin Higgins, Ashby made *Harold and Maude* (1971), a witty treatment of a young man's faux-existentialist crisis, solved by an affair with a woman who could be his grandmother. Such a gentle send-up of conventional pieties is managed expertly in *Shampoo* (1975), whose political themes limn the situation for a touching comedy of manners with the hip hair stylist as modern hero; and in *Being There* (1979), a witty meditation on the theme of the emperor's new clothes.

Coming Home (1978), much applauded for its sensitivity to second-stage feminism and paraplegia, has not aged quite so well. The heavy hand of star Jane Fonda is in evidence, as unconventional sex becomes the solution for the problems of plot and society alike. *The Last Detail* (1973), which avoids melodramatic reassurance, is Ashby's best film, an understated portrayal of the military's unconsciously unjust crushing of individuality. By the 1980s Ashby's output was in decline. He became unreliable because of his alcohol and drug habit. He collapsed while making the Rolling Stones concert film *Let's Spend the Night Together* (1983), and made only a few more films. **BP**

Top Takes...

8 Million Ways to Die 1986
The Slugger's Wife 1985
Let's Spend the Night Together 1983
Lookin' to Get Out 1982
Second-Hand Hearts 1981
Being There 1979
Coming Home 1978
Bound for Glory 1976
Shampoo 1975
The Last Detail 1973
Harold and Maude 1971
The Landlord 1970

1920s

"If I had it all to do over again, I would rather go at it a different way."

VITTORIO AND PAOLO TAVIANI

Vittorio: Born September 20, 1929 (San Miniato di Pisa, Tuscany, Italy).
Paolo: Born November 8, 1931 (San Miniato di Pisa, Tuscany, Italy).

Directing style: Makers of early documentaries, and later melodramas; political and historical themes dealing with power and corruption; skillful storytelling.

Forget the Cohens. Forget the Farrellys. You can even forget the Wachowskis. These guys are just new *fratelli* on the block. Before them all, the two-seated directorial chair was thoroughly warmed by Italian brothers Vittorio and Paolo Taviani who became purveyors of a very distinct form of modern Italian cinema. Their early forays culminated in a collaboration with both Cesare Zavattini and Valentino Orsini on *San Miniato, luglio '44* (1954), a very personal film that explored Nazi atrocities carried out in the brothers' own village just ten years before. It was the first in a series of pictures that would explore the political in the historical, and the historical in the political.

Their feature breakthrough came with *I Sovversivi* (1967) (*The Subversives*), although it was *Padre padrone* (1977) (*Father and Master*), the first film ever to win both the Palme d'Or and Critics Prize at Cannes Film Festival, that brought them international fame. A grim but tender adaptation of Gavino Ledda's novel, it traced the arduous real-life journey of a Sardinian child who escapes his father's brutal treatment to finally graduate as a university professor. The later *La notte di San Lorenzo* (1982) (*Night of the Shooting Stars*) was also typical, exploring as it did the hopes and fears of Tuscan peasants during World War II awaiting the arrival of liberation, for which the brothers again triumphed at Cannes, winning another two awards. Like much of their work, *Night of the Shooting Stars* was political and it was direct, placing history and resistance within a very Italian context. The Tavianis are a true family unit, sharing writing duties and even alternating direction of scenes, yet never falling foul to petty squabbles. In interviews their individual remarks are often not even attributed: they are simply the Tavianis. **RH**

"It is the cinema's job to show it—not just to emphasize dramatic camera angles."—Vittorio

JOHN CASSAVETES

Born: John Nicholas Cassavetes, December 9, 1929 (New York City, New York, U.S.); died 1989 (Los Angeles, California, U.S.).

Directing style: Prolific pioneering director of U.S. independent film; improvisation advocate; creative partnership with Gena Rowlands; naturalistic dialogue.

John Cassavetes was one of the founding fathers of U.S. independent cinema, using the proceeds from a successful Hollywood acting career to finance his own defiantly different films as writer and director. Different in that, from his hugely influential debut *Shadows* (1959) up until the glorious, albeit unintended, summation of his life's work in *Love Streams* (1984), he consistently favored character, milieu, mood, and theme over plot. Indeed, so wayward were his narratives in terms of arc and pacing, so naturalistic his dialogue and the performances he elicited from his actors, that many mistook his films as improvised. His first feature resulted from extensive improvisations with the cast, but was scripted before shooting began; his subsequent work, with casts that usually included wife Gena Rowlands and close friends such as Peter Falk and Seymour Cassel, was carefully written and rehearsed.

 Shadows is more tightly plotted than its successors, as it explores the tensions between two brothers, their sister, and their friends as they do the rounds of the jazzy New York bohemian world of the late 1950s. Later, *Faces* (1968), *Husbands* (1970), *A Woman Under the Influence* (1974), *The Killing of a Chinese Bookie* (1976), and *Opening Night* (1977) left greater room for longueurs in their attempt to give honest accounts of everyday behavior. These films mainly depict crises in relationships between people of limited articulateness seeking understanding and love; the impression of verisimilitude is enhanced by the almost documentary rawness of the camerawork, with close-ups going in and out of focus. Most notable is the edgy acting: not only Cassavetes's prime tool for investigating humanity, but a metaphor for the masks people adopt in communicating with each other. **GA**

Top Takes...

Big Trouble 1986
Love Streams 1984
Gloria 1980
Opening Night 1977
The Killing of a Chinese Bookie 1976
***A Woman Under the Influence* 1974** ☆
Minnie and Moskowitz 1971
Husbands 1970
Faces 1968
A Child Is Waiting 1963
A Pair of Boots 1962
My Daddy Can Lick Your Daddy 1962
Too Late Blues 1961
Shadows 1959

1920s

"As an artist, I feel that we must try many things—but above all we must dare to fail."

FREDERICK WISEMAN

Born: Frederick Wiseman, January 1, 1930 (Boston, Massachusetts, U.S.).

Directing style: Master documentary maker; use of fly-on-the-wall footage; often controversial topics with political undercurrents; lengthy run time; champion of the underdog.

Top Takes…

1930s

A master of nonfiction filmmaking, specifically what has been deemed "direct cinema," Frederick Wiseman is a documentary maker in the most literal sense. In each of his works, from the most modest to the epic, Wiseman strives to make himself invisible, eschewing the interviews, narration, and narrative style common to many of his peers in favor of stories that tell themselves strictly through fly-on-the-wall footage.

Wiseman studied to be a lawyer, but abandoned the profession for filmmaking. His first feature, *Titicut Follies* (1967), set in a state hospital for the insane, was quickly hailed as a masterpiece of the form, but also banned for nearly 30 years for its controversial depiction of the hospital's staff and patients. Subsequent works, such as *High School* (1968), *Law and Order* (1969), and *Hospital* (1970), quickly solidified his reputation as a dedicated chronicler of quotidian subjects, although often presented with a political undercurrent intended to give voice to those oppressed or suppressed by society's various imposed preferences in matters of class, race, gender, and the like.

Wiseman's films continued to grow longer and more ambitious, even if his techniques remained largely hands-off, with his works finding their final shape in the editing room rather than from a script or traditional narrative arc. *Belfast, Maine* (1999), for example, was a four-hour meditation on life in the small town, down to the tiniest detail, whereas *Domestic Violence* (2001) turned out to be Wiseman's most striking work in years, taking place in and around a battered women's shelter in Florida. Due to their nontraditional nature, many of Wiseman's films have not received theatrical distribution, instead often finding a home on public TV. **JK**

"…the most compassionate of all the Wiseman films."

—*New York Times,* on *Domestic Violence*

JOHN FRANKENHEIMER

Born: John Michael Frankenheimer, February 19, 1930 (New York City, New York, U.S.); died 2002 (Los Angeles, California, U.S.).

Directing style: Creator of masterful thrillers and dramas; the king of car-chase scenes; innovative low-angle shots and deep-focus compositions; fast editing.

John Frankenheimer was one of the few TV pioneers who strived to compose innovative and striking visuals. Soon he was applying these techniques to features, making his big-screen debut with *The Young Stranger* (1957). It led to a string of classics such as *Birdman of Alcatraz* (1962), *Seven Days in May* (1964), and *The Train* (1964). His aptitude for unconventional visuals helped *The Manchurian Candidate* (1962) and *Seconds* (1966) gain a cult following.

After Frankenheimer moved to Europe, his films mostly sank into obscurity. By the 1970s he was primarily a hired-hand director, but he still managed to generate enough thrills and suspense to make *French Connection II* (1975) and *Black Sunday* (1977) box-office hits.

Though still a busy director throughout the 1980s and early 1990s, most often on political thrillers or stories that touched on sociological issues, it was not until he directed *Ronin* (1998) that his reinvention of thrilling and magnificently shot car-chase scenes reminded audiences that he was still a great craftsman. Replacing open roads with narrow streets and orange fireball crashes with relentless speed, Frankenheimer—then in his late sixties—proved he had not lost his ability to inject new approaches to familiar genres.

In retrospect it seems a shame that John Frankenheimer was not afforded more opportunities to demonstrate his considerable talents. It is interesting to remember that, besides his persistent ability to excite and entertain audiences, the action in *Birdman of Alcatraz* was mostly restricted to a prison cell, as was the much-admired detoxification scene in *French Connection II*. Only a great talent could create compelling cinema in such simple settings. **DW**

Top Takes...

Reindeer Games 2000
Ronin 1998
The Island of Dr. Moreau 1996
The Fourth War 1990
Black Sunday 1977
French Connection II 1975
The Iceman Cometh 1973
The Gypsy Moths 1969
The Fixer 1968
Seconds 1966
The Train 1964
Seven Days in May 1964
The Manchurian Candidate 1962
Birdman of Alcatraz 1962
The Young Stranger 1957

1930s

"I feel that my job is to create an atmosphere where creative people can do their best work."

RICHARD DONNER

Born: Richard D. Schwartzberg, April 24, 1930 (New York City, New York, U.S.).

Directing style: Craftsman who moves between various genres; masterful storytelling and credible characterizations; often amusing and heartwarming in tone; attention to detail.

Top Takes...

16 Blocks 2006
Timeline 2003
Conspiracy Theory 1997
Assassins 1995
Maverick 1994
Radio Flyer 1992
Scrooged 1988
Lethal Weapon 1987
The Goonies 1985
Ladyhawke 1985
The Toy 1982
Inside Moves 1980
Superman II 1980
Superman 1978
The Omen 1976
X-15 1961

"I'm here to fight for truth, and justice, and the American way."

—Superman, *Superman*

There's always a spirit of fun when watching a Richard Donner film. Whether a character is a protagonist or antagonist, Donner consistently strives to imbue him or her with a sense of charm. His overriding understanding of the importance of story, tone, and pacing has allowed him to move easily from horror movies, such as *The Omen* (1976), to cartoon adventures, such as *Superman* (1978), to action movies, such as *Lethal Weapon* (1987), and to comedies, such as *Scrooged* (1988).

Donner spent nearly 20 years directing TV before being hired to helm *The Omen*. Eliminating many of the devil-worship elements of the script, he focused on the horror of a father being convinced that he should kill his son. The film was a blockbuster hit and led the way to his most influential film, *Superman*. With *Superman*, Donner knew that if audiences were to take his characters seriously, they had to believe a man could fly. Unfortunately the effect ended up taking a year to perfect, and production delays forced him to suspend filming of *Superman II* (1980), which was being shot simultaneously.

The producers were not pleased with these slowdowns and, despite the fact that his efforts paid off and *Superman* was a huge hit, Donner was not allowed to complete *Superman II*.

Although capable of epic filmmaking, Donner has subsequently focused more on modestly budgeted films, generating at least one cult favorite with *Scrooged*, which extracted an unlikely sweetness from its sadomasochistic script. But his most popular accomplishment has been the *Lethal Weapon* series, in which the characters have evolved into a lovable bunch. Their lives may be filled with violence and death, but the impression is clear that friends and family make life worth living. **DW**

PAUL MAZURSKY

Born: Irwin Mazursky, April 25, 1930 (Brooklyn, New York, U.S.).

Directing style: Actor turned director of wry dramas and bittersweet romantic comedies; themes often revolve around contemporary U.S. family life, the changing values of the United States, and aging.

Paul Mazursky has directed an impressively varied body of work that reflects the rapidly changing values of the United States in the late twentieth century. *Bob & Carol & Ted & Alice* (1969) brilliantly captures the ambivalent complexity of the sexual revolution of the late 1960s. A much-celebrated first feature, it was followed by *Alex in Wonderland* (1970), an interesting, if failed, attempt to remake Italian director Federico Fellini's *8½* (1963). Mazursky returned to the same theme in one of his later productions, *The Pickle* (1993).

Harry and Tonto (1974) demonstrated that Mazursky could empathize with the sense of liberation and sadness that characterize the first stages of aging, with a lonely widower taking to the road to find new meaning for his life. A new beginning is also the subject of *An Unmarried Woman* (1978), which explores a newly divorced wife's initial panic at abandonment, then poignant recovery of equilibrium and confidence. *Next Stop, Greenwich Village* (1976) offers a nostalgic, finely detailed homage to 1950s beat culture.

An accomplished actor himself, Mazursky has had great success handling star performers. He ably directed the uniquely energetic Robin Williams in *Moscow on the Hudson* (1984), then both directed and acted in the comedy *Scenes from a Mall* (1991), starring Woody Allen and Bette Midler as a couple whose marriage disintegrates, renews itself, and disintegrates again—a wry commentary on life and what constitutes well-being in the contemporary United States. Mazursky also directed and acted in *Down and Out in Beverly Hills* (1986), a comedy that comments perceptively on social trends, here the yawning economic divide between the nouveau riche and those left behind by the "American Dream." **BP**

Top Takes…

Yippee 2006
Faithful 1996
The Pickle 1993
Scenes from a Mall 1991
Enemies: A Love Story 1989
Moon Over Parador 1988
Down and Out in Beverly Hills 1986
Moscow on the Hudson 1984
Tempest 1982
An Unmarried Woman 1978 ☆
Next Stop, Greenwich Village 1976
Harry and Tonto 1974
Blume in Love 1973
Alex in Wonderland 1970
Bob & Carol & Ted & Alice 1969
Last Year at Malibu 1962

"First, we'll have an orgy. Then we'll go see Tony Bennett."

—Ted, *Bob & Carol & Ted & Alice*

CLINT EASTWOOD

Born: Clinton Eastwood Jr., May 31, 1930 (San Francisco, California, U.S.).

Directing style: Actor turned director; maker of dramas, thrillers, and, most notably, Westerns; exploration of morality; outsider themes; use of shadow lighting; often acts in his own movies.

Top Takes...

Letters from Iwo Jima **2006** ☆
Flags of Our Fathers 2006
Million Dollar Baby **2004** ★
Mystic River **2003** ☆
Blood Work 2002
Space Cowboys 2000
True Crime 1999
Absolute Power 1997
The Bridges of Madison County 1995
Unforgiven **1992** ★
Bird 1988
Heartbreak Ridge 1986
Pale Rider 1985
Sudden Impact 1983
Honkytonk Man 1982
Firefox 1982
Bronco Billy 1980
The Gauntlet 1977
The Outlaw Josey Wales 1976
The Eiger Sanction 1975
Breezy 1973
High Plains Drifter 1973
Play Misty for Me 1971
The Beguiled: The Storyteller 1971

In the beginning was The Man With No Name, the role that made Clint Eastwood an international star. Combining his squint of squints, tall physique, and generally inscrutable features, the type proved iconic and earned him the freedom to move beyond it and become an all-around movie artist.

He learned from two masters, Sergio Leone and Don Siegel, with whom he frequently worked until his directorial debut, *The Beguiled: The Storyteller* (1971), which was followed by *Play Misty for Me* (1971), *High Plains Drifter* (1973), *Breezy* (1973), and *The Eiger Sanction* (1975), each of which traded on his star power to earn distribution. Then came his first masterpiece, *The Outlaw Josey Wales* (1976), a revisionist Western that reexamined the U.S. Civil War through the bankruptcy of the frontier myth, organized around a domestic melodrama and tale of revenge. Significantly, the picture also paired him with Sondra Locke, his offscreen companion from the late 1970s into the 1980s, a pairing that yielded memorable work in *The Gauntlet* (1977), *Bronco Billy* (1980), and *Sudden Impact* (1983).

As the 1980s began, Eastwood stretched the age limits of action stardom, especially in *Firefox* (1982) and *Heartbreak*

RIGHT: *Unforgiven,* Eastwood's critically-lauded effort to debunk the Wild West myth.

ABOVE: The World War II film *Letters from Iwo Jima* is told from a Japanese perspective.

Ridge (1986), but he was also moving behind the camera, without appearing before it, for the first time in *Bird* (1988). He continued to cross generic divides, doing a drama, *Honkytonk Man* (1982), and a second masterwork in the Western *Pale Rider* (1985). By 1992, Eastwood hit his stride, winning his first Best Director Oscar for *Unforgiven* (1992). He went on to embrace themes of loss and aging in *The Bridges of Madison County* (1995), *Absolute Power* (1997), *Blood Work* (2002), and the science fiction adventure *Space Cowboys* (2000), leading to his offscreen handling of two remarkable war films, *Flags of Our Fathers* (2006) and its sequel *Letters from Iwo Jima* (2006).

His *Mystic River* (2003) showcased Sean Penn and Tim Robbins as working-class Bostonians destroyed through a neighborhood murder. Then *Million Dollar Baby* (2004) repeated *Unforgiven*'s awards-season sweep, albeit with far less of a stamp on cinema history. **GCQ**

Unforgiven

For many, Eastwood's reputation rests on *Unforgiven* (1992), his Oscar-winning, Directors Guild of America-winning, and Golden Globe Award-winning film about the false myths of the West and pioneer life. Images and sounds from this singular work reflect on the whole of the Western tradition, cutting through the virtues of stark morality with the awesome vistas of Montana, a simple musical theme Eastwood himself composed, and a tale of highly ritualized violence. It exposed how the latter was formidably adjusted through newspapers and the first Western histories were based on sensationalism.

CLAUDE CHABROL

Born: Claude Chabrol, June 24, 1930 (Paris, France).

Directing style: "The French Hitchcock;" key figure of the French New Wave; suspenseful thrillers; explores the underbelly of bourgeois society and its moral conundrums.

Top Takes...

L'ivresse du pouvoir 2006
  (*The Comedy of Power*)
La demoiselle d'honneur 2004
  (*The Bridesmaid*)
Rien ne va plus 1997 (*The Swindle*)
La cérémonie 1995
L'enfer 1994
Madame Bovary 1991
Une affaire de femmes 1988 (*Story of Women*)
Le cri du hibou 1988
Violette Nozière 1978
Le boucher 1970
La femme infidèle 1969
Les biches 1968
Les cousins 1959 (*The Cousins*)
Le beau serge 1958

Sometimes dubbed "The French Hitchcock," Claude Chabrol made his name as a director of mystery and crime thrillers that were really studies in character psychology as well as explorations of the social and class backgrounds of his protagonists. For Chabrol, brutality could erupt at any time within the most banal and everyday of settings, and his films frequently take a jaundiced, but keenly political, look at society. His movies are characterized by sudden, abrupt shifts in tone, and are permeated by a restless, menacing sense that the norms and laws of civility can break down without warning.

A leading exponent of the French New Wave emerging between the late 1950s and the early 1960s, Chabrol was part of a group of French directors including Jean-Luc Godard, Eric Rohmer, and François Truffaut, all of them writing for the influential journal *Cahiers du cinéma*, and all of them carrying the lessons, ideas, and passions of film criticism into their work as film directors.

In movies such as *Les biches* (1968) and *La femme infidèle* (1969), Chabrol explored disruptions and deviations within bourgeois life, and this phase of his work reached its arguable peak with *Le boucher* (1970). The latter is a classic creation of a suspense-filled, brooding atmosphere, that is as indebted to Henri-Georges Clouzot as it is to Alfred Hitchcock. Chabrol has continued directing up to the present day, amassing a truly significant body of work and adding to his reputation as one of the world's leading suspense-thriller directors. *La cérémonie* (1995) successfully adapts a Ruth Rendell novel, whereas *Rien ne va plus* (1997) (*The Swindle*), starring Isabelle Huppert, shows Chabrol combining a lighter touch with some old-school shock moments. **MH**

> "I am a Communist ... but that doesn't mean I have to make films about the wheat harvest."

KINJI FUKASAKU

Born: Kinji Fukasaku, July 3, 1930 (Mito, Japan); died 2003 (Tokyo, Japan).

Directing style: Japanese writer and director of crime, science-fiction, and action movies; innovator within the *yakuza* genre by using it as a mode of social criticism.

Kinji Fukasaku was a Japanese writer and director known for violent gangster films that challenged the nation's social conventions. He enrolled at Nihon University in Tokyo to study cinema and, upon graduation, he began working at Toei Studios in 1953 as an assistant director. Fukasaku made his directorial debut with the gangster tale *Hakuchu no buraikan* (1961) (*Greed in Broad Daylight*), and for the next two decades his *yakuza* crime films would characterize his career.

Fukasaku's *Jingi naki tatakai* (1973) was a defining film for the *yakuza* genre. Utilizing a neorealist aesthetic, he demystifies the honorable gangster image, portraying gangsters instead as reprehensible criminals. The film was a huge hit, leading to a five-part series that was so successful that Toei Studios demanded another three films. By challenging traditions, Fukasaku paved the way for contemporary *yakuza* filmmakers such as Takeshi Kitano and Takashi Miike. He is also well known for directing the Japanese scenes in *Tora! Tora! Tora!* (1970), and science-fiction films including *Uchu kara no messeji* (1978) (*Return to Jelucia*), *Fukkatsu no hi* (1980) (*Day of Resurrection*), and *Satomi hakken-den* (1983) (*Legend of the Eight Samurai*).

Fukasaku's final film, *Batoru rowaiaru* (2000) (*Battle Royale*), is a dark satire on the relationship among generations and the complicity of a society that accepts violence as entertainment. The film created an uproar among Japanese politicians; as a result, it was released with a rating restricting it to audiences over the age of fifteen. Despite this limitation, the movie was an enormous success and finally brought Fukasaku international acclaim. At the time of his death in 2003, Fukasaku had begun work on a sequel, which was completed by his son Kenta Fukasaku. **WW**

Top Takes...

Batoru rowaiaru 2000 (*Battle Royale*)
Chushingura gaiden totsuya kaidan 1994
Itsuka giragirasuruhi 1992 (*Double Cross*)
Satomi hakken-den 1983
  (*Legend of the Eight Samurai*)
Fukkatsu no hi 1980 (*Day of Resurrection*)
Uchu kara no messeji 1978 (*Return to Jelucia*)
Yagyû ichizoku no inbô 1978
  (*The Shogun's Samurai*)
Jingi no hakaba 1975 (*Graveyard of Honor*)
Jingi naki tatakai 1973
Bakuto gaijin butai 1971
  (*Gambler: Foreign Opposition*)
Tora! Tora! Tora! 1970
The Green Slime 1968
Hakuchu no buraikan 1961
  (*Greed in Broad Daylight*)

> "You just have to fight for yourself. That's just life."
> —Mitsuko, *Battle Royale*

1930s

JEAN-LUC GODARD

Born: Jean-Luc Godard, December 3, 1930 (Paris, France).

Directing style: Revolutionary French director of landmark films of the French New Wave; jerky jump cuts; left-wing political content; later poetic meditations.

Top Takes…

A symbol of the liberal consciousness of the 1960s, Godard shares with Che Guevara and John F. Kennedy a passionate belief in changing the world, an intellectual profundity, a knack for rhetoric, and a reputation as a radical. Such was his impact that no film now can claim political innocence.

In the 1950s Godard started writing for the renowned magazine *Cahiers du cinéma*. He and fellow critics François Truffaut, Claude Chabrol, and Eric Rohmer, impatient with the rules and formulas of mainstream cinema, decided to discard conventions and emphasize direct human emotions and impulsive action. The movement became the New Wave.

Godard's debut feature, *À bout de souffle* (1960) (*Breathless*), hit like a rocket at the Cannes Film Festival. At base a petty gangster story, it was frivolous in its evocation of swinging, existentialist Paris, with its mix of a cool jazz soundtrack, the dynamic rhythm of furious chases, jerky jump cuts, sudden bursts of violence, casual sex, smooth traveling shots, and an air of philosophical contemplation. The film oozed spontaneous immediacy, embodied in the lovely scene where Jean Seberg

RIGHT: Jean-Paul Belmondo looks glum in a scene from Godard's *Breathless*.

and Jean-Paul Belmondo stroll flirtingly along the Champs Élysées. Instantly famous, Godard became a left-wing hero, a symbol for the youthful, progressive, antiwar movement. *Le petit soldat* (1963) (*The Little Soldier*) and *Les carabiniers* (1963) (*The Riflemen*) are activist films. The first was banned because of its criticism of the war in Algeria and an infamous torture scene; the latter was a sharp satire of war, in bleached, pseudo-found footage tones of black and white.

ABOVE: Michel Piccoli and a tousled Brigitte Bardot in bed on the set of *Contempt*.

Une femme est une femme (1961) (*A Woman is a Woman*) and *Vivre sa vie: film en douze tableaux* (1962) (*My Life to Live*) were the first films to criticize consumerism (the characters are a stripper and a prostitute), but they also exhibit a tender belief in love. The dystopian *Bande à part* (1964) and *Alphaville, une étrange aventure de Lemmy Caution* (1965) deconstruct the

"What I want . . . is to destroy the idea of culture. Culture is an alibi of imperialism."

Breaking the Mold

According to Jean-Luc Godard, "A story should have a beginning, a middle, and an end, but not necessarily in that order"—a quote that neatly sums up Godard's revolutionary attitude to movie making and the unconventional approach adopted by advocates of the French New Wave movement.

- Godard was the second of four children in a bourgeois French-Swiss family.
- When studying at the Sorbonne, he met François Truffaut, Jacques Rivette, and Eric Rohmer. They established the *Gazette du cinéma*, for which Godard wrote film reviews.
- After his family cut off financial support, Godard adopted a bohemian lifestyle.
- In 1953, he went to Switzerland to work on a dam project as a construction worker. With the money he earned, he made a short film about the dam.
- Godard's writing for publications such as *Cahiers du cinéma*, *Arts*, and *Temps de Paris*, as well as writing film scenarios, established him in the forefront of the French New Wave movement. This was consolidated by his film *Breathless*, which was a great success with the public and critics alike.
- Since the late 1960s Godard has largely abandoned mainstream cinema in favor of films tackling political, sociological, and humanitarian themes.

RIGHT: Poster for Godard's *Pierrot le fou*, a crime drama about a couple on the run.

genres of road movie and science fiction. *Le mépris* (1963) (*Contempt*) is Godard's most Hollywood film, and also a vicious attack on it. With lush colors and exotic locations, containing nudity, guns, and big stars Brigitte Bardot, Jack Palance, and Fritz Lang, it is a film about filming Homer's *Odyssey*, which of course is unfilmable—and that is its point.

The personal becomes political

In 1965, Godard bid farewell to plot-driven stories in favor of a Marxist recruitment of cinema as a revolutionary weapon. *Pierrot le fou* (1965), *La Chinoise* (1967), and *Week End* (1967) use a narrative framework for their ideological criticisms, and because of that their overtly political metaphors retain a sharp edge: the *route du soleil* littered with burning cars in *Week End* is the most damning criticism of leisure society thus far.

Once Godard left narration behind, his films became agit-prop manifestos through which he participated in the 1968 upheavals. He worked on a number of pamphlets advocating the proletarian revolution and deconstructing film language to its bare bones. The dismantling was so thorough that it was 1979 before Godard composed a story again. *Sauve qui peut (la vie)* (1980) (*Every Man for Himself*) heralded a return to narrative filmmaking, away from politics into art and philosophy. *Passion* (1982), *Prénom Carmen* (1983) (*First Name: Carmen*), *King Lear* (1987), *Nouvelle vague* (1990), and *Hélas pour moi* (1993) slowly established him as a wise old veteran. Fitting the part, his idiosyncratic eight-volume *Histoire(s) du Cinéma* (1988–1998) gave a most personal account of a century of cinema's role in society.

Eloge de l'amour (2001) (*Praise of Love*) and *Notre musique* (2004) framed his adoration for literature and classical music into introspective vignettes, difficult to digest, but with spurts of brilliance. As the saying goes: if one is not a Marxist at twenty, one does not have a heart; if one is still one at forty, one does not have a brain. Godard's films have altered the course of cinema history single-handedly, giving it a political consciousness when it was in dire need of one. After that, he simply made films, full of wisdom and beauty. **EM**

LA SOCIÉTÉ NOUVELLE DE CINÉMATOGRAPHIE
présente
JEAN-PAUL BELMONDO

ﾍNS UN FILM DE
EAN-LUC GODARD

NNA KARINA
ZIELLA GALVANI
K SANDERS
GER DUTOIT

LA PARTICIPATION EXCEPTIONNELLE DE
AYMOND DEVOS
THN LA PHOTOGRAPHIE RAOUL COUTARD
A ANTOINE DUHAMEL ÉDITIONS HORTENSIA

Pierrot LE Fou

SNC

KING HU

Born: Hu Jingquan, April 29, 1931 (Beijing, China); died 1997 (Taipei, Taiwan).

Directing style: Auteur and director of Hong Kong martial-arts movies; masterful swordplay sequences; often female heroine as the central protagonist; themes of chivalry.

Top Takes…

" . . . a tour de force of editing and action choreography . . . *"*

—Stephen Teo on *The Valiant Ones*

King Hu's status as the unchallenged master of the *wuxia pian* (swordplay) film is based predominantly around three magnificent works he produced between 1966 and 1969: *Long men ke zhen* (1966) (*Dragon Gate Inn*), *Da zui xia* (1966) (*Come Drink with Me*), and *Hsia nu* (1969) (*A Touch of Zen*). Often distributed on the art-theater circuit and in subtitled versions, these films, for many foreign audiences, were strange, dreamy, even mystical representations of Chinese culture—a far cry from the dubbed, reedited, frenetic swordplay films that would soon swamp inner-city grindhouse cinemas across the world.

Hu would not prove to be as prolific a director as many of his contemporaries within the Hong Kong film industry, but he did make a number of significant pictures after these three, including other masterful swordplay works such as *Ying chun ge zhi Fengbo* (1973) (*The Fate of Lee Khan*) and *Chung lieh t'u* (1975) (*The Valiant Ones*). However, the dominant genre in Hong Kong in this period was the kung fu film, which tended to increase the feeling that Hu was something of an outsider.

It has only been in recent years that Hu's influence has perhaps been most keenly felt. When the older genres of Hong Kong cinema were being revived in the 1990s, producer Hark Tsui turned to Hu to contribute to his reinvention of the swordplay film, *Xiao ao jiang hu* (1990) (*Swordsman*). The influence of his approach to the subject matter and his visual style continues to be felt by anyone making swordplay films. Perhaps most strikingly—although it may have gone unnoticed by many of those who experienced it—this can be seen in Ang Lee's *Wo hu cang long* (2000) (*Crouching Tiger, Hidden Dragon*), which seems to have the spirit of Hu etched into almost every frame. **AW**

ETTORE SCOLA

Born: Ettore Scola, May 10, 1931 (Trevico, Avellino, Italy).

Directing style: Italian director of satirical comedies of manners, and later provocative socially conscious political dramas; biting political awareness; celebration of the underdog.

Ettore Scola is a classic example of a director whose career was born out of his exceptional talent for writing. After studying law, he drifted toward writing film scripts in the mid-1950s. Seen as a key figure in the emergence of the *commedia all'italiana* tradition, he made his directing debut with the episodic film *Se permettete parliamo di donne* (1964) (*Let's Talk About Women*), and often worked with leading postwar Italian actors, including Alberto Sordi, Ugo Tognazzi, and Vittorio Gassman. Consistent commercial success soon followed in a genre that he did so much to help create, his comedies of manners usually underlined with social satire and biting political awareness.

Scola's celebration of the underdog and his social-political insight became more focused with his later work, which was generally more provocative. A significant change of direction came with *Trevico-Torino (viaggio nel Fiat-Nam)* (1973). The film dealt with Italy's "southern question," which surrounded the migration of workers from the south to Fiat factories in northern Italy. After this, Scola's work seemed to take on greater seriousness, moving away from the more comedic and addressing instead issues of greater substance. Some of it tended toward the more cerebral such as *La terrazza* (1980) (*The Terrace*), whereas his talent for comedy was ever-present in the internationally successful *C'eravamo tanto amati* (1974) (*We All Loved Each Other So Much*). A regular award winner at the Cannes Film Festival, Scola's semiautobiographical *La famiglia* (1987) (*The Family*) won him a second Oscar nomination for Best Foreign Language Film, after his earlier *Una giornata particolare* (1977) (*A Special Day*) had garnered the same honor ten years earlier. **RH**

Top Takes…

Gente di Roma 2003
Lettere dalla Palestina 2002
　(*Letters from Palestine*)
La cena 1998 (*The Dinner*)
Il viaggio de Capitan Fracassa 1990
　(*Captain Fracassa's Journey*)
Che ora è? 1989 (*What Time Is It?*)
La famiglia 1987 (*The Family*)
La nuit de Varennes 1982
　(*That Night in Varennes*)
La terrazza 1980 (*The Terrace*)
Una giornata particolare 1977 (*A Special Day*)
C'eravamo tanto amati 1974
　(*We All Loved Each Other So Much*)
Trevico-Torino (viaggio nel Fiat-Nam) 1973
Se permettete parliamo di donne 1964
　(*Let's Talk About Women*)

"Scola's place in humanist film history is unassailable."

—Lillian Schiff, *Film Reference*

ERMANNO OLMI

Born: Ermanno Olmi, July 24, 1931 (Bergamo, Italy).

Directing style: Italian director of realistic, subtle dramas; master storyteller of everyday life; use of nonprofessional actors; documentary approach; long takes; slow pace.

Top Takes...

"Olmi is a filmmaker nurtured by postwar neorealism."

—P. Adams Sitney, *Film Reference*

Like his mother, Ermanno Olmi worked for many years as a clerk at the Edison-Volta electric plant, his father, an avowed antifascist, having been killed in World War II. Between 1953 and 1961, Olmi directed corporate documentaries for Edison-Volta before eventually heading the corporation's film section.

After penning and directing his first feature, *Il tempo si è fermato* (1959) (*Time Stood Still*), Olmi left Edison to become a full-time filmmaker. Of his subsequent work, *Il posto* (1961) (*The Job*) and *I fidanzati* (1963) (*The Fiancés*) are typical, focusing sensitively on the everyday nature of the aspirations of young, working-class Italians. Stretching low budgets to good effect, he continued to utilize the documentary approach that was to characterize his work, maintaining the low-key, fuss-free technical style for which he was famed, and employing his preferred technique of using nonprofessional actors.

Olmi's sensitive biopic of Pope John Paul XXIII, *E venne un uomo* (1965), was well made but a commercial failure, adding weight to the feeling that Olmi was at his best telling simple tales of everyday folk, stories that showed how complicated the small things in life could be. Although he was to win the Golden Lion at the Venice Film Festival for *La leggenda del santo bevitore* (1988) (*The Legend of the Holy Drinker*), his later work lacked the quiet introspection of his earlier period. Olmi's epic, *L'albero degli zoccoli* (1978) (*The Tree of Wooden Clogs*), which won a Palme d'Or at Cannes, was a critical success, focusing on the lives of a group of peasants in Lombardy, and is the work for which he will perhaps be best remembered. Olmi is the rarest of creatures: a critically-acclaimed filmmaker as little known outside his own shores as within them. **RH**

1930s

RUY GUERRA

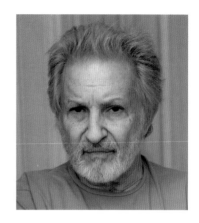

Born: Ruy Guerra, August 22, 1931 (Maputo, Mozambique).

Directing style: Versatile director of Cinema Novo dramas that subtly critique socio-politics of contemporary Brazilian society; edgy dialogue; innovative use of sound.

After studying cinema at Paris's Institut des Hautes Études Cinématographiques, Ruy Guerra has made most of his films in Brazil, where he joined the Cinema Novo movement. His first feature, *Os Cafajestes* (1962) (*The Unscrupulous Ones*), provoked a scandal for showing the first frontal nudity in Brazilian cinema. Quite different from other Cinema Novo films of that time, which openly criticized the living conditions of the poor in Brazil, *Os Cafajestes* makes a more subtle, indirect critique of capitalist society vis-à-vis the middle class of Rio de Janeiro.

Os Fuzis (1964) (*The Guns*), a classic of political cinema, is set in the *sertão*, Brazil's poor northeast. It deals with starving peasants during a drought, unable to obtain food from the wealthy landowner's warehouse, which is protected by soldiers. A clear-cut stylistic difference between the representation of the peasants and the soldiers emphasizes the insurmountable barrier between the two. In the sequel, *A Queda* (1976) (*The Guns*), the soldiers of *Os Fuzis* are now exploited construction workers in Rio de Janeiro. *A Queda* alternates between present and past, between the slow rhythm of *Os Fuzis* and the rapid pace of the urban setting, disclosing the social contradictions in Brazil. *Ternos Caçadores* (1969) (*Sweet Hunters*) is set on an island where several isolated characters wait for something that never arrives. *Os Deuses e os Mortos* (1970) (*Of God and the Undead*) is a complex allegorical movie on power struggle in Brazil. From the 1980s onward, Guerra has made strongly varying films, such as *Eréndira* (1983), a cinematic approach to magic realism; *Ópera do Malandro* (1986) (*Malandro*), a musical about stylish gangsters in Rio de Janeiro; and *Estorvo* (2000) (*Turbulence*), which is narrated from the perspective of a paranoid character. **PS**

Top Takes...

O Veneno da Madrugada 2004
Portugal S.A. 2004
Estorvo 2000 (*Turbulence*)
Kuarup 1989
Fábula de la Bella Palomera 1988
   (*The Fable of the Beautiful Pigeon Fancier*)
Ópera do Malandro 1986 (*Malandro*)
Eréndira 1983
Mueda, Memoria e Massacre 1980
   (*Mueda, Memory and Massacre*)
A Queda 1976 (*The Fall*)
Os Deuses e os Mortos 1970
   (*Of God and the Undead*)
Ternos Caçadores 1969 (*Sweet Hunters*)
Os Fuzis 1964 (*The Guns*)
Os Cafajestes 1962 (*The Unscrupulous Ones*)
Quand le soleil dort 1954

> "*Eréndira* has a kind of dreamy if monotonous charm to it."
> —*New York Times*

1930s

MÁRTA MÉSZÁROS

Born: Márta Mészáros, September 19, 1931 (Kispest, Hungary).

Directing style: Hungarian director of documentaries and dramas; incorporation of newsreel footage; autobiographical content; themes of political oppression; exploration of women's role in society.

Top Takes…

1930s

Born in Hungary, Márta Mészáros's success as a filmmaker and an individual can be attributed to the hardships suffered early in her life. Five years after her birth, her family moved to Russia, during a period when Joseph Stalin's government welcomed outsiders. Her father was later taken to a concentration camp, following a change in Stalin's attitude toward immigrants, and Mészáros lost her mother to typhoid. She was not able to confirm her father's death until 60 years later.

Mészáros's colorful, yet undeniably horrible past became the inspiration behind her most successful and internationally acclaimed films. These were her series of "Diary" films, released during the 1980s, including *Napló gyermekeimnek* (1984) (*Diary For My Children*), *Napló szerelmeimnek* (1987) (*Diary For My Loved Ones*), and *Napló apámnak, anyámnak* (1990) (*Diary For My Father and Mother*). *Diary For My Children* was kept from distribution for two years because of its use of actual newsreel clips and content. These politically charged movies changed the face of Hungarian cinema with their insightful illustrations of young spirited rebellion, memory, and historical fact.

Mészáros began her career making documentaries in the 1950s, and her first major film to receive recognition was *Eltávozott nap* (1968) (*The Girl*). Her career accelerated in the 1970s with such pictures as *Szabad lélegzet* (1973) (*Riddance*) and *Örökbefogadás* (1975) (*Adoption*), which touch on psychosexual relationships in a social realm of multiple generations. More recently, *A Temetetlen halott* (2004) (*The Unburied Man*) told the story of Nagy Imre, former Prime Minister of Hungary, who fought for peasants' rights but eventually lost his life in the effort to gain Hungary independence from the Soviet Union. **ES**

> "I captured the ordinary lives of these people and their problems. I did it many times."

MIKE NICHOLS

Born: Michael Igor Peschkowsky, November 6, 1931 (Berlin, Germany).

Directing style: Versatile director; notable for tragicomedies and dramas that explore family life, domesticity, and the dynamics of male and female relationships; sharp wit and sense of theatricality.

Born into a Russian-Jewish family in Berlin in 1931, Mike Nichols fled Germany with his family in 1939 to escape Nazi persecution. As an improvisational comedian, he was half of a famed duo with Elaine May. He had a notable career as a stage director, including Broadway hits such as *Plaza Suite* (1968), *Uncle Vanya* (1973), and *The Real Thing* (1984). His more than 20 films include several explorations of sexual relationships popular in their day: *Closer* (2004), about love and abandonment; *Carnal Knowledge* (1971), from the work of Jules Feiffer; the homosexual-themed carnival, *The Birdcage* (1996); and the legendary *The Graduate* (1967).

Nichols brings a sense of theatricality, a sharp wit, and a keen, European intelligence toward a penetratingly critical view of contemporary culture, often with a sleight of hand that makes his filmmaking appear effortless, even magical. *Catch-22* (1970), based on the antiwar novel by Joseph Heller, ridicules military organization, but also offers a shocking portrait of the human devastation war produces. *Regarding Henry* (1991) tackles the issue of mental retardation in a love story starring Harrison Ford and Annette Bening; *Silkwood* (1983) explores the medical underside of plutonium processing in a politically challenging way; and *Postcards from the Edge* (1990) presents an unbearably painful generational conflict between an aging show-business trooper, played by Shirley MacLaine, and her talented but alienated daughter.

Much of Nichols's work is impressive, but his best film may be his first, *Who's Afraid of Virginia Woolf?* (1966), in which Elizabeth Taylor and Richard Burton gave virtuoso performances as a couple whose marriage has become like living in purgatory. **MP**

Top Takes...

Closer 2004
Primary Colors 1998
The Birdcage 1996
Regarding Henry 1991
Postcards from the Edge 1990
Working Girl 1988 ☆
Biloxi Blues 1988
Silkwood 1983 ☆
Carnal Knowledge 1971
Catch-22 1970
The Graduate 1967 ★
Who's Afraid of Virginia Woolf? 1966 ☆

"I'm loud and I'm vulgar . . . but I am not a monster, I'm not."

—Martha, *Who's Afraid of Virginia Woolf?*

1930s

FRANÇOIS TRUFFAUT

Born: François Roland Truffaut, February 6, 1932 (Paris, France); died 1984 (Neuilly-sur-Seine, Hauts-de-Seine, France).

Directing style: Director of French New Wave; Hitchcockian influence; poetical romances; autobiographical themes; exploration of women, love, and childhood.

Top Takes…

Vivement dimanche! 1983 (*Confidentially Yours*)

La femme d'à côté 1981

Le dernier métro 1980 (*The Last Metro*)

L'amour en fuite 1979 (*Love on the Run*)

La chambre verte 1978 (*The Green Room*)

L'homme qui aimait les femmes 1977

L'argent de poche 1976 (*Pocket Money*)

L'histoire d'Adèle H. 1975 (*The Story of Adele H.*)

La nuit américaine 1973 (Day for Night) ☆

Une belle fille comme moi 1972
(*A Gorgeous Bird Like Me*)

Les deux anglaises et le continent 1971
(*Two English Girls*)

Domicile conjugal 1970 (*Bed & Board*)

L'enfant sauvage 1970 (*The Wild Child*)

La sirène du Mississippi 1969
(*Mississippi Mermaid*)

Baisers volés 1968 (*Stolen Kisses*)

La mariée était en noir 1968
(*The Bride Wore Black*)

La peau douce 1964 (*The Soft Skin*)

Jules et Jim 1962

Les quatre cents coups 1959
(*The Four Hundred Blows*)

Les mistons 1957 (*The Kids*)

In his late teens François Truffaut began to idolize French film critic and theorist André Bazin, who became a kind of adoptive father, and by 1953 he was one of the first editors of *Cahiers du cinéma*. Adopting a vitriolic tone toward the typical romantic literary cinema of the day, and championing the Hollywood films of Howard Hawks, Nicholas Ray, Samuel Fuller, and Anthony Mann in an inspired onslaught of critical pieces, Truffaut helped found the French New Wave. By 1957, the desire to make movies had virtually eclipsed his need to write critically about them, although he always retained a sharp critical perspective. He made a small film about delinquent kids, *Les mistons* (1957) (*The Kids*), and followed this with a quartet about the waywardly charming French youth: the poetic *Les quatre cents coups* (1959) (*The Four Hundred Blows*), *Baisers volés* (1968) (*Stolen Kisses*), *Domicile conjugal* (1970) (*Bed & Board*), and *L'amour en fuite* (1979) (*Love on the Run*). Here, and in his other films, he explored the fragilities and contingencies of young love in contemporary Parisian life.

Exploring the dark side of human relationships, *Jules et Jim* (1962) centers on a tragic threesome. *L'enfant sauvage* (1970)

RIGHT: Jeanne Moreau shares a laugh with Henri Serre and Oskar Werner in *Jules et Jim*.

(*The Wild Child*) recounts the nineteenth-century story of the wild boy of Aveyron, raised from infancy by wolves and then discovered by a linguist, who works patiently to civilize him.

La chambre verte (1978) (*The Green Room*) celebrates the idea of memorializing one's dead, and in a key scene Truffaut memorializes his own. *Le dernier métro* (1980) (*The Last Metro*), set during the Nazi occupation of France, showed Truffaut at the top of his game and won ten Césars. Truffaut's final film was a modernist murder mystery, *Vivement dimanche!* (1983) (*Confidentially Yours*), shot in stunning black and white.

Truffaut played the linguist Claude Lacombe, who first communicates with aliens in Steven Spielberg's *Close Encounters of the Third Kind* (1977). It was a poignant cameo and an homage from Spielberg: it was the last time that Truffaut acted on the big screen before his early demise from cancer at the age of fifty-two. **MP**

ABOVE: Catherine Deneuve and Gérard Depardieu in the war drama *The Last Metro*.

Truffaut and Hitchcock

François Truffaut was an avid reader and correspondent, penning tautly energetic and sincere letters to friends, production associates, and actors whose work he had seen. In 1962 he wrote what was to become a legendary letter to Alfred Hitchcock, calling him "the greatest film director in the world." This was the beginning of an intensive collaboration in which Truffaut conducted interviews with Hitchcock between July and September of that year. The results of the interviews were presented in a celebrated book, *Le Cinéma Selon Alfred Hitchcock* (*Hitchcock/Truffaut*) (1962).

ALEXANDER KLUGE

Born: Alexander Kluge, February 14, 1932 (Halberstadt, Germany).

Directing style: Member of the Oberhausen Group; social criticism and exploration of national psyche; masterful storytelling; innovative use of montage with photographs and archive footage.

Top Takes...

Vermischte Nachrichten 1986
  (*Miscellaneous News*)

Die Macht der Gefühle 1983
  (*The Power of Emotion*)

Krieg und Frieden 1982 (*War and Peace*)

Biermann-Film 1982

Der Kandidat 1980 (*The Candidate*)

Die Patriotin 1979 (*The Patriotic Woman*)

Deutschland im Herbst 1978
  (*Germany in Autumn*)

Der Starke Ferdinand 1976
  (*Strongman Ferdinand*)

Die Artisten in der Zirkuskuppel: Ratlos 1968
  (*The Artist in the Circus Dome: Clueless*)

Abschied von Gestern—(Anita G.) 1966
  (*Yesterday Girl*)

Brutalität in Stein 1961 (*Brutality in Stone*)

"These days you can't choose how you want to express yourself anymore."

RIGHT: A scene from Kluge's symbolic, avant-garde drama, *The Patriotic Woman*.

Alexander Kluge was a major force behind the transition that changed German cinema from irrelevant *Heimat* (German identity) and quasihistorical movies to rich explorations of national history and psyche. His modernist aesthetic paved the way for the later, superior works of Werner Herzog, Rainer Werner Fassbinder, and Hans-Jürgen Syberberg. The 1962 Oberhausen Manifesto, "The old film is dead. We believe in the new one," was Kluge's credo and motivation for directors' revisions and reinterpretations. The whole complex of unresolved problems concerning German culture and politics became his focus of interest. Kluge's style was based on the proposition that if you want to achieve cathartic encounters with new reality, first you must make necessary interventions inside film form itself.

This transformation is already evident in Kluge's debut film, *Abschied von Gestern—(Anita G.)* (1966) (*Yesterday Girl*). Anita is a Jew from East Germany, who escapes to West Germany only to find disillusionment and another kind of entrapment. Her story is treated not only as an allegory about a general denial of traumatic moments, but also as an example of a new social cinema with a strong poetic foundation. In *Die Artisten in der Zirkuskuppel: Ratlos* (1968) (*The Artist in the Circus Dome: Clueless*), Kluge's collage turns politics almost into abstraction. The director's most accessible movie is also his most satiric work: in *Der Starke Ferdinand* (1976) (*Strongman Ferdinand*), Kluge shows how, in the face of a terrorist threat, an obsession with total safety can be the main danger for the system. Nothing here is unexpected or plainly perverse: to prove his point, security expert Ferdinand Rieche, played by Heinz Schubert, will himself—according to the film's inherent logic—commit a terrorist act. **AB**

MILOS FORMAN

Born: Jan Tomáš Forman, February 18, 1932 (Cáslav, Czech Republic).

Directing style: Maker of early Czech New Wave comedies, and later Hollywood dramas and biopics about unpopular historical figures; themes of the outsider, liberty, and freedom of speech.

Top Takes...

Milos Forman has directed an impressive oeuvre of films about rebels, eccentrics, and iconoclasts. Many of them, such as *One Flew Over the Cuckoo's Nest* (1975), which earned him his first Oscar for Best Director, and *The People vs. Larry Flint* (1996), pit outcasts against institutional authority, and inspire audiences to question their own societal and moral assumptions.

After helping to launch the Czech New Wave with such movies as *Lásky jedné plavovlásky* (1965) (*The Loves of a Blonde*), Forman came to the United States in the early 1970s. Here he had a major break with *One Flew Over the Cuckoo's Nest*, the Oscar-sweeping story which makes an antiestablishment hero of petty crook Randle Patrick McMurphy.

This was followed by an anticlimactic adaptation of 1960s stage-musical smash *Hair* (1979). Forman had tried to make a film version when first arriving in the United States, but could not get the rights until long after the once cutting-edge hippie paean had lost much of its impact. *Ragtime* (1981) was an eclectic depiction of the United States in the early 1900s centered on the powerful story of Coalhouse Walker Jr. seeking justice in a white man's world. Although Forman managed to

RIGHT: Tom Hulce as Mozart, the man of the moment, in Forman's Oscar-winning *Amadeus*.

1930s

entice James Cagney into a riveting performance in what was the final role of his legendary career, the film's canvas was too broad to earn large box-office success.

Forman struck gold again with *Amadeus* (1984), which landed him his second Oscar for Best Director. This biopic was a homecoming for Forman, as location shooting was in his native Prague. His facility with provocative characterizations gave his audience an acute and unexpected look into the working of genius in the form of Tom Hulce's boorish Wolfgang Amadeus Mozart as well as the prosaic world of ordinary men, represented by the Oscar-winning performance of F. Murray Abraham as Antonio Salieri.

Forman has also made a significant mark in academia, working at Columbia University's film program since the 1970s. He continues to develop and occasionally direct film scripts, although none has returned him to his former glory. **WSW**

ABOVE: Jack Nicholson causes a stir in *One Flew Over the Cuckoo's Nest*.

Forman and Freedom

Milos Forman lost his parents to facism and later fled to the United States to escape communism. His childhood led him to a perennial search for freedom.

- Both of Forman's parents died in the Nazi concentration camp at Auschwitz.

- Forman's own trouble with the authorities started with *The Fireman's Ball* (1968)—he was accused of making fun of good communist workers.

- His move to the United States meant leaving his family, including his twin sons.

- He has fought against film censorship and copyright laws in the United States.

NAGISA OSHIMA

Born: Nagisa Oshima, March 31, 1932 (Okayama, Japan).

Directing style: Vanguard director of Japanese New Wave, and documentary filmmaker; radical political energy; merging of documentary and surrealist aesthetics; often themes of postwar Japan.

Top Takes...

Gohatto 1999 (Taboo)

Kyoto, My Mother's Place 1991

Max mon amour 1986 (Max My Love)

Merry Christmas Mr. Lawrence 1983

Ai no borei 1978 (Empire of Passion)

Ai no corrida 1976 (In the Realm of the Senses)

Tokyo senso sengo hiwa 1970
(He Died After the War)

Shonen 1969 (Boy)

Koshikei 1968 (Death by Hanging)

Hakuchu no torima 1966 (Violence at Noon)

Nihon no yoru to kiri 1960
(Night and Fog in Japan)

Seishun zankoku monogatari 1960
(Cruel Story of Youth)

Ai to kibo no machi 1959
(A Street of Love and Hope)

"My hatred for Japanese cinema includes absolutely all of it."

From his earliest works, such as *Ai to kibo no machi* (1959) (*A Street of Love and Hope*), Oshima established himself as an innovative artist concerned not only with depicting Japan's rapid industrialization and Westernization, but also as a director determined to infuse Japanese cinema with a radical political energy that he found lacking in the motion pictures of classical Japanese directors. Although he populated his earliest films with alienated youth living on society's margins, his narratives never romanticized these subjects or environments. Rather, he used his films to advance the notion that cinema could instigate social change.

As his career developed, Oshima continued to experiment with cinema's formal and narrative structures, merging documentary and surrealist aesthetics while maintaining an interest in outlaw characters. *Hakuchu no torima* (1966) (*Violence at Noon*) and *Tokyo senso sengo hiwa* (1970) (*He Died After the War*) are two of his best-known works from this period, but it was his sexually explicit tale of carnal obsession, *Ai no corrida* (1976) (*In the Realm of the Senses*), that brought Oshima international renown. Loosely based on a true story about a violent affair between a prostitute and an innkeeper, the film met with both censorship and critical acclaim for its stifling representation of a couple seeking to purge themselves of responsibility through sadomasochistic bouts of lovemaking. *In the Realm of the Senses* marked the first of several coproductions, including *Ai no borei* (1978) (*Empire of Passion*) and *Max mon amour* (1986) (*Max My Love*). Oshima's most recent film, *Gohatto* (1999) (*Taboo*), won several national and international film awards, and was nominated for the Palme d'Or at the Cannes Film Festival. **JM**

RIGHT: A scene from Nagisa Oshima's critically acclaimed *In the Realm of the Senses*.

ANDREI TARKOVSKY

Born: Andrei Arsenyevich Tarkovsky, April 4, 1932 (Zavrazhe, Ivanono, Russia); died 1986 (Paris, France).

Directing style: Innovative science-fiction movies; long takes where it seems time stands still; metaphysical themes; beautiful, dreamy, poetic imagery.

Top Takes…

Offret 1986 (*The Sacrifice*)

Nostalghia 1983

Tempo di viaggio 1983 (*Voyage in Time*)

Stalker 1979

Serkalo 1975 (*The Mirror*)

Solyaris 1972 (*Solaris*)

Andrey Rublyov 1969

Ivanovo detstvo 1962 (*My Name is Ivan*)

Katok i skripka 1960
   (*The Steamroller and the Violin*)

Segodnya uvolneniya ne budet 1959
   (*There Will be No Leave Today*)

Ubiytsy 1958 (*The Killers*)

Son of Arseny Tarkovsky, an eminent Russian poet, Andrei Tarkovsky studied music and Arabic before training for more than five years at the All-Union State Institute of Cinematography (VGIK) in Moscow. Tarkovsky is responsible for what may very well be the greatest science-fiction movie ever made, *Solyaris* (1972) (*Solaris*), which is based on a novel by Stanislaw Lem. Like Stanley Kubrick in *2001: A Space Odyssey* (1968), Tarkovsky is unafraid to use a more measured and ponderous pace to explore the worlds of both outer and inner space. And, as in *2001*, there's a very real maturity and depth to *Solaris*. Although it was remade by writer and director Steven Soderbergh in 2002, the twenty-first-century version converts what was a thoughtful meditation on emotional loss and mortality into a slightly more generic affair.

Preeminently moody and haunting, Tarkovsky's *Solaris* uses science fiction to ask big questions about the nature of humanity and alienation. A hybrid of art-theater sensibility and genre-led storytelling, the film takes science fiction's reputation as a literature of ideas seriously, while also lending a strong emotional punch to the proceedings.

RIGHT: Alexander Kaidanovsky in the title role of the science-fiction thriller *Stalker*.

Tarkovsky is also famous for his work on the film *Stalker* (1979), which is again based on a science-fiction source novel. This movie mines the genre once more for philosophical and metaphysical consequences, although it is, if anything, rather more surreal than *Solaris*.

Tarkovsky repeatedly demonstrates in his films that he is unafraid of the poetry and the genuine art of cinema. In *Nostalghia* (1983), he is not afraid to focus on a single character carrying a lighted candle for many minutes without ever cutting away. The film was shot in Italy and after its completion Tarkovsky decided not to return to Russia.

An auteur's auteur—and strongly opposed to the notion of film as being mere entertainment—Tarkovsky's vision and his thoughtful, beautiful, and philosophical slowing-down of cinema are pretty much unrivaled in the Russian movie world and beyond. **MH**

ABOVE: A psychologist finds an alternate reality on the *Solaris* space station.

Soviet Film School

Andrei Tarkovsky studied cinematography at VGIK, the All-Union State Institute of Cinematography in Moscow.

- The institute was renamed in 1986, becoming the Gerasimov All-Russian State Institute of Cinematography in tribute to the Russian film director and actor Sergei Gerasimov.

- Founded by Vladimir Gardin in 1919, it is the world's oldest educational institution teaching cinematography.

- Among its most distinguished professors are Sergei M. Eisenstein, Vsevolod Pudovkin, and Aleksey Batalov.

1930s

JEAN-PAUL RAPPENEAU

Born: Jean-Paul Rappeneau, April 8, 1932 (Auxerre, Yonne, Bourgogne, France).

Directing style: Lavish historical dramas and light romantic comedies; elaborate attention to detail; notable artistic collaborations with actor Gérard Depardieu.

Top Takes…

Bon voyage 2003
Le hussard sur le toit 1995
 (*The Horseman on the Roof*)
Cyrano de Bergerac 1990
Tout feu, tout flamme 1982 (*All Fired Up*)
Le sauvage 1975 (*The Savage*)
Les mariés de l'an II 1971
 (*The Scarlet Buccaneer*)
La vie de château 1966
 (*A Matter of Resistance*)
Chronique provinciale 1958

French screenwriter turned director Jean-Paul Rappeneau scored an unlikely international hit with his faithful adaptation of the play *Cyrano de Bergerac* (1990). Starring Gérard Depardieu as the self-conscious wit who fears his super-sized snout will foil his love for the gorgeous Roxanne, the movie reaped a clutch of awards including ten Césars, a handful of Oscar nominations, and one Oscar win for Best Costume Design. Born in 1932, Rappeneau first fell in love with the movies as a fifteen-year-old when he saw *Citizen Kane* (1941). He then organized a film club in his home town to show the U.S. movies flooding into France after World War II.

After a flirtation with law, Rappeneau began his film career as an assistant and screenwriter, penning *Signé arsène lupin* (1959), and collaborating with Louis Malle on *Zazie dans le métro* (1960). In 1966, he made his directorial debut using his own script with the wartime romantic comedy *La vie de château* (*A Matter of Resistance*), a major box-office draw and critical hit. Subsequent self-directed offerings included *Les mariés de l'an II* (1971) (*The Scarlet Buccaneer*) with Jean-Paul Belmondo, *Le sauvage* (1975) (*The Savage*) with Yves Montand, and *Tout feu, tout flamme* (1982) (*All Fired Up*), with Belmondo and Isabelle Adjani. Rappeneau is best known for his elaborate treatment of *Cyrano de Bergerac*. Generally considered Depardieu's greatest role, no effort or expense was spared in the film's production; the English subtitles were provided by *A Clockwork Orange* (1971) writer Anthony Burgess, and the film ranks as one of the costliest French productions ever. Rappeneau went on to direct *Le hussard sur le toit* (1995) (*The Horseman on the Roof*) and the lighthearted World War II drama *Bon voyage* (2003), which also starred Depardieu. **TE**

> "I made a mess of everything, even my death."
>
> —Cyrano, *Cyrano de Bergerac*

MONTE HELLMAN

Born: Monte Hellman, July 12, 1932 (New York City, New York, U.S.).

Directing style: Controversial auteur maker of offbeat, existential Westerns and cult dramas; beautiful and moody locations; gritty visuals; sardonic humor; collaboration with Jack Nicholson on early films.

If talent and individuality counted for anything, Monte Hellman would have enjoyed a stellar career. Instead, he has scraped a living making a sporadic handful of intriguing cult movies, interspersed with years in the wilderness.

Like many of his generation, Hellman learned his craft in the rough-and-ready exploitation school of Roger Corman. He became friends with Jack Nicholson and together they made two spare, existential Westerns, shot back-to-back on a derisory budget in the Utah desert: *Ride in the Whirlwind* (1965) and *The Shooting* (1967). Nicholson scripted *Ride in the Whirlwind* and acted in both. Neither film attracted much notice in the United States or Britain, but the French took to them with enthusiasm and they ran in Paris for months.

No director used Warren Oates's edgy, hair-trigger persona better than Hellman, who starred him in his next three films. *Two-Lane Blacktop* (1971) captured the disenchanted wind-down of the 1960s. *Cockfighter* (1974), with Oates as a drifter wandering the Southern states, hit distribution problems owing to its subject matter. *Amore, piombo e furore* (1978) (*China 9, Liberty 37*)—the U.S. title refers to a signpost, not an ideological sporting score—was a sardonic take on Spaghetti Westerns. After several projects fell through, Hellman was reduced to the secondhand fare of *Silent Night, Deadly Night 3: Better Watch Out!* (1989). For a while he survived by acting as an uncredited editor rescuing other people's films until, in 2006, he edited one episode of Dennis Bartok's horror film *Trapped Ashes*. Rumors of a comeback, possibly funded by Quentin Tarantino as a quid pro quo for Hellman's help as executive producer on *Reservoir Dogs* (1992), continue to circulate. **PK**

Top Takes...

Trapped Ashes 2006
Stanley's Girlfriend 2006
Iguana 1988
Inside the Coppola Personality 1981
Amore, piombo e furore 1978
  (*China 9, Liberty 37*)
The Greatest 1977
Cockfighter 1974
Two-Lane Blacktop 1971
The Shooting 1967
Ride in the Whirlwind 1965
Flight to Fury 1964
The Terror 1963
Beast from Haunted Cave 1959

1930s

> "Performance and image, that's what it's all about."
> —G.T.O., *Two-Lane Blacktop*

MELVIN VAN PEEBLES

Born: Melvin Peebles, August 21, 1932 (Chicago, Illinois, U.S.).

Directing style: "The Grandfather of Blaxploitation," the genre begun with his *Sweet Sweetback's Baadasssss Song*; pioneering and controversial director whose movies explore notions of race and racism in a humorous way.

Top Takes...

The Real Deal 2003

Le conte du ventre plein 2000 *(Bellyful)*

Tales of Erotica (Vroom Vroom Vroom) 1996

Gang in Blue 1996

Identity Crisis 1989

Don't Play Us Cheap 1973

Sweet Sweetback's Baadasssss Song 1971

Watermelon Man 1970

The Story of a Three-Day Pass 1968

Cinq cent balles 1963

Three Pickup Men for Herrick 1957

Sunlight 1957

"The Grandfather of Blaxploitation," Melvin Van Peebles is also a novelist, memoirist, musician, composer, actor, editor, director, producer, options trader, icon, and playwright. Van Peebles is active today, most recently as the subject of his son Mario Van Peebles's *How to Get the Man's Foot Outta Your Ass* (2003), and as the centerpiece of the documentary *How to Eat Your Watermelon in White Company (and Enjoy It)* (2005).

Melvin Van Peebles started out producing short films, *Three Pickup Men for Herrick* (1957) and *Sunlight* (1957), but failed to break into Hollywood. Frustrated, he moved to Europe, added the "Van" to his name, and made his debut feature, *The Story of a Three-Day Pass* (1968)—an interracial love story with tragic edges and New Wave conceits. Filmed in France, and selected as the French entry in the San Francisco Film Festival, it was awarded the top prize. For a black director to receive an award from America during this period was groundbreaking.

Based on this success, Van Peebles landed a contract with Columbia Pictures for the comedy *Watermelon Man* (1970), the story of a white man who turns black. This experience of working in the mainstream industry was unpleasant, so his third feature was produced independently, shooting guerrilla style on the streets of Los Angeles, and without regard for conventional taste. *Sweet Sweetback's Baadasssss Song* (1971) fomented the late 1960s U.S. civil rights struggles and became a hit, despite not being distributed through mainstream channels. Its basic premise about a black man pulling one over on the authorities was immediately taken in by Hollywood, transforming a nascent political theme into an action-adventure staple in the Blaxploitation cycle of the early 1970s. **GCQ**

> "... a maverick spirit and multi-talented creative force."
>
> —*Senses of Cinema*

YASH CHOPRA

Born: Yash Chopra, September 27, 1932 (Lahore, Punjab, Pakistan).

Directing style: "The King of the Bollywood romance"; maker of melodramas, action movies, and sentimental musicals; creative collaborations with actor Amitabh Bachchan.

Yash Chopra is, without doubt, one of the most significant directors to emerge from the Hindi popular cinema—or, as it is now more commonly known, "Bollywood."

Chopra began his career in the late 1950s making the romantic *Dhool Ka Phool* (1959) (*Blossom of Dust*), and throughout the 1960s made a number of impressive features such as *Waqt* (1965) (*Time*) and *Ittefaq* (1969) (*Coincidence*). However, his career did not really take off until the 1970s, with his first collaboration with Hindi superstar Amitabh Bachchan on the film *Deewaar* (1975) (*I'll Die for Mama*). This film was a runaway success and subsequently the two collaborated on a number of projects that again utilized Bachchan's "angry young man" persona. These included *Trishul* (1978) (*Trident*) and *Kaala Patthar* (1979) (*Black Stone*). Chopra also had notable success during this period with other films that drew more on the star's romantic side with works such as *Kabhi Kabhie—Love is Life* (1976) (*Sometimes*) and *Silsila* (1981) (*The Affair*).

With the huge success of *Chandni* (1989) (*Moonlight*), Chopra became known as the "King of the Bollywood romance." As the 1990s progressed he turned away from directing films and moved more toward producing. In this role he has encouraged a number of young filmmakers who have written or directed some of the most successful films in the history of Indian cinema. These include *Mohabbatein* (2000) (*Love Stories*) and *Dhoom* (2004) (*Blast*). One of the most striking things about Chopra's later films is his obvious awareness of the potential profit to be made from the Indian diaspora. As such, many of his recent productions have been set all over the globe and have helped Hindi cinema reach screens well beyond the Indian subcontinent. **AW**

Top Takes...

Veer-Zaara 2004
Dil To Pagal Hai 1997 (*The Heart is Crazy*)
Darr 1993 (*A Violent Love Story*)
Parampara 1992 (*Tradition*)
Lamhe 1991
Chandni 1989 (*Moonlight*)
Vijay 1988
Faasle 1985
Silsila 1981 (*The Affair*)
Kaala Patthar 1979 (*Black Stone*)
Trishul 1978 (*Trident*)
Kabhi Kabhie—Love is Life 1976 (*Sometimes*)
Deewaar 1975 (*I'll Die for Mama*)
Ittefaq 1969 (*Coincidence*)
Waqt 1965 (*Time*)
Dhool Ka Phool 1959 (*Blossom of Dust*)

1930s

"Films have been my only passion .... I have never made a movie I have not believed in."

LOUIS MALLE

Born: Louis Malle, October 30, 1932 (Thumeries, Nord, France); died 1995 (Beverly Hills, California, U.S.).

Directing style: Versatile director of French New Wave who aimed to continually reinvent himself; sometimes controversial sexual content; taboo-breaking themes.

Top Takes...

"The longer I live, the less I trust ideas, the more I trust emotions."

Of the French New Wave directors who achieved lasting success, Louis Malle and Eric Rohmer perhaps stand furthest apart. Rohmer discovered early what he could do and has carried right on doing it. Malle, however, seemed determined never to repeat himself and explored different genres, styles, and countries. It was a risky strategy and Malle had his share of fiascos. *Vie privée* (1962) (*A Very Private Affair*), with Brigitte Bardot as a put-upon sex symbol, proved trite and sentimental; but at least it scored at the box office, unlike *Black Moon* (1975), a bizarre private fantasy. *Crackers* (1984) was an ill-advised attempt to transplant Mario Monicelli's classic crime comedy *I Soliti Ignoti* (1958) (*Big Deal*) to San Francisco, and *Damage* (1992), a study in sexual obsession, never found the right tone.

But against these can be set those films where Malle's eclecticism and audacity paid off, as in the stylishly cool and assured thriller *Ascenseur pour l'échafaud* (1958) (*Frantic*).

Some of Malle's most accomplished and deeply felt films concern adolescence: the semiautobiographical *Le souffle au coeur* (1971) (*Dearest Heart*); *Lacombe Lucien* (1974), in which a loutish peasant lad joins the fascists in occupied France; and the moving *Au revoir, les enfants* (1987) (*Goodbye Children*). In an utterly different register, *Viva Maria!* (1965) teamed Bardot and Jeanne Moreau in a high-spirited Western, whereas *Atlantic City* (1980) made elegiac use of Burt Lancaster as an aging, has-been minor mobster, and *My Dinner with Andre* (1981) proved that two men talking in a restaurant for 95 minutes could be utterly engrossing. But perhaps Malle's most internationally famous movie is *Pretty Baby* (1978), which set Brooke Shields on the road to stardom, playing a twelve-year-old New Orleans prostitute. **PK**

JEAN-MARIE STRAUB

Born: Jean-Marie Straub, January 8, 1933 (Metz, Moselle, Lorraine, France).

Directing style: Half of a directing duo with his wife Danièle Huillet, at the vanguard of New German Cinema; sparsely minimalist films; use of long takes and fixed camera positions or slowly moving dolly shots.

One of the key figures of the New German Cinema, Jean-Marie Straub worked most of his life with his wife and artistic partner, Danièle Huillet. As a teenager, Straub was already infatuated with the cinema and left Metz for Paris where he met Huillet.

Straub and Huillet moved to Germany in 1958 and made their first short film, a satire of German military authority, *Machorka-Muff* (1963). This was followed by the landmark movie *Nicht versöhnt oder Es hilft nur Gewalt wo Gewalt herrscht* (1965) (*Not Reconciled*), which strips plot and incident to an absolute minimum and requires the actors to recite their lines in a monotone. Next came the ambitious *Chronik der Anna Magdalena Bach* (1968) (*The Chronicle of Anna Magdalena Bach*), which was photographed on many of the actual locations of Johann Sebastian Bach's life. Narrated by Bach's wife Anna (played by Christiane Lang), the film was an international success. The duo followed with a series of increasingly challenging films, including *Geschichtsunterricht* (1972) (*History Lessons*) and *Moses und Aron* (1975) (*Moses and Aaron*). These are austere and sparsely minimalist films that demand intense concentration and patience from audiences.

In the early 1970s, Straub and Huillet moved to Rome. Their later films, such as *Dalla nube alla resistenza* (1979) (*From the Clouds to the Resistance*), relied increasingly on an intricate network of grants, state subsidies, and patronage for financing. Jean-Marie Straub will probably not make another film without his wife and longtime collaborator, who died in 2006. Nevertheless, Straub and Huillet's films offer the audience a transcendent and clarifying experience, and are deeply admired internationally for their purity, clarity, and sincerity of purpose. **WWD**

Top Takes...

Sicilia! 1999 (*Sicily!*)

Dalla nube alla resistenza 1979
    (*From the Clouds to the Resistance*)

Moses und Aron 1975 (*Moses and Aaron*)

Geschichtsunterricht 1972 (*History Lessons*)

Les yeux ne veulent pas en tout temps se fermer, ou Peut-être qu'un jour Rome se permettra de choisir à son tour 1970 (*Eyes Do Not Want to Close at All Times, or, Perhaps One Day Rome Will Allow Herself to Choose in Her Turn*)

Der Bräutigam, die Komödiantin und der Zuhälter 1968 (*The Bridegroom, the Comedienne and the Pimp*)

Chronik der Anna Magdalena Bach 1968
    (*The Chronicle of Anna Magdalena Bach*)

Nicht versöhnt oder Es hilft nur Gewalt wo Gewalt herrscht 1965 (*Not Reconciled*)

Machorka-Muff 1963

> "*Machorka-Muff* is the story of the rape of a country on which an army has been imposed."

1930s

LILIANA CAVANI

Born: Liliana Cavani, January 12, 1933 (Carpi, Modena, Italy).

Directing style: Italian documentary maker and director of provocative and controversial antitotalitarian movies; period dramas exploring Nazism; minimalist feel; often sexual themes.

Top Takes…

Ripley's Game 2002

Dove siete? Io sono qui 1993
   (Where Are You? I'm Here)

Francesco 1989 (St. Francis of Assisi)

The Berlin Affair 1985

Oltre la porta 1982 (Beyond the Door)

La pelle 1981 (The Skin)

Al di là del bene e del male 1977
   (Beyond Good and Evil)

Il portiere di notte 1974 (The Night Porter)

Milarepa 1974

L'ospite 1972 (The Guest)

I Cannibali 1970 (The Year of the Cannibals)

Galileo 1969 (Galileo Galilei)

Francesco d'Assisi 1966 (Francis of Assisi)

Primo Piano: Philippe Pétain
   processo a Vichy 1965

"I'm a creation. A gifted improviser."

—Tom Ripley, Ripley's Game

After studying classical literature in Bologna, Liliana Cavani went to Rome and completed a film course with two short films, both dealing with intercultural problems and racism. At the TV station RAI, Cavani had success with several documentaries on the Third Reich and she soon became established as a specialist for this historical period. Her fictional debut was a Marxist reinterpretation of *Francesco d'Assisi* (1966) (*Francis of Assisi*), executed in a very minimalist style. In 1989, Cavani made a more mystical remake of this film. *Francesco d'Assisi* also created her first scandal due to its ideological content, and it came as no surprise that the antitotalitarian gesture has marked most of her films.

Her first international production *Il portiere di notte* (1974) (*The Night Porter*) caused Cavani's second scandal: this *amour fou* between an ex-Schutzstaffel officer and his concentration-camp victim was based on real events, but widely considered a tasteless pornographic fantasy. Luchino Visconti and Pier Paolo Pasolini supported the petition to show the film despite the censor's judgment. With the Buddhist mystery drama *Milarepa* (1974), Cavani turned to religion, but completed her German trilogy (begun with *The Night Porter*) with *Al di là del bene e del male* (1977) (*Beyond Good and Evil*) and *The Berlin Affair* (1985). *La pelle* (1981) (*The Skin*), starring Burt Lancaster, Claudia Cardinale, and Marcello Mastroianni was Cavani's most expensive film to date. Condemned by the critics as exploitative, it still has to be reevaluated. The auteur Cavani will at least be remembered for her intense cult film *The Night Porter*—in which Charlotte Rampling gained iconic status—and for her strong artistic ability and will to morally provoke and stimulate her audience. **MS**

STAN BRAKHAGE

Born: Robert Sanders, January 14, 1933 (Kansas City, Missouri, U.S.); died 2003 (Victoria, British Columbia, Canada).

Directing style: Experimental filmmaker of visual poetry; silent films; use of collage; scratched emulsion; metaphysical themes; meditations on nature and war.

Stan Brakhage made nearly 380 films, each lasting between nine seconds and four hours. Most of his work was done in 16mm, and he often handpainted the film or scratched the image directly on to the film emulsion, sometimes using collage techniques. Even within the highly individualist scene of experimental cinema, Brakhage remained an outsider, advocating an irrational, heartfelt approach. His first films, biographical in nature and observing the awkwardness of the human body, have a direct, visceral impact. When he reminisces about youth home-movie style in *Sirius Remembered* (1959), or when he films the birth of his first child in *Window Water Baby Moving* (1962), the viewer feels empathy. When one sees the dead man hanging in *Anticipation of the Night* (1962) or the ghoulish graveyards in *The Dead* (1960), it provokes unease. Witnessing the chillingly clinical autopsy dissection in *The Act of Seeing With One's Own Eyes* (1971), is truly disturbing. The sight of a dead person changing, before one's eyes, into parts and props is tough to digest even for seasoned film students; this discomfort is reinforced by the lack of comforting sound.

Brakhage gradually drifted away from such macabre diaries into pure form: colors, movements, lights, specks, and flecks, like the shapes seen when one rubs one's eyes hard. In the hallucinatory *The Dante Quartet* (1987) Brakhage achieved a poetry that was abstract and illuminating and he makes poetic use of the stunning natural beauty of the Pacific Northwest coast in *Creation* (1979), . . . *Reel* (1998) series, *A Child's Garden and the Serious Sea* (1991), and *The Mammals of Victoria* (1994). Sensitive and sensorial, Brakhage was perhaps the first, and last, filmmaker ever to try and film the inside of one's eyes—the true perception of what one really sees. **EM**

Top Takes…

The God of Day Had Gone Down Upon Him 2000
The Mammals of Victoria 1994
Study in Color and Black and White 1993
A Child's Garden and the Serious Sea 1991
I . . . Dreaming 1988
The Dante Quartet 1987
Creation 1979
The Stars Are Beautiful 1974
The Act of Seeing With One's Own Eyes 1971
Dog Star Man 1964
Anticipation of the Night 1962
Window Water Baby Moving 1962
The Dead 1960
Sirius Remembered 1959
Wedlock House: An Intercourse 1959

> "[His] films . . . are stunningly, even ravishingly beautiful."
> —Fred Camper, *Senses of Cinema*

1930s

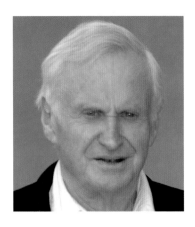

JOHN BOORMAN

Born: John Boorman, January 18, 1933 (Shepperton, Surrey, England).

Directing style: British director whose dramas can make the ordinary alien; mythic themes of quest and survival; creative collaborations with actor Lee Marvin.

Top Takes…

The Tiger's Tail 2006
Country of My Skull 2004
The Tailor of Panama 2001
The General 1998
Lumière et compagnie 1995
Hope and Glory 1987 ☆
The Emerald Forest 1985
Journey Into Light 1985
Excalibur 1981
Exorcist II: The Heretic 1977
Zardoz 1974
Deliverance 1972 ☆
Leo the Last 1970
Hell in the Pacific 1968
Point Blank 1967
Catch Us If You Can 1965

"Legends are templates for human behavior … a myth is a story that has survived."

Born in 1933 in the suburban outskirts of London, John Boorman recounted his experience of growing up during the Blitz of World War II in his award-winning *Hope and Glory* (1987). After completing his national service, Boorman earned a living in postwar London writing and broadcasting. Eager to become a filmmaker, in 1955 he landed a post at Independent Television News, where he learned the rudiments of filmmaking by becoming an assistant editor. Two years later he moved to Southern Television, where he was promoted to director and editor. He eventually accepted a position at the BBC, where he directed several provocative documentaries.

During a leave of absence from the BBC, Boorman directed his first feature, *Catch Us If You Can* (1965) about the British pop scene. In late 1966, he resigned from the BBC to make *Point Blank* (1967) with Lee Marvin, one of the best films of the 1960s, a stylish, hallucinatory story of a man who, betrayed by his wife and close friend, in his dying moment imagines his vengeance upon them. He followed this with another evocative film featuring Marvin, *Hell in the Pacific* (1968).

For *Leo the Last* (1970), set in London's small West Indian community, Boorman won the Best Director award at Cannes. Films such as *Zardoz* (1974) and the Arthurian *Excalibur* (1981) reveal that his subject matter is consistently drawn from myths and archetypes. Boorman's biggest commercial success, however, was a brutal story of atavistic violence set in the backwoods—the landmark movie *Deliverance* (1972). A classic tale about surviving in the wilderness, memorable for its male rape scene, the film's disturbing sense of menace leaves many wondering whether they'll ever again enjoy a stroll in the woods. **SU**

JACK HILL

Born: Jack Hill, January 28, 1933 (Los Angeles, California, U.S.).

Directing style: "The Howard Hawks of exploitation filmmaking"; cult B-movie director of early blaxploitation films, and innovator of women-in-prison genre; introduced Pam Grier as a leading exploitation player.

Jack Hill is a U.S. writer and director known for his thrilling contributions to the exploitation genre in the early 1970s. Growing up, he gravitated toward music and took a degree in music composition from the University of California, Los Angeles (UCLA). Hill also studied film there and scored student projects. After graduation, Hill was utilized as a musician on several major studio soundtracks. He then began work at Roger Corman's New World Pictures, working alongside UCLA alumnus Francis Ford Coppola in various capacities as editing supervisor, dialogue writer, and uncredited director.

Hill made his recognized debut in 1964 with the horror movie *Spider Baby or, The Maddest Story Ever Told* (1968) which, despite sitting in distribution limbo for four years, became the first of several cult hits for the director. In the early 1970s, Hill journeyed to the Philippines to make the women-in-prison duo *The Big Doll House* (1971) and *The Big Bird Cage* (1972) for Corman. Despite the exploitive subject matter, both films feature a nice combination of humor and subtle political subtext. Hill followed up on these successes by moving to American International Pictures to film the blaxploitation pair *Coffy* (1973) and *Foxy Brown* (1974), both starring Pam Grier.

The female juvenile-delinquent film *Switchblade Sisters* (1975) followed. Hill said of the movie, "The idea of doing a realistic movie about street gangs with beautiful blondes in hot pants was preposterous, so we tried to make it a wacky fantasy." Despite being an exciting success, it is the last film on which Hill was officially credited. In 1996, his career saw a rebirth thanks to supporter Quentin Tarantino, who has described Hill as "The Howard Hawks of exploitation filmmaking." **WW**

Top Takes...

Sorceress 1982
Switchblade Sisters 1975
Foxy Brown 1974
Coffy 1973
The Big Bird Cage 1972
The Big Doll House 1971
The Winner 1969
Spider Baby or, The Maddest Story Ever Told 1968
House of Evil 1968
Blood Bath 1966
Mondo Keyhole 1966
The Terror 1963
The Wasp Woman 1960
The Host 1960

1930s

"You'd better keep your ass off our turf, or we'll blow it off!"

—Maggie, *Switchblade Sisters*

COSTA-GAVRAS

Born: Konstantinos Gavras, February 12, 1933 (Loutra-Iraias, Greece).

Directing style: Greek director who revolutionized the genre of the political thriller; ethical and political themes that both entertain and challenge; dark tone; commentary on media feeding frenzy inspired by sensational events.

Top Takes...

Costa-Gavras's third film, *Z* (1969), was an international sensation, winning the Jury Prize at the Cannes Film Festival and an Oscar for Best Foreign Language Film. It redefined the genre of the political thriller, jettisoning the sub-Hitchcockian emphasis on picaresque adventure and improbable romance that glamorized and trivialized even many of the most riveting realistic examples of the genre. *État de siège* (1972) (*State of Siege*) and *Missing* (1982) exposed the malevolence of antidemocratic power structures and the failure of the United States and other Western governments to avoid complicity in terror, torture, and suppression of freedom around the world.

Costa-Gavras's later work, however, soon fell into the same melodramatic traps he had so deftly avoided. *Betrayed* (1988), like *Z*, meditates on real events, in this instance the brutal murder of a left-wing, Jewish talk-radio host, but it is more interested in spinning the plot out with suspense built up around the possibility that the undercover agent might be discovered before he can be put into custody.

Music Box (1989), rather like Hitchcock's *Stage Fright* (1950), uses a trial format to put into question the identity of the heroine's father, an accused Nazi collaborator complicit in the brutal murder of Jews, whose protestations of innocence are startlingly overturned by his daughter's discovery of a totemic object, a device that implausibly contains photographs that put his guilt beyond question. *Mad City* (1997) completes this turn toward standard screen drama. The film is a virtual remake of Billy Wilder's *Ace in the Hole* (1951) and offers, albeit deftly and with dark humor, much the same kind of biting commentary on sensational events, and the media feeding frenzy they inspire. **BP**

> "Concurrently, the military banned ... the letter 'Z'...."
>
> —Narrator, *Z*

1930s

BOB RAFELSON

Born: Bob Rafelson, February 21, 1933 (New York City, New York, U.S.).

Directing style: Wunderkind director of the 1970s; creator of the pop group and TV series "The Monkees"; notable artistic collaborations with Jack Nicholson, who starred in several of the director's films.

Like other directors who found their voice in the maverick, movie-brat Hollywood of the 1970s, Bob Rafelson seemed to lose his way as that decade receded into history. But for a few years he and the films he made were seamlessly in tune with the disruptive, disenchanted zeitgeist of the period.

Rafelson started out in TV where, together with producer Bert Schneider, he created The Monkees, the ersatz pop group welded together to emulate the appeal of The Beatles, and then proceeded to destroy them in his first feature film, *Head* (1968), sending up and exposing the whole charade. With Schneider and Steve Blauner he formed the influential indie outfit BBS Productions (short for Bert, Bob, and Steve), which produced *The Last Movie* (1971) and Rafelson's next film, *Five Easy Pieces* (1970).

Five Easy Pieces, which starred Jack Nicholson as a former classical pianist in downwardly mobile flight from his cultured middle-class background, used its dysfunctional family to reflect the sense of disillusionment and burnt-out rebellion that closed the 1960s. *The King of Marvin Gardens* (1972), set in a decaying, out-of-season Atlantic City, explored similar themes with an even bleaker tone, making *Stay Hungry* (1976) seem almost upbeat by comparison.

Rafelson's remake of *The Postman Always Rings Twice* (1981) added in a lot of sex but missed the parched quality of the earlier version; *Black Widow* (1987) was a well-made but unexceptional thriller. *Mountains of the Moon* (1990), about Captain Richard Francis Burton and Lieutenant John Hanning Speke's search for the source of the Nile, was handsomely staged but lacked focus. Since then, Rafelson's films have grown steadily less frequent and less individual. **PK**

Top Takes...

The House on Turk Street 2002
Poodle Springs 1998
Blood and Wine 1996
Tales of Erotica 1994
Wet 1995
Man Trouble 1992
Mountains of the Moon 1990
Black Widow 1987
The Postman Always Rings Twice 1981
Modesty 1981
Brubaker 1980
Stay Hungry 1976
The King of Marvin Gardens 1972
Five Easy Pieces 1970
Head 1968

> "... I'm getting away from things that get bad if I stay."
> —Bobby, *Five Easy Pieces*

PHILIPPE DE BROCA

Born: Phillipe Claude Alex de Broca de Ferrussac, March 15, 1933 (Paris, France); died 2004 (Neuilly-sur-Seine, France).

Directing style: Member of French New Wave movement; cheerful, fast-paced boudoir comedies and farces; collaborations with actor Jean-Paul Belmondo.

Top Takes...

Vipère au poing 2004 (*Viper in the Fist*)

Amazone 2000 (*Amazon*)

Le jardin des plantes 1994 (*Tales From the Zoo*)

La gitane 1986 (*The Gypsy*)

L'Africain 1983 (*The African*)

On a volé la cuisse de Jupiter 1980 (*Jupiter's Thigh*)

Tendre poulet 1978 (*Dear Inspector*)

L'incorrigible 1975 (*Incorrigible*)

Le magnifique 1973 (*Greatest Secret Agent*)

Le roi de coeur 1966 (*King of Hearts*)

L'homme de Rio 1964 (*That Man From Rio*)

Les sept péchés capitaux 1962 (*The Seven Deadly Sins*)

Les jeux de l'amour 1960

Le Farceur 1960 (*The Joker*)

> "Life's a bubble. When it touches earth, it's over."
> —Claire, *Five Day Lover*

A master of lightweight comedies and escapist films, Philippe de Broca broke into the film business as a cameraman. He became a member of the French New Wave, although he was at heart more of a traditionalist, and served as an assistant to such directors as François Truffaut and Claude Chabrol. His first feature, *Les jeux de l'amour* (1960), was a spirited farce that won critical and commercial favor and de Broca soon began to pursue a career as a highly successful director of comedies, romances, and fast-paced action films with a light edge.

International success for de Broca came with *L'homme de Rio* (1964) (*That Man From Rio*), shot in dazzling color, edited to a percussive samba beat, and starring Jean-Paul Belmondo. He also contributed to the anthology film *Les sept péchés capitaux* (1962) (*The Seven Deadly Sins*), which he codirected with Chabrol, Jean-Luc Godard, and Roger Vadim, among others, contributing a short section on the theme of *La Gourmandise*.

De Broca's later work was more frankly commercial and he never developed a great international following, preferring to create his films strictly for Gallic audiences. His later films, such as *Tendre poulet* (1978) (*Dear Inspector*) and *La gitane* (1986) (*The Gypsy*), are almost throwbacks to the classical cinema of the 1950s, characterized by slick execution and a major studio sensibility. Often working with French stars Belmondo and Jean-Pierre Cassel, the director started his own production company, Fildebroc, to facilitate the creation of his works. De Broca's films may be slight, but in their cheerful energy and vulnerable good mood they offer a tonic to the cares of everyday existence, and offer the viewer a world in which even the slums of Rio de Janeiro can become a magical playground of exotic glamour. **WWD**

IVAN PASSER

Born: Ivan Passer, July 10, 1933 (Prague, Czech Republic).

Directing style: Known for early Czech New Wave output focusing on the realities of everyday life; has directed successful films across a variety of genres; black humor.

Ivan Passer started out in the film industry as a scriptwriter, and worked as assistant director to fellow Czech director Milo Forman on films such as *Cerný Petr* (1964) (*Black Peter*). He went on to make his debut with the short *Fádní Odpoledne* (1964) (*A Boring Afternoon*), which looked at the lives of soccer fans. His feature debut came with one of the key works of the Czech New Wave, *Intimni Osvetleni* (1966) (*Intimate Lighting*), a tragicomic tale of two musicians facing up to their lost dreams as a successful symphony musician visits an old friend who teaches music at a small-town school. The film captured international attention for its gentle story of everyday life and use of music, winning two awards from the U.S. National Society of Film Critics. Passer's success on home ground was cut short, however, when the Soviets invaded Czechoslovakia in 1968. He moved to the United States, where he has lived and worked ever since, switching from one genre to another.

Cutter's Way (1981) is Passer's most successful film in his adopted country, achieving almost cult status. The movie stars John Heard as a one-eyed, one-armed, one-legged, drunk and abusive Vietnam War veteran who gets a new lease of life when his gigolo beach-bum friend, played by Jeff Bridges, witnesses a body being dumped. The duo try to expose what looks to be a high-powered murderer in a move toward their own redemption. The thriller is a good example of Passer's masterful way of satirizing the absurdities of life through his camera lens. Since then he has garnered most praise for his TV biopic of the Soviet dictator *Stalin* (1992). A recent venture into historical epic territory, *Nomad* (2005), is set in eighteenth-century Kazakhstan, and was the country's entry for the Best Foreign Language Film Oscar. **CK**

Top Takes...

Nomad 2005
The Wishing Tree 1999
Pretty Hattie's Baby 1991
Haunted Summer 1988
Creator 1985
Cutter's Way 1981
Silver Bears 1978
Ace Up My Sleeve 1976
Law and Disorder 1974
Born to Win 1971
Intimni osvetleni 1966 (*Intimate Lighting*)
Fádni odpoledne 1964 (*A Boring Afternoon*)

"One of the ten films that have most affected me."—Krzyzstof Kieslowski on *Intimate Lighting*

ROMAN POLANSKI

Born: Roman Liebling, August 18, 1933 (Paris, France).

Directing style: Dramas, thrillers, literary adaptations, and horror movies; cameo appearances; masterful storytelling; psychological exploration and insights.

Top Takes...

Born in Paris but raised in Poland, Roman Polanski studied at Łódź Film School. Following his feature debut *Nóz w wodzie* (1962) (*Knife in the Water*), he moved to France, where he collaborated with writer Gérard Brach on *Repulsion* (1965) and *Cul-de-sac* (1966).

The bizarre horror pastiche *The Fearless Vampire Killers* (1967) caught the attention of producer Robert Evans, who chose Polanski to helm the supernatural thriller *Rosemary's Baby* (1968), a massive hit with critics and audiences alike. In the wake of its success, Polanski's wife Sharon Tate was brutally murdered in one of the most infamous crimes in U.S. history.

Polanski next adapted William Shakespeare's *The Tragedy of Macbeth* (1971) and reunited with Brach for the detour *What?* (1972) before making what many consider his masterpiece, *Chinatown* (1974), an award-winning film noir classic starring Jack Nicholson. *Le locataire* (1976) (*The Tenant*) was overshadowed by accusations that Polanski drugged and raped a thirteen-year-old girl, a charge hardly tempered when he entered a guilty plea for unlawful sexual intercourse with a minor. Polanski fled the United States to Europe, and has never

RIGHT: Mia Farrow and John Cassavetes in a scene from the horror *Rosemary's Baby*.

returned. Needless to say, his crime and later absence put a damper on his career, and after the release of *Tess* (1979) it would be decades before Polanski's critical and commercial success resumed. Follies such as *Pirates* (1986) did not help, and small steps toward artistic rehabilitation were stymied by some strange and poorly received films.

Polanski's fortunes changed once again with *The Pianist* (2002), arguably his most personal film due to its setting: the Polish ghettos orchestrated and imposed by the Nazis during World War II. The film earned Polanski his first and only Oscar as Best Director, as well as an Oscar for the screenplay.

Riding high on this new adulation, Polanski returned with a workmanlike adaptation of *Oliver Twist* (2005), an oddly mundane follow-up to such a powerful and well-received film; but given the controversial twists and turns of his career, maybe the choice was not so strange after all. **JK**

ABOVE: Jack Nicholson is accosted by Roman Polanski in the thrilling *Chinatown*.

Polanski's Baby

Polanski's 1968 hit *Rosemary's Baby* forms a loose trilogy with *Repulsion* (1965) and *Le locataire* (1976) (*The Tenant*), depicting the horrors of urban life.

- The Dakota building on Manhattan's Upper West Side was renamed The Bramford for the film. John Lennon was later assassinated outside the building.
- The color red, symbolizing the devil, is used throughout the film.
- One year after the movie's release, Polanski's pregnant wife Sharon Tate was murdered by the Charles Manson "family."

LUCIAN PINTILIE

Born: Lucian Pintilie, November 9, 1934 (Tarutino, Ukraine).

Directing style: Romanian director of comedies, dramas, and thrillers; controversial subject matter; themes examine the moral dilemmas faced by individuals living under a totalitarian regime.

Top Takes…

Tertium non datur 2005

Niki Ardelean, colonel în rezerva 2003
  (*Niki and Flo*)

Dupa-amiaza unui tortionar 2001
  (*The Afternoon of a Torturer*)

Terminus paradis 1998 (*Next Stop Paradise*)

Prea târziu 1996 (*Too Late*)

Un été inoubliable 1994
  (*An Unforgettable Summer*)

Balanta 1992 (*The Oak*)

De ce trag clopotele, Mitica? 1981
  (*Why Are the Bells Ringing, Mitica?*)

Paviljon VI 1978

Reconstituirea 1968 (*Reconstruction*)

Duminica la ora 6 1965 (*Sunday at Six*)

Lucian Pintilie was born in what was Romania and is now the Ukraine, and graduated from Bucharest's Institute of Theater and Cinematographic Art. After graduating he worked in TV, and also began working in the theater, directing both classical and contemporary plays. It was not until *Duminica la ora 6* (1965) (*Sunday at Six*) that he made his film debut as a director with a romance set in World War II following a couple's lives under the boot of fascism.

His thriller *Reconstituirea* (1968) (*Reconstruction*) tells the tale of two students who get drunk and attack a bar owner. They later have to reconstruct the events of their crime with grotesque results. The film got Pintilie into trouble with the Romanian authorities who viewed its examination of bureaucracy as subversive, but it was his stage career that got him into deeper trouble. His production of Nikolai Gogol's *The Inspector General* in 1972 was eventually forbidden, and he moved to Paris where he concentrated on theater work.

His fifth film, the fast-paced comedy *De ce trag cloptele, Mitica* (1981) (*Why Are the Bells Ringing, Mitica?*) set in a small town preparing for a carnival, fell foul of the censors because of Pintilie's characteristic sideswipes at the consequences of living in a totalitarian state, and he only returned to the big screen after the fall of Romanian President Nicolae Ceauşescu's regime in 1989. Two of the director's later movies, *Un été inoubliable* (1994) (*An Unforgettable Summer*) and *Prea târziu* (1996) (*Too Late*), were nominated for the Palme d'Or at the Cannes Film Festival. *An Unforgettable Summer* examines the issue of ethnic cleansing, and both films see Pintilie portray the ethical dilemmas faced by individuals against a backdrop of murky politics. **CK**

> "I do not accuse, I only describe things. And this is obvious in [*Reconstruction*]."

BRUCE CONNER

Born: Bruce Conner, November 18, 1933 (McPherson, Kansas, U.S.).

Directing style: Influential artist and avant-garde filmmaker of shorts; use of still photography; skilful editing of found or stock footage; challenges issues of authorship.

Born in Kansas in 1933, Conner earned a Bachelor of Fine Arts from Nebraska University and moved to New York City before gradually relocating westward, first through Colorado and then on to San Francisco, where he established himself, falling in with the Beat movement in the mid-1950s.

Conner first grew to prominence as a fine artist: a sculptor known for his assemblages of "found objects." He would later use this skill in his filmmaking. By the end of the decade he had moved into cinematography, making short movies. His debut, *A Movie* (1958), was a collage of found footage; the film commented on human violence, U.S. consumerism, and self-reflection moviemaking. This concern for using found or stock footage, edited to prove a point-of-view in opposition to the source's original intent, fueled his masterwork *Report* (1967), which was an examination of the aftermath of the assassination of President John F. Kennedy.

Bruce Conner has always bristled under the political restrictions of the art world, and he has never fit into the movie marketplace, although many of his shorts—such as *Mongoloid* (1978)—are precursors to modern music videos. Occupying a space somewhere in the midst of several art forms, although not beholden to any one of them, Conner both excites and confounds audiences. Many of his projects begin in the real world but are not about objectively investigating real events, something that can be seen in his *Take the 5:10 to Dreamland* (1976). Although his acclaim is limited, Conner remains influential for challenging notions of what constitutes cinema; for example, in *Ten Second Film* (1965) the relationship between fiction and documentary is deliberately blurred. **GCQ**

Top Takes...

Looking for Mushrooms 1996
Television Assassination 1995
America is Waiting 1981
Mongoloid 1978
Valse Triste 1977
Crossroads 1976
Take the 5:10 to Dreamland 1976
Marilyn Times Five 1973
Permian Strata 1969
Looking for Mushrooms 1967
Report 1967
The White Rose 1967
Ten Second Film 1965
Vivian 1965
Cosmic Ray 1962
A Movie 1958

"I like music a whole bunch. Probably more than any of the visuals."

1930s

DONALD CAMMELL

Born: Donald Seaton Cammell, January 17, 1934 (Edinburgh, Scotland); died 1996 (Hollywood, California, U.S.).

Directing style: Influential, experimental Scottish director of cult pop-culture classics; stunning visuals; movies often violent, sexually explicit, and disturbing.

Top Takes...

Wild Side 1995
White of the Eye 1987
Demon Seed 1977
Performance 1970

Donald Cammell, the son of Charles Richard Cammell (poet, critic, heir to the Cammell-Laird shipbuilding fortune, and biographer of satanist Aleister Crowley), was born in Edinburgh. From a young age he demonstrated great artistic talent and by the time he was nineteen years old was enjoying a studio in the exclusive London area of Chelsea, where he was a highly sought-after portrait painter. He soon became restless and disillusioned with society portraiture, however, abandoning his career in the early 1960s to take up residence in Paris.

Prompted by his love of the movies, Cammell began writing screenplays. In 1965, after the sale of his first work for the screen, *Avec Avec,* filmed as *Duffy* (1968), he met the Rolling Stones, becoming friends with both Brian Jones and Mick Jagger. His friendship with Jagger led to the latter's role as Turner in *Performance* (1970)—now considered a masterpiece of world cinema—which Cammell wrote and then codirected with Nicolas Roeg. In 1972 Cammell moved to Hollywood, where his filmmaking ambitions were frequently frustrated.

Over time, however, he managed to direct some stylish and disturbing pictures, including the science-fiction film *Demon Seed* (1977) and the horror-thriller *White of the Eye* (1987). In the late 1970s he collaborated with Marlon Brando on a proposed film project, *Fan-Tan,* an epic adventure about female pirates. In 1982, with the film realization scuttled, Cammell transformed *Fan-Tan* into a novel. Brando blocked the novel's publication, but it was eventually published after the actor's death in 2005. Cammell's erotic thriller *Wild Side* (1995), was restored posthumously in 1999. He committed suicide in 1996 at the age of sixty-two by shooting himself. **SU**

"You're a comical little geezer. You'll look funny when you're fifty."—Chas to Turner, *Performance*

JOÃO CÉSAR MONTEIRO

Born: João César Monteiro, February 2, 1934 (Figueira da Foz, Portugal); died 2003 (Lisbon, Portugal).

Directing style: Daring and controversial writer/director of bizarre satires; spiritual, philosophical, sexual, and taboo themes; frequently starred in his own movies.

Born in rural Portugal to an antifascist family, João César Monteiro won a grant to study cinema in England. On his return to Portugal he began making documentaries and shorts. He often wrote and starred in his films, and took years to craft them, which led to a sporadic output. But he is known as a master of Portuguese cinema with a knack for anarchic yet lyrical visual comedies with a self-indulgent and esoteric twist.

Monteiro made his feature film debut with the comedy *Fragmentos de um Filme-Esmola: A Sagrada Família* (1972), an adaptation of short stories by various authors, including James Joyce and surrealist André Breton. However, the director is perhaps most famous for his portrayal of his alter ego character, the gaunt-looking João de Deus, meaning John of God, who first hit the screen in his comedy *Recordações da Casa Amarela* (1989) (*Recollections of the Yellow House*) as a middle-aged man thrown out of his lodgings after making advances toward his landlady's daughter. The character reappears as the main protagonist in Monteiro's best known movie, *A Comédia de Deus* (1995) (*God's Comedy*), which is about a manager of an ice cream parlor owned by a former prostitute. De Deus is again a lusty, lonely pervert, this time given to collecting female pubic hair and with a penchant for teenage girls.

Monteiro took a starring role in his next film, *Le Bassin de J. W.* (1997) (*The Hips of J. W.*), playing God. This is a bizarre antireligious comedy that tells the story of two rivals performing in an adaptation of August Strindberg's novel *Inferno* (1897), one of whom has an obsession with actor John Wayne and his swaggering walk. Monteiro's films often shock audiences, yet he remains loved by art theatergoers for his almost plotless, philosophical musings that never fail to provoke. **CK**

Top Takes…

Vai E Vem 2003 (*Come and Go*)
Branca de Neve 2000 (*Snow White*)
As Bodas de Deus 1999 (*God's Wedding*)
Le Bassin de J. W. 1997 (*The Hips of J. W.*)
A Comédia de Deus 1995 (*God's Comedy*)
Passeio com Johnny Guitar 1995
Recordações da Casa Amarela 1989
  (*Recollections of the Yellow House*)
À Flor do Mar 1986 (*Flower of the Sea*)
Silvestre 1982
Amor de Mãe 1975
Fragmentos de um Filme-Esmola:
  A Sagrada Família 1972
Sophia de Mello Breyner Andresen 1969

"I am not part of groups and I do not have any cultural affinities with colleagues . . . ."

1930s

SYDNEY POLLACK

Born: Sydney Pollack, July 1, 1934 (Lafayette, Indiana, U.S.).

Directing style: Actor turned director of classic, star-studded Hollywood period dramas, thrillers, romances, and comedies; strong acting; artistic collaborations with actor Robert Redford.

Top Takes...

The Interpreter 2005
Random Hearts 1999
Sabrina 1995
The Firm 1993
Havana 1990
Out of Africa 1985 ★
Tootsie 1982 ☆
Absence of Malice 1981
The Electric Horseman 1979
Bobby Deerfield 1977
Three Days of the Condor 1975
The Way We Were 1973
Jeremiah Johnson 1972
They Shoot Horses, Don't They? 1969 ☆
This Property Is Condemned 1966
The Slender Thread 1965

Sydney Pollack began his career as an actor, clocking up many TV appearances from 1959 to 1962. He has kept his hand in, too, playing bit parts in his own films, and substantial supporting roles in such movies as Woody Allen's *Husbands and Wives* (1992) and Stanley Kubrick's *Eyes Wide Shut* (1999). In the early 1960s he shifted focus to directing, handling episodes on TV shows such as *The Alfred Hitchcock Hour* (1962–1963).

His first feature was *The Slender Thread* (1965), a suspenseful social-issue drama with Sidney Poitier and Anne Bancroft. It set the tone for Pollack's directorial career: editorial wrapped up in entertainment with awards-worthy star performances. In *This Property Is Condemned* (1966) Pollack cast Robert Redford, with whom he had acted in *War Hunt* (1962). The two friends made seven films together, including *Jeremiah Johnson* (1972), *The Way We Were* (1973), *Three Days of the Condor* (1975), *The Electric Horseman* (1979), and *Out of Africa* (1985), for which Pollack won an Academy Award for Best Director.

Pollack has directed many stars in showpiece roles: Jane Fonda as a marathon dancer in *They Shoot Horses, Don't They?* (1969), Al Pacino as an emotionally stunted racing driver in *Bobby Deerfield* (1977), Paul Newman and Sally Field in the press ethics drama *Absence of Malice* (1981), and Tom Cruise in legal trouble in *The Firm* (1993), among others. One of his best-loved movies, the comedy *Tootsie* (1982), features Dustin Hoffman as an actor who dresses in drag to stay in a soap opera. Pollack, who hadn't been in front of the camera for some years, was persuaded by Hoffman to play his character's agent in the movie. The pair famously argued on and offscreen during the film's making, garnering themselves Oscar nominations in the process. **KN**

"I don't value a film I've enjoyed making. If it's good, it's damned hard work."

RIGHT: Robert Redford and Meryl Streep looking sultry in the acclaimed *Out of Africa*.

JAN ŠVANKMAJER

Born: Jan Švankmajer, September 4, 1934 (Prague, Czech Republic).

Directing style: Czech master of animated shorts and features; surrealist and bizarre literary adaptations; fairy tale horror; Gothic imagery; use of stop-motion technique.

Top Takes…

"For me, objects are more alive than people, more permanent, and more expressive."

Jan Švankmajer is a Czech master of animated shorts, later equally celebrated for his feature films. A natural-born surrealist, Švankmajer was largely inspired by classic literature of the *fantastique*, as evidenced in his short films *Otrantský zámek* (1977) (*Castle of Otranto*), *Zánik domu Usheru* (1981) (*The Fall of the House of Usher*), and *Kyvadlo, jáma a nadeje* (1983) (*The Pit, The Pendulum and Hope*), as well as in his feature-length version of Lewis Carroll's masterpiece, *Neco z Alenky* (1988) (*Alice*). The influence of folk tales can be seen in *Otesánek* (2000) (*Little Otik*), about an infertile couple who adopt a lump of wood as their son. His version of *Faust* (1994) (*Lesson Faust*) owes more to medieval folklore than to either Christopher Marlowe or Johann Wolfgang Goethe.

Like a cinematic alchemist, Švankmajer uses animation techniques to reach the "soul" of apparently inanimate objects, stressing their tactile, sensual nature and enticing grotesque metamorphoses of wood, clay, or iron with live matter such as meat, eggs, and vegetables. Food comes alive unpredictably, human faces appearing out of fruit in *Moznosti dialogu* (1982) (*Dimensions of Dialogue*) and characters adopting weird table manners in *Jídlo* (1992) (*Food*). Polymorphous sexuality is derived from the fictions of the Marquis de Sade and Sigmund Freud in *Spiklenci slasti* (1996) (*Conspirators of Pleasure*) and *Šílení* (2005) (*Lunacy*). Švankmajer's imagery often relies on Gothic motifs and body horror, but is rooted in archetypal childhood fears, as in *Do pivnice* (1983) (*Down to the Cellar*), where darkness, animated coal, potatoes, and a cat conspire against a little girl. It is a fairy tale horror film with a Middle-European sensibility: playful, irrational, bizarre, but also grimly humorous. **DO**

1930s

KIRA MURATOVA

Born: Kira Georgiyevna Korotkova, November 5, 1934 (Soroki, Moldova).

Directing style: Ukrainian auteur of controversial, emotionally intense, poetic melodramas and later absurd tragicomedies; themes exploring family life; use of close-ups, flashbacks, and handheld camera.

Kira Muratova entered the film industry as a pupil of director Sergei Gerasimov. She codirected the short, *U krutogo yara* (1962) (*On the Steep Cliff*) with her then husband, Aleksandr Muratov. The film follows a hunter who seeks two wolves that have been preying upon sheep in Siberia. Her independent directorial debut came with *Nash chestnyy khleb* (1964) (*Our Honest Bread*), and she followed it up with *Korotkiye vstrechi* (*Brief Encounters*), made in 1967 but not officially released until 1987. The picture tells the story of a country girl who moves to the city and becomes the maid of a member of the District Soviet, only to find herself entangled in a love triangle.

Despite its black and white format, *Dolgie provody* (1971) (*A Long Goodbye*) enjoyed considerable success. But the majority of Muratova's works suffered the same fate as *Brief Encounters*: the increased censorship laws of the Soviet government prevented their release. These laws were repealed in 1987.

In 1989, Muratova rammed heads with the government with her satire, *Astenichesky sindrom* (*The Asthenic Syndrome*): she refused to remove a scene containing obscene language and its screening was halted. However, in 1990, the picture was historically released in its uncut format, celebrating the new liberal standards in Soviet cinema.

Her films feature feisty women, and examine women's role in society under communist rule and the *perestroika* era. They examine the harshness of everyday family life, and present the emotional turmoil of her characters by the use of experimental film techniques. Only her fine comedic sense of the absurd provides relief for her audience. Muratova's later films, such as *Tri istorii* (1997) (*Three Stories*), have enjoyed international recognition, as well as widespread releases. **ES**

Top Takes...

Nastroyshchik 2004 (*The Tuner*)
Chekhovskie motivy 2002 (*Chekhov's Motifs*)
Vtorostepennyye lyudi 2001
  (*Second Class Citizens*)
Tri istorii 1997 (*Three Stories*)
Uvlecheniya 1994 (*Passions*)
Astenicheskiy sindrom 1989
  (*The Asthenic Syndrome*)
Peremena uchasti 1987 (*Change of Fortune*)
Poznavaya belyy svet 1979
  (*Getting to Know the Big Wide World*)
Russia 1972
Dolgie provody 1971 (*A Long Goodbye*)
Korotkie vstrechi 1967 (*Brief Encounters*)
Nash chestnyy khleb 1964 (*Our Honest Bread*)
U krutogo yara 1962 (*On the Steep Cliff*)

"It's up to you or anyone who speaks or writes to characterize the atmosphere of the film."

1930s

YVONNE RAINER

Born: Yvonne Rainer, November 24, 1934 (San Francisco, California, U.S.).

Directing style: Avant-garde director of experimental films; themes addressing gender, social, and political issues, and the nature of performance; sequences of choreographed minimalist dance.

Top Takes…

1930s

Born in San Francisco in 1934, Rainer was raised in an atmosphere thick with art and activism. She studied acting, met abstract painter and future husband Al Held at the Beat-friendly Six Gallery, and followed him to New York in 1956. The marriage was brief and acting did not pan out, but in New York Rainer discovered modern dance, studying at the Martha Graham Center of Contemporary Dance, and performing with modern dance pioneer Merce Cunningham. A cofounder of the influential Judson Dance Theater, Rainer was quickly recognized as a charismatic performer and innovative choreographer who rejected technical virtuosity in favor of everyday movement charged with autobiographical, feminist, and political meaning.

By the late 1960s, Rainer was experimenting with multimedia works, adding "filmed choreographic exercises" to her dance pieces. Rainer's first feature, *Lives of Performers* (1972), was the logical next step, a kind of deconstructed backstage musical that alternates real rehearsal footage of her own dance pieces *Walk, She Said* (1972) with a scripted romantic triangle, and ends with lengthy shots mimicking stills from *Die Büchse der Pandora* (1929) (*Pandora's Box*). Rainer's later work, including *Privilege* (1990) and *MURDER and murder* (1996), situates issues of race, class, age, power, and female sexuality within somewhat more accessible narratives. Although claimed by the queer film community, Rainer has consistently mined all aspects of her own life for material, from same-sex relationships to cancer (her mastectomy figures in *MURDER and murder*), and the inevitable decay of the flesh, all filtered through the prism of her uncompromising intelligence. **MM**

> "My films always were meant to confound in a certain way."

SHYAM BENEGAL

Born: Shyam Benegal, December 14, 1934 (Andhra Pradesh, India).

Directing style: Indian maker of ironic dramas that explore themes of the disadvantaged in contemporary society; master storyteller; complex characterizations; narrative ambivalence.

At the start of his career, when his films *Ankur* (1974) (*The Seedling*) and *Manthan* (1976) (*The Churning*) were released to international acclaim, Shyam Benegal was widely seen as Indian cinema's heir apparent to Satyajit Ray. Although his sympathies are essentially leftist, Benegal has never adopted the Marxist perspective of Mrinal Sen or Ritwik Ghatak; like Ray, his standpoint is classically liberal-humanist. In placing himself in opposition to the all-singing, all-dancing kitsch of Bollywood, Benegal questions not so much its aesthetic practices, which on occasion he has been willing to borrow, as what he sees as its underlying political assumptions. "My films are all about conflict," he notes. "In mainstream [Indian] cinema, the values projected are status quo. Hindi commercial cinema constantly tells you that change is not possible!"

Over the years, the naturalism of Benegal's early work has gradually widened to take in elements of fantasy, visual stylization, and narrative ambivalence, particularly a penchant for multiple viewpoints. But his overriding concern has been to give expression to the disadvantaged: women above all, but also *Dalits*, or "untouchables," and members of religious minorities, those elements so often denied a voice within Indian society. These two strands come together in perhaps his finest film yet: *Suraj Ka Satvan Ghoda* (1993) (*Seventh Horse of the Sun*), an ironic, densely layered drama that attacks the discrimination that continues to disfigure modern-day India.

Benegal's weakness is for issue-driven films made to dramatize a thesis. The quality of his output has suffered from its sheer bulk: 23 feature-length films in 30 years. Had Benegal made fewer but more considered movies, his reputation would probably stand far higher. **PK**

Top Takes…

Chamki Chameli 2006

Zubeidaa 2001

Samar 1999 (*Conflict*)

The Making of the Mahatma 1996

Sardari Begum 1996

Suraj Ka Satvan Ghoda 1993
    (*Seventh Horse of the Sun*)

Nehru 1985

Kalyug 1981 (*The Machine Age*)

Junoon 1978

Bhumika: The Role 1977

Manthan 1976 (*The Churning*)

Nishaant 1975 (*Night's End*)

Ankur 1974 (*The Seedling*)

Gher Betha Ganga 1962
    (*Ganges at Your Doorstep*)

1930s

"I totally subscribe to the idea that cinema's primary purpose is to entertain."

THEODOROS ANGELOPOULOS

Born: Theodoros Angelopoulos, April 17, 1935 (Athens, Greece).

Directing style: Greek director of dramas; exploration of themes of Greek cultural identity; use of extremely long, sinuous sequence shots; use of monochrome camerawork.

Top Takes…

Endlessly reworking themes, stories, and characters from Greek myth and tragedy in order to reflect on the last century or so of Greek and Balkan history, Theodoros Angelopoulos has built up a wholly personal body of work concerned with exile and return, conflict and reconciliation, oppression, and longing. From *Anaparastasi* (1970) (*Reconstruction*), it was clear not only that he had a distinctive visual style but that, in terms of narrative, he was more than happy to blur the lines dividing fact and fantasy, truth and falsehood, past and present.

Made, miraculously, under "the Colonels' regime" (when Greece was under military rule), *O Thiassos* (1975) (*The Travelling Players*), about a theatrical troupe's experiences during a period of murderous civil war and unrest, was a magisterial epic, a meditation on myth, time, politics, and history. Later films such as *O Melissokomos* (1986) (*The Beekeeper*) and *Topio stin Omichli* (1988) (*Landscape in the Mist*) focused more intimately on a handful of characters to reflect on the problematic state of Greek cultural identity. In *Landscape in the Mist*, two children search for a father they have been led to believe left home to seek work in Germany. Angelopoulos's recent films, *To Vlemma tou Odyssea* (1995) (*Ulysses' Gaze*), *Mia Aioniotita kai mia Mera* (1998) (*Eternity and A Day*), and *Trilogia I: To Livadi pou Dakryzei* (2004) (*Trilogy: The Weeping Meadow*), have witnessed a slight mellowing of vision, with righteous anger replaced by a melancholy awareness of man's capacity for cruelty, violence, greed, and negligence. However, his long, sinuous sequence shots—usually gliding to the lilt of Eleni Karaindrou's poignant music—locate the actions of individuals within the wider contexts of politics, history, geography, and culture. **GA**

"Prizes are prizes, but I still need to tell that story. And being simple is the hardest thing."

1930s

WILLIAM FRIEDKIN

Born: William Friedkin, August 29, 1935 (Chicago, Illinois, U.S.).

Directing style: Oscar-winning New Hollywood director who revolutionized the crime thriller and horror genres; use of handheld camera for thrilling, gritty action sequences.

William Friedkin was a central figure in the "New Hollywood" movement of the 1970s. Subsequent work has been patchy, both critically and commercially, but has proved provocative and, sometimes, distinctive.

Working in the 1950s, Friedkin established himself in live TV, a format that had some bearing on the edgy immediacy of much of his film work. After the TV documentary, *The People vs. Paul Crump* (1962)—instrumental in the release of a death-row prisoner—early features were undistinguished, although *The Boys in the Band* (1970) was notable for its dramatization of homosexual issues largely ignored by Hollywood.

His two major successes, *The French Connection* (1971), which won him an Academy Award for Best Director; and *The Exorcist* (1973), which received ten Oscar nominations, including Best Director and Best Picture, reinvigorated the crime thriller and horror film respectively. *The French Connection* drew from Friedkin's documentary experience, a street-level *policier* troubling in its fascistic undertones but exhilarating in its hugely influential car-chase sequence. *The Exorcist* was shaped around a narrative of Roman Catholic angst and redemption, the central motif of childhood innocence under diabolic attack proving potent worldwide.

Sorcerer (1977) was a costly remake of Henri-Georges Clouzot's *Il Salario della Paura* (1953) (*The Wages of Fear*) and, despite some impressive set pieces, was a box office failure. Since then, Friedkin's best films have proved at odds with commercial trends. *Cruising* (1980) and *To Live and Die in L.A.* (1985) are crime narratives fascinating for their presentation of masculinity in crisis, whereas *Jade* (1995) is despairing in its evocation of exploitation and corruption. **NJ**

Top Takes...

Bug 2006
The Hunted 2003
Rules of Engagement 2000
Jade 1995
Blue Chips 1994
The Guardian 1990
Rampage 1988
To Live and Die in L.A. 1985
Deal of the Century 1983
Cruising 1980
Sorcerer 1977
The Exorcist 1973 ☆
The French Connection 1971 ★
The Boys in the Band 1970
The Birthday Party 1968
Good Times 1967

"... the greatest thrill in the world, is getting 20 seconds onscreen that really gas you."

1930s

ALAN CLARKE

Born: Alan Clarke, October 28, 1935 (Birkenhead, Cheshire, England); died 1990 (London, England).

Directing style: Gritty, realistic dramas; edgy acting; exploration of social conditions among the contemporary male working classes; lengthy tracking shots.

Top Takes...

Elephant 1989
The Firm 1988
Christine 1987
Road 1987
Rita, Sue and Bob Too 1986
Contact 1985
Billy the Kid and the Green Baize Vampire 1985
Made in Britain 1982
Baal 1982
Scum 1979

1930s

Alan Clarke honed his directorial skills crafting teleplays for the BBC series *The Wednesday Play* (1969–1970), and *Play for Today* (1970–1981). The films he went on to create remain as important and influential now as they were at the time of their creation. A social realist director akin to fellow *cineastes* such as Ken Loach, Mike Leigh, and Stephen Frears, Clarke's works focused on marginalized and economically disadvantaged young males struggling to survive in a culture in which social institutions designed to relieve poverty and reduce labor exploitation have failed.

Yet to conceptualize Clarke's films as documents fashioned for the sole purpose of rigidly detailing social conditions in Britain would be to overlook his skills as a storyteller and a visual artist. One need only view his final film, *Elephant* (1989) to realize how Clarke was willing to break from strict realist conventions to articulate his aesthetic and political vision. Chronicling eighteen consecutive, ambiguously motivated killings, *Elephant* presents a meditation upon, rather than an explanation of, cycles of violence in Northern Ireland.

Among Clarke's other more celebrated works are *Made in Britain* (1982), starring a young Tim Roth as a racist skinhead caught up in the British judicial system, and *The Firm* (1988), a film about soccer hooliganism starring Gary Oldman. One of the greatest strengths of Clarke's work is his reluctance to provide a reductivist solution to the myriad social concerns raised in his narratives. Instead, his movies are skillfully crafted fictions that hold a proverbial mirror up to life. Audiences may not always feel comfortable with what they see in the looking glass, but it is a reflection society ignores at its own risk. **JM**

> "If you was an undertaker people'd stop dying."—The One,
>
> *Billy the Kid and the Green Baize Vampire*

PETER WATKINS

Born: Peter Watkins, October 29, 1935 (Norbiton, Surrey, England).

Directing style: British director of controversial, realistic docudramas that examine historical events of the past, present, and possible future; faux newsreel style; use of nonprofessional actors.

British director Peter Watkins is best known for igniting a political firestorm when his docudrama *The War Game* (1965) was banned by the BBC for its graphic portrayal of nuclear war. The film, using a quasi-newsreel style and nonprofessional actors, was due to be shown on August 6, 1966—the anniversary of Hiroshima—but was pulled by the corporation as it was judged "too horrifying for the medium of broadcasting." The film was eventually released in cinemas the same year, and won an Oscar for Best Documentary, Features.

Born in 1935, Watkins studied acting at London's prestigious Royal Academy of Dramatic Art before working in advertising as an assistant producer. He turned to amateur filmmaking in the late 1950s, and was commissioned by the BBC to make the TV feature *Culloden* (1964). A portrayal of the 1745 Jacobite uprising at the Battle of Culloden, it used a grainy, docudrama technique similar to those of Vietnam War news broadcasts to bring a sense of familiarity to its scenes. It drew critical acclaim and Watkins began work on *The War Game*. After the furor that film generated, he directed *Privilege* (1967), a faux documentary following the life of an iconic pop star played by Paul Jones.

In 1969 Watkins made the science-fiction drama *Gladiatorerna*, and later offerings included the antiauthoritarian *Punishment Park* (1971), and the TV biopic *Edvard Munch* (1974). His 15-hour epic *Resan* (1987) (*The Journey*) dealt with the arms race and global hunger, whereas *La Commune (Paris, 1871)* (2000) offered a glimpse into the world of the nineteenth-century Paris Communards. More recently, Watkins has concerned himself with criticism of the dominance of the authoritarian Hollywood-style news reporting he has branded "monoform." **TE**

Top Takes...

La Commune (Paris, 1871) 2000
Resan 1987 (*The Journey*)
Aftenlandet 1977 (*Evening Land*)
Punishment Park 1971
Gladiatorerna 1969
Privilege 1967
The War Game 1965
The Forgotten Faces 1961
The Diary of an Unknown Soldier 1959
The Field of Red 1958
The Web 1956

"Those who were once able to work critically within the media have been marginalized."

1930s

WOODY ALLEN

Born: Allen Stewart Konigsberg, December 1, 1935 (Brooklyn, New York, U.S.).

Directing style: Prolific king of comedy; satirical take on Jewish life; fascination with neurotic characters; stars in many of his films; themes of love, romance, and family life.

Top Takes...

Match Point 2005

Sweet and Lowdown 1999

Deconstructing Harry 1997

Everyone Says I Love You 1996

Mighty Aphrodite 1995

Bullets Over Broadway 1994 ☆

Manhattan Murder Mystery 1993

Husbands and Wives 1992

Crimes and Misdemeanors 1989 ☆

Another Woman 1988

September 1987

Radio Days 1987

Hannah and Her Sisters 1986 ☆

The Purple Rose of Cairo 1985

Broadway Danny Rose 1984 ☆

Zelig 1983

A Midsummer Night's Sex Comedy 1982

Manhattan 1979

Interiors 1978 ☆

Annie Hall 1977 ★

Love and Death 1975

Sleeper 1973

*Everything You Always Wanted to Know About Sex * But Were Afraid to Ask* 1972

Bananas 1971

RIGHT: Woody Allen and Louise Lasser
in the farcical political comedy *Bananas*.

Woody Allen has become an icon of filmography, equally renowned for his directing style and his unique acting ability. Although Manhattan has been the playground for generations of musicians, designers, urban planners, gardeners, novelists, and politicians, today the island is famed as the main setting of Woody Allen's films, his protagonist at the margins of every frame, and the source of life for comedy after comedy. Having thus stamped this singular landscape, Allen has contributed his own mythology to the neighborhoods, landmarks, sports teams, and social fabric of the metropolis, but especially the rarefied environs of the Upper East Side.

Taking as his subject the largely irreligious, upwardly mobile, highly educated New York Jew, his films have demonstrated the very stereotype he seems somehow to both embody and transcend. His being Jewish is embraced and celebrated, not just for the sake of commercial and secular affirmation required in a world scarred by the Holocaust, but because U.S. Jewishness, and the affinities and habits the identity implies, is exactly where Allen's humor originates.

1930s

Born Allen Konigsberg in Brooklyn, he chose the nickname "Woody" while in his teens and changed his named legally in 1952. He started selling jokes at fifteen years old and within a couple of years they were being bought by commercial stations to be used by such famous names as Bob Hope and Danny Kaye. Allen also worked as a stand-up comedian, honing his timing and craft, before working for actor Sid Caesar on TV. His first produced feature screenplay was Clive Donner's *What's New Pussycat?* (1965), which led to his first codirecting credit with Senkichi Taniguchi on *What's Up, Tiger Lily?* (1966) and his eventual first solo credit on *Take the Money and Run* (1969). Thereafter, Allen has produced virtually a feature film a year for nearly 40 years, many of which have become cult icons. Their titles are as familiar as Allen's own name and their

ABOVE: Diane Keaton and Woody Allen in *Annie Hall*, the film that made Keaton a star.

"The worst that you can say about [God] is that basically he's an underachiever."

Up Close and Personal

The heart of Woody Allen's creativity is forever connected with his physique and personality. Slightly built, nervous, wordy, glasses-wearing, wildly gesturing, easily excitable, and a wit, Allen is often the star or costar of his films. This presence in front of, and behind, the camera makes his work both familiar and personal.

It is common for Allen to be confused with his characters, especially those in situations similar to Allen's real and private life, for example his marriage to Soon-Yi Previn, the adopted daughter of his long-term lover Mia Farrow. The situation was uncannily presaged by Mariel Hemingway in *Manhattan* (1979).

- Woody Allen made eight movies with his one-time muse and former partner Diane Keaton. These include *Annie Hall* (1977), *Love and Death* (1975), *Manhattan Murder Mystery* (1993), *Radio Days* (1987), and *Sleeper* (1973).
- Actress Mia Farrow was also Allen's muse and long-term lover. The couple had three children together—two of whom were adopted—and she starred in 13 of his pictures. These include *Broadway Danny Rose* (1984), *Crimes and Misdemeanors* (1989), *Hannah and Her Sisters* (1986), *The Purple Rose of Cairo* (1985), *Husbands and Wives* (1992), *A Midsummer Night's Sex Comedy* (1982), and *Zelig* (1983).

RIGHT: A displeased Martin Landau with Woody Allen in *Crimes and Misdemeanors*.

jokes and plot premises have passed into cinematic legend. In addition to his own prodigious workload, Allen has made guest appearances or provided a voice for other directors' films, including Paul Mazursky's *Scenes from a Mall* (1991) and Eric Darnell and Tim Johnson's *Antz* (1998).

A writer as well as director, for many years Allen has been a regular contributor to *The New Yorker*. In addition, his prolific movie output has been the stamping ground for various established stars, such as Sean Penn and Goldie Hawn, as well as the launch pad for then-emerging stars including Mia Farrow, Dianne Wiest, and Mira Sorvino.

Private and public life

Allen's famously mixed-up personality means that, despite working in a very public arena, he attempts to remain aloof from the Hollywood celebrity circuit. He gives very few public appearances—aside from his standing gig playing jazz clarinet at Manhattan's Carlyle Hotel on Monday nights. He has been married three times and divorced twice, which means that, in spite of what can sometimes amount to an obsessive desire for privacy, his personal life has hit the papers with regularity.

Allen also has a remarkable history with film critics and the movie establishment. He has achieved the following: three Directors Guild of America nominations, with one win, and a Lifetime Achievement Award; four Golden Globe Award nominations for writing, alongside one win, one nomination for acting, and four nominations for director; twelve Academy Award nominations for writing with two wins, one nomination for acting, and five nominations for director with one win.

Woody Allen has become the gold standard for comic writing and situational humor. His characters become flesh and blood through their individual settings and the way his people talk their way into, and out of, problems has become a classic hallmark of his oeuvre. In the end, the magic of Allen's cinema is found in the wry distinctions between tragic human relations that often tip toward horror, but are relieved by the saving grace of serendipitous timing. **GCQ**

JAROMIL JIREŠ

Born: Jaromil Jireš, December 10, 1935 (Bratislava, Slovak Republic); died 2001 (Prague, Czech Republic).

Directing style: Leading director of Czech New Wave; dramas exploring the moral issues faced in everyday life; stunning, surreal visual imagery; masterful storytelling.

Top Takes…

Ucitel tance 1995 (*The Dance-Master*)

Labyrinth 1991

Lev s bílou hrívou 1986

Prodlouzený cas 1984

Katapult 1983

Neúplné zatmení 1982 (*Incomplete Eclipse*)

Opera ve vinici 1981

Úteky domu 1980

Mladý muz a bílá velryba 1978
   (*The Young Man and Moby Dick*)

Kasar 1973 (*The Safe Cracker*)

… a pozdravuji vlastovky 1972
   (*And Give My Love to the Swallows*)

Valerie a týden divu 1970
   (*Valerie and Her Week of Wonders*)

Zert 1969 (*The Joke*)

Krik 1963 (*The Cry*)

> "[I] wanted to explore the connections between reality and dream, horror and humor."

One of the key players of the Czech New Wave, director and screenwriter Jaromil Jireš will be remembered for a range of innovative movies including *Krik* (1963) (*The Cry*) and *Zert* (1969) (*The Joke*). He studied at the Prague Film School with contemporaries such as Milos Forman and Ivan Passer, and began his career with a series of shorts before making the critically acclaimed *The Cry*. Eschewing traditional dramatic structure, its fresh, highly personal approach consisted of fragmentary recollections of a husband and wife. The husband's unflattering reflections on what kind of world his child is being born into brought him into conflict with the authorities, and he did not make another film for years; instead he made documentaries. Finally, he was able to make *The Joke*, an adaptation of the Milan Kundera novel, and a harsh critique of Stalinist totalitarianism. Ironically, its release coincided with the Soviet invasion sparked by President Alexander Dubček's attempt to give "socialism a human face."

Under the harsh new regime, the film industry was rigidly controlled. Jireš was one of the few directors to remain, and his first project was the surreal *Valerie a týden divu* (1970) (*Valerie and Her Week of Wonders*). At first glance the film appears apolitical, but given its fairy tale horror feel, it was a subtle critique of the regime. Adapting to the authoritarian dictates, Jireš's wartime drama . . . *a pozdravuji vlastovky* (1972) (*And Give My Love to the Swallows*) exhibited a spiritual quality via a safe subject. With the political upheavals of the late 1980s, censorship was relaxed but state subsidies were withdrawn, obliging Jireš to diversify into documentaries for cinema and TV. He died in 2001 from complications arising after a road accident. **TE**

IM KWON-TAEK

Born: Im Kwon-taek, May 2, 1936 (Changsong, Cheollanam-do, Korea).

Directing style: Korean director of sentimental, epic, and autobiographical dramas; exploration of modern Korean cultural identity and beliefs; visual beauty; spiritual themes.

In true fairy tale fashion, Im Kwon-taek embodies the rags-to-riches fantasies that most dream of and rarely experience. Born in 1936, the Korean native grew up in the southern city of Kwangju. After the Korean War, however, Kwon-taek was forced to move elsewhere with his family to look for work. He toiled as a laborer until moving to Seoul, where his big break came in the form of work as a film production assistant.

With the aid of director Chung Chang-Hwa, *Dumanganga jal itgeola* (1962) (*Farewell to the Duman River*) was his first film to be released. The black and white picture told the story of college kids who left home to fight against Japanese forces in China. It was films such as these that helped to establish Kwon-taek as a commercial filmmaker: Korea profited from his efficient nature, as he would complete around eight films each year. In reaction to this apparent mass production of entertainment, Kwon-taek began to pay more attention to artistically challenging and stimulating films, which can be seen in *Jokbo* (1979) (*Genealogy*).

The next wave of critical acclaim came with *Mandala* (1981), a film detailing the process one must undergo to become Buddha. With success came the honor of being considered one of Korea's most influential directors, and with *Mandala*'s release, Kwon-taek's movies began to be seen in festivals, and entered the category of art theater cinema.

The director has retained his popularity by producing films that remain constant to the subject areas of Korea's essence, culture, and military history. Additionally, Kwon-taek and his movies have won every prize in contention in Korea's three annual film ceremonies, and *Seopyeonje* (1993) is the most recognized Korean film ever made. **ES**

Top Takes…

Haryu insaeng 2004 (*Low Life*)

Chihwaseon 2002 (*Painted Fire*)

Chunhyang 2000

Seopyeonje 1993

Yeonsan ilgi 1988 (*Diary of King Yonsan*)

Sibaji 1987 (*The Surrogate Woman*)

Ticket 1986

Gilsoddeum 1986

Angae maeul 1983 (*Village in the Mist*)

Mandala 1981

Jokbo 1979 (*Genealogy*)

Nakdongkaneun heureuneunga 1976 (*Commando on the Nakdong River*)

Jeungeon 1974 (*The Testimony*)

Dumanganga jal itgeola 1962 (*Farewell to the Duman River*)

"This is my life—to produce films that contain universal messages."

KEN LOACH

Born: Kenneth Loach, June 17, 1936 (Nuneaton, Warwickshire, England).

Directing style: British director of gritty, bleak, socialist realist dramas; visual naturalism; themes often tackle controversial social issues; focus on the underdog; frequent collaboration with scriptwriter Jim Allen.

Top Takes...

1930s

Ken Loach is considered one of the elder statesmen of the British film industry. This has not, however, blunted his ongoing commitment to bringing social and political issues to the screen. A socialist, Loach has built a reputation for making films that offer a sympathetic, and yet unpatronizing, view of the lives of Britain's working class.

His career began in TV, where he made a number of landmark dramas such as *Up the Junction* (1965) and *Cathy Come Home* (1966). His first collaboration with scriptwriter Jim Allen was a drama about a group of striking Liverpool dockers, *The Big Flame* (1969). Allen would subsequently contribute scripts for a number of Loach's key works, including the feature films *Hidden Agenda* (1990) and *Land and Freedom* (1995).

In the 1960s Loach met producer Tony Garnett, and together they made Loach's first feature *Kes* (1969). Shot on location, and using a number of nonprofessional performers alongside his actors, *Kes* introduced to the cinema the understated visual style Loach had been perfecting on TV. Although still a predominantly TV director, Loach found work increasingly hard to come by as the right-wing government of Margaret Thatcher changed the political landscape of Britain in the 1980s. By the 1990s, however, Loach was established at the forefront of British filmmaking. He returned triumphantly with the popular *Riff-Raff* (1990), set on a construction site, and has subsequently delivered several consistently strident, yet moving tales of hardship in Britain, and beyond. His recent work, such as *My Name is Joe* (1998), *Bread and Roses* (2000), *Ae Fond Kiss . . .* (2004), and *The Wind that Shakes the Barley* (2006), has been marked by his continued collaboration with the screenwriter Paul Laverty. **AW**

> "A movie isn't a political movement . . . . At best it can add its voice to public outrage."

JAN NĚMEC

Born: Jan Němec July 12, 1936 (Prague, Czech Republic).

Directing style: Czech New Wave director; maker of documentaries and surreal features that investigate the psychological effects of life under totalitarian rule; unconventional narrative; use of handheld camera.

Czech director Jan Němec attended Prague's Film and TV School of The Academy of Performing Arts at a time when Czechoslovakia operated under strict censorship laws and standards imposed by the Soviet Union. As a result, underground revolutionary groups and movements developed in Prague during the era, and Němec became one of the many caught up by what became known as the Czech New Wave.

Němec made his professional debut when he received a prize for his student film short, *Sousto* (1960) (*The Loaf of Bread*), in Amsterdam. He released his documentary *Pamet naseho dne* (1963) (*The Memory of Our Day*) while serving in the military. His feature debut came with *Démanty noci* (1964) (*Diamonds of the Night*), a charged Holocaust film that set the groundwork for his political tendencies.

His best known film, *O slavnosti a hostech* (1966) (*A Report on the Party and the Guests*), presented a satirical look at the chilling views of communism in the face of reality as a group of friends engage in a picnic. Němec's objective was to create a political allegory, but instead he was banned for life as a director. The ban only increased the popularity and desire for his works, however, as he was now a forbidden commodity. In this way, Němec continued to create films as part of the underground networks.

In the year that the Soviets invaded Czechoslovakia, Němec created his second most important work, *Oratorio for Prague* (1968), a documentary that denounced the Soviets' actions. So as to avoid conflict with the authorities, the film was released without credits, to protect those who worked with him. He did not make another film until 1975, and then worked in France and West Germany. He continues to direct films in the Czech Republic. **ES**

Top Takes...

Toyen 2005
Krajina mého srdce 2004
  (*Landscape of My Heart*)
Nocní hovory s matkou 2001
  (*Late Night Talks with Mother*)
Jmeno kodu: Rubin 1997 (*Code Name: Ruby*)
Strahovská demonstrace 1990
Das Rückendekolleté 1975
Oratorio for Prague 1968
Mucedníci lásky 1966 (*Martyrs of Love*)
Perlicky na dne 1966 (*Pearls of the Deep*)
O slavnosti a hostech 1966
  (*A Report on the Party and the Guests*)
Démanty noci 1964 (*Diamonds of the Night*)
Pamet naseho dne 1963
  (*The Memory of Our Day*)
Sousto 1960 (*The Loaf of Bread*)

"We would have had no chance of making [*A Report . . .*] if it had been more concrete."

ROBERT REDFORD

Born: Charles Robert Redford Jr., August 18, 1936 (Santa Monica, California, U.S.).

Directing style: Superstar actor turned Oscar-winning director of dramas and romances; often themes of family disintegration; soft-focus visuals; interest in the environment.

Top Takes...

Aloft 2007
Lions for Lambs 2007
The Legend of Bagger Vance 2000
The Horse Whisperer 1998
Quiz Show 1994 ☆
A River Runs Through It 1992
The Milagro Beanfield War 1988
Ordinary People 1980 ★

The incredibly handsome and boyishly blond Robert Redford worked as an actor on TV in the early 1960s, made his big screen debut alongside frequent collaborator Sydney Pollack in *War Hunt* (1962), and soon rose to prominence as a golden boy film star with *Barefoot in the Park* (1967), *Butch Cassidy and the Sundance Kid* (1969), *The Sting* (1973), *All the President's Men* (1976), *Out of Africa* (1985), *Indecent Proposal* (1993), and others. Not content to be a smiling pinup, Redford took on more varied roles, with mixed success. He was outstanding for Michael Ritchie in *Downhill Racer* (1969) and *The Candidate* (1972), and disappointing as *The Great Gatsby* (1974).

He established secondary careers as a director and, via his Sundance Festival and Institute, as a patron of independent filmmaking. *Ordinary People* (1980), his debut directorial feature, won him an Academy Award as Best Director.

A chilly, intense family drama with poised performances from Donald Sutherland, Mary Tyler Moore, and Timothy Hutton, *Ordinary People* surprised audiences, who thought they knew Redford through his acting, but didn't associate this type of film with their perceived image of him. The cinema-going public preferred Redford's romantic, outdoorsy *The Milagro Beanfield War* (1988), *A River Runs Through It* (1992), *The Horse Whisperer* (1998), in which he also stars, and *The Legend of Bagger Vance* (2000). These mostly soft-focus pictures suggest he has learned a great deal from working with Pollack and George Roy Hill. Redford's best picture to date, *Quiz Show* (1994), earned him another Best Director Oscar nod, with Ralph Fiennes taking what would have been the Redford role as the apparent winner gnawed at by a sense of his own hollowness. **KN**

> "As a director, I wouldn't like me as an actor. As an actor, I wouldn't like me as a director."

YILMAZ GÜNEY

Born: Yilmaz Pütün, April 1, 1937 (Adana, south Anatolien, Turkey); died 1984 (Paris, France).

Directing style: Turkish-Kurdish actor turned director of Young Turkish Cinema; maker of epic melodramas; often political themes and exploration of Kurdish life.

One of the most eccentric directors of the Turkish cinema, Yilmaz Güney had a penchant for getting into trouble, and attracted unwanted attention for his fiery, polemical articles and short stories. He was arrested for the first time in 1957.

Even as he developed a reputation as a political firebrand, Güney was also nursing a passionate love for the cinema. By 1970 he was making films that more directly addressed the political situation in Turkey, especially the marginal existence of the poor and working class. *Baba* (1971) (*The Father*) is one of his most accomplished films in this vein, shot on a shoestring budget in color on location, yet infused with a passion and energy that reflected Güney's social conscience.

But Güney was falsely arrested in 1975 for the murder of a local judge. Despite his innocence, he was sentenced to 19 years in jail. Incredibly, this did not slow him down, and he was soon producing a torrent of novels, scripts, and articles from his cell. His production company, Güney Filmcilik, continued to flourish, and he ghost directed two of his most popular films, *Sürü* (1978) (*The Herd*), and *Düsman* (1979) (*The Enemy*), using detailed storyboards to guide Zeki Ökten.

In 1979, he began work on his most famous film, *Yol* (1982) (*The Way*), which he wrote in jail. (The film was ghost directed by Şerif Gören.) In 1981, Güney escaped from prison and moved to Paris, where he made his last film, the sentimental *Duvar* (1983) (*The Wall*).

His best pictures are simultaneously romantic and overtly political. His vision is epic, sweeping, and ineffably visionary. Under more favorable circumstances, Güney's work would have had a much wider international audience in his lifetime, but today it remains as resonant and compelling as ever. **WWD**

Top Takes...

Duvar 1983 (*The Wall*)
Yol 1982 (*The Way*)
Düsman 1979 (*The Enemy*)
Sürü 1978
Zavallilar 1975 (*The Poor*)
Arkadas 1974 (*Friend*)
Endise 1974 (*Anxiety*)
Agit 1972 (*Elegy*)
Aci 1971 (*Pain*)
Baba 1971 (*The Father*)
Ibret 1971
Piyade Osman 1970 (*Private Osman*)
Umut 1970 (*Hope*)
Pire Nuri 1968
Seyyit Han 1968 (*Bride of the Earth*)
Bana kursun islemez 1967

1930s

"History is not only full of victories; it is also made up of defeats, errors, and deceptions."

FRANCIS VEBER

Born: Francis Veber, July 28, 1937 (Neuilly-sur-Seine, Hauts-de-Seine, Île-de-France, France).

Directing style: Writer turned director of satirical situation comedies and witty farces; mistaken identity scenarios; artistic collaborations with Gérard Depardieu.

Top Takes…

La Doublure 2006 (The Valet)
Tais-toi! 2003 (Ruby & Quentin)
Le Placard 2001 (The Closet)
Le dîner de cons 1998 (The Dinner Game)
Le Jaguar 1996
Three Fugitives 1989
Les Fugitifs 1986
Les Compères 1983 (ComDads)
La Chèvre 1981 (The Goat)
Le Jouet 1976 (The Toy)

Francis Veber is a French screenwriter, playwright, producer, and director known for his satirical situation comedies. Born into a family of writers, Veber originally anticipated being a journalist and, following a period in the army, found work as a radio reporter. In the late 1960s, he began his professional writing career with successful work in TV and theater. This led to screenwriting jobs, the earliest being crime stories.

Veber's first big screenwriting achievement was *Le grand blond avec une chaussure noire* (1973) (*The Tall Blond Man with One Black Shoe*), which established his penchant for comedy of errors and mistaken identity scenarios. Throughout the 1970s, he wrote several successful comedies, including the adaptation of *La cage aux folles* (1978) (*Birds of a Feather*), for which he received an Oscar nomination for Best Adapted Screenplay.

Veber made his directorial debut with *Le Jouet* (1976) (*The Toy*). He followed with the trio *La Chèvre* (1981) (*The Goat*), *Les Compères* (1983) (*ComDads*), and *Les Fugitifs* (1986), all three centering on the mismatched comic pair of Pierre Richard and Gérard Depardieu. Remarkably, Veber's first four films as a director were all remade in the United States, with Veber relocating to Hollywood to direct *Three Fugitives* (1989). After the unsuccessful *Out on a Limb* (1992), Veber spent his time in the United States, ironically rewriting a French film for the Depardieu vehicle *My Father the Hero* (1994). Splitting his time between Los Angeles and Paris, Veber returned to French-language cinema with *Le Jaguar* (1996). He received his biggest commercial and critical success with *Le dîner de cons* (1998) (*The Dinner Game*), an adaptation of his own play that was nominated for six César Awards, and won three. **WW**

> "You're asking me to come out of a closet I've never been in!"
>
> —François Pignon, *Le Placard*

CLAUDE LELOUCH

Born: Claude Lelouch, October 30, 1937 (Paris, France).

Directing style: French director of crime capers and romances; fast-paced transitions; tinting of black and white film; slick writing; collaborations with composer Françis Lai.

Born in Paris in 1937, Claude Lelouch brought training in editing and cinematography to filmmaking with a sense of throbbing, fast-paced transitions, swooping neodocumentary camerawork, and slick writing that could convey situations sharply and without delay. Filming since 1962, his first major success was the internationally heralded, yet very simple, *Un homme et une femme* (1966) (*A Man and a Woman*), in which Anouk Aimée and Jean-Louis Trintignant carry on a hesitant love affair against the currents of contemporary Parisian life. Juxtaposition of color with black and white scenes and tinting of black and white film characterize this work, as does an acclaimed and very popular score by Françis Lai, whose music backed many of Lelouch's subsequent pictures.

The drama of the crime chase centers some of Lelouch's best work: *L'aventure, c'est l'aventure* (1972) (*Money Money Money*), in which a team of gangsters formulate an elaborate plot to kidnap the pope; *La bonne année* (1973) (*Happy New Year*), about jewel thieving on the Riviera; and *Le chat et la souris* (1975) (*Cat and Mouse*), where to prove a possible motive a police inspector races from Paris to the countryside and back.

All of Lelouch's work skirts the issue of romance, sometimes infusing it with an extraterrestrial chill as in *Viva la vie!* (1984) (*Long Live Life*), sometimes with exquisitely stunning historical resonance as in *Toute une vie* (1974) (*And Now My Love*), and sometimes with breathtaking, if somewhat overcontrolled, harmony and organization as in *Les uns et les autres* (1981) (*Bolero*) which climaxes with a Red Cross concert on the Eiffel Tower. *Un homme et une femme, 20 ans déjà* (1986) (*A Man and a Woman, 20 Years Later*) reunited Trintignant and Aimée, but without commercial success. **MP**

Top Takes…

11'09"01—September 11 2002
Les Misérables 1995
Tout ça … pour ça! 1993 (*All That … for This?!*)
Viva la vie! 1984 (*Long Live Life*)
Les uns et les autres 1981 (*Bolero*)
C'était un rendez-vous 1976
Le chat et la souris 1975 (*Cat and Mouse*)
Toute une vie 1974 (*And Now My Love*)
La bonne année 1973 (*Happy New Year*)
L'aventure, c'est l'aventure 1972
  (*Money Money Money*)
Le Voyou 1970 (*The Crook*)
Un homme et une femme 1966 ☆
  (***A Man and a Woman***)
Une fille et des fusils 1964 (*To Be a Crook*)
L'amour avec des si 1962 (*In the Affirmative*)

1930s

"Filmmaking is like spermatozoa. Only one in a million makes it."

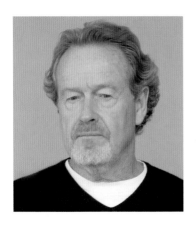

RIDLEY SCOTT

Born: Ridley Scott, November 30, 1937 (South Shields, Tyne and Wear, England).

Directing style: Premier visual stylist; innovator of cyberpunk; pioneer of the director's cut version of films; maker of innovative special effects epics; atmospheric lighting.

Top Takes...

A brilliant image-maker by trade as an advertising man, Sir Ridley Scott has since managed to successfully translate lustrous pictures into big-screen stories. This jump from producing desire to constructing narrative is no small issue, because making beautiful pictures is one thing whereas building plot is quite another. But from his early work using simple and beautifully photographed imagery of a boy on a bicycle to advertise Hovis bread, to an alien bursting from the abdomen of John Hurt in *Alien* (1979), Scott's sense of visual impact has been extraordinary.

Having graduated from art school, Scott made his way to Hollywood via advertising campaigns and TV, finally directing his feature debut, *The Duellists* (1977). Stylish and impressive, but relatively unseen, the title led to Scott's breakout, *Alien*. Featuring the biological nightmare of an acid-bleeding, irrational alien on a rampage, the film made space travel blue collar and dirty, and elevated Sigourney Weaver to stardom.

Scott then directed the classic science-fiction movie *Blade Runner* (1982), and *Legend* (1985), a fantasy now remembered for Tim Curry's incarnation of the devil, as well as being an early

RIGHT: William Sanderson, Daryl Hannah, and Rutger Hauer star in *Blade Runner*.

Tom Cruise outing. *Black Rain* (1989) was Scott's mid-career resurrection, proving he was capable of directing glossy action films, then *Thelma & Louise* (1991) made him the critics' darling with the buddy tale of two women on the lam.

Scott's latest streak of commercially successful films began with Russell Crowe in *Gladiator* (2000), with stunning visuals, intense battle scenes, an impressive set, and five Oscars, and continued through *Hannibal* (2001) and *Black Hawk Down* (2001). He teamed with Crowe again for *A Good Year* (2006).

Scott is now preparing for his fourth decade in movies. Detractors consider him a stylish hack, someone capable of dressing up feces. But supporters contend that it is this same talent for rendering the everyday extraordinary that lends him truly awesome storytelling power. Never a shy filmmaker, Scott's cinema reveals characters and situations that are never what they appear at first glance. **GCQ**

ABOVE: Russell Crowe gets feisty in the film that made him a huge star, Scott's *Gladiator*.

For Better or Worse?

So, does the director's cut of a film provide the opportunity to enhance the original work or is it merely a marketing tool? Certainly Ridley Scott's dystopian view of twenty-first-century Los Angeles, *Blade Runner* (1982), opened mostly to critical and popular yawns. However, the director's cut elevated it to cult status and the film is today cited as influential in the emergence of the cyberpunk genre, and greatly admired for its fantasy cityscape and groundbreaking special effects. Whether the re-release is better or worse than the original version though will always fuel a heated debate.

LARISA SHEPITKO

Born: Larisa Yefimovna Shepitko, January 6, 1938 (Artyomovsk, now Ukraine); died 1979 (Tver Province, Russia).

Directing style: Ukrainian director of controversial political dramas; narrative slow burn; heightened, almost surreal style; use of Christian iconography.

Top Takes...

Voskhozhdeniye 1976 (*Ascent*)

Ty i ya 1971 (*You and Me*)

Nachalo nevedomogo veka 1967 (*Beginning of an Unknown Era*)

Krylya 1966 (*Wings*)

Znoy 1963 (*Heat*)

Zhivaya voda 1957 (*Living Water*)

Slepoy kukhar 1956 (*The Blind Cook*)

Larisa Shepitko attended the State Institute for Cinematography (VGIK) in Moscow, and worked under the tutelage of Alexander Dovzhenko. When she graduated, she received critical acclaim for her diploma film, *Znoy* (1963) (*Heat*), which depicts the clash between a Stalinist farm leader and an idealistic youth in a small community in central Asia in the mid-1950s.

Shepitko's next film was *Krylya* (1966) (*Wings*), the story of a female fighter pilot in World War II who becomes a teacher and struggles to communicate with a generation she does not understand. The film was highly regarded, as was Shepitko's only color film, *Ty i ya* (1971) (*You and Me*), which details the existential crisis of two surgeons forced to consider the viability of hope within the context of constantly compromised ideals.

Shepitko's final completed work, *Voskhozhdeniye* (1976) (*Ascent*), was also her most widely recognized and artistically accomplished. The film is set in 1942 and documents the story of a group of Russian partisans captured by the Nazis. Over the course of the narrative, they are interrogated and executed. What this synopsis cannot well articulate, however, is the profundity of Shepitko's vision, particularly her approach to depicting seemingly simple events. She skillfully transforms a familiar scenario into a serious reflection upon ideas of loyalty and devotion. The manner in which both transcendence and truth are communicated through a visual template owes much to traditional Christian iconography, as well as the cinematic portraiture of Robert Bresson.

> "The color sphere of the film was new to me—I entered it with trepidation and curiosity."

In 1979 Shepitko and several members of her crew were killed in a car accident. She had been in the process of shooting *Proshchanie* (1983) (*Farewell to Matyora*), and her husband, the filmmaker Elem Klimov, completed the work. **NC**

ISTVÁN SZABÓ

Born: István Szabó, February 18, 1938 (Budapest, Hungary).

Directing style: Hungarian director of dramas exploring the effect of World War II on Hungary; auteur; cameo appearances; collaborations with actor Klaus Maria Brandauer.

István Szabó was awarded an Oscar for Best Foreign Language Film for *Mephisto* (1981), the only Hungarian director to have won such an accolade. The movie, with Klaus Maria Brandauer as an actor in a moral dilemma concerning his friendship with a Nazi officer, was the first in Szabó's signature trilogy dealing with World War II's effects on his country. *Oberst Redl* (1985) (*Colonel Redl*), which chronicled the rise and fall of a closet homosexual officer facing blackmail, came next, and *Hanussen* (1988), which featured Brandauer as a soldier who becomes clairvoyant after being shot in the head, concluded the series and won Szabó another Oscar nomination.

Szabó distinguished himself as an auteur in the Hungarian New Cinema of the 1960s before the Oscar-nominated short *Koncert* (1963) (*The Concert*) gave him the opportunity to branch out. After *Hanussen*, he switched to English-language films with *Meeting Venus* (1991); the historical drama *Sunshine* (1999), which traced the tragic lives of a Hungarian Jewish family over three generations; and *Taking Sides* (2001) featuring Harvey Keitel as a U.S. officer instructed to convict the renowned conductor of a Berlin orchestra for being a Nazi. *Being Julia* (2004), a comedy drama, landed a Best Actress Oscar nomination for lead Annette Bening.

On a less savory note and in a striking parallel to some of his own cinematic themes, it was revealed in 2006 that Szabó, while a film student, had informed on his classmates, including director Lajos Koltai, for the post-revolutionary communist regime. Szabó insisted he was blackmailed and complied to save the lives of himself and a fellow student. Ironically, Koltai, who has since forgiven Szabó, worked on many of Szabó's movies, including the acclaimed *Rokonok* (2006) (*Relatives*). **TE**

Top Takes...

Rokonok 2006

Being Julia 2004

Taking Sides 2001

Sunshine 1999

Meeting Venus 1991

Hanussen 1988

Oberst Redl 1985 (*Colonel Redl*)

Mephisto 1981

Bizalom 1980 (*Confidence*)

Apa 1966 (*Father*)

Álmodozások kora 1964 (*Age of Illusions*)

Koncert 1963 (*The Concert*)

1930s

"I want to show people they can be liberated from the mask given to them by society."

JIŘÍ MENZEL

Born: Jiří Menzel, February 23, 1938 (Prague, Czech Republic).

Directing style: Award-winning Czech New Wave director of dark, satirical comedies; often anticommunist themes; appears as an actor in many of his movies.

Top Takes...

The stalwart of the Czech New Wave, and occasional tightrope walker, Jiří Menzel scored a memorable international hit with the Best Foreign Language Film Oscar-winning *Ostre sledované vlaky* (1966) (*Closely Watched Trains*). The sex comedy-cum-social satire told the story of a stationmaster's assistant more concerned with losing his virginity than promoting Hitler's New Order. The film showcased Menzel's trademark strengths of humanity and sarcasm.

Menzel studied at Prague Film School and worked as an assistant to Vera Chytilova before becoming a director. He made an episode for the feature anthology *Perlicky Na Dne* (1965) (*Pearls on the Ground*). Menzel followed up his Oscar success with the nostalgic comedy *Rozmarné léto* (1968) (*Capricious Summer*), in which he played a tightrope walker. He made the gritty drama *Skrivánci na niti* (1990) (*Skylarks on a String*) in 1969. It featured prison laborers working in a scrapyard, and its anticommunist stance landed him in trouble. It was banned until 1990, after which it played internationally.

Menzel was prevented from making films until he declared his support for communism. He directed *Kdo hledá zlaté dno* (*Who Looks for Gold?*) in 1974, a movie he has since disowned due to the oppressive circumstances of its creation. Subsequent offerings have included nonpolitical comedies, including the critically acclaimed, Oscar-nominated *Vesnicko má stredisková* (1985) (*My Sweet Little Village*), a satire set in World War I. In the late 1980s, his political activism was reactivated but his output was undistinguished. In front of the camera, Menzel has enjoyed a minor acting career with a leading role in Costa-Gavras's comedy drama *La petite apocalypse* (1992) (*The Little Apocalypse*). **TE**

> "It sure is a relief to be famous ... except that I'm beginning to lose my sense of humor."

1930s

JERZY SKOLIMOWSKI

Born: Jerzy Skolimowski, May 5, 1938 (Łódź, Poland).

Directing style: Polish director of poetic comedies and dramas; often autobiographical themes; focus on the obsessed loner in society; use of improvisation.

When examining the films of Jerzy Skolimowski, it seems he enjoys probing loner characters with unusual obsessions. Out of place in their surroundings, much like immigrants in a new land, these seemingly benign, nonthreatening kooks often turn out to be dangerous—even deadly—to those they befriend. Considering Skolimowski was born in Poland (he cowrote *Nóz w wodzie* (1962) (*Knife in the Water*) with Roman Polanski) yet made his most influential films elsewhere, such as England, it is a curious tendency.

Deep End (1971) focuses on Mike, a fifteen-year-old boy who works in a public bathhouse in late-1960s London. The setting is one oozing in sexual decadence, and for an immature lad such as Mike, it only feeds his obsession for an older, very attractive coworker. Unwittingly she toys with him, and inflames his delusions, a situation which ultimately triggers her tragic end. *The Shout* (1978) follows the story of a married couple who take in a vagabond claiming to have learned some extraordinary Aboriginal magic. Finding themselves intrigued instead of repulsed, their curiosity results in a conclusion that is apocalyptic in nature. Skolimowski began the script for *Moonlighting* (1982) on December 13, 1981, the day martial law was established in Poland. Six months later the completed film debuted at Cannes Film Festival. The story is powerful in its simplicity. On the surface it is about a group of Polish workers who are hired to renovate a London house. What evolves is a unique parable that is open to many interpretations. The wild card is Jeremy Irons, who plays foreman to the workers. As with earlier Skolimowski characters he seems quite benevolent, but gradually his selfish desires lead to disaster for everyone. **DW**

Top Takes...

America 2006
Ferdydurke 1991
Torrents of Spring 1989
The Lightship 1986
Success is the Best Revenge 1984
Moonlighting 1982
Rece do góry 1981 (*Hands Up!*)
The Shout 1978
King, Queen, Knave 1972
Deep End 1971
The Adventures of Gerard 1970
Le Départ 1967
Bariera 1966 (*Barrier*)
Walkower 1965 (*Walkover*)
Boks 1961 (*Boxing*)

"I feel safe with a story that tempts you to believe or disbelieve."

LARRY COHEN

Born: Lawrence G. Cohen, July 15, 1938 (Kingston, New York, U.S.).

Directing style: Independent U.S. director across a range of genres, particularly inventive low-budget horror movies; dark comedy mixed with social commentary.

Top Takes...

Larry Cohen is a U.S. writer, producer, and director known for his fiercely independent filmmaking. Working with undersized budgets in order to retain complete creative control, Cohen has worked in various genres including comedy, drama, horror, mystery, science fiction, and the Western.

Cohen attended the City College of New York as a film student. He entered the entertainment industry as a page at NBC studios and quickly advanced to writing for TV shows, eventually creating several series including the cult hit science-fiction series *The Invaders* (1967). Cohen made his feature debut with the comedy drama *Bone* (1972). A satirical look at racism and class anxiety in Beverly Hills, the film did not fare well financially but established Cohen's penchant for dark comedy mixed with social commentary.

Cohen joined the blaxploitation craze with his second film, *Black Caesar* (1973). It was a financial success that paved the way for the horror feature *It's Alive* (1974). Gleefully over the top and harshly attacking societal norms, *It's Alive* showcases Cohen's talent for creating innovative scenarios within the horror genre. The movie proved to be a huge box-office success and spawned two sequels, *It Lives Again* (1978) and *It's Alive III: Island of the Alive* (1987). Cohen continued to work primarily in the horror and science-fiction genres. This allowed him extraordinary license for social commentary on diverse subjects such as corporations, the film industry, inner cities, and police brutality. And as an independent, his messages are rarely diluted by the Hollywood studio system. As Cohen slowed his output as a director, he ironically found himself in demand as a writer of high-concept thrillers, such as *Phone Booth* (2002), for major studios. **WW**

> "If Hitchcock were alive he would have wanted to direct *Phone Booth*."—Steven Spielberg

RIGHT: The public go crazy for the "stuff" in Cohen's comic mock-horror movie.

PAUL VERHOEVEN

Born: Paul Verhoeven, July 18, 1938 (Amsterdam, Noord-Holland, Netherlands).

Directing style: Dutch director of action and science-fiction movies; often features nudity and misogyny; artistic collaborations with actor Rutger Hauer and screenwriter Joe Eszterhas.

Top Takes...

Zwartboek 2006 (*Black Book*)
Hollow Man 2000
Starship Troopers 1997
Showgirls 1995
Basic Instinct 1992
Total Recall 1990
RoboCop 1987
Flesh + Blood 1985
De vierde man 1983 (*The Fourth Man*)
Spetters 1980
Soldaat van Oranje 1977 (*Soldier of Orange*)
Turks fruit 1973 (*Turkish Delight*)
Een Hagedis teveel 1960 (*A Lizzard Too Much*)

"People seem to have this strange idea that films can influence people to be violent."

Despite the excess of nudity and full-on sex that decorates several of his films, Paul Verhoeven's movies, like Old Dutch Masters, reveal themselves as sophisticated criticisms of hypocrisy, capitalist commerce, and gung-ho zealotry.

Verhoeven first entered the spotlight with *Turks fruit* (1973) (*Turkish Delight*), criticized for its frankness but the most profitable Dutch film ever. Its story of *l'amour fou* between Rutger Hauer and Monique van de Ven is a damning attack on the bourgeoisie. Hauer and Verhoeven would make three more films together: *Soldaat van Oranje* (1977) (*Soldier of Orange*) was a surprisingly balanced account of heroes and villains in the war-torn Netherlands; *Spetters* (1980) chronicled the sexual awakenings of the Netherlands's youth; and the underrated *Flesh+Blood* (1985) portrayed mercenary warfare and religious sanctimony in a medieval Europe ravaged by the plague.

Verhoeven reached Hollywood in the mid-1980s, where he became noted for violent science-fiction parables with *RoboCop* (1987), an anticapitalist metaphor of Christ's suffering; and *Starship Troopers* (1997), which equated the U.S. army's attitude toward alien invaders with Nazi ideology. He also received a lot of press for two collaborations with screenwriter Joe Eszterhas. Both *Basic Instinct* (1992) and *Showgirls* (1995) were ostracized because of their misogyny and nudity—Sharon Stone's lack of underwear and Elizabeth Berkeley's pool orgasm to be precise. After his brashness made him an outcast in Hollywood, Verhoeven returned to his native Netherlands, where *Zwartboek* (2006) (*Black Book*) demonstrates how he continues to expose dishonest practices that put manners, routine, and efficiency before sincerity, with World War II as the backdrop. **EM**

RALPH BAKSHI

Born: Ralph Bakshi, October 29, 1938 (Haifa, then Palestine, now Israel).

Directing style: Legendary pioneering animator of X-rated adult comic and fantasy cartoons, and live-action features; often controversial nonpolitically correct content; use of rotoscoping.

While he was still a baby, Ralph Bakshi's family fled to the United States to escape World War II. In the 1960s, he worked as a cel polisher and cel painter at Terrytoons, during a time when TV animation was at its height. He toiled on characters such as Mighty Mouse and Deputy Dawg, before moving to Paramount Pictures and supervising a clutch of animation shows based on *Marvel Comics* superheroes.

Fritz the Cat (1972), Bakshi's first feature, was based on Robert Crumb's underground comics, and hyped as the first X-rated animated film. A talking animal film with a counterculture backdrop, and plentiful sex and drug references, *Fritz the Cat* was condemned by Crumb but successful enough with the college crowds to enable Bakshi to make more original films in the same style: *Heavy Traffic* (1973) and *Coonskin* (1975). Hogarthian in their crudeness and exaggeration, these films attracted criticism for supposed racism, although the white pig cops are at least as outrageous as the black crow pimps.

It was not much of a stretch for Bakshi to move into the sword-and-sorcery genre which, in the pre-computer-generated graphics era, was far better suited to animation than live action. After *Wizards* (1977), he ambitiously embarked on *The Lord of the Rings* (1978), which adapts the first two books in the trilogy. It was left to Jules Bass and Arthur Rankin Jr. to make *The Return of the King* (1980) as a TV movie to complete the story. Heavily committed to the mixed blessing of rotoscoping, Bakshi has stayed with fantasy, making films such as *Fire and Ice* (1983), and music with *American Pop* (1981). He has essayed an unsuccessful cartoon and live-action hybrid *Cool World* (1992), and a lone live-action feature, *The Cool and the Crazy* (1994). **KN**

Top Takes…

1930s

"Cartooning is a low-class, for-the-public art, just like graffiti art and rap music."

JEAN ROLLIN

Born: Jean Michel Rollin Le Gentil, November 3, 1938 (Neuilly-sur-Seine, Paris, France).

Directing style: Director of pornography and cult horror movies; nudity, graphic violence, and gory, sadistic rituals; bizarre beauty; often vampire themes.

Top Takes…

La fiancée de Dracula 2002

Les deux orphelines vampires 1997
(*Two Orphan Vampires*)

La morte vivante 1982
(*The Living Dead Girl*)

Fascination 1979

Les raisins de la mort 1978
(*The Raisins of Death*)

Lèvres de sang 1975 (*Lips of Blood*)

Phantasmes 1975

Le frisson des vampires 1971

Vierges et vampires 1971
(*Requiem for a Vampire*)

Le viol du vampire 1967
(*The Rape of the Vampire*)

Les amours jaunes 1958

Spawned in the 1970s, the decade in which cinema was at its naughtiest and taste was under sustained attack, Jean Rollin's oeuvre of gorgeous Gallic gore and lesbian virgin vampires stands out for its sensual, surreal beauty, and bizarre, sadistic rituals. Part of exploitation cinema, Rollin's work only received limited theatrical exposure, but at genre festivals around the world it still attracts cult celebrations.

Rollin's first feature, *Le viol du vampire* (1967) (*The Rape of the Vampire*), in stark black and white against a barren background, tells the tale of four nymphettes chased by a vampire—it is always nymphettes versus vampires. The plot is pointless—it is actually a short with an added hour and different actors—but the nudity, graphic violence, and decadent atmosphere were, for the time, sensational. Always consistent, Rollin revisited this theme endlessly, with *Vierges et vampires* (1971) (*Requiem for a Vampire*) and *Lèvres de sang* (1975) (*Lips of Blood*) as highlights, bathed in visually striking compositions (often using extreme angles, invited by the châteaux locations), with lush colors and strange, suspenseful silences. Even in his parallel career as a porn director, Rollin always returned to these methods. His most famous features are *Les raisins de la mort* (1978) (*The Raisins of Death*), *Fascination* (1979), and *La morte vivante* (1982) (*The Living Dead Girl*), not solely for the otherworldly beauty of Brigitte Lahaie, Rollin's most famous waif (her scythe-wielding elegance in *Fascination* is unforgettable), but because of the

> "The story is always made, it is an alibi for me to shoot some [visuals] that I want to shoot."

desperate, dreamy lyricism with overtones of the Marquis de Sade. Since the mid-1980s Rollin's career has slowed, but with films such as *Le fiancée de Dracula* (2002), he has confirmed that he is still unsurpassed as underground's *le roi vampire*. **EM**

JEAN EUSTACHE

Born: Jean Eustache, November 30, 1938 (Pessac, France); died 1981 (Paris, France).

Directing style: French director of documentaries, shorts, and dramas; often critical self-portraits; themes of rural life, love, despair, and relationships.

Only one of his films is widely known internationally, but in France, Jean Eustache is often cited as the most important post-New Wave director and a vital influence on contemporary figures such as Catherine Breillat and Benoît Jacquot.

Eustache arrived in Paris in the 1950s and transformed himself into an urban dandy. A fringe member of the *Cahiers du cinema* crowd, he began making documentaries and short films in the early 1960s. These two branches to his art were linked yet qualitatively distinct. Documentaries such as *La rosière de Pessac* (1968) (*The Virgin of Pessac*) and *Le Cochon* (1970) (*The Pig*) were sympathetic portraits of rural communities, whereas short films *Les mauvaises fréquentations* (1963) and *Le Père Noël a les yeux bleus* (1966) (*Santa Claus Has Blue Eyes*) concerned dissolute, sexually predatory young men and were merciless self-portraits.

Running nearly four hours, *La maman et la putain* (1973) (*The Mother and the Whore*), Eustache's defining film, charts the relationship between the narcissistic Alexandré (played by one of the iconic leading men of the New Wave, Jean-Pierre Léaud), the older woman he lives with, and the promiscuous younger girl he seduces. Encapsulating the disillusionment felt by his generation in the 1970s, the film was both a summation of the New Wave and a decisive break with it. Eustache's only standard-length feature film, *Mes petites amoureuses* (1974), follows a boy's growth into a gauche adolescent and delinquent. A more lighthearted movie, it was nevertheless suffused with his pervasive sense of despair. Perhaps Eustache's bleak outlook would have mellowed with age, but in 1981, having been immobilized by a car accident, despair finally overwhelmed him and he took his own life. **RB**

Top Takes...

Les photos d'Alix 1980
La rosière de Pessac 1979 (*The Virgin of Pessac*)
Mes petites amoureuses 1974
La maman et la putain 1973
  (*The Mother and the Whore*)
Numéro zéro 1971
Le Cochon 1970 (*The Pig*)
La rosière de Pessac 1968 (*The Virgin of Pessac*)
Le Père Noël a les yeux bleus 1966
  (*Santa Claus Has Blue Eyes*)
Les mauvaises fréquentations 1963
  (*Bad Company*)

1930s

"The films I made are as autobiographical as fiction can be."

BERTRAND BLIER

Born: Bertrand Blier, March 14, 1939 (Boulogne-Billancourt, Hauts-de-Seine, Île-de-France, France).

Directing style: French director of dark, satirical, surreal farces; themes of sex, society, and gender roles; artistic collaborations with actor Gérard Depardieu.

Top Takes...

In 1939 Bertrand Blier entered both the world and the entertainment industry as the son of French actor Bernard Blier. The younger Blier's foray into French cinema began in the form of documentaries. His first feature film, *Hitler, connais pas* (1963) (*Hitler—Never Heard of Him*) centered upon disillusioned youth following the insanity of World War II. The success of this movie brought Blier into the international spotlight, and he went on to direct his famous father in *Si j'étais un espion* (1967) (*If I Were a Spy*).

Blier then turned to dark comedy in the form of satire, in films such as *Les valseuses* (1974) (*Going Places*), a comment on the operation of sexuality within society. Four years later, Blier received an Academy Award for Best Foreign Film, for his picture *Préparez vos mouchoirs* (1978) (*Get Out Your Handkerchiefs*) starring Gérard Depardieu and Patrick Dewaere. An exposé of the materialistic values of the bourgeoisie, Blier's film follows two quirky thugs as they worm their way out of trouble in pursuit of luxuries.

Blier is also known for his *Buffet froid* (1979) (*Cold Cuts*); *Beau-père* (1981), a version of the classic Lolita story; *Tenue de soirée* (1986) (*Ménage*); and the poignant comedy about adultery, *Trop belle pour toi* (1989) (*Too Beautiful For You*). Collaborations with actress Anouk Grinberg produced other popular films such as *Un, deux, trois, soleil* (1993) (*1, 2, 3, Sun*) and *Mon homme* (1996) (*My Man*), and he teamed again with Gérard Depardieu for *Les Acteurs* (2000) (*Actors*) and *Combien tu m'aimes?* (2005) (*How Much Do You Love Me?*). Bertrand Blier's dark, humorous, and satiric style continues to both enrapture—and divide—critics and audiences from all over the world. **ES**

> "It disappoints me when my films fail to provoke indignation."

1930s

GLAUBER ROCHA

Born: Glauber Rocha, March 14, 1939 (Vitória da Conquista, Bahia, Brazil); died 1981 (Rio de Janeiro, Brazil).

Directing style: Director of Cinema Novo; anticolonial themes; fusion of Afro-Brazilian mysticism with Brechtian alienation effects; folklore; poetic narratives.

Glauber Rocha was the polemical spokesman of the Cinema Novo and one of the most prominent political filmmakers of the 1960s. Rocha wrote extensively on film, reflecting on an anticolonial cinema that combines leftist subject matters with a new and complex aesthetics, epitomized in his famous essay, *Eztetyka da Fome* (1965) (*The Aesthetic of Hunger*).

Barravento (1962) (*The Turning Wind*) deals with a poor Afro-Brazilian fishing village, and is already an example of Rocha's original and highly ambivalent style. *Deus e o Diabo na Terra do Sol* (1964) (*God and the Devil in the Land of the Sun*) shows the life of a poor cowherd and his wife in the *sertão*, the poorest region in Brazil. Rocha makes use of a form of Brazilian poetry, *literatura de cordel*, or string literature, to structure the narrative of the film, which ends with a cut from the *sertão* to the sea as a metaphor of a revolutionary transformation. *Terra em Transe* (1967) (*Land in Anguish*) is an allegory of the right-wing military coup d'état in Brazil in 1964 that ironically takes place in a land called Eldorado. Narrated from the perspective of the mortally wounded protagonist, the film includes a long fragmented flashback, a delirious visual stream of consciousness about the events that had led to the coup. *O Dragão da Maldade contra o Santo Guerreiro* (1969) (*Antônio das Mortes*) won the Best Director Award at Cannes.

From 1970 on, Rocha made various films in exile: *Cabezas cortadas* (1970) (*Cutting Heads*) in Spain, *Der Leone have sept cabeças* (1971) (*The Lion has Seven Heads*) in the Congo, and *Claro* (1975) in Panama. His swan song, *A Idade da Terra* (1980) (*The Age of the Earth*), Rocha's legacy, is one of the most enigmatic and iconoclastic works in film history, dealing with a polymorphic, multiracial revolutionary Christ of the Third World. **PS**

Top Takes…

1930s

"An idea in one's head and a camera in one's hand should be enough for a film."

VOLKER SCHLÖNDORFF

Born: Volker Schlöndorff, March 31, 1939 (Wiesbaden, Hessen, Germany).

Directing style: German director of dramas and literary adaptations; often tackles themes of totalitarianism; artistic collaborations with director and actress Margarethe von Trotta.

Top Takes…

Der Neunte Tag 2004 (*The Ninth Day*)

Die Stille nach dem Schuss 2000 (*Legend of Rita*)

The Handmaid's Tale 1990

Death of a Salesman 1985

Un amour de Swann 1984 (*Swann in Love*)

Die Blechtrommel 1979 (*The Tin Drum*)

Deutschland im Herbst 1978 (*Germany in Autumn*)

Der Fangschuss 1976 (*Coup de grâce*)

Die Verlorene Ehre der Katharina Blum oder: Wie Gewalt entstehen und wohin sie führen kann 1975 (*The Lost Honor of Katharina Blum*)

Michael Kohlhaas—Der Rebell 1969 (*Man on Horseback*)

Mord und Totschlag 1967 (*Degree of Murder*)

Der Junge Törless 1966 (*Young Torless*)

"Producers always tend to underestimate the audience, and their curiosity."

Volker Schlöndorff is best known for his film version of Günter Grass's allegorical novel *The Tin Drum* (1959). He was a stalwart of West Germany's postwar cinema, and is widely respected for his inspired adaptations of classic literary works. After studying economics and political science in Paris, he worked as an assistant director for both Louis Malle and Alain Resnais. He made his feature debut with *Der Junge Törless* (1966) (*Young Torless*), a parable dealing with the rise of Nazism. It won the critics' prize at the Cannes Film Festival, and is credited with paving the way for New German Cinema directors such as Rainer Werner Fassbinder and Wim Wenders.

A few years after the hard-hitting *Die Verlorene Ehre Der Katharina Blum Oder: Wie Gewalt Entstehen Und Wohin Sie Führen Kann* (1975) (*The Lost Honor of Katharina Blum*) came *Die Blechtrommel* (1979) (*The Tin Drum*). The latter is the story of a young boy who refuses to grow up as a reaction to Adolf Hitler's regime; it won a Best Foreign Film Oscar, and the Palme d'Or at Cannes. He then made the intense drama *Un amour de Swann* (1984) (*Swann in Love*), starring Jeremy Irons as the Parisian *bon viveur*, and went on to make his U.S. debut with the TV version of Arthur Miller's *Death of a Salesman* (1985), starring Dustin Hoffman. Schlöndorff scored one of his greatest successes with *The Handmaid's Tale* (1990), an adaptation of Margaret Atwood's chilling vision of a future ruled by religious fundamentalists. Subsequent work was intermittent and included the mystery thriller *Palmetto* (1998) and *Die Stille Nach Dem Schuss* (2000) (*Legend of Rita*). Offscreen, he has been the chief executive of the German production company Babelsberg Studios, and teaches film and literature at the European Graduate School in Switzerland. **TE**

LINO BROCKA

Born: Catalino Ortiz Brocka, April 7, 1939 (Pilar, Sorsogon, Luzon, Philippines); died 1991 (Quezon City, Metro Manila, Luzon, Philippines).

Directing style: Controversial low-budget melodramas and film noirs; critiques of Ferdinand Marcos's government; themes of homosexuality and social injustice.

In the United States, Lino Brocka equals *Macho Dancer* (1988), a homoerotic melodrama set against the backdrop of Manila's gay go-go clubs and brothels. But before his death in a car accident at age fifty-two, Brocka made more than 50 films, successfully navigating the political minefield of the era of Ferdinand Marcos's presidency (1965–1986), and spiking genre cinema with bold statements about poverty, unemployment, and social injustice in the Philippines. Although Brocka was gay, *Macho Dancer* is less concerned with issues of queer identity than with the pragmatic intersection of brutal privation and marketable youth.

As a scholarship student at the University of the Philippines Manila, he abandoned prelaw studies for liberal arts and theater, entering the film business as an assistant to exploitation filmmaker Eddie Romero. Brocka then took a spiritual detour: he became one of the first Filipino converts to The Church of Jesus Christ of Latter-day Saints, and went to Hawaii as a Mormon missionary. Brocka returned in the 1960s, and joined the Philippine Educational Theater Association. He made his directing debut with *Wanted: Perfect Mother* (1970), based on a popular comic strip. His revenge melodrama *Insiang* (1976) was the first Filipino feature shown at the Cannes Film Festival, and the neonoir *Jaguar* (1979) was nominated for the Palme d'Or. In 1983 Brocka founded Concerned Artists of the Philippines to encourage creative individuals to address political and social issues in their work. The shallow and sex-obsessed comedies of Brocka's nephew, U.S.-based Quenton Allan Brocka, embody the sensibilities of a less politicized, more comfortably mainstream generation of gay filmmakers. **MM**

Top Takes...

Comment vont les enfants 1993
   (*How Are the Kids?*)
Lucia 1992
Gumapang ka sa lusak 1990 (*Dirty Affair*)
Macho Dancer 1988
Bayan ko: Kapit sa patalim 1985
   (*Bayan Ko: My Own Country*)
Angela Markado 1980
Jaguar 1979
Insiang 1976
Maynila: Sa mga kuko ng liwanag 1975
   (*The Nail of Brightness*)
Tinimbang ka ngunit kulang 1974
   (*You Are Weighed in the Balance
   But Are Found Wanting*)
Tubog sa ginto 1971 (*Dipped in Gold*)
Wanted: Perfect Mother 1970

"[The city of Manila] exerts an invisible force on the lives of its people."

FRANCIS FORD COPPOLA

Born: Francis Ford Coppola, April 7, 1939 (Detroit, Michigan, U.S.).

Directing style: *Il capo* of organized crime epics; the godfather of family-themed dramas; family cameo appearances; magnificent handling of leading male actors to create iconic figures.

Top Takes…

The Rainmaker 1997

Jack 1996

Dracula 1992

The Godfather: Part III 1990 ☆

Peggy Sue Got Married 1986

Captain EO 1986

The Cotton Club 1984

Rumble Fish 1983

The Outsiders 1983

One from the Heart 1982

Apocalypse Now 1979 ☆

The Godfather: Part II 1974 ★

The Conversation 1974

The Godfather 1972 ☆

The Rain People 1969

Finian's Rainbow 1968

You're a Big Boy Now 1966

Dementia 13 1963

The Bellboy and the Playgirls 1962

Artists and athletes enjoy streaks of brilliance. For Francis Ford Coppola, the streak starts in 1970 and continues through 1979. Before that and afterward, there are memorable moments, but in this decade he directed impressive, award-winning pictures with unprecedented frequency.

Coppola grew up as part of a creative Italian-American family. He apprenticed for Roger Corman and made a handful of shorts, including *The Bellboy and the Playgirls* (1962), and his feature debut, *Dementia 13* (1963). It didn't take long for Coppola to become dissatisfied with Hollywood, and in 1969 he established his independent studio, American Zoetrope. That year he released *The Rain People* (1969), telling a trademark Coppola journey of self-discovery in which Natalie Ravenna heads off across the States in search of happiness.

Back in Hollywood, Coppola made *The Godfather* (1972), affirming his personal brilliance and redefining the gangster film by putting a Mafioso family at the center of an allegory about the immigrant experience. For his efforts he won Golden Globes and an Oscar for the screenplay, and helped usher in the blockbuster revolution of the 1970s.

RIGHT: *Apocalypse Now* was premiered at the 1979 Cannes Film Festival.

Flush with influence and prestige, he backed George Lucas on *American Graffiti* (1973), which also earned Coppola a Best Picture Academy Award nomination in 1973, and prepared two films, *The Conversation* (1974) and *The Godfather: Part II* (1974)—they won him three Oscars. After three years' work, he finally released the ambitious and highly acclaimed Vietnam War epic *Apocalypse Now* (1979) at Cannes Film Festival, thereby confirming his position atop the directors' hierarchy.

The 1980s saw him mount titles that were not particularly well-received, but the epics *One from the Heart* (1982) and *The Cotton Club* (1984), and a pair of independently minded youth films, *The Outsiders* (1983) and *Rumble Fish* (1983) remain important works. Although Coppola's later work was sporadic, it should be noted that he is one of only five people to win the Academy Award for Best Picture, Best Director, and Best Screenplay in the same year. **GCQ**

ABOVE: The movie that defined an era of cult filmmaking, *The Godfather*.

Coppola Family Values

Francis Ford Coppola is clearly fascinated by the dynamics within families and by what holds them together or causes them to fall apart. He often casts relatives in his own movies (daughter Sofia Coppola, nephew Nicolas Cage, sister Talia Shire) and has many extended family members working within the film industry. It is not surprising then that Coppola is perhaps best known for directing the intense and tragic saga of the Corleone family in *The Godfather* trilogy. Made over 18 years, the films display a unique talent for narrative and Coppola's often overlooked prowess for cinematic technique.

PETER BOGDANOVICH

Born: Peter Bogdanovich, July 30, 1939 (Kingston, New York, U.S.).

Directing style: Actor turned director across a range of genres; homages to Hollywood classics; notable screwball comedies; writer; producer; documentary filmmaker.

Top Takes...

Like the French New Wave directors, Peter Bogdanovich began as a critic before going on to make movies. His films are heavily influenced by his passion for the directorial work of Orson Welles, Howard Hawks, and Sir Alfred Hitchcock, and are imbued with a poignant sense of loss.

One of his first films as a director, *Targets* (1968), is a thoughtful and brilliantly tense thriller, a love letter to the past, and a poison pen letter to the present. It is an elegy for Hollywood's golden age, and, for its star Boris Karloff, the kind of loving valediction of which all actors must dream.

He followed this up with *The Last Picture Show* (1971), a film that filtered bittersweet sentiments through a beautifully observed portrait of small-town life in 1950s Texas. The plot played out in and around a rundown movie theater. Comparisons were made with *Citizen Kane* (1941) and the film won a number of awards. He followed it with two smash-hit pastiches of classical Hollywood formulae: *What's Up, Doc?* (1972), an exhausting screwball comedy closely modeled on the 1938 hit *Bringing Up Baby*, and *Paper Moon* (1973), a Depression-era fable with something of the flavor of John Ford or early Frank Capra. The films that followed reflect not so much a decline in achievement as a sense of being left behind by fashion. Although they were major commercial and critical failures, there is still much to recommend in *At Long Last Love* (1975) and *Nickelodeon* (1976); their only clear fault, perhaps, being central miscasting. Their failure, however, resulted in Bogdanovich spending the rest of his career in the wilderness. In the final analysis, *Targets* remains his best film, but he certainly returned to form with the excellent *The Cat's Meow* (2001). **MC**

> "The end of the studio system signaled the end of the great screen stars."

RIGHT: Tatum O'Neal won an Oscar for her role in *Paper Moon*—she was ten years old.

WES CRAVEN

Born: Wesley Earl Craven, August 2, 1939 (Cleveland, Ohio, U.S.).

Directing style: Visionary king of nightmare horror and slasher movies; innovative makeovers of the horror genre placing fear in the heart of ordinary U.S. suburbia.

Top Takes…

Initially making an impact in the exploitation field of the early 1970s, Wes Craven is a resourceful writer and director known as one of the horror genre's most creative, innovative, and resilient visionaries.

Craven studied literature and psychology at Wheaton College in Illinois and earned a Master's Degree in philosophy from John Hopkins University in Maryland. This academic background in psychology perhaps explains his fascination with fear and its effect on the psyche. Craven's interest in cinema also began at college because he was forbidden to watch anything other than Disney films as a child by his Baptist parents. Following graduation, Craven began teaching but was intent on breaking into the film industry.

He moved to New York and began working at various jobs on low-budget movies to gain experience. Craven soon found himself on the end of an offer from a group of cinema investors who wanted a scary movie. The resulting film, *The Last House on the Left* (1972), struck a nerve with both audiences and critics alike. A shocking and violent retelling of Ingmar Bergman's *Jungfrukällan* (1960) (*The Virgin Spring*), *The Last*

RIGHT: The man who spawned nighmares, Robert Englund as Freddy Krueger.

House on the Left gained an instant unsavory reputation that temporarily hindered Craven's directing ambitions and career.

Craven returned with *The Hills Have Eyes* (1977). Like his debut, it is a brutal affair repeating the theme of normal people driven to violent behavior. The film was a success and finally opened doors for Craven in Hollywood. Working steadily, but financially unfulfilled, Craven delivered with his eighth film, *A Nightmare on Elm Street* (1984). With its heavy doses of violence, surrealist dreamscapes, and the spine-chilling character Freddy Krueger, the film became a worldwide success spawning seven sequels; Craven himself helmed *New Nightmare* (1994).

Craven mirrored this success a decade later with *Scream* (1996), a familiar tale of a psychopathic serial killer stalking teenagers in an ordinary California town. Craven's postmodern teen-slasher film satirized the genre, wowed the critics, and led him to make two successful sequels. **WW**

ABOVE: Jada Pinkett Smith shares the screen with scary masks, in *Scream 2.*

Come to Freddy . . .

Rumor has it that Wes Craven's Freddy Krueger character was named for a boy who bullied him in high school. Rumors aside, the character has certainly entered film history as one of the arch villains of all time. Complete with clawed spiked-metal gloved hand, burnt face, fedora hat, striped jumper, dirty overcoat, and creepy rendition of the *One, Two, Buckle My Shoe* nursery rhyme, Krueger is the fictional invincible child serial killer. He eerily haunts the inhabitants of Elm Street, able to torment his victims by making them dream of their own death after being slashed by his glove.

JOEL SCHUMACHER

Born: Joel Schumacher, August 29, 1939 (New York City, New York, U.S.).

Directing style: Premier maker of Brat Pack genre, action-packed dramas and controversial Caped Crusader movies; surreal imagery; artistic collaborations with Irish actor Colin Farrell.

Top Takes...

The Phantom of the Opera 2004
Veronica Guerin 2003
Phone Booth 2002
Tigerland 2000
8MM 1999
Batman & Robin 1997
A Time to Kill 1996
Batman Forever 1995
The Client 1994
Falling Down 1993
Dying Young 1991
Flatliners 1990
The Lost Boys 1987
St. Elmo's Fire 1985
The Incredible Shrinking Woman 1981

Joel Schumacher is a fashion designer by trade. After making costumes for TV, he wrote the screenplays for *Sparkle* (1976) and *Car Wash* (1976), two small films with lasting impact on African-American cinema. In 1978 he wrote *The Wiz*, adapting William F. Brown's Broadway stage musical of *The Wonderful Wizard of Oz*, into an African-Americanized version.

His debut as director was a comic vehicle for Lily Tomlin, *The Incredible Shrinking Woman* (1981). It was well received, but Schumacher really made his mark with the Brat Pack actors Emilio Estevez, Rob Lowe, and Demi Moore, and the coming-of-age drama, *St. Elmo's Fire* (1985). The director's ease with presenting young performers in crisis made way for a lasting theme, first confirmed in the vampire story *The Lost Boys* (1987) and followed by the science-fiction thriller *Flatliners* (1990) and the drama *Dying Young* (1991).

The early 1990s saw Schumacher step away from youth for the story of a man unhinged, *Falling Down* (1993), and two successful John Grisham adaptations, *The Client* (1994) and *A Time to Kill* (1996). In 1995 Schumacher stamped on pop culture forever with his flamboyant *Batman Forever* (1995) and then *Batman & Robin* (1997). Trouble centered on perceptions that Schumacher's homosexuality "polluted" one of the most beloved of comic book fables. In reality, the series had run its course and Schumacher's excesses were but an easy scapegoat for an extremely limited franchise. Since then, Schumacher has kept busy with the disturbing *8MM* (1999), the low-budget films *Tigerland* (2000) and *Phone Booth* (2002), a minor miracle in the biopic of the murdered Irish journalist *Veronica Guerin* (2003), and an adaptation of *The Phantom of the Opera* (2004). **GCQ**

"... it is show business, and it's more business now than it is show ...."

RIGHT: A contemplative moment for the masked villain in *The Phantom of the Opera*.

HARRY KÜMEL

Born: Harry Kümel, January 27, 1940 (Antwerp, Belgium).

Directing style: Belgian director of cult horror films, erotica, and costume dramas; dramatic colors; dazzling cinematography; often vampire themes; injection of style and attitude into Belgian cinema.

Top Takes...

Eline Vere 1991

The Secrets of Love 1986

Een dag in Viaanderen 1986

Draadvariaties 1980

Het verloren paradijs 1978 (Paradise Lost)

De komst van Joachim Stiller 1976
  (The Arrival of Joachim Stiller)

Repelsteeltje 1973 (Rumplestiltskin)

Les lèvres rouge 1971 (Daughters of Darkness)

Malpertuis 1971 (The Legend of Doom House)

Monsieur Hawarden 1969

Waterloo 1965

De Grafbewaker 1965

Claudia Cardinale 1965

Hendrick Conscience 1963

Erasmus 1963

"I know things no
one knows I know!"

—Cassavius, *The Legend of Doom House*

Among cult connoisseurs, Harry Kümel is famous for two prodigal pictures. *Les lèvres rouges* (1971) (*Daughters of Darkness*) started off as a gamble to make a film featuring 700 vestal virgins in Belgium, without state support, only to become the most sophisticated lesbian vampire film ever made—erotically charged, lavishly decorated, and with a superbly languishing Delphine Seyrig as the ultimate *mère vampire*. *Malpertuis* (1971) (*The Legend of Doom House*) is, at surface level, a baroque, haunted house thriller, but the themes of terror, torture, and betrayal give it a mythological profundity, underpinned by claustrophobic decor, dramatic colors, and dazzling cinematography. What drew cinephiles' attention was Orson Welles's part as a *pater familias*, lording over captured Greek gods—a small ruler of the world.

Kümel was still a young man when he directed these renowned movies, an angry autodidact bursting with ideas. In 1969 he delighted critics with the mysterious puzzle of identity and period cross-dressing, *Monsieur Hawarden*, a film dedicated to Josef von Sternberg in a style reminiscent of F. W. Murnau and François Truffaut. And even before that, he had directed a dozen short films as well as several TV shows. The strict film policies of Belgium and the Netherlands hampered Kümel's efforts considerably after *The Legend of Doom House*. *De komst van Joachim Stiller* (1976) (*The Arrival of Joachim Stiller*), the soft erotic film *The Secrets of Love* (1986), and his last feature film, *Eline Vere* (1991), still found acclaim in niche markets, but above all they showed restraint. Kümel retired in 2005 and, even if there will never be a new Kümel movie, his bravura injected Belgian cinema with a much-needed dose of style and attitude. **EM**

GEORGE A. ROMERO

Born: George Andrew Romero, February 4, 1940 (New York City, New York, U.S.).

Directing style: U.S. director of cult horror films; king of zombie themes; innovative use of horror genre as political commentary on the state of the nation; depiction of consumerism as a monstrous force.

Despite having worked on a range of other notable films, such as *Martin* (1977), George Romero will forever be linked in film fans' minds with one image—the lumbering, shuffling zombie. Responsible for bringing a newfound seriousness to the zombie subgenre, Romero has directed *Night of the Living Dead* (1968), *Dawn of the Dead* (1978), *Day of the Dead* (1985), and *Land of the Dead* (2005).

But these films do much more than feature a kind of monster. *Night of the Living Dead* has been celebrated by critics for bringing horror into the homes of its U.S. characters and showing a bleak world where ties of family and nation can be lethally undermined. Here, the zombie threat is not easily overcome by a group of heroes. Romero's horror focuses on an escalating threat rather than on magical solutions, first introducing a note of weariness and nihilism into the genre at a time when, politically, the United States was facing a crisis in confidence. Making reference to the civil rights movement, Romero also included an African-American character as his male lead Ben, played by Duane Jones, suggesting at the film's conclusion that it was not just zombies Ben needed to fear.

Romero's use of the horror genre to offer a social commentary has distinguished his zombie films for generations of viewers. *Dawn of the Dead* focuses on zombies as consumers rampaging through a shopping mall, casting consumerism as a monstrous force; *Day of the Dead* reduces humanity to the survivors of a zombie apocalypse, reflecting the nuclear fears of the era. And Romero's return to the *Land of the Dead* depicts a polarized world of economic haves and have-nots, suggesting that the zombies themselves may be sentient and deserving of audience sympathy. **MH**

Top Takes…

Land of the Dead 2005
Bruiser 2000
The Dark Half 1993
Due occhi diabolici 1990 (*Two Evil Eyes*)
Monkey Shines 1988
Day of the Dead 1985
Creepshow 1982
Knightriders 1981
Dawn of the Dead 1978
Martin 1977
The Crazies 1973
Hungry Wives 1972
There's Always Vanilla 1971
Night of the Living Dead 1968

1940s

"I'm seen as a genre guy. I've made several nongenre films, but nobody went to see them."

BERNARDO BERTOLUCCI

Born: Bernardo Bertolucci, March 16, 1940 (Parma, Emilia-Romagna, Italy).

Directing style: Italian director of lavish epics and literary adaptations; breathtaking visuals; themes of sex and politics, often with a Marxist or Freudian twist; exploration of the human condition.

Top Takes...

The Dreamers 2003

Ten Minutes Older: The Cello 2002

Besieged 1998

Stealing Beauty 1996

Little Buddha 1993

The Sheltering Sky 1990

12 registi per 12 città 1989

The Last Emperor 1987 ★

L'addio a Enrico Berlinguer 1984

Tragedy of a Ridiculous Man 1981

La luna 1979 (Luna)

Novocento 1976 (1900)

Ultimo tango a Parigi 1972 ☆
(Last Tango in Paris)

La salute è malata 1971

Strategia del ragno 1970
   (The Spider's Stratagem)

Il conformista 1970 (The Conformist)

Partner 1968

Il canale 1966

Prima della rivoluzione 1964
   (Before the Revolution)

La commare secca 1962 (The Grim Reaper)

One of the most respected figures of Italian cinema, Bernardo Bertolucci is responsible for some of the most vibrant and provocative films the medium has ever seen. He remains, after 40 years, as controversial as he is revered.

Bertolucci began his career as a poet before gravitating toward film, assisting Pier Paolo Pasolini on his film *Accattone* (1961), before directing *La commare secca* (1962) (*The Grim Reaper*) and *Prima della rivoluzione* (1964) (*Before the Revolution*). His adaptation of Alberto Moravia's novel *Il conformista* (1970) (*The Conformist*) made Bertolucci the toast of the foreign cinema set. A highly stylized work, it is as well known for its striking design and astounding cinematography as it is for its themes of sexuality and violent fascism.

Bertolucci's reputation exploded with the release of the controversial *Ultimo tango a Parigi* (1972) (*Last Tango in Paris*), for which he received an Oscar nomination for Best Director. The film is notorious for its then relatively explicit sex scenes, but is also considered a masterpiece by many, its drama anchored by revelatory performances from stars Maria Schneider and Marlon Brando.

RIGHT: Stunning visuals enhance a scene from the unique thriller *The Conformist*.

The same good fortune did not shine upon the epic *Novecento* (1976) (*1900*), which focused on the lives of two boys and their flirtation with fascism and communism. The film was a commercial disappointment, but a decade later another epic, *The Last Emperor* (1987), won numerous awards, including an Oscar for Bertolucci. Since then, Bertolucci has chosen smaller films with intimate stories to tell, even if their themes and settings sometimes seem suited for epic treatment. *Little Buddha* (1993) was a surprisingly grounded take on Buddhist theology whereas *Stealing Beauty* (1996) and *Besieged* (1998) captured the subjects of lust and lost love from adolescent and embattled adult perspectives, respectively.

The Dreamers (2003) was perhaps Bertolucci's most personal film to date, as well as his most provocative in decades. It concerned an unusual love triangle composed of three film buffs, set against the Paris student revolts of 1968. **JK**

ABOVE: A scene from the lavish drama *The Last Emperor,* which won nine Oscars.

An Epic Movie

The Last Emperor (1987), a biopic about the life of Pu Yi, the last Emperor of China, was a huge hit for Bernardo Bertolucci.

- It was the first feature film allowed by the Chinese government to be shot within the Forbidden City.
- 19,000 extras were used in the film.
- The film's producer, Jeremy Thomas, singlehandedly raised $25 million to finance the film.
- Pu Yi's eldest brother Pu Chieh and other people from his life were brought in to act as advisers on the film.

PAUL COX

Born: Paulus Henriqus Benedictus Cox, April 16, 1940 (Venlo, Limburg, Netherlands).

Directing style: Award-winning auteur; recurring themes of hope, isolation, love, loss, and human survival; simple visual style with few special effects.

Top Takes...

Human Touch 2004
The Diaries of Vaslav Nijinsky 2001
Innocence 2000
Molokai: The Story of Father Damien 1999
Lust and Revenge 1996
Exile 1994
A Woman's Tale 1991
Golden Braid 1990
Island 1989
Vincent 1987
Cactus 1986
My First Wife 1984
Man of Flowers 1983
Lonely Hearts 1982
Illuminations 1976
The Island 1975

The Dutch-born director Paul Cox is a leading light of alternative, fiercely independent cinema in his adopted Australia. Dealing exclusively with the human condition, his low-budget movies feature ordinary, forgotten people facing up to the pressures of everyday life.

After attending art school, Cox took up photography and arrived in Australia in 1963 to attend Melbourne University. As a hobby he began making short films and documentaries. From the beginning his movies have stuck to a rigid template: he never auditions actors; scripts are left free for improvisation; and complicated production setups are avoided. It would be eleven years before he made his first feature, the drama *Illuminations* (1976). He went on to enjoy critical acclaim for his 1982 low-key romantic drama *Lonely Hearts*. The following year *Man of Flowers* (1983) flickered between fantasy and reality to tell the story of a rich eccentric, and in *My First Wife* (1984), John Hargreaves plays a self-centered musician whose marriage falls apart. Blindness was the theme of *Cactus* (1986), starring Isabelle Huppert, whereas *Vincent* (1987) ambitiously told the story of the painter van Gogh in an animated feature. In 1999, Cox broke from his traditional use of familiar players to employ an international cast—including Sam Neill, Derek Jacobi, and Peter O'Toole—for *Molokai: The Story of Father Damien*, the biopic of a priest devoted to lepers. The following year *Innocence*—a tale of two seventy-year-olds embarking on an affair—showed Cox had held fast to his desire not to opt for pat solutions. A stern critic of Hollywood fare, Cox has remained true to his humanist ideals and never compromised his vision of film as "the ideal way of expressing myself." **TE**

> "I have no system at all. I work totally on instinct, at random. I don't know anything."

JAMES L. BROOKS

Born: James L. Brooks, May 9, 1940 (North Bergen, New Jersey, U.S.).

Directing style: Prolific writer, producer, and director of comedies of manners and dramas on the big and small screen; strong characterizations within an ensemble cast.

For some filmmakers, TV serves only as a stepping stone to the silver screen. But for James L. Brooks, the two forms have always stood on equal tiers. He is a giant of both camps: having won 19 Prime Time Emmy awards and being one of only five directors who have won Oscars for Best Picture, Best Director, and Best Screenplay (Original/Adapted) for the same film.

Raised in New York, Brooks worked as a writer for CBS News in the late 1960s before heading over to the fiction-minded side of the TV world. His early successes included *The Mary Tyler Moore Show* (1970–1973) and *Rhoda* (1974–1975), which established his credentials as a TV writer and producer.

Brooks's first forays into film were tentative, beginning with *Starting Over* (1979). The movie was well received but hardly a smash. Not so the tearjerker *Terms of Endearment* (1983), which Brooks wrote, produced, and directed, and which won Best Picture at the Academy Awards as well as statues for actors Jack Nicholson and Shirley MacLaine, and Brooks himself for writing and directing. Brooks next returned to the big screen four years later with the popular *Broadcast News* (1987), another box-office hit that garnered seven Oscar nominations.

He continued working as a producer on such TV hits as *The Simpsons* (1989–2007), and feature films including *Big* (1988), in the meantime directing the ill-conceived musical *I'll Do Anything* (1994), a notorious flop. Yet its disastrous reception was nearly erased by the accolades that met his next film, *As Good as It Gets* (1997), which reunited Brooks with Nicholson, and earned Oscars for both the actor and his costar Helen Hunt. Following the hit-or-miss pattern that seems to mark his career, Brooks next wrote and directed the poorly received comedy drama *Spanglish* (2004). **JK**

Top Takes...

Spanglish 2004
As Good as It Gets 1997
Broadcast News 1987
***Terms of Endearment* 1983 ★**

> "I love it if comedy reflects real life . . . it's more reassuring that we'll get through."

1940s

CARLOS DIEGUES

Born: Carlos Diégues, May 19, 1940 (Maceió, Alagoas, Brazil).

Directing style: Vanguard director of Brazil's Cinema Novo movement; maker of poetic dramas and witty comedies; tackles historical themes such as slavery.

Top Takes...

O Maior Amor do Mundo 2006
  (*The Greatest Love of All*)
Deus É Brasileiro 2003 (*God is Brazilian*)
Orfeu 1999
Dias Melhores Virão 1989 (*Better Days Ahead*)
Un Trem para as Estrelas 1987
Quilombo 1984
Bye Bye Brasil 1979
Chuvas de Verão 1978 (*Summer Showers*)
Xica da Silva 1976
Joana Francesa 1975
Quando o Carnaval Chegar 1972
  (*When Carnival Comes*)
Os Herdeiros 1970 (*The Heirs*)
A Grande Cidade 1966 (*The Big City*)
Ganga Zumba 1963

Carlos Diegues is one of the key directors of the Brazilian Cinema Novo, and by the end of the early 1970s, he was the most popular director of the movement.

Ganga Zumba (1963), Diegues's first feature film, deals with the neglected history of slavery in Brazil and reevaluates Afro-Brazilian culture. The film tells the story of a slave revolt on a sugar-cane plantation in 1641 and the flight to Palmares—a *quilombo*, or free community, established by runaway slaves.

A Grande Cidade (1966) (*The Big City*) focuses on the life of Rio de Janeiro's poor immigrants from rural Brazil. It is Diegues's formally most radical film, in which he breaks with illusion, already apparent in the first take: *The Big City* begins with a postcard view of modern Rio de Janeiro, ironically combined with a seventeenth-century quotation about the beauty of the place. *Os Herdeiros* (1970) (*The Heirs*), meanwhile, tells the story of a bourgeois family from 1930 to 1964, and focuses on the political and cultural history of that period.

Quando o Carnaval Chegar (1972) (*When Carnival Comes*) follows the tradition of the *chanchada*, a Brazilian musical comedy, and marks the beginning of Diegues's more commercial productions, although he still maintained his criticism of topics such as slavery, which he turned to once more in *Quilombo* (1984). *Bye Bye Brasil* (1979) is an allegorical road movie leading through all of Brazil. In 1999, Diegues filmed *Orfeu*, a remake of Marcel Camus's classic *Orfeu Negro* (1959). In the original French film, Rio de Janeiro's *favelas* serve as a picturesque background for the Greek myth, whereas *Orfeu* shows the social and political dimensions of life in the slums. *Deus É Brasileiro* (2003) (*God is Brazilian*) is a witty comedy about God taking a journey through Brazil. **PS**

"*Xica* is too intelligent and too exotic to be boring."
—*New York Times*

ABBAS KIAROSTAMI

Born: Abbas Kiarostami, June 22, 1940 (Teheran, Iran).

Directing style: Iconic independent Iranian filmmaker; documentaries and neorealist dramas; poetic, allegorical storytelling; frequent child protagonists; use of stationary cameras; exploration of the nature of film as fiction.

At the end of the 1990s, an international poll of influential critics and curators named Abbas Kiarostami that decade's most important filmmaker—no mean feat for a self-taught cineaste whose earliest movies were shorts made for Iran's Centre for the Intellectual Development of Children and Young Adults. But those films display breathtaking originality in their fresh, free-wheeling approach to storytelling and in their upfront, witty use of cinematic form, in which Kiarostami plays with sound, image, dramatic structure, and point of view to draw attention to the films' status as manipulative artifice.

Only at the end of the 1980s did Kiarostami begin to garner the international acclaim he deserved. His award-winning *Khane-ye doust kodjast?* (1987) (*Where Is the Friend's Home?*) was the turning point, but it was *Nema-ye Nazdik* (1990) (*Close Up*) and *Zendegi va digar hich* (1991) that displayed the full sophistication and complexity of Kiarostami's methods. Not only was Kiarostami taking events from real life and turning them into urgent, poetic, emotionally affecting fables, he was also offering reflections on the nature of the films he was making in particular and on the cinematic medium in general.

Digital technology enabled greater experimentation. *Ten* (2002) is a moving, relevant, and richly resonant look at the plight of women in Iran. It was shot wholly within the confines of a car, using two digital cameras fixed to the dashboard, and pointed at the driver and her passengers. *Five Dedicated to Ozu* (2003) was very experimental, consisting of five seemingly single-shot shorts filmed by the Caspian Sea. It is minimalist, metaphorical, and nearly abstract, but also witty, lyrical, and imbued—as is all of Kiarostami's work—with a profound, contemplative love of life's mysteries. **GA**

Top Takes...

Five Dedicated to Ozu 2003
Ten 2002
ABC Africa 2001
Bad ma ra khahad bord 1999
 (*The Wind Will Carry Us*)
Ta'm e gilass 1997 (*A Taste of Cherry*)
Lumière et compagnie 1995
Zire darakhatan seyton 1994
 (*Through the Olive Trees*)
Zendegi va digar hich 1991
Nema-ye Nazdik 1990 (*Close Up*)
Khane-ye doust kodjast? 1987
 (*Where Is the Friend's Home?*)
Hamsarayan 1982 (*The Chorus*)
Be Tartib ya Bedoun-e Tartib 1981
 (*Orderly or Unorderly*)
Mossafer 1974 (*The Traveler*)

1940s

"Good cinema is what we can believe and bad cinema is what we can't believe."

VICTOR ERICE

Born: Victor Erice Aras, June 30, 1940 (Karrantza, Vizcaya, País Vasco, Spain).

Directing style: Spanish director of lyrical dramas and documentaries; painterly use of color; meditative explorations of transience and the nature of cinema; the relationship between creativity and time.

Top Takes…

La morte rouge 2006

Ten Minutes Older: The Trumpet 2002

El sol del membrillo 1992
  (*Quince Tree of the Sun*)

El sur 1983

El espíritu de la colmena 1973
  (*The Spirit of the Beehive*)

Los sesafios 1970 (*The Challenges*)

Entre vias 1966

Los dias perdidos 1963

Páginas de un diario perdido 1962

En la terraza 1961 (*On the Terrace*)

Although Victor Erice has completed few films, he is one of the most distinctive artists working in the medium today. A former critic, he won international acclaim with his first feature *El espíritu de la colmena* (1973) (*The Spirit of the Beehive*), an elliptical, densely allusive work about a small girl growing up in rural Spain just after the Civil War. Depicting Franco's divided nation as blighted by memories and dashed dreams too painful to be mentioned, Erice seeks hope in the child's innocent mind. A subtle exploration of fear, inertia, and notions of monstrosity, the film has the meticulous beauty of a painting by Diego Velázquez or Francisco de Zurbarán.

A decade passed before the release of Erice's next feature, *El sur* (1983). It was as fine as *El espíritu de la colmena*, this time looking at life in northern Spain during the 1950s, through the eyes of a teenage girl. Again, Erice captures a moment in time through painterly use of color, light, and movement.

The relationship between creativity and time was the subject of *El sol del membrillo* (1992) (*Quince Tree of the Sun*), a documentary featuring the Hyperrealist artist Antonio López García as he paints a tree in his Madrid garden; so painstaking are his attempts to represent reality that time takes its inevitable toll on the fruit, and he has to start a second painting. A wise, witty meditation on transience, perfectionism, and pragmatism, the film, which is partly a self-portrait and essay on cinema, is another Erice masterpiece. Sadly, several Erice projects have never been filmed. Recently, however, he has turned to digital filmmaking with *La morte rouge* (2006), a half-hour foray into autobiographical reminiscence, as richly poetic a contemplation on life, death, and art as anything else he has made. **GA**

> "… a tribute to the beauty and mutability of nature."—On *Quince Tree of the Sun, New York Times*

BRUCE BERESFORD

Born: Bruce Beresford, August 16, 1940 (Sydney, New South Wales, Australia).

Directing style: Prolific Australian New Wave director of satirical comedies and period dramas; often exploration of sexual relationships, history, race, and nationality.

In the early 1970s, Australia's film industry was still only in its earliest stages, but director Bruce Beresford was there to help usher in a new era of antipodean moviemaking.

After studying at Sydney University, Beresford traveled to Britain where he found work producing documentaries for the British Film Institute production board. He returned to Australia in 1971 and quickly set to work writing and directing his first features—*The Adventures of Barry McKenzie* (1972) and *Barry McKenzie Holds His Own* (1974), both starring Australian icons Barry Crocker and Barry Humphries.

By the early 1980s, Beresford's reputation had spread beyond his native shores, in no small part due to the impact of *'Breaker' Morant* (1980), a rousing, provocative take on the politically muddled aftermath of Australia's involvement in the Boer War. The film was shown at the Cannes Film Festival where it was nominated for a number of awards.

Beresford used the acclaim to gain entrée into Hollywood, directing the well-received *Tender Mercies* (1983), starring Robert Duvall, before entering into an erratic period of hits and misses, topped at the end of the decade by his across-the-board success with *Driving Miss Daisy* (1989). Based on a play by Alfred Uhry, the critically acclaimed drama won four Academy Awards, including Best Picture and Best Actress for star Jessica Tandy at the age of eighty-one.

Yet the 1990s found Beresford struggling once again with a series of mostly forgettable flops and failures. The female prisoner-of-war film *Paradise Road* (1997) was a rare artistic success, and the crowd-pleasing feminist revenge thriller *Double Jeopardy* (1999) was a box-office hit despite taking a critical drubbing. **JK**

Top Takes…

The Contract 2006
Evelyn 2002
Bride of the Wind 2001
Double Jeopardy 1999
Paradise Road 1997
Last Dance 1996
A Good Man in Africa 1994
Silent Fall 1994
Black Robe 1991
Driving Miss Daisy 1989
***Tender Mercies* 1983** ☆
'Breaker' Morant 1980
Money Matters 1978
Don's Party 1976
Barry McKenzie Holds His Own 1974
The Adventures of Barry McKenzie 1972

> "It's a new kind of war … a new war for a new century."
> —Harry Morant, *'Breaker' Morant*

1940s

DARIO ARGENTO

Born: Dario Argento, September 7, 1940 (Rome, Italy).

Directing style: Leading Italian director of heart-stopping horror movies and mystery thrillers; acts as narrator in his films; vibrant color; painterly visuals; inventive use of wild music.

Top Takes...

Il cartaio 2004 (*The Card Player*)
Non ho sonno 2001 (*Sleepless*)
Il fantasma dell'opera 1998
   (*The Phantom of the Opera*)
La sindrome di Stendhal 1996
   (*The Stendhal Syndrome*)
Due occhi diabolici 1990 (*Two Evil Eyes*)
Opera 1987
Phenomena 1984 (*Creepers*)
Tenebre 1982 (*Unsane*)
Inferno 1980
Suspiria 1977
Profondo rosso 1975 (*The Deep Red*)
Le cinque giornate 1973 (*The Five Days*)
L'uccello dalle piume di cristallo 1970
   (*The Bird with the Crystal Plumage*)

Dubbed "The Italian Hitchcock" by U.S. critics trying to wrestle his baroque, dreamlike thrillers into a familiar niche, Dario Argento grew up in the industry. His father, Salvatore Argento, produced his early movies and his younger brother, Claudio Argento, produced many later ones. Argento began his career as a critic and graduated to screenplays, contributing to Italian director Sergio Leone's classic Western *C'era una volta il West* (1968) (*Once Upon a Time in the West*) and a mix of war films, crime movies, and sex comedies.

An admirer of pioneering horror stylist Mario Bava, who contributed effects to Argento's horror fantasy *Inferno* (1980), Argento made his directing debut with *L'uccello dalle piume di cristallo* (1970) (*The Bird with the Crystal Plumage*). An accomplished mystery characterized by elaborate murder sequences, it set the course for his career. Excepting the darkly comic historical outing *Le cinque giornate* (1973) (*The Five Days*), he has never strayed from thrillers, although *Suspiria* (1977) and *Inferno*—hallucinatory haunted-house films deeply indebted to eighteenth-century writer Thomas de Quincey's drug-induced visions—have added supernatural elements to the mix. Argento's films are characterized by bold use of color, massive close-ups, flamboyant camera movement, and insinuating scores—many made by his longtime collaborator Claudio Simonetti's band Goblin. He has also collaborated with his partner, actress and screenwriter Daria Nicolodi, on films such as *Tenebre* (1982) (*Unsane*) and *Opera* (1987). Argento is more than an "Italian Hitchcock:" he brings a contemporary Italian sensibility to the thriller genre, and his heart-stopping horror movies, with their dreamlike sequences and inventive use of music, make him an original. **MM**

"*The Deep Red* is my favorite movie. [Marcus] is very much based on my own personality."

RIGHT: Cristina Marsillach is gagged and bound in Argento's horrifying *Opera*.

BRIAN DE PALMA

Born: Brian Russell De Palma, September 11, 1940 (Newark, New Jersey, U.S.).

Directing style: Premier maker of gangster movies and live-action films; homages to Sir Alfred Hitchcock; master of filmic techniques to induce spine-tingling suspense.

Top Takes...

RIGHT: Sissy Spacek feels trapped as the mousy but gifted title character in *Carrie*.

Brian De Palma has often been criticized for imitating Sir Alfred Hitchcock but, for modern audiences, De Palma is the superior master of suspense. His best cinematic moments—often grand, slow-moving vistas of tension and violence—are some of the most memorable in film history.

De Palma's early films were not very slick, although *Greetings* (1968) and *Hi, Mom!* (1970) were indie hits. They were intentionally sloppy-looking pictures, reflecting their low budgets and the counter-culture influences of the time. But it was not until he demonstrated his Hitchcock affection, with the use of split screen in *Sisters* (1973) and *Phantom of the Paradise* (1974), that De Palma began to shine.

What really grabbed audiences was his adaptation of Stephen King's *Carrie* (1976). His use of slow-motion, split-screen editing, close-ups, music, and isolated sounds during the prom sequence in *Carrie* demonstrated how he could combine all these filmic elements and generate suspense. He perfected this technique in many of his later scripted films, most notably *Dressed to Kill* (1980), *Blow Out* (1981), and *Femme Fatale* (2002), all of which feature plentiful suspense-driven set

1940s

pieces. Even the much-criticized *Mission To Mars* (2000) features the virtuoso meteorites scene that is as mesmerizing as the staircase sequence in *The Untouchables* (1987).

It is when De Palma moves into gangster movies and action films that his talents shine brightest. He is also aided when he can tap into scriptwriting talent, such as that of Oliver Stone in *Scarface* (1983), David Mamet in *The Untouchables*, and David Koepp in *Carlito's Way* (1993) and *Mission: Impossible* (1996). The results of such collaborations have created iconic movie moments. Who can forget the Cuban immigrant turned Mafioso played by Al Pacino snorting from a cocaine mountain in *Scarface*? Or Robert De Niro as mob boss Al Capone meting out punishment in *The Untouchables*? Or Tom Cruise as the *Mission: Impossible* secret agent who can hover above a floor suspended by, it seems, a mere thread? These are the moments that De Palma is not just good at—he is par excellence. **DW**

ABOVE: Al Pacino stars as a paranoid drug dealer in the crime drama *Scarface*.

Kings of Suspense

The first of Stephen King's novels to be adapted for a movie, *Carrie* helped forge Brian De Palma's reputation for spine-tingling suspense.

- For the dizzying prom sequence, William Katt and Sissy Spacek were placed on a revolving platform, while the camera dollied in the opposite direction.

- The school is named Bates High—a reference to Norman Bates in *Psycho*.

- The "pig's blood" dropped on Sissy Spacek was karo syrup with food coloring. She had to be hosed down when it became gluey under the lights.

PANTELIS VOULGARIS

Born: Pantelis Voulgaris, October 2, 1940 (Athens, Greece).

Directing style: Greek director of historical dramas and romantic melodramas; themes examine everyday life and personal sacrifice under a totalitarian regime; emphasis on emotional lives of characters.

Top Takes...

Nyfes 2004 (*Brides*)

Ola einai dromos 1998 (*It's a Long Road*)

Acropol 1995

Isiches meres tou Avgoustou 1991
(*Quiet Days in August*)

I Fanella Me To 9 1988

Petrina Chronia 1985 (*Stone Years*)

Eleytherios Venizelos: 1910–1927 1980

Haroumeni Imera 1976 (*Happy Day*)

O megalos erotikos 1973
(*The Great Love Songs*)

To proxenio tis Annas 1972
(*The Engagement of Anna*)

Jimis o tigris 1966

Pantelis Voulgaris studied at Stavrakou Film School and worked as an assistant director before making his debut with the short *Jimis o tigris* (1966). His first feature was set in 1970s Athens, *To proxenio tis Annas* (1972) (*The Engagement of Anna*). It wryly observes the fortunes of a servant girl and the matchmaking efforts of her employers against the stifling backdrop of Athenian life and mores. It brought Voulgaris international plaudits at a time when his country was culturally isolated. But this was the era of the Greek military junta, and the political climate forced Voulgaris into exile for six months in 1973.

After he returned to Greece he made *Haroumeni Imera* (1976) (*Happy Day*), an Orwellian allegory about political prisoners detained in a concentration camp. He continued his examination of Greek politics with the historical drama *Eleftherios Venizelos: 1910–1927* (1980), and again in *Petrina Chronia* (1985) (*Stone Years*). The latter was based on true life and relates the love story of two communists during the Greek Civil War. The melodrama of the couple's fight against the authorities, life in prison, and determination to hold on to love again won Voulgaris awards at the Venice Film Festival. His next film, *I Fanella Me To 9* (1988), saw Voulgaris head for the soccer pitch in what has become a Greek classic examining the nature of power. It charts the efforts of a soccer player to reach the major league, and what happens when he hits the big time. *Isyhes meres tou Avgoustou* (1991) (*Quiet Days in August*) follows the lives of three individuals, and tackles the themes of isolation and communication in city life. Despite the zigzagging arc of Voulgaris's subject matter, what unites his oeuvre is his capacity to depict the emotional lives of his characters within their sociohistoric context. **CK**

"The reason we keep making films is because we feel that the next one will be even better."

TERRY GILLIAM

Born: Terence Vance Gilliam, November 22, 1940 (Minneapolis, Minnesota, U.S.).

Directing style: Legendary Monty Python member turned director; fantastical sets; surreal storylines; wacky, dark humor; characters often in a struggle against authority.

Born in Minnesota, Gilliam landed a job at *Help!* magazine, where he met future Monty Python costar John Cleese. Moving to England, he worked with Eric Idle, Terry Jones, and Michael Palin, whom he would soon join to found *Monty Python's Flying Circus* (1969–1974). Gilliam's contributions were largely behind the scenes, his distinctive cartoons offering yet another degree of playful anarchy to the production.

Gilliam's feature debut, *Monty Python and the Holy Grail* (1975) found the troupe in fine form even as it wound down. It was followed by Gilliam's first solo credit, *Jabberwocky* (1977), based on the Lewis Carroll poem, but it was the oddball hit *Time Bandits* (1981), about a group of time-traveling dwarves, that indicated Gilliam would never be at a loss for fresh ideas.

Following his final *Python* foray, *The Meaning of Life* (1983), Gilliam directed *Brazil* (1985), an ingenious satire set in a dystopian, bureaucratic future. Despite conflict with the studio, the film won numerous awards from Gilliam's supportive fans in the critical community. The ambitious *The Adventures of Baron Munchausen* (1988) was a notorious failure, though *The Fisher King* (1991) and *Twelve Monkeys* (1995) showed Gilliam could be commercial and creatively viable when he really wanted to, but those two movies were his last real flirtation with the mainstream.

Fear and Loathing in Las Vegas (1998) was a controversial adaptation of Hunter S. Thompson's book and an aborted attempt at his dream project, *The Man Who Killed Don Quixote*, went nowhere. *The Brothers Grimm* (2005) seemed like another stab at commercial success, but lacked the spark that made Gilliam's other movies so special. Critics were divided over *Tideland* (2005) and it failed to land wide distribution. **JK**

Top Takes…

Tideland 2005
The Brothers Grimm 2005
Fear and Loathing in Las Vegas 1998
Twelve Monkeys 1995
The Fisher King 1991
The Adventures of Baron Munchausen 1988
Brazil 1985
The Meaning of Life 1983
Time Bandits 1981
Jabberwocky 1977
Monty Python and the Holy Grail 1975
Storytime 1968

1940s

"There's a side of me that always fell for manic things, frenzied . . . performances."

HAYAO MIYAZAKI

Born: Hayao Miyazaki, January 5, 1941 (Tokyo, Japan).

Directing style: Leading Japanese director of animations; often environmental and magical themes; depicts youthful characters resolving a moral dilemma; stunning hand-drawn visuals.

Top Takes...

Mizugumo monmon 2006

Hauru no ugoku shiro 2004
(Howl's Moving Castle)

Koro no dai-sanpo 2002

Mei to Koneko basu 2002
(Mei and the Kitten Bus)

Sen to Chihiro no kamikakushi 2001
(Spirited Away)

Mononoke-hime 1997 (Princess Mononoke)

Kurenai no buta 1992 (Porco Rosso)

Majo no takkyûbin 1989 (Kiki's Delivery Service)

Tonari no Totoro 1988 (My Neighbor Totoro)

Tenkû no shiro Rapyuta 1986 (Castle in the Sky)

Kaze no tani no Naushika 1984
(Nausicaä of the Valley of the Winds)

Rupan sansei: Kariosutoro no shiro 1979
(Arsene Lupin and the Castle of Cagliostro)

Hayao Miyazaki is often called "The Japanese Walt Disney," but whether in style, substance, or sensibility, that myopic comparison ends beyond the two directors' shared vocation of animation. In common with many animators, Miyazaki began work on the sidelines, assisting in a series of animated TV shows and films, before his first feature, *Rupan sansei: Kariosutoro no shiro* (1979) (*Arsene Lupin and the Castle of Cagliostro*). He soon crossed paths with director Isao Takahata, and, following the success of his next feature *Kaze no tani no Naushika* (1984) (*Nausicaä of the Valley of the Winds*), the two would cofound Studio Ghibli, an outlet for directors to create animated films of both a personal and independent nature.

Nausicaä of the Valley of the Winds introduced themes that would run through most of Miyazaki's pictures, including childhood fantasy and environmental messages. Each film has benefited greatly from his impeccable craftsmanship and dedication to traditional animation. The Disney studios noted these achievements and quickly snatched several of Miyazaki's films for distribution, dubbing the Japanese dialogue with name actors but trying to remain true to Miyazaki's vision at the same time. After all, the director seemed to be on the right track. *Mononoke-hime* (1997) (*Princess Mononoke*) was a huge international success and a breakthrough film for Miyazaki, garnering him more acclaim than ever before. It set the stage for the even greater success of *Sen to Chihiro no kamikakushi* (2001) (*Spirited Away*), which won the freshly minted Oscar for Best Animated Feature, and became the highest-grossing movie of all time in Japan. After threatening retirement, Miyazaki directed *Hauru no ugoku shiro* (2004) (*Howl's Moving Castle*), and is still at work. **JK**

"... children's souls are the inheritors of historical memory from previous generations."

MICHAEL APTED

Born: Michael Apted, February 10, 1941 (Aylesbury, Buckinghamshire, England).

Directing style: British director of documentaries and Hollywood dramas; strong female protagonists, including the first James Bond female villain; often themes tackle an ethical, social, or political issue.

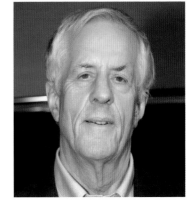

Michael Apted worked at Granada Television in 1964, where he was a researcher on *Seven Up!* (1964), a documentary examining the lives of British seven-year-olds from various socioeconomic backgrounds for Granada's *World in Action* series. The program was a success, and seven years later Apted returned to direct *7 Plus Seven* (1970), catching up with the subjects at age fourteen, and he has stayed with the series as director for further installments. Although Apted has had a wide-ranging career in the British and U.S. film industry, with box-office successes to his credit, this series of documentaries, which stands as a valuable—and sometimes hideous—social document, may stand as his most significant work.

Apted made his film debut with *The Triple Echo* (1972), from H. E. Bates's novel. In the 1970s, he seesawed between quality TV such as the Film 4 production *P'tang, Yang, Kipperbang* (1982), and interesting British films such as *Stardust* (1974), an evocative, barbed portrait of a pop star who is cracking up through a combination of drugs, excess, and pretension.

Always professional, Apted moved into international movies, specializing in strong leading ladies who have won Academy Award nominations for their efforts: Sissy Spacek as Loretta Lynn in *Coal Miner's Daughter* (1980), Sigourney Weaver as Dian Fossey in *Gorillas in The Mist: The Story of Dian Fossey* (1988), and Jodie Foster as a wild child in *Nell* (1994). He transferred his strength as a women's director to *The World Is Not Enough* (1999), the first of the James Bond franchise to have a female character as the arch villain.

Apted has also made films with a strong ethical bias, such as the political thriller *Gorky Park* (1983), which deals with police corruption in the former Soviet Union. **KN**

Top Takes...

Amazing Grace 2006
Lipstick 2002
Enough 2002
Married in America 2002
Enigma 2001
The World Is Not Enough 1999
Me & Isaac Newton 1999
Nell 1994
Gorillas in The Mist: The Story of Dian Fossey 1988
Gorky Park 1983
P'tang, Yang, Kipperbang 1982
Coal Miner's Daughter 1980
Stardust 1974
The Triple Echo 1972
7 Plus Seven 1970

> "Exactly, and me a Siberian. I'm used to the cold."
>
> —Irina Asanova, *Gorky Park*

ADRIAN LYNE

Born: Adrian Lyne, March 4, 1941 (Peterborough, Cambridgeshire, England).

Directing style: English director of sexually provocative dramas; themes of marital infidelity, obsession, desire, and the nature of love; erotically charged atmosphere.

Top Takes…

Unfaithful 2002
Lolita 1997
Jacob's Ladder 1990
Fatal Attraction 1987 ☆
9½ Weeks 1985
Flashdance 1983
Foxes 1980
Mr. Smith 1976

Adrian Lyne is part of a prominent wave of directors that emerged from the British advertising industry of the 1970s. His films have a glossy veneer, helping to define the commercial aesthetic of 1980s Hollywood. Moreover, they have often tackled sexually provocative themes that tap into the contemporary sexual zeitgeist.

The teen drama *Foxes* (1980) achieved moderate success, but it was with *Flashdance* (1983) that Lyne established a commercial foothold, utilizing modish pop-video stylistics in service of its female underdog narrative. It is perhaps more notable as a template for the methods of its production team: Don Simpson and Jerry Bruckheimer.

Lyne's *9½ Weeks* (1985) has become a cultural benchmark for designer erotica that drew in the crowds, but the film itself is a tepid affair. Reducing a supposedly sadomasochistic relationship to a process of tease and suggestion, any exploration of the dual dynamic of *eros* and *Thanatos* is drowned in a flood of self-conscious, artfully designed poses. Turning again to sexual obsession, *Fatal Attraction* (1987) was another major hit for Lyne, although it was manipulative in its punishment of female sexual independence. Read widely as a metaphor for the dangers of promiscuity in the AIDS era, the film is ruthless in its attack upon its female monster. His *Jacob's Ladder* (1990) is a highly effective supernatural chiller, however, *Indecent Proposal* (1993) was a frankly idiotic reprise of all of Lyne's worst directorial instincts, and his adaptation of Nabokov's *Lolita* (1997) is stymied by a soft-focus sheen. Fortunately, *Unfaithful* (2002) saw Lyne return successfully to the arena of modern sexuality in its evocation of infidelity and jealousy. **NJ**

> "I'll pity you … I'll pity you. I'll pity you because you're sick."
>
> —Dan Gallagher, *Fatal Attraction*

WOLFGANG PETERSEN

Born: Wolfgang Petersen, March 14, 1941 (Emden, Lower Saxony, Germany).

Directing style: German director of big-budget, star-studded action films and suspense-packed thrillers; abundant special effects; fast-paced action; intelligent scripts; themes about fears of terrorism and disaster.

Despite an extensive Hollywood career taking in major hits and mammoth budgets, it is for his TV offerings that Wolfgang Petersen is best remembered. His 16mm adaptation of Alexander Ziegler's autobiographical novel of pederastic love, *Die Konsequenz* (1977) (*The Consequence*), caused a stir when it was first broadcast nationwide in Germany—and the local Bavarian network turned off the transmitters rather than broadcast it. His World War II German submarine TV drama was an international success in its feature-length version, *Das Boot* (1983) (*The Boat*), winning two Academy Award nominations.

After *The Boat*, Petersen handled the international fantasy *Die Unendliche Geschichte* (1984) (*The Neverending Story*), the German-shot, U.S.-backed science-fiction film *Enemy Mine* (1985), and then went to the United States for the tricky amnesia thriller *Shattered* (1991).

Petersen's first critical and commercial Hollywood success was *In the Line of Fire* (1993), a picture about a professional hired gunman, with the presidential bodyguard played by Clint Eastwood. The film was a hit, with Eastwood striking different types of sparks off would-be assassin John Malkovich and heroine Rene Russo. Having proved himself a capable pair of hands, Petersen has been given more big stars to work with, including Dustin Hoffman, Harrison Ford, George Clooney, and Brad Pitt, as well as sizable special-effects budgets. He has made expansive films about small, desperate groups isolated by the elements and hostile activity. This has led to the viral techno-thriller *Outbreak* (1995), the U.S. president hostage movie *Air Force One* (1997), the working-class disaster movie *The Perfect Storm* (2000), and the remake *Poseidon* (2006). **KN**

Top Takes...

Poseidon 2006

Troy 2004

The Perfect Storm 2000

Air Force One 1997

Outbreak 1995

In the Line of Fire 1993

Shattered 1991

Enemy Mine 1985

Die Unendliche Geschichte 1984
  (*The Neverending Story*)

Das Boot 1983 (The Boat) ☆

Schwarz und weiss wie Tage und Nächte 1978

Die Konsequenz 1977 (*The Consequence*)

Einer von uns beiden 1974 (*One or the Other*)

Ich werde dich toten, Wolf 1971
  (*I Will Kill You, Wolf*)

"Look at these new heroes. All wind and smoke."

—Captain, *The Boat*

1940s

BERTRAND TAVERNIER

Born: Bertrand Tavernier, April 25, 1941 (Lyon, Rhône, France).

Directing style: Versatile French director across an extensive range of genres; themes of family relationships and ideological issues, informed by left-wing political view; ironic humor.

Top Takes...

Holy Lola 2004
Laissez-passer 2002 (*Safe Conduct*)
Ça commence aujourd'hui 1999
   (*It All Starts Today*)
L'appât 1995 (*Fresh Bit*)
Daddy Nostalgie 1990 (*Daddy Nostalgia*)
'Round Midnight 1986
Un dimanche à la campagne 1984
   (*A Sunday in the Country*)
Phlippe Soupault 1982
Coup de torchon 1981 (*Clean Slate*)
La mort en direct 1980 (*Deathwatch*)
Des enfants gâtés 1977 (*Spoiled Children*)
Le juge et l'assassin 1976
   (*The Judge and the Assassin*)
L'horloger de Saint Paul 1974
   (*The Clockmaker of St. Paul*)

"I want to deal with social and political issues . . . they are organic to the jobs of people."

RIGHT: Dexter Gordon looks the worse for wear with his tenor sax in *'Round Midnight*.

Bertrand Tavernier started directing in the early 1970s, midway between the French New Wave and the Cinéma du Look, yet he has little in common with either group. His extensive output covers a range of genres, but common to them all is an alert intelligence and a refusal to patronize his audience.

Tavernier signaled his indifference to cinematic fashion by having the script of his first feature—*L'horloger de Saint Paul* (1974) (*The Clockmaker of St. Paul*)—written by Jean Aurenche and Pierre Bost, a veteran team whose work had been dismissively trashed by François Truffaut and the French New Wave. The Georges Simenon adaptation provided a political dimension that was lacking in the original novel.

All of Tavernier's films have been informed by his leftist politics, including the film noir *Coup de torchon* (1981) (*Clean Slate*), which skillfully transposed a grungy Jim Thompson novel to French colonial Africa. Yet it is family relationships and the ravages of time that most often figure in Tavernier's work. *Un dimanche à la campagne* (1984) (*A Sunday in the Country*) subtly explores the tensions between an aging Impressionist painter and his extended family. In *Daddy Nostalgie* (1990) (*Daddy Nostalgia*), a man nearing death attempts a reconciliation with his daughter. The director's most notable international success is *'Round Midnight* (1986), which won Dexter Gordon an Oscar nomination for Best Actor, in what was seen as a depiction of a musician who was a mixture of himself, Lester Young, and Bud Powell.

Tavernier's films, unsentimental and shrewd, never offering easy solutions to the complexity of life, are in danger of being undervalued, but their honesty, ironic humor, and clear-eyed intelligence deserve wider exposure. **PK**

STEPHEN FREARS

Born: Stephen Arthur Frears, June 20, 1941 (Leicester, England).

Directing style: Versatile English director across a range of genres, in cinema and TV, in the United States and Britain; consistently captures the national mood and concerns of the moment; wry humor.

Top Takes…

For most of his career, Stephen Frears has straddled several worlds: British and U.S. films, big and low budget, cinema and TV, and any number of different genres. Even more remarkably, he seems to be at home in all of them. His breakthrough film about an Asian guy and his white male lover set in a laundromat, *My Beautiful Laundrette* (1985), is utterly British in its tone, its politics, and its use of South London locations. Yet his Jim Thompson adaptation, the twisty thriller *The Grifters* (1990), never feels less than authentically American.

Frears learned his craft at London's Royal Court Theatre, and in TV, working with Lindsay Anderson and Karel Reisz. His film debut, *Gumshoe* (1971), a loving pastiche of private-eye movies set in Liverpool, was a hit with the critics but not the box office. The same went for a tougher thriller, *The Hit* (1984). *My Beautiful Laundrette* and its follow-up, *Sammy and Rosie Get Laid* (1987), both scripted by Hanif Kureishi, attracted some right-wing bile, which did not prevent Frears from securing his first international hit, the erotic drama *Dangerous Liaisons* (1988).

Since then Frears has continued his unpredictable and varied career, taking in a Western, *The Hi-Lo Country* (1998); a surprisingly effective transposition of Nick Hornby's North London novel, *High Fidelity* (2000), to Chicago; a hard-hitting view of immigrant life in London, *Dirty Pretty Things* (2002); and a period comedy drama set in a World War II London strip joint, *Mrs. Henderson Presents* (2005). Frears's hit *The Queen* (2006), which won an Oscar for Helen Mirren, was incisively scripted by Peter Morgan. It centers on the relationship between the British monarch and Prime Minister Tony Blair during the week following the death of Diana, Princess of Wales, in 1997. **PK**

> "… Prime Minister to be. I haven't asked him yet."
>
> —HM Queen Elizabeth II, *The Queen*

1940s

DENYS ARCAND

Born: Denys Arcand, June 25, 1941 (Deschambault, Québec, Canada).

Directing style: French-Canadian filmmaker of documentaries, comedies, and dramas; exploration of moral issues; themes regarding the nature of sexual and national politics.

The career of Denys Arcand has traced a roller-coaster pattern, swooping from the depths of official disfavor to the heights of international acclaim, and down again to the doldrums of neglect. He began as a maker of short documentaries; but even into such anodyne subjects as *Volleyball* (1966) and *Parcs atlantiques* (1967) (*Atlantic Parks*), Arcand contrived to slip elements of his skepticism and pessimistic humor. Trouble erupted over his first feature-length documentary, *On est au coton* (1976) (*Cotton Mill, Treadmill*), an exposé of the working conditions in Québec's textile industry. The National Film Board, which had financed the film, suppressed it until 1976.

Undeterred, Arcand moved into features. *Réjeanne Padovani* (1973) and *Gina* (1975), which used the thriller format to explore questions of sexual and national politics, were well received. But Arcand was still the object of official suspicion and was reduced to directing episodes of TV miniseries.

He bounced back with his international breakthrough, *Le déclin de l'empire américain* (1986) (*The Decline of the American Empire*), a witty, sardonic comedy about sex and alienation. It was nominated for a Best Foreign Language Film Oscar, as was the passionately ironic fable *Jésus de Montréal* (1989) (*Jesus of Montréal*). Yet his first English-language film, *Love & Human Remains* (1993), flopped badly, and *Joyeux Calvaire* (1996) and *Stardom* (2000) failed to impress. Unexpectedly, Arcand re-emerged into the spotlight with *Les invasions barbares* (2003) (*The Barbarian Invasions*), a follow-up to *The Decline of the American Empire* that featured the same characters at a later stage of their lives. Ironic, erudite, elegiac, and emotionally generous, it won the Best Foreign Language Film Oscar. Arcand, it seems, is back in form. **PK**

Top Takes...

Les invasions barbares 2003
  (*The Barbarian Invasions*)
Stardom 2000
Joyeux Calvaire 1996
  (*Poverty and Other Delights*)
Love & Human Remains 1993
Jésus de Montréal 1989 (*Jesus of Montreal*)
Le déclin de l'empire américain 1986
  (*The Decline of the American Empire*)
Confort et l'indifférence 1982
  (*Comfort and Indifference*)
On est au coton 1976 (*Cotton Mill, Treadmill*)
Gina 1975
Réjeanne Padovani 1973
Parcs atlantiques 1967 (*Atlantic Parks*)
Volleyball 1966
Champlain 1964

> "I'm the worst possible writer. I have no method. I've never learned it."

1940s

KRZYSZTOF KIEŚLOWSKI

Born: Krzysztof Kieślowski, June 27, 1941 (Warsaw, Poland); died 1996 (Warsaw, Poland).

Directing style: Giant of the Polish "cinema of moral anxiety"; documentary maker; dramas of everyday life; examines the nature of prevailing ideologies.

Top Takes…

Trois couleurs: Rouge **1994** ☆
  (*Three Colors: Red*)

Trzy kolory: Bialy 1994 (*Three Colors: White*)

Trois couleurs: Bleu 1993 (*Three Colors: Blue*)

La double vie de Véronique 1991
  (*The Double Life of Veronique*)

Krótki film o milosci 1988
  (*A Short Film About Love*)

Krótki film o zabijaniu 1988
  (*A Short Film About Killing*)

Siedem dni w tygodniu 1988
  (*Seven Days a Week*)

Przypadek 1987 (*Blind Chance*)

Bez konca 1985 (*No End*)

Dworzec 1980 (*Railway Station*)

Gadajace glowy 1980 (*Talking Heads*)

Amator 1979 (*Camera Buff*)

Z punktu widzenia nocnego portiera 1978
  (*Night Porter's Point of View*)

Siedem kobiet w róznym wieku 1978
  (*Seven Women of Different Ages*)

Nie wiem 1977

Blizna 1976 (*The Scar*)

Personel 1976 (*Personnel*)

Szpital 1976 (*Hospital*)

RIGHT: A thoughtful Irène Jacob in
The Double Life of Veronique.

One of a select few filmmakers whose works stand not just as art, but as starting points for rigorous philosophical discussion and debate, Krzysztof Kieślowski started out a prominent voice of Polish cinema before becoming an international film icon.

After graduating from Łódź Film School, Kieślowski gravitated toward documentary. However, political interference and censorship sent him to narrative filmmaking, which he felt gave him more freedom, given the symbolic tools fiction affords. His earliest films, *Personel* (1976) (*Personnel*) and *Blizna* (1976) (*The Scar*), were transitional, still utilizing documentary techniques, but *Amator* (1979) (*Camera Buff*) and *Przypadek* (1987) (*Blind Chance*) showed a distinctive voice and introduced several key trademarks. Kieślowski still faced government censorship, but he was somehow able to skirt its paranoia to produce political films such as *Bez konca* (1985) (*No End*).

Kieślowski's movies took a turn for the profound with the release of his Polish TV miniseries *Dekalog* (1989–1990) (*The Decalogue*), ten short films loosely structured around the biblical Ten Commandments. The series was hailed as a masterpiece, and helped Kieślowski draw French funding.

La double vie de Véronique (1991) (*The Double Life of Veronique*) continued to address the ambitious themes of *The Decalogue*, but in some ways the picture merely set the stage for the "Three Colors Trilogy"—*Trois couleurs: Bleu* (1993) (*Three Colors: Blue*), *Trzy Kolory: Bialy* (1994) (*Three Colors: White*), and *Trois couleurs: Rouge* (1994) (*Three Colors: Red*). Each was visually distinct, yet equally fascinating and complex.

Sadly, those films would also prove to be Kieślowski's swan song, as he died during open-heart surgery in 1996. However, in 2000 Jerzy Stuhr directed *Duze Zwierze*, based on an unfinished Kieślowski script; and in 2003 Tom Tykwer based *Heaven* on a Kieślowski screenplay; it was intended to be the start of another trilogy. Neither of these tributes resonated quite as loudly as Kieślowski's own projects, but in the years since their release his films have, by and large, all become major staples of international cinema. **JK**

ABOVE: Juliette Binoche grieves in the first of Kieślowski's trilogy, *Three Colors: Blue*.

1940s

Cinema of Moral Anxiety

Two important strands emerged in Polish cinema from the 1950s onward: the "Polish school" of 1956–1961 and the "cinema of moral anxiety" of 1975–1981. The latter movement developed from the Polish documentaries of the 1960s and 1970s, which strove to depict reality as it was, rather than the authorized version. Kieślowski, along with other Polish directors, including Janusz Kijowski, Andrzej Wajda, and Agnieszka Holland, belonged to the movement, which sought to employ documentary techniques in feature films. Kieślowski made *Camera Buff* and *Blind Chance* during this period.

WALTER HILL

Born: Walter Wesley Hill, January 10, 1942 (Long Beach, California, U.S.).

Directing style: Maker of action movies; includes items such as revolvers, rifles, and cowboy hats in his films as an homage to the Western; tough films with rugged, outsider tone.

Top Takes...

Broken Trail 2006
The Prophecy 2002
Undisputed 2002
Last Man Standing 1996
Wild Bill 1995
Geronimo: An American Legend 1993
Trespass 1992
Another 48 Hrs. 1990
Johnny Handsome 1989
Red Heat 1988
48 Hrs. 1982
Southern Comfort 1981
The Long Riders 1980
The Warriors 1979
Hard Times 1975

Despite receiving only modest recognition from mainstream critics, Walter Hill has proven to be one of the more versatile filmmakers in the United States over the last three decades, with a series of explosive films to his credit.

Hill originally intended to be a cartoonist but, after a brief period studying art in Mexico, he eventually took a degree in journalism from Michigan State University. He then entered the entertainment business through the director's training program at the Director's Guild of America. This led to work as a second-unit director in the late 1960s and screenwriting engagements for several thrillers in the early 1970s.

Hill's first film, *Hard Times* (1975), was a Depression-era tale of a bare knuckle boxer. With its depiction of a tough man fighting against even tougher situations, the film conveys Hill's distinctly rugged and outsider tone that informs most of his work. Two subsequent features, *The Warriors* (1979) and *Southern Comfort* (1981), extend this approach to a group of individuals. Skilled at mixing genres, Hill's teaming of Eddie Murphy and Nick Nolte for the comedy action movie *48 Hrs.* (1982) led to his most commercially successful film. An avowed Western fan, Hill has made several Westerns, such as *The Long Riders* (1980), *Geronimo: An American Legend* (1993), and *Wild Bill* (1995), over his career. However, his work on the HBO Western TV series *Deadwood* (2004) earned Hill his highest industry recognition with an Emmy win for Best Director, as well as a host of wins and nominations for the series. In addition to his work as a director, Hill is known for his active role as a producer, most notably for the successful *Alien* (1979–2007) franchise, and the *Tales from the Crypt* (1989–1996) TV series. **WW**

"... you've got a 500-dollar suit and you're still a low-life."

—Jack, *48 Hrs.*

DEREK JARMAN

Born: Michael Derek Elworthy Jarman, January 31, 1942 (London, England); died 1994 (London, England).

Directing style: Giant of "Queer Cinema"; surreal, painterly visuals; experimental dramas; playful literary adaptations; themes exploring mainstream prejudices.

Derek Jarman made an almost bewildering array of anarchic and experimental films across his distinguished career. He directed music videos for pop groups, such as The Smiths, Suede, and The Pet Shop Boys, alongside many radical, "queer" movies such as the erotically charged *Sebastiane* (1976), the first film to be made entirely in Latin. In the 1970s Jarman also embraced the energies and anticapitalist, antimainstream tendencies of the punk movement. In *Jubilee* (1977), various punk performers participate in a demented narrative involving Queen Elizabeth I being transported forward in time to a ruined twentieth-century London.

By the time of *Caravaggio* (1986), Jarman had also incorporated a painterly aesthetic that was very much appropriate to the film's subject matter. In pictures such as this, and especially in *Edward II* (1991), with its attacks on homophobia, Jarman expressed his political commitments to "queer" activism. His films were always political statements as well as experiments in form and expressions of surrealism.

In *Wittgenstein* (1993)—created like *Edward II* while he was aware of being HIV-positive—Jarman explored the life of the groundbreaking philosopher Ludwig Wittgenstein while combining elements of theater and film in interesting ways to create some stunning iconography. His characteristic interests in sexuality, repression, and combating prejudice also shone through in this film.

Toward the end of his life, and losing his sight, Jarman directed *Blue* (1993), which made use of one shot of the title color. What could have been a gimmick in other contexts was, for Jarman, a poignant expression of the importance of the visual, and a reminder of how film can express so much through so little. **MH**

Top Takes...

Glitterbug 1994
Blue 1993
Wittgenstein 1993
The Next Life 1993
Edward II 1991
The Garden 1990
War Requiem 1989
The Last of England 1987
Aria 1987
Caravaggio 1986
The Angelic Conversation 1985
Imagining October 1984
Jubilee 1977
Sebastiane 1976
Miss Gaby 1972
Studio Bankside 1970

1940s

" . . . to use the word 'queer' is a liberation. It was a word that frightened me, but no longer."

MARGARETHE VON TROTTA

Born: Margarethe von Trotta, February 21, 1942 (Berlin, Germany).

Directing style: German director of feminist dramas; themes of sexual politics and the camaraderie of women; sensitive approach to complexity of female bonds; artistic collaborations with director Volker Schlöndorff.

Top Takes...

Hailed as one of the greatest female directors, and credited with presenting some of the first real female characters in film, Margarethe von Trotta's feminist legacy owes much perhaps to her unorthodox upbringing: she was raised single-handedly by her mother in Düsseldorf in an atmosphere of strong female solidarity. After completing her education, von Trotta moved to Paris where she soon became involved with the New German Cinema movement, starring in films by Rainer Werner Fassbinder and Volker Schlöndorff. The latter invited her to codirect a number of films, and the pair married in 1971. However, it was years before von Trotta made her solo directorial debut with *Das Zweite Erwachen der Christa Klages* (1978) (*The Second Awakening of Christa Klages*), in which her authorial vision was realized through the introduction of many themes that recur in her later work.

Detailing the complexities of female bonds, the film tells the true story of a kindergarten teacher who commits a bank robbery. A trilogy of films followed, all preoccupied with female ties and with an understated, distinctly feminine, political sensitivity. These included *Schwestern oder Die Balance des Glücks* (1979) (*Sisters, or the Balance of Happiness*), a personal work that has been recognized as a flag-bearer for mainstream feminist cinema. However, widespread critical acclaim did not come until her masterpiece, *Die Bleierne Zeit* (1981) (*Marianne and Julianne*), made her the first woman ever to win a Venice Festival Golden Lion. Still working today, von Trotta continues to make an impact on German cinema. However, her personal disapproval of the "feminist" label suggests that she should be celebrated for her sensitivity rather than for the gender of her characters. **LC**

> "... narrative cinema's foremost feminist filmmaker."
>
> —Ben Andac, *Senses of Cinema*

MICHAEL HANEKE

Born: Michael Haneke, March 23, 1942 (Munich, Bavaria, Germany).

Directing style: German director of sophisticated, challenging dramas; use of long, static takes; absence of film score; exploration of cinema and violence; cool, precise direction.

Benny's Video (1992) and *Funny Games* (1997) earned Michael Haneke an erroneous reputation as a provocateur aiming primarily to shock. But his desire that audiences engage on an intellectual level has come, in time, to be better understood. That *Funny Games*—a nightmarish story of two young men entering uninvited the home of a family they plan to murder—shows almost no violence testifies to Haneke's seriousness of purpose; his cool, precise direction is worlds away from the overkill favored in mainstream thrillers.

That much was clear in Haneke's little-seen feature debut, *Der Siebente Kontinent* (1989) (*The Seventh Continent*), whose elliptical narrative fragments and tightly framed compositions provide no easy explanations for a middle-class family's decision to commit suicide together. In *71 Fragmente einer Chronologie des Zufalls* (1994) (*71 Fragments in a Chronology of Chance*), Haneke presents intriguing images, sounds, and scenes, but never makes fully clear how they relate in terms of cause and effect. The audience is invited to become participants in the construction of the film's meaning.

Even the more linear stories of *La Pianiste* (2001) (*The Piano Teacher*), about a pianist's masochistic obsession with a student, and *Caché* (2005) (*Hidden*), about a liberal intellectual haunted by fears of the exposure of a shameful childhood act, refuse the comforts of conventional narrative closure or psychological motivation. The audience is left asking questions that illuminate moral issues and social, political, and historical contexts. This could be dry or uninvolving, but Haneke is skilled at constructing suspenseful narratives and working with actors. He is one of modern Europe's most important filmmakers. **GA**

Top Takes...

Caché 2005 (*Hidden*)
Le temps du loup 2003 (*The Time of the Wolf*)
La Pianiste 2001 (*The Piano Teacher*)
Code inconnu: Récit incomplet de divers voyages 2000 (*Code Unknown: Incomplete Tales of Several Journeys*)
Das Schloss 1997 (*The Castle*)
Funny Games 1997
Lumière et compagnie 1995 (*Lumière and Company*)
71 Fragmente einer Chronologie des Zufalls 1994 (*71 Fragments in a Chronology of Chance*)
Benny's Video 1992
Der Siebente Kontinent 1989 (*The Seventh Continent*)

"My films are intended as polemical statements against American 'barrel-down' cinema."

PETER GREENAWAY

Born: Peter Greenaway, April 5, 1942 (Newport, Gwent, Wales).

Directing style: Welsh director of sophisticated, fantastical, fairy-tale dramas with a macabre Gothic twist; high-art puzzles that are visual and aural feasts for an audience.

Top Takes…

Nightwatching 2007

A Life in Suitcases 2005

The Tulse Luper Suitcases: Parts 1–3 2003–2004

8½ Women 1999

The Pillow Book 1996

Lumière et compagnie 1995
  (Lumière and Company)

The Baby of Mâcon 1993

M is for Man, Music, Mozart 1991

Prospero's Books 1991

The Cook, the Thief, His Wife & Her Lover 1989

Drowning by Numbers 1988

The Belly of an Architect 1987

A Zed & Two Noughts 1985

The Draughtsman's Contract 1982

H is for House 1973

"[Critics] … are like haughty, barren spinsters lodged in a maternity ward."

Peter Greenaway's graphic, allegorical films are visibly influenced by fine art. Layer upon layer, frame within frame, they are virtuosic and dazzling, mazes of meaning overloaded with symbols and metaphors. His films are above all, sensual sophisticated films to be savored.

Trained as a painter and film editor, Greenaway started out with funny shorts such as *H is for House* (1973). Tied around visual motifs and facts such as words starting with H, it replaced narrative logic with encyclopedic or alphabetic order. Such structures would become Greenaway's trademark. In a string of beautiful, stunning films, such as *The Draughtsman's Contract* (1982) and *Drowning by Numbers* (1988), visual design and elaborate mise-en-scène take precedence over anything as mundane as plot. Greenaway's dry wit gave these films an edge and an adoring audience.

The baroque, Jacobean inquisition tale *The Cook, the Thief, His Wife & Her Lover* (1989), color-coded around taste palettes and menus, was his first film without that sardonic tone. The William Shakespeare adaptation, *Prospero's Books* (1991), the gruesome critique of religion, *The Baby of Mâcon* (1993), and the complex ode to calligraphy, *The Pillow Book* (1996) were mind-blowing but hermetic high art. Although this eclecticism diminished Greenaway's wider appeal, it also liberated him. His most personal project, the trilogy *The Tulse Luper Suitcases* (2003–2004), a multimedia venture, combined biography and international history. The Rembrandt van Rijn biopic *Nightwatching* (2007) seems to bring Greenaway full circle and back to the terrain where he started—a movement fitting his career-long obsession with perfectly shaped images. **EM**

BARRY LEVINSON

Born: Barry Levinson, April 6, 1942 (Baltimore, Maryland, U.S.).

Directing style: Writer turned director of classic dramas and comedies; diverse range of subjects; semiautobiographical themes with movies often set in his native Baltimore, Maryland.

One of America's most versatile filmmakers, Barry Levinson got into showbiz as a comedy writer, winning multiple Emmy Awards for *The Carol Burnett Show* (1967), and working with Mel Brooks on the scripts for *Silent Movie* (1976) and *High Anxiety* (1977). He made his debut as a writer and director with *Diner* (1982), an autobiographical movie set in Levinson's home town of Baltimore during the late 1950s. Brilliantly written and cast with unknowns who all went on to become stars, *Diner* is one of the key films of the 1980s and remains Levinson's most distinctive piece of work. He followed up with an exercise in mythmaking, filming Bernard Malamud's baseball-themed novel, *The Natural* (1984), and the adventure romp *Young Sherlock Holmes* (1985), before returning to Baltimore for the *Diner*-like *Tin Men* (1987).

With *Good Morning, Vietnam* (1987), featuring Robin Williams, and *Rain Man* (1988) with Dustin Hoffman and Tom Cruise, Levinson erased his own personality sufficiently to become a skilled manufacturer of audience-pleasing, awards-bid pictures, although his subsequent efforts along those lines—such as *Bugsy* (1991), *Disclosure* (1994), *Sleepers* (1996), *Sphere* (1998), and *Bandits* (2001)—proved more resistible.

Like director Rob Reiner, Levinson has settled into high-profile Hollywood professionalism, but he has never quite relinquished his hustling roots. The personal project *Toys* (1992) is a fascinating fiasco, but the scurrilous political satire *Wag the Dog* (1997) is funny and pointed. Levinson returned to Baltimore again for *Avalon* (1990) and *Liberty Heights* (1999), the outstanding *Homicide: Life on the Street* (1993–1995) TV cop show, and a documentary, *Original Diner Guys* (1999). **KN**

Top Takes…

Bandits 2001
Liberty Heights 1999
Original Diner Guys 1999
Sphere 1998
Wag the Dog 1997
Sleepers 1996
Disclosure 1994
Toys 1992
***Bugsy* 1991** ☆
***Rain Main* 1988** ★
Good Morning, Vietnam 1987
Tin Men 1987
Young Sherlock Holmes 1985
The Natural 1984
Diner 1982

1940s

"Everybody deserves a fresh start every once in a while."
—"Bugsy" Siegel, *Bugsy*

WERNER HERZOG

Born: Werner Stipetic, September 5, 1942 (Munich, Germany).

Directing style: Dramas and documentaries focusing on humans at the mercy of nature; confronting humans with their arrogance; sublime imagery of the world's most impressive landscapes; often cast Klaus Kinski.

Top Takes...

Rescue Dawn 2006

The Wild Blue Yonder 2005

Grizzly Man 2005

The White Diamond 2004

Wheel of Time 2003

Invincible 2001

Mein liebster Feind—Klaus Kinski 1999
  (My Best Fiend)

Lektionen in Finstemis 1992
  (Lessons of Darkness)

Cerro Torre: Schrei aus Stein 1991
  (Scream of Stone)

Cobra Verde 1987 (Slave Coast)

Fitzcarraldo 1982

Woyzeck 1979

Nosferatu: Phantom der Nacht 1979
  (Nosferatu the Vampyre)

Herz aus Glas 1976 (Heart of Glass)

Jeder fürsich und Gott gegen alle 1974
  (Every Man for Himself and God Against All)

Aguirre, der Zom Gottes 1972
  (Aguirre, The Wrath of God)

Fata Morgana 1971

Auch Zwerge haben klein angefangen 1970
  (Even Dwarfs Started Small)

The thread through Werner Herzog's oeuvre is ecstatic truth: the romantic belief in meaning beyond the material surface, celebrations of madness messing up methodic determination. Often shooting under extreme conditions, with a bare script, Herzog's films have dragged him to the most remote and barren corners of the world. Besides sublime imagery of the world's most impressive landscapes, his approach has given his films an adventurous revolutionary spirit and emotional accuracy no travel report could deliver.

Herzog's most notorious film is *Aguirre, der Zorn Gottes* (1972) (*Aguirre, The Wrath of God*), a literal reliving of the search for El Dorado by a band of sixteenth-century Spanish conquistadors. Filmed in the Andes highlands, on rafts on the Amazon River, with cast and crew sharing hardship, it is as much a document of perseverance as it is a feverish portrayal of greed. *Aguirre, The Wrath of God* was Herzog's first collaboration with actor Klaus Kinski.

In 1982 Herzog and Kinski revisited the area for *Fitzcarraldo*. The production's troubles, captured on film in the attempt to haul a huge paddle boat up a hill via primitive means, fittingly

RIGHT: Klaus Kinski leads a desperate quest for gold in *Aguirre, The Wrath of God.*

reflected the story's themes of impulse and irrationality. Herzog made another two films with Kinski: an uncanny remake of *Nosferatu: Phantom der Nacht* (1979) (*Nosferatu the Vampyre*) and *Woyzeck* (1979), about a hapless soldier, alone and powerless in society. Herzog's last duet with Kinski was the superb slave trade epic *Cobra Verde* (1987) (*Slave Coast*).

Since *Cerro Torre: Schrei aus Stein* (1991) (*Scream of Stone*), Herzog has mostly stuck to documentaries; but the raw intensity of the apocalyptic, burning oil fields in *Lektionen in Finsternis* (1992) (*Lessons of Darkness*) and the brutally honest tribute to Kinski, *Mein liebster Feind—Klaus Kinski* (1999) (*My Best Fiend*), show that while he may have become more anthropological, Herzog's commitment to film has remained the same. His movies still put people under extreme endurance, confronting mankind with its own arrogance, at the mercy of a beautifully cruel nature; a most ecstatic truth indeed. **EM**

ABOVE: An unconventional journey for a river boat through the jungle in *Fitzcarraldo*.

A Grizzly Tale

Interest in Werner Herzog has escalated since the release of his controversial 2005 documentary *Grizzly Man*, which consists of footage shot by Timothy Treadwell, an amateur grizzly bear expert and wildlife preservationist who lived and died among the bears in Alaska. Treadwell and his girlfriend were found dead in October 2003, killed by the bears he loved—and killed as predicted by Treadwell himself in his recorded monologue, which opens the film. Treadwell was a perfect subject for Herzog, who is attracted to individuals who pitch themselves against extreme conditions in search of "ecstatic truth."

1940s

MARTIN SCORSESE

Born: Martin Luciano Scorsese, November 17, 1942 (Queens, New York, U.S.).

Directing style: King of gangster movies; legendary creative collaborations with Robert De Niro; explores issues of Italian-American identity; religious themes with characters seeking redemption.

Top Takes...

The Departed 2006 ★
The Aviator 2004 ☆
Gangs of New York 2002 ☆
Bringing Out the Dead 1999
Il mio viaggio in Italia 1999 (*My Voyage to Italy*)
Kundun 1997
Casino 1995
The Age of Innocence 1993
Cape Fear 1991
Goodfellas 1990 ☆
The Last Temptation of Christ 1988 ☆
Bad 1987
After Hours 1985
The King of Comedy 1983
Raging Bull 1980 ☆
The Last Waltz 1978
New York, New York 1977
Taxi Driver 1976
Alice Doesn't Live Here Anymore 1974
Mean Streets 1973
Boxcar Bertha 1972
I Call First 1967
The Big Shave 1967

Martin Scorsese is the ultimate movie director. He may not be successful in every project he undertakes, nor be beloved by everyone, but even his most passionate critics concede that his work has elevated the public appraisal of the director more than any other contemporary figure (with the possible exception of Steven Spielberg.)

The attention-getting techniques that run through Scorsese's work are either the first tip-off to genius, or the opening indications of artistic excess. Most obviously, there are moving cameras into and away from close-ups, typically to reveal character and mood. It is with this trait of formally acknowledging the audience, of making his audience coconspirators in the revelation of story and plot, that Scorsese sinks or swims, because many moviegoers crave seamless entertainment without having the process of filmmaking itself presented to them. To that extent, Scorsese is a showboat. That he also recognizes the specific limitations and strengths of the cinematic medium suggests a mind carefully organized around the frame, not just as a device for telling stories but as the passageway into psychological experiences. Unarguably,

RIGHT: Harvey Keitel and Robert De Niro stick together in Scorsese's *Mean Streets*.

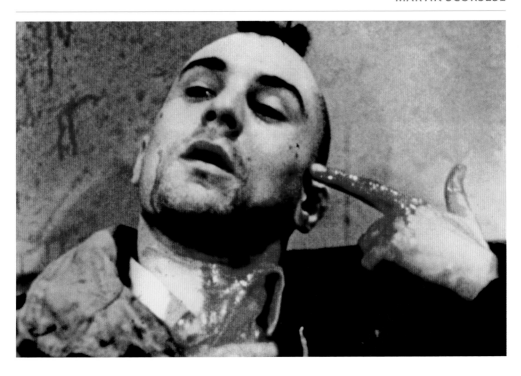

Scorsese's movies, which now stretch across five decades, leave indelible fingerprints on the corpus of cinema.

ABOVE: Robert De Niro stars as the lonely insomniac turned gunman in *Taxi Driver*.

1940s

Along the way, Scorsese has made actors into stars and made key behind-the-scenes collaborators into celebrities. He has received the American Film Institute Lifetime Achievement Award; had six Academy nominations for Best Director; has been nominated for five Emmys; and was nominated for five Golden Globes as director, one for screenwriter, and had two Best Director wins for *Gangs of New York* (2002) and *The Departed* (2006).

"I am difficult and angry . . . the only thing that gets me through is a sense of humor."

Born in Queens, New York, into a devoutly Roman Catholic Italian family, Scorsese was an asthmatic child who early on discovered a passion for movies. He studied initially for the priesthood, but opted out and enrolled instead in film school, where he made short films such

Crime Pays

Martin Scorsese won a long overdue Oscar for Best Director with his 2006 film *The Departed*, which marked his return to the crime genre. The film also earned the Academy Award for Best Motion Picture of 2006, Best Adapted Screenplay, and Best Film Editing; a Golden Globe for Best Director; a Critic's Choice Award; and the Director's Guild of America Award.

- The film was based on the Hong Kong police drama *Infernal Affairs*.
- It marked Scorsese's third consecutive collaboration with Leonardo DiCaprio.
- Most of the film was shot in New York City, doubling for Boston, with two three-week stints in Boston.
- When accepting his Oscar, Scorsese said, "This is the first movie I have ever done with a plot."
- Many of Jack Nicholson's scenes were improvised, to add to the tension.
- Retired Boston detective Thomas B. Duffy acted as technical adviser on the film. He also appeared onscreen as the Governor of Massachusetts, swearing in the new Police Academy graduates.
- Newcomer Vera Farmiga was chosen to play Madolyn amidst an all-star cast.
- Jack Nicholson wore his New York Yankees hat during filming, having refused to wear a Boston Red Sox hat.
- *The Departed* is Scorsese's highest grossing film to date.

as *What's a Nice Girl Like You Doing in a Place Like This?* (1963) and worked for Roger Corman's machine on *Boxcar Bertha* (1972). *Mean Streets* (1973) followed, establishing him in the mainstream, which he supported with *Alice Doesn't Live Here Anymore* (1974), the brilliant *Taxi Driver* (1976), *New York, New York* (1977), and the critically lauded but commercially unsuccessful *Raging Bull* (1980).

The 1980s were a difficult time when Scorsese's acclaim petered out, forcing him into new creative channels. Some of the results are extraordinary, as in *The King of Comedy* (1983) and *The Last Temptation of Christ* (1988), while some are kitsch, such as the video for Michael Jackson's *Bad* (1987) and the segment "Life Lessons" from *New York Stories* (1989).

Back in the game

Goodfellas (1990) re-established Scorsese at the top of his game, fully in control of cathartic violence and tales of male loyalty. A box-office draw again, he remade *Cape Fear* (1991), directed the period drama *The Age of Innocence* (1993), then the mob tale *Casino* (1995). *Kundun* (1997) was widely viewed as beautiful but slight. In the new century, Scorsese helmed *Gangs of New York*, finally managed a blockbuster in *The Aviator* (2004), and reworked a Hong Kong movie for an ensemble cops-and-robbers flick, *The Departed* (2006), his biggest commercial hit yet. **GCQ**

ABOVE: Jack Nicholson thinks he knows who his friends are in *The Departed*.

1940s

SUBHASH GHAI

Born: Subhash Ghai, January 24, 1943 (Nagpur, Maharashtra, India).

Directing style: Hindi director of Bollywood blockbuster musical dramas; opulent color; breathtaking locations; Rajasthani song-and-dance numbers; entertaining comic action; cameo appearances.

Indian native Subhash Ghai began his film career after completing his education at the Film and Television Institute of India in Pune, Maharashtra. His first picture to receive critical recognition was *Kalicharan* (1976). It told the story of a police officer who goes undercover to investigate a socially connected individual with ties to crime; the movie became one of the director's biggest hits.

After forming Mukta Arts in 1982, Ghai won the National Award for *Karma* (1986), an action-adventure story that portrayed a man who unwittingly finds himself on the wrong side of a crime boss in a struggle to protect the welfare of his family, and exact revenge against the evil regime. It was hailed by India's president as the best film on antiterrorism.

Pardes (1997) confronted the difficulties of Westernization, whereas *Taal* (1999) paired two unlikely lovers in a struggle to find personal and public acceptance of their bond, while fighting against the socially acceptable boundaries and expectations of their world. Both had international releases and were well received in the United States. Other popular films directed by Ghai include *Saudagar* (1991), which he also wrote, and *Kisna: The Warrior Poet* (2005), which he cowrote.

Associated with exceptional grandeur and epic proportions, Ghai's pictures became most successful in the 1990s, as he strove to outdo himself with each coming release, ultimately resulting in *Pardes*. Each of these films feature a song-and-dance number placed near the climax. Ghai's unique style and unwavering standard of excellence has earned him a place as one of the most successful and prolific Hindi directors and, although he is known for hyping his own epics, he remains "The Showman" of Bollywood. **ES**

Top Takes…

Kisna: The Warrior Poet 2005
Yaedein 2001 (*Cherished Memories*)
Taal 1999
Pardes 1997
Khal Nayak 1993
Saudager 1991
Ram Lakhan 1989
Karma 1986
Meri Jung 1985
Hero 1983
Vidhaata 1982
Krodhi 1981
Kaz 1980
Gautam Govinda 1979
Vishwanath 1978
Kalicharan 1976

"History will judge *Kisna: The Warrior Poet* differently. In time it will be considered a classic."

1940s

TOBE HOOPER

Born: Tobias Paul Hooper, January 25, 1943 (Austin, Texas, U.S.).

Directing style: Cult master of gritty horror movies and science-fiction epics; use of jarring editing to disorientate and create atmosphere of terror; brutal imagery and terrifyng soundtrack.

Top Takes...

"You've got to send a physical sensation through and not let them off the hook."

Tobe Hooper is a writer and director responsible for some of the horror genre's best work, including classics *The Texas Chainsaw Massacre* (1974) and *Poltergeist* (1982).

With his father owning a movie theater, Hooper was raised on a steady diet of films and EC Comics, and began making 8mm movies in high school. As a documentary cameraman, he made a series of shorts in the mid-1960s and then made his feature debut with the hallucinogenic *Eggshells* (1969), an allegorical statement on the death of the peace movement.

For his follow-up, Hooper looked to the true story of 1950s cannibal and murderer Ed Gein. The original *The Texas Chainsaw Massacre* terrified audiences with its gritty documentary feel, brutal imagery, jarring editing, and terrifying soundtrack, all of which establish a sense of terror previously unmatched in film. The movie was a box-office hit and led Hooper to Hollywood. Before the 1970s were over, he had created another showpiece in the TV adaptation of Stephen King's *Salem's Lot* (1979).

The strength of *The Texas Chainsaw Massacre* led Steven Spielberg to select Hooper to direct the haunted-house project *Poltergeist*. The film, although a meld of Hooper's style with Spielberg's PG-sensibilities, resulted in the biggest success of Hooper's career. He then signed a three-film contract with the Cannon Group, resulting in the big-budget science-fiction epics *Lifeforce* (1985) and *Invaders from Mars* (1986), and the sequel to his 1974 hit, *The Texas Chainsaw Massacre 2* (1986). Since then, Hooper has worked steadily on features for theaters and TV, and in 2005 founded his own low-budget horror franchise, TH Nightmare; yet he has failed to rise above his cult standing as the director of one of the scariest films ever made. **WW**

MICHAEL MANN

Born: Michael Kenneth Mann, February 5, 1943 (Chicago, Illinois, U.S.).

Directing style: Master of action movies; characterization to show the similar mind sets of cops and criminals; stylish, finger-on-the-pulse look; likes to operate the camera himself for much of the photography.

A moviemaker with a clear eye about the importance of look and feel, Michael Mann first made his mark as a director on TV with *Police Woman* (1977), and as a writer on *Starsky and Hutch* (1975–1977). This led to his Emmy Award-winning TV prison drama *The Jericho Mile* (1979) and his feature debut, *Thief* (1981). He then created the TV series *Miami Vice* (1984), with a hip idea about how the police both control and mirror criminals.

The series launched a fashion movement for rolled-up sleeves, and helped Mann create two more TV series, *Crime Story* (1986–1987) and *Private Eye* (1987), while establishing a cinematic tone with his Thomas Harris-inspired *Manhunter* (1986). Now eclipsed by the success of the Hannibal Lecter franchise, this earlier work is in many ways more satisfying for the way it compares law and chaos, good and evil.

Mann wrote, produced, and directed the TV movie *L.A. Takedown* (1989); but it was his version of *Last of the Mohicans* (1992) that made him commercially viable after so many box-office missteps. He then remade *L.A. Takedown* into the more satisfying and successful *Heat* (1995).

By the time of *Heat*'s release, Mann had hit the big time and had command of a superstar cast that placed Al Pacino and Robert De Niro opposite each other for the first time, playing the lead cop and criminal. Once again, Mann successfully showed the parallels between those camps.

Mann followed up with the critically lauded (and Academy Award-nominated) *The Insider* (1999), the biopic *Ali* (2001), and experimented with digital camcorders for a spectacular result in *Collateral* (2004). He most recently adapted *Miami Vice* (2006) for the big screen, to provide what was great summer entertainment. **GCQ**

Top Takes...

Miami Vice 2006
Collateral 2004
Ali 2001
The Insider 1999 ☆
Heat 1995
The Last of the Mohicans 1992
L.A. Takedown 1989
Manhunter 1986
The Keep 1983
Thief 1981
17 Days Down the Line 1972
Jaunpuri 1971

1940s

"A 65-ft.-wide screen and 500 people reacting . . . there is nothing like that experience."

MIKE LEIGH

Born: Mike Leigh, February 20, 1943 (Salford, Greater Manchester, England).

Directing style: British maker of stark, working-class dramas; heightened realism; often themes of family secrets and tackling social taboos; improvised scripts; acutely observed observation of British class system and family life.

Top Takes...

Vera Drake 2004 ☆
All or Nothing 2002
Topsy-Turvy 1999
Career Girls 1997
Secrets & Lies **1996** ☆
Naked 1993
Life Is Sweet 1990
Bleak Moments 1971

In a filmmaking career lasting more than 30 years, Mike Leigh has completed just nine features. This is not due to laziness or fastidiousness—rather that Leigh, one of Britain's most admired directors, still has trouble getting his films funded.

Producers are often disconcerted by Leigh's unconventional approach to filmmaking. He never starts with a script or even an idea for a story; instead, he assembles a group of actors and asks them to develop characters and improvise situations based on them. On this foundation he creates a text that after further rehearsals becomes the script of the film.

Seventeen years elapsed between Leigh's first feature film, *Bleak Moments* (1971), and his second, *High Hopes* (1988), during which time he was limited to working in TV and the theater. Since then, while remaining fiercely independent and staunchly left-wing in his attitudes, Leigh has built up a body of work that anatomizes Britain's class system and everyday family life. The best of them, *Life Is Sweet* (1990), *Secrets & Lies* (1996), *All or Nothing* (2002), *Vera Drake* (2004), and his most abrasive film, *Naked* (1993), articulate a subversive critique of English life that is often funny and often acutely painful. Despite the paucity of his output, Leigh has garnered many awards, and both *Secrets & Lies* and *Vera Drake* gained Oscar nominations; yet it was a surprising addition to his filmography, a Victorian period film about Gilbert and Sullivan, *Topsy-Turvy* (1999), which finally won Oscars, albeit for Best Costume Design and Best Makeup. But Leigh, a Gilbert and Sullivan fan from his childhood, observed that *Topsy-Turvy*, like all of his films, is still about people and relationships, and the film focuses on the relationship between the two directors at a time when they are struggling. **PK**

"Given the choice of Hollywood or poking steel pins in my eyes, I'd prefer steel pins."

ANDRÉ TÉCHINÉ

Born: André Téchiné, March 13, 1943 (Valence d'Agen, Tarn-et-Garonne, Midi-Pyrénées, France).

Directing style: Creator of Gallic tales of the travails of the human heart; woman's director; artistic collaborations with actress Catherine Deneuve.

The Gallic penchant for creating dramas that explore the intricacies of human relationships and complexities of people's emotions without a sentimental Hollywood ending is well known, and French writer and director André Téchiné falls squarely in that tradition. He has also given some of France's leading actresses, including grande dame Catherine Deneuve, some of their most memorable screen moments.

When Téchiné's application to film school was rejected he followed in the footsteps of predecessors, such as François Truffaut, and became a film critic for *Cahiers du cinéma*. Téchiné made his directorial debut with *Paulina s'en va* (1970) (*Paulina Is Leaving*), but this tale of prostitution and insanity failed to find a sympathetic audience and Téchiné returned to writing.

The director's determination finally paid off, however, and the romantic thriller *Barocco* (1976), starring heavyweight French actors Gérard Depardieu and Isabelle Adjani, won him a César nomination for Best Director. The story of unlikely lovers and the transformational psychological road of turmoil traveled by the film's characters are themes Téchiné returned to throughout his career, most notably in *Ma saison préférée* (1993) (*My Favorite Season*), and *Les roseaux sauvages* (1994) (*The Wild Reeds*). *My Favorite Season* stars Deneuve as a middle-aged woman attempting to reconcile with her estranged brother, whereas *The Wild Reeds* is a coming-of-age drama about the nature of love and the attraction of opposites, seen from the viewpoint of a homosexual adolescent.

Téchiné's films do not provide easy answers for audiences; rather they are observations of the everyday dilemmas of people tangling with the consequences of their emotions, and the bittersweet nature of human relationships. **CK**

Top Takes...

Les temps qui changent 2004 (*Changing Times*)
Les Égarés 2003 (*Strayed*)
Loin 2001 (*Far Away*)
Alice et Martin 1998 (*Alice and Martin*)
Les Voleurs 1996 (*Thieves*)
Les roseaux sauvages 1994 (*The Wild Reeds*)
Ma saison préférée 1993 (*My Favorite Season*)
J'embrasse pas 1991 (*I Don't Kiss*)
Le lieu du crime 1986 (*Scene of the Crime*)
Rendez-vous 1985
Les innocents 1984 (*The Innocents*)
Hôtel des Amériques 1981 (*Hotel America*)
Les soeurs Brontë 1979 (*The Brontë Sisters*)
Barocco 1976
Paulina s'en va 1970 (*Paulina Is Leaving*)

1940s

"The death of a brother is tough. I thought I'd die."

—Serge Bartolo, *The Wild Reeds*

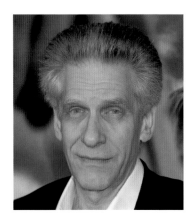

DAVID CRONENBERG

Born: David Paul Cronenberg, March 15, 1943 (Toronto, Ontario, Canada).

Directing style: "The Baron of Blood" and inventor of the body-horror genre; fascination with the dark side of the human body; gore-filled splatter schlock; meditations on the dysfunctions of the nuclear family.

Top Takes…

No wonder Martin Scorsese was terrified when he had to meet David Cronenberg. After all, the affectionately nicknamed "Dave Deprave" invented the genre of body-horror, which locates mankind's monstrous enemy inside its own body.

Cronenberg debuted with two odd films, *Stereo* (1969) and *Crimes of the Future* (1970), centering around sex, science, and experiments on human subjects, then explored these views further through the commercial horror format. The apocalyptic, science-induced, deadly sex virus-themed *Shivers* (1975) caused outrage and broke box-office records, and was the start of a series of successful gore-filled splatter movies. It made Cronenberg the champion of a new generation of horror fans.

The Brood (1979) was Cronenberg's *Kramer vs. Kramer*, but with female rage embodied by external wombs breeding murderous dwarves. In the masterful and messy cult classic *Videodrome* (1983), Cronenberg turned his cold, analytic attention toward the exploitation of the human body through media technologies, examining the visceral effects of violence onscreen, media terrorism, and pornography. *Videodrome* also marked the beginning of a more thoughtful approach.

RIGHT: Peter Weller has a drink and a smoke with a bizarre creature in *Naked Lunch*.

Cronenberg's subsequent films saw him tackle such topics as mutating and transferable diseases (cancer and AIDS) in *The Fly* (1986), gynecology and genetics in *Dead Ringers* (1988), and drug addiction and paranoia in *Naked Lunch* (1991). These films were acclaimed for their metaphoric value for contemporary culture. At the top of that line is the nihilistic fusion of sex and cars, *Crash* (1996), which in spite of its philosophical attitude profoundly disturbed audiences and critics.

Since 2000, *Spider* (2002) and *A History of Violence* (2005) have shown a more meditative Cronenberg, fascinated still by the dark side of human bodies, but politically more relevant. *A History of Violence*'s deconstruction of "The American Dream"— in the form of its investigation of socially acceptable violence, gun abuse, and community vigilance—elevated Cronenberg into the canon of contemporary cinema, completing his move from "The Baron of Blood" to cultural hero. **EM**

ABOVE: Holly Hunter takes an unhealthy interest in car accidents in *Crash*.

Crash Landing

Adapted from the book by J. G. Ballard, *Crash* (1996) inspired controversy because of its subject matter of people who derive sexual pleasure from car accidents.

- Six vintage Lincolns were used: three for driving, one for smashing, one cut in half for studio shots, and one converted to a pick-up with a rear camera mounted.
- The film has been banned in several cities in the United Kingdom, including the City of Westminster in London.
- *Crash* won a special prize at the Cannes Film Festival thanks to its daring audacity and originality.

1940s

JON JOST

Born: Jon Jost, May 16, 1943 (Chicago, Illinois, U.S.).

Directing style: Maverick independent filmmaker and digital-video auteur of features, shorts, and essays; psychedelic composition; insightful social critique of U.S. issues; experimental narratives.

Top Takes...

Jon Jost has assembled an extraordinary body of work that challenges filmmakers and spectators alike to re-examine the aesthetic and ideological functions of sound and image. He taught himself filmmaking soon after being expelled from college, completing his first work, a short film *Repetition* in 1963. In 1965, Jost refused to cooperate with the U.S. Selective Service System, which administers military conscription, and he was imprisoned for two years and three months. His incarceration, however, did not quell his creative energies.

During the last 40 years, Jost has written and directed more than 20 shorts and 14 features, the latter ranging from essay films such as *Speaking Directly* (1973) and *Stagefright* (1981), to experimental genre exercises such as *Angel City* (1977) and *Frameup* (1993), to dramatic narratives that skillfully wed insightful social critique with daring avant-garde practices as in *Last Chants for a Slow Dance* (1977) and *Slow Moves* (1983). Jost's best known fiction films are undoubtedly *All the Vermeers in New York* (1990), which won both the Caligari Film Award at the Berlin Film Festival and the Los Angeles Critics Award for Best Independent Film, and *The Bed You Sleep In* (1993), a critical exposé of "The American Dream." In 1996, Jost switched to a new medium, leaving celluloid behind for digital video and the potential of electronic media. Rather than cling to practices specific to film, Jost embraced video's unique aesthetic, crafting impressionistic and often hallucinatory compositions that remind spectators that cinema is first and foremost a visual art. Over the last decade, Jost has created a dozen digital features and numerous shorts, with more works on the way. There is much people can learn from this underappreciated visionary. **JM**

"Jon Jost is not a traitor to the movies. He makes them move."

—Jean-Luc Godard

TERRENCE MALICK

Born: Terrence Malick, November 30, 1943 (Waco, Texas, U.S.).

Directing style: Maker of meditative dramas; painterly visuals; lingering shots of nature; aural beauty; collective narrative; attention to period detail; culture clash themes.

Terrence Malick remains one of Hollywood's last true mysteries. The son of an oil executive, Malick was born in Texas, where he played football and worked in the oil fields before heading off to Harvard University, and later the University of Oxford as a Rhodes Scholar. Following a stint teaching philosophy, he got his Master of Fine Arts from Hollywood's American Film Institute Conservatory and soon made the short film *Lanton Mills* (1969). His feature debut *Badlands* (1973), loosely based on the notorious Charlie Starkweather murders, emerged around the same time as other masterpieces from the usual 1970s luminaries, but *Days of Heaven* (1978) soon proved Malick was another breed of moviemaker.

Top Takes...

The New World 2005
***The Thin Red Line* 1998** ☆
Days of Heaven 1978
Badlands 1973
Lanton Mills 1969

"Soon," of course, is relative. *Days of Heaven* followed a five-year gap—but that was nothing compared with the 20-year wait for *The Thin Red Line* (1998), during which time the reclusive Malick practically vanished, his absence the subject of countless rumors. The film, perhaps due to high expectations, was met with a mixed reception, though even its detractors treated it with respect, wondering whether the oft-mentioned hours upon hours of unused footage would ever see the light in a new, longer cut. At the time of the *The Thin Red Line*'s release, Malick refused to participate in the film's promotion, denying interview requests and photographs. His next film, *The New World* (2005), arrived relatively quickly, its speedy production possible thanks to the fact that the film's script dated back to the 1970s, and also because

> "We're living in a world that's blowing itself to hell . . . ."
> —First Sgt. Welsh, *The Thin Red Line*

a rumored Che Guevara biopic fell through. The movie itself shares much in common with *The Thin Red Line*, especially its notions of a collective narrative and its lingering nature shots, which have become Malick's directorial trademarks. **JK**

ARTURO RIPSTEIN

Born: Arturo Ripstein Rosen, December 13, 1943 (Mexico City, Mexico).

Directing style: Godfather of independent Mexican cinema; somber, slow-paced, macabre melodramas that explore existential loneliness; sense of the grotesque; close collaborations with authors.

Top Takes…

La virgen de la lujuria 2002

La perdición de los hombres 2000
(The Ruination of Men)

Así es la vida 2000 (Such Is Life)

El Coronel no tiene quien le escriba 1999
(No One Writes to the Colonel)

Profundo carmesí 1996 (Deep Crimson)

La mujer del puerto 1991 (Woman of the Port)

Mentiras piadosas 1987 (Love Lies)

La Seducción 1980 (Seduction)

El lugar sin límites 1978 (Hell Without Limits)

La viuda negra 1977 (The Black Widow)

Foxtrot 1976

El santo oficio 1974 (The Holy Office)

El castillo de la pureza 1973 (Castle of Purity)

Tiempo de morir 1966 (Time to Die)

"In Mexico, melodrama is employed frequently because there is no public voice."

Mexico has produced a number of internationally recognized filmmakers, but Arturo Ripstein is generally acknowledged to be the country's most respected living director, and one of the godfathers of independent Mexican cinema.

The son of legendary producer Alfredo Ripstein Jr., Arturo grew up on film sets and formed a close friendship with Luis Buñuel, whose work was to have a profound influence on his own. With the help of his father, Arturo directed his first feature at the age of twenty-two. *Tiempo de morir* (1966) (*Time to Die*), a violent revenge Western coscripted by Gabríel Garcia Márquez and Carlos Fuentes, was the first of many collaborations with Latin American authors.

However, difficulties in raising finance and escaping the shadow of his famous father meant that it wasn't until the mid-1970s that Ripstein truly began to establish himself. *El castillo de la pureza* (1973) (*Castle of Purity*) is a powerfully claustrophobic family melodrama, whereas *El santo oficio* (1974) (*The Holy Office*), concerning the ordeals of a Jewish family in Mexico, reflects Ripstein's own ethnic roots.

Foxtrot (1976), his only English-language film to date, starred Peter O'Toole and Charlotte Rampling and is a study in sexual politics on an isolated island. *El lugar sin límites* (1978) (*Hell Without Limits*) was a pioneering look at homosexuality in an aggressively macho culture. During the 1980s and 1990s Ripstein supported personal films with television work and commissions, but his dark, somber oeuvre continued to grow and the mid-1990s saw the release of some of his most celebrated films, notably *Profundo carmesí* (1996) (*Deep Crimson*). It is perhaps his most unflinching portrayal of the destructive nature of l'amour fou. **RB**

ALAN PARKER

Born: Alan William Parker, February 14, 1944 (Islington, London, England).

Directing style: British director across a variety of genres; known for hard-hitting dramas with messages on issues of social justice; lavish spectacle; literary adaptations and musicals.

Sir Alan Parker came to the cinema after directing British TV commercials. From this medium, he learned to punch over every point at least twice, getting close to dramatic moments and working hard to rid the screen of anything like ambiguity. Like his sometime collaborator and later nemesis, Oliver Stone, Parker favors very loud statements—and his films often shout at the tops of their voices. He has stated that it is his intention to make a film in every imaginable genre: so far, he has tackled the prison film with *Midnight Express* (1978), the family melodrama with *Shoot the Moon* (1982), an economical combination of private-eye picture and horror film with *Angel Heart* (1987), and crazy, fact-based, period black comedy with *The Road to Wellville* (1994).

Parker most frequently returns to the musical, delivering films as varied as the gangster pastiche *Bugsy Malone* (1976) and the biopic of Eva Peron, *Evita* (1996). He is also known for films on broad-stroke social issues: delivering messages on the problems of racism with *Come See the Paradise* (1990); the misery of poverty with *Angela's Ashes* (1999); and the thorny issue of capital punishment with *The Life of David Gale* (2003).

Parker's best work tends to come in his smaller scale efforts, based on good books, such as the intense, excellently acted *Birdy* (1984) from William Wharton's novel about traumatized Vietnam War veterans, and the lively, engaging *The Commitments* (1991) from Roddy Doyle's book about a foul-up Dublin soul band. Otherwise, he is most likely to be remembered for the Grand Guignol tongue-ripping, foot-bashing, and behind-bars buggery of *Midnight Express* and the Southern Gothic antics of hideously ugly Ku Klux Klansmen in the crime thriller *Mississippi Burning* (1988). **KN**

Top Takes...

The Life of David Gale 2003
Angela's Ashes 1999
Evita 1996
The Road to Wellville 1994
The Commitments 1991
Come See the Paradise 1990
Mississippi Burning 1988 ☆
Angel Heart 1987
Birdy 1984
Pink Floyd The Wall 1982
Shoot the Moon 1982
Fame 1980
Midnight Express 1978 ☆
Bugsy Malone 1976
Our Cissy 1974

"I was once described by one of my critics as an aesthetic fascist."

1940s

JONATHAN DEMME

Born: Jonathan Demme, February 22, 1944 (Baldwin, Long Island, New York, U.S.).

Directing style: Influential director across a range of genres; trademark use of characters looking directly into the camera; challenging insights into human behavior; strong women characters.

Top Takes...

In 1973, Jonathan Demme signed to make his directorial debut on a low-budget British sex film, *Secrets of a Door-to-Door Salesman*. He was fired after a few days' shooting and replaced by Wolf Rilla, although some Demme footage remains in. Less than 20 years later, Demme accepted the Academy Award for Best Director for *The Silence of the Lambs* (1991), which also won Best Picture and Best Writing, plus Best Actor and Actress Awards for its leads. Few can claim such an arc.

Demme began in exploitation for Roger Corman as a writer and producer on *Angels Hard As They Come* (1971), and made his completed directorial debut with the lively women-in-prison picture *Caged Heat* (1974). Although he handled straight action with *Fighting Mad* (1976), and a Hitchcockian thriller with *Last Embrace* (1979), Demme specialized in quirky, blackly comic road movies such as *Crazy Mama* (1975), *Melvin and Howard* (1980), and *Something Wild* (1986). He gravitated toward mainstream comedy with *Swing Shift* (1984) and *Married to the Mob* (1988), while maintaining a sideline in performance films such as *Stop Making Sense* (1984).

The Silence of the Lambs, an influential horror thriller based on Thomas Harris's novel, was a rare film to sweep both the Oscars and Fuse Fangoria's Chainsaw Awards. It introduced Anthony Hopkins as Harris's bogeyman Hannibal Lecter to pop culture and elevated the director to the A list. Demme stayed awards-friendly with *Philadelphia* (1993), an early mainstream AIDS movie, and *Beloved* (1998), a commercial disappointment based on the Toni Morrison novel. He then gravitated to acceptable but needless remakes such as *The Manchurian Candidate* (2004), while keeping up with music films such as *Neil Young: Heart of Gold* (2006). **KN**

"I don't think it's sacrilegious to remake any movie, including a good or even great movie."

CHARLES BURNETT

Born: Charles Burnett, April 13, 1944 (Vicksburg, Mississippi, U.S.).

Directing style: Director of New Black Cinema; maker of dramas focusing on themes of African-American identity and upward mobility; fly-on-the-wall documentary technique.

Educated at the University of California and the recipient of a MacArthur Fellowship "Genius Grant," Charles Burnett is one of the most widely regarded but little-known movie directors in what has been called the "New Black Cinema." Upstaged by more commercial filmmakers such as Spike Lee, Burnett draws on Italian neorealism and documentary techniques, and tends to favor issues of African-American identity and the general struggle toward upward mobility. His world view is not particularly violent or propped up by action adventure tropes, nor is he particularly didactic or overtly political. Instead, his dramas focus on individuals placed at crossroads between the "American Dream" and the realities of daily experience inside a racially divided United States.

Burnett's early masterpiece is *Killer of Sheep* (1977). The movie tells the story of an African-American, working-class, Los Angeles family, and is a study in closely observed domestic circumstances and a snapshot of urban life in the mid-1970s. It remains Burnett's most celebrated film, and in 1990 it was declared a national treasure by the Library of Congress, and was one of the first fifty films placed on the U.S. National Film Registry. Since then his career has been disappointingly patchy, mixing occasional short films, such as *When It Rains* (1995) and *Olivia's Story* (2000), with successful work on TV, including the well-regarded movies *Nightjohn* (1996), *The Wedding* (1998), and family drama *Finding Buck McHenry* (2000).

His feature film work has also been inconsistent following the success of *Killer of Sheep*, save for his most respected mature work, *To Sleep with Anger* (1990), and his most commercial title to date, *The Glass Shield* (1994), starring rapper turned actor Ice Cube. **GCQ**

Top Takes...

Nujoma: Where Others Wavered 2006
Nat Turner: A Troublesome Property 2003
Olivia's Story 2000
The Annihilation of Fish 1999
Selma, Lord, Selma 1999
Dr. Endesha Ida Mae Holland 1998
When It Rains 1995
The Glass Shield 1994
America Becoming 1991
To Sleep with Anger 1990
My Brother's Wedding 1983
Killer of Sheep 1977
The Horse 1973
Several Friends 1969

1940s

"You have to be able to tell your stories and share them with the rest of the world."

GEORGE LUCAS

Born: George Walton Lucas Jr., May 14, 1944 (Modesto, California, U.S.).

Directing style: Emperor and myth maker of science-fiction epic morality tales of good versus evil; innovator of special effects; pioneer of film merchandising; creator of the *Star Wars* franchise.

Top Takes…

Star Wars: Episode III—Revenge of the Sith 2005

Star Wars: Episode II—Attack of the Clones 2002

Star Wars: Episode I—The Phantom Menace 1999

Star Wars 1977 ☆

American Graffiti 1973 ☆

THX 1138 1971

Filmmaker 1968

6-18-67 1967

Electronic Labyrinth THX 1138 4EB 1967

The Emperor 1967

1:42:08: A Man and His Car 1966

Freiheit 1966

Herbie 1966

Look at Life 1965

Born in 1944, George Lucas grew up in the 1950s, admiring fast cars. After a serious car accident in his late teens ended Lucas's dreams of becoming a professional drag racer, he attended the University of Southern California film school, and produced a number of attention-grabbing shorts, especially *Electronic Labyrinth THX-1138 4EB* (1967). This film led to a Warner Brothers scholarship where he met Francis Ford Coppola, and the two formed the production company American Zoetrope. Coppola produced and Lucas directed his semiautobiographical *American Graffiti* (1973), which was a smash hit and critically lauded. Lucas earned Academy Award nominations for directing and writing, and collected the necessary cachet to produce his space opera *Star Wars* (1977).

The project was considered a terrible risk, both financially and for combining kitsch influences such as 1930s movie serials with mythological symbolism. During production Lucas was regularly at odds with his crew. He lost weight, went over budget, and was left exhausted. But *Star Wars* surpassed even the wildest expectations, making Lucas a legendary cultural figure, always seen in plaid shirts with a beard.

RIGHT: Director Ron Howard's first role in the movies was in Lucas's *American Graffiti*.

ABOVE: The original *Star Wars* crew contemplate grimly what lies ahead.

He spent the next two decades being a writer and producer, helping originate *Raiders of the Lost Ark* (1981) and its sequels with Steven Spielberg, seeing his *Star Wars* franchise develop two sequels and untold numbers of tie-in products, and earning the Irving Thalberg Award. An entire generation learned about movies through his influence, so it was with considerable anticipation that he returned to the director's chair, making three more *Star Wars* movies, *Star Wars: Episode I—The Phantom Menace* (1999), *Star Wars: Episode II—Attack of the Clones* (2002), and *Star Wars: Episode III—Revenge of the Sith* (2005). Unfortunately, the once charming magic of fairy tales writ large over science-fiction settings proved spectacular but not as satisfying as the originals.

Now a billionaire, Lucas busies himself with film education. Perhaps one day he'll return to highly personal filmmaking and discover the artist buried beneath a rich man's burden. **GCQ**

Merchandising Madness

Aside from a vibrant strand of expressive works meant for small audiences, the cinema has always been a commercial enterprise. But *Star Wars* (1977) changed not just the profit-making impulse behind the movies but the very nature of the film industry. That single film confirmed the idea of the blockbuster, and advanced the idea of movies being part of an entire cultural movement characterized by mass merchandising. Although the project was considered risky at the time, Lucas will never rue the day he gave up his salary for *Star Wars* in exchange for a share of the profits and merchandising licenses.

TONY SCOTT

Born: Anthony Scott, June 21, 1944 (Stockton-on-Tees, England).

Directing style: British maker of stylish thrillers and action dramas; use of quick cuts and colored filters for a dark, glamorous feel; lush photography; opulent production design.

Top Takes...

1940s

The younger brother of director Ridley Scott, Tony Scott made his name through a group of stylish thrillers that combine his background in TV commercials with a penchant for violence-prone dramas about people at the edge of life. Beginning with his revisionist cult vampire tale *The Hunger* (1983), his craftsmanship has been centrally organized around two main ideas: quick cuts and overproduced production design.

The Tom Cruise vehicle *Top Gun* (1986) was his star turn, showcasing a sexy young cast with fast airplanes, a best-selling soundtrack album, and pro-military imagery. *Beverly Hills Cop II* (1987) cemented his popular appeal, this time showcasing Eddie Murphy in his signature role, while combining high fashion, gun play, comedy, and action adventure, all to big box-office success and another hit soundtrack album.

Come the 1990s, Scott directed a Kevin Costner dud *Revenge* (1990) and another successful Cruise vehicle, *Days of Thunder* (1990), which established a regular pattern in his career: alternating oddly irritating hits, such as *Crimson Tide* (1995), with interesting but overlooked gems such as *Domino* (2005). Importantly, and despite all the technical precision lavished on each of his films, Scott has yet to direct a masterpiece. Hints of brilliance litter his filmography, but the clear priority has always been form over content. At his best, Scott is a stylish dramatist, as with the cult pulp road movie *True Romance* (1993) that was no doubt helped by Quentin Tarantino's violent but comic screenplay. And often enough, he has managed to successfully weave complex stories (*Spy Game*, 2001) with exciting imagery to entertain audiences (*Deja Vu*, 2006), over and above more idiosyncratic questions of art. **GCQ**

> "I told him, come work with me and within a year you'll have a Ferrari. And he did."—Ridley Scott

RIGHT: Tom Cruise wants to be the best of the bunch in the action drama *Top Gun*.

PETER WEIR

Born: Peter Lindsay Weir, August 21, 1944 (Sydney, New South Wales, Australia).

Directing style: Australian maker of dramas and thrillers; themes explore the outsider trying to make sense of strange new worlds; sense of natural landscape; cinematography.

Top Takes…

Master and Commander: The Far Side of the World 2003 ☆
The Truman Show 1998 ☆
Fearless 1993
Green Card 1990
Dead Poets Society 1989 ☆
The Mosquito Coast 1986
Witness 1985 ☆
The Year of Living Dangerously 1982
Gallipoli 1981
The Last Wave 1977
Picnic at Hanging Rock 1975
The Cars That Ate Paris 1974
Homesdale 1971

Peter Weir helped spearhead the Australian New Wave with a handful of shorts and his feature debut, the sideways thriller *The Cars That Ate Paris* (1974). But it was the haunting and enigmatic *Picnic at Hanging Rock* (1975) that introduced Weir to wider audiences. The plot was inspired by true events and focuses on a girls school field trip to the outback, where several students mysteriously, and perhaps magically, go missing.

Average people cast into odd or often unusual circumstances is a theme Weir would gravitate toward again and again in future projects, with his protagonists often outsiders trying to make sense of strange new worlds. That was certainly the case with *The Last Wave* (1977), about a lawyer's immersion in ominous, Aboriginal folklore; *Gallipoli* (1981), which starred a young Mel Gibson in a story of Australians fighting in Turkey in World War I; and *The Year of Living Dangerously* (1982), about a journalist in the middle of Indonesian political upheaval.

However, Weir's jump to Hollywood with *Witness* (1985) showcased his cinematographic skills and allowed him to hone his themes for a mainstream audience, with Harrison Ford starring as a police officer living in an Amish commune. More unconventional and less commercial, films such as *Fearless* (1993) and *The Mosquito Coast* (1986) have alternated with thoughtful crowd-pleasers such as *Dead Poets Society* (1989) and *The Truman Show* (1998), the latter film about a man who discovers his life has been the subject of a much-watched TV show, and his home basically an elaborate set. Weir adapted the first installment of Patrick O'Brian's beloved maritime novels, *Master and Commander: The Far Side of the World* (2003), a film that earned him his fourth Best Director nomination at the Academy Awards. **JK**

"It takes the littlest thing to reveal the chaos underneath."

GEORGE MILLER

Born: George Miliotis, March 3, 1945 (Chinchilla, Queensland, Australia).

Directing style: Key player in the Australian New Wave; collaboration with Byron Kennedy; director of the *Mad Max* movies that made actor Mel Gibson a star; children's films.

Originally the slightly unhinged mind behind *Mad Max* (1979), Australian filmmaker George Miller has broadened his palette to take in mischievous porkers (*Babe*, 1995) and idealistic penguins (*Happy Feet*, 2006). As a youngster Miller developed twin passions—medicine and cinema. He and his brother John jointly enrolled at the New South Wales Medical School and went on to produce and direct a one-minute short together. It came first in a local competition and the prize was a summer film school workshop in Melbourne. Miller hooked up with future collaborator Byron Kennedy and, moonlighting from his job as a doctor, churned out scripts. Their first offering was the short gory spoof *Violence in the Cinema, Part 1* (1971).

However, it was *Mad Max*, Miller's hi-octane blockbuster that brought international acclaim and catapulted actor Mel Gibson to stardom. Inevitably, it spawned a sequel, *Mad Max 2: The Road Warrior* (1981), and an invitation in 1983 from Steven Spielberg to direct one of the more successful segments of *Twilight Zone: The Movie* (1983).

Miller utilized his industry clout as a producer to push the careers of directors John Duigan (*The Year My Voice Broke*, 1987; *Flirting*, 1991) and Philip Noyce (*Dead Calm*, 1989). In 1987, he was persuaded against his better judgment to direct the hugely successful *The Witches of Eastwick* in the United States. More artistically satisfying was the Oscar-nominated *Lorenzo's Oil* (1992), but then Miller struck box-office gold with *Babe* (1995), his delightful tale of a talking piglet, based on the children's book by Dick King-Smith. It was eight years after the sequel—*Babe: Pig in the City* (1998)—that Miller would direct an Oscar-winning feature, the computer-generated animation *Happy Feet*. **TE**

Top Takes…

Happy Feet 2006
Babe: Pig in the City 1998
40,000 Years of Dreaming 1997
Lorenzo's Oil 1992
The Witches of Eastwick 1987
Mad Max Beyond Thunderdome 1985
Twilight Zone: The Movie 1983
Mad Max 2: The Road Warrior 1981
Mad Max 1979
Violence in the Cinema, Part 1 1971

1940s

"I just really follow my nose … I don't make many films, and I'm driven by curiosity."

RAINER WERNER FASSBINDER

Born: Rainer Werner Fassbinder, May 31, 1945 (Bad Wörishofen, Bavaria, Germany); died 1982 (Munich, Bavaria, Germany).

Directing style: Dynamic, enfant terrible of German New Wave; controversial social melodramas of sexuality and passion; themes of life in postwar Germany.

Top Takes…

Querelle 1982

Die Sehnsucht der Veronika Voss 1982
  (Veronika Voss)

Lili Marleen 1981

Die Ehe der Maria Braun 1979
  (The Marriage of Maria Braun)

In einem Jahr mit 13 Monden 1978
  (In a Year of 13 Moons)

Despair 1978

Deutschland im Herbst 1978
  (Germany in Autumn)

Bolwieser 1977 (The Stationmaster's Wife)

Satansbraten 1976 (Satan's Brew)

Faustrecht der Freiheit 1975
  (Fox and His Friends)

Angst essen Seele auf 1974 (Fear Eats the Soul)

Die Bitteren Tränen der Petra von Kant 1972
  (The Bitter Tears of Petra von Kant)

Händler der vier Jahreszeiten 1972
  (The Merchant of Four Seasons)

Whity 1971

Der Amerikanische Soldat 1970
  (The American Soldier)

Warum läuft Herr R. Amok? 1970
  (Why Does Herr R. Run Amok?)

Liebe ist kälter als der Tod 1969
  (Love Is Colder Than Death)

RIGHT: A poignant moment from
The Bitter Tears of Petra von Kant.

The youngest, most precocious, and controversial of the directors whose dynamism resurrected the moribund German cinema in the 1960s, Rainer Werner Fassbinder was also the most prolific. His early films were frequently experimental and arduous to watch; a more accessible work from this period is *Der Amerikanische Soldat* (1970) (*The American Soldier*).

Just as Fassbinder often worked with a stock company of players and technicians, so he also returned to certain themes and concerns, especially the various forms that sexual passion and frustration can take, of which *Satansbraten* (1976) (*Satan's Brew*) and *Bolwieser* (1977) (*The Stationmaster's Wife*) are striking examples. If his studies of lesbianism, *Die Bitteren Tränen der Petra von Kant* (1972) (*The Bitter Tears of Petra von Kant*), and of gay men, *Querelle* (1982), are highly stylized and often deliberately unrealistic, both nevertheless show Fassbinder's interest in domination, humiliation, and masochism in ways that cruelly highlight the social nature of any sexual relation. Thus he is less concerned with showing men dominating women than with the way people believe they need to behave in order to draw some sexual, psychological, and/or financial

advantage. So it is not surprising that prostitution figures in his films in every possible combination of character and situation.

This dimension of domination is patent in his film on transsexuality, *In einem Jahr mit 13 Monden* (1978) (*In a Year of 13 Moons*), and the multifaceted nature of desire finds its most intense, implacable, and tragic expression in *Händler der vier Jahreszeiten* (1972) (*The Merchant of Four Seasons*). Fassbinder's radicalism is also uppermost in the splendid *Angst essen Seele auf* (1974) (*Fear Eats the Soul*), where racism is excoriated in the controversial context of guest laborers, here the Moroccan worker who becomes the love object of a middle-aged widow. This is also the film in which the director makes his most explicit tribute to classic Hollywood.

Ultimately, however, the lessons to be learned from this exceptional body of films lie in Fassbinder's uncompromising approach to his material. **ReH**

ABOVE: The marriage in *The Marriage of Maria Braun* lasted less than 24 hours.

Personal and Political

Fassbinder pilloried the conservatism and corruption of postwar Germany in his most mainstream work *Die Ehe der Maria Braun* (1979) (*The Marriage of Maria Braun*). His resolve not to allow Germans to repress the Nazi past or politicians to hide their complicity made him a target for right-wing activists. He was openly homosexual, and he dealt best with this theme by distancing himself as in *The Bitter Tears of Petra von Kant*, or creating a patently fantasy world as in *Querelle*. When he cast himself as the gay victim in *Faustrecht der Freiheit* (1975) (*Fox and His Friends*), the result was less satisfying.

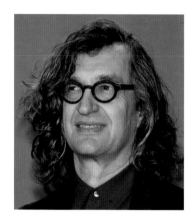

WIM WENDERS

Born: Ernst Wilhelm Wenders, August 14, 1945 (Düsseldorf, North Rhine-Westphalia, Germany).

Directing style: Poetical dramas; slow pace; Expressionist use of color; improvisation; long monologues; artistic collaborations with Robby Müller.

Top Takes...

Born in Düsseldorf in 1945, Wim Wenders was attracted to Hollywood's golden age. He came to prominence with *Alice in den Städten* (1974) (*Alice in the Cities*), about an improbable friendship between a journalist and a little girl, and *Der Amerikanische Freund* (1977) (*The American Friend*), based on one of Patricia Highsmith's Ripley novels. Wenders's directness and willingness to expose raw emotion onscreen earned him a loyal following among cinephiles. In a cinephilic spirit, *Lightning Over Water* (1980) celebrates the life and career of movie director Nicholas Ray.

In *Der Stand der Dinge* (1982) (*The State of Things*), his crew stymied in the midst of a shoot, a director must leave his Portuguese location for a fateful meeting with the producer in Hollywood. The pulse of the story is cyclical, even hypnotic, the cinematography expressive, and the performances minimalist. *Der Himmel über Berlin* (1987) (*Wings of Desire*), possibly the director's most famous movie, poetically assumes the point of view of two angels hovering over the desperations of humanity. Made with a minimal script, the film shifts from color to monochrome to distinguish between the points of view of humans and angels, and won Wenders the Best Director award at the Cannes Film Festival. Also of particular note are *Die Angst des Tormanns beim Elfmeter* (1972) (*The Goalie's Anxiety at the Penalty Kick*), where an athlete responsible for his team's loss commits a horrid murder; and the cult drama *Paris, Texas* (1984), which uses a haunting soundtrack by Ry Cooder and crystalline cinematography by Robby Müller to follow a lonely man searching for his alienated wife. It is Wenders's most critically acclaimed movie and deservedly won the Palme d'Or at Cannes. **MP**

"Sex and violence was never my cup of tea; I was always more into sax and violins."

RIGHT: Nastassja Kinski stars in the cult movie *Paris, Texas,* Wenders's most acclaimed film.

ROGER DONALDSON

Born: Roger Donaldson, November 15, 1945 (Ballarat, Australia).

Directing style: Influential Australian director of early eccentric New Zealand genre pieces and later popular Hollywood action movies; often concentrates on U.S. foreign policy.

Top Takes…

1940s

Australian Roger Donaldson immigrated to New Zealand and began his directing career there. *Sleeping Dogs* (1977), a near-future thriller with actor Sam Neill persecuted by an Orwellian police state, broke a 15-year hiatus on New Zealand feature filmmaking, and established Donaldson as an important local director with international potential. He used his new standing to lobby the New Zealand government to set up the New Zealand Film Commission, which he cofounded in 1978.

He followed up with a comic gangster movie *Nutcase* (1980), and *Smash Palace* (1981), an intense family drama with Bruno Lawrence expressing his anger in a demolition derby. These films are very much in the vein of 1970s Australian cinema: odd genre pieces with a great deal of character, a self-critical eye for the worst elements of local culture, and an eccentric streak that has been squeezed out of his subsequent U.S. work.

Donaldson went international with a conventional version of *The Bounty* (1984), starring Anthony Hopkins and Mel Gibson, and ended up in Hollywood where he specialized in films a lot of people saw, although few could name the director. He has essayed serious, fact-based pictures such as *Marie* (1985) and *Thirteen Days* (2000), but most often turned out solidly commercial entertainment such as *No Way Out* (1987), *Cocktail* (1988), *Species* (1995), *Dante's Peak* (1997), and *The Recruit* (2003). His few box-office misses include the misjudged Robin Williams comedy drama *Cadillac Man* (1990). Early in his career, Donaldson directed *Burt Munro: Offerings to the God of Speed* (1971), a documentary for New Zealand TV. *The World's Fastest Indian* (2005), his feature film return to New Zealand, is similarly based on Burt Munro's biography, and stars Hopkins. **KN**

"Sometimes you have to lick your wounds and just move on."

ROLAND JOFFÉ

Born: Roland Joffé, November 17, 1945 (London, England).

Directing style: British director of hard-hitting, unflinching historical dramas; themes tackling issues of politics, sexual politics, and Western colonization; breathtaking cinematography.

British director Roland Joffé first came to international prominence with the critical success of his two David Puttnam-produced features, *The Killing Fields* (1984) and *The Mission* (1986). Both of these films tackled the effects of Westernization on colonial and postcolonial settings, and added a visual gloss to the political content familiar to many from his early work in the theater, and later work in TV. Both movies also won Joffé Academy Award nominations for Best Director.

The Killing Fields centers on a *New York Times* journalist, played by Sam Waterston, who, helped by a local representative, played by Oscar winner Haing S. Ngor, is covering some of the tragedy and madness of the struggle of the civil war in Cambodia. *The Mission*, meanwhile, features Jeremy Irons as a Spanish Jesuit and Robert De Niro as a converted slave hunter who join forces to defend their mission in the South American wilderness against the Portuguese aggressors.

During his earlier period in TV, Joffé had developed a reputation for directing works with strong left-wing sympathies. These included collaborations with Marxist writers Trevor Griffiths and Jim Allen, as well as the controversial documentary drama *The Legion Hall Bombing* (1978), based on the trial of a suspected IRA bomber. After his initial strong impact, Joffé has struggled to find pictures that enable him to engage with the social and political issues so germane to his earlier output. High-profile works with major stars, such as *Fat Man and Little Boy* (1989) with Paul Newman, *City of Joy* (1992) with Patrick Swayze, and *The Scarlet Letter* (1995) with Demi Moore, have proved to be a series of hit-or-miss affairs, whereas smaller films, such as *Goodbye Lover* (1998), have struggled to find an appreciative audience. **AW**

Top Takes…

Vatel 2000
Goodbye Lover 1998
The Scarlet Letter 1995
City of Joy 1992
Fat Man and Little Boy 1989
The Mission 1986 ☆
The Killing Fields 1984 ☆

"I try to address my audiences intelligently. The man in the street counts …."

1940s

DAVID LYNCH

Born: David Keith Lynch, January 20, 1946 (Missoula, Montana, U.S.).

Directing style: Innovative maker of enigmatic and unsettling dramas that make viewers feel like they are stepping into a surreal, circular nightmare; painterly cinematography; perplexing Borgesian narratives; vibrant color.

Top Takes...

Inland Empire 2006
Darkened Room 2002
Rabbits 2002
Mulholland Dr. 2001 ☆
The Straight Story 1999
Lost Highway 1997
Twin Peaks: Fire Walk with Me 1992
Wild at Heart 1990
Blue Velvet 1986 ☆
Dune 1984
The Elephant Man 1980 ☆
Eraserhead 1977
The Grandmother 1970
Six Figures Getting Sick 1966

If high hair is an indication of genius, then David Lynch's plumage outclasses that of his contemporaries—steeper than Jim Jarmusch and wilder than David Cronenberg. The same goes for his oeuvre. With their steep and wild puzzle narratives, Lynch's films are to be experienced instead of explained— never good with words, he is more of a preverbal philosopher than an evangelist, questioning instead of answering.

A true obsessive, it took Lynch six years to complete his first feature. Surreal, romantic, and harsh, in raw black and white with a subterranean industrial noise soundtrack, *Eraserhead* (1977) is inimitable and profoundly unsettling. No wonder it became an immediate midnight cult classic. The wide acclaim of the similarly downbeat but fact-based biopic *The Elephant Man* (1980), still in black and white but more lush, seemed to pave the way for large-scale Hollywood-friendly projects; instead the science-fiction epic *Dune* (1984) failed to satisfy.

Blue Velvet (1986) tells of a teenager's exploration of abuse, sexual decadence, and drug-crazed violence underneath the surface of a white suburban paradise, and was a ruthless antidote to sweet 1950s coming-of-age dramas. Road movie

RIGHT: "I am not an animal! I am a human being! I . . . am . . . a man!" (*The Elephant Man*)

and Elvis Presley tribute *Wild at Heart* (1990), for which Lynch received the Palme d'Or at Cannes Film Festival, completed his fixation with small-town America.

Increasingly unconcerned with narrative logic, and shifting from realism to gory violence and surreal hallucination within the frame of a few scenes, *Lost Highway* (1997) is more feverish than before; paranoid and noir, it is Lynch's version of free jazz. Helped by an incredibly cool soundtrack provided by David Bowie and Trent Reznor, *Lost Highway* convinced audiences to take the required large leap of faith into Lynch's unfathomable universe. The very similar *Mulholland Dr.* (2001) continued that appeal, but then the momentum dropped slightly and Lynch branched out into the Internet, animation, and digital video. The intensely self-reflexive *Inland Empire* (2006), however—in which actors' lives begin to mirror those of the characters they play—was as hair-raising and Lynchian as ever. **EM**

ABOVE: Nothing is as it seems in the Hollywood dream of *Mulholland Dr.*

1940s

Weird on Top

Away from the bright lights of Hollywood, David Lynch created the unexpectedly successful TV phenomenon *Twin Peaks* (1990–1991). The series soon acquired a cult following and gave rise to various tie-in enterprises such as *The Secret Diary of Laura Palmer* written by Lynch's daughter. The drama extended Lynch's small-town interest—this time unearthing the underground secrets and shenanigans of a windswept lumber town under Federal Bureau of Investigation examination. The second series lost viewers rapidly, however, and the movie *Twin Peaks: Fire Walk With Me* (1992) was a flop.

HECTOR BABENCO

Born: Héctor Eduardo Babenco, February 7, 1946 (Mar del Plata, Buenos Aires, Argentina).

Directing style: Latin American filmmaker of daring dramas with a social conscience; themes frequently tackle the plight of the marginalized in society.

Top Takes…

Carandiru 2003
Corazón iluminado 1996 (*Foolish Heart*)
At Play in the Fields of the Lord 1991
Ironweed 1987
Kiss of the Spider Woman 1985 ☆
A terra é redonda como uma laranja 1984
Pixote: A lei do mais fraco 1981
  (*Pixote, the Law of the Weakest*)
Lúcio Flávio, o passageiro da agonia 1977
  (*Lucio Flavio*)
O rei da noite 1975 (*King of the Night*)
O Fabuloso Fittipaldi 1973

1940s

Hector Babenco won international acclaim for the wrenching drama *Kiss of the Spider Woman* (1985), which landed William Hurt a Best Actor Oscar for his powerhouse role as a homosexual prisoner. His visceral prison drama *Carandiru* (2003) has been noted for reinvigorating the Brazilian film industry with its raw, trademark themes of social inequality.

Born to Russian and Polish Jewish immigrants, Babenco quit Argentina because of anti-Semitism, moved to Brazil, and became an impoverished globetrotter. He spent seven years working as house painter, kitchen servant, and even as an extra in Spanish and Italian spaghetti Westerns.

Returning to Brazil in the early 1970s, he learned his film craft quietly as the military regime was heavily censoring the industry. He made his feature debut with *O rei da noite* (1975) (*King of the Night*), while *Lúcio Flávio, o passageiro da agonia* (1977) (*Lucio Flavio*), with its withering social commentary on the military dictatorship, attracted death threats for the director but helped kick-start the domestic film industry.

Babenco first gained international acclaim with *Pixote: A lei do mais fraco* (1981) (*Pixote, the Law of the Weakest*), a heartrending tale using street children. Although his first U.S. feature, *Kiss of the Spider Woman*, brought global acclaim, his experience of the Hollywood system with *Ironweed* (1987) drove him back to Brazil. By a quirk of fate he was treated by oncologist Drauzio Varella who, having tackled a prison AIDS epidemic, wrote a book about São Paulo's notorious convicts, which became the basis for Babenco's sublimely sprawling drama *Carandiru*. The movie chronicled anarchic life in the festering jail, and became one of the most successful Brazilian films of all time. **TE**

> "I fed off his enthusiasm when my enthusiam was nil. [Varella] became a kind of alter ego."

JÚLIO BRESSANE

Born: Júlio Bressane, February 13, 1946 (Rio de Janeiro, Brazil).

Directing style: Radical Brazilian filmmaker of the underground Cinema Marginal movement; scathing political commentary on Brazilian society; long takes; fragmentary narrative.

Júlio Bressane is one of Brazil's most radical and prolific directors, and has made more than 20 experimental feature-length films since the late 1960s. He was involved in Cinema Marginal, an underground film movement that began in 1968 and targeted the rigid conventions within Brazilian cinema. After his first feature, *Cara a Cara* (1967) (*Face to Face*), Bressane made two of the most important films of Cinema Marginal, *Matou a Família e Foi ao Cinema* (1969) (*Killed the Family and Went to the Movies*) and *O Anjo Nasceu* (1969) (*The Angel Was Born*). The former film depicts various cases of family murder without establishing any causal connection between them. The highly fragmented story is full of images of horror. Screams, seas of blood, and a detailed torture scene give evidence of the abyss of existence vis-à-vis the military regime in Brazil without directly referring to it. *The Angel Was Born* deals with two misfits who wander about Rio de Janeiro. The film is replete with very long takes, and a dramatic development is absent—epitomized in the last scene, in which a static take shows an empty road, where occasionally a car passes by.

In 1970, Bressane was accused by the military of practicing subversion and left Brazil for a three-year exile in London, where he continued making movies. Back in Brazil, Bressane directed *O Rei do Baralho* (1973), which experiments with a form of Brazilian musical comedy, the *chanchada*.

In the twenty-first century, Bressane's *Filme de Amor* (2003) (*A Love Movie*) confirms his uncompromising approach to experimental film as well as his intense intermedial dialogue with painting, music, and literature. Inspired by the Greek myth of "The Three Graces," the movie deals with eroticism in a highly artificial and stylized manner. **PS**

Top Takes...

Filme de Amor 2003 (*A Love Movie*)
Dias de Nietzsche em Turim 2001
  (*Days of Nietzche in Turin*)
São Jerônimo 1999
Miramar 1997
Brás Cubas 1985
Tabu 1982
O Rei do Baralho 1973
O Anjo Nasceu 1969 (*The Angel Was Born*)
Matou a Família e Foi ao Cinema 1969
  (*Killed the Family and Went to the Movies*)
Cara a Cara 1967 (*Face to Face*)

"It was easy to chase the public away from the cinema; it's difficult to bring it back."

1940s

JOHN WATERS

Born: John Waters, April 22, 1946 (Baltimore, Maryland, U.S.).

Directing style: The duke of disgust; comic camp; cult bad-taste movies; transgressive themes that know no limits; trash-pop iconography; sexually explicit; often cast cross-dressing actor Divine.

Top Takes...

1940s

If lack of taste is a virtue, John Waters is a saint. Asked for his guilty pleasure once, Waters admitted that he secretly enjoys art films, against his better judgment. The turning of the taste tables is typical of his attitude, and oeuvre. Waters's first feature, *Mondo Trasho* (1969), sets the tone with its insane plot and the deliciously outrageous drag queen, Divine, a high school friend of Waters, in sexual, blasphemous, and filthy actions.

Stepping up his efforts, Waters's next films, *Multiple Maniacs* (1970) and *Pink Flamingos* (1972), quickly became midnight classics in grind houses. With lethal chicken sex, *Pink Flamingos* excels as an exercise in poor taste, and Divine is the constantly costume-changing, foul-mouthed blizzard at its center. Most famous is the concluding scene, where Divine scoops up fresh dog excrement, eats it, gags, and smiles for Waters's camera.

Female Trouble (1974), *Desperate Living* (1977), and *Polyester* (1981) confirmed Waters's status as the duke of disgust, although his films gradually moved from glue-sniffing porn and foot fetishes to serious undertones, such as fascism, and fashion in the face of tolerance. As his fame spread, Waters became broader in his appetites, even campy, a move indicated by *Hairspray* (1988), filled with trash-pop iconography.

Ironically, the reverence for Waters and the growing appeal of paracinematic counter-taste attitudes popularized bad taste to the degree that his subsequent films almost look respectable. *Cry-Baby* (1990), with Iggy Pop, Ricki Lake, and a young Johnny Depp; *Serial Mom* (1994); and *Pecker* (1998) received wide acclaim as reflexive comedies without the shock value. But rest assured, the sexually explicit and disgustingly trashy *A Dirty Shame* (2004) proves that Waters still reigns on his side of the taste border. **EM**

> "Some call me director, producer, filmmaker. I prefer to call myself pube-king."

LASSE HALLSTRÖM

Born: Lars Hallström, June 2, 1946 (Stockholm, Sweden).

Directing style: Swedish director of early indie movies, and later star-studded Hollywood dramas and romantic comedies; faithful literary adaptations; lavish visuals.

Although he made his name working in Sweden, Lasse Hallström wasted little time making the leap to Hollywood and specifically its niche of popular, semi-independent art theater fare that often courted and earned Oscars, commercial success, and critical praise in equal measure.

After several successful Swedish projects, Hallström directed the coming-of-age film *Mitt liv som hund* (1985) (*My Life as a Dog*), based on the novel by Reidar Jönsson, which earned Hallström Oscar nominations for writing and directing. He initially remained in Sweden, but eventually gravitated to the United States to direct. *What's Eating Gilbert Grape* (1993), based on a novel by Peter Hedges, was an early splash, starring Johnny Depp and a young Leonardo DiCaprio. *Something to Talk About* (1995), a rote romantic comedy, led to a quiet four-year gap without a feature film.

Hallström returned with a sentimental adaptation of John Irving's *The Cider House Rules* (1999), and later the popular—and some might argue middlebrow—*Chocolat* (2000), adapted from the novel by Joanne Harris. It was a sign to many that the indie studio and longtime Hallström benefactor Miramax had moved well beyond its scruffy roots and into the mainstream.

Hallström's touch faltered with *The Shipping News* (2001) adapted from the novel by E. Annie Proulx, *An Unfinished Life* (2005), and *Casanova* (2005), films with an impeccable technical pedigree featuring A-list actors that nonetheless failed to gain much critical support. His next film, *The Hoax* (2006) was inspired by the real story of a scam artist's near-successful attempt to sell a fabricated autobiography of Howard Hughes as the real thing. Some already consider the picture a return to form for Hallström. **JK**

Top Takes...

The Hoax 2006
The Shipping News 2001
Chocolat 2000
The Cider House Rules 1999 ☆
Something to Talk About 1995
What's Eating Gilbert Grape 1993
Once Around 1991
Mitt liv som hund 1985 ☆
  (My Life as a Dog)
Två killar och en tjej 1983 (*Happy We*)
Tuppen 1981 (*The Rooster*)
Jag är med barn 1979 (*Father to Be*)
ABBA: The Movie 1977
En kille och en tjej 1975 (*A Guy and a Gal*)

> "I have an affinity for eccentrics and outsiders, portraying them and not being judgmental . . . ."

GEOFF MURPHY

Born: Geoff Murphy, June 13, 1946 (New Zealand).

Directing style: New Zealand director across a variety of genres; action sequences; themes tackle the politics of imperialism; wry comedy; specialized in making sequels.

Top Takes...

1940s

Geoff Murphy began his career with a run of excellent, ambitious New Zealand genre films starring local actor Bruno Lawrence. He and Lawrence knew each other from their days as founding members of Bruno Lawrence's Electric Revelation and Traveling Apparition (Blerta) musical and theatrical cooperative formed in the 1970s. The best known of Murphy's early films is *Goodbye Pork Pie* (1981), a good-humored and exciting road movie that became a cult classic in the vein of *Easy Rider* (1969) in his native New Zealand. The low-budget film was put together by a crew and cast of only twenty-four. Such was its shoestring budget that the Holden police cars used in the film doubled as transport for crew and towing vehicles, and Murphy performed some of the stunts himself.

Murphy followed this up successfully with what was a big-budget movie for its time, *UTU* (1983), a historical drama about nineteenth-century clashes between imperialist British settlers and the native Maori. *The Quiet Earth* (1985) is an intelligent science-fiction film based on a novel by Craig Harrison about the few people who are left behind when most of humankind disappears after an apocalyptic event. It gave Lawrence and Murphy the opportunity to vent some anti-U.S. sentiments.

Murphy then went to the United States to make a TV movie, *Red King, White Knight* (1989), and stayed there as a gun for hire. He has specialized in by-the-book sequels such as *Young Guns II* (1990), *Under Siege 2: Dark Territory* (1995), and *Fortress 2* (1999); Westerns such as *The Last Outlaw* (1994); and science-fiction films such as *Race against Time* (2000). Murphy returned to New Zealand where he made *Blerta Revisited* (2001), a documentary about the Blerta cooperative, and the conspiracy thriller *Spooked* (2004). **KN**

> "I could build a radio station out of a milk carton and two condom wrappers."—*Fortress 2*

PAUL SCHRADER

Born: Paul Joseph Schrader, July 22, 1946 (Grand Rapids, Michigan, U.S.).

Directing style: Film critic turned successful screenwriter turned movie director of often brutal film noirs and dramas; existential and sexual themes; neo-Expressionist feel.

Paul Schrader was raised in a strict Dutch Calvinist environment with restricted access to filmed entertainment. In the 1960s his ambition was to be a minister, but a chance meeting with film critic Pauline Kael provided him with an introduction to University of California, Los Angeles (UCLA) film school, where he fervently watched films, and under Kael's mentoring became critic for *LA Weekly*. In the early 1970s Schrader worked as editor for *Cinema* magazine, and published *Transcendental Style in Film: Ozu, Bresson, Dreyer* (1972).

Schrader's first success as a screenwriter came with *The Yakuza* (1974), and his script output included *Obsession* (1976), *Taxi Driver* (1976), and *Raging Bull* (1980). He made his directorial debut with *Blue Collar* (1978), and went on to make such films as *American Gigolo* (1980), *Cat People* (1982), *Patty Hearst* (1988), *Light Sleeper* (1992), and *Auto Focus* (2002).

Like other directors who began in the ranks of cinephile critic, Schrader loads his work with reference and allusion. His college years were mostly informed by the films of Ingmar Bergman, but at UCLA his influences included Jean Renoir, Robert Bresson, John Ford, and Alfred Hitchcock. Schrader counts *The Searchers* (1956) and *Vertigo* (1958) among the greatest films ever made. Additionally, Schrader's interest in film noir is evident in works from the neo-Expressionist *Taxi Driver* through *Light Sleeper* to the film noir romance of *Forever Mine* (1999). Schrader acknowledges, too, the legacy of his upbringing; John Calvin's endeavor to reduce the window of faith to the smallest of apertures is expressed through an emotionally blinding moment in the prison sequences of *American Gigolo* and *Light Sleeper*, and in the suicidal endings of *Taxi Driver* and *Mishima* (1985). **CV**

Top Takes...

Dominion: Prequel to the Exorcist 2005
Auto Focus 2002
Forever Mine 1999
Affliction 1997
Light Sleeper 1992
The Comfort of Strangers 1990
Patty Hearst 1988
Light of Day 1987
Mishima: A Life in Four Chapters 1985
Cat People 1982
American Gigolo 1980
Hardcore 1979
Blue Collar 1978

"I killed more characters in the first four films I wrote than I have since. I realized I had to stop . . . ."

1940s

GORAN MARKOVIC

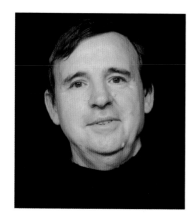

Born: Goran Markovic, July 24, 1946 (Belgrade, Yugoslavia).

Directing style: Serbian director of satirical comedies frequently with a fantasy horror edge; examination of the effect of socialism on ordinary people; often merged genres.

Top Takes…

Kordon 2002 (*The Cordon*)
Serbie, année zéro 2001 (*Serbia, Year Zero*)
Urnebesna tragedija 1994
Tito i ja 1992 (*Tito and Me*)
Sabirni centar 1989 (*The Meeting Point*)
Vec vidjeno 1987 (*Reflections*)
Variola vera 1981
Majstori, majstori 1980 (*All That Jack's*)
Nacionalna klasa 1979
   (*National Class Category Up to 785 ccm*)
Specijalno vaspitanje 1977 (*Special Education*)
Bez názvu 1970 (*Without a Name*)

The son of actors, Goran Markovic studied directing in Prague. His first feature, *Specijalno vaspitanje* (1977) (*Special Education*) was a critical and commercial success, and he is among a select few Serbian directors who have been equally awarded at the festivals and the box office. Markovic's debut introduced the dominant theme of his opus: the effect of socialism on common people's souls; his approach, a satire; and his mise-en-scène, an isolated group as a microcosm reflecting the ills of society. This was elaborated upon in *Majstori, majstori* (1980) (*All That Jack's*), a tragicomedy about alienated elementary level teachers whose school celebration turns into a nightmare.

Markovic was the first Serbian director to merge the social concerns of auteur cinema with the motifs and style of genre film. His urban comedy *Nacionalna klasa* (1979) (*National Class Category Up to 785 ccm*) mixed a strong youth appeal with clever satire, and gained cult status as a result. In *Variola vera* (1981), based on a real event, a Belgrade hospital is quarantined after an outbreak of smallpox. Structured as a disaster movie verging on horror, it is a powerful parable of a dysfunctional and diseased society. Genre horror is more evident in *Vec vidjeno* (1987) (*Reflections*), about a disturbed piano teacher who, after a lifetime of abuse, snaps and goes on a killing spree. Fantasy, comedy, and horror also merge in *Sabirni centar* (1989) (*The Meeting Point*), a satire about attempts of the deceased to come back to life and rectify certain wrongs. Markovic's most famous film remains *Tito i ja* (1992) (*Tito and Me*), a bleakly comic tale of a boy's obsession with the communist dictator who ruled Yugoslavia from 1945 to 1980. His later films, often dealing with another dictator, Slobodan Milošević, have been less successful. **DO**

> "[*Tito and Me*] is refreshingly free of things folkloric and picturesque."—*New York Times*

OLIVER STONE

Born: William Oliver Stone, September 15, 1946 (New York City, New York, U.S.).

Directing style: Political filmmaker of dramas and biopics; frequently tackles controversial issues; examines the nature of power and individual morality; antiwar themes.

Oliver Stone dropped out of the Ivy League to enlist in the Vietnam War, in which he was injured and highly decorated. He attended New York University, began writing scripts, and directed the horror movie, *Seizure* (1974). His script for *Midnight Express* (1978) earned him an Oscar, and he soon afterward directed another horror film, *The Hand* (1981).

He went on to write and direct *Salvador* (1986) and *Platoon* (1986), which established the tone of his best work, largely focused on Vietnam or sociopolitical issues. *Salvador* uncovers the sordid truth of relations between the United States and Central America, whereas *Platoon*, his first Oscar-winning turn as director, is an autobiographical story of Vietnam and provoked a national catharsis. His second masterpiece and another Oscar winner, *Born on the Fourth of July* (1989), translates antiwar Vietnam veteran Ron Kovic's story for the screen. He followed this up with the story of the rock band *The Doors* (1991), and then *JFK* (1991), which exposed competing theories about Kennedy's assassination and caused lasting controversy.

Thereafter, Stone was inconsistent. *Heaven & Earth* (1993) was a disappointment but *Natural Born Killers* (1994) became a violent tour de force. Criticized for being over the top, the film reflects the way current society is in fact intrigued by violence. His biopic *Nixon* (1995) was fascinating, and *U Turn* (1997) neat but not up to his usual high standard. In the new millennium, Stone made several shorts about Cuban leader Fidel Castro before directing his dream epic *Alexander* (2004), which was an utter failure. Thankfully Stone has turned a corner, directing *World Trade Center* (2006), a reflection on 9/11, which encouraged former detractors to join in celebrating the triumph of individual heroism in the face of disaster. **GCQ**

Top Takes...

World Trade Center 2006
Comandante 2003
Any Given Sunday 1999
U Turn 1997
Nixon 1995
Natural Born Killers 1994
***JFK* 1991** ☆
The Doors 1991
***Born on the Fourth of July* 1989** ★
Talk Radio 1988
Wall Street 1987
***Platoon* 1986** ★
Salvador 1986
The Hand 1981
Seizure 1974
Last Year in Viet Nam 1971

"They say I'm unsubtle. But we need above all, a theater that wakes us up: nerves and heart."

1940s

JOHN WOO

Born: Yusen Wu, September 23, 1946 (Guangzhou, China).

Directing style: Maker of early Hong Kong gangster movies in the "Heroic Bloodshed" style, and later Hollywood action blockbusters; balletically choreographed violent action sequences.

Top Takes...

Paycheck 2003
Hostage 2002
Mission: Impossible II 2000
Face/Off 1997
Hard Target 1993
Laat sau sen taan 1992
Zong heng si hai 1991
  (*Criss-Cross Over Four Seas*)
Die xue jie tou 1990 (*Bloodshed in the Streets*)
Dip hyut shueng hung 1989 (*The Killer*)
Ying hung boon sik 1986 (*A Better Tomorrow*)
Xiao jiang 1984 (*The Time You Need a Friend*)
Tie han rou qing 1974 (*Ninja Kids*)
Ouran 1968 (*Accidentaly*)

One of the leading action directors working today, John Woo is the most successful of the filmmakers to emerge from Hong Kong cinema's international recognition during the late 1980s and early 1990s.

Growing up in the slums of Hong Kong, Woo's family could not afford to send him to school. Thanks to the support of a U.S. family, however, he was able to attend one and began making short films with friends. He entered the film industry in 1969 as a production assistant at Cathay Studios, and moved to Shaw Brothers studios in 1971, where he assisted legendary martial arts director Cheh Chang. Woo made his directorial debut with the kung fu film *Tie han rou qing* (1974) (*Ninja Kids*). Over the next decade, he established himself as a reliable director, working in every genre but becoming best known for comedies.

This reputation changed dramatically when Woo joined Tsui Hark's Film Workshop. Influenced by Jean-Pierre Melville and Sam Peckinpah, Woo crafted the gangster opus *Ying hung boon sik* (1986) (*A Better Tomorrow*). Showcasing his now trademark "Heroic Bloodshed" style of operatic violence, the film was a huge homeland success. However, worldwide recognition came with *Dip hyut shueng hung* (1989) (*The Killer*), which won awards in Hong Kong, and is now considered a classic of the genre. Hollywood soon called, and Woo made the transition with *Hard Target* (1993). But the adjustment proved to be rough: the film suffered major cuts by the Motion Picture Association of America because of its violent content. However, the hardship was temporary and Woo quickly recovered, directing a number of big-budget action vehicles, including the box-office hits *Face/Off* (1997) and *Mission: Impossible II* (2000). **WW**

"[Doves] look so beautiful, like a woman. For me they represent peace and love and purity."

JOE DANTE

Born: Joseph Dante Jr., November 28, 1946 (Morristown, New Jersey, U.S.).

Directing style: Maker of darkly humorous horror and science-fiction films; films often contain cartoon homages and cinematic references; notable collaborations with director Steven Spielberg.

Joe Dante is a U.S. director best known for his darkly comic horror and science-fiction films, including *Piranha* (1978), *The Howling* (1981), and the monster hit *Gremlins* (1984).

Dante started out as a cartoonist on magazines, before focusing on filmmaking. An avid movie fan, Dante wrote film reviews for several publications prior to his first job in the film industry as an editor at New World Pictures. He worked his way up from cutting trailers to features and, eventually, a codirecting credit on *Hollywood Boulevard* (1976).

Dante made his solo directing debut with *Piranha*, a variation on *Jaws* (1975) scripted by John Sayles, which became a cult hit. The duo teamed up again for the werewolf entry *The Howling* (1981). Both films provided enough evidence of Dante's talent at storytelling and special effects for Steven Spielberg to hire him to direct a segment of *Twilight Zone: The Movie* (1983), and the creature feature *Gremlins*. The latter turned into a worldwide phenomenon and Dante followed it with a sequel. He capped this with another Spielberg production, the science-fiction comedy *Innerspace* (1987), which won an Academy Award for Best Effects, Visual Effects.

As evidenced by *Gremlins*, Dante's work combines humor with horror. He reached his dramatic peak with *Matinee* (1993), a coming-of-age story where B-movie terrors merge with real-life panic in the form of the Cuban missile crisis. Dante's love of cinema is also evident onscreen, as his films often feature cinematic references, and stars from the B movies of yesteryear. In addition to his big-screen work, Dante has consistently directed for TV, working on *The Twilight Zone* (1985), Spielberg's *Amazing Stories* (1986), *Eerie, Indiana* (1991–1992), and *Masters of Horror* (2005–2006). **WW**

Top Takes…

Trapped Ashes 2006
Haunted Lighthouse 2003
Small Soldiers 1998
Matinee 1993
Gremlins 2: The New Batch 1990
Innerspace 1987
Explorers 1985
Gremlins 1984
Twilight Zone: The Movie 1983
The Howling 1981
Piranha 1978
Hollywood Boulevard 1976

1940s

"Each director, given any given project, is going to make a different movie out of it."

STEVEN SPIELBERG

Born: Steven Allan Spielberg, December 18, 1946 (Cincinnati, Ohio, U.S.).

Directing style: Titan of Hollywood; genius of storytelling; depictions of ordinary people in extraordinary circumstances; powerful war dramas; uplifting science fiction; masterful action adventures.

Top Takes...

Munich **2005** ☆
War of the Worlds 2005
Catch Me If You Can 2002
Minority Report 2002
Artificial Intelligence: AI 2001
Saving Private Ryan **1998** ★
Schindler's List **1993** ★
Jurassic Park 1993
Hook 1991
Indiana Jones and the Last Crusade 1989
Empire of the Sun 1987
The Color Purple 1985
Indiana Jones and the Temple of Doom 1984
Twilight Zone: The Movie 1983
E.T. the Extra-Terrestrial **1982** ☆
Raiders of the Lost Ark **1981** ☆
1941 1979
Close Encounters of the Third Kind **1977** ☆
Jaws 1975
The Sugarland Express 1974
The Last Gun 1959

Steven Spielberg was imagining movies in childhood, and filming them on 8mm around the age of twelve. With a background in television direction for shows such as *Marcus Welby, M.D.* (1970), his first serious film work came with *Duel* (1971), in which a mild-mannered commuter businessman, played by Dennis Weaver, is harassed by a diabolical tractor-trailer on an open road. He then filmed another road story, *The Sugarland Express* (1974), about an escaped convict racing across country with his wife and child while the police, some well-intentioned and some not, give chase in a long and increasingly malevolent caravan.

It was in 1975, however, that Spielberg exploded on to the movie scene around the world. Working with Peter Benchley's book of the same name, he directed *Jaws* (1975), about a giant rogue shark and three somewhat incompatible men who sail out to kill it. The film captured audiences with its wittily edited and chillingly scored narrative, and its energizing concentration on visual storytelling. Spielberg was hailed as a wunderkind. Over the next ten years he triumphed with *Close Encounters*

RIGHT: A "hold on to the edge of your seat" moment from the classic horror film *Jaws*.

1940s

of the *Third Kind* (1977), *1941* (1979), *Raiders of the Lost Ark* (1981), *E.T. the Extra-Terrestrial* (1982), *Indiana Jones and the Temple of Doom* (1984), and an adaptation of Alice Walker's best-selling novel, *The Color Purple* (1985), which is a richly photographed story of slavery, emancipation, and womanhood. All of these movies emphasize a sentimental view of the world perfectly attuned to audiences' bourgeois sensibility, and feature gracefully swooping camerawork, meticulous mise-en-scène in realistic settings, and evocative performances from perfectly cast actors, some of whom, typically, were young or just youthfully innocent on camera.

ABOVE: A tender and iconic image from the alien tearjerker, *E.T. the Extra-Terrestrial.*

"I don't drink coffee. That's something you probably don't know about me."

   E.T. the Extra-Terrestrial has become iconic in many ways. The story of a young boy befriending a goofy extra-terrestrial who has inadvertently been abandoned on Earth, the film explores

Facts and Figures

Steven Spielberg is now regarded as the most financially successful filmmaker in history, a leading figure in his generation, and a blockbuster force in Hollywood film production through his Amblin Entertainment and DreamWorks SKG. He has directed more than 20 feature films to date, and has produced numerous films for himself and others, including *Back to the Future* (1985), which made Michael J. Fox an instant superstar, and *Flags of Our Fathers* (2006).

- *E.T. the Extra-Terrestrial* grossed more than $1 billion on a shooting budget of $10 million.
- Spielberg spent almost a year on Martha's Vineyard filming *Jaws*. The movie made back $7 million of its $12 million budget on the first weekend, and proceeded to gross more than $500 million worldwide.
- *Jurassic Park* broke the record for the highest grossing movie of all time. Spielberg reputedly made $250 million from the film. The two sequels were also financially successful but did not receive the critical acclaim of the original.
- Although he produced and directed *Schindler's List*, Spielberg did not make any money from the film. He asked not to be paid.
- Steven Spielberg is one of the richest producer/directors in the world.

a child's capacity for wonder in the context of a malevolent adult world. The alien creature, a robot created by Carlo Rambaldi, endeared itself to viewers because of its thirst for beer, its ability to cure wounds at a touch, and its longing for home: "E.T. phone home!"

Success after success

Empire of the Sun (1987) has a stunning symphonic quality as it recounts the imprisonment of a young British boy, James "Jamie" Graham (played by Christian Bale in an extraordinary performance), near Shanghai in the days before the explosion of the first atomic bomb. Mixing location and studio shots with aplomb, conceiving and executing complicated action shots—especially one where Jamie sees his favorite airplane swoop past him—and drawing out the pain of the child's separation from his parents, his canny survival skills in various prison camps, his near starvation, and his final reconciliation in his mother's arms, Spielberg creates an evocative, harmonious, and visually centered film of great power and attractiveness.

In two 1990s films based on Michael Crichton's *Jurassic Park* novel, Spielberg plays out a self-reflexive adventure in a commercial funland inhabited by clones of prehistoric beasts. *Artificial Intelligence: AI* (2001) also explores cloning, as does the Tom Cruise box-office hit *Minority Report* (2002), in which punishment precedes crime—an allegorical slap at contemporary right-wing political maneuvers in the wake of 9/11. His later work has had a more lukewarm reception, but his finest could still be to come.

Spielberg has a passionate interest in World War II that is reflected in the subject matter of films such as *Saving Private Ryan* (1998). One of his finest movies, the film wowed critics and audiences but surprisingly missed out on the Best Picture Oscar. Most controversial of his films is *Schindler's List* (1993), the story of a man who saved Jews from the extermination camps; Spielberg was accused of maudlin misrepresentation as much as for bravely bringing the Holocaust to light in the context of mainstream entertainment. **MP**

RIGHT: Movie poster for Spielberg's hugely disconcerting war drama *Schindler's List*.

1940s

A FILM BY STEVEN SPIELBERG
SCHINDLER'S LIST
UNIVERSAL PICTURES PRESENTS AN AMBLIN ENTERTAINMENT PRODUCTION "SCHINDLER'S LIST" LIAM NEESON · BEN KINGSLEY
RALPH FIENNES · CAROLINE GOODALL · JONATHAN SAGALLE · EMBETH DAVIDTZ MUSIC BY JOHN WILLIAMS CO-PRODUCER LEW RYWIN PRODUCTION DESIGNER ALLAN STARSKI
FILM EDITED BY MICHAEL KAHN, A.C.E. DIRECTOR OF PHOTOGRAPHY JANUSZ KAMINSKI EXECUTIVE PRODUCER KATHLEEN KENNEDY BASED ON THE NOVEL BY THOMAS KENEALLY SCREENPLAY BY STEVEN ZAILLIAN
AMBLIN
R RESTRICTED
PRODUCED BY STEVEN SPIELBERG GERALD R. MOLEN BRANKO LUSTIG DIRECTED BY STEVEN SPIELBERG A UNIVERSAL PICTURE
UNIVERSAL

TAKESHI KITANO

Born: Takeshi Kitano, January 18, 1947 (Tokyo, Japan).

Directing style: Actor and director across a diversity of genres; unpredictable; often plays the cool protagonist himself; careful composition; immaculate framing; deadpan humor.

Top Takes…

Takeshi Kitano began directing on *Sono otoko, kyôbô ni tsuki* (1990) (*Violent Cop*), a film in which he played precisely such a character. He brought much visceral violence and deadpan humor to the picture, and so began a career that has alternated between enormously inventive and delightfully playful variations on the crime genre, such as *3–4x juugatsu* (1990) (*Boiling Point*) and the successful *Hana-bi* (1997) (*Fireworks*).

He has also directed a variety of more unusual works. *Ano Natsu, ichiban shizukana umi* (1991) (*A Scene at the Sea*) is a witty, poignant tale of a young deaf couple getting into surfing. *Minnâ-yatteruka!* (1995) (*Getting Any?*) is boisterous madcap comedy. *Dolls* (2002) is a visually sumptuous and strange triptych of love stories inspired by *bunraku* puppet theater. *Takeshis'* (2005) is an audaciously complex, experimental reflection upon Kitano's career, in which he plays both a famous star-cum-director and a would-be movie star.

What unites the diverse strands in Kitano's unpredictable oeuvre is his distinctive approach to composition, color, and cutting. Just as his performances tend toward the laconic and deadpan, so he shows only what is essential to his overall purpose. The framing is immaculate; establishing and linking shots that would be used by most directors are often omitted, and what shots are included are held just long enough to make their point. This lean aesthetic never feels forced because there is too much humor in Kitano's work for portentousness to arise. Rather, it is appropriate to the character of his existential protagonists, who (usually played by Kitano himself) give the impression of being inwardly preoccupied by questions of how to live, and die, in a manner that is true to themselves. **GA**

> "… to show violence realistically, you need stamina. It's not easy."

ROB REINER

Born: Robert Reiner, March 6, 1947 (Bronx, New York City, New York, U.S.).

Directing style: Actor turned director; maker of romantic comedies and dramas; focus on idiosyncrasies of the human character, and the dynamic of power in relationships.

Rob Reiner's career as a director has been highly successful, both commercially and critically, starting with the cult classic rock-mockumentary, *This Is Spinal Tap* (1984). His film output has fallen off in recent years, in both quantity and quality, as he has become a high-profile political advocate.

Reiner was born the son of comedy legend Carl Reiner, and has directed an impressive string of hit romantic comedies and dramas. Among the comedies, *When Harry Met Sally* (1989) was the most successful. Its exploration of how, or if, women and men can be nonsexual friends was highlighted by Meg Ryan's iconic fake orgasm in a restaurant. It also demonstrates Reiner's focus on the idiosyncrasies and intricacies of humankind.

This focus is most compelling in his dramas, which also concentrate on the dynamic of power in individual and institutional relationships. Reiner uses a realistic style with few technical frills to get to the heart of how people interact, particularly as expressed in the uniquely U.S. experience.

Misery (1990) gets inside the head of an obsessed fan, played by Kathy Bates, whose passive-aggressive adoration of James Caan's Stephen King alter ego becomes violently malevolent. *A Few Good Men* (1992) and *Ghosts of Mississippi* (1996) dissect two U.S. cultural phenomena: a professional military torn by the moral dilemma concerning questions of loyalty, and, secondly, black-white racism with its continuing ramifications in the U.S. South.

The paradox of U.S. obsession with both morality and can-do pragmatism that so often characterizes Reiner's work is best summed up in the infamous rebuke by the old-school Colonel (Jack Nicholson) to the prima donna Judge Advocate Lawyer (Tom Cruise) in *A Few Good Men*: "You can't handle the truth!" **WSW**

Top Takes...

Rumor Has It . . . 2005
Alex & Emma 2003
The Story of Us 1999
Spinal Tap: The Final Tour 1998
Ghosts of Mississippi 1996
The American President 1995
A Few Good Men 1992
Misery 1990
When Harry Met Sally 1989
The Princess Bride 1987
Stand by Me 1986
The Sure Thing 1985
This Is Spinal Tap 1984

1940s

"I like writing because you can make things happen . . . the way they never do in real life."

HSIAO-HSIEN HOU

Born: Hsiao-hsien Hou, April 8, 1947 (Meixian, Guangdong, China).

Directing style: Director of the Taiwanese New Wave; graceful storytelling; exploration of the impact of the historical upon the human; themes of generational conflict.

Top Takes…

Zui hao de shi guang 2005 (Three Times)

Kôhî jikô 2003 (Café Lumière)

Qianxi manbo 2001 (Millennium Mambo)

Hai shang hua 1998 (Flowers of Shanghai)

Nanguo zaijan, nanguo 1996
  (Goodbye South, Goodbye)

Haonan haonu 1995
  (Good Men, Good Women)

Hsimeng jensheng 1993 (The Puppetmaster)

Beiqing chengshi 1989 (A City of Sadness)

Niluohe nuer 1987 (Daughter of the Nile)

Lianlian fengchen 1986 (Dust in the Wind)

Tong nien wang shi 1985
  (A Time to Live and a Time to Die)

Dongdong de jiaqi 1984
  (A Summer at Grandpa's)

"Art movies and commercial movies are [in Taiwan considered] opposites . . . ."

Hsiao-hsien Hou is frequently heralded as one of the premier auteurs of the Taiwanese New Wave. His work engages themes of political, cultural, and personal transition, frequently through oblique narratives grounded upon generational conflicts. Like the films of Yasujiro Ozu, Hou's minimalist yet meticulous mise-en-scène depicts not only life's seemingly insignificant details, but the impact of time and light upon the understanding of character and history. Hou's film, Kôhî jikô (2003) (Café Lumière) is a loving tribute to the Japanese master.

In his early years, Hou witnessed a series of transformations: the establishment of a Chinese nationalist government after World War II, decades of Japanese occupation, the impact of the economic boom and rapid Western-style urbanization, and the infusion of electronic information technologies.

Perhaps no film better illuminates the impact of the historical upon the human in Hou's cinema than Zui hao de shi guang (2005) (Three Times), a trio of love stories. Three Times's settings encapsulate the approximate historical moments and material landscapes upon which the majority of his films are based. "A Time for Love" is reminiscent of the locations in Tong nien wang shi (1985) (A Time to Live and a Time to Die); "A Time for Freedom" evokes the subtle machinations of two of his most critically acclaimed films, Hsimeng jensheng (1993) (The Puppetmaster) and Hai shang hua (1998) (Flowers of Shanghai); and the love triangle and contemporary urban technoculture of "A Time for Youth" recall Qianxi manbo (2001) (Millennium Mambo). A hugely talented visionary, Hou is one of the greatest storytellers of this, or any, age. Six of his films have been nominated for the Palme d'Or and he has received numerous awards. **JM**

THE QUAY BROTHERS

Born: Stephen and Timothy Quay, June 17, 1947 (Norristown, Pennsylvania, U.S.).

Directing style: Avant-garde stop-motion animators; absence of spoken content; surreal, nightmarish, and erotic imagery; allusions to literature and myth; maze-like narrative.

Identical twin brothers Stephen and Timothy Quay moved to London to study at the Royal College of Art, and are now based there; but their imaginations and sensibilities roam a mythic, phantasmagorical world of Mitteleuropa. In their intricate animations, pieces of discarded junk such as rusty screws, fragments of broken mirror, pulleys, half-dismembered dolls, feathers, and balls of fluff take on an urgent, obsessive life of their own and play out obscure rituals and enigmatic dramas.

To date the Quays have made two feature-length films: *Institute Benjamenta, or This Dream People Call Human Life* (1995) and *The Piano Tuner of Earthquakes* (2005). The first is set in a school for servants deep in a Germanic forest, the second in a remote island asylum where a sinister doctor keeps a beautiful catatonic opera singer whom he kidnapped on the eve of her marriage. Both are dreamlike, surrealist, and remote, and show scant concern for narrative pacing or logic.

But it is in the Quays's short animated films that the essence of their oddball genius is distilled. Narrative here is even less in evidence, although obscure literary sources often underlie the films: the Epic of Gilgamesh for *This Unnameable Little Broom* (1985), the Polish writer Bruno Schulz for *Street of Crocodiles* (1986), and the Swiss essayist Robert Walser for *Stille Nacht I* (1988) and *The Comb* (1990). Franz Kafka is an all-pervasive influence throughout their work. *The Cabinet of Jan Svankmajer* (1984) pays tribute to the great Czech animator whose work bears the closest affinities to theirs.

Attempting to extract meaning from the Quays's films would be futile. But watching them, it is almost impossible not to succumb to their sinister, melancholy, haunting, and strangely erotic imagery. **PK**

Top Takes...

The Piano Tuner of Earthquakes 2005
In Absentia 2000
Duet 2000
Institute Benjamenta, or This Dream People Call Human Life 1995
Stille Nacht IV 1993
Are We Still Married 1992
Tales from the Vienna Woods 1992
De Artificiali Perspectiva 1991 (*Anamorphosis*)
The Comb 1990
Stille Nacht I 1988
Street of Crocodiles 1986
This Unnameable Little Broom 1985
The Cabinet of Jan Svankmajer 1984
Nocturna Artificialia 1979

1940s

"What happens in the shadow, in the gray regions, interests us—all that is elusive . . . ."

ROSS McELWEE

Born: Ross McElwee, July 21, 1947 (Charlotte, North Carolina, U.S.).

Directing style: Independent filmmaker of nonfiction features and shorts; autobiographical and sociopolitical content; subjective narratives; appears in his own movies.

Top Takes...

1940s

Ross McElwee refers to his filmmaking as "nonfiction" rather than "documentary." He made several films before completing the work that signaled his artistic path, *Charleen or How Long Has This Been Going On?* (1980), about Charleen Swansea, an eccentric poetry teacher who also happened to be his former high school mentor. *Charleen* anticipated the direction McElwee's approach to nonfiction filmmaking would take: he began to experiment with a personal or autobiographical approach to his subject, often using friends and members of his family, filming simply as a one-person crew and weaving into the completed film a subjective narration along with serendipitous, nonintentional on-camera experiences.

Sherman's March (1986) was the film that brought him acclaim, winning numerous awards and honors. In this amusing and frequently funny film, his strikingly original inventive strategy was to retrace General William Tecumseh Sherman's destructive U.S. Civil War route, juxtaposing his own, highly subjective meditations on love and life against the lives of seven Southern women he meets along the way. Its success led to an autobiographical sequel, *Time Indefinite* (1993), in which McElwee happily gets married, confronts his father's sudden death, and subsequently becomes a father himself. His next film, *Six O'Clock News* (1996), was for the TV documentary series *Frontline* (1983–), and interweaves his thoughts on exploitive news with the narrative of the lives of people who have been the subjects of sensational news stories. *Bright Leaves* (2003), about the tobacco industry in his home state, was nominated for Best Documentary by both the Director's Guild of America and the Writer's Guild of America. McElwee teaches filmmaking at Harvard University. **SU**

> "It seems I'm filming my life in order to have a life to film, like some primitive organism. . . ."

EDWARD YANG

Born: Te-Chang Yang, November 6, 1947 (Shanghai, China).

Directing style: Auteur of the Taiwanese New Wave; multiple narratives; exploration of the impact of Westernization upon the individual; themes of urban life.

Along with Hsiao-hsien Hou and Ming-liang Tsai, Edward Yang is one of the most important directors to have emerged from Taiwan. His first films to attract attention abroad were *Qingmei Zhuma* (1985) (*Taipei Story*) in which Hou played the lead role, and *Kongbu fenzi* (1986) (*The Terroriser*), multistranded narratives capturing the complexity of life in a city undergoing considerable changes, and so experiencing some confusion in terms of its sense of identity.

But it was *Guling jie shaonian sha ren shijian* (1991) (*A Brighter Summer Day*) that established Yang's reputation as one of the most interesting filmmakers of the 1990s. It is a beautifully measured, elliptical account of a boy's experiences of violent gang rivalry and first love in 1960s Taipei, and deals with the social and psychological effects of Taiwan's separation from mainland China, and its concomitant Westernization. Reflecting Yang's interest in how individuals relate to society, it also favors medium and long shots over the close-up, just as costume and décor are used to suggest class background and aspiration, and lighting and color to evoke mood.

Although *Duli shidai* (1994) (*A Confucian Confusion*) was a foray into the domain of comic irony, as opposed to the sober, understated drama that is Yang's specialty, and although his satire *Mahjong* (1996) was flawed by one poorly cast character, Yang has continued to create intelligent, compassionate, and witty works of considerable mastery. His three-hour epic *Yi yi* (2000) is a recent example of his ability to deal with a large social tapestry while drawing the audience into intimate dramas of great emotional and psychological authenticity. The film won favor with audiences and critics alike, and Yang won Best Director at the Cannes Film Festival. **GA**

Top Takes…

The Wind 2007
Yi yi 2000
Mahjong 1996
Duli shidai 1994 (*A Confucian Confusion*)
Guling jie shaonian sha ren shijian 1991 (*A Brighter Summer Day*)
Kongbu fenzi 1986 (*The Terroriser*)
Qingmei Zhuma 1985 (*Taipei Story*)
Haitan de yitian 1983 (*That Day, on the Beach*)
Guangyinde gushi 1982 (*In Our Time*)

1940s

"… no one was willing to give us any money, but we shared all these idealistic thoughts."

PATRICE LECONTE

Born: Patrice Leconte, November 12, 1947 (Paris, France).

Directing style: Gallic director of surreal romantic comedies; use of bizarre situational humor; themes of sexuality, mental health, and obsession; witty dialogue.

Top Takes...

Mon meilleur ami 2006 (*My Best Friend*)

Confidences trop intimes 2004
  (*Intimate Strangers*)

L'homme du train 2002 (*The Man on the Train*)

Félix et Lola 2001 (*Felix and Lola*)

La fille sur le pont 1999 (*The Girl on the Bridge*)

Ridicule 1996

Le batteur du boléro 1992

Le mari de la coiffeuse 1990
  (*The Hairdresser's Husband*)

Monsieur Hire 1989 (*M. Hire*)

Tandem 1987

Les spécialistes 1985

Les bronzés 1978 (*French Fried Vacation*)

Les vécés étaient fermés de l'interieur 1976

Known for his tendencies to stray from the norm, it is not surprising that Patrice Leconte took the unconventional path of becoming a cartoonist for *Pilote* magazine. His first feature, *Les vécés étaient fermés de l'interieur* (1976), is based on the French police mysteries that were popular in the 1950s. The movie displays the director's bizarre sense of humor and tells the story of a man blown up in a restroom.

Leconte first found success with *Les bronzés* (1978) (*French Fried Vacation*), a comedy that pokes fun at Club Med vacations. It was well received and he went on to make two sequels. Leconte changed his comedic approach with *Les spécialistes* (1985) about two escaped prisoners on the run. The film proved to be his most successful yet and had commercial appeal. The movie that first brought Leconte international recognition was *Monsieur Hire* (1989) (*M. Hire*), which tells the story of the voyeuristic nature of a relationship between neighbors and was nominated for the Palme d'Or at the Cannes Film Festival. He followed this up with the international hit *Le mari de la coiffeuse* (1990) (*The Hairdresser's Husband*) about a man's love for haircuts—and a hairdresser. Leconte's versatility was displayed in his period romantic comedy *Ridicule* (1996) that re-created the social games and complexities of the eighteenth-century court of Versailles. It was widely acclaimed and received an Oscar nod for Best Foreign Language Film. His taste for wacky situational humor was again apparent in the romantic comedy *La fille sur le pont* (1999) (*The Girl On The Bridge*) about a knife thrower who employs suicidal female assistants. Other popular films include *L'homme du train* (2002) (*The Man on the Train*) and *Mon meilleur ami* (2006) (*My Best Friend*). **ES**

"... like John Huston, I'd like to become very old and go on and make films until I die."

JOHN CARPENTER

Born: John Howard Carpenter, January 16, 1948 (Carthage, New York, U.S.).

Directing style: Slasher horror maestro; maker of urban action thrillers and science-fiction movies; composes his own synthesizer-based soundtracks; artistic collaborations with actor Kurt Russell.

Across a career spanning more than three decades, "The Master of Terror" John Carpenter can surely number many achievements. He has been credited with inventing the commercial version of the slasher film with *Halloween* (1978), and has overseen the outer reaches of prosthetic and latex special effects in *The Thing* (1982). Carpenter has also given new life to the urban action thriller, *Assault on Precinct 13* (1976), and combined occult themes with a scientific twist in *Prince of Darkness* (1987).

Perhaps the thinking genre fan's favorite director, Carpenter made his name with a string of huge Hollywood successes. Although his output tailed off somewhat by the 1990s, his body of work as a popular genre auteur remains stunning. Despite his evident affinity with horror-based material, he has shown an ability to work across different genres such as science fiction and comedy. And as have many directors, Carpenter has worked repeatedly with favored actors: Kurt Russell features in a number of his films, among them *The Thing*, *Escape From New York* (1981), and *Big Trouble in Little China* (1986).

Carpenter is especially well known for writing musical scores, and he has composed the dramatic scores for 16 of his own movies. His use of eerie and insistent synthesizer sounds lends much to the impact of films such as *Halloween* and *The Fog* (1980). Indeed, the *Halloween* music has almost taken on a life of its own thanks to its iconic status among horror film aficionados. Carpenter's earlier successes have started to become the subject of remakes, with Rupert Wainwright's *The Fog* (2005) and Jean-François Richet's *Assault on Precinct 13* (2005) reinventions for contemporary audiences, without improving much on the originals. **MH**

Top Takes...

Ghosts of Mars 2001
Vampires 1998
Village of the Damned 1995
In the Mouth of Madness 1995
Memoirs of an Invisible Man 1992
They Live 1988
Prince of Darkness 1987
Big Trouble in Little China 1986
Christine 1983
The Thing 1982
Escape from New York 1981
The Fog 1980
Halloween 1978
Assault on Precinct 13 1976
Dark Star 1974
Revenge of the Colossal Beasts 1962

"In France, I'm an auteur; . . . in Britain, a genre film director; and, in the USA, a bum."

NICK BROOMFIELD

Born: Nicholas Broomfield, January 30, 1948 (London, England).

Directing style: British documentary maker; cinéma vérité and later reflexive filmmaking; use of minimal crew; subjects include famous personalities and important current events.

Top Takes...

Ghosts 2006
Aileen: Life and Death of a Serial Killer 2003
Kurt & Courtney 1998
Aileen Wuornos: The Selling
   of a Serial Killer 1992
The Leader, His Driver and the Driver's Wife 1991
Diamond Skulls 1989
Driving Me Crazy 1988
Lily Tomlin 1986
Chicken Ranch 1983
Soldier Girls 1981
Who Cares 1971

"I'd never use 'middle class' as a term for describing someone. It's so meaningless. So bland."

The son of a photographer, Nick Broomfield became interested in photography as a teenager. He originally studied law before switching to film at the National Film and Television School in London in the early 1970s. His first documentary, *Who Cares* (1971), was partially funded by the British Film Institute. In 1975, Broomfield began both a personal and professional relationship with fellow filmmaker Joan Churchill. The duo has codirected five features, and they have a son together.

Broomfield abandoned the voyeuristic style of cinéma vérité for a more intrusive first-person approach in *Driving Me Crazy* (1988). By injecting himself into his documentaries with this reflexive style of filmmaking, Broomfield questions the idea that a filmmaker is not considered part of the scenario, and is able to truly capture a situation intuitively. Filmmakers who use this style have become known as *Les Nouvelles Egotistes*. Broomfield went on to focus on the dynamic between celebrity, media, and reality. Subjects varied wildly from former British Prime Minister Margaret Thatcher to rock star Kurt Cobain.

Broomfield then made his most recognized work, focusing on a female murderer in *Aileen Wuornos: The Selling of a Serial Killer* (1992). He revisited the case a decade later with *Aileen: Life and Death of a Serial Killer* (2003). This film was to be the pinnacle of Broomfield's commentary on the filmmaker as participant and his original documentary was introduced as evidence during a new trial, and Broomfield himself was called as a witness. He has also directed two documentary-style features, *Diamond Skulls* (1989) about South African Eugene Terreblanche, and *Ghosts* (2006), inspired by the Morecambe Bay tragedy where 23 Chinese cockle pickers drowned after being cut off by the tides. **WW**

ERROL MORRIS

Born: Errol Morris, February 5, 1948 (Hewlett, Long Island, New York, U.S.).

Directing style: Maker of stylish investigative documentaries and feature films; themes of crime and politics; conversational tone and use of monologues in narratives.

Errol Morris straddles the wide divide between nonfiction approaches and fictional technique. Not a documentary maker content to avoid manipulating his subject, but still journalistic enough to develop stories from fact and not fantasy, he is also a respected commercial director, having produced dozens of ads for companies such as Apple Computer, Miller Brewing Company, and Sharp Corporation.

His debut film was *Gates of Heaven* (1980), a glimpse at a pet cemetery and its proprietors, followed by *Vernon, Florida* (1982), a view of that town's residents originally intended to focus on amputees who disfigure themselves in pursuit of insurance money. *The Dark Wind* (1991) followed, and then Morris returned to form with *A Brief History of Time* (1991), a tie-in to Stephen Hawking's book. Offering a look at four men—a lion tamer, topiary gardener, mole-rat specialist, and a robotics designer—*Fast, Cheap & Out of Control* (1997) added humor to the palette of Morris's production technique.

Actively involved with investigating a police officer's murder, *The Thin Blue Line* (1988) re-enacts crime scenes and conducts numerous interviews, and helped free an innocent man. This achievement established new ground for documentary films and suggested how their evidentiary capacity can be utilized, as in Morris's later film about an execution device inventor and Holocaust denier, *Mr. Death: The Rise and Fall of Fred A. Leuchter, Jr.* (1999). Yet because documentary is often most meaningful when recording historical evidence, Morris turned his eye on an icon of the Vietnam War and finally won an Oscar for Best Documentary, Features with *The Fog of War: Eleven Lessons from the Life of Robert S. McNamara* (2003). **GCQ**

Top Takes…

The Fog of War: Eleven Lessons from the Life of Robert S. McNamara 2003

Mr. Death: The Rise and Fall of Fred A. Leuchter, Jr. 1999

Fast, Cheap & Out of Control 1997

A Brief History of Time 1991

The Thin Blue Line 1988

Vernon, Florida 1982

Gates of Heaven 1980

> "*[The Thin Blue Line]* is the first murder mystery that actually solves a murder."

1940s

MIKE FIGGIS

Born: Michael Figgis, February 28, 1948 (Carlisle, Cumbria, England).

Directing style: British maker of edgy, often experimental dramas and thrillers; use of cutting-edge digital film techniques; acting improvisation; psychological exploration of characters.

Top Takes...

Co/Ma 2004
Hotel 2001
Timecode 2000
Miss Julie 1999
The Loss of Sexual Innocence 1999
One Night Stand 1997
Flamenco Women 1997
Leaving Las Vegas 1995 ☆
The Browning Version 1994
Mr. Jones 1993
Liebestraum 1991
Internal Affairs 1990
Stormy Monday 1988

"Film is very important to our culture—it is the main storytelling medium."

Mike Figgis made his feature debut with *Stormy Monday* (1988), a derivative British thriller set in Newcastle with U.S. imports Melanie Griffith and Tommy Lee Jones mingling with locals Sean Bean and Sting. The sort of film no one really likes but that leads to opportunities, it landed Figgis a good U.S. picture, *Internal Affairs* (1990), which was a stronger thriller with better cast leads—Richard Gere and Andy Garcia as crooked and straight cops respectively—and some thematic meat.

A jazz musician with a tendency to experiment, Figgis has hopped between conventional and unusual projects, and works so well with actors that he often attracts Altman-style casts to low- or mid-budget films. For example, Saffron Burrows and Julian Sands, who have been weak in other directors' work, have been very impressive in Figgis films. After *Internal Affairs*, he helmed a murky mystery, *Liebestraum* (1991). He then made a compromised Gere vehicle, *Mr. Jones* (1993), and reported that when studio executives realized it was the somber story of a manic depressive they asked for cuts that served to make the protagonist appear one-dimensional.

The experience prompted Figgis to seek more independence. He played straight with a remake of *The Browning Version* (1994), then fast and loose in a successful study of alcoholism, *Leaving Las Vegas* (1995), which won its lead, Nicolas Cage, a Best Actor Oscar. Figgis then spent some quality time on cheaply shot fringe pictures: *The Loss of Sexual Innocence* (1999), *Timecode* (2000), and *Hotel* (2001). All of them tackled a lot of thematic material and permitted their casts to play around with both structure and cinematic method. He returned to the mainstream with a disappointingly ordinary thriller, *Cold Creek Manor* (2003). **KN**

CLAIRE DENIS

Born: Claire Denis, April 21, 1948 (Paris, France).

Directing style: French maker of exquisite dramas; themes of sensual psychological rifts and alienation from society; poetic, erotic imagery; slow, languorous pace.

After working as an assistant director for giants Wim Wenders, Costa-Gavras, and Jim Jarmusch, Claire Denis directed her first film, the drama *Chocolat* (1988), at the age of forty. *Chocolat* is a French woman's remembrance of her youth in Cameroon, particularly her mother's relationship with an African houseboy toward whom she feels an attraction. It anticipates themes of Denis's later work—sensual psychological rifts, alienation from society—but shows little sign of the abstracted style characteristic of the later Denis.

In *Beau travail* (1999) (*Good Work*), an adaptation of Herman Melville's *Billy Budd* (1886), the Denis style becomes apparent: accretion of poetic images instead of expository dialogue, and a true love of narrative ellipses. But her films are not exquisite compositions for cinematic beauty's sake; few directors take you so directly within a character's subjectivity, and Denis does it with imagistic tactility rather than overt psychology. This is true of *L'Intrus* (2004) (*The Intruder*): on the surface it is an almost wordless, globe-spanning narrative of a man's heart transplant, but it is actually a paean to the broken-down beauty of a bearish Michel Subor who plays the patient. Denis flirts with the visually ridiculous: one of the first shots of *The Intruder* is of Subor lounging in the nude in a quintessential pastoral scene, flanked by his two dogs, showing his sensuality and vulnerability. But these risks succeed.

Denis has composed some of the most ecstatic yet enigmatic shots in recent film history: who can forget the ending of *Good Work* when the ostracized officer Galoup dances alone in a disco? It would be a pure pop moment, other than the fact that the audience has just seen him contemplating suicide. He is truly dancing like his life depended on it. **HB**

Top Takes...

Vers Mathilde 2005
L'Intrus 2004 (*The Intruder*)
Ten Minutes Older: The Cello 2002
Vendredi soir 2002 (*Friday Night*)
Trouble Every Day 2001
Beau travail 1999 (*Good Work*)
Nénette et Boni 1996 (*Nenette and Boni*)
À propos de Nice, la suite 1995
J'ai pas sommeil 1994 (*I Can't Sleep*)
Boom-Boom 1994
Keep It for Yourself 1991
Man No Run 1989
Chocolat 1988

1940s

"A screenplay is a kind of take-off . . . the best moment is to see the characters taking off."

CATHERINE BREILLAT

Born: Catherine Breillat, July 13, 1948 (Bressuire, Deux-Sèvres, Poitou-Charentes, France).

Directing style: Controversial auteur of adult dramas; non-naturalistic dialogue; themes of erotic desire and female sexuality; explicit depictions of sex and violence.

Top Takes...

Une vieille maitresse 2007
Barbe bleue 2006
Anatomie de l'enfer 2004 (*Anatomy of Hell*)
Sex Is Comedy 2002
Brève traversée 2001 (*Brief Crossing*)
À ma soeur! 2001 (*Fat Girl*)
Romance 1999
Parfait amour! 1996 (*Perfect Love*)
À propos de Nice, la suite 1995
Sale comme un ange 1991 (*Dirty Like an Angel*)
36 fillette 1988 (*Virgin*)
Tapage nocturne 1979 (*Nocturnal Uproar*)
Une vraie jeune fille 1976 (*A Real Young Girl*)

It would be easy but erroneous to dismiss Catherine Breillat as a *provocateuse* whose unusually explicit emphasis on sex is designed primarily to shock and scandalize. True, since the start of her directorial career, when *36 fillette* (1988) (*Virgin*) dealt with the teasing, tumescent relationship between a girl in her mid-teens and a lustful older playboy, she has focused relentlessly on the seductive but treacherous topography of erotic desire, shying away neither from its physical dimensions nor from its often sadomasochistic psychological aspects.

Hence, the ironically titled *Parfait amour!* (1996) (*Perfect Love*) chronicles the power shifts in the relationship between a divorcee and a younger man, and measures how his initial curiosity about her greater sexual experience first feeds insecurity and jealousy, then a murderously pathological resentment. *Romance* (1999) went further, charting a young woman's forays into masochistic transgression and experimentation. For all its explicit imagery, the film is reminiscent of Walerian Borowczyk, Luis Buñuel, and Nagisa Oshima in its consideration of passion and yet resolutely philosophical in its tone and approach.

Romance may be some kind of masterpiece, but *À ma soeur!* (2001) (*Fat Girl*) is easier to digest as a plausible study in the psychology of sex as practiced and discussed by two teenage sisters: the older beautiful and ready to give herself to a boy, the younger dumpy and profoundly resentful. A shockingly violent coda does nothing to undermine the rigor of Breillat's characterizations; indeed, her seriousness of purpose was again discernible in *Sex Is Comedy* (2002), in which she revisits, as fiction, the filming of a scene in *Fat Girl* to examine the politics and ironies of representation in the filming of sex, faked or otherwise. **GA**

"By trying to protect us [censors] form an absurd concept of what is obscene."

BILLE AUGUST

Born: Bille August, November 9, 1948 (Brede, Denmark).

Directing style: Danish director of sensitive dramas; themes of familial relationships; faithful literary adaptations; a keen eye for period detail; use of stunning landscapes.

Danish photographer turned director Bille August has applied his considerable talents to projects that range from collaborating with veteran Swedish director Ingmar Bergman to helming episodes of *The Young Indiana Jones Chronicles* (1993). With an uncanny eye for detail, he has produced acclaimed features including *Pelle erobreren* (1987) (*Pelle the Conquerer*) and *Smilla's Sense of Snow* (1997).

Top Takes...

Goodbye Bafana 2007
Return to Sender 2004
En Sång för Martin 2001 (*A Song for Martin*)
Smilla's Sense of Snow 1997
Jerusalem 1996
Den Goda viljan 1992 (*The Best Intentions*)
Pelle erobreren 1987 (*Pelle the Conqueror*)
Tro, håb og kærlighed 1984 (*Twist and Shout*)
Busters verden 1984 (*Buster's World*)
Zappa 1983
Honning måne 1978 (*Honeymoon*)

August worked in TV after graduating from the Danish Film Institute. He moved into films as a cinematographer on *Hemåt i natten* (1977) (*Homeward in the Night*) before taking the director's chair and writing *Honning måne* (1978) (*Honeymoon*). After directing the TV drama *Maj* (1982), a brace of movies, *Zappa* (1983) and *Tro, håb og kærlighed* (1984) (*Twist and Shout*), did well both inside and outside Denmark. Then *Pelle the Conquerer*, a tale of Swedish emigrants settling on a Danish island, landed August a Best Foreign Language Film Oscar.

Bergman penned the script for August's next directorial effort, the biographical tale of Bergman's own parents, *Den Goda viljan* (1992) (*The Best Intentions*). August followed it with the lackluster star-studded *The House of the Spirits* (1993), starring Meryl Streep and Jeremy Irons, but was back on form with the atmospheric thriller *Smilla's Sense of Snow*, a mystery woven around the death of a young boy that he directed at the instigation of the author of the novel it was based on, fellow Dane Peter Høeg.

August was less successful with his big screen adaptation of *Les Misérables* (1998), but *En Sång för Martin* (2001) (*A Song For Martin*), an affecting tale of the ravages of Alzheimer's disease, again showed his strengths. Recent work includes the drama *Return to Sender* (2004), starring Connie Nielsen and Kelly Preston. **TE**

> "The only thing that makes me truly happy is mathematics. Snow, ice, and numbers."—Smilla

1940s

AGNIESZKA HOLLAND

Born: Agnieszka Holland, November 28, 1948 (Warsaw, Poland).

Directing style: Prominent Polish New Wave director of dramas; themes of dislocation, loss, and betrayal; explorations of communism and the effect of World War II.

Writer and Polish New Wave director Agnieszka Holland has made films in Europe and the United States, switching among theater, TV, and feature films. Her credits range from the war drama *Bittere Ernte* (1985) (*Angry Harvest*) to the children's story *The Secret Garden* (1993) to *Shot in the Heart* (2001), about a spree killer. However, she regularly returns to themes of dislocation, loss, and betrayal, all of which colored her youth.

Holland's parents were left-leaning journalists, and her father was Jewish; he died in police custody in Poland when she was thirteen years old. She studied film at the Prague Film and TV Academy, and was in Czechoslovakia in 1968 when Soviet tanks crushed the short-lived Prague Spring. Two years later, she was arrested, imprisoned without being charged, and released six weeks later without explanation.

Holland began writing screenplays that were regularly rejected by Polish government censors, but found a mentor in director Andrzej Wajda, who invited her to join his production company. They collaborated on scripts, and Holland was finally allowed to make the TV drama *Niedzielne dzieci* (1976) (*Sunday Children*) about illegal adoption, and her feature debut *Aktorzy prowincjonalni* (1979) (*Provincial Actors*) about the state of contemporary Polish politics. She left Poland for France two years later, just before martial law was declared, nipping the fledgling Solidarity Movement in the bud. Holland's best-known films include *Angry Harvest* and the sly psychological thriller *Olivier, Olivier* (1992). But her crowning glory is *Europa Europa* (1990) based on the true life story of Solomon Perel, a Jewish youth who survived World War II by joining the Hitler Youth. The film won a bevy of awards including an Oscar nod for Holland's screenplay. **MM**

Top Takes...

Catherine and Peter 2007
Copying Beethoven 2006
Julie Walking Home 2002
Total Eclipse 1995
The Secret Garden 1993
Olivier, Olivier 1992
Europa Europa 1990
To Kill a Priest 1988
Bittere Ernte 1985 (*Angry Harvest*)
Goraczka 1981 (*Fever*)
Aktorzy prowincjonalni 1979 (*Provincial Actors*)
Obrazki z zycia 1975 (*Pictures from Life*)
Hrich boha 1970 (*Jesus Christ's Sin*)

"Although women are important in my films feminism is not the central theme . . . ."

MARLEEN GORRIS

Born: Marleen Gorris, December 9, 1948 (Roermond, Limburg, Netherlands).

Directing style: Controversial Dutch feminist filmmaker of provocative dramas exploring gender and queer politics; uncompromising depictions of relationships between men and women.

One of the Netherlands's most important filmmakers, Marleen Gorris is known for making uncompromisingly feminist films that privilege the female experience, and explore gender and gay and lesbian politics. She began writing film scripts at the age of thirty with almost no previous experience in cinema, and her debut feature, *De Stilte rond Christine M.* (1982) (*A Question of Silence*), caused controversy upon its release. A less ambiguous predecessor to Virginie Despentes's *Baise-moi* (2000) (*Rape Me*), *A Question of Silence* is in many ways typical of its time, being a feminist role-reversal tale about the violence perpetrated against women in a patriarchal society and the women's silent reactions to such violence. In the story, three unacquainted women beat a random male stranger to death. A female psychiatrist concludes that the women's suppressed rage generated by a male-dominated society led to their crime.

Gorris's follow-up, *Gebroken spiegels* (1984) (*Broken Mirrors*), which told the harrowing story of prostitutes in an Amsterdam brothel, examined similar themes. *The Last Island* (1990) was highly acclaimed, although once more proved controversial for its portrayal of men as unsuccessful, ignorant, and violent.

Gorris is perhaps best known for writing and directing *Antonia* (1995), which won a number of awards, including an Oscar for Best Foreign Film. The film revolves around the lives of an unconventional matriarch and her descendants in a Dutch village, and perhaps offered more hope in its message than Gorris's earlier work. Gorris also directed the less radical literary adaptations *Mrs. Dalloway* (1997), based on Virginia Woolf's novel, and her first feature with a male protagonist, *The Luzhin Defence* (2000), about a psychologically tormented grandmaster of chess. **KM**

Top Takes...

Heaven and Earth 2007
Rosa 2006
Carolina 2003
The Luzhin Defence 2000
Mrs. Dalloway 1997
Antonia 1995
The Last Island 1990
Gebroken spiegels 1984 (*Broken Mirrors*)
De Stilte rond Christine M. 1982
   (*A Question of Silence*)

1940s

"I'd like to do a comedy and a thriller and I can easily do that whether I'm a feminist or not."

JIM SHERIDAN

Born: Jim Sheridan, February 6, 1949 (Dublin, Ireland).

Directing style: Leading director and producer of Irish film; maker of biopics and dramas examining Irish life and politics; artistic collaborations with actor Daniel Day-Lewis.

Top Takes...

Get Rich or Die Tryin' 2005
In America 2002
The Boxer 1997
***In the Name of the Father* 1993** ☆
The Field 1990
***My Left Foot* 1989** ☆

Born in Dublin, Ireland, the son of a stage director, Jim Sheridan worked his way up the cinematic ladder—including some time spent at New York University's film school—before establishing himself as one of the preeminent voices of Irish film. It's no coincidence that he helped solidify that reputation with *My Left Foot* (1989), a movie about the paraplegic poet and painter Christy Brown, one of Ireland's preeminent voices.

The Field (1990) was a less flashy follow-up to *My Left Foot*, although it did earn star Richard Harris much notice, but *In the Name of the Father* (1993), which reunited Sheridan with *My Left Foot* star Daniel Day-Lewis, proved a more popular achievement with its fictionalized retelling of the case of the Guildford Four. Sheridan and Lewis worked together one more time for *The Boxer* (1997), but the story did not connect with audiences or critics as strongly as its predecessor. Perhaps that explains Sheridan's decision to draw from his own experience as an Irish immigrant in New York for the sentimental but undeniably moving *In America* (2002), the tale of an Irish immigrant family attempting to make a life in New York.

The same year Sheridan produced the docudrama *Bloody Sunday* (2002), about one of Ireland's darkest and most violent clashes between public and police, but he subsequently surprised fans with his left-turn follow-up as director, *Get Rich or Die Tryin'* (2005). The film was an uneven adaptation of the early life and struggles of hip-hop star Curtis "50 Cent" Jackson, and lacked the heart, passion, and personal touch on display throughout Sheridan's earlier works. Sheridan has since signed on to direct a remake of Akira Kurosawa's 1952 masterpiece, *Ikiru* (*Doomed*), and he has reported several other projects in the pipeline. **JK**

> "It is good and exciting to go outside your own little society and do something different."

SALLY POTTER

Born: Sally Potter, September 19, 1949 (London, England).

Directing style: Maker of dramas dealing with art, the British class system, sexuality and gender; use of dance; writes lyrics and composes soundtracks; wry humor.

Sally Potter left school at the age of sixteen to become a filmmaker, and joined the London Filmmakers Co-op. Sometimes, regardless of how many or how few films a director has made, one title will forever be associated with them. This is certainly true of Potter, who marked herself out as a filmmaker of note with *Orlando* (1992), starring Tilda Swinton. *Orlando* is an ambitious, unusual, art theater movie that draws on the work of English modernist and feminist writer Virginia Woolf. Potter attempts to adapt and film one of Woolf's novels, setting herself the unenviable task of conveying Woolf's prose, fluidity of writing, and narrative style in a fully cinematic manner.

Orlando seeks to achieve this in a variety of ways. The novel it is based on involves an ageless title character, who is able to move across cultures, times, and even genders. Potter's *Orlando* endeavors to work more narrative into this, at least giving Orlando's "gift" some basic rationale, and trying to drive on and motivate the story, rather than allowing it to meander and simply change. The film is interesting not just for its gender swapping, but also for its use of direct-to-camera comments that aim to emulate and imitate Woolf's use of narration. Although capturing such a piece of literature on film can never just be about staying faithful to the original, Potter's *Orlando* can nevertheless be fairly described as imbued with the spirit and politics of Woolf's writing. It attacks the English class system as much as it criticizes the subordination of women.

After the achievement and arty ambitions of *Orlando*, Potter has written, directed, and appeared as the character Sally in *The Tango Lesson* (1997), another highly unusual and distinctive piece of film commentary dealing with art and gender. **MH**

Top Takes...

Yes 2004
The Man Who Cried 2000
The Tango Lesson 1997
Orlando 1992
*I Am an Ox, I Am a Horse, I Am a Man,
   I Am a Woman* 1988
The Gold Diggers 1983
London Story 1980
Thriller 1979

"The language of cinema as it has evolved has excluded vast swathes of human experience."

PEDRO ALMODÓVAR

Born: Pedro Almodóvar Caballero, September 24, 1949 (Calzada de Calatrava, Ciudad Real, Castilla-La Mancha, Spain).

Directing style: Auteur; outrageously comic melodramas; sensual use of color and kitsch; themes of romantic and family relationships; strong female characters.

Top Takes...

Volver 2006 (*To Return*)

La mala educación 2004 (*Bad Education*)

Hable con ella 2002 (*Talk to Her*) ☆

Todo sobre mi madre 1999
   (*All About My Mother*)

La flor de mi secreto 1995
   (*The Flower of My Secret*)

Kika 1993

Tacones lejanos 1991 (*High Heels*)

¡Átame! 1990 (*Tie Me Up! Tie Me Down!*)

Mujeres al borde de un ataque de nervios 1988
   (*Women on the Verge of a Nervous Breakdown*)

La ley del deseo 1987 (*Law of Desire*)

Matador 1986

Entre tinieblas 1983 (*Dark Habits*)

Laberinto de pasiones 1982
   (*Labyrinth of Passion*)

Pepi, Luci, Bom y otras chicas del montón 1980
   (*Pepi, Luci, Bom and Other Girls on the Heap*)

Folle . . . folle . . . fólleme Tim! 1978

Salomé 1978

Blancor 1975

El sueño, o la estrella 1975

Film político 1974

Pedro Almodóvar is often compared to Luis Buñuel, but Almodóvar is both more of a populist and a humanist filmmaker. Almodovar himself has remarked, "The characters in my films are assassins, rapists, and so on, but I don't treat them as criminals, I talk about their humanity." And that is true, but he does so in the most playfully outrageous ways imaginable. Almodóvar's films are very much movies that are filled with color and spectacular moments, and that revel in the sheer joy of filmmaking. Many of his early films are set in Madrid but things that happen in his films are invariably glamorized into the fabulous à la Hollywood form. Sometimes these aspects become subversive statements, as in a scene in *Matador* (1986) where the camera lingers on the crotches of the young men training to be matadors—a slyly satirical scene that would pass without comment were the focus on jiggling breasts. If it makes some viewers uneasy, perhaps that is the point.

Almodóvar's work has been highly influential in the liberation of Spanish cinema post-Franco and, importantly, he achieved huge international acclaim with the comedy *Mujeres al borde de un ataque de nervios* (1988) *Women on the Verge of a*

RIGHT: One of Almodóvar's favorite actors, Antonio Banderas, starring in *Matador*.

Nervous Breakdown. It established Almodóvar as a "women's director" and set a high level of expectation for future work. His movies from *Laberinto de pasiones* (1982) (*Labyrinth of Passion*) through to *Volver* (2006) (*To Return*) are outrageous, unashamedly melodramatic soap operas amped to a spectacular degree. They are the kind of movies that revisionists insist Hollywood director Douglas Sirk made in the 1950s: trashy stories that subvert the very genre that contains them. But in Almodóvar's case, there is no need for revisionism. All the evidence is right there on the screen. It is a world full of homosexual filmmakers with busty, transsexual, movie star sisters and oddly sympathetic psychotic stalkers, as in *La ley del deseo* (1987) (*Law of Desire*). Boy meets girl can be redefined in terms of attempted rape in a story involving serial killers, religious fanaticism, and a would-be bullfighter who faints at the sight of blood. Is it art? If not, it is what art should be. **KH**

ABOVE: Penelope Cruz wows her audience with a fine performance in *To Return*.

Almodóvar's Favorites

Pedro Almodóvar has always cast a handful of favorite actresses to play his strong female protagonists. For example:

- Carmen Maura has collaborated with Almodóvar on five movies, including his first feature, *Pepi, Luci, Bom and Other Girls on the Heap*, and his most recent, *To Return*.

- Penelope Cruz has had plum roles in *Todo sobre mi madre* (1999) (*All About My Mother*) and *To Return*.

- Victoria Abril began her fruitful collaboration with Almodóvar in *¡Átame!* (1989) (*Tie Me Up! Tie Me Down!*).

HARK TSUI

Born: Tsui Man-Kong, February 15, 1950 (Vietnam).

Directing style: Visionary director of Hong Kong New Wave; master of kung fu movies and *wuxia* genre; superbly crafted, fast-paced action sequences; themes of effects of Westernization on China.

One of Hong Kong's most versatile and acclaimed film figures, "The Steven Spielberg of Asia," Hark Tsui has served as actor, director, producer, or writer on more than 50 films.

Born in Vietnam, Tsui was raised in Saigon and moved to Hong Kong as a teenager to study. During this period, he began making experimental short films in 8mm, and drew comic books. Tsui relocated to the United States in the early 1970s and began studying filmmaking at the University of Texas. After a brief sojourn in New York, he returned to Hong Kong in 1977 and started working in the TV industry.

Tsui made his debut with the Mario Bava-style horror thriller *Die bian* (1979) (*The Butterfly Murders*), which caused a stir. He made several more films before transforming the industry with his feature *Suk san: Sun Suk saan kim hap* (1983) (*Zu: Warriors from the Magic Mountain*). Inspired by a Chinese fairy tale, it showcased Tsui's affinity for utilizing explosions of color, lightning-fast pacing, and Hollywood-style special effects. In 1984, Tsui formed his own production company, Film Workshop, a haven for filmmakers seeking to achieve their artistic visions. The early 1990s saw a peak for Tsui as he directed more than a dozen films in five years including the popular *Wong Fei Hung* (1991–1994) (*Once Upon a Time in China*) series. A hands-on producer, Tsui is known to codirect or handle second-unit photography. Tsui answered Hollywood's request in the late 1990s with a pair of distinct, yet unsatisfying Jean-Claude Van Damme offerings. Following this disappointing foray, Tsui returned to Hong Kong but displayed a slower pace. Embracing digital technology, Tsui produced a series of special effects films including the epic *Chat gim* (2005) (*Seven Swords*). **WW**

Top Takes…

Chat gim 2005 (*Seven Swords*)

Shu shan zheng zhuan 2001 (*Zu Warriors*)

Seunlau ngaklau 2000 (*Time and Tide*)

Leung juk 1994 (*Butterfly Lovers*)

Wong Fei Hung ji yi: Naam yi dong ji keung 1992 (*Once Upon a Time in China II*)

Long xing tian xia 1989 (*The Master*)

Do ma daan 1986 (*Peking Opera Blues*)

Da gung wong dai 1985 (*Working Class*)

Shanghai zhi ye 1984 (*Shanghai Blues*)

Suk san: Sun Suk saan kim hap 1983 (*Zu: Warriors from the Magic Mountain*)

Di yi lei xing wei xian 1980 (*Don't Play with Fire*)

Die bian 1979 (*The Butterfly Murders*)

> "[*Wuxia* movies] give a refreshed view of the values … and the way we looked at life."

JOHN HUGHES

Born: John Hughes II, February 15, 1950 (Lansing, Michigan, U.S.).

Directing style: Inspirational director of the Brat Pack genre of movies; maker of 1980s teen comedies that grapple with coming-of-age themes; keen sense of fashion.

A baby boomer who worked for *National Lampoon Magazine* in the 1970s, John Hughes wrote scripts for various films such as the National Lampoon movie *Class Reunion* (1982) and *Mr. Mom* (1983) before making his debut as writer and director on *Sixteen Candles* (1984). Focused on Molly Ringwald's vulnerable super teen, Hughes portrayed the difficult world of adolescence and found his first star, who also anchored his ensemble piece, *The Breakfast Club* (1985). In both films, he successfully recognized the knowingness of adolescence, while churning out pop-rock soundtracks. This clever move helped identify the movies with youth culture and led to box-office success.

Another comedy, *Weird Science* (1985), followed the story of two nerds who manufacture "a perfect woman." Hughes then proved he could not be defined by his past; he turned to adult comedy starring John Candy and Steve Martin in *Planes, Trains & Automobiles* (1987), returned to youth-oriented fare with *She's Having a Baby* (1988), savaged nuclear families with the use of Candy in *Uncle Buck* (1989), and ended his directorial career with the kid comedy *Curly Sue* (1991).

Since then, Hughes has been writing movies for other directors, including *Home Alone* (1990) and *Maid in Manhattan* (2002), alongside adaptations such as *101 Dalmatians* (1996). Most of his career has been devoted to comedy, but he is best remembered for defining what it was to be a teenager in the 1980s and setting cultural benchmarks. With a clear eye for describing the pratfalls of aging, a keen sense of fashionable clothing and music, and a knack for telling stories that his audience could identify with, Hughes gave a generation of Americans a set of references for growing up without PCs or cell phones. **GCQ**

Top Takes...

Curly Sue 1991
Uncle Buck 1989
She's Having a Baby 1988
Planes, Trains & Automobiles 1987
Ferris Bueller's Day Off 1986
Weird Science 1985
The Breakfast Club 1985
Sixteen Candles 1984

1950s

"I'm not really a digital effects/ sci-fi kinda guy; it's not really my cup of tea as a filmmaker."

NEIL JORDAN

Born: Neil Jordan, February 25, 1950 (Sligo, Ireland).

Directing style: Visionary Irish filmmaker; imaginative teller of stories that span the fantastical to the realistic to the political; opulent visuals; themes of morality; sexual motifs.

Top Takes...

1950s

"I'm fascinated by monsters and monstrous people and . . . with illogic and irrationality."

That Neil Jordan's career has lasted for more than 20 years is very nearly as remarkable as his filmography. In a business that rarely has much use for quirky visionaries, Jordan has somehow managed to craft a body of work that is wholly his own, and often dwells most comfortably in art theater cinema, while also keeping one foot tentatively in the mainstream.

When his first notable film *The Company of Wolves* (1984) appeared, Jordan was cited as someone to watch. His follow-up work, *Mona Lisa* (1986), placed him at the forefront of Irish filmmakers. Unfortunately *High Spirits* (1988) was so mangled by the studio that it tanked, although some scenes, combined with the performances of Peter O'Toole, Jennifer Tilly, and Peter Gallagher, suggest it may once have been a good movie. It might have killed Jordan's career, had not the underrated *The Miracle* (1991) stood him on firmer ground, while the surprise hit *The Crying Game* (1992) put him back on top.

Though less than ideally cast, his big-budget movie version of *Interview with the Vampire: The Vampire Chronicles* (1994) was a stylish work that cemented his reputation as a commercially viable filmmaker. The clout of this success allowed him to make *Michael Collins* (1996), a more personal project that never quite gelled and that bombed at the box office. His next film, *The Butcher Boy* (1997), however, is an extraordinary work that ushered in Jordan's richest, most personal period artistically. Later films, even the stylish horrors of *In Dreams* (1999) and the crime-caper thrills of *The Good Thief* (2002), have all evidenced an increasing depth of purpose and vision, and a fascination with the concept of original sin, which found full expression in the brilliant quirkiness of *Breakfast on Pluto* (2005). **KH**

PHILLIP NOYCE

Born: Phillip Noyce, April 29, 1950 (Griffith, New South Wales, Australia).

Directing style: Maker of early experimental films, docudramas, iconic realistic Australian dramas, and Hollywood political thrillers; artful storytelling; investigations of colonialism.

Phillip Noyce began experimenting with an 8mm camera in his teens. Inspired by U.S. experimental films, he began making shorts of his own such as *Better to Reign in Hell* (1968).

Noyce enrolled in the newly founded Australian National Film School in 1973, and made more short films, such as *Castor and Pollux* (1973). He made his breakthrough with the staged documentary *God Knows Why, But It Works* (1975). It chronicled the work of an altruistic doctor working with poverty-stricken Aboriginal patients, and Noyce parlayed the success of that film into his first true feature, *Backroads* (1977), about racial strife in Australia, followed by *Newsfront* (1978), a historical docudrama about the Australian newsreel industry.

In 1989 he directed the thriller *Dead Calm* (1989), which starred Nicole Kidman in a very early role. The movie was an international success and Noyce was able to break out of the limited budgets of Australian productions by accepting work in Hollywood. Since that time, Noyce has fluctuated between deeply personal and utterly commercial films. The pulp action movie *Patriot Games* (1992), which starred Harrison Ford, was his first U.S. assignment and a huge commercial success; he returned to thriller territory with *Clear and Present Danger* (1994).

Astonishingly, Noyce rebounded from the abysmal *The Saint* (1997) with a brilliant version of Graham Greene's novel *The Quiet American* (2002) about a dissolute reporter in 1950s Indochina. This was followed by the drama *Rabbit-Proof Fence* (2002), which marked a return to the concerns of his native land. Noyce's curiously uneven career to date nevertheless offers distinct promise for tomorrow; he has created some brilliant films, and it seems he will keep surprising his audiences for some time to come. **WWD**

Top Takes…

American Pastoral 2007
Catch a Fire 2006
The Quiet American 2002
Rabbit-Proof Fence 2002
The Bone Collector 1999
Clear and Present Danger 1994
Patriot Games 1992
Dead Calm 1989
Echoes of Paradise 1987
Heatwave 1982
Newsfront 1978
Backroads 1977
That's Showbiz 1973
Castor and Pollux 1973

1950s

"Directors spend most of their lives caught up in telling stories. It's a lifelong passion."

CHANTAL AKERMAN

Born: Chantal Anne Akerman, June 6, 1950 (Brussels, Belgium).

Directing style: Belgian maker of feminist dramas; themes of daily ritual; minimalist narrative; obsessive attention to detail; use of static camera; dark humor.

Top Takes...

Là-bas 2006

De l'autre côté 2002 (*From the Other Side*)

La Captive 2000 (*The Captive*)

Un divan à New York 1996
  (*A Couch in New York*)

Nuit et jour 1991 (*Night and Day*)

Histoires d'Amérique 1988
  (*Family and Philosophy*)

Les rendez-vous d'Anna 1978
  (*The Meetings of Anna*)

*Jeanne Dielman, 23 Quai du Commerce,
  1080 Bruxelles* 1976

Je, tu, il, elle 1974 (*I, You, She, He*)

Hôtel Monterey 1972

Saute ma ville 1968 (*Blow Up My Town*)

Arguably the most important European director of the 1970s and 1980s, Chantal Akerman has a spare visual style that is matched only by the uncompromising ferocity of her individual vision as a filmmaker. Her upbringing was anything but privileged and this hardscrabble beginning encouraged Akerman to have compassion for the disenfranchised, a theme that runs through all her work.

After education in Brussels and Paris, she became a devotee of the works of director Jean-Luc Godard, and made her first short film, *Saute ma ville* (1968) (*Blow Up My Town*) at the age of eighteen. In 1971, the film was a surprise hit at the Oberhausen International Short Film Festival, and Akerman subsequently left for New York, where she took a variety of odd jobs to fund her time making the spare documentary *Hôtel Monterey* (1972), a silent feature about the denizens of a Manhattan welfare hotel. This was followed by her first sound feature, the sexually graphic *Je, tu, il, elle* (1974) (*I, You, She, He*). She then created what is generally considered her most ambitious work, *Jeanne Dielman, 23 Quai du Commerce, 1080 Bruxelles* (1976) chronicling the life of a middle-class housewife and prostitute with unsparing accuracy, and almost manic attention to detail.

Her subsequent films have been equally audacious, such as *Les rendez-vous d'Anna* (1978) (*The Meetings of Anna*), which follows a young director across Europe in typically minimalist fashion, and the more accessible *Un divan à New York* (1996) (*A Couch in New York*) and *La Captive* (2000) (*The Captive*). Although Akerman's films seldom play outside the festival circuit, her dry, acerbic vision of human existence has proven deeply influential for a younger generation of feminist filmmakers. **WWD**

> "I still like to work relatively simply with long takes and medium close-ups."

JOHN LANDIS

Born: John Landis, August 3, 1950 (Chicago, Illinois, U.S.).

Directing style: Innovative director who changed the face of the pop music video industry; cult master of knockabout comedies and comedy horror genre; hip use of music; cameo appearances by directors.

John Landis worked on a few sets in various menial capacities but went outside the industry to assemble his first feature, the parodic monster movie *Schlock* (1973), in which he also dons a suit made by genius Hollywood makeup artist Rick Baker to play The Banana Monster. The scattershot sketch comedy *The Kentucky Fried Movie* (1977) led to a directing assignment on the breakout hit *Animal House* (1978).

With *Animal House* star John Belushi and *Saturday Night Live* (1975–2003) alumnus Dan Aykroyd, Landis then made the gargantuan comedy musical *The Blue Brothers* (1980). It was much loved for its then fashionable car crash stunts as well as for its homage to rhythm 'n' blues music. In *An American Werewolf in London* (1981), Landis returned to his genre roots, with Baker again providing memorable effects, and essayed a pop-tragic monster movie without entirely abandoning knockabout comedy or backlist hit tunes.

The 1980s saw Landis change the face of the pop music industry. He made the groundbreaking music video *Thriller* (1983), the first he would make for pop legend Michael Jackson. The video changed the face of music videos forever, and gave TV stations such as MTV meat they had never had before. He also worked with comedian Eddie Murphy in *Trading Places* (1983), *Coming to America* (1988), and *Beverly Hills Cop III* (1994). More satisfying than these high-profile efforts is a run of underrated, busy comedies that are often packed with cameos from fellow directors, including *Into the Night* (1985), *Spies Like Us* (1985), *¡Three Amigos!* (1986), and *Oscar* (1991).

In the 1990s, Landis reprised some of his hits to little effect and, after a hiatus, returned to directing unexpectedly with a documentary about a used-car salesman, *Slasher* (2004). **KN**

Top Takes...

Slasher 2004
Susan's Plan 1998
The Stupids 1996
Black or White 1991
Coming to America 1988
¡Three Amigos! 1986
Spies Like Us 1985
Into the Night 1985
Twilight Zone: The Movie 1983
Trading Places 1983
An American Werewolf in London 1981
The Blues Brothers 1980
Animal House 1978
The Kentucky Fried Movie 1977
Schlock 1973

1950s

"I've done every job there is to do on a movie set, except hairdressing."

JOHN SAYLES

Born: John Sayles, September 28, 1950 (Schenectady, New York, U.S.).

Directing style: Writer and director of offbeat dramas; themes of social responsibility, and explorations of societal values; masterful creation of credible characters.

Top Takes...

1950s

"I've always felt like I was on the margins . . . that's what independent used to mean."

Movies that avoid happy endings are not necessarily doomed. It is possible to mix social responsibility with entertainment, and no U.S. filmmaker does it better than John Sayles.

He started out writing short stories, novels, and also scripts for director Roger Corman, and with earnings saved from these projects made *Return of the Secaucus 7* (1980), the story of a college reunion. Considered an artistic success, the film nonetheless revealed a problem that has haunted Sayles ever since: how to arrange financing for projects with limited commercial appeal. The answer was writing for hire on Hollywood scripts, and pumping his salary into much smaller productions. The only exception to this tack is *Baby It's You* (1983), a trying experience that led to exclusively directing his movies outside the system.

Twice nominated for screenwriting Oscars with his story of a one-time soap opera star in *Passion Fish* (1992) and the Western *Lone Star* (1996), Sayles's best works build from ensemble casts placed in complicated settings, such as *Matewan* (1987) and *Sunshine State* (2002). The style does not always work, but there are notable experiments: the tale of a lesbian love affair *Lianna* (1983); the science-fiction adventure *The Brother from Another Planet* (1984); the Irish folk tale *The Secret of Roan Inish* (1994); a Spanish-language film made for the U.S. market, *Men with Guns* (1997) (*Hombres Armados*) about the fate of the indigenous people of Guatemala; and the adoption drama *Casa de los babys* (2003). Altogether, the Sayles movie experience emphasizes context over individuality, and thoughtful consideration over solution. His work lacks spectacle, and can tend toward the pedantic. But his best work is magic. **GCQ**

AMOS GITAI

Born: Amos Weinraub, October 11, 1950 (Haifa, Israel).

Directing style: Controversial Israeli director of dramas that explore questions of Jewish identity and culture; themes of exile and Middle East politics; documentary maker.

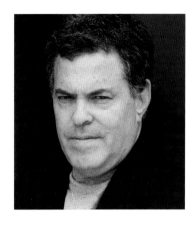

"It's a pity Israelis don't speak Arabic like Palestinians speak Hebrew. If they do, I think things will change." This quote, from Amos Gitai's film *Free Zone* (2005) provides a valuable point of entry into the works of one of world cinema's most prolific and controversial directors. Spoken by a Palestinian woman, played by Hiam Abbass, to a female taxi driver from Israel, played by Hana Laszlo, these deceptively simple lines succinctly articulate the most important recurring theme in Gitai's oeuvre: the importance of communication and mutual understanding as a necessary instrument for breaking cycles of oppression.

A creative visual artist, Gitai was studying architecture when the Yom Kippur War began in 1973. He served on a helicopter rescue crew that was shot down by a Syrian missile over Gaza, an experience he revisited in his gritty war drama, *Kippur* (2000). During military service, Gitai began shooting films on an 8mm camera. He soon embarked upon a career as a documentary filmmaker, creating both short films and features that tackled complex issues such as the Israeli occupation of Palestine in *Bayit* (1980) (*The House*) and the Lebanon War in *Yoman Sadeh* (1982) (*Field Diary*). These works, however, were frequently censored, and Gitai spent the next few years in exile.

Back in Israel, Gitai continued making documentaries, but he also began crafting fiction films every bit as critical of social and cultural institutions. Often featuring long takes and meticulous mise-en-scène, these films engaged issues ranging from exile and identity as in *Golem, l'esprit de l'exil* (1992) (*Golem, the Spirit of the Exile*); patriarchal and sexual oppression as in *Kadosh* (1999) (*Sacred*) and *Promised Land* (2004); and the impact of political ideologies upon personal relationships as in *Esther* (1986) and *Kedma* (2002). **JM**

Top Takes...

Free Zone 2005
Promised Land 2004
Alila 2003
11'09"01—September 11 2002
Kedma 2002
Eden 2001
Kippur 2000
Kadosh 1999 (*Sacred*)
Yom Yom 1998
Zion, Auto-Emancipation 1998
Golem, l'esprit de l'exil 1992
  (*Golem, the Spirit of the Exile*)
Berlin-Yerushalaim 1989 (*Berlin-Jerusalem*)
Esther 1986
Yoman Sadeh 1982 (*Field Diary*)
Bayit 1980 (*The House*)

"How do you direct chaos? Directing is usually about making order."—On *Kippur*

1950s

GILLIAN ARMSTRONG

Born: Gillian May Armstrong, December 18, 1950 (Melbourne, Victoria, Australia).

Directing style: Trailblazing Australian maker of period dramas and literary adaptations; strong female protagonists; powerful storytelling; rich use of landscape; intelligent handling of actors.

Top Takes...

Death Defying Acts 2007

Unfolding Florence: The Many Lives of Florence Broadhurst 2006

Charlotte Gray 2001

Oscar and Lucinda 1997

Little Women 1994

The Last Days of Chez Nous 1992

High Tide 1987

Mrs. Soffel 1984

Starstruck 1982

Touch Wood 1980

My Brilliant Career 1979

The Singer and the Dancer 1977

Smokes and Lollies 1975

Gretel 1973

Old Man and Dog 1970

"I think documentary filmmaking is very, very hard. It doesn't suit my personality."

RIGHT: Cate Blanchett, an ordinary woman in an extraordinary time in *Charlotte Gray*.

Gillian Armstrong formed part of the Australian New Wave, a group of performers and filmmakers who emerged at the end of the 1970s and beginning of the 1980s. Her early work, such as the adaptation of Miles Franklin's novel, *My Brilliant Career* (1979), marked her out as a director interested just as much in the emotional lives of her characters as in capturing a powerful sense of time and place. It was also the first Australian feature film to be directed by a woman in 46 years.

This style of lush cinematography and emotive storytelling was later developed in Armstrong's all-star Hollywood version of Louisa May Alcott's nineteenth-century novel *Little Women* (1994). The movie boasted sumptuous visuals and poignancy of narrative; Armstrong was undoubtedly by this time cementing her reputation for making popular quality cinema in the heritage or classic drama tradition. *Oscar and Lucinda* (1997) featured Australian actress Cate Blanchett and was based on Peter Carey's prize-winning novel, once again furnishing the director with a sense of literary prestige. Armstrong was reunited with Blanchett on *Charlotte Gray* (2001), another film adaptation with a historical setting, this time based on the novel by contemporary author Sebastian Faulks. Armstrong's work has been repeatedly characterized by aesthetic, graceful, and artful direction, this frequently being combined with a focus on unusual love stories and strong central female characters. Having worked with a range of Hollywood A-list stars, Armstrong has also recurrently cast leading Australian actors in her films, including Geoffrey Rush as the narrator of *Oscar and Lucinda*, and Guy Pearce as magician and escape artist Harry Houdini, in *Death Defying Acts* (2007). **MH**

JEAN-PIERRE AND LUC DARDENNE

Jean-Pierre: Born Carl Higgans, April 21, 1951 (Engis, Liège, Belgium).
Luc: Born Eric Higgans, March 10, 1954 (Awirs, Belgium).

Directing style: Independent filmmakers of poignant, everyday dramas; gritty portrayals of society's underprivileged; sparse dialogue; absence of musical score.

Top Takes...

Often, the best material lies in the small struggles of everyday reality, the daily dramas parents, kids, and teens overcome to carve out a decent life. Brothers Jean-Pierre and Luc Dardenne have turned these tiny tales into compelling cinema. Operating from a decayed working-class slagheap town in Belgium, they moved from documentary to fiction for their stories of socially excluded individuals confronted with moral choices.

With the tale of an unemployed steel worker *Je pense à vous* (1992), and a tale of immigration *La Promesse* (1996) (*The Promise*), the Dardennes developed a direct style that reflected the grim social situation of their subjects. That stark style found perfection in *Rosetta* (1999), a story centered on the teenage outcast and daughter of an alcoholic mother, Rosetta, who struggles for a job and respect. The use of a constantly close, always moving camera gives the film an authentic immediacy, pushing the viewer on to, and into, Rosetta's plight.

Le Fils (2002) (*The Son*), about a reclusive carpenter and his on-probation apprentice who may have killed the carpenter's son, takes this confrontational style even further. The camera is never more than a foot away from the characters, forcing us to see them as they are: frightened and insecure. In *L'Enfant* (2005) (*The Child*), which won them worldwide acclaim, the Dardennes' camera is more restrained. But the story of welfare-reliant Bruno and Sonia, and their newborn baby, is all the more urgent, and a humbling indictment of the way industrialized society treats the poor. The Dardennes' films hardly have dialogue; their characters don't make big speeches. Instead, their camera says it all, simple and effective, with respect. In doing so they achieve the pressing social relevance that all realist cinema aims for. **EM**

> "Filmmakers in Belgium are seen as arts and crafts makers. It is a small country."

ROLF DE HEER

Born: Rolf de Heer, May 4, 1951 (Heemskerk, Noord-Holland, Netherlands).

Directing style: Independent filmmaker of low-budget, eccentric, science-fiction movies, and thoughtful dramas; themes questioning the nature of childhood and Australian culture; innovative use of sound.

Rolf de Heer is an Australian writer, producer, and director known for his eclectic subjects and showcasing of the Australian outback.

Following graduation in 1980, de Heer directed his first feature, *Tail of a Tiger* (1984) about a young boy fascinated with model planes. He then made the eccentric science-fiction comedy *Encounter at Raven's Gate* (1988), featuring a perplexing ending. His next film, the musical *Dingo* (1991), marked the beginning of de Heer's critical reception and was nominated for several Australian Film Institute (AFI) awards. It won Best Original Score for the work of musician costar Miles Davis.

Rather than rest on critical plaudits, de Heer returned two years later with the bizarre cult movie *Bad Boy Bubby* (1993). The story of a man entering the unknown world after 30 years of isolation, the film sharply divided critics. It is notable for using dozens of cinematographers and the innovation of recording in binaural sound, which means that each scene was recorded in stereo from the perspective of the main character to convey the experience of seeing and hearing the world anew. The film won de Heer an AFI Best Director award.

De Heer returned to science fiction with *Epsilon* (1997), having changed direction with the drama *The Quiet Room* (1996). International critical approval greeted *The Tracker* (2002) and *Alexandra's Project* (2003). *Ten Canoes* (2006), the first film shot in the native Australian Aboriginal language, swept the AFI awards, and won de Heer his second Best Director award. Set before the arrival of colonialists, it tells the story of a group of Aboriginal tribesman, and reveals the workings of the indigenous Australian culture, while making an argument for its relevance and validity today. **WW**

Top Takes...

Ten Canoes 2006
Alexandra's Project 2003
The Tracker 2002
The Old Man Who Read Love Stories 2001
Dance Me to My Song 1998
Epsilon 1997
The Quiet Room 1996
Bad Boy Bubby 1993
Dingo 1991
Encounter at Raven's Gate 1988
Tale of a Tiger 1984

"The world is funny and tragic, ugly and beautiful, spiteful and forgiving, loving and hateful."

1950s

ALEKSANDR SOKUROV

Born: Aleksandr Nikolayevich Sokurov, June 14, 1951 (Podorvikha, Russia).

Directing style: Independent auteur of Russian avant-garde cinema; abstract meditations on war and military service; painterly visuals; use of nonprofessional actors; father and son themes; slow pace.

Top Takes…

Solntse 2005 (*The Sun*)

Otets i syn 2003 (*Father and Son*)

Russkiy kovcheg 2002 (*Russian Ark*)

Elegiya dorogi 2002 (*Elegy of a Voyage*)

Telets 2001

Molokh 1999

Mat i syn 1997 (*Mother and Son*)

Vostochnaya elegiya 1996 (*Oriental Elegy*)

Kamen 1992 (*The Stone*)

Krug vtoroy 1990 (*The Second Circle*)

Spasi i sokhrani 1989 (*Rescue and Save*)

Dni zatmeniya 1988 (*The Days of Eclipse*)

Skorbnoye beschuvstviye 1987
  (*Mournful Insensibility*)

Odinokiy golos cheloveka 1987
  (*The Lonely Human Voice*)

"Russia is the land of inspiration and illumination. Europe is the domain of disciplined intellect."

"Happy are those near to us who die before us" is the epitaph that ends Sokurov's film, *Krug vtoroy* (1990) (*The Second Circle*), and it serves as a virtual *leitmotif* for much of his work.

Aleksandr Sokurov was born the son of a former military officer, and it is perhaps from this relationship that much of his later, highly stylized, and contemplative meditations on war and military service have their origins. His first film, *Odinokiy golos cheloveka* (1987) (*The Lonely Human Voice*) won several awards, but Soviet censors suppressed much of his early work.

Since the late 1980s Sokurov has emerged as a world-class auteur, often placed alongside his mentor Andrei Tarkovsky. They certainly share a predilection for the metaphysical, but Sokurov's work is more consistently grounded in material struggle. This often emerges as the struggle with death, as seen best in his masterpiece, *Mat i syn* (1997) (*Mother and Son*), which is fixated on the ebb of life and the unavoidable dissolution of physical attachment.

This theme is pursued within Sokurov's historical films. *Telets* (2001) relates the slow fade of Vladimir Lenin and *Russkiy kovcheg* (2002) (*Russian Ark*) laments the passing of cultural history itself. Though Sokurov may be best known for *Russian Ark*, his unique aesthetic is more consistent and distinctive than that. He has relied much on a painterly cinematographic technique in which figures are distorted or elongated, and the image is softened. This approach is perhaps best exemplified by *Kamen* (1992) (*The Stone*), which is so heavily filtered that it is almost impossible to make out images and objects. Sokurov continues to expand boundaries, particularly in the field of digital video, which has become his medium of choice for many of his documentary projects. **NC**

ABEL FERRARA

Born: Abel Ferrara, July 19, 1951 (The Bronx, New York, U.S.).

Directing style: Cult director of exploitation movies, and violent crime dramas; use of New York City as a location; Roman Catholic religious themes of guilt and redemption.

Born in The Bronx and based in New York City, Abel Ferrara is that brand of New York filmmaker who creates truly unsettling, regional entertainments, occasionally skirting Hollywood long enough to produce another uncompromising vision set in his native city. Having begun making Super-8 movies as a teenager, his coming-of-age film was *The Driller Killer* (1979). Then followed his acclaimed *Ms. 45* (1981), and thereafter an apprenticeship, as he directed a string of bigger budget features such as *Fear City* (1984) and *Cat Chaser* (1989).

His breakthrough came with the stylish and ultraviolent *King of New York* (1990). It is a modern-day Robin Hood story of a drug lord released from jail, out to regain his turf, and hand over his profits to the city's poor. The cops 'n' robbers tale also came with a scintillating cast including David Caruso, Laurence Fishburne, Wesley Snipes, and headliner Christopher Walken.

The movie's success also persuaded Harvey Keitel to star in *Bad Lieutenant* (1992). Keitel produced a memorable performance as a depraved, drug-using, corrupt cop who eventually gets the opportunity for redemption. Ferrara concluded this golden period with two gems, a vampire story, *The Addiction* (1995), and *The Funeral* (1996), a second Walken vehicle, which centered on a 1950s New York mobster family. The latter was also Ferrara's last collaboration with long-time screenwriter and friend Nicholas St. John.

More recently Ferrara helmed *The Blackout* (1997) and *Mary* (2005). Always, his mythology stems from Roman Catholicism and his technique runs to handheld, grainy, and amateurish. The combination is often difficult, but at its best, as in *Bad Lieutenant*, Ferrara marches his audience through a sewer and keeps them asking for more. **GCQ**

Top Takes...

Mary 2005
'R Xmas 2001
New Rose Hotel 1998
The Blackout 1997
The Funeral 1996
The Addiction 1995
Dangerous Game 1993
Body Snatchers 1993
Bad Lieutenant 1992
King of New York 1990
Cat Chaser 1989
China Girl 1987
Fear City 1984
Ms. 45 1981
The Driller Killer 1979
Nicky's Film 1971

1950s

"Don't sleep with your leading actress: it isn't conducive to good filmmaking."

MAMORU OSHII

Born: Mamoru Oshii, August 8, 1951 (Tokyo, Japan).

Directing style: Titan of Japanese anime; use of cutting-edge 3D graphics; sophisticated and cynical cyberpunk animations; philosophical reflections on what constitutes sentience; engaging narratives.

Top Takes…

Tachiguishi retsuden 2006
  (*Amazing Lives of the Fast Food Grifters*)

Inosensu: Kôkaku kidôtai 2004
  (*Ghost in the Shell 2: Innocence*)

Avalon 2001

Kôkaku kidôtai 1995 (*Ghost in the Shell*)

Kidô keisatsu patorebâ: The Movie 2 1993
  (*Patlabor 2*)

Talking Head 1992

Jigoku no banken: kerubersu 1991 (*Stray Dogs*)

Kidô keisatsu patorebâ: The Movie 1989
  (*Patlabor 1*)

Jigoku no banken: akai megane 1987
  (*The Red Spectacles*)

Tenshi no tamago 1985 (*Angel's Egg*)

Urusei Yatsura 1: Onri yû 1983
  (*Urusei Yatsura 1: Only You*)

> "Whether it's background material or the characters, the source material is hand drawn."

Mamoru Oshii is considered one of the reigning giants of Japanese animation, or anime. His philosophical and aesthetic vision skillfully weds meticulous compositions with an understanding of the simultaneously liberating and destructive potentials of mechanical and information technologies.

Oshii's direction embraces technological innovations, while acknowledging and, at times, exposing cinema's fundamental artifice. This latter strategy is perhaps most evident in his live-action films, including *Talking Head* (1992) and *Avalon* (2001). *Talking Head* uses the premise of an anime production in crisis as the springboard for a frequently satirical commentary upon the process of creating mass entertainments, whereas *Avalon* immerses spectators in a world in which online gaming—beautifully rendered through a striking combination of 3D computer animation and live action—has become an addictive and rewarding alternative to mundane daily life.

However, it is for his animated features that Oshii is best known, specifically *Kôkaku kidôtai* (1995) (*Ghost in the Shell*), and its sequel *Inosensu: Kôkaku kidôtai* (2004) (*Ghost in the Shell 2: Innocence*). Building upon the success of his science-fiction anime features, *Kidô keisatsu patorebâ: The Movie* (1989) (*Patlabor 1*) and *Kidô keisatsu patorebâ: The Movie 2* (1993) (*Patlabor 2*), *Ghost in the Shell* solidified Oshii's reputation for crafting narratives that raise vital questions on what it means to be human. Oshii continues to explore the boundaries of contemporary animation. His feature, *Tachiguishi retsuden* (2006) (*Amazing Lives of the Fast Food Grifters*), combines conventional 2D animation, 3D computer graphics, and photography to evoke a universe every bit as surreal as the one humans occupy. **JM**

YIMOU ZHANG

Born: Zhang Yimou, November 14, 1951 (Xi'an, Shaanxi, China).

Directing style: Maker of martial arts movies; graceful, breathtaking action; sequences of people flying; lush use of color; flamboyant, extravagant costumes; strong female characters.

Known for his intimate personal dramas and lavish action period pieces, Yimou Zhang is one of the most prominent and critically acclaimed directors to emerge from the Fifth Generation of Chinese filmmakers who began making films after the Cultural Revolution. In 1979, he applied to the Beijing Film Academy but was rejected. After meeting the Minister of Culture, he was accepted and graduated in 1982.

Zhang entered the film industry as a cinematographer and actor. His directorial debut, *Hong gao liang* (1987) (*Red Sorghum*), established Zhang's reputation internationally, and showcases his early meditative manner employing strong female protagonists. The film also marked the beginning of a personal and professional relationship with actress Li Gong that would last through seven films. Zhang experienced political hardships with *Ju Dou* (1990) and *Da hong deng long gao gao gua* (1991) (*Raise the Red Lantern*) when Chinese censors banned both films. After performing well internationally, and receiving Academy Award nominations, the films were reinstated by the Chinese government.

Recently, Zhang made a major directorial shift with the period wushu martial arts films *Ying xiong* (2002) (*Hero*), *Shi mian mai fu* (2004) (*House of Flying Daggers*), and *Man cheng jin dai huang jin jia* (2006) (*Curse of the Golden Flower*). Although they retain Zhang's visual storytelling artistry, with its trademark use of flamboyant color as a motif, extravagant costumes, and graceful action sequences, the films drew criticism for glamorizing Eastern society for Western consumption. In addition to his film work, Zhang has also directed the opera *Turandot* in Florence and China, and prepared a ballet version of *Raise the Red Lantern*. **WW**

Top Takes...

Man cheng jin dai huang jin jia 2006
 (*Curse of the Golden Flower*)
Shi mian mai fu 2004 (*House of Flying Daggers*)
Ying xiong 2002 (*Hero*)
Xingfu shiguang 2000 (*Happy Times*)
Yi ge dou bu neng shao 1999 (*Not One Less*)
Wo de fu qin mu qin 1999 (*The Road Home*)
You hua hao hao shuo 1997 (*Keep Cool*)
Yao a yao yao dao waipo qiao 1995
 (*Shanghai Triad*)
Huozhe 1994 (*Living*)
Qiu Ju da guan si 1992 (*The Story of Qiu Ju*)
Da hong deng long gao gao gua 1991
 (*Raise the Red Lantern*)
Ju Dou 1990
Hong gao liang 1987 (*Red Sorghum*)

"The objective of any form of art is not political . . . I am not interested in politics."

KATHRYN BIGELOW

Born: Kathryn Ann Bigelow, November 27, 1951 (San Carlos, California, U.S.).

Directing style: Intellectual female maker of provocative action movies; explorations of gender and the seductiveness of violence in cinematic form; blurring of genres.

Top Takes…

K-19: The Widowmaker 2002
The Weight of Water 2000
Strange Days 1995
Point Break 1991
Blue Steel 1990
Near Dark 1987
The Loveless 1982
The Set-Up 1978

"There should be more women directing . . . there's just not the awareness that it's possible."

Kathryn Bigelow is a Hollywood paradox: a female action director whose films demonstrate sharp intelligence, dazzling style, and impressive technical innovation, yet whose work has never received the popular or critical recognition it deserves.

With a distinguished academic background in conceptual art and film theory, she made her first short, *The Set-Up* (1978), in which two men beat each other up while two philosophers discuss violence on the soundtrack. Subsequent films, such as the stylized biker movie *The Loveless* (1982), explored the intersection of gender, genre, and violence while celebrating a group of outsiders. But it was the genre-deconstructing vampire Western and cult favorite *Near Dark* (1987), shot primarily at night in deep blues, blacks, and contrasting light, that established Bigelow's visual style and characteristic pairing of a streetwise heroine with a vulnerable protagonist.

The testosterone and adrenaline-charged *Point Break* (1991) became Bigelow's single unqualified hit, whereas her subsequent edgier and more intellectually ambitious films have been box-office disappointments. With its riveting POV sequences, dazzling visuals, and layered subplots, the tech-noir *Strange Days* (1995) addressed the related issues of violence and voyeurism head on, implicating and sabotaging its audience. Her one film to explore feminist subject matter, *The Weight of Water* (2000), interweaves a true nineteenth-century double-murder case with a contemporary story, and explores dysfunctional relationships, repressed jealousy, claustrophobia, and desire. It was received politely if not warmly, as was her subsequent study of men under duress and confinement, the Russian submarine movie *K-19: The Widowmaker* (2002). **LB**

ROBERTO BENIGNI

Born: Roberto Benigni, March 27, 1952 (Misericordia, Arezzo, Tuscany, Italy).

Directing style: Italian actor and director of tragicomedies; themes of the lost outsider facing a dilemma in a hostile, unknown environment; highbrow literary allusions.

The films of Italian actor and director Roberto Benigni may seem as light and frothy as a cappuccino, but beneath the froth lies substance: Benigni may often play the fool, but he is not one. His films are tragicomedies, rich with highbrow allusions from Dante to William Shakespeare, and peppered with wry digs at Italian society and politics.

Benigni made his directorial debut with *Tu mi turbi* (1983) (*You Disturb Me*), costarring with his wife and muse, Nicoletta Braschi. This set Benigni on the path to a number of comedies that became box-office gold in Italy. *Non ci resta che piangere* (1985) (*Nothing Left to Do But Cry*) is a surreal trip back in time to the Italian Renaissance worthy of Woody Allen. *Il piccolo diavolo* (1988) (*The Little Devil*) sees Benigni incarnated as a devil lost in a modern world. In the Shakespearean style comedy of errors, *Johnny Stecchino* (1991) (*Johnny Toothpick*), in which he plays a care worker who is the doppelganger of a Sicilian Mafia boss, Benigni focuses on the Italian view of the island and assumptions about criminality.

But his tour de force so far has been *La vita è bella* (1997) (*Life Is Beautiful*) that saw him pick up a Best Actor Oscar, along with another for Best Foreign Language Film. It starts out as a romance set against the backdrop of fascism and turns into a haunting tale of a father and son, and their life in a Nazi concentration camp. And as much as Benigni incredibly finds a way to play it for laughs, it asks the viewer to imagine how parents explained the Holocaust to their children. Ultimately it is a story of familial love, but one that avoids a saccharine ending. Few directors can achieve such a feat, and it set Benigni alongside those predecessors he admires most: Groucho Marx and Sir Charles Chaplin. **CK**

Top Takes...

La tigre e la neve 2005 (*The Tiger and the Snow*)
Pinocchio 2002
La vita è bella 1997 ☆
  (Life Is Beautiful)
Il Mostro 1994 (*The Monster*)
Johnny Stecchino 1991 (*Johnny Toothpick*)
Il piccolo diavolo 1988 (*The Little Devil*)
Non ci resta che piangere 1985
  (*Nothing Left to Do But Cry*)
L'Addio a Enrico Berlinguer 1984
Tu mi turbi 1983 (*You Disturb Me*)

1950s

"Charlie Chaplin used his ass better than any actor . . . his ass is practically the protagonist."

ROBERT ZEMECKIS

Born: Robert Lee Zemeckis, May 14, 1952 (Chicago, Illinois, U.S.).

Directing style: Wizard of special effects; maker of dramas and comedies; pioneering performance capture techniques; use of match moving; trademark long opening shots.

Top Takes…

Beowulf 2007

The Polar Express 2004

Cast Away 2000

Contact 1997

Forrest Gump 1994 ★

Death Becomes Her 1992

Back to the Future Part III 1990

Back to the Future Part II 1989

Who Framed Roger Rabbit 1988

Back to the Future 1985

Romancing the Stone 1984

Used Cars 1980

I Wanna Hold Your Hand 1978

A Field of Honor 1973

The Lift 1972

Friend, colleague, and collaborator of director Steven Spielberg since the late 1970s, Robert Zemeckis eventually established himself as a pioneer and box-office breadwinner on a par with his old friend and mentor. He has made a number of well-crafted dramas and comedies that are notable for their use of cutting-edge special effects, but at the same time tell a story in an entertaining fashion, proving that special effects can be used as a narrative-enhancing device.

From the well-received shorts *The Lift* (1972) and *A Field of Honor* (1973) Zemeckis graduated to the fictional take on Beatlemania *I Wanna Hold Your Hand* (1978) and the cult satire *Used Cars* (1980), before the action adventure *Romancing the Stone* (1984) catapulted him to the mainstream. His next films were also smash hits, including the Spielberg-produced *Back to the Future* (1985), its two sequels, and the technologically groundbreaking *Who Framed Roger Rabbit* (1988) that combined live action seamlessly with traditional animation.

Then came *Forrest Gump* (1994), another pioneering film that saw Zemeckis place lead Tom Hanks in scenes with well-known historical figures such as former U.S. President John F. Kennedy. It won six Oscars, including a Best Director statue for Zemeckis. However, his homage to Sir Alfred Hitchcock, *What Lies Beneath* (2000), took a critical drubbing before Zemeckis inevitably bounced back with *Cast Away* (2000), another major Academy Awards contender. The film was set almost entirely on a desert island, with Hanks the sole actor in a modern take on Daniel Defoe's novel, *Robinson Crusoe*. In 2004 Zemeckis directed the children's book adaptation *The Polar Express*, which pioneered a new style of hyperrealistic animation. **JK**

> "The only thing I had that was inspirational was television— and it actually was."

GUS VAN SANT

Born: Gus Van Sant Jr., July 24, 1952 (Louisville, Kentucky, U.S.).

Directing style: Maker of early independent cult movies and later Hollywood dramas; often gay themes or characters; artistic collaborations with actors Keanu Reeves and Matt Damon.

Gus Van Sant is one of cinema's most consistently experimental mainstream filmmakers. Often drastically reinventing himself over the course of his career, he has managed to bounce back from failures, and work the fluid, voracious, creative curiosity that characterizes his short films into virtually every feature he has directed. This has not made him bankable box-office fare, but Van Sant's pain is inevitably the viewers' gain.

After *Mala Noche* (1985) put him on the critical map, Van Sant hit the big time with *Drugstore Cowboy* (1989). A quasi-Warholian breath of fresh air for 1980s moviegoers weary of action movies, it saw Matt Dillon put in a tour de force performance as a junkie. Its follow-up, *My Own Private Idaho* (1991), overreached somewhat with a surfeit of Shakespearean pretensions, but its rambling dexterity and gay sex scenes presaged a change of direction.

His new phase initially stumbled with the overpadded *Even Cowgirls Get the Blues* (1993), but quickly recovered with its lean neo-noir counterpart, *To Die For* (1995). *Good Will Hunting* (1997) put Ben Affleck and Matt Damon on the map, and earned several Academy Award nominations, including one for Van Sant as Best Director. *Finding Forrester* (2000) saw Van Sant struggling in Hollywood's tar pit, although it paired him with cinematographer Harris Savides, so all was not lost. Beginning with the excessively non-commercial experimental *Gerry* (2002), where Van Sant worked again with Damon and Savides, he recovered his equilibrium, and went on to do his best work yet. *Elephant* (2003) made up for its occasional platitudinizing with a daring humanism, while *Last Days* (2005) remains the definitive movie statement on the obliterative confluence of art, fame, and identity. **MH**

Top Takes...

Paris, je t'aime 2006
Last Days 2005
Elephant 2003
Gerry 2002
Good Will Hunting 1997 ☆
Ballad of the Skeletons 1997
To Die For 1995
My Own Private Idaho 1991
Thanksgiving Prayer 1991
Drugstore Cowboy 1989
Five Ways to Kill Yourself 1987
My New Friend 1987
Mala Noche 1985

"I'm thinking of remaking *Psycho* again . . . we're talking about a Punk rocker setting."

JIM JARMUSCH

Born: James R. Jarmusch, January 22, 1953 (Akron, Ohio, U.S.).

Directing style: Independent filmmaker of intelligently crafted vignettes of contemporary U.S. life and its myths; themes of communication; wry humor; use of stationary camera.

Top Takes...

1950s

With his shock of white hair and droll demeanor, Jim Jarmusch has long been one of the most recognizable faces of U.S. independent cinema. Yet the director himself has often pointed to fellow filmmakers such as Yasujiro Ozu and Jean-Pierre Melville as primary influences in addition to such domestic icons as Samuel Fuller. Indeed, Jarmusch's films reflect a pan-global mindset that deftly merges the pop cultural highs and lows of international cinema, with life in general.

A long-time New York City resident, Jarmusch studied film in New York, and later France, working on *Lightning Over Water* (1980) with iconic director Nicholas Ray and peer Wim Wenders. His low-budget first film, *Permanent Vacation* (1980), won him enough attention to earn greater financing for *Stranger Than Paradise* (1984), a galvanizing independent film that introduced a theme that resonates through nearly all of Jarmusch's later films, namely the collision and unlikely intersection of people of different backgrounds, and the difficulty of communication.

Down by Law (1986) was about a trio of cellmates, *Mystery Train* (1989) a series of stories set in the oddball corners of Memphis, and the even more ambitious *Night on Earth* (1991) was set in five international cities. The postmodern Western *Dead Man* (1995) found Jarmusch exploring the depths of movie myths and legends, something he achieved to a different degree with the unconventional Neil Young documentary *Year of the Horse* (1997). The samurai hit man movie *Ghost Dog: The Way of the Samurai* (1999) returned Jarmusch to New York, and *Coffee and Cigarettes* (2003) compiled a series of shorts he had been working on for decades. *Broken Flowers* (2005) stars Bill Murray as a man in crisis on a cross-country search for his former lovers. **JK**

> "I don't let the Money give me notes on my scripts. I don't allow the Money on the set."

FRIDRIK THÓR FRIDRIKSSON

Born: Fridrik Thór Fridriksson, May 12, 1953 (Reykjavik, Iceland).

Directing style: Director of literary dramas; wry humor; narratives in the Icelandic saga storytelling tradition; stunning cinematography; issues of identity; use of Icelandic New Wave music.

Director, producer, writer, and actor, Fridrik Thór Fridriksson is one of Iceland's best-known filmmakers. He grew up with 1960s Hollywood movies, but his key influences also include Akira Kurosawa, John Ford, and Nicholas Ray.

Fridriksson started his career making documentaries and experimental films such as *Brennu-njálssaga* (1980) (*The Saga of Burnt Njal*) and *Kúrekar norðursins* (1984) (*Icelandic Cowboys*). In 1987 he founded The Icelandic Film Corporation, which has gone on to become his country's premier production company. Fridriksson's work is strongly rooted in the saga storytelling tradition, and he has collaborated with some of Iceland's most lauded writers. With novelist Einar Kárason he made *Skytturnar* (1987) (*White Whales*), *Fálkar* (2002) (*Falcons*), and *Djöflaeyjan* (1996) (*Devil's Island*). The latter revolves around a community of outcasts living in barracks left by U.S. forces after World War II, and Fridriksson attempts to show a hidden world of Iceland and the effects of Americanization on its culture.

Fridriksson's films have an appealing wit and whimsy, and viewers are invited to feel a great solidarity for his characters. In the Oscar-nominated, life-affirming *Börn náttúrunnar* (1991) (*Children of Nature*), an old man has to move into a retirement home in Reykjavik. He meets an old female friend, and they set off together on a wild adventure. *Cold Fever* (1995) is a striking Japanese and Icelandic road movie exploring the problems of upholding Japanese tradition in the unforgiving yet stunningly beautiful Icelandic terrain. Although he has been criticized for being overly sentimental, Fridriksson has resisted becoming a propagandist, arguing that Icelandic culture is strong enough not to need political polemic in order to make a point. **KM**

Top Takes...

Niceland (Population. 1.000.002) 2004
Fálkar 2002 (*Falcons*)
Englar alheimsins 2000 (*Angels of the Universe*)
On Top Down Under 2000
Djöflaeyjan 1996 (*Devil's Island*)
Cold Fever 1995
Bíódagar 1994 (*Movie Days*)
Börn náttúrunnar 1991 (*Children of Nature*)
Skytturnar 1987 (*White Whales*)
Hringurinn 1985
Kúrekar norðursins 1984 (*Icelandic Cowboys*)
Rokk í Reykjavík 1982
Eldsmiðurinn 1981 (*The Blacksmith*)
Brennu-njálssaga 1980 (*The Saga of Burnt Njal*)

"I prefer that people don't try to understand my film, but rather to feel it."

1950s

NANNI MORETTI

Born: Giovanni Moretti, August 19, 1953 (Brunico, Bolzano, Trentino-Alto Adige, Italy).

Directing style: Marxist director of eccentric, neurotic comedies; autobiographical themes; ironic observations of Italian politics and middle-class existence.

Top Takes…

Il Caimano 2006 (The Caiman)

The Last Customer 2003

La stanza del figlio 2001 (The Son's Room)

Aprile 1998 (April)

L'unico paese al mondo 1994

Caro diario 1993 (Dear Diary)

La Cosa 1990 (The Thing)

Palombella rossa 1989 (Red Wood Pigeon)

La messa è finita 1985 (The Mass Is Ended)

Sogni d'oro 1981 (Sweet Dreams)

Ecce Bombo 1978

Io sono un autarchico 1976 (I Am Self Sufficient)

Paté de bourgeois 1973

"I fix images of our country for myself. In Italy, we have a short memory. I freeze moments."

Italy's favorite art theater export, writer, actor, and director, Nanni Moretti has developed a small but loyal following. After gaining note with a Super-8mm film, *Io sono un autarchico* (1976) (*I Am Self Sufficient*), commercial success followed with his first feature *Ecce Bombo* (1978). Little known outside his native land, Moretti is a true maverick of Italian cinema, balancing the cerebral tone of his work with large doses of irony. Although often quirky and individualistic in style, in many ways Moretti is the middle classes' poster boy for Italy's post-1968 generation, continually confronting their inner turmoils of faith and spirit.

Best known outside of Italy for his semiautobiographical *Caro diario* (1993) (*Dear Diary*), where his riffs on contemporary Italian life won him the Palme d'Or and Best Director awards at the Cannes Film Festival, his label "The Italian Woody Allen" underplays Moretti's own significance as an original and pointedly political filmmaker. Like Allen, his films are always witty, and more often than not cuttingly acerbic, yet they also display a harder political underbelly. For Moretti the personal is political, and the political can get very personal. A self-confessed Marxist, he has not been afraid to attack the Italian political elite, constantly displaying a burrowing and unending political neurosis in films such as *La Cosa* (1990) (*The Thing*). His *Palombella rossa* (1989) (*Red Wood Pigeon*) is typical, using a water polo match as a metaphor to explore tensions within the post-*glasnost* Italian Communist Party. *La stanza del figlio* (2001) (*The Son's Room*) , for which he won the Palme d'Or again, took a more personal turn, but by *Il Caimano* (2006) (*The Caiman*) he had returned to his favorite cinematic sport: baiting Italy's political establishment. **RH**

JEAN-PIERRE JEUNET

Born: Jean-Pierre Jeunet, September 3, 1953 (Roanne, Loire, France).

Directing style: French visionary storyteller of eccentric black comedies, romantic fables, and fantastical dramas; eye-opening sets and costumes; frequent use of short lens.

France's answer to Terry Gilliam, Jean-Pierre Jeunet is a visionary whose eye and instinct for fantastic, fascinating imagery does not intrude on his ability to tell a story.

Jeunet embarked on his first film endeavors with designer Marc Caro. They began with a series of shorts before Jeunet and Caro created *Delicatessen* (1991), a dark comedy set in an apartment complex during a post-apocalyptic food shortage, where the butcher landlord creates cannibalistic meals for his odd tenants. The film's surreal comedy and fantastically bizarre set that gave the apartment a feel of crumbling chaotic decay found favor at home and abroad. The even more ambitious, *La cité des enfants perdus* (1995) (*The City of Lost Children*), about a doctor who kidnaps children in order to steal their dreams, was wildly inventive and eye-catching, featuring costumes by Jean-Paul Gaultier and huge, astounding sets.

Capitalizing on his popularity, Jeunet helmed *Alien: Resurrection* (1997) in the United States, but it was a creative misfire. Back in France he made the smaller scale, but significantly more successful, *Le fabuleux destin d'Amélie Poulain* (2001) (*Amélie*), an unusual fable starring Audrey Tautou. The fantastical romantic comedy set in the charming district of Abbesses in Paris won various Oscar nominations including Best Screenplay.

Jeunet next set about adapting a World War I novel by Sébastien Japrisot, *Un long dimanche de fiançailles* (2004) (*A Very Long Engagement*). The award-winning romantic mystery saw France reexamine its past, and Tatou star as a woman obsessed with finding her fiancé, one of five French soldiers who wound themselves to escape the fighting on the Somme and are abandoned in no-man's land as a punishment. **JK**

Top Takes...

Un long dimanche de fiançailles 2004
  (*A Very Long Engagement*)
Le fabuleux destin d'Amélie Poulain 2001
  (*Amélie*)
Alien: Resurrection 1997
La cité des enfants perdus 1995
  (*The City of Lost Children*)
Delicatessen 1991
Foutaises 1989
  (*Things I Like, Things I Don't Like*)
Pas de repos pour Billy Brakko 1984
Le bunker de la dernière rafale 1981
  (*The Bunker of the Last Gunshots*)
Le Manège 1980
L'Évasion 1978 (*The Escape*)

"Cinema since the New Wave always seems to be about a couple fighting in the kitchen."

1950s

ANTHONY MINGHELLA

Born: Anthony Minghella, January 6, 1954 (Ryde, Isle of Wight, England).

Directing style: British director of romantic epics and literary adaptations; subtle and intelligent handling of actors; collaborations with Jude Law; alluring use of landscape.

Top Takes...

Breaking and Entering 2006
Cold Mountain 2003
Play 2000
The Talented Mr. Ripley 1999
The English Patient 1996 ★
Mr. Wonderful 1993
Truly Madly Deeply 1991

Anthony Minghella began his career in the 1980s script editing the popular BBC TV children's series *Grange Hill* (1983–1988). He then wrote and directed his first feature, the deliriously sad tragicomedy *Truly Madly Deeply* (1991). A story of a young widow who has not yet found a way to grieve, the film catapulted Juliet Stevenson and Alan Rickman to new heights and brought Minghella a wide and attentive audience.

He moved on to *Mr. Wonderful* (1993) and cast Matt Dillon and Annabella Sciorra as a divorced couple thrown together through a banker's irony. Then came his stellar hit, *The English Patient* (1996) adapted from the celebrated novel by Michael Ondaatje. The Oscar Best Picture winner stars Ralph Fiennes as a badly burned World War II crash victim and, as in *Truly Madly Deeply*, Minghella shows his capacity for sober and evocative pacing, mature characterization, precisely structured and aesthetically resonant mise-en-scène, and musical phrasing in both the story structure and editing. *The English Patient* has a sweeping quality without ever descending into bathos.

Minghella then made a minor masterpiece with *The Talented Mr. Ripley* (1999). Matt Damon is an insuperable confection of unctuous sweetness and casual, murderous ferocity in the title role and the film perfectly balances strong supporting performances along with sumptuous location filming to make a haunting story of murder and love. *Cold Mountain* (2003) attempts a large canvas in a tale set at the end of the U.S. Civil War, with a wounded soldier played by Jude Law braving the elements, strange and hostile people, and fate in order to be reunited with his lost love. Despite faultless mise-en-scène, the film was not particularly successful financially, but garnered seven Oscar nominations. **MP**

"The only lesson to extract from any civil war is that it's pointless and futile and ugly."

RIGHT: The layers of deceipt mount up for Matt Damon in *The Talented Mr. Ripley*.

IDRISSA OUEDRAOGO

Born: Idrissa Ouedraogo, January 21, 1954 (Banfora, Burkina Faso).

Directing style: Maker of African fables of village life; use of indigenous oral traditions of storytelling; explorations of traditional values, home, and community.

Top Takes...

"For African cinema to grow, it is vital for African movies to reach African audiences."

Idrissa Ouedraogo makes stories, both modern and ancient, indigenous to his native African culture. He uses a constantly emerging, even urgent, development of narrative against a background whose simplicity is often deceptive. He steers his characters, and their often strained relationships, to weave a deft picture of the complexity of contemporary African life.

Ouedraogo was born in Burkina Faso, and went to France to study film. He made his directorial debut with the short *Poko* (1981), and his first feature was *Yam Daabo* (1986) (*The Choice*). His subsequent effort, *Yaaba* (1989), depicts the trials of African village life as two children become friends with an older woman who is an outcast of the village because she is suspected of being a witch. It won the director international attention, and was awarded the FIPRESCI Prize at the Cannes Film Festival. Ouedraogo returns to village life with *Samba Traoré* (1992). Its title character has been away from his village and returns a rich man. But soon the locals wonder how he got all his money and start asking questions. Before long he is running for his life, as his sordid past is revealed.

Tilai (1990) (*The Law*) is set in precolonial days. A young man, Saga, returns to his village to discover that his promised bride has been married to his father while he has been away. The young couple are still in love and consummate their passion. Saga is condemned, but his brother only pretends to execute him and the lovers flee, erroneously thinking they will have a new future. A masterpiece of elegant simplicity, it won the Jury's Grand Prize at Cannes. In *Kini and Adams* (1997), the director depicts two friends dreaming of a new life in Zimbabwe, as once again Ouedraogo is drawn to themes of life both in and beyond the village. **MP**

1950s

RON HOWARD

Born: Ronald William Howard, March 1, 1954 (Duncan, Oklahoma, U.S.).

Directing style: Child actor turned director of blockbuster Hollywood dramas and lighthearted comedies; artistic collaborations with actor Tom Hanks; family cameo appearances.

Ron Howard was born into an acting family and was in his first movie, *Frontier Woman* (1956), at only eighteen months old. He went on to spend his childhood in front of cameras, on TV shows such as *Dennis the Menace* (1959–1960), and later as Richie Cunningham on *Happy Days* (1974). An early serious role came in George Lucas's *American Graffiti* (1973).

The actor soon turned his hand to directing, and his skill with light comedic material was established with *Splash* (1984) about a mermaid found at the Statue of Liberty. *Cocoon* (1985) posited a group of octogenarians who tumble into the swimming pool of youth, and brought such respected actors as Don Ameche, Hume Cronyn, Jack Gilford, Jessica Tandy, and Gwen Verdon back to the screen. *Parenthood* (1989), a skillfully wrought romp through the story of a confusing and enormous family, showed Howard's comedic talent as did *How the Grinch Stole Christmas* (2000), starring the irrepressible Jim Carrey.

With *Apollo 13* (1995), Howard turned serious. Based on Henry S. F. Cooper's account of the almost fatal space mission, this taut thriller recreated conditions in a space capsule during an equipment malfunction. The director then continued to show he had a flair for drama, resulting in his crowning glory *A Beautiful Mind* (2001), which sensitively explored autism and mathematical genius, and won him an Oscar for Best Director.

Howard also bravely took up the gauntlet of producing the film version of Dan Brown's contentious pulp thriller *The Da Vinci Code* (2006). The film had a star-studded cast headed by Tom Hanks, and was shot on location in Europe for $125 million. Despite high hopes, the film did not compare with the greatest triumphs of Hollywood, although it was a sound financial success. **MP**

Top Takes...

The Da Vinci Code 2006
Cinderella Man 2005
The Missing 2003
A Beautiful Mind 2001 ★
How the Grinch Stole Christmas 2000
Ransom 1996
Apollo 13 1995
The Paper 1994
Far and Away 1992
Backdraft 1991
Parenthood 1989
Cocoon 1985
Splash 1984
Old Paint 1969

"There is something inherently tough about Americans. They will not accept defeat."

1950s

MICHAEL MOORE

Born: Michael Moore, April 23, 1954 (Flint, Michigan, U.S.).

Directing style: Controversial social activist and guerrilla filmmaker of documentaries that attack and subvert contemporary U.S. corporate life and politics; ambush-style interviews.

Top Takes...

Fahrenheit 9/11 2004
Bowling for Columbine 2002
The Big One 1997
Canadian Bacon 1995
Roger & Me 1989

Michael Moore arrived with *Roger & Me* (1989), inspired by his return home to Flint, Michigan, to discover a General Motors-created wasteland. He financed the film by running bingo games in his home. The documentary saw him chasing General Motors's chief executive Roger Smith with ambush interviews, and placing himself as his movie's central subject. It established Moore as a working-class hero. Significantly, he also combined self-promotion and objective presentation of fact to redirect documentary form at the precise moment when relatively inexpensive video cameras made truly guerrilla filmmaking possible for the masses.

Moore continued attacking corporate elites on the TV show, *TV Nation* (1994–1995), for which he won an Emmy. He directed John Candy in his only fiction feature to date, *Canadian Bacon* (1995), and returned to documentary with *The Big One* (1997), before the small screen *The Awful Truth* (1999).

Following the Littleton, Colorado, massacre at Columbine High School, Moore focused on the military industrial complex, the National Rifle Association, and teen violence to make the documentary *Bowling for Columbine* (2002), which won an Academy Award for Best Documentary, Features. *Bowling for Columbine*, the first blockbuster documentary in history, made Moore's technique a litmus test of the distinction between journalistic accuracy and mass entertainment. It was followed by *Fahrenheit 9/11* (2004), about the September 11, 2001 terrorist attacks on the United States. This confirmed Moore's status as a gifted political artist commenting on the nature of U.S. national identity. He does so with an ironic black humor that manages to make nightmare scenarios palatable to his audience. **GCQ**

"We live in a time where we have a man sending us to war for fictitious reasons."

JANE CAMPION

Born: Jane Campion, April 30, 1954 (Wellington, New Zealand).

Directing style: Auteur storyteller of insightful feminist dramas; exploration of the dark side of romance; issues of gender and identity; striking visuals and costume dramas.

Jane Campion is most famous for writing and directing lyrical drama *The Piano* (1993) about an immigrant to New Zealand. Its stunning imagery and haunting score helped it become an international hit at art theaters, and it proved a successful crossover to the mainstream. *The Piano* won Academy Awards for Best Actress (Holly Hunter), Best Supporting Actress (Anna Paquin), and Best Writing, Screenplay Written Directly for the Screen for Campion (she was the second woman ever to be nominated for this award).

Campion first came to international attention with her directorial debut, the allegorical short *An Exercise in Discipline —Peel* (1982), which won the Palme d'Or for Best Short Film at Cannes Film Festival, and revealed her gift for storytelling. Her first feature, *Sweetie* (1989), a dark fiction about the twisted psychologies of two sisters, also proved an award winner. She followed this up with the TV series, *An Angel at My Table* (1990), the story of New Zealand writer Janet Frame.

Following the success of *The Piano*, Campion turned her hand to filming a Henry James novel, *The Portrait of a Lady* (1996). Then Campion departed intriguingly from the costume drama genre with *In the Cut* (2003), a contemporary character study adopting the genre conventions of the police crime thriller. In a stark move away from her typical romantic comedy roles, Meg Ryan played a woman attracted to danger, and to a homicide detective. With both the female lead and the female director playing against type, *In the Cut* is not just daring for its graphic depictions of sex, it represents a rare occasion where a female star and auteur are united in challenging audiences to view them, and their work, in radically new ways. **MH**

Top Takes...

The Water Diary 2006
In the Cut 2003
Holy Smoke 1999
The Portrait of a Lady 1996
***The Piano* 1993** ☆
Sweetie 1989
After Hours 1984
A Girl's Own Story 1984
Passionless Moments 1983
An Exercise in Discipline—Peel 1982

"To deny women directors, as I suspect is happening, . . . is to deny the feminine vision."

1950s

AMY HECKERLING

Born: Amy Heckerling, May 7, 1954 (The Bronx, New York City, New York, U.S.).

Directing style: Inventive writer and director of lighthearted, screwball comedies; innovative take on the teen movie genre; fast-fire gags; strong female characters in mainstream films.

Top Takes...

1950s

"I think that *Clueless* was very deep ... deep in the way that it was very light."—Alicia Silverstone

The 1980s teen movie *Fast Times at Ridgemont High* (1982) gave Amy Heckerling her first step into feature-length, mainstream movie direction. Written by a young Cameron Crowe, the comedy looks at the lives of teenagers at high school and the mall, and saw a youthful Sean Penn make his feature debut in a hilarious performance as a stoned surfer.

Heckerling has since been responsible for writing and directing a string of popular Hollywood hits, among them the feel-good comedy inspired by her own experience of pregnancy and motherhood, *Look Who's Talking* (1989) and its rapid-fire sequel *Look Who's Talking Too* (1990).

Heckerling is best known for her work on another teen movie, the satire *Clueless* (1995). It made its lead, Alicia Silverstone, into a star, and became a talking point thanks to Heckerling's super-sharp screenplay, its depiction of teenagers' slang, and its audacious—and successful—transplant of the plot from a Jane Austen novel, *Emma,* to the setting of a contemporary U.S. West Coast high school. The radical move from literary classic to popular film meant that *Clueless* could be enjoyed equally by audiences who appreciated how it was toying with a literary classic, and those who responded to it as a slick high school movie. Its knowingness, playful blurring of both highbrow and pop culture, and sense of encouraging laughter both with, and at, some of its characters, combined to bring it critical and intellectual respectability. Arguably Heckerling has yet to recapture the heights of inventiveness and sheer verve shown in *Clueless*. Her subsequent projects have lacked the immediate appeal and startling uniqueness of vision that she displayed in some of her earlier films, but her best may lie ahead. **MH**

JAMES CAMERON

Born: James Francis Cameron, August 16, 1954 (Kapuskasing, Ontario, Canada).

Directing style: Guru of cutting-edge special effects; maker of action-packed science fiction and dramas; underwater filming sequences; themes of man and technology.

A former special-effects whiz, James Cameron achieved his big break by directing a quickie sequel for B-movie maven Roger Corman. Cameron quickly translated the low-budget acumen displayed in *Piranha Part Two: The Spawning* (1981) into his pet project, *The Terminator* (1984), a film that catapulted its creator, and star Arnold Schwarzenegger, to international fame.

Cameron followed that cult science-fiction smash by developing fellow visionary Ridley Scott's science-fiction masterpiece *Alien* (1979) into a monstrously popular action franchise, with its sequel *Aliens* (1986). His following project, *The Abyss* (1989), was better known for its pioneering special effects than its box-office performance. Not so *Terminator 2: Judgment Day* (1991), Cameron's reunion with Schwarzenegger and the first $100 million movie. It kicked special effects, particularly the nascent process of morphing, several years into the future, while breaking theatrical records.

Schwarzenegger returned for the light action film *True Lies* (1994), another smash hit, albeit a crass one. But Cameron had an ace already hidden up his sleeve for his next project: *Titanic* (1997), the first $200 million movie. The subject of much conjecture and derision before its release, *Titanic* silenced all the naysayers by becoming the highest-grossing film of all time and cleaning up at the Academy Awards, including winning Cameron the Best Director title.

But how can one follow such a film? In Cameron's case, so far he has not. Although he has directed a pair of underwater documentaries, and extolled the virtues of 3D filmmaking, no feature films have emerged. To date, Cameron has spent the post-*Titanic* years attaching himself to, and detaching himself from, several potential projects. **JK**

Top Takes...

Aliens of the Deep 2005
Ghosts of the Abyss 2003
***Titanic* 1997 ★**
Terminator 2: 3-D 1996
True Lies 1994
Terminator 2: Judgment Day 1991
The Abyss 1989
Aliens 1986
The Terminator 1984
Piranha Part Two: The Spawning 1981

"I had pictured myself as a filmmaker, but I had never pictured myself as a director."

1950s

ANG LEE

Born: Ang Lee, October 23, 1954 (Pingtung, Taiwan).

Directing style: Incredibly versatile and innovative director who refuses to be pigeonholed by genre, language, or culture; masterful storytelling of dramas involving secrets and lies.

Top Takes...

Brokeback Mountain 2005 ★

Hulk 2003

Chosen 2001

***Wo hu cang long* 2000** ☆
  (Crouching Tiger, Hidden Dragon)

Ride with the Devil 1999

The Ice Storm 1997

Sense and Sensibility 1995

Yin shi nan nu 1994 (*Eat Drink Man Woman*)

Hsi yen 1993 (*The Wedding Banquet*)

Tui shou 1992

After his first three films, *Tui shou* (1992) (*Pushing Hands*), *Hsi yen* (1993) (*The Wedding Banquet*), and *Yin shi nan nu* (1994) (*Eat Drink Man Woman*), most people thought they had Ang Lee pegged as a maker of delicately funny Taiwanese family comedies, wryly observing the dilemma when filial duty collides with personal satisfaction. Upon which he started zigzagging off into one unexpected genre after another.

Slipping unpredictably into classic English literature mode, Lee directed his first mainstream Hollywood movie, *Sense and Sensibility* (1995), one of the liveliest and most stylish Jane Austen adaptations yet made. The same acute sense of time, place, and social convention informed *The Ice Storm* (1997), adapted from Rick Moody's novel, a study of sexual and family tensions in wintry 1970s New England suburbia. As if to prove he could move out of family-sized dramas and tackle a wider canvas, Lee took his first foray into action movies with *Ride with the Devil* (1999), a gritty U.S. Civil War saga.

Nostalgically harking back to his Taiwanese moviegoing childhood, and shooting his first Chinese-language film since *Eat Drink Man Woman*, Lee permanently raised the bar for martial arts films with the elegant, visually stunning period fantasy epic *Wo hu cang long* (2000) (*Crouching Tiger, Hidden Dragon*). The film set a precedent that Yimou Zhang for one has gratefully followed, but Lee as ever scorned to repeat himself. *Hulk* (2003) had a mixed reception, but nonetheless mapped out new territory for comic-book movies. Lee soon redeemed himself with the acclaimed, Oscar-winning gay Western, *Brokeback Mountain* (2005), once again showing how unobtrusively he could insinuate himself into, and subvert, the tribal conventions of different cultures. **PK**

"Now I'm kind of established as a director, I much prefer directing to writing."

EMIR KUSTURICA

Born: Emir Kusturica, November 24, 1954 (Sarajevo, Bosnia and Herzegovina).

Directing style: Controversial Serbian maker of lyrical dramas, poignant romances, and farcical comedies; absurdist humor; themes of Serbian cultural identity and the effects of war.

Serbian Emir Kusturica is one of only a handful of directors to receive multiple Palme d'Or Awards at the Cannes Film Festival. His work has developed over the years in a true auteurist fashion emphasizing the discipline of an individual vision, and the ferociousness of an untethered imagination.

Specifically, Kusturica is fascinated by the inner workings of tribes of people, whether they be obvious family groups as in *Otac na sluzbenom putu* (1985) (*When Father Was Away on Business*); the unorthodox loose families of social malcontents as in his first English-language film *Arizona Dream* (1993); or perhaps most suggestively, tribes defined by ethnic identity as in *Crna macka, beli macor* (1998) (*Black Cat, White Cat*).

These groups' traditions and rituals are depicted with a communicative, irreverent insouciance. Yet, even at their most benign, the free-wheeling characters Kusturica depicts never fully escape the pressures of social contextualization. The frenetic, Fellini-esque burlesques of his most anarchic and chaotic comedies seem attuned to the harried insanity of a larger, often incoherent social order disintegrating into disorder, usually as a result of war and strife. *Underground* (1995) still stands as his most masterful assessment of the culmination of these themes. Accentuated by a consistent, absurdist humor, the movie's two main characters, Marko and Blacky, struggle to assert their opposing cultural identities within the Balkan wars.

Perhaps Kusturica's lasting legacy will be his unique intuitive ability to mirror the reality of war in the guise of a wild artifice. In particular, viewers will remember his hyperkinetic comic sensibility, a perspective precisely attuned to the tragic horrors of a bombastic and all too true reality. **NC**

Top Takes…

Maradona 2006

All the Invisible Children 2005

Zivot je cudo 2004 (*Life Is a Miracle*)

Super 8 Stories 2001

Crna macka, beli macor 1998
 (*Black Cat, White Cat*)

Underground 1995

Arizona Dream 1993

Dom za vesanje 1988 (*Time of the Gypsies*)

Otac na sluzbenom putu 1985
 (*When Father Was Away on Business*)

Sjecas li se, Dolly Bell 1981
 (*Do You Remember Dolly Bell?*)

Guernica 1978

"I will not cut my film because, because, because, because of the wonderful Wizard of Oz."

1950s

JOEL AND ETHAN COEN

Born: Joel Coen, November 29, 1954 (Minneapolis, Minnesota, U.S.).
Born: Ethan Coen, September 21, 1957 (Minneapolis, Minnesota, U.S).

Directing style: Innovative dynamic duo of comedy of errors dramas; homages to film noir; black humor; use of landscape as a motif; themes of miscommunication.

Top Takes...

Paris, je t'aime 2006 (*Paris, I Love You*)
The Ladykillers 2004
Intolerable Cruelty 2003
The Man Who Wasn't There 2001
O Brother, Where Art Thou? 2000
The Big Lebowski 1998
***Fargo* 1996** ☆
The Hudsucker Proxy 1994
Barton Fink 1991
Miller's Crossing 1990
Raising Arizona 1987
Blood Simple 1984

The only way to define the writing and directing duo of the Coen Brothers is through their resistance to definition itself. Geeky, quirky, and postmodern, their movies are among the most remarkable in post-1980s U.S. independent cinema. The hilarious *Blood Simple* (1984) and the pyrotechnic *Raising Arizona* (1987) were so unlike any previous film that they made the brothers' names an instant cult topic. Although not instantly mainstream, these first two films led on to a major breakthrough, with the Palme d'Or winner *Barton Fink* (1991). The movie was written while Joel and Ethan were struggling with their deliberately convoluted gangster thriller *Miller's Crossing* (1990), a film that looked into the mind of a Hollywood screenwriter suffering from writer's block, and is a cleverly complex labyrinth of symbols and genres. *The Hudsucker Proxy* (1994) explored similar genre mixing in an excellent tribute to screwball comedies.

With *Fargo* (1996), the Coen Brothers rose above such references. Set in the snowy north, it was a bare-boned, disarming tale of misfits and failed crime. *The Big Lebowski* (1998) also presented clumsy crooks and obsessive, obnoxious,

RIGHT: Frances McDormand takes aim in the homespun murder story *Fargo*.

and opinionated losers, but details such as a German band of anarchist terrorists and a devotion to White Russian cocktails made it a cult phenomenon.

The wickedly funny *O Brother, Where Art Thou?* (2000) took up the postmodern referencing again, transposing Homer's ancient classic *The Odyssey* and *The Wizard of Oz* (1939) onto a Great Depression-era prison-break comedy. Since then, the sophisticated parable of gender politics, *Intolerable Cruelty* (2003), has been suitably slick, but *The Man Who Wasn't There* (2001) and the remake of Alexander Mackendrick's crime caper *The Ladykillers* (2004) were bland by Coen standards.

The Coen Brothers have always stressed how small people and little things—details like a toad named Pete or a ruined rug—are in fact crucial to understanding the world. Perhaps in a decade or so their oeuvre will be as neatly explained as so-called classical cinema, but hopefully not. **EM**

ABOVE: Is the game over for the players in the crime comedy *The Big Lebowski*?

O Brother, Who Art Thou?

Sometimes referred to as the "two-headed director," Ethan and Joel Coen have had the final say on every feature film they've directed. They are frequently credited under the name Roderick Jaynes.

- Ethan studied philosophy at college.
- Joel is married to actor Frances McDormand.
- Ethan is also a published author. In 1999 he produced a book of short stories, entitled *Gates of Eden*.
- A young Joel was an assistant editor on *The Evil Dead* (1983), while still a student.

1950s

SU FRIEDRICH

Born: Su Friedrich, December 12, 1954 (New Haven, Connecticut, U.S.).

Directing style: Avant-garde maker of experimental shorts and docudramas; striking black and white cinematography; feminist and lesbian themes; analysis of private rituals and social conventions.

Top Takes...

New York filmmaker Su Friedrich studied art and art history at the University of Chicago and Oberlin College before becoming a photographer and writer. After attending New York's Millennium Film Workshop she made her directorial debut with *Hot Water* (1978), an experiment in sound. She continues to produce 16mm shorts, many of which have received international acclaim. Her movies are notable for their experimental nature, black and white cinematography, feminist and lesbian themes, analysis of the private and intimate, and a depiction of how emotions and rituals function within social convention. Such films include *Cool Hands, Warm Heart* (1979). Set in a busy outdoor market, it depicts various women on stages performing intimate rituals such as shaving their legs and brushing their hair. Another woman attempts to disrupt their activities, but eventually joins in, as Friedrich portrays the pull of social convention and the herd instinct.

Friedrich's oeuvre often draws on her own life. *The Ties That Bind* (1985) illustrates the life of Friedrich's mother, who lived in Germany during the Nazi regime. In a series of interviews, her mother describes life during this period, and the subsequent relationship she developed with a U.S. soldier who became her husband. *Sink or Swim* (1990) describes, through 26 short stories, the childhood events that shaped Friedrich's concepts of parenthood, family, and work, and in particular her difficult relationship with her father. Groundbreaking docudrama *Hide and Seek* (1996) was nominated for the Grand Jury Prize at the Sundance Film Festival. It mixes interviews with adult lesbians discussing their teenage years with the tale of a twelve-year-old girl exploring her sexuality in the 1960s, and the sense of alienation she experiences. **ES**

"The Ties That Bind breaks with the usual format of war documentaries."

1950s

KIYOSHI KUROSAWA

Born: Kiyoshi Kurosawa, July 19, 1955 (Kobe, Hyogo, Japan).

Directing style: Japanese maker of satiric comedies, *yakuza* films, and J-Horror movies; frequently casts actor Kôji Yakusho; ambient sound; hypnotic pacing; chaotic narratives.

Winner of a scholarship to Robert Redford's Utah Sundance Institute, Kiyoshi Kurosawa is Japanese cinema's foremost enigmatist. He has flirted with Western fame since the release of his warped cop thriller, *Kyua* (1997) (*Cure*), but his movies are too unapologetically oblique to ensure mainstream appeal. Despite a predilection for pulp, and occasional forays into J-Horror, Kurosawa is a versatile, delightfully morose satirist and an adventurous stylist who consistently scares the bejesus out of his audiences. Only the haunted house shocker *Suito homu* (1989) (*Sweet Home*) and *Kairo* (2001) (*Pulse*) indulge in stock-genre shenanigans. His customary palette inclines more toward uneasy ambient sounds, hypnotic pacing, and jumbled, fuguelike narratives. These complement his dogged interrogation of existential progress, exemplified by *Cure* and its follow-ups: *Karisuma* (1999) (*Charisma*), in which a disgraced cop becomes the steward of a planet-menacing tree; and *Dopperugengâ* (2003) (*Doppelganger*), a sly comedy about robot wheelchairs and creative self-sabotage.

Other Kurosawa highlights include *Hebi no michi* (1998) (*Serpent's Path*) and *Kumo no hitomi* (1998) (*Eyes of the Spider*), a complementary pair of *yakuza* films that showcase his astonishing range. The made-for-TV *Kôrei* (2000) (*Séance*), based on Mark McShane's novel, forgoes the baroque rationalism of Bryan Forbes's 1964 adaptation in favor of a more psychologically ambiguous approach; and *Akarui mirai* (2003) (*Bright Future*), a surprisingly sympathetic study of disaffected youth, reveals the director's covert humanism. The latter features a neck-hair-raising climactic tracking shot that, like the rest of Kurosawa's oeuvre, implies there is nothing quite so apocalyptic as coming to terms with oneself. **MH**

Top Takes…

Sakebi 2006 (*Retribution*)
Rofuto 2005 (*Loft*)
Ghost Cop 2004
Dopperugengâ 2003 (*Doppelganger*)
Akarui mirai 2003 (*Bright Future*)
Kairo 2001 (*Pulse*)
Kôrei 2000 (*Séance*)
Oinaru genei 1999 (*Barren Illusions*)
Karisuma 1999 (*Charisma*)
Ningen gokaku 1998 (*License to Live*)
Hebi no michi 1998 (*Serpent's Path*)
Kumo no hitomi 1998 (*Eyes of the Spider*)
Kyua 1997 (*Cure*)
Abunai hanashi mugen monogatari 1989
Suito Homu 1989 (*Sweet Home*)

"Kurosawa's films are unique in the film world . . . . [He] is a bold new voice."—*New York Times*

1950s

BÉLA TARR

Born: Béla Tarr, July 21, 1955 (Pécs, Hungary).

Directing style: Hungarian maker of darkly comic dramas; claustrophobic mise-en-scène; long takes; often films in black and white; themes of maintaining human dignity.

Top Takes...

"When [my wife and I] are making a movie . . . we never talk about art or God."

Béla Tarr began making films as a teenager, completing his first feature-length work, *Családi tüzfészek* (1979) (*Family Nest*), before enrolling in film school. Combining social realism with darkly comic elements reminiscent of late-nineteenth-century Scandinavian drama, *Family Nest*, with its handheld cameras, uncomfortable close-ups, and emotional dialogue, set the tone for *Szabadgyalog* (1981) (*The Outsider*) and *Panelkapcsolat* (1982) (*The Prefab People*). The film's intimacy and immediacy resonated with critics, drawing comparisons with John Cassavetes, whom Tarr recognizes as a profound influence.

Tarr's TV adaptation of Shakespeare's *Macbeth* (1982) and his feature, *Öszi almanach* (1985) (*Almanac of Fall*) are crucial transitional works. Comprised of only two shots—one lasting 5 minutes; the other an astounding 67 minutes—*Macbeth* marked the director's developing preoccupation with long takes that challenge and redefine cinema. *Almanac of Fall*, with its selfish characters, Impressionistic color schemes, and copious tracking shots, further reveals Tarr's aesthetic.

This focus upon maintaining human dignity amid dire social conditions and a transforming cultural landscape informs *Kárhozat* (1988) (*Damnation*), *Sátántangó* (1994) (*Satan's Tango*), and *Werckmeister harmóniák* (2000) (*Werckmeister Harmonies*). Adapted from novels by László Krasznahorkai, the films feature narrative recursions, intricate dolly shots, and high-contrast lighting that conduct audiences through extraordinary physical and psychological landscapes. A radical departure from his earliest works, these films have had a profound influence on cinema, most notably upon Gus Van Sant, whose *Gerry* (2002), *Elephant* (2003), and *Last Days* (2005) borrow directly from Tarr. **JM**

1950s

FERNANDO MEIRELLES

Born: Fernando Meirelles, November 9, 1955 (São Paulo, São Paulo, Brazil).

Directing style: Brazilian filmmaker of dramas and comedies exploring human behavior; rich storytelling; themes examining the plight of the poor with glimpses of hope and optimism.

Brazilian Fernando Meirelles's *Cidade de Deus* (2002) (*City of God*) struck like an arrow. Violent, fast-moving, and emotionally involving, it told the story of crime lords in the *favelas* surrounding Rio de Janeiro, and perfectly captured the viciousness of poverty within a picaresque coming-of-age story using unknown actors and local children. From the opening shots, *City of God* set a high mark for technical brilliance through a sometimes grueling plot about two boys: one making good in a career in photo-journalism in order to escape the slums, and the other embracing a criminal lifestyle.

His work combined the aesthetics of video games and advertising with gangster films, and the film earned Meirelles an Academy Award nomination for Best Director and an invitation to direct the film of John le Carré's novel, *The Constant Gardener* (2005). This title explored the contradictions in seemingly civilized society, substituting NGOs and big pharmaceutical companies for the class distinctions among the poor, to expose moral bankruptcy and often fleeting glimpses of hope and optimism. *The Constant Gardener* was also a rigorously complicated narrative driven by strong performances; this time by international stars, Ralph Fiennes and Rachel Weisz. The impact is the same: a critical swipe at hypocritical behavior when wealth and power are concerned.

Born to a middle-class family in São Paulo, Meirelles does not seem a natural fit for the subjects he tackles. He studied archicture, then spent several years working in TV and advertising, before cofounding O2 Filmes in the early 1990s. O2 produced his first feature films: family movie *Menino Maluquinho 2: A Aventura* (1998) (*The Nutty Boy 2*) and satirical comedy *Domésticas* (2001) (*Maids*). **GCQ**

Top Takes...

The Constant Gardener 2005
Cidade de Deus 2002 ☆
  (City of God)
Golden Gate (Palace II) 2002
Domésticas 2001 (*Maids*)
Menino Maluquinho 2: A Aventura 1998
  (*The Nutty Boy 2*)

"I'd like to make Brazilian films for international audiences that are not big-budget."

1950s

VINCENT WARD

Born: Vincent Ward, January 1, 1956 (Greytown, New Zealand).

Directing style: New Zealand maker of independent movies and Hollywood blockbusters; period dramas; exploration of themes of cultural identity; poetic imagery; opulent color.

Top Takes...

River Queen 2005
What Dreams May Come 1998
Map of the Human Heart 1993
The Navigator: A Mediaeval Odyssey 1988
Vigil 1984
In Spring On Plants Alone 1980
A State of Siege 1978

Vincent Ward is a writer and director who, despite a small body of work, consistently delivers films featuring poetic images and consummate visions. He studied painting and sculpture at the Ilam School of Fine Art in Christchurch, New Zealand. While there, he changed from artist to filmmaker, completing the short film *A State of Siege* (1978). Ward then spent two years living with a Maori family to compile his documentary *In Spring One Plants Alone* (1980). His feature film debut was *Vigil* (1984), a rustic coming-of-age tale; it became the first movie from New Zealand to be screened at Cannes Film Festival.

Ward spent four years preparing his second feature, which was partially inspired by his own nomadic life. *The Navigator: A Mediaeval Odyssey* (1988) is about fourteenth-century peasants seeking to escape the Black Death, who dig their way to modern-day New Zealand. Contrasting stark black and white scenes with radiant colors, Ward delivered a visually imaginative film that drew international acclaim and recognition. Hollywood noticed and Ward was courted to make the third *Alien* film. His vision, featuring lead Ripley encountering a wooden spaceship built by monks, proved to be too unique and he left the project. However, he retains a story credit.

> "Every film is, in a way, a meeting with reality."

Ward returned with a surreal World War II love story, *Map of the Human Heart* (1993). It follows an Inuit boy and his life in the Royal Canadian Air Force and was notable for its scenes of the bombing of Dresden. *What Dreams May Come* (1998) portrays the afterlife as a lavish canvas and won an Oscar for Best Effects, Visual Effects. *River Queen* (2005) is a story of colonialism inspired by Ward's time with the Maori. The film suffered a tumultuous shoot that included accidents and floods, and Ward was fired and then rehired. **WW**

1950s

MEL GIBSON

Born: Mel Columcille Gerard Gibson, January 3, 1956 (Peekskill, New York, U.S.).

Directing style: Leading man of action movies turned controversial experimental filmmaker; spectacular action adventures marrying history and legend; brash violence; craftsmanlike storytelling.

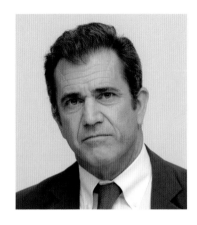

Disregarding conservative religious interests and his apparent alcoholism, Mel Gibson has emerged from his past as sexiest man in the world to become one of the more controversial filmmakers of his generation, drawing comparisons to Werner Herzog. Interestingly, his turn from star to director has not followed the usual progression of aging Adonis running away from the limelight. Although this is usually self-effacing, Gibson's journey has instead been marked by enhanced celebrity due to courted controversy and effective technique.

Gibson's directorial debut, *The Man Without a Face* (1993), is the story of a boy trying to make good on his education with the help of a disfigured neighbor. Influenced by Peter Weir's *Dead Poets Society* (1989), it was little more than a pleasant storytelling exercise. His next film was the Kubrickian riff on Scottish history, *Braveheart* (1995), which he produced, directed, and starred in, as Scottish hero William Wallace. The epic won him two Oscars for Best Picture and Best Director.

Then Gibson performed a minor miracle, making an experimental film about the Bible. *The Passion of the Christ* (2004) describes the final hours of Christ's life. The draw for this well-trodden story was Gibson's use of the dead language Aramaic. That the resulting film captured worldwide attention, turning many Christians to their faith, is part of the evangelical vision. That it was also a well-crafted display of human cruelty is equally in keeping with the lowest common denominator demands of moviegoers. Gibson courted controversy again with *Apocalypto* (2006), depicting the sixteenth-century Mayan kingdom. It angered Mayan people with its violent depiction of the demise of their ancestors, but won favor with the critics and audiences. **GCQ**

Top Takes...

Apocalypto 2006
The Passion of the Christ 2004
***Braveheart* 1995 ★**
The Man Without a Face 1993

"The main ingredient for me as a director on [*The Man Without a Face*] was patience."

GUY MADDIN

Born: Guy Maddin, February 28, 1956 (Winnipeg, Manitoba, Canada).

Directing style: Consummate craftsman of features and shorts; re-creates the mood of silent movies; films often feature autobiographical elements; frequent use of moving shots.

Top Takes…

1950s

"I'm used to behaving kind of recklessly in my film projects."

Canadian director and writer Guy Maddin graduated from the University of Winnipeg with a degree in economics. No film studies schools existed in Winnipeg, so he worked as a house painter and a bank teller, while fueling his ambition of working in the film industry. Like his influences Werner Herzog and David Lynch, and peers the Brothers Quay, Maddin works outside the mainstream and has established his own, self-contained cinematic universe that often draws on his own life.

His first feature, *Tales from the Gimli Hospital* (1988), draws on silent German expressionist cinema and *Archangel* (1990) is modeled on early sound films shot as visually fluent silents, and then recut to make room for technically awkward sound sequences. He uses this deliberately stilted style in *Careful* (1992), set in an Alpine village where even the most intense conversations have to be whispered for fear of avalanches.

He has occasionally used other filmmakers such as Paul Cox in *Careful*, and familiar actors such as Shelley Duvall, in *Twilight of the Ice Nymphs* (1997); most notably Maddin's short about Roberto Rossellini, *My Dad Is 100 Years Old* (2005), stars Rossellini's daughter, Isabella Rossellini. Maddin has been sparing in delivering fully-fledged features, but all are relishable. *Twilight of the Ice Nymphs* experiments with pale pastel colors. *The Saddest Music in the World* (2003) and *Brand Upon the Brain!* (2006) are unforgettable features of bizarre, deadpan humor, and cardboard melancholia. *Dracula: Pages from a Virgin's Diary* (2002), a filming of a preexisting ballet production, is among the most striking film versions of Bram Stoker's novel. Between features, Maddin has directed a great many shorts, some highly wrought and extremely powerful. **KN**

WALTER SALLES

Born: Walther Moreira Salles Jr., April 12, 1956 (Rio de Janeiro, Rio de Janeiro, Brazil).

Directing style: Brazilian maker of dramas; often road movies; themes of exile and Latin American identity; uses composition and cutting to suggest physical and psychological distance traveled.

A crucially important and influential figure in the recent revival of interest in Latin American cinema, Walter Salles started out as a documentary maker before attracting attention with *Terra Estrangeira* (1996) (*Foreign Land*), an impressive noir-inflected road movie centered primarily on a young Brazilian's efforts to visit his late mother's Basque homeland. The film's successful blending of social, historical, and political concerns with suspenseful, emotionally resonant drama has become a hallmark of Salles's style.

The road movie *Central do Brasil* (1998) (*Central Station*) used an elderly woman and an orphan in her charge to reflect on Brazil's past cynicism, and its potential for a better future; *O primeiro dia* (1998) (*Midnight*) was a millennial thriller-cum-love story that cast light on Brazil's shameful prisons; and *Abril Despedaçado* (2001) (*Behind the Sun*), a murderous fable reminiscent of Greek tragedy, echoed divisions in Brazilian society in the early 1900s. *Diarios de motocicleta* (2004) (*The Motorcycle Diaries*) an epic variation on the road movie inspired by the journal-recorded travels of the young revolutionary fighter Ernesto "Che" Guevara, dealt with the changes, and lack of changes, in Latin America during the previous 50 years.

Salles's films are notable not only for the clarity he brings to complex narratives, but for their assured sense of pace, and their bold but precise visual style. Where *Behind the Sun*, for example, stressed the elements to evoke the timelessness of a cyclical blood-feud story, *Central Station* and *The Motorcycle Diaries* use composition, camera movement, and cutting to convey a very real sense of scale and size in suggesting the moral and spiritual distances traveled by their protagonists. **GA**

Top Takes...

Paris, je t'aime 2006 (*Paris, I Love You*)
Dark Water 2005
Diarios de motocicleta 2004
 (*The Motorcycle Diaries*)
Castanha e caju contra o encouraçado titanic 2002
Armas e paz 2002 (*Guns and Peace*)
Abril Despedaçado 2001 (*Behind the Sun*)
Somos todos filhos da terra 1998
O primeiro dia 1998 (*Midnight*)
Central do Brasil 1998 (*Central Station*)
Terra Estrangeira 1996 (*Foreign Land*)
Socorro Nobre 1995 (*Life Somewhere Else*)
A Grande Arte 1991 (*High Art*)

"I wouldn't like turning anything Brazilian into a North American narrative."

1950s

LARS von TRIER

Born: Lars Trier, April 30, 1956 (Copenhagen, Denmark).

Directing style: Avant-garde director of surreal, experimental melodramas and comedies; subversion and reinvention of Hollywood classic genre; self-referencing trilogy series; use of handheld camera.

Top Takes…

Direktøren for det hele 2006 (*The Boss of It All*)

Manderley 2005

Dogville 2003

Dancer in the Dark 2000

Idioterne 1998 (*The Idiots*)

Breaking the Waves 1996

Europa 1991 (*Zentropa*)

Epidemic 1987

Forbrydelsens Element 1984

Befrielsesbilleder 1982 (*Images of Relief*)

Nocturne 1980

Orchidégartneren 1977 (*The Orchid Gardener*)

A leading figure in European avant-garde, Danish filmmaker Lars von Trier is as happy when being as reviled as admired. A flamboyant figure, his films are acts of provocation, alternately exhilarating and dismaying, and unmatched in their bold experimentation, stylistic range, conceptual rigor, and disturbing intensity. They include *Idioterne* (1998) (*The Idiots*) about yuppie dropouts who pretend to be mentally disabled; *Dancer in the Dark* (2000), a musical about a blind, immigrant mother who sings "My Favorite Things" on death row; and the three-hour epic *Dogville* (2003) made without sets or props.

Von Trier has made most of his films in English, premiered all but one at Cannes and, like Ingmar Bergman, has organized his career into trilogies ("Europe," "Golden Heart," and "USA").

Lending a revolutionary, anti-Hollywood edge to the late 1990s, Dogme coincided with von Trier's handheld camera "Golden Heart" trilogy. *Breaking the Waves* (1996) and *Dancer in the Dark* reconceived the woman's picture with transcendent performances from Emily Watson and Björk.

Although von Trier's eternal theme is misguided idealism or holy idiocy, his signature strategy may be his 180-degree turns between trilogies, between films, and even within films. Since 1998, von Trier's choices have followed on Dogme's challenge to global Hollywood with an overtly political stance. Three of his films set in the United States subvert Hollywood genres, and both *Dogville* and *Manderlay* (2005) are shot on an empty, chalk-lined stage to reflect the director's opinion of what the United States's real face is in a minimalist European mirror. The absurdist screwball comedy *Direktøren for det hele* (2006) (*The Boss of It All*), was an experiment made in the wake of the Mohammed cartoon controversy. **LB**

> "If you tell a man what to do in real life, to which extent is it reality?"

1950s

GIUSEPPE TORNATORE

Born: Giuseppe Tornatore, May 27, 1956 (Bagheria, Sicily, Italy).

Directing style: Maker of heart-tugging dramas; depictions of small-town Sicilian life; observations on prejudice and the nature of community; collaborations with composer Ennio Morricone.

An autodidact, Sicilian-born Giuseppe Tornatore's early career was spent working as a freelance photographer, before eventually gravitating toward film. In 1979 he began a long-term collaboration with the national Italian TV network RAI, where he was to specialize in documentary filmmaking.

After acting as cowriter and second unit director on Giuseppe Ferrara's *Cento giorni a Palermo* (1984), Tornatore's feature film debut came with *Il camorrista* (1986) (*The Professor*). However, it is for *Nuovo cinema Paradiso* (1988) (*Cinema Paradiso*) that he is best known, and it won him an Oscar for Best Foreign Language Film. The director's use of the metaphor of the changing fortunes of a local cinema, as seen through the eyes of young Salvatore, who together with his friend Alfredo ran the projection booth, to reflect the changing face of his homeland is typical of Tornatore; its Spielbergian tugging of the heartstrings charmed audiences and critics worldwide.

What followed was darker. Small-town life was now viewed through a different lens, cautioning against the dangers of envy, gossip, and greed. This approach can be seen in both *L'uomo delle stelle* (1995) (*The Star Maker*) and *Malèna* (2000), focusing on the repressive strictures of a small community.

Underlying much of Tornatore's work is a recurring theme of the ways the system can corrupt the individual, his characters often desperate people struggling to survive in times of personal and social instability. Although his success has been forged with films that touch the soul of Sicily, Tornatore has moved into English-language films and away from his beloved island. He is not prolific in output, but Tornatore has crafted himself a key place among Italy's premier contemporary filmmakers. **RH**

Top Takes...

La Sconosciuta 2006

Malèna 2000

La leggenda del pianista sull'oceano 1998
  (*The Legend of the Pianist on the Ocean*)

L'uomo delle stelle 1995 (*The Star Maker*)

Una pura formalità 1994 (*A Pure Formality*)

La domenica specialmente 1991
  (*Especially on Sunday*)

Stanno tutti bene 1990 (*Everybody's Fine*)

Nuovo cinema Paradiso 1988
  (*Cinema Paradiso*)

Il camorrista 1986 (*The Professor*)

1950s

"Life isn't like in the movies. Life is much harder."

—Alfredo, *Cinema Paradiso*

DANNY BOYLE

Born: Danny Boyle, October 20, 1956 (Radcliffe, Lancashire, England).

Directing style: British maker of cult hard-hitting dramas, social satires, and black comedies; literary adaptations with verve; Scottish locations; often casts actor Ewan McGregor.

Top Takes...

Sunshine 2007
Millions 2004
28 Days Later 2002
Alien Love Triangle 2002
The Beach 2000
A Life Less Ordinary 1997
Trainspotting 1996
Shallow Grave 1994

After stints in the theater and for BBC TV, the early 1990s saw Danny Boyle directing two episodes of the hit British detective show *Inspector Morse* (1990–1992) before directing the BBC's critically acclaimed miniseries *Mr. Wroe's Virgins* (1993).

His quirky, low-budget first feature *Shallow Grave* (1994) was a witty and offbeat comedy that demonstrated Boyle's ability to explore the darker side of human nature while retaining a penchant for black humor. It also launched Scottish actor Ewan McGregor to fame, and initiated a string of collaborations between the actor and director. Despite its perturbing premise—the effects of heroin addiction on a group of Glaswegian friends—*Trainspotting* (1996) proved to be one of the highest grossing British films of all time, the movie's iconic posters adorning the walls of countless students in the late 1990s. Its powerfully creative visuals and nihilistic attitude, perversely underpinned by a doggedly vivacious spirit, seemed to tap perfectly into the prevailing zeitgeist. In short, it was all that is good about its director.

At his best with social satire, it has often been said of Boyle that the further he travels from Hollywood the better he gets. His toe-dip into the realm of U.S. filmmaking would seem to bear this out, with both *A Life Less Ordinary* (1997) and *The Beach* (2000) hitting a flat note with the critics and appearing limp in comparison with his earlier, harder hitting, red-hot subject matter. TV has always provided a structuring backbone to Boyle's career, and returning home he again found work directing several projects for the BBC. Indeed, Boyle himself has said he prefers working on smaller, off-the-radar projects, and the massive commercial success of *28 Days Later* (2002) can only have reinforced this belief. **RH**

> "I learned with *The Beach* that I'm a bit better lower down the radar."

SOGO ISHII

Born: Sogo Ishii, January 15, 1957 (Hakata, Fukuoka, Japan).

Directing style: Pioneer of Japanese New Wave; shifts between genres; use of rapid-fire cutting for visceral cyberpunk feel; often violent content; hyperactive camerawork.

Sogo Ishii participated in Japan's punk revolution as a singer and guitarist, and as a director of concert videos. His motto was: "To experience the video not with just the eye and the ear, but to feel it through the whole body."

His first two movies dealt with biker gangs, and introduced a visceral style in which a restless camerawork in fast motion, aided by rapid-fire cutting, created a cinematic equivalent of punk music. It culminated in *Bakuretsu toshi* (1982) (*Burst City*), which put the "punk" in "cyberpunk." The film is a vivid document of an era, and its fresh attitude to moviemaking pioneered the New Wave of Japanese film, influencing works by Shinya Tsukamoto, Kazuhiro Kitano, and Takashi Miike.

Ishii's later films showed versatility outside the underground sensibility: *Gyakufunsha kazoku* (1984) (*The Crazy Family*) is an absurdist satire on contemporary Japanese values, whereas *Enjeru dasuto* (1994) (*Angel Dust*) is a thinking man's serial killer thriller that frightens with its Cronenbergian iciness of urban alienation tinged with an ambiguity similar to Kiyoshi Kurosawa's works. *Mizu no naka no hachigatsu* (1995) (*August in the Water*) is permeated by a similar, hypnotic style, introducing science-fiction overtones into Japan's countryside, whereas *Gojo reisenki: Gojoe* (2000) (*Gojoe: Spirit War Chronicle*) reimagines the samurai fights as stylized abstractions laced with a contemplative mood. The latter movie starred Ishii's fellow band member, Tadanobu Asano, who was also in *Electric Dragon 80.000 V* (2001), about a duel between guitarist super heroes, and in *Dead End Run* (2003).

Ishii transcends his chosen genre with uncanny ease, with his innate sense for rhythm and mood, and delivers unique experiences, felt rather than merely seen. **DO**

Top Takes...

Kyoshin 2005 (*Mirrored Mind*)

Dead End Run 2003

Electric Dragon 80.000 V 2001

Gojo reisenki: Gojoe 2000
  (*Gojoe: Spirit War Chronicle*)

Yume no ginga 1997 (*Labyrinth of Dreams*)

Mizu no naka no hachigatsu 1995
  (*August in the Water*)

Enjeru dasuto 1994 (*Angel Dust*)

Shiatsu Oja 1989 (*The Master of Shiatsu*)

Gyakufunsha kazoku 1984 (*The Crazy Family*)

Ajia no gyakushu 1983 (*Asia Strikes Back*)

Bakuretsu toshi 1982 (*Burst City*)

Shuffle 1981

Kuruizaki sanda rodo 1980
  (*Crazy Thunder Road*)

"Ishii . . . has an astoundingly elegant understanding of the pleasures of film."—*Ninth Art*

1950s

SPIKE LEE

Born: Shelton Jackson Lee, March 20, 1957 (Atlanta, Georgia, U.S.).

Directing style: Leading voice of New Black Cinema; socially conscious dramas; often casts Denzel Washington; issues of African-American identity and racial politics; autobiographical themes; movies often span the events of one day.

Top Takes...

Inside Man 2006

Jesus Children of America 2005

She Hate Me 2004

25th Hour 2002

Ten Minutes Older: The Trumpet 2002

Come Rain or Come Shine 2001

The Original Kings of Comedy 2000

Summer of Sam 1999

4 Little Girls 1997

Girl 6 1996

Lumière et compagnie 1995
   (Lumière and Company)

Clockers 1995

Malcolm X 1992

Jungle Fever 1991

Mo' Better Blues 1990

Do the Right Thing 1989

School Daze 1988

She's Gotta Have It 1986

Joe's Bed-Stuy Barbershop: We Cut Heads 1983

Last Hustle in Brooklyn 1977

Spike Lee reached adulthood with a Student Academy Award for his Master of Fine Arts thesis film *Joe's Bed-Stuy Barbershop: We Cut Heads* (1983). After several years of aborted projects, freelance work, family donations, and careful saving, he manage to edit, produce, write, direct, and costar in his landmark feature debut, *She's Gotta Have It* (1986). A comedy about dating, sexuality, loyalty, and a strong African-American woman, it made millions on an investment of $160,000 and established Lee as the voice of a New Black Cinema, and a leading figure of a nascent independent cinema movement.

Never far from holding a mirror up to his own life's experience, virtually all Lee's films reflect on his family, his upbringing, the creative professions, New York City, and being a wicked smart African-American artist in a whitewashed world. The themes of autobiography and race quickly become useful for understanding Lee's work.

School Daze (1988), a comedy drama set in a historically African-American Southern college, was followed by early masterwork, *Do the Right Thing* (1989), which took place on the hottest day of the year in racially inflamed Bed-Stuy, New

RIGHT: Denzel Washington is focused on the job as civil rights icon Malcolm X.

IN MEMORY OF

DENISE MC NAIR   CYNTHIA WESLEY   ADDIE MAE COLLINS   CAROL ROBERTSON

THEIR LIVES WERE TAKEN BY UNKNOWN PARTIES ON SEPTEMBER 15, 1963 WHEN THE SIXTEENTH STREET BAPTIST CHURCH WAS BOMBED.

"MAY MEN LEARN TO REPLACE BITTERNESS AND VIOLENCE WITH LOVE AND UNDERSTANDING"

ABOVE: In memory of the four girls at the center of Lee's hate-crime documentary.

York—Lee grew up in Brooklyn. *Mo' Better Blues* (1990) starred Denzel Washington as a jazz musician (like Lee's father) and *Jungle Fever* (1991) squared widowed Wesley Snipes against interracial romance and adultery (Lee's father married a white woman). *Malcolm X* (1992), also starring Washington, showcased Lee's attitude toward U.S. civil rights agitation.

Since Lee's career shift to being a more ambitious producer, his work has been uneven. Certain projects are fantastically good, and sometimes commercially successful, whereas others are disastrous, from conception to execution, eliciting shrugs of confusion that someone so great might be brought so low. Brilliant is as brilliant does, however, and movies such as *Clockers* (1995), the Emmy and Academy Award-nominated documentary *4 Little Girls* (1997), *The Original Kings of Comedy* (2000), and the documentary *When the Levees Broke: A Requiem in Four Acts* (2006) prove Lee is a filmmaker for the ages. **GCQ**

Keeping It in the Family

Shelton Jackson Lee is the son of a school teacher, Jacquelyn Lee, and jazz musician, Bill Lee. The nickname "Spike" started in childhood and stuck.

- Spike's brother David has worked as a stills director on four of Spike's films.
- Another brother, Chris, has also worked for Spike, but is best known for a long-running feud with the director over a disputed land claim.
- Spike's younger sister Joie is a well-respected actress, appearing regularly on TV and in films, including four of her brother's movies.

1950s

AKI KAURISMÄKI

Born: Aki Olavi Kaurismäki, April 4, 1957 (Orimattila, Finland).

Directing style: Prolific director of Finnish cinema; themes of working-class life and aspirations; sparse dialogue; use of live music; low-key humor; Helsinki locations and subject matter.

Top Takes...

Laitakaupungin valot 2006 (Lights in the Dusk)
Mies vailla menneisyyttä 2002
  (The Man Without a Past)
Kauas pilvet karkaavat 1996 (Drifting Clouds)
Välittäjä 1996 (Employment Agent)
Leningrad Cowboys Meet Moses 1994
La vie de bohème 1992 (Bohemian Life)
These Boots 1992
Those Were the Days 1992
I Hired a Contract Killer 1990
Tulitikkutehtaan tyttö 1990
  (The Match Factory Girl)
Leningrad Cowboys Go America 1989
Ariel 1988
Varjoja paratiisissa 1986 (Shadows in Paradise)

"Why should people pay to see bad films when they can see bad television for nothing?"

Aki Kaurismäki's films can be described as black comedies, with the actors delivering their lines deadpan, while immersed in coffee and cigarettes. Initially collaborating with his brother Mika, Kaurismäki made his own directorial debut with the Fyodor Dostoyevsky adaptation *Rikos ja rangaistus* (1983) (*Crime and Punishment*). The film already showcased several of his latter day trademarks: seemingly stilted performances, the inclusion of live music, and working-class characters seeking a more purposeful existence in an urban Finnish environment.

His two trilogies include his most acclaimed works. The first trilogy, encompassing *Varjoja paratiisissa* (1986) (*Shadows in Paradise*), *Ariel* (1988), and *Tulitikkutehtaan tyttö* (1990) (*The Match Factory Girl*), presents various blue-collar Helsinki residents yearning for love and understanding, while struggling to make ends meet in an indifferent everyday life. In the first two films, the protagonists obtain a certain form of happiness by leaving Finland, but *The Match Factory Girl* ends with the main character facing imprisonment.

The later trilogy of *Kauas pilvet karkaavat* (1996) (*Drifting Clouds*), *Mies vailla menneisyyttä* (2002) (*The Man Without a Past*), and *Laitakaupungin valot* (2006) (*Lights in the Dusk*) is concerned with the position of the working class within Finnish society. Kaurismäki observes his native country through the economic depression of the early 1990s, the search for an identity at the dawn of the new millennium, and starting out life anew in a country that's now grown colder than ever before. Yet although Kaurismäki does not seem to think that Finland's spiritual vacuum might be filled in the near future, even his bleaker pictures tend to leave the audience with a glimmer of hope. **LL**

CLARA LAW

Born: Clara Law, May 29, 1957 (Macao, China).

Directing style: Independent director of dramas; poetic narratives; themes of immigration, isolation, and cultural identity; imagistic use of lavish color and landscape.

Clara Law was born in China and studied filmmaking at The National Film and Television School in London. Although her roots are in China, Law relocated to Australia prior to the 1997 transition of power in Hong Kong. Because of this life-altering event, Law's films tend to carry with them similar themes of relocation, disengagement, and isolation in the form of her characters' quest for identity and belonging.

Her first film was *They Say the Moon Is Fuller Here* (1985), but it was not until her production, *Ai zai taxiang de jijie* (1990) (*Farewell China*), that Law began to receive significant international attention. Set in New York City, a man embodies the foreign dream of success in the United States as he follows his wife to the unknown land of opportunity. Similarly, *Qiuyue* (1992) (*Autumn Moon*) solidified Law's presence as an international director when it received honors at the Locarno International Film Festival. The film is about a Japanese tourist, who, although he travels to Hong Kong in search of divine edibles, finds himself a part of an unlikely friendship.

In Australia, Law directed *Floating Life* (1996) and *The Goddess of 1967* (2000) with her partner and collaborator Eddie Ling-Ching Fong. *Floating Life* was awarded numerous prizes at festivals around the world. Critics were drawn to the movie's narrative of relocation and its subsequently isolating tendencies. *The Goddess of 1967* is a road movie that shows a Japanese man on a mission to find the car of his dreams, but when he travels to meet the seller in Australia, events turn horribly wrong. Law's recent film *Letters to Ali* (2004) tells the story of an Afghan refugee. It openly confronts Australia's refugee situation and the issues faced by asylum seekers globally. **ES**

Top Takes...

Letters to Ali 2004
The Goddess of 1967 2000
Floating Life 1996
Erotique 1994
Xi chu bawang 1994 (*King of Western Chu*)
You Seng 1993 (*Temptation of a Monk*)
Qiuyue 1992 (*Autumn Moon*)
Yes! yi zu 1991 (*Fruit Punch*)
Ai zai taxiang de jijie 1990 (*Farewell China*)
Pan Jin Lian zhi qian shi jin sheng 1989
  (*The Reincarnation of Golden Lotus*)
Wo ai tai kong ren 1988
  (*The Other Half & the Other Half*)
They Say the Moon Is Fuller Here 1985

"With *The Goddess of 1967,* I wanted to create a mysterious and ambiguous atmosphere."

1950s

MOHSEN MAKHMALBAF

Born: Mohsen Makhmalbaf, May 29, 1957 (Tehran, Iran).

Directing style: Controversial visual poet of Iranian New Wave; autobiographical and childhood themes; chronicles the history of Iran state and its people; often works with family members.

Top Takes...

Sex & Philosophy 2005
The Chair 2005
Alefbay-e afghan 2002 (The Afghan Alphabet)
Safar e Ghandehar 2001 (Kandahar)
Tales of an Island 2000
Ghessé hayé kish 1999 (Tales of Kish)
Sokout 1998 (The Silence)
Nun va Goldoon 1996 (A Moment of Innocence)
Gabbeh 1996
Salaam Cinema 1995
Honarpisheh 1993 (The Actor)
Shabhaye Zayendeh-Rood 1991
    (The Nights of Zayendeh-Rood)
Nobat e Asheghi 1990 (Time of Love)
Baykot 1985 (Boycott)
Tobeh Nosuh 1983

1950s

"A lot of people love cinema because they find it a way of expressing themselves."

With its repressive political environment, Iran may seem an unlikely spot for a film renaissance, but that is just what has emerged in the country over the course of the past few years. One of the leaders of Iran's modern film movement is writer and director Mohsen Makhmalbaf.

Born in Tehran, Makhmalbaf grew up to become an anti-Shah activist and was subsequently jailed for four years for his political beliefs. Finally released after the 1979 Islamic Revolution, Makhmalbaf moved away from politics and into filmmaking, although his features still often reveal a strong political undercurrent. Indeed, several have been banned under Iran's regime, even though the director and his films draw praise from around the globe.

One of Makhmalbaf's earliest breakthroughs was Gabbeh (1996), which coincided with the recognition of all the great films being made in Iran. His Cannes Film Festival Palme d'Or winner Safar e Ghandehar (2001) (Kandahar), coincidentally released shortly before the events of the September 11 terrorist attacks, captured the difficulties of life in Afghanistan under the waning but oppressive rule of the Taliban, and work on that film helped inspire Makhmalbaf's ongoing dedication to humanitarian aid around Central Asia. Makhmalbaf is in the rare position of being able to call both his wife Marzieh Meshkini and his daughter Samira Makhmalbaf his peers, as well as his students, as each has proven, in part thanks to Makhmalbaf's tutelage and instruction, a successful and acclaimed filmmaker in her own right. Makhmalbaf continues to work closely with his talented family members, often collaborating with them in the role of either editor or screenwriter. **JK**

CAMERON CROWE

Born: Cameron Bruce Crowe, July 13, 1957 (Palm Springs, California, U.S.).

Directing style: Writer and director of feel-good romantic teen comedies and dramas; autobiographical themes; use of rock music; frequently casts superstar Tom Cruise.

Cameron Crowe started out writing for the U.S. rock music bible *Rolling Stone Magazine* when he was just fifteen years old and at high school. He then segued into his Hollywood career as a screenwriter, writing the classic teen movie *Fast Times At Ridgemont High* (1982). The comedy was a knockout success for Crowe and his fellow first-time feature colleagues, director Amy Heckerling and actor Sean Penn.

Crowe then graduated to writing and directing his own take on the teen romantic comedy, *Say Anything* (1989). His work as a director has generally been sharply commercial, imbued with populist, feel-good energy and warmth. Perhaps Crowe's finest hour in this respect was the major hit, and Tom Cruise vehicle, *Jerry Maguire* (1996), about the life of a hard-nosed sports agent who discovers that he does have a heart and a conscience. Cruise's infamous line as Jerry Maguire, "Show me the money!" took on a life of its own outside the film, and the movie's portrayal of romance, sentiment, and moral values winning out over raw moneymaking cynicism struck a chord with the moviegoing public.

Crowe's love for rock music is evident in the soundtracks of all of his movies, but is most obvious in *Almost Famous* (2000). Drawing on his own experiences of life on the road with a rock band, Crowe's comedy is a coming-of-age tale of a high school student who gets the opportunity to write for *Rolling Stone Magazine* about an up-and-coming rock band on tour. He then reaffirmed his status with another Cruise movie, *Vanilla Sky* (2001). A remake of Alejandro Amenábar's thriller *Abre los ojos* (1997) (*Open Your Eyes*), it was notable for developing the original's themes and motifs by fusing them with big, iconic, and emotive sequences. **MH**

Top Takes...

Elizabethtown 2005
Vanilla Sky 2001
Almost Famous 2000
Jerry Maguire 1996
Singles 1992
Say Anything 1989

1950s

"When I was trying to write memorable stuff as a journalist people just ran for the hills."

STANLEY KWAN

Born: Jinpang Guan, October 9, 1957 (Hong Kong).

Directing style: Daring Hong Kong director of powerhouse dramas and documentaries; themes of women's role in society; exploration of gender and sexual identity.

Top Takes...

Changhen ge 2005 (*Everlasting Regret*)

Lan yu 2001

You shi tiaowu 1999 (*The Island Tales*)

Yue kuai le, yue duo luo 1997 (*Hold You Tight*)

Yang ± Yin: Gender in Chinese Cinema 1996

Hong meigui, bai meigui 1994
  (*Red Rose White Rose*)

Kin chan no Cinema Jack 1993

Yuen Ling-yuk 1992 (*The Actress*)

*Leung goh nuijen, yat goh leng, yat goh
  m leng* 1992 (*Too Happy for Words*)

Ren zai Niu Yue 1990 (*Full Moon in New York*)

Yin ji kau 1987 (*Rouge*)

Nu ren xin 1985 (*Women*)

"My stance is that if I am moved by . . . a story or a group of characters, I will film it."

Stanley Kwan's debut feature, *Nu ren xin* (1985) (*Women*), starred movie icon Yun-Fat Chow and was a box-office hit. Kwan followed this with a series of films centering on female protagonists and their struggles within society, including the romantic ghost story *Yin ji kau* (1987) (*Rouge*), the biopic of silent-screen star Lingyu Ruan, *Yuen Ling-yuk* (1992) (*The Actress*), and the epic melodrama *Changhen ge* (2005) (*Everlasting Regret*). Kwan investigates methods of presentation: the ways in which people frame and see members of society, and thereby allocate them to designated positions within it.

His fascination with the overtly artificial aspects of filmmaking led him to self-reflexive experiments such as *The Actress*, in which documentary footage of Ruan speaking in the present is intercut with re-enactments of scenes from her films. This cinematic deconstruction, while maintaining a palpable emotional capacity, is a trait he shares with Korea's Sang-soo Hong. Similarly, the acting in Kwan's films recalls the highly stylized films of his countryman Kar Wai Wong.

Kwan is one of only a few openly gay directors in Asia and has examined homosexuality within Chinese society with more freedom since coming out in 1996. His documentary *Yang ± Yin: Gender in Chinese Cinema* (1996) looks at the history of Chinese language film and its confinement of characters by preconceived notions of gender and sexual identity. His *Lan yu* (2001) is a gay love story based on a novel first published on the Internet. Shot without permits in Beijing, the central narrative plays out against the 1989 protests in Tiananmen Square. Kwan establishes a relationship between historical actuality and emotional immediacy, while continuing to leave space for what is indeterminate and irresolvable. **NC**

MIRA NAIR

Born: Mira Nair, October 15, 1957 (Bhubaneshwar, Orissa, India).

Directing style: Indian maker of documentaries, romantic comedies, and dramas; exploration of immigrant integration issues; outsider themes; artful storytelling of the lives of complex characters.

Mira Nair came to international prominence with a successful first feature *Salaam Bombay!* (1988). She had begun her career as a documentary maker and brought the immediacy of that genre to her debut, which focused on a group of street kids forging a meager existence on the streets of Mumbai. The film's success meant Nair was able to secure a high-profile cast, including Denzel Washington, for her next outing, *Mississippi Masala* (1991). Both this film and the subsequent *The Perez Family* (1995) engaged with issues facing immigrants to the United States and their attempts to find acceptance. The former is concerned with an Indian expelled from Uganda, and the latter with Cuban refugees settling in Miami.

Following critical indifference to *Kama Sutra: A Tale of Love* (1996), Nair returned to her ongoing interest in the South Asian diaspora, beginning with the TV movie *My Own Country* (1998). Her focus perhaps found its most potent expression in her best-known film, *Monsoon Wedding* (2001). A huge worldwide success, it tells the story of a middle-class Delhi family who return to their native city from across the globe for a wedding.

With a clear desire to avoid stereotyping, Nair followed the success of *Monsoon Wedding* with the classic literary adaptation of William Thackeray's novel *Vanity Fair* (2004). Despite once again attracting an impressive cast, including Reese Witherspoon as Becky Sharp, the film was not a major success. Nair returned to more familiar material with *The Namesake* (2006), a film that relates the struggle of the son of Indian immigrants to fit into New York life without losing sight of his traditional ways. Nair's career so far reveals a director who, perhaps more than any other working today, can be best described as transnational. **AW**

Top Takes...

The Namesake 2006
Vanity Fair 2004
11'9"01—September 11 2002
Monsoon Wedding 2001
Kama Sutra: A Tale of Love 1996
The Perez Family 1995
The Day the Mercedes Became a Hat 1993
Mississippi Masala 1991
Salaam Bombay! 1988
So Far from India 1983
Jama Masjid Street Journal 1979

"I am an independent filmmaker first and foremost. I have always cut my own cloth."

1950s

MING-LIANG TSAI

Born: Ming-liang Tsai, October 27, 1957 (Kuching, Malaysia).

Directing style: Taiwanese New Wave director; themes of transformation exploring tradition and modernity; water motifs; long takes; sparse dialogue; ensemble troupe of actors.

Top Takes...

Hei yan quan 2006 (*I Don't Want to Sleep Alone*)

Tian bian yi duo yun 2005 (*The Wayward Cloud*)

Bem-Vindo a São Paulo 2004
  (*Welcome to São Paulo*)

Bu san 2003 (*Good Bye, Dragon Inn*)

Tianqiao bu jianle 2002 (*The Skywalk Is Gone*)

Ni neibian jidian 2001 (*What Time Is It There?*)

Fish, Underground 2001

Dong 1998 (*The Last Dance*)

He liu 1997 (*The River*)

Aiqing wansui 1994 (*Vive L'Amour*)

Ch'ing shaonien na cha 1992
  (*Rebels of the Neon God*)

Xiao hai 1991 (*Boys*)

"I think European films are closer to me because they are about modern life."

Ming-liang Tsai was born in Malaysia, but grew up in Taiwan. He graduated from the Drama and Cinema Department of the Chinese Cultural University before working in theater and TV. A fan of European cinema, especially François Truffaut, Tsai welcomed the opportunity to shift from directing teleplays to fashioning feature-length films for theatrical release.

His films show a preoccupation with transitional spaces and transformational structures and his most conspicuous motif is water: it flows and stagnates, floods and drains, gushes and drips. Tsai's films reveal a preoccupation with temporal flows: watches and clocks permeate his narratives, as do images of urban alienation.

Tsai is a visual artist with a singular, unique vision that does not shy away from critiquing long-established social hierarchies and behavioral codes. His focus on transformation deepens his audience's understanding of the aesthetic, psychological, and cultural impact of his world. He uses visuals such as elevators, escalators, and corridors, and shifting notions of gender, disease, passion, and the pornographic mise-en-scène.

Like Truffaut, Tsai has assembled a troupe of talented, naturalistic performers. Kang-sheng Lee, for example, has played the lead in almost all Tsai's films. In *Ni neibian jidian* (2001) (*What Time Is It There?*), Tsai twice pays direct homage to his French predecessor including having Lee's character watch a scene from Truffaut's *Quatre cents coups* (1959) (*The 400 Blows*). Perhaps Tsai's most assessable work, *What Time Is it There?* explicitly extends his themes of alienation, transience, and urban ennui beyond the borders of millennial Taiwan. The film also explores the importance of human connection on a national and global stage. **JM**

ROBERT LEPAGE

Born: Robert Lepage, December 12, 1957 (Québec City, Québec, Canada).

Directing style: Canada's "Renaissance Man"; visionary writer and director; challenging reinventions of genres; metaphysical themes; explorations of sexual identity, politics, and power.

French-Canadian actor, playwright, and director Robert Lepage has distinguished himself by creating a number of epic theatrical plays and intricate and cerebral films, leading him to be hailed as "Canada's Renaissance Man." His directorial debut drama *Le confessionnal* (1995) (*The Confessional*) paid homage to Sir Alfred Hitchcock by carefully constructing parallels between its characters and Hitchcock's filming of *I Confess* (1953) in Québec City. Interweaving these different narratives, and working across two different time periods, *The Confessional* is complicated but always highly rewarding. Where other Canadian directors such as David Cronenberg have elevated the horror genre to full artistic integrity, Lepage seemingly wants to craft an intellectual thriller. His emerging body of work has frequently been marked by a certain emotional coolness or air of directorial detachment.

Lepage's ambition to turn established genres into film art is equally evident in his first English-language feature film, *Possible Worlds* (2000). This time it is science fiction that is worked over, being combined with the philosophy of possible worlds that speculates on the existence of multiple realities where everything that can happen, has happened. Versions of this reality splitting theme have occupied European cinema via films such as *Lola rennt* (1998) (*Run, Lola, Run*), but Lepage refuses to resolve his exploration of parallel worlds into neat patterns. *Possible Worlds* sets up a number of mysteries and puzzles, but to describe the film simply as a science-fiction thriller fails to capture its deliberate strangeness. Lepage has consistently been willing to frustrate audiences who want easy solutions: his movies set out from recognizable genres, but invariably arrive at unexpected places. **MH**

Top Takes…

La face cachée de la lune 2003
   (*The Far Side of the Moon*)
Possible Worlds 2000
Nô 1998
Le Polygraphe 1996 (*Polygraph*)
Le confessionnal 1995 (*The Confessional*)

"I like being kind of vague in how I define myself and I believe in chaos very much."

KAR WAI WONG

Born: Kar Wai Wong, July 17, 1958 (Shanghai, China).

Directing style: Cult Asian director of romantic dramas; exploration of love, sex, betrayal, and repression; intriguing storytelling; stunning cinematography; strong female characters; attention to period detail.

Top Takes…

> "I hate movies with labels like 'gay film'… there are only good films and bad films."

The New Wave of Asian cinema has produced several notably ambitious eccentrics and iconoclasts. That the inimitable and mysterious Kar Wai Wong still stands out as particularly distinctive underscores his unconventional approach and uniquely accomplished output.

Born in Shanghai but raised in Hong Kong, Wong began his career in TV before graduating to features with *Wong gok ka moon* (1988) (*As Tears Go By*) and later *A Fei jing juen* (1991) (*Days of Being Wild*), two relatively conventional works that preceded his breakthrough *Chung hing sam lam* (1994) (*Chungking Express*). That film introduced many of the trademarks that remain pronounced in Wong's work, namely gorgeous cinematography and elliptical plots, often held together with tenuous, tentative romance stories.

Dung che sai duk (1994) (*Ashes of Time*) marked a throwback to action films, but *Duo luo tian shi* (1995) (*Fallen Angels*), about a contract killer trying to find a cure for his unrequited love in Hong Kong's seedy underworld, *Cheun gwong tsa sit* (1997) (*Happy Together*) about a gay love affair set in Argentina, and in particular the powerful and evocative tale of thwarted and unrequited passion, *Fa yeung nin wa* (2000) (*In the Mood for Love*), solidified his critical reputation as well as his established habits, foremost among them relying on largely improvised scripts and the impulsive camerawork of cinematographer Christopher Boyle. *2046* (2004) was a loose sequel of sorts to *In the Mood for Love* and marked the director's return to the world of vague plots and oblique storytelling. Wong also contributed to the tripartite anthology of love and sex, *Eros* (2004), along with Steven Soderbergh and Michelangelo Antonioni. **JK**

DAVID O. RUSSELL

Born: David Owen Russell, August 20, 1958 (New York City, New York, U.S.).

Directing style: Auteur maker of quirky, cult, existentialist comedies; metaphysical and antiwar themes; use of handheld camera and Steadicam; improvisation of actors.

One of the most original and eccentric voices in independent film, David O. Russell has steadfastly refused to make the same kind of movie twice, let alone downplay his pronounced interest in politics and philosophy, or his disinterest in the energy-sapping machinations of Hollywood.

None of these qualities were on obvious display, however, throughout the exceedingly neurotic *Spanking the Monkey* (1994), a very low-budget, dark comedy about an incestuous mother and son relationship, or *Flirting with Disaster* (1996), a road trip farce about an adopted man's search for his birth parents. Instead, Russell's creative voice came to the fore with *Three Kings* (1999), a prescient and provocative antiwar movie set in the waning days of the first Gulf War and one of the first movies to address the complexities of combat in that particular arena. It was also the movie that set tongues wagging based on rumors that Russell and George Clooney had come to blows on the set, reportedly because Clooney objected to Russell shouting at the extras.

But maybe *Three Kings* was the exception. Notorious for his work ethic and control issues, Russell took his time returning to the big screen, and when he did it was with the strange, leftfield *I ♥ Huckabees* (2004), an almost uncategorizable comedy whose themes of existential crisis resulted in praise, criticism, and head-scratching, in equal measure. In 2004 Russell helped direct *Soldiers Pay*, a follow-up documentary to *Three Kings* intended as a critique of current U.S. foreign policy to be included on a proposed DVD rerelease of *Three Kings*. To Russell's dismay, politics stepped in and stopped the release. The film was subsequently screened on TV and put on sale by an independent company. **JK**

Top Takes...

Soldiers Pay 2004
I ♥ Huckabees 2004
Three Kings 1999
Flirting with Disaster 1996
Spanking the Monkey 1994
Hairway to the Stars 1990
Bingo Inferno 1987

> "I cast people who I think feel real and [I] think feel right for the part."

1950s

TIM BURTON

Born: Timothy William Burton, August 25, 1958 (Burbank, California, U.S.).

Directing style: Gothic king of the bizarre; fairy-tale dramas and fantastical comedies; homages to early expressionist horror movies; frequently casts Johnny Depp.

Top Takes…

Tim Burton's first job was for Disney, where he directed shorts such as *Vincent* (1982) about a boy who wanted to be Vincent Price (the actor obligingly provided a voice-over). The attention they drew made it possible for Burton to move his rich, visual universe into features. The burlesque *Pee-wee's Big Adventure* (1985) and the horror comedy *Beetle Juice* (1988) showcased Burton's talent for sketching outré gore and slapstick situations with limited means—showing that weirdness works well.

Their success landed Burton in the driver's seat of the highly hyped, caped crusader franchise. Burton turned *Batman* (1989) into a Gothic, sinister tale of personal revenge and moral corruption in a doomed Gotham City reminiscent of *Metropolis* (1927). The movie's massive box-office appeal saved Burton from the frowns of studio executives, who feared his vision might stand in the way of revenue.

The sequel, *Batman Returns* (1992), did less well, but Burton had already moved on to *Edward Scissorhands* (1990), the first of several collaborations with Johnny Depp. It shows a sweet young girl helping a lonely creature escape into a real world that looks thoroughly fabricated. The sympathetic biopic of

RIGHT: Michael Keaton as Beetlejuice tries to scare off some troublesome tenants.

the world's worst director *Ed Wood* (1994) and science-fiction bonanza *Mars Attacks!* (1996) demonstrated Burton's reach, while evidencing its visual coherence, and the century was topped off by the intimate and creepy *Sleepy Hollow* (1999).

Burton's remake of *Planet of the Apes* (2001) was a mistake, however: a visualist, he could not bring the racial and environmental politics to life. After the uncharacteristically optimistic and small-scale *Big Fish* (2003), Burton returned with another remake, *Charlie and the Chocolate Factory* (2005). Its huge success was followed by *Corpse Bride* (2005) and the musical *Sweeney Todd* (2007).

Depp once said that no one so obviously out of place in Hollywood fits in so right as Burton. Maybe that explains why misfit director Burton remains in the unique position of a chameleon whose movies appeal to mainstream and cultish fringe audiences alike. **EM**

ABOVE: Johnny Depp contemplates his actions as Edward Scissorhands.

Homage to Horror

Tim Burton attributes his fascination with the horror genre to the gory Saturday afternoon films he watched regularly on TV as a child.

- *Sleepy Hollow* pays obvious homage to the Hammer House of Horror movies.
- *Edward Scissorhands* is Burton's excellent attempt to make a 1930s-style Gothic horror movie. The genre is made implicit with the deliberate casting of horror maestro Vincent Price as a Dr. Frankenstein-type character.
- *Beetle Juice* harks back to the spoof horror films of the 1950s.

1950s

ALEKSEI BALABANOV

Born: Aleksei Oktyabrinovich Balabanov, February 25, 1959 (Yekaterinburg, Russia).

Directing style: Controversial Russian maker of low-budget and blockbuster dramas; themes of life in contemporary Russia and the rise of violence and organized crime.

Top Takes…

Gruz 200 2007 (*Freight 200*)

Mne ne bolno 2006 (*It Doesn't Hurt*)

Zhmurki 2005 (*Blind Man's Bluff*)

Voyna 2002 (*War*)

Brat 2 2000 (*Brother 2*)

Pro urodov i lyudey 1998 (*Of Freaks and Men*)

Brat 1997 (*Brother*)

Pribytiye poyezda 1995 (*The Arrival of a Train*)

Zamok 1994 (*The Castle*)

Shchastlivyye dni 1991 (*Happy Days*)

From the History of Aerostatics in Russia 1990

Yegor and Nastya 1989

"[*Brother*] is a work of great cinematic confidence."

—British Film Institute

Aleksei Balabanov is a Russian writer, producer, and director who is seen as one of the most influential filmmakers in postcommunist Russia. His films tackle life in contemporary Russia, and in particular the rise of its new criminal class after the fall of the Iron Curtain, and have been criticized for what some perceive as their anti-American sentiments.

As a young man, Balabanov studied in Gorky at the Institute of Foreign Languages and spent time in the Soviet army working as a translator. In the early 1980s, he took film courses in Moscow and began work as an assistant director. He made his directorial debut with the documentary shorts *Yegor and Nastya* (1989) and *From the History of Aerostatics in Russia* (1990), the latter earning him a directorial diploma.

Balabanov's feature debut was *Shchastlivyye dni* (1991) (*Happy Days*), followed by *Zamok* (1994) (*The Castle*). Turning from literary adaptations, he then made the violent low-budget movie *Brat* (1997) (*Brother*). Chronicling the rise of gangsters in free-market Russia, *Brother* earned Balabanov international attention and was Russia's top box-office draw that year.

Next, Balabanov went unconventional with *Pro urodov i lyudey* (1998) (*Of Freaks and Men*), a nineteenth-century story of pornography and deformity obsession recalling early David Lynch. The film created a scandal at its premiere in St. Petersburg. Despite the controversy, the picture received seven Nika nominations, winning Best Director and Best Film. His *Brat 2* (2000) (*Brother 2*), following Russian gangster Danila to the United States, was a huge box-office hit. Balabanov later poked fun at the criminal landscape with *Zhmurki* (2005) (*Blind Man's Bluff*). His realistic Chechen war film *Voyna* (2002) (*War*) earned five Nika nominations. **WW**

1950s

LUC BESSON

Born: Luc Besson, March 18, 1959 (Paris, France).

Directing style: Stunning visual stylist of French Cinéma du look; maker of dramas, action films, and science-fiction movies; collaborations with actor Jean Reno.

Beginning with his action breakthrough *La Femme Nikita* (1990) (*Nikita*), an unlikely story of a beautiful assassin, Luc Besson has become one of the world's most visible and bankable creators of expensive action movies and would-be blockbusters.

Originally, Besson wanted to become a marine biologist specializing in dolphins. But a teen diving accident meant he was no longer able to dive, and the aquatic world's loss was the film world's gain. Before *Nikita*, he directed a few art theater films, including cult thriller *Subway* (1985), and the visually impressive ocean fest *Le grand bleu* (1988) (*The Big Blue*). *Léon* (1994) (*The Professional*) marked his first foray into all-English-language cinema. It helped introduce French film staple Jean Reno to the United States and started the career of Natalie Portman, who put in a powerhouse performance as an orphan taken in—and then smitten by—a hit man.

The Fifth Element (1997) was more perplexing. A fast-paced science-fiction romantic comedy, it cemented Besson's reputation as some kind of skewed auteur, campy and over the top in equal degrees. Starring Bruce Willis and Besson's future second wife, Milla Jovovich, it has since become a cult hit, noted for its astounding visuals. The same cannot be said for *The Messenger: The Story of Joan of Arc* (1999), which was criticized as being a largely inscrutable film, rife with ego, insipidity, and historical inaccuracy. Its failure sent Besson back behind the scenes as a writer and producer on a number of diverse projects. He returned to the director's chair with *Angel-A* (2005), a film he claimed would be his last as a director, although he then went on to direct the family animation adventure movie, *Arthur et les Minimoys* (2006) (*Arthur and the Invisibles*). **JK**

Top Takes...

Arthur et les Minimoys 2006
  (*Arthur and the Invisibles*)

Angel-A 2005

The Fifth Element 1997

Léon 1994 (*The Professional*)

De Serge Gainsbourg à Gainsbarre de 1958–1991 1994

Atlantis 1991

La Femme Nikita 1990 (*Nikita*)

Le grand bleu 1988 (*The Big Blue*)

Subway 1985

Le dernier combat 1983 (*The Final Combat*)

L'avant dernier 1981

"It's always the small people who change things. It's never the politicians or the big guys."

1950s

TODD SOLONDZ

Born: Todd Solondz, October 15, 1959 (Newark, New Jersey, U.S.).

Directing style: Controversial maker of morally challenging, angst-ridden, dark comedies tackling taboo subjects; harsh humor; themes of middle-class suburban life.

Top Takes…

Palindromes 2004
Storytelling 2001
Happiness 1998
Welcome to the Dollhouse 1995
Fear, Anxiety & Depression 1989
Schatt's Last Shot 1985

"I don't want the controversy to overwhelm the experience of watching the movie itself."

RIGHT: Cynthia Stevenson and Dylan Baker only appear to be happy in *Happiness*.

Todd Solondz's rarely seen first feature, *Fear, Anxiety & Depression* (1989), tells the tale of a playwright who sends his work to Samuel Beckett in the hope they can collaborate. The film's title could have served for any one of his films to date. With *Welcome to the Dollhouse* (1995) and *Happiness* (1998), Solondz established himself as the cinematic bard of squirming, self-despising, middle-class misery. Swimming determinedly against the feel-good, consolatory mainstream of U.S. cinema, he has persisted with a personal brand of anguished comedy.

Solondz's refusal to resort to simplistic moral judgments has often led to trouble. *Happiness*, one of whose characters is a pederast who is nonetheless shown as a loving husband and father, was dropped by its original distributors and came in for outraged critical comment. Yet *Welcome to the Dollhouse*, which takes an even more despairing view of humankind, was widely praised. Most bleakly pessimistic of the "high school is hell on earth" genre, it contains not one likable character. Solondz claims he tries to get under the skin of characters who are bleeding souls. His films, never comfortable to watch, tread a knife-edge line between comedy and contempt. A certain self-consciousness mars Solondz's two subsequent features, *Storytelling* (2001) and *Palindromes* (2004). Upset by the critical attacks on *Happiness*, he seems to have set out to justify himself and, at the same time, lay his methods open to scrutiny. As a result, the films seem at times muddled, and oddly tentative. Their subject matter includes rape, sodomy, racism, abortion, underage sex, disability, and the Holocaust. It is clear, Solondz has lost none of his propensity for airing taboo subjects, or for pulling the moral rug out from under his audience. **PK**

SAM RAIMI

Born: Samuel Marshall Raimi, October 23, 1959 (Royal Oak, Michigan, U.S.).

Directing style: Cult slapstick horror moviemaker; graphic violence; later move to big-budget blockbusters in a variety of genres; frequently casts actor Bruce Campbell.

Top Takes...

Spider-Man 3 2007
Spider-Man 2 2004
Spider-Man 2002
The Gift 2000
For Love of the Game 1999
A Simple Plan 1998
The Quick and the Dead 1995
Army of Darkness: Evil Dead III 1992
Darkman 1990
Evil Dead II 1987
Crimewave 1985
The Evil Dead 1981
Clockwork 1978
Within the Woods 1978
It's Murder! 1977

"Heroic stories . . . show us the way. They remind us of the good we are capable of."

Like contemporaries such as Peter Jackson, Sam Raimi has moved on from a movie background in slapstick cult horror to directing big-budget blockbusters.

In Raimi's case, he has graduated to helming the highly successful *Spider-Man* franchise (2002–2007). Although his roots lie partly in the superhero subgenre with films such as *Darkman* (1990), they also take in the slapstick gore fest of *The Evil Dead* (1981) and its sequels. *The Evil Dead*'s graphic violence proved controversial in the United States and Europe, and he had difficulties getting it aired. The film was caught up in the 1980s "video nasties" panic in Britain—becoming the subject of legal action aimed at preventing its distribution. This helped to make it even more of a horror genre cause célèbre, cementing Raimi's reputation as a daring cult filmmaker. *The Evil Dead* is much loved by genre fans, but for its impressive use of cinematic techniques as much as for its gore: Raimi makes artistic and adrenaline-pumping use of swooping cameras and point-of-view shots to indicate unseen evil.

Evil Dead II (1987) was pretty much a bigger-budget remake of its predecessor, but the later sequel *Army of Darkness: Evil Dead III* (1992) developed a time-traveling aspect by placing the hero Ash, played by Raimi's childhood friend Bruce Campbell, in a medieval setting. It also shifted tone, moving away from extreme slapstick horror to a more reassuring out-and-out comedic approach. Raimi's work has arguably been at its most potent when seamlessly fusing humor with horror. Despite that, his versatility in working across lighter horror and comedy probably prepared him well to step up to a blockbuster franchise such as *Spider-Man*, with its moments of darkness but its overall lighter tone. **MH**

1950s

HAL HARTLEY

Born: Hal Hartley, November 3, 1959 (Lindenhurst, Long Island, New York, U.S.).

Directing style: Cult auteur U.S. independent filmmaker; composes music for his films; witty dialogue; deadpan acting; films shot in his native Long Island; often casts same actors.

Hal Hartley was born in the Long Island suburb of Lindenhurst—a location he returns to frequently in his movies. Initially enrolling in Boston's Massachusetts College of Art, Hartley transferred to the State University of New York to study film.

Following two early shorts, *The Cartographer's Girlfriend* (1987) and *Dogs* (1988), Hartley's debut feature *The Unbelievable Truth* (1989) introduces the terse, lucid dialogue that has become the signature of his early cycle of feature work. Examining themes of love and art through disaffected yet inquiring characters who find themselves in improbable situations, Hartley has achieved critical recognition as a leading figure in the 1990s U.S. independent movement. He has also employed and introduced a cast of regular actors including Martin Donovan, Robert John Burke, Elina Lowensohn, Bill Sage, and Parker Posey.

The highly stylized nature of his work has attracted comparisons to Jean-Luc Godard, whom Hartley acknowledges as a significant influence. Hartley has largely avoided the tendency of other directors associated with the 1990s movement to direct bigger-budget films. He followed *Henry Fool* (1997) with a series of nonnarrative shorts including *The Book of Life* (1998) and *Kimono* (2000). His feature work since 1997 has included the monster film *No Such Thing* (2001) and *The Girl From Monday* (2005); both make clear the critique of modern-day humanity that always subtends Hartley's narratives and continue his practice of composing music for his films under the pseudonym Ned Rifle. Hartley describes his recent movie *Fay Grim* (2006) as something like a sequel to *Henry Fool*. The film picks up the story of the original characters ten years later.   **CP**

Top Takes…

Fay Grim 2006
The Girl from Monday 2005
No Such Thing 2001
Kimono 2000
The Book of Life 1998
Henry Fool 1997
Flirt 1995
Amateur 1994
Iris 1994
Flirt 1993
Simple Men 1992
Theory of Achievement 1991
Trust 1990
The Unbelievable Truth 1989
Dogs 1988
The Cartographer's Girlfriend 1987

"I'm always compromising. I just don't compromise on . . . my films."

1950s

SHINYA TSUKAMOTO

Born: Shinya Tsukamoto, January 1, 1960 (Shibuya, Tokyo, Japan).

Directing style: Highly influential cult Japanese auteur across a range of genres; artistic collaborations with Tomoroh Taniguchi; frequently acts in own films; own brand of garish sophistication.

Top Takes…

Akumu tantei 2006 (*Nightmare Detective*)

Haze 2005

Vital 2004

Rokugatsu no hebi 2002 (*A Snake of June*)

Sôseiji 1999 (*Gemini*)

Bullet Ballet 1998

Tokyo Fist 1995

Tetsuo 1989 (*Tetsuo: the Iron Man*)

"I always wanted to make a film in which every image is infused with eroticism."

Shinya Tsukamoto first gained notice with the low-budget, 16mm black and white movie *Tetsuo* (1989) (*Tetsuo: the Iron Man*). A raucous synthesis of biomechanized rutting and urban angst, it was essentially a glorified student film. It paved the way for his subsequent, more mature movies that have influenced the films of others both at home and abroad.

After the forgettable, for-hire horror movie *Yokai Hanta—Hiruko* (1990) (*Hiruko the Goblin*) and lesser *Tetsuo II: Body Hammer* (1992), Tsukamoto applied his singular style to the risky, hyperviolent *Tokyo Fist* (1995) and his breakthrough film, *Bullet Ballet* (1998), a deeply personal exploration of repression and—as always—uproarious transformation.

The operatic *Sôseiji* (1999) (*Gemini*), adapted from a story by Japanese detective novelist Rampo Edogawa, and Tsukamoto's sole period piece, extended this thread beautifully. Like *Tetsuo: the Iron Man*, it pivots on an outrageously fetishistic depiction of alienation, but the mayhem is tempered by Tsukamoto's wry, sympathetic grasp of the irony of human intimacy.

Rokugatsu no hebi (2002) (*A Snake of June*), a study of therapeutic voyeurism championed by French director Catherine Breillat, synthesizes this pet theme nicely, and its relatively sedate tone gave way to the even more uncharacteristically restrained *Vital* (2004). The film, along with its wrenching short-form follow-up, *Haze* (2005), showed Tsukamoto sharpening his focus and underscored his most impressive trait as an artist: a body of work that exhibits amazing progression. For this reason and the fact that he also writes, shoots, choreographs, edits, and frequently acts in his films, Tsukamoto is among the few working directors who can truly be called an auteur. **MH**

ATOM EGOYAN

Born: Atom Yeghoyan, July 19, 1960 (Cairo, Egypt).

Directing style: Independent Canadian filmmaker; use of voice-over and flashback; explorations of Armenian history; themes of unconventional relationships, distressed family units, and isolation.

Born in Cairo, Egypt, but of Armenian descent and raised in Canada, Atom Egoyan rose to prominence as one of the most critically respected, challenging, and intriguing filmmakers of Canada's burgeoning independent movie scene. Several well-received short films and experiments led to his feature debut *Next of Kin* (1984) and for the next several years Egoyan would continue to explore that film's themes of unconventional relationships, distressed family units, and alienation.

A trio of striking and well-reviewed films, *Family Viewing* (1987), *Speaking Parts* (1989), and *The Adjuster* (1991), led to what many consider to be Egoyan's first masterpiece, *Calendar* (1993)—also his first film shot in Armenia—which was told in a series of complex but never convoluted flashbacks and leaps forward. That time-shifting style became even more prominent in Egoyan's breakthrough, the puzzle box drama *Exotica* (1994), a movie that won him further international acclaim. That praise was validated with *The Sweet Hereafter* (1997), a powerful adaptation of the Russell Banks novel about the aftermath of a horrible school bus accident that earned Egoyan two Oscar nods (for directing and writing) and a much wider audience.

Yet Egoyan shifted tack with the unconventional and enigmatic serial killer film *Felicia's Journey* (1999) and *Ararat* (2002), a movie that further explored his roots in its treatment of the Armenian genocide from 1915 to 1917. He returned to more familiar themes and styles with *Where the Truth Lies* (2005), a movie whose racy content set Egoyan at odds with the Motion Picture Association of America. He made cuts to the film but was forced to release it with an NC-17 rating, significantly limiting its potential audience, yet making him something of a free-speech martyr in the process. **JK**

Top Takes...

Where the Truth Lies 2005
Ararat 2002
The Line 2000
Felicia's Journey 1999
***The Sweet Hereafter* 1997** ☆
Exotica 1994
Calendar 1993
The Adjuster 1991
Speaking Parts 1989
Family Viewing 1987
Next of Kin 1984
Open House 1982
Peep Show 1981
After Grad with Dad 1980
Howard in Particular 1979

"I'm not working in some sort of vacuum, I do know exactly what my options are."

1960s

RICHARD LINKLATER

Born: Richard Stuart Linklater, July 30, 1960 (Houston, Texas, U.S.).

Directing style: Independent U.S. filmmaker of dramas; Texan locations; frequently action takes place in a day; examinations of youth culture; often casts Ethan Hawke.

Top Takes...

A Scanner Darkly 2006
Fast Food Nation 2006
Bad News Bears 2005
Before Sunset 2004
The School of Rock 2003
Live from Shiva's Dance Floor 2003
Tape 2001
Waking Life 2001
Before Sunrise 1995
Dazed and Confused 1993
Slacker 1991
Woodshock 1985

Did Richard Linklater's indie breakthrough *Slacker* (1991) reflect the culture it came from, or did it actively help give that slacker subculture shape? Linklater would no doubt argue that he is just the one making movies, and leaves the analysis to others. Perhaps that is why he followed *Slacker* with *Dazed and Confused* (1993), a relatively commercial film steeped in 1970s nostalgia. But it was *Before Sunrise* (1995), a film that depicted a full day in the life of two would-be lovers who meet on a train that best revealed Linklater's almost literary aspirations, his scripts always full of heady philosophical discussions that are sometimes at odds with their deceptively breezy delivery.

After two relative failures, the teenage drama *SubUrbia* (1996) and the more unlikely *The Newton Boys* (1998), Linklater returned to familiar ground with the pioneering *Waking Life* (2001), a stream of consciousness animated film whose trippy visual look was at least as important as the rapid-fire discussions that filled it. If *Tape* (2001) saw Linklater retreat even further toward indulgent indie film tropes, *The School of Rock* (2003) proved him to be surprisingly adept at overtly mainstream material. In fact, *Before Sunset* (2004), a belated sequel to *Before Sunrise,* and *Bad News Bears* (2005) showed Linklater more than willing to balance more outré or independent fare with bankable material. It remains to be seen whether his adaptation of Eric Schlosser's muck-raking book *Fast Food Nation* (2006) does better than his take on Philip K. Dick's paranoid science-fiction masterpiece *A Scanner Darkly* (2006), but no one can accuse Linklater of refusing to take risks. In truth, given his reputation in the indie world, he is the rare director for whom accepting a commercial project is the real risk. **JK**

"If you can't say something nice you shouldn't say anything at all."—On film critics

TAKASHI MIIKE

Born: Takashi Miike, August 24, 1960 (Yao, Osaka, Honshu, Japan).

Directing style: Cult Japanese director across a variety of genres; controversial depictions of bizarre sex; ultraviolent, taboo-breaking content; elusive endings; examinations of family relationships.

Impressively prolific Takashi Miike is not so much a director as an industry unto himself; his nonstop products range erratically but proudly and energetically from artful dramas to surreal dark comedies, to gut-churning horror and explosive action. No genre earns his particular allegiance, and no film reveals any limitations to Miike's ambitions. Of course, Miike's ambitions are often as muddy as his aesthetics, but it is ultimately hard to go wrong with an anything-goes mentality.

Miike was taught by Shohei Imamura and first worked in TV. In the wake of Japan's "V-Cinema" or direct-to-video boom, he took advantage of the less stringent censorship and more creative freedom afforded by such a financially viable format. In the West, Miike first gained notice outside his small but fervent cult with *Ôdishon* (1999) (*Audition*), a predictably shocking affair whose twisted narrative ends with a protracted bout of graphic torture and dismemberment that had as many moviegoers enthralled as appalled.

Even as discussion of the film lingered, Miike had moved on with his *yakuza* series, beginning with *Dead or Alive: Hanzaisha* (1999) (*Dead or Alive*) and the perverse serial killer movie *Koroshiya 1* (2001) (*Ichi the Killer*), which encountered problems with censors worldwide because of its depiction of violence toward women. He then contributed a segment to *Saam gaang yi* (2004) (*Three . . . Extremes*), a collection of horror shorts from Asian directors, and made the bizarre samurai film *Izo* (2004). The U.S. TV series *Masters of Horror* (2006) did not air an episode by Miike titled "Imprint" because of concerns over its disturbing scenes of violence.

By some counts Miike has made more than 60 films since 1991, and the list is surely to grow a few titles longer. **JK**

Top Takes...

Taiyo no kizu 2006 (*Sun Scarred*)

Izo 2004

Saam gaang yi 2004 (*Three . . . Extremes*)

Katakuri-ke no kôfuku 2001
(*The Happiness of the Katakuris*)

Araburu tamashii-tachi 2001 (*Agitator*)

Koroshiya 1 2001 (*Ichi the Killer*)

Bijitâ Q 2001 (*Visitor Q*)

Dead or Alive 2: Tôbôsha 2000
(*Dead or Alive 2: Birds*)

Dead or Alive: Hanzaisha 1999 (*Dead or Alive*)

Ôdishon 1999 (*Audition*)

Chûgoku no chôjin 1998
(*The Bird People in China*)

Gokudô sengokushi: Fudô 1996
(*Fudoh: The New Generation*)

> "Violence is an easy tool for expressing or conveying certain problems or emotions."

1960s

KENNETH BRANAGH

Born: Kenneth Charles Branagh, December 10, 1960 (Belfast, Northern Ireland).

Directing style: British actor and director of dramas; frequent Shakespeare adaptations; often acts in his own movies; artistic collaborations with actress Emma Thompson.

Top Takes...

The Magic Flute 2006
As You Like It 2006
Listening 2003
Love's Labour's Lost 2000
Hamlet 1996
In the Bleak Midwinter 1995
Frankenstein 1994
Much Ado About Nothing 1993
Peter's Friends 1992
Swan Song 1992
Dead Again 1991
Henry V 1989 ☆

Acclaimed actor and stage director Kenneth Branagh showed ambition and hubris with his screen directorial debut, William Shakespeare's *Henry V* (1989). By directing, adapting, and starring in the film, Branagh invited comparison with Sir Laurence Olivier, who had done exactly the same in 1944. Branagh won Oscar nominations for Best Director and Best Actor, the same as Olivier had. However, Branagh's approach differs from Olivier's stuffy embalming of the play: Branagh spent a third of the budget on a single, impressive battlefield tracking shot, making the Battle of Agincourt a blood-and-mud World War I vista.

Branagh has several times returned to Shakespeare, although *In the Bleak Midwinter* (1995), a black and white comedy about an amateur dramatic staging of *Hamlet*, is more distinctive than the star-studded, slightly plodding adaptations of *Much Ado About Nothing* (1993), *Hamlet* (1996), *Love's Labour's Lost* (2000), and *As You Like It* (2006). Wary of being pigeonholed, Branagh demonstrated versatility by directing the Hitchcockian private eye and reincarnation drama *Dead Again* (1991); a popular British variant on *The Big Chill* (1983) titled *Peter's Friends* (1992); and a filmed opera, *The Magic Flute* (2006). *Frankenstein* (1994) is an interesting, super-produced disappointment. Robert De Niro's incarnation of the monster is a particular missed opportunity, and Branagh's shirtless, buff romantic poet of a mad scientist also fails to take advantage of the richness of Mary Shelley's novel, and its place in cinema mythology. Continuing to work as a busy actor, Branagh distinctly gives the impression that, again like Olivier, being a movie director comes about halfway down his list of priorities. **KN**

> "I resist being appropriated as the current repository of Shakespeare on the planet."

KI-DUK KIM

Born: Ki-Duk Kim, December 20, 1960 (Bonghwa, South Korea).

Directing style: South Korean director of experimental, poetic dramas; lack of dialogue; themes of communication, prostitution, and crime; graphic sex and violence.

Ki-Duk Kim is a controversial South Korean director of unique, unpredictable films imbued with a rare visceral force. He bravely explores the big issues, such as sin, guilt, shame, love, jealousy, revenge, punishment, redemption, and sacrifice. The central theme of Kim's entire opus is communication, and the lack of it. His best works are centered on moody characters, scarred by unknown sorrow. The communion between souls is never verbal: it can be established through violence as in *Nabbeun namja* (2001) (*Bad Guy*); eroticism as in *Samaria* (2004) (*Samaritan Girl*); sadomasochism as in *Seom* (2000) (*The Isle*); or music as in *Bin-jip* (2004) (*3-Iron*). It can even be established in silence as in *Hwal* (2005) (*The Bow*).

Kim's films' existential love affairs are intriguing, painful, spiritual, and thought provoking. Religious symbolism is eclectic and unobtrusive: Buddhism in *Bom yeoreum gaeul gyeoul geurigo bom* (2003) (*Spring, Summer, Fall, Winter . . . and Spring*) and Roman Catholicism in *Samaria* provide the archetypes, making his characters' concerns universal. Physical cruelty and mental anguish are followed by sentimental passages of touching beauty: lyrical scenes precede surprising acts of bloodshed—and all of them, as a whole, reveal a profound insight into the human condition. It is precisely in extreme acts that his characters are revealed, unmasked, and only in their attempts at communication does the audience realize who these characters really are. Kim's semi-abstract style of surgical distance and ambiguity may alienate some viewers. But the pleasure of his films is in the sense of exploration, in the fascinating walk on shaky ground, and in sharing thoughts, emotions, fears, and insecurities with a genuine artist. **DO**

Top Takes...

Shi gan 2006 (*Time*)

Hwal 2005 (*The Bow*)

Bin-jip 2004 (*3-Iron*)

Samaria 2004 (*Samaritan Girl*)

Bom yeoreum gaeul gyeoul geurigo bom 2003 (*Spring, Summer, Fall, Winter . . . and Spring*)

Hae anseon 2002 (*The Coast Guard*)

Nabbeun namja 2001 (*Bad Guy*)

Suchwiin bulmyeong 2001 (*Address Unknown*)

Seom 2000 (*The Isle*)

Shilje sanghwang 2000 (*Real Fiction*)

Yasaeng dongmul bohoguyeog 1996 (*Wild Animals*)

Ag-o 1996 (*Crocodile*)

"My movies are lamentable for uncovering the genitals that everyone wants to hide."

1960s

TODD HAYNES

Born: Todd Haynes, January 2, 1961 (Los Angeles, California, U.S.).

Directing style: Influential director of new queer cinema; maker of period melodramas; examinations of environment as disease, and the repressive nature of societal conventions.

Top Takes...

I'm Not There 2007
Far from Heaven 2002
Velvet Goldmine 1998
Safe 1995
Poison 1991
Superstar: The Karen Carpenter Story 1987
Assassins: A Film Concerning Rimbaud 1985

A key figure in the new queer cinema of the 1990s, Todd Haynes became infamous years before the movement was named when he used Barbie dolls instead of actors in his short *Superstar: The Karen Carpenter Story* (1987), and the film was banned after the Carpenter family and the Mattel Corporation objected. Haynes's films reflect his background in art and semiotics, and *Superstar* juxtaposed the squeaky-clean plasticity of the singer's public image against archival footage of the invasion of Cambodia and the Watergate crisis, and played alternately and knowingly like a disease-of-the-week documentary, family melodrama, and musical biopic.

Haynes flirted with controversy once again with the award-winning triptych *Poison* (1991), which explored AIDS as a metaphor for contamination by intercutting between films. With its chilling silences and dehumanizing blank spaces, *Safe* (1995), a movie about a housewife whose affluent late 1980s environment turns on her, ushered in a new phase in Haynes's ever-deepening examination of environment as disease. Another departure and return, the gorgeously phantasmagorical *Velvet Goldmine* (1998) was a coming-of-age story that traced the David Bowie and Iggy Pop glam rock era to the sexual and identity politics of Oscar Wilde. It was in *Far from Heaven*'s (2002) revisit to 1950s female melodrama, however, that Haynes's methods synchronized perfectly. Replicating the lush color and lighting and poignant symbolism of the weepies of Douglas Sirk—its complete lack of irony a revelation—the film brought once taboo issues of racism and sexuality to the surface in a way that deconstructed and disarmed its audience's postmodern nostalgia. **LB**

> *"Superstar* gave me the reputation that enabled me to continue making films."

1960s

ALEXANDER PAYNE

Born: Alexander Papadopoulos, February 10, 1961 (Omaha, Nebraska, U.S.).

Directing style: Witty writer and director of satirical comedies; Omaha, Nebraska locations; commentary on U.S. suburban life; uses non-actors to play minor roles.

Writer and director Alexander Payne is one of the brightest talents to emerge in Hollywood recently, with a distinctive style of comedy. After some student films, he worked at Universal Pictures and wrote unproduced screenplays. He then made contributions to two segments of the *Inside Out* (1992) portmanteau films, before completing his first feature, *Citizen Ruth* (1996). The film stars Laura Dern as an improvident drug user and single mother, who can only be saved from jail if she terminates her latest pregnancy. Befriended by a pro-life supporter, Dern finds herself in a tug of war between both sides of the abortion debate. From this unlikely material Payne fashioned a comedy that satirized both sides of the fence.

He followed this with *Election* (1999), starring Reese Witherspoon as an ambitious high school student determined at all costs to secure election as school president. It is a sharp and funny satire on high school life and small-town mores. In Payne's next film, *About Schmidt* (2002), Jack Nicholson plays a curmudgeonly widower who senses that life has passed him by, and makes a cross-country journey in his Winnebago to visit his daughter. The director presents a pitiless dissection of suburban ennui, and the laughter he generates keeps the audience one jump ahead of despair.

In *Sideways* (2004), Payne cast two relatively unknown actors as friends who embark on a tour of the California vineyards prior to one of them getting married. A series of disasters ensues, each more embarrassingly hilarious than the last. Payne varies the mix, successfully combining slapstick with verbal humor, and comedy based on character. The film won an Oscar for Best Writing, Adapted Screenplay for Payne and his writing partner Jim Taylor. **EB**

Top Takes...

Paris, je t'aime 2006 (*Paris, I Love You*)
***Sideways* 2004** ☆
About Schmidt 2002
Election 1999
Citizen Ruth 1996
The Passion of Martin 1991
Carmen 1985

"It shouldn't be an epic aspiration to make simple human stories, but it is."

1960s

MICHAEL WINTERBOTTOM

Born: Michael Winterbottom, March 29, 1961 (Blackburn, Lancashire, England).

Directing style: British filmmaker across a multiplicity of genres; often literary adaptations; use of improvisation; sexual imagery; frequently casts actor Christopher Eccleston.

Top Takes…

The diversity and often confounding variety of Michael Winterbottom's projects are in some sense a throwback to Hollywood's contract days, when a director was treated as little more than a hired hand and was forced to make the most of the material given to him. However, the comparison ends when you account for Winterbottom's risky subject matter and apparent aversion to repetition and conformity.

A graduate of Oxford University, Winterbottom subsequently went to film school at Bristol University. He then worked in TV, directing shows such as the detective series *Cracker* (1993). Winterbottom launched his film career with the psychological thriller *Butterfly Kiss* (1995), and has kept up a brisk production clip ever since. His subjects have ranged from literary adaptations such as Thomas Hardy's classic novel, *Jude* (1996); to political satire including *Welcome to Sarajevo* (1997); to pornography such as *9 Songs* (2004), which is notorious for its sequences of unsimulated sex.

Frustratingly for fans of the auteur theory, few of Winterbottom's films have much in common thematically or stylistically, besides the fact that each has been generally well accomplished in its own right. No matter how successful each individual film is, Winterbottom moves swiftly on to his next surprising story. *9 Songs*, for example, was quickly followed by another literary adaptation, this time of a supposedly unfilmable novel, *A Cock and Bull Story* (2005), and then by *The Road to Guantanamo* (2006), a neodocumentary polemic drawn straight from contemporary news headlines about three spirited British Muslims who suffered a lengthy imprisonment in Guantánamo Bay after being falsely accused of terrorism. **JK**

> "You could say that what inspired *9 Songs* were all the films that avoid sex."

HIDEO NAKATA

Born: Hideo Nakata, July 19, 1961 (Okayama, Japan).

Directing style: Japanese master of J-Horror and plot-led thrillers; innovative use of soundtrack to send chills down the spine; dark, eerie lighting; use of suspense over gore.

The man who made *Ringu* (1998) (*Ring*), and helped resuscitate the moribund world of Japanese cinema, got his start making porn movies. Hideo Nakata began his film career as an apprentice at Nikkatsu Studios in 1980, cranking out full-length feature films in less than a week for the raincoat crowd. Setting aside the aesthetics of the works, it was good practice for an aspiring filmmaker to learn how to stretch the limits of budgets, and how to hint at things that could not be shown.

As Nikkatsu Studios started to sink into the quagmire that claimed so many Japanese studios in the dark days of the 1980s, Nakata made the move to London. There he developed a fascination for blacklisted British director and communist, Joseph Losey, and a determination to memorialize the man in a documentary, *Joseph Losey: The Man with Four Names* (1998).

To finance this Losey biopic, Nakata returned to Tokyo to take whatever directing gigs came his way: movies such as *Honto ni atta kowai hanashi: jushiryou* (1992) (*Curse Death & Spirit*) and *Joyû-rei* (1996) (*Don't Look Up*). These were landmark works of J-Horror, combining ancient symbols of Asian folklore with contemporary fears and urban legends in a restrained, muted style that emphasized suspense over gore. Thanks to this track record, Hideo Nakata was hired to helm the 1998 feature adaptation of Kôji Suzuki's best-selling horror novel *Ringu*, about a cursed videotape that spreads its evil like a contagion. *Ring* broke global box-office records, and Nakata became famous. He resists the "horror director" label, but his best-known films are thrillers in the *Ring* mold such as *Honogurai mizu no soko kara* (2002) (*Dark Water*), as well as less supernatural suspense thrillers such as the superb *Kaosu* (1999) (*Chaos*). **DK**

Top Takes…

Kaidan 2007
The Ring Two 2005
Last Scene 2002
Honogurai mizu no soko kara 2002 (*Dark Water*)
Sotohiro 2000
Garasu no nou 2000 (*Sleeping Bride*)
Sadistic and Masochistic 2000
Ringu 2 1999 (*Ring 2*)
Kaosu 1999 (*Chaos*)
Joseph Losey: The Man with Four Names 1998
Ringu 1998 (*Ring*)
Joyû-rei 1996 (*Don't Look Up*)

"I don't want to put myself in a small box. I think I can make different kinds of movies."

1960s

PETER JACKSON

Born: Peter Jackson, October 31, 1961 (Pukerua Bay, North Island, New Zealand).

Directing style: Lord of the fantasy epic; early cult splatstick horror movies; extensive use of special effects; films on location in New Zealand; multiple camera angles; cameo appearances.

Top Takes…

The Lovely Bones 2007

King Kong 2005

The Lord of the Rings:
The Return of the King 2003 ★

The Lord of the Rings: The Two Towers 2002

The Lord of the Rings:
The Fellowship of the Ring 2001 ☆

The Frighteners 1996

Heavenly Creatures 1994

Braindead 1992

Meet the Feebles 1989

Bad Taste 1987

The Valley 1976

Now best known for blockbusters such as the multiple Oscar-winning *The Lord of the Rings* trilogy (2001–2003), and a *King Kong* remake (2005), New Zealander Peter Jackson's career has taken in a wide range of very different movies. He started out as a writer and director of cult bad-taste films; appropriately enough coming up with a splatstick horror movie titled *Bad Taste* (1987) that featured dangerously vomiting aliens and won him international acclaim at Cannes Film Festival. This was followed by the mind-boggling musical comedy *Meet the Feebles* (1989)—essentially the Muppets puppets reimagined in an adult and deliberately vile way.

After this filth fest, Jackson calmed himself and started to build on his early successes with major pictures such as the Michael J. Fox vehicle *The Frighteners* (1996). Still displaying his interest in slapstick and a little crazy gore, films such as this showed that Jackson could handle the trappings of bigger budget mainstream movies, and thus provided him with a launch pad into the realms of blockbusterdom. Achieving the clout to mount *The Lord of The Rings: The Fellowship of the Ring* (2001) also meant that Jackson could help put New Zealand on the industry map and remain based there for the filming of the trilogy. In a curious way, Jackson's career had moved full circle by the 1990s: he had shifted from making low-budget, cult New Zealand movies to crafting high-budget, cult New Zealand movies. Not only are his latter day films in much better taste than his early bad taste outings, but by adapting Tolkien's cult novels, and remaking a Hollywood cult movie of the 1930s, Jackson has cleverly guaranteed that he can conform to the mainstream, yet can still maintain a loyal cult following. **MH**

"I doubt I could ever control myself sufficiently to make a serious horror film."

ALFONSO CUARÓN

Born: Alfonso Cuarón Orozco, November 28, 1961 (Mexico City, Distrito Federal, Mexico).

Directing style: Director of New Mexican Cinema; visceral dramas and literary adaptations, particularly of children's novels; well-choreographed action sequences.

Like his fellow directors of the New Mexican Cinema, Guillermo del Toro and Alejandro González Iñárritu, Alfonso Cuarón seems able to move fluently among cultures, exploring those of other countries with a sure touch while remaining rooted in his native country. His best-known Mexican film, *Y tu mamá también* (2001) (*And Your Mother Too*), succeeded in taking a seemingly banal, adolescent tale of two lusty teenage boys on a road trip with a sexy older woman, and transforming it into a meditation on maturity, sex, and death, seasoned with acute insights into the condition of twenty-first-century Mexico.

At the same time, Cuarón has shown a strong affinity for English literature, and children's literature in particular. His first English language film was an adaptation of Frances Hodgson Burnett's Victorian classic *A Little Princess* (1995), filmed with an exact feeling for period that avoided excess sentimentality. *Great Expectations* (1998), an updating of Charles Dickens's novel to the modern-day United States, worked better than might have been expected, though the film lost its grip in the later New York scenes. Cuarón's entry in the adaptations of J. K. Rowling's novels, *Harry Potter and the Prisoner of Azkaban* (2004), was the darkest and most powerful yet of the cycle.

Cuarón's apocalyptic thriller *Children of Men* (2006) is a radical reworking of P. D. James's dystopian novel. Making potent use of London locations, it extrapolates from present-day concerns such as terrorism and climate change, to create a scarily convincing picture of a beleaguered Britain two decades hence, while at the same time deploying virtuoso camera technique to ratchet up the tension. Cuarón's versatility, growing technical assurance, and acute sense of tone suggest a career still promisingly in the ascendant. **PK**

Top Takes...

The Possibility of Hope 2007
Children of Men 2006
Harry Potter and the Prisoner of Azkaban 2004
Y tu mamá también 2001
  (*And Your Mother Too*)
Great Expectations 1998
A Little Princess 1995
Sólo con tu pareja 1991
  (*Love in the Time of Hysteria*)
Cuarteto para el fin del tiempo 1983
  (*Quartet for the End of Time*)
Who's He Anyway 1983

"If I care to connect with anybody, it's young people … they keep you relevant."

1960s

RAM GOPAL VARMA

Born: Ram Gopal Varma, April 7, 1962 (Hyderabad, India).

Directing style: Innovative Hindi director who has reinvented Bollywood; pioneer of Mumbai noir; maker of dramas and thrillers; homages to Hollywood movies.

Top Takes...

Sholay 2007
Shiva 2006
Sarkar 2005
Bhoot 2003
Company 2002
Jungle 2000
Prema Katha 1999
Satya 1998
Daud: Fun on the Run 1997
Anaganaga Oka Roju 1997
Deyyam 1996
Great Robbery 1996
Gaayam 1993
Raat 1992
Shiva 1989

Ram Gopal Varma is one of the most interesting and challenging directors working within popular Hindi cinema. He began his career within the Southern Indian film industry, making pictures such as his debut *Shiva* (1989) in the local Telugu language. After a number of consistently impressive films in a variety of genres, including *Raat* (1992), the suspenseful horror movie and homage to William Freidkin's *The Exorcist* (1973), Varma reached another level of creativity with his highly stylized and commercially successful gangster film *Satya* (1998). *Satya* showed a serious tone and a concern with the social reality of the poor in Mumbai that was lacking in many other Bollywood successes of the period. Again unusual for popular Hindi cinema, *Satya* attempted to place its musical numbers into the context of the film's narrative.

After the success of *Satya*, Varma moved to the highest echelons of the Bombay film industry, having formed his own production house, Varma Corporation, which produces low-budget movies. He has also forged a reputation for making pictures in a variety of genres but always attempting to create works that push the boundaries of Bollywood convention. Typical of his willingness to work with influences from outside India, *Company* (2002) drew on the popular gangster films being produced in Hong Kong and the United States, without losing its context of Bombay at the time. Indeed, Varma is credited with helping to create the "Mumbai noir" style that brings psychological depth to characters, and a sense of realism uncommon to earlier Bollywood output. The director also began an ongoing collaboration with Ajay Devgan, who has appeared in a number of Varma's subsequent films, including his remake of the Hindi classic *Sholay* (2007). **AW**

> "Bollywood became trapped into thinking that without songs, a film couldn't work."

DAVID FINCHER

Born: David Leo Fincher, August 28, 1962 (Denver, Colorado, U.S.).

Directing style: Director of dynamic Hollywood blockbusters and cult action films; maker of dark, violent dramas that tap into contemporary society's anxieties and obsessions.

David Fincher trained at George Lucas's Industrial Light and Magic doing visual effects on movies such as *Star Wars: Episode VI—Return of the Jedi* (1983). He then moved on to make TV commercials and pop music videos.

Cofounding the production company Propaganda Films, Fincher made his feature debut with *Alien³* (1992). Living up to the franchise reputation proved difficult, however, and he was repulsed by Hollywood. He returned to music videos, making *Dangerous: The Short Films* (1993), *Aerosmith: Big Ones You Can Look at* (1994), *The Best of Sting: Fields of Gold 1984–1994* (1994), when *Se7en* (1995) dropped in his lap.

Top Takes...

Zodiac 2007
Panic Room 2002
Fight Club 1999
The Game 1997
Se7en 1995
Alien³ 1992
The Beat of the Live Drum 1985

The resulting picture, about a serial killer enacting the seven deadly sins, replete with sinister settings and a pessimistic view of human nature, was a blockbuster masterpiece. Next was *The Game* (1997), which was not particularly well received, followed by a second masterpiece, *Fight Club* (1999), about a schizophrenic who founds a men's no-holds-barred fight club as cover for revolution. Due to its brutality and dead-on observations about consumer society, audiences largely stayed away, making *Fight Club* an acquired taste and a cult favorite. Fincher then directed *Panic Room* (2002), a stylish film about a home invasion, and then there was *Zodiac* (2007) concerning the notorious late-1960s serial murderer of the same name.

There is always a tendency toward flashy technique in Fincher's output. While impressive, it can add up to genius, as in *Fight Club*, or echo emptily, as in *Panic Room*. A matter of subjective perception, yes, but the brilliance is in manipulating movie form and technology to tell stories filled with nihilism and violence, which nevertheless describe a journey to redemption. **GCQ**

"The thing I love about *Jaws* is the fact that I've never gone swimming in the ocean again."

1960s

BAZ LUHRMANN

Born: Mark Anthony Luhrmann, September 17, 1962 (New South Wales, Australia).

Directing style: Australian director of dramas and comedies; "The Bazmanian Devil"; modernizer of the musical; lavish colors; loving attention to detail; flamboyant costumes; fast-paced editing.

Top Takes…

Moulin Rouge! 2001
Romeo + Juliet 1996
Strictly Ballroom 1992

Nicknamed "The Bazmanian Devil" for both his Antipodean birthplace and his distinctive frenetic style, Australian Baz Luhrmann discovered and embraced movies at a young age thanks to his father, who owned a theater. Luhrmann would look to his father as well as his mother, who enjoyed ballroom dancing, as inspiration for his first film, *Strictly Ballroom* (1992), a low-budget romantic comedy about Australian dance competitions that became a sleeper hit.

Romeo + Juliet (1996), however, introduced Luhrmann to even wider acclaim and, in some circles, to controversial disdain. The film took William Shakespeare's timeless play and set it against a postmodern collision of action, melodrama, and nearly incessant camera motion. Despite its utterly idiosyncratic nature, the movie (starring Leonardo DiCaprio and Claire Danes as the star-crossed lovers) somehow clicked, even if some argued that it never gelled. It was a huge hit, and declared Luhrmann one of the most promising directors in the industry.

Yet if anyone thought they knew what to expect from Luhrmann, *Moulin Rouge!* (2001) proved them wrong. His third, most grandiose romance, *Moulin Rouge!* was even more maddeningly busy than its predecessors, featuring an anachronistic soundtrack of contemporary pop songs reimagined for the film's late nineteenth-century setting. Yet as sly as the movie may be, the love story at its heart is Luhrmann's most conventionally sincere and least ironic to date, creating some real waves of cognitive dissonance. Lurhmann has since flirted with several follow-up projects, even adding his distinctive directorial eye for lavish detail to the world's most expensive advertisement, for Chanel No. 5, the four-minute short *No. 5: The Film* (2004), starring Nicole Kidman. **JK**

> "The films I make are about 60 percent of what I imagine them to be."

STEVEN SODERBERGH

Born: Steven Soderbergh, January 14, 1963 (Atlanta, Georgia, U.S.).

Directing style: Prolific director of existentialist dramas and crime capers; themes of friendship and communication; frequent artistic collaborations with superstar George Clooney.

The oeuvre of versatile busybody Steven Soderbergh is held together by a refusal, or inability, to commit. Existentialist, ironic, and amoral, all his characters want is to connect; in a world without family ties, they all crave friendship.

Soderbergh's sensational debut *Sex, Lies, and Videotape* (1989) symbolized the hedonist, cynical, and media-savvy Generation X, and catapulted him into fame. The Expressionist *Kafka* (1991), the introverted *King of the Hill* (1993), and the self-obsessed *Gray's Anatomy* (1996) all contain characters in search of companionship . . . a search they all fail.

The success of Soderbergh's first collaboration with George Clooney, *Out of Sight* (1998), made him lots of buddies inside Hollywood, especially since he delivers on time and on budget. The duo formed their own company, Section Eight Productions, and he has since been bouncing like a yo-yo between Hollywood and independent cinema. The studio-backed *Erin Brockovich* (2000) and the independent *Traffic* (2000) earned him Best Director Oscar nominations, and a win for the latter.

Soderbergh seems to have access to more inspiration and hours in a day than his contemporaries, directing at least a film per year. The light-footed heist movie *Ocean's Eleven* (2001) pivoted around the trust among eleven gangsters and the dynamics of a tight, ensemble cast. In contrast, the moody *Solaris* (2002) highlights the desolateness of isolation. The difficulty of fleeting friendships is also a theme in the World War II film noir *The Good German* (2006).

Soderbergh has been good to his real-life pals, producing Clooney's films and endorsing many others. Friendship may not last forever, but for now Soderbergh seems on a continuous high, and having a swell time. **EM**

Top Takes...

Ocean's Thirteen 2007
The Good German 2006
Bubble 2005
Ocean's Twelve 2004
Solaris 2002
Full Frontal 2002
Ocean's Eleven 2001
Traffic 2000 ★
Erin Brockovich 2000 ☆
Out of Sight 1998
Gray's Anatomy 1996
King of the Hill 1993
Kafka 1991
Sex, Lies, and Videotape 1989
Winston 1987

"A part of you has to be scared, it keeps you alert; otherwise you become complacent."

1960s

QUENTIN TARANTINO

Born: Quentin Jerome Tarantino, March 27, 1963 (Knoxville, Tennessee, U.S.).

Directing style: King of cool cult action films; graphic violence; unconventional narratives; use of veteran actors of cult fame; homages to Asian movies; cameo appearances.

Top Takes...

Grindhouse 2007
Sin City 2005
Kill Bill: Vol. 2 2004
Kill Bill: Vol. 1 2003
Jackie Brown 1997
Four Rooms 1995
Pulp Fiction 1994 ☆
Reservoir Dogs 1992
My Best Friend's Birthday 1987

The popular myth is legendary, whereby unknown talent catapults from obscurity into the limelight. So it was that the twenty-nine-year-old Quentin Tarantino, an occasional actor, video store clerk, and pop-culture enthusiast, wrote and directed his debut feature, *Reservoir Dogs* (1992), in which he costarred as one of a group of bank robbers involved in a caper that goes terribly wrong. The film made it to the Sundance Film Festival and almost overnight the name Tarantino was on everyone's lips. *Reservoir Dogs,* a partial rewrite of the Hong Kong movie, *Lung fu fong wan* (1987) (*City on Fire*), became an instant cult classic, changing the scope of star Harvey Keitel's career, popularizing compilation soundtrack albums with a flair for nostalgia, and making profanity-laden scripts with hip references, sexual metaphor, brutal violence, and showcase parts for ensemble casts the stuff of important art.

First a screenwriter, Tarantino sold two notable scripts, *True Romance* (1993) and *Natural Born Killers* (1994); this exposure enhanced his reputation, made him influential friends, and allowed him to collect an all-star cast for one of independent cinema's most ambitious projects, *Pulp Fiction* (1994).

RIGHT: Tarantino favorites, John Travolta and Samuel L. Jackson, star in *Pulp Fiction.*

Winner of a Golden Globe and an Oscar for his *Pulp Fiction* script and nominated for Best Director at both ceremonies, Tarantino's brand of melodrama, non-chronological narrative, and violence-prone set pieces made *Pulp Fiction* a rare piece. Placed at the film's center is the story of two hit men who witness a possibly divine miracle, forcing each of them to reconsider their path in life.

Tarantino went into general seclusion to hatch what many consider his most provocative and ambitious project yet, *Kill Bill: Vol. 1* (2003) and *Kill Bill: Vol. 2* (2004). Combining anime, horror, chop socky, and action-adventure to tell a story of extraordinarily obsessive revenge, the two-part movie is divided along stylistic lines; the first edition is more devoted to action; the second to drama; the results of which brought veteran David Carradine back from a marginal retirement, and again proved the writer/director's connection to cool. **GCQ**

ABOVE: Brandishing a sword, Uma Thurman eyes up the opposition in *Kill Bill: Vol. 1.*

Tarantino Trademarks

Quentin Tarantino's films are renowned for their various trademarks, both blatant and more subtle:

- Characters sing along to the soundtrack.
- Copious amounts of blood ooze, spurt, and flow from the wounded.
- The Mexican Standoff—three characters point a gun at each other at the same time.
- A black suit, white shirt, and black tie is the standard outfit—male and female.
- Quick cuts of rapid hand movements in close-up have been widely imitated.

1960s

MICHEL GONDRY

Born: Michel Gondry, May 8, 1963 (Versailles, France).

Directing style: French writer and director; influential visual trickster of pop music videos and surreal, fantastical whimsical dramas; innovator of bullet-time, slow-motion special effects.

Top Takes...

A fantasist in the truest sense, art school graduate Michel Gondry draws literally from nightmares and daydreams to create surreal, albeit somewhat sentimental, flights of whimsy.

Not surprisingly, Gondry found his initial outlet in music videos, first for his own band Oui Oui, and then for Icelandic star Björk, who saw his work and invited him to make the first of five videos for her. Gondry is credited for reinventing the pop music video and has since worked with such receptive, bands as The Chemical Brothers, the Rolling Stones, and The White Stripes. He also did groundbreaking work on TV commercials for brands such as GAP and Smirnoff.

Following in the footsteps of his friend Spike Jonze, Gondry hooked up with screenwriter Charlie Kaufman for his first foray into film, the not quite fully realized satire *Human Nature* (2001). Another collaboration with Kaufman, *Eternal Sunshine of the Spotless Mind* (2004), was a much better picture, and although it wasn't as successful financially as some had no doubt hoped or expected, it continues to resonate as one of the strongest films in recent memory, winning an Academy Award for Best Writing, Original Screenplay. Gondry then filmed a live hip hop concert, starring well-known artists and organized by comedian Dave Chappelle on the streets of Brooklyn, and it was up to Gondry to successfully find a creative way to present such a happening with *Block Party* (2005). *La science des rêves* (2006) (*The Science of Sleep*), based on an original script by Gondry, once again displayed his gift for practical effects and trick camera shots that give the illusion of something much more complex but never step in the path of emotions in the way distracting computer effects often do. **JK**

> "Two thousand years ago, some guy died and still today everyone's crazy about it."

ALEJANDRO GONZÁLEZ IÑÁRRITU

Born: Alejandro González Iñárritu, August 15, 1963 (Mexico City, Distrito Federal, Mexico).

Directing style: Mexican prodigy of morality tale dramas; themes examine cultural assumptions; intertwining stories reveal the cause and effect of people's actions.

A radio disc jockey and TV prodigy in his twenties, Alejandro González Iñárritu quickly rose through the ranks of international cinema to become one of the leading voices of the Mexican film world. Iñárritu studied film in the unlikely locale of Maine, as well as Los Angeles, before returning home to Mexico to work in TV. Beginning with *Amores perros* (2000) (*Love Dogs*), his increasingly ambitious features have proven to be some of the few films not only to cross cultural barriers, but also to capture life on a global scale. About the intersection of three very different stories set in Mexico City, *Love Dogs* earned a Best Foreign Language Film nomination at the Academy Awards, and it also introduced the distinctively nonlinear narrative approach Iñárritu would take in collaboration with screenwriter Guillermo Arriaga.

Iñárritu made a striking and shocking entry in the *11'09"01—September 11* (2002) anthology, which featured long stretches of black screen interrupted with flashes of bodies falling from the World Trade Center. His next film *21 Grams* (2003) starred Sean Penn, Naomi Watts, and Benicio Del Toro in another chopped-up tragedy whose meaning and power becomes more apparent the closer the movie comes to its conclusion.

Iñárritu produced *Nine Lives* (2005) for Colombian director Rodrigo García, before embarking on his most ambitious film to date, *Babel* (2006), a tale of intertwining lives and the parallel cultures set in several different countries, which starred Brad Pitt and Cate Blanchett alongside a host of newcomers, nonprofessional actors, and unfamiliar faces. The film won extensive international acclaim, including the Best Director prize at Cannes Film Festival, but a public falling out between Iñárritu and Arriaga tainted its success. **JK**

Top Takes...

Babel 2006 ☆
21 Grams 2003
11'09"01—September 11 2002
Powder Keg 2001
Amores perros 2000 (*Love Dogs*)
El Timbre 1996

"Money isn't a big problem .... When there's a good script, everybody circles."

1960s

CHAN-WOOK PARK

Born: Chan-wook Park, August 23, 1963 (Tanyan, South Korea).

Directing style: South Korean maker of violent, dark psychological thrillers; vivid colors; black humor; themes of vengeance; explorations of identity and moral choice.

Top Takes...

Bakjwi 2007 (*Evil Live*)

Saibogujiman kwenchana 2006
  (*I'm a Cyborg, But That's OK*)

Chinjeolhan geumjassi 2005 (*Lady Vengeance*)

Saam gaang yi 2004 (*Three . . . Extremes*)

Oldboy 2003

Yeoseot gae ui siseon 2003 (*If You Were Me*)

Boksuneun naui geot 2002
  (*Sympathy for Mr. Vengeance*)

Gongdong gyeongbi guyeok JSA 2000
  (*Joint Security Area*)

Simpan 1999 (*Judgement*)

Saminjo 1997

Moon is the Sun's Dream 1992

Although he exploded on to the international movie scene in 2004, Chan-wook Park had been directing feature films in South Korea for some time. Known for his sleek, dark thrillers, Park is one of the most unique and recognized talents to emerge from South Korean New Wave filmmakers.

Growing up under military government, Park had only a modest exposure to the cinema, mostly watching U.S. Westerns on TV. He entered the film industry in the late 1980s, working as an assistant director, and made his directorial debut feature with the romantic thriller *Moon is the Sun's Dream* (1992).

Park's first hit arrived with *Gongdong gyeongbi guyeok JSA* (2000) (*Joint Security Area*), a drama focusing on a murder in the demilitarized zone, and the volatile political relationship between North and South Korea. His next film, the revenge thriller *Boksuneun naui geot* (2002) (*Sympathy for Mr. Vengeance*) was the start of a trilogy. It features a consciously darker approach that utilizes sinister psychological undertones, black humor, extreme violence, and clever plot twists. Despite tepid local box-office returns, this style change would help define Park's career. The seond in the trilogy was the dark and poignant film noir *Oldboy* (2003), which tells the tale of a man who has been incarcerated in a room for fifteen years, and who on his release tries to determine the identity of his captor and why he has been imprisoned. Mirroring the aesthetic of *Sympathy for Mr. Vengeance*, *Oldboy* became the most significant film of Park's career, playing at film festivals worldwide, and winning the Grand Prix at the Cannes Film Festival. Park completed his *Vengeance* trilogy with the beautifully photographed thriller *Chinjeolhan geumjassi* (2005) (*Lady Vengeance*). **WW**

> "There is nothing wrong with fantasizing about revenge . . . . You just shouldn't act on it."

1960s

ALEX PROYAS

Born: Alex Proyas, September 23, 1963 (Egypt).

Directing style: Director of pop music videos and big-budget, dark, science-fiction movies with a detective thriller edge; use of cutting-edge special effects; moody, futuristic cityscapes.

A distinct visual stylist, Australian-based Alex Proyas is best known for his gloomy and polished science-fiction movies.

He attended the Australian Film Television and Radio School, and formed Meaningful Eye Contact Films. He eventually directed hundreds of cutting-edge pop music videos—for bands including Crowded House, INXS, Yes, and Fleetwood Mac—as well as short films, and TV commercials for companies such as American Express and Nike. With partial financing from the Australian Film Commission, Proyas made his feature debut with the futuristic thriller *Spirits of the Air, Gremlins of the Clouds* (1989).

His debut earned him little recognition, but Proyas traveled to Hollywood where, on the strength of his music videos, he landed his next project, the comic-book adaptation *The Crow* (1994). The film galvanized audiences, partly due to the tragic death of lead actor Brandon Lee, son of Bruce Lee, but mainly because Proyas delivered an inimitable vision of the future along with an emotional balance to the pulpy source material.

Proyas changed direction with his next film, the science-fiction noir *Dark City* (1998). He fused advanced technology with the influence of moody German Expressionism, predating the similarly dark paranoia and stylistic trappings of *The Matrix* (1999). Despite a poor showing at the box office, *Dark City* acquired a considerable following on video, and is Proyas's most original work to date. He returned to Hollywood with the big-budget science-fiction smash *I, Robot* (2004). The film continued Proyas's love for large-scale special effects with its futuristic cityscape, and starred Will Smith as a skeptical detective investigating a murder committed by a robot. **WW**

Top Takes...

I, Robot 2004
Garage Days 2002
Dark City 1998
Book of Dreams: "Welcome to Crateland" 1994
The Crow 1994
Spirits of the Air, Gremlins of the Clouds 1989
Spineless 1987
Strange Residues 1981
Groping 1980

"It took two years to convince my dad to buy me a camera—two years of whining."

1960s

GASPAR NOÉ

Born: Gaspar Noé, December 27, 1963 (Buenos Aires, Argentina).

Directing style: Controversial writer and director of shocking dramas; investigations of rape, revenge, violence, and justice; use of handheld camera; often casts Philippe Nahon.

Top Takes...

8 2007

Destricted 2006

Irréversible 2002 (*Irreversible*)

Seul contre tous 1998 (*I Stand Alone*)

Sodomites 1998

Carne 1991

Pulpe amère 1987

Tintarella di luna 1985

Little known outside France, where his films are a *scandale du prestige*, Argentine-born Gaspar Noé is infamous for directing the tour de force *Irréversible* (2002) (*Irreversible*). Having previously made short films such as *Carne* (1991), the story of a butcher on a vengeance kick, and the feature *Seul contre tous* (1998) (*I Stand Alone*), an expanded story about *Carne*'s butcher, *Irreversible* is a story of conception, rape, and destruction. It is also a rigorously executed exercise in style (camera movements are often handheld and out of focus); emotional manipulation (the opening is scored with a low-frequency hum intended to make audiences sick); and thematic realization (evil acts are irreversible and cannot be avenged).

Centered on the character of Alex, played by Monica Bellucci, a woman in terrible circumstances through accidents of timing, *Irreversible* is also effective as an investigation into chronology, cause and effect, and justice. Told backward in a series of chapters that focus on the events of a single day, Alex's rape motivates the men in her life to commit murder. That her boyfriend and their friend Pierre kill the wrong man is precisely the film's point. "Time destroys everything," says a character in the film, and this is the dominant message. For as the audience watches the plot unfold, from failed vengeance, to rape, to arguments at a party, to friends traveling by metro, to the central couple making love, viewers finally learn that Alex is pregnant. Having passed through one of cinema's most brutal depictions of rape, then seeing that violence reflected through the lens of pending motherhood, *Irreversible* is an astonishingly brave film that depicts the violation of both innocent womanhood and potential life in a single step. **GCQ**

> "I thought if *Irreversible* was to be useful I should portray [violence] as raw as it can be."

GUILLERMO DEL TORO

Born: Guillermo del Toro, October 9, 1964 (Guadalajara, Jalisco, Mexico).

Directing style: Writer and director of dramas, comic-book adaptations, and fantasy horror movies; themes of the Spanish Civil War; magical realism feel; fascination with the monster within.

Guillermo del Toro's films juxtapose the world of the fantastic with horrific reality. He began showcasing the esoteric with *Cronos* (1993), in which an old man transforms into a vampire in front of his granddaughter. Children witnessing the brutal realities of life are often pivotal to his plots. His first Hollywood film, *Mimic* (1997), dealt with a hive of huge insects underneath a Gothic metropolis. Children were instrumental in solving the mystery, with some of them meeting an unpleasant end.

At a young age, through meeting exiles from Spanish dictator Francisco Franco's regime, del Toro developed an awareness of the Spanish Civil War. This later inspired his Spanish epoch film, *El espinazo del diablo* (2001) (*The Devil's Backbone*), set in an orphanage haunted by a boy's ghost. A few years later, del Toro traveled to Spain to film the Arthur Rackham-influenced fable *El laberinto del fauno* (2006) (*Pan's Labyrinth*), in which a young girl living under Franco's rule meets an ancient deity. This carefully woven tale of life under fascism won del Toro an Academy Award nomination for Best Writing, Original Screenplay. One of his intervening movies, *Hellboy* (2004), showed the eponymous diabolic investigator Hellboy battling modern-day Nazis and Lovecraftian monsters.

All del Toro's films thus far employ a certain form of magical realism, available to particular age groups, occupations, creeds, or forms. Yet the nature of these worlds is always related to the protagonists entering them. Thus vampire hunters and scientists are met with damp sewers in an urban underworld, whereas children and humanity-friendly demons see a broader spectrum of creatures good, bad, and ambivalent. Del Toro's coda appears to be that monsters exist in the eye of the beholder. **LL**

Top Takes...

El laberinto del fauno 2006 (*Pan's Labyrinth*)

Hellboy 2004

Blade II 2002

El espinazo del diablo 2001 (*The Devil's Backbone*)

Mimic 1997

Cronos 1993

Geometria 1987

Doña Lupe 1985

> *"Hellboy* is the first movie where both ends of the spectrum are combined."

1960s

TOM TYKWER

Born: Tom Tykwer, May 23, 1965 (Wuppertal, Germany).

Directing style: German director of dramas and thrillers; innovative subversion of narrative; luscious, striking imagery; vibrant use of color; strong narrative; attention to period detail.

Top Takes...

Perfume: The Story of a Murderer 2006
Paris, je t'aime 2006 (*Paris, I Love You*)
True 2004
Heaven 2002
Der Krieger und die Kaiserin 2000
  (*The Princess and the Warrior*)
Lola rennt 1998 (*Run, Lola, Run*)
Winterschläfer 1997 (*Winter Sleepers*)
Die Tödliche Maria 1993 (*Deadly Maria*)
Epilog 1992
Because 1990

Tom Tykwer came to international prominence for his intriguing *Lola rennt* (1998) (*Run, Lola, Run*). Starring his former girlfriend Franka Potente in the title role, along with a thumping techno soundtrack, this dazzling speed-rush of a movie was notable for its three-part storyline. Lola has just 20 minutes to acquire a large sum of money and save her petty criminal boyfriend from an unpleasant fate—hence her constant, frantic running—but before she reaches this strict deadline, the audience is shown three different versions, and three different outcomes, of the crucial 20 minutes.

Partly a meditation on chance and fate and on how small events can have big consequences, *Run, Lola, Run* still manages to be tense, thrilling, and terse. Despite the fact that audiences are presented with various futures, which according to convention should destroy the film's tension and realism, the narrative device works by adding another level of intricacy, and of entertainment. *Run, Lola, Run* intentionally and artistically plays with the three-act structure of screenplay writing.

Tykwer's interest in cinematic art, playing with genres such as horror and the thriller, is also displayed in *Heaven* (2002), based on an outline by the revered late Polish director Krzysztof Kieslowski, and *Perfume: The Story of a Murderer* (2006). The latter is based on Patrick Süskind's novel, and is a story that many—including the legendary director Stanley Kubrick—thought was unfilmable. Tykwer renovates the genre traditions he exploits, twisting the serial killer motif toward a synesthesia of seeing smells in *Perfume*, and lending the crime thriller an existential energy in *Run, Lola, Run*. Not just art theater cinema, Tykwer's best films represent smart cinema for cinephiles expecting that little bit extra. **MH**

"I'm not this separated director, I am the audience, I go to see films, if it's possible, every day."

BRYAN SINGER

Born: Bryan Jay Singer, September 17, 1965 (New York City, New York, U.S.).

Directing style: Maker of dramas and science fiction; adaptations of the comic-book genre; themes of alienation; political comment; often uses music by composer John Ottman.

Bryan Singer has doggedly worked his way up from the ranks of the independent film world to the top of the box-office mountain. A short film, *Lion's Den* (1988), earned him attention from a Japanese production company, and encouraged Singer to reconnect with a high school friend, Christopher McQuarrie. With the Japanese investment the two made *Public Access* (1993), a political satire about the darkness that lurks behind the safe veneer of the suburbs. It was their next film, however, that made Singer a behind-the-camera star. *The Usual Suspects* (1995) was a sleeper hit that won McQuarrie an Oscar for Best Writing, Screenplay Written Directly for the Screen.

Singer's next project was *Apt Pupil* (1998), an adaptation of a Stephen King story, which turned out to be a rare, early misstep, but Singer bounced back—and then some—by helming the first two films of the *X-Men* franchise. *X-Men* (2000) approached its comic-book material with a welcome maturity, and *X-Men 2* (2003) was praised not just as a superhero film but as one of the rare sequels that bested the original.

In 2004, Singer helped with a new version of the TV show *Battlestar Galactica*. His company, Bad Hat Harry Productions, also jump-started the medical television drama *House M.D.*, with Singer directing some early episodes.

After toying with the idea of a third *X-Men* film, Singer surprised many by switching studios and swapping projects, moving on with his most ambitious and expensive project to date, a reimagining of the *Superman* franchise titled *Superman Returns* (2006). Despite costing upward of $300 million to make, the film was met with mixed critical response and relatively disappointing box-office returns. Unbowed, Singer quickly signed up to direct the film's proposed sequel. **JK**

Top Takes…

Superman Returns 2006
X-Men 2 2003
X-Men 2000
Apt Pupil 1998
The Usual Suspects 1995
Public Access 1993
Lion's Den 1988

"I love filmmaking and I love the process and I would rather do nothing else. It's a privilege."

1960s

LUCRECIA MARTEL

Born: Lucrecia Martel, December 14, 1966 (Salta, Argentina).

Directing style: Writer and director of New Argentina Cinema; maker of moving, mysterious, erotic dramas; ideas of transcendence; use of characters' physical gestures to convey and enhance meaning and mood.

Top Takes…

La niña santa 2004 (*The Holy Girl*)
La ciénaga 2001 (*The Swamp*)
Rey muerto 1995
Besos rojos 1991
Piso 24 1989
El 56 1988

Lucrecia Martel grew up in a large Roman Catholic family in a heavily conservative part of Argentina; elements of this upbringing figure prominently in her films. After studying at Buenos Aires's Escuela Nacional de Experimentación y Realización Cinematográfica, she directed a number of TV documentaries and short films. Her first feature was *La ciénaga* (2001) (*The Swamp*), which won international awards. Her follow-up, *La niña santa* (2004) (*The Holy Girl*), was selected for competition at Cannes Film Festival.

What distinguishes Martel is her extraordinary attention to detail and nuance. In *The Swamp*, she explores the seemingly off-hand moments of communication between members of a family, recognizing the resonance and revelations in such moments of intimacy. She is profoundly sensitive to the impact of silence, as well as the organic cohesion of sound and image. Nothing is frivolous within her finely composed frames. She shares a respect for gesture and expression with contemporary Mexican director Julián Hernández. Furthermore, Martel's inclination toward organic unity extends to the manner in which she shoots locations, eschewing traditional notions of establishing shots or transitions. *The Holy Girl*, about the struggle of a young Roman Catholic girl to reconcile her burgeoning sexuality with spiritual desires, pays homage to Luc Besson with the idea of transcendence firmly rooted in the physical. Such transcendence is, in fact, determined by the parameters of the material world.

> "I am interested in the Catholic religion because . . . it is where I learned a way of thinking."

Martel's work is also inspired by that of Béla Tarr. In so thoroughly acknowledging and inhabiting a corporeal universe, Martel transmutes it into something unknowable, with its essence veiled from us. **NC**

FRANÇOIS OZON

Born: François Ozon, November 15, 1967 (Paris, France).

Directing style: Daring French auteur maker of delicately crafted dramas; themes of sexual identity and gender; satirical humor; frequently casts actress Charlotte Rampling.

François Ozon studied at Paris's La Fémis film school and began filming shorts in 1988, early on plunging into sexual themes in a delicate and profound way. For example, in *Une rose entre nous* (1994) a young hairdresser is picked up by an older British woman in Paris; in *La petite mort* (1995), a young gay man wants to photograph men's faces during orgasm. The story of an Ozon film is often substantially in the viewer's imagination, as in *X 2000* (1998), where a man wanders through an apartment filled with sleeping lovers.

Sous le sable (2000) (*Under the Sand*) began an ongoing collaboration between Ozon and British actress Charlotte Rampling. Here, Rampling's character loses her husband of 25 years while sunbathing on a beach. Not knowing whether he has drowned or walked out on her, she pretends he is still there. In *Swimming Pool* (2003), Rampling plays a mystery author vacationing with her typewriter at her publisher's home in southern France; she is unprepared for the deliciously uncloseted behavior of his teenage daughter.

In *8 femmes* (2002) (*8 Women*), the octet of the title are suspects in the murder of an industrialist. As the women, including characters played by Catherine Deneuve, Isabelle Huppert, Danielle Darrieux, Fanny Ardant, Ludivine Sagnier, and Emmanuelle Béart, hunt among themselves for the murderer, they discover many other, and dirtier, secrets. The ensemble won a Silver Bear at the Berlin Film Festival. *Le temps qui reste* (2005) (*Time to Leave*) centers on a dying man and his rejection of his condition, whereas *5 x 2* (2004) dissects a romance, moving backward in time from the signing of divorce papers, through the disintegration of the union, to the happy meeting. **MP**

Top Takes...

Angel 2007
Un lever de rideau 2006
Le temps qui reste 2005 (*Time to Leave*)
5 x 2 2004
Swimming Pool 2003
8 femmes 2002 (*8 Women*)
Sous le sable 2000 (*Under the Sand*)
Les amants criminels 1999 (*Criminal Lovers*)
Scènes de lit 1998
Sitcom 1998
X 2000 1998
Regarde la mer 1997 (*See the Sea*)
L'homme idéal 1996
Une robe d'été 1996 (*A Summer Dress*)
La petite mort 1995
Une rose entre nous 1994

"I wanted moments, expressions, very few words, an atmosphere, some sensations."

1960s

ROBERT RODRIGUEZ

Born: Robert Anthony Rodriguez, June 20, 1968 (San Antonio, Texas, U.S.).

Directing style: Enfant terrible of low-budget action films, and later Hollywood blockbusters and children's movies; numerous collaborations with Quentin Tarantino; often casts Antonio Banderas; innovative special effects.

Top Takes...

The Adventures of Sharkboy
   and Lavagirl 3-D 2005
Sin City 2005
Once Upon a Time in Mexico 2003
Spy Kids 3-D: Game Over 2003
Spy Kids 2: Island of Lost Dreams 2002
Spy Kids 2001
The Faculty 1998
From Dusk Till Dawn 1996
Four Rooms 1995
Desperado 1995
El Mariachi 1992
Bedhead 1991

Taking do-it-yourself methods to inspiring extremes, Robert Rodriguez helped revolutionize low-budget filmmaking with *El Mariachi* (1992) before ultimately recalibrating the notion of independence as a one-man writer, director, producer, editor, composer, and special effects man. With *El Mariachi* Rodriguez used invention to surmount seeming limitations; ironically the limitations of the story hampered that film's big-budget remake *Desperado* (1995). On *Four Rooms* (1995) Rodriguez worked with Quentin Tarantino; he then filmed a Tarantino script, *From Dusk Till Dawn* (1996). A rote Hollywood science-fiction movie, *The Faculty* (1998), sent Rodriguez in the other direction, making films fit for kids, including his own, beginning with *Spy Kids* (2001), and its two sequels.

Rodriguez then set up shop in Texas at his own studio-ranch production company, working on *Once Upon a Time in Mexico* (2003), a film that served as a testing ground for the aptly named Troublemaker Studios. His next project, the dark comic-book adaptation *Sin City* (2005), was Rodriguez's most ambitious film to date. Shot digitally and made free from Hollywood interference, *Sin City* created an almost entirely computer-designed, special-effects world that allowed shooting on a shoestring budget around the busy schedule of the famous cast. Rodriguez also famously dropped out of the Directors Guild of America because the organization refused permission for comic-book artist and *Sin City* creator Frank Miller to have a codirecting credit. Another kids movie, *The Adventures of Sharkboy and Lavagirl 3-D* (2005), followed before Rodriguez started work on another Tarantino collaboration, *Grindhouse* (2007), an homage to the trashy genre films they devoured while growing up. **JK**

> "I always ask for less money than we need so that you have to be more creative."

LUKAS MOODYSSON

Born: Karl Frederik Lukas Moodysson, October 17, 1969 (Malmö, Sweden).

Directing style: Swedish writer and director of tragicomedies; religious themes; explorations of the nature of community and human dignity; often stories of coming-of-age teenagers.

Lukas Moodysson has developed into one of the most important contemporary Swedish filmmakers since Ingmar Bergman. His breakthrough hit was *Fucking Åmål* (1998) (*Show Me Love*), in which two girls cope with the boredom of small-town life and their budding sexuality in ways that cause consternation to their parents and neighbors. In addition to getting superb performances out of his neophyte actors, Moodysson displayed a keen ear for dialogue, and a knack for moving between tragedy and comedy at a moment's notice.

This was followed by the comedy drama *Tillsammans* (2000) (*Together*), chronicling the life of a commune during the 1970s, and the attendant personal and romantic struggles of the various members of this supposedly utopian social experiment. *Lilja 4-ever* (2002) is another compelling drama, in which sixteen-year-old Lilja is abandoned by her mother in a shabby apartment in the former Soviet Union, and is subsequently reduced to prostitution as a result. A way out seems to present itself when a young man offers to take her to Sweden with him, but as Lilja finds out, the dream of freedom that the move represents comes with a high price. Moodysson has since moved into far more experimental territory with the film *Container* (2006), shot in stark black and white, an almost inaccessible personal allegory, which was indifferently received by both critics and audiences. *Container* would seem to be a detour from Moodysson's more humanistic work and, for many, the film is all but unwatchable. But Moodysson's career is just beginning, and the impact of his three key movies indicates that he will return to the human dimension of his earlier works, and expand upon them in the years to come. **WWD**

Top Takes...

Ett hål i mitt hjärta 2004 (*A Hole in My Heart*)
Terrorister—en film om dom dömda 2003 (*Terrorists: The Kids They Sentenced*)
Lilja 4-ever 2002
Tillsammans 2000 (*Together*)
Fucking Åmål 1998 (*Show Me Love*)
Bara prata lite 1997 (*Talk*)
En uppgörelse i den undre världen 1996
Det var en mörk och stormig natt 1995

"Rehearsing can make things stale, you lose the natural and spontaneous energy."

1960s

DARREN ARONOFSKY

Born: Darren Aronofsky, December 2, 1969 (Brooklyn, New York, U.S.).

Directing style: Maker of surrealistic psychological dramas and thrillers; intellectual content; use of camera rigged to the body of the actor; hip-hop montage technique.

Top Takes...

The Fountain 2006
Requiem for a Dream 2000
Pi 1998
Protozoa 1993
Fortune Cookie 1991
Supermarket Sweep 1991

Darren Aronofsky studied anthropology, live-action film, and animation at Harvard. He burst on to the cinephile scene with *Pi* (1998). Sometimes described as a thriller, the film's depiction of obsession and its black and white artistry marked it out as indie surrealism fused with offbeat philosophizing. Despite its super-low budget, the film creates a weirdly compelling world in which mathematics threatens to reveal the ultimate, unifying order of life. In the end, this quest for a perfect order is shown to be a kind of madness.

Aronofsky is drawn to characters in the grip of compulsion and addiction. *Requiem for a Dream* (2000), like *Pi*, is powered by its protagonists' desperation and their descent into various private hells. It examines drug addiction through a range of characters, and succeeds in producing an impressively intense and visceral sense of how these addictions degrade not only bodies, but also peoples' minds, their perceptions, and ultimately their self-worth. With its powerfully rhythmic, repetitive editing, there is something alluring about the poster-boy druggies of *Requiem for a Dream*. Hard-hitting content is combined with an aesthetic glaze and a surrealist edge, producing a buzz of cinematic art, as well as being a cautionary tale. *The Fountain* (2006) returns to the intense territory of people who can't fit in, who will not ever fit in. Here, the difference separating the male lead, played by Hugh Jackman, from those around him is not mathematical obsession or drug addiction, but potential immortality. Like *Pi* and *Requiem for a Dream*, *The Fountain* centers on the self-isolation of a character trapped in his own bubble of existence. Whether by choice or compulsion, Aronofsky's films ask if everyone is fatally trapped in their own private worlds. **MH**

> "I'm godless. I've had to make my own God, and my God is narrative filmmaking."

1960s

WES ANDERSON

Born: Wesley Wales Anderson, May 1, 1969 (Houston, Texas, U.S.).

Directing style: Auteur maker of quirky comedies; underwater shots; themes of communication; often casts Bill Murray; artistic collaborations with actor and writer Owen Wilson.

King of literary geek chic on the silver screen, Wes Anderson emerged from the U.S. movie underground an almost ready-made savant. Remarkably quickly, his quirky, off-kilter films neatly established Anderson almost as a genre unto himself.

Anderson studied philosophy at the University of Texas, where he met frequent future collaborator Owen Wilson. The two worked together to make a short version of what was to become Anderson's feature debut, *Bottle Rocket* (1996), which starred and was cowritten by Wilson. The film did not do well at the box office, but its cult success gave Anderson a big career boost—director Martin Scorsese, among others, often claims to be a huge fan.

Anderson's next film, also written with Owen Wilson, was *Rushmore* (1998), the story of an unusual love triangle between a school teacher, her student, and a businessman that earned comedian Bill Murray numerous accolades and brought Anderson his most acclaim to date. The absurdist comedy *The Royal Tenenbaums* (2001) followed, telling the tale of a family of disillusioned young geniuses who are reunited with their estranged father, played by Gene Hackman. If the film featured an expanded A-list ensemble cast, it was still reminiscent of the style of Anderson's earlier works—perhaps this was the result of having also been cowritten with Wilson. Wilson costarred in but did not write Anderson's next movie, the Murray starrer *The Life Aquatic with Steve Zissou* (2004), the director instead teaming with friend and fellow filmmaker Noah Baumbach. The results were noticeably weaker although no less quirky. Anderson's upcoming projects are *The Darjeeling Limited*, with Roman Coppola, and an adaptation of Roald Dahl's children's book, *Fantastic Mr. Fox*. **JK**

Top Takes...

The Life Aquatic with Steve Zissou 2004
The Royal Tenenbaums 2001
Rushmore 1998
Bottle Rocket 1996

> "I like characters when they're aspiring to something beyond their grasp."

1960s

THOMAS VINTERBERG

Born: Thomas Vinterberg, May 19, 1969 (Copenhagen, Denmark).

Directing style: Cofounder of Danish Dogme Brethren and maker of dramas; emphasis on purity of location; use of handheld camera; intoxicating action sequences; forgoing of special effects.

Top Takes...

Dear Wendy 2005

It's All About Love 2003

The Third Lie 2000

Festen 1998 (*The Celebration*)

De største helte 1996 (*The Biggest Heroes*)

Drengen der gik baglæns 1994
  (*The Boy Who Walked Backwards*)

Sidste omgang 1993 (*Last Round*)

Sneblind 1990

Coauthor of Dogme95, Thomas Vinterberg made Dogme's first and most influential film and became a figurehead for the independent renaissance of the 1990s. Raised in a commune, Vinterberg was the youngest student accepted to the Danske Filmskole. He had made only one feature before *Festen* (1998) (*The Celebration*) won the Cannes Film Festival Jury Prize.

Less radical than anti-bourgeois, the film was constructed around a wealthy patriarch's sixtieth birthday, when the elder son exposes the honoree as an incestuous child abuser. A brilliant cast and Vinterberg's inspired approach lent a quasipolitical edge to this family melodrama. Discomfortingly intimate digital-camera work and an increasingly grainy, decomposing image complemented the struggle within a deteriorating patriarchal regime.

It's All About Love (2003), a mix of science fiction, fantasy, romance, and thriller in English with international stars, left Dogme behind, fusing formal elements such as color, lighting, and jarring sound in place of special effects. Inspired by the publicity-crazed detachment of Vinterberg's post-Dogme years, the film literalized a concept of the twenty-first century as an emotional ice age—and regrettably left audiences cold.

With *Dear Wendy* (2005), about West Virginian teenagers with a gun fetish who unsuccessfully attempt to remain pacifists, Vinterberg collaborated with his Dogme brother Lars von Trier. Vinterberg's direction brought warmth, realism, and chracteristic action sequences to von Trier's cerebral screenplay, but the film is often discredited as a European diatribe against U.S. gun culture. More accurately, it is divided between critique and celebration, and between von Trier's and Vinterberg's varied strengths. **LB**

"I was raised to be humble, but this business doesn't allow for that kind of thing."

SPIKE JONZE

Born: Adam Spiegel, October 22, 1969 (Rockville, Maryland, U.S.).

Directing style: Director of pop music videos and commercials, documentaries, and quirky dramas; playful, puzzling narratives; striking visuals; artistic collaborations with screenwriter Charlie Kaufman.

Born in suburban Maryland, the freshly minted Spike Jonze dabbled in low-key journalism and skateboarding culture before finding his calling directing several clever, noteworthy, and now, iconic music videos and commercials, among them clips for Weezer, Björk, the Beastie Boys, and Fatboy Slim. Several of Jonze's videos have even since eclipsed the songs and artists they were intended to support.

Top Takes…

Adaptation 2002
***Being John Malkovich* 1999** ☆
Torrance Rises 1999
Amarillo by Morning 1998
How They Get There 1997

Following several short films, documentaries, experiments, and pranks, Jonze connected with screenwriter Charlie Kaufman for the highly acclaimed *Being John Malkovich* (1999). The film has been rightly praised as one of the most inventive in recent memory, although Jonze's handling of such unique material was surprisingly restrained. Around the same time Jonze married fellow filmmaker Sofia Coppola (although they divorced in 2003), and appeared as an actor in his friend David O. Russell's Gulf War adventure *Three Kings* (1999), while all the time managing to maintain his ties to the cool underground.

Jonze's second film, *Adaptation* (2002), drawn from another puzzle box of a script by Kaufman—a confusing and amusing tale of a screenwriter struggling to adapt a book about orchids into a film—made him the go-to guy for hip projects. The critics were divided, despite the movie's stellar cast—including Nicolas Cage—and great performances, but the public was more enthusiastic. Since *Adaptation* Jonze has appeared to be taking his time making careful career choices. He is currently at work on a third Kaufman collaboration, as well as a big-screen adaptation of Maurice Sendak's classic children's book *Where the Wild Things Are* (1963), a hybrid of live action and animation in collaboration with writer Dave Eggers. **JK**

> "I try to figure out the idea of the film we are making and let the style be dictated by that."

PAUL THOMAS ANDERSON

Born: Paul Thomas Anderson, June 26, 1970 (Studio City, California, U.S.).

Directing style: Writer and director of character-driven dramas; nostalgic themes recalling the 1970s and 1980s; Altman-like use of ensemble cast; interweaving storylines of characters.

Top Takes...

There Will Be Blood 2007
Punch-Drunk Love 2002
Magnolia 1999
Boogie Nights 1997
Sydney 1996
Cigarettes & Coffee 1993
The Dirk Diggler Story 1988

Paul Thomas Anderson is a writer and director of ensemble pictures filled with moving cameras, multi-layered plots, suburban angst, unusual views of everyday situations, and the collision of unrelated people forced into life-changing confrontation. He experimented with moviemaking as a teenager, making the documentary short *The Dirk Diggler Story* (1988), about the rise and fall of the 1970s porn movie star of the title. Anderson then enrolled in the New York University film school, but dropped out after only two days to make the short *Cigarettes & Coffee* (1993) before crewing on TV commercials and pop music videos.

Developed through The Sundance Lab, Anderson's feature debut was *Sydney* (1996), the story of a wise guy looking out for a simpleton. Not widely released, *Sydney* nonetheless led to *Boogie Nights* (1997), the director's breakout hit about the 1970s world of pornography seen through the eyes of a dysfunctional professional family, and the feature adaptation of his earlier short about Diggler.

Anderson became heir apparent to the style of Robert Altman, and has affirmed this thematic connection in the long, difficult, and brilliant *Magnolia* (1999), a community snapshot of a day in many people's lives connected by a series of coincidences. Featured players in the Anderson family reappeared, but it was Tom Cruise's acid turn as Frank T. J. Mackey that set audiences talking. Anderson then directed *Punch-Drunk Love* (2002), a darkly comic take on an eccentric salesman who falls in love and is played, against type, by Adam Sandler. Based on the broader appeal of his star vehicles, Anderson is now more bankable, although his slice of cinema remains devoted to character-driven dramas. **GCQ**

"I guess the way I feel is that *Magnolia* is, for better or worse, the best movie I'll ever make."

CHRISTOPHER NOLAN

Born: Christopher Johnathan James Nolan, July 30, 1970 (London, England).

Directing style: British director of character-driven dramas; narrative trickery and surprising endings; frequently casts actor Larry Holden; use of flashback; often antiheroic characters.

British director Christopher Nolan broke through as a director of note with his film *Memento* (2000). The star of this movie is really its story, told in a fractured and backward nonlinear way that emphasizes the fact that its antihero cannot form any new memories. All of this could have been desperately gimmicky, but Nolan put it to work in the service of a carefully orchestrated thriller. The film's themes more than justified its tricksy telling, and from its opening frames—played in reverse, of course—*Memento* offered that rare thing: style and substance in consummate harmony. Some of *Memento*'s narrative tricks were prefigured in Nolan's earlier film *Following* (1998), which also wedded the viewer to one character's perspective.

In the wake of *Memento*'s success, Nolan developed his core directorial interests, choosing to focus on the dark character-driven psychologies and damaged masculinities on show in remake *Insomnia* (2002), and franchiser *Batman Begins* (2005), which was notable for his attempts to shirk special effects and concentrate on character development.

If "The Dark Knight" himself represents the furthest Nolan has yet pushed his line in antiheroic, dangerous male characters while still achieving commercial success, then the dramatic thriller *The Prestige* (2006) set in Victorian England offers up another characteristic interest: the director as a kind of magician. Whereas *Memento* plays an audacious trick on its audiences because of its surprising ending, *The Prestige* directly takes trickery and magic as its storyline's starting points. Magic as a metaphor for film direction has fascinated others across the history of cinema but perhaps here those same connections are being reimagined for a new generation of film lovers. **MH**

Top Takes...

The Prestige 2006
Batman Begins 2005
Insomnia 2002
Memento 2000
Following 1998
Doodlebug 1997

> "There's a very limited pool of finance in the UK . . . it's a very clubby kind of place."

1970s

M. NIGHT SHYAMALAN

Born: Manoj Nelliyattu Shyamalan, August 6, 1970 (Mahé, Pondicherry, India).

Directing style: Writer and director of shocking dramas with a horror movie feel; surprise endings; frequently casts Bruce Willis; cameo appearances in his films; uses child actors.

Top Takes...

Lady in the Water 2006
The Village 2004
Signs 2002
Unbreakable 2000
The Sixth Sense 1999 ☆
Wide Awake 1998
Praying with Anger 1992

The son of two doctors, M. Night Shyamalan began making movies in boyhood and modeled his career on idols such as Steven Spielberg. After two independent, autobiographically motivated but barely seen films, *Praying with Anger* (1992) and *Wide Awake* (1998), he wrote and directed the smash hit that melded drama, horror, and thriller, *The Sixth Sense* (1999). He was twenty-eight years old and managed to successfully write a trick narrative, whereby a critical detail is left out of the screen story until an important, climactic revelation uncovers this provocative and meaningful truth—shocking audiences, and changing the movie's meaning in an instant. Centered on the story of a boy who sees ghosts, the movie also remade the flagging career of Bruce Willis and put the phrase "I see dead people" in the popular lingo.

For his efforts, Shyamalan earned Golden Globe and Oscar nominations for writing and directing, and was thereafter able to establish a moviemaking empire in his home state of Pennsylvania, which has been the setting for each of his subsequent features. *Unbreakable* (2000), the story of an ordinary man with superhuman durability, was followed by *Signs* (2002), the story of a Midwestern farmer whose lands become the epicenter of an otherworldly invasion. Both movies saw him reprise his previous collaboration with Willis. Audiences were disappointed by the former but delighted with the latter. The confusion over whether to embrace Shyamalan continued with *The Village* (2004), the story of a community beset by evil demons. *Lady in the Water* (2006) tells the story of a water nymph's troubles spilling over into the lives of a resort hotel's inhabitants, but was a commercial failure. **GCQ**

> "The idea is to always go for the thing that's risky. I want to be courageous and original."

RIGHT: What can Bruce Willis and Haley Joel Osment see in *The Sixth Sense*?

1970s

ALEJANDRO AMENÁBAR

Born: Alejandro Fernando Amenábar Cantos, March 31, 1972 (Santiago de Chile, Chile).

Directing style: Writer and director of horror movies and dark, psychological thrillers; composes film scores; uses nightmarish flashbacks; surprise endings.

Top Takes...

Mar adentro 2004 (*The Sea Inside*)
The Others 2001
Abre los ojos 1997 (*Open Your Eyes*)
Tesis 1996 (*Thesis*)
Luna 1995
Himenóptero 1992

Chilean-born Alejandro Amenábar has rapidly established himself as a writer and director of note. Whether working on Spanish genre titles such as the horror thriller *Tesis* (1996) (*Thesis*), or the fantasy of *Abre los ojos* (1997) (*Open Your Eyes*), Amenábar has brought sophistication and ambition to a range of projects. *Thesis* features students mysteriously disappearing from university as one particular film student, Angela, investigates the appeal of horror movies for her thesis. The film combines a movie fan's knowingness with edge-of-your-seat scares. At the same time, it sides with Angela's investigation into screen violence, commenting on its own status as a horror movie. *Thesis* shows Amenábar's willingness to challenge and entertain audiences; something that *Open Your Eyes* develops by playing with the idea of what is real within its storyline.

The Others (2001), a vehicle for Nicole Kidman, carried Amenábar into the Hollywood system, and achieved notoriety thanks to its jaw-dropping twist ending.

Amenábar has proven his credentials outside the horror genre, taking an emotive and intelligent style of storytelling into the mainstream with *Mar adentro* (2004) (*The Sea Inside*). This won an Oscar for Best Foreign Language Film, and tells the tale of real-life quadriplegic, Spaniard Ramón Sampedro, who wishes to take his own life, even though this is against Spanish law. As Sampedro fights for his right to determine his own fate, *The Sea Inside* represents a moving exploration of some difficult issues, displaying Amenábar's trademark interest in dark subject matter. Yet this darkness tends to be combined in his films with a surprisingly mannered approach, whether in the stylized setting of *The Others*, or via the student investigation storyline of *Thesis*. **MH**

"If this story doesn't deserve to be told, that's the end of movie making to me."—On *The Sea Inside*

DAVID GORDON GREEN

Born: David Gordon Green, April 9, 1975 (Little Rock, Arkansas, U.S.).

Directing style: Writer and director of graceful, Southern Gothic coming-of-age dramas; themes of life in small-town and rural communities, and the effects of economic deprivation.

David Gordon Green studied directing at the North Carolina School of the Arts. During this time he made several short films, including *Pleasant Grove* (1996) and *Physical Pinball* (1998). These early pieces evidenced Green's interest in the ways small towns or rural environments, along with economic impoverishment, can impact people's lives. They also reveal Green's fascination with the natural optimism of children.

His technique was further refined in his first feature film, the much celebrated *George Washington* (2000) about a group of teenagers in the Deep South. The critical adulation was not misplaced because Green's accomplishment was quite significant. He managed to blend and balance a number of seemingly conflicting styles and influences. These include Charles Burnett's *Killer of Sheep* (1977), with its emphasis on the tolls of poverty upon an African-American urban family; Terrence Malick's first features, with their self-conscious poetic naturalism; and the surreal vistas of Harmony Korine, which seek to explore the extremes of social maladjustment. Green successfully emerged with his own unique vision.

What has made that vision distinctive and has carried through into his later work, *All the Real Girls* (2003) and *Undertow* (2004), is his sincerely felt sympathy toward his characters. Certainly, his work has tended to center on characters on the social fringe and continues to draw clear inspiration from William Faulkner's Southern Gothic literature. It comes as little surprise then that Green's name has been circulated in connection with a possible adaptation of John Kennedy Toole's *A Confederacy of Dunces* (1980), a novel highly regarded for its detailed and humane portrait of social misfits. **NC**

Top Takes...

Snow Angels 2007
Undertow 2004
All the Real Girls 2003
George Washington 2000
Physical Pinball 1998
Pleasant Grove 1996

"It's probably my knee-jerk reaction . . . to go find the oddball version."

1970s

CONTRIBUTORS

Geoff Andrew (GA) is Head of Film Programme at London's National Film Theatre and Contributing Editor to *Time Out London* magazine. He has written studies of Nicholas Ray and the U.S. "indie" filmmakers of the 1980s and 1990s, and monographs on Kiarostami's *10* and Kieslowski's *Three Colours* trilogy.

Linda Badley (LB), a professor of English at Middle Tennessee State University, has published widely on horror and science-fiction film, coedited *Traditions in World Cinema*, and is currently at work on books on Lars von Trier and American commercial-independent film.

Aleksandar Becanovic (AB) is a Montenegrin writer and film critic.

Richard Bell (RB) studied Visual Cultures at the University of Derby and Publishing at the London College of Printing. He currently works for an educational publisher and as a freelance writer.

Heidi Bollich (HB) writes on books and film and lives in New York.

Edward Buscombe (EB) has written several books on the American Western and is Visiting Professor of Film at the University of Sunderland.

Nathaniel Carlson (NC) is a film critic for *Fever Pitch* magazine.

Garrett Chaffin-Quiray (GCQ) is a writer and teacher living in San Diego County.

Laura Clayton (LC) is a freelance writer and avid cinemagoer based in London.

Matthew Coniam (MC) is a freelance writer specializing in vintage cinema, culture, science, philosophy, and other disreputable topics.

Guy Crucianelli (GC) is a graduate of the University of Wisconsin-Parkside. He has written for the anthology, *Monstrous Adaptations: Generic and Thematic Mutations in Horror Film*.

Wheeler Winston Dixon (WWD) is the James Ryan Endowed Professor of Film Studies, Professor of English at the University of Nebraska–Lincoln, and coeditor-in-chief of the *Quarterly Review of Film and Video*.

Tim Evans (TE) is reviews editor for Skymovies. com. Born in London, he worked as a British Rail signals technician before becoming a journalist specializing in news and latterly film.

Ken Hanke (KH) is an award-winning film critic for the *Mountain Xpress* (Asheville, NC) and has written books on Ken Russell, Tim Burton, and the films of Charlie Chan, as well as serving as associate editor for *Scarlet Street* magazine.

Bernd Herzogenrath (BH) teaches American Studies at the University of Cologne, Germany, and, in 2006, has finally returned Edgar G. Ulmer to his birth home in Olomouc, Czech Republic.

Matt Hills (MH) is a Reader in Media & Cultural Studies at Cardiff University, Wales, and author of *The Pleasures of Horror* (Continuum).

Reynold Humphries (ReH) has authored *Fritz Lang: Genre and Representation in His American Films*, *The American Horror Film: An Introduction*, and *The Hollywood Horror Film, 1931-1941: Madness in a Social Landscape*. His new book is *Hollywood's Blacklists: A Political and Cultural History*.

Russ Hunter (RH) is a Doctoral candidate at the University of Wales, Aberystwyth. He is currently researching the cross-cultural reception of the films of Dario Argento.

Neil Jackson (NJ) has a PhD from the University of Westminster. He has contributed to *Critical Guides to Contemporary North American Directors* and *British and Irish Directors* (Wallflower Press), and to *Post Script* and *Video Watchdog*.

David Kalat (DK) is a film historian, author, and DVD producer with All Day Entertainment, an independent DVD label dedicated to "movies that fell through the cracks."

Alexia Kannas (AK) is a PhD candidate at Monash University. Her research areas include American and European exploitation cinema and genre theory.

Philip Kemp (PK) is a freelance reviewer and film historian, and contributor to *Sight & Sound*, *Total Film*, and *DVD Review*. He teaches Film Journalism at Leicester and Middlesex Universities.

Carol King (CK) is a freelance writer and editor who fell in love with cinema on her first trip to the movies to see *Snow White*. She graduated in English Literature from the University of Sussex, and also studied Fine Art at Central St. Martin's.

Joshua Klein (JK) writes regularly for the *Chicago Tribune*, *Time Out Chicago*, and *Pitchfork Media*.

Frank Lafond (FL), PhD, teaches Film Studies in Lille, France, and has published a book on Jacques Tourneur.

Lauri Loytokoski (LL) is a Finnish film writer and researcher with a penchant for horror.

Ernest Mathijs (EM) writes on cult cinema. He is Assistant Professor of Film and Drama at the University of British Columbia. He is the author of *The Cult Film Reader*, *The Cinema of David Cronenberg*, and *Watching The Lord of the Rings*.

Maitland McDonagh (MM) is the senior movies editor for TVGuide.com and the author of *Broken Mirrors/Broken Minds: The Dark Dreams of Dario Argento* and *Movie Lust: Recommended Viewing for Every Mood, Moment and Reason*.

Jay McRoy (JM) is Associate Professor of English and Cinema Studies at the University of Wisconsin-Parkside. He is the editor of *Japanese Horror Cinema* (Edinburgh UP), coeditor of *Monstrous Adaptations: Generic and Thematic Mutations in Horror Film* (Manchester UP), and author of *Nightmare Japan* (Rodopi).

Karen Morden (KM) is a writer and editor. She has a PhD in Media and Cultural Studies and works at an art gallery.

Kim Newman (KN) is a novelist, critic, and broadcaster. He is a contributing editor to *Sight & Sound* and *Empire*.

Dejan Ognjanovic (DO) has published two books (on the devil in cinema, and on Serbian horror films), contributed to the BFI's *100 European Horror Films*, and writes regularly about Asian cinema for www.kfccinema.com.

R. Barton Palmer (BP) is Calhoun Lemon Professor of Literature and Director of Film Studies at Clemson University. He is the author or editor of numerous books on film and literary subjects.

Claire Perkins (CP) is completing a PhD on contemporary American commercial-independent filmmaking at Monash University, Australia.

Murray Pomerance (MP) has written extensively on film and is the author of *An Eye for Hitchcock*, *Johnny Depp Starts Here*, and editor of *City That Never Sleeps: New York and the Filmic Imagination*.

Peter Schulze (PS) teaches Cinema at the Department of Film Studies at the University of Mainz, Germany. His publications include a book on Glauber Rocha from a postcolonial perspective.

Erica Sheerin (ES) is a Mass Communications major at the University of California, Berkeley.

Aaron Smuts (AS) earned his PhD in philosophy at the University of Wisconsin-Madison, where he also studied film. He primarily works in metaethics and the philosophy of art.

Marcus Stiglegger (MS) is lecturer of film studies at the University of Mainz, Germany, and has written and edited several books on film history, aesthetics, and theory.

Samuel J. Umland (SU) is Professor of English and Film Studies at the University of Nebraska at Kearney. He is coauthor with Rebecca Umland of *Donald Cammell: A Life on the Wild Side*.

Constantine Verevis (CV) is senior lecturer in Film & Television Studies at Monash University, Melbourne. He is the author of *Film Remakes*.

Mark Wall (MW) is a film critic and enthusiast based in Middlesbrough, North East England.

Wm. Scott Whited (WSW) is a veteran of the film & television industry in Los Angeles. Earning his B.A. in Theatre at the University of Iowa and his M.A. in English from the University of California, he now teaches film and theater at Colorado State University–Pueblo.

Darryl Wiggers (DW) is a BFA graduate of York University and most recently Director of Programming for the horror channel SCREAM in Canada.

Andy Willis (AW) teaches film and media studies at the University of Salford, England.

William Sean Wilson (WW) is a film writer who currently resides in Williamsburg, Virginia. He graduated from The College of William & Mary with a degree in Literary and Cultural Studies.

GLOSSARY

Anime
A popular style of Japanese animation that originates from comic book cartoon drawings. Although it is used across many genres, anime is often associated with children's fantasy films and adult science fiction.

Avanspettacolo
Translates literally as "curtain raiser" and is a successful style of Italian musical revue that predated television. It has its roots in variety theater and takes the shape of a short, often poorly presented performance that nevertheless thrills its audiences.

Bullet-time
A computer-generated slow motion effect that enables a shot to be slowed down enough to follow the path of a bullet, for example, while the point-of-view shot continues at a normal pace.

Chanchada
Brazilian musical comedy popular between the 1930s and 1960s. *Chanchada* gets its name from the slang for "trash" or "trick," and later became an umbrella term for all lightweight Brazilian comedy.

Cinéma vérité
French term meaning "cinema of truth." The genre has its roots in documentary filmmaking, using "real" people in "real" locations, and employs stylized camera techniques. Often filmmakers endeavor to provoke reactions from their subjects.

Close-up
A camera shot used to emphasize the importance of its subject or to show detail. The close-up tightly frames the subject, typically an actor's face.

Commedia all'italiana
A genre of Italian comedy films popular during the 1950s, commonly threaded with an element of morality. The term was used, by some, in contempt.

Crosscutting
Term for an editing technique used to interweave between action shots that occur simultaneously. The pace of cutting between the shots is varied to enhance a theme or to create dramatic tension.

Cut-up technique
A random cutting technique through which a conventional storyline is given a new and less obvious interpretation. First used in feature films by Nicolas Roeg and Donald Cammell.

Dissolve
Term for a smooth editing technique whereby one scene gradually fades out and is replaced by another. The pace of the transition often determines the time frame of the action.

Dolly shot
Also known as a tracking shot, the camera is mounted on a truck that is moved along rails

while the shot is being filmed. The technique is commonly used to focus in on or pull away from the action. It is subtly different from a zoom shot.

Flashback
A scene that appears out of chronological sequence and depicts an event that occurred earlier in the narrative. Flashbacks are frequently used to fill in background information.

Giallo
Italy's particular twist on the mystery genre, dominated by elaborate, show-stopping murder sequences and an overwhelming air of perversity.

Hays Code
Also known as the Production Code, the Hays Code was a set of regulatory guidelines drawn up in the 1930s to censor the film industry. The regulations were strict and made clear that the depiction of sex, crime, violence, and other such activities was not morally acceptable onscreen. Enforcement of the Code was abandoned in the late 1960s.

Hip-hop montage technique
Sequence of images shown in fast motion with accompanying sound effects, usually shown to simulate a certain action, for example, taking drugs.

House Un-American Activities Committee
A committee of the House of Representatives that, in 1947, investigated alleged incidences of communist propaganda within the film industry. Many artists were blacklisted and subsequently dropped by their respective studios, some never to resurrect their careers.

Iris shot
A lens-masking technique used to focus attention on a specific element of a scene. Much of the shot is blacked out to leave a limited view through a keyhole or chink in the door, as defined by the director.

J-Horror
A Japanese horror genre that focuses on psychological drama and high levels of tension. The films are often remakes of classic horror movies and tell tales of ghosts and spirits rather than blood and gore.

Match moving
A special effects technique that tracks the movement of the camera during a shot. The movement is replicated in a computer program to allow two- or three-dimensional computer-generated images to be inserted into live action footage.

Method acting
Pioneered by Konstantin Stanislavski and made popular by Lee Strasberg, Method acting is a demanding technique that requires actors to analyze the emotional motivation of their character to facilitate a more realistic performance. Performers are encouraged to draw parallels with their own life experiences to inform their characterization.

Mise-en-scène
The artistic elements that contribute to the visual appearance of a scene, including the set, props, costumes, and types of camera shots used. Also used to describe a scene whose appearance conveys the mood of a character or situation without the need for dialogue and in a nonrealistic manner.

Pinku eiga (Pink film)
A style of Japanese soft-core pornographic film that follows strict censorship rules in Japan. Popular in the 1970s and 1980s.

Pre-Code
Movies made in the 1920s and 1930s before the Hays Code was enforced in 1934. Typically the films enjoyed risqué subject matter and a liberal attitude to moral correctness.

Rotoscoping
A precision animation technique in which live action is traced either by hand or more commonly in a computer program. It brings a realistic element to animated movies and can be used as a special effects technique.

Splatstick
A hybrid of the splatter movie and the slapstick style, this genre uses excessive blood and gore to comedic effect within a horror remit.

Stop trick
A simple and highly effective special effect whereby an object seems to disappear from view. The technique was discovered accidentally by George Méliès whose camera malfunctioned and lost a few frames, thus creating the illusion that the object of the shot vanished.

Time-lapse photography
Used to portray the development of a typically slow process, for example the growth of a plant. Frames are captured at regular intervals but at a slow rate, and then projected at a normal cinematic speed to give the impression of time lapsing.

The Kuleshov Effect
A montage technique pioneered in 1918 by Lev Kuleshov to demonstrate the importance of movie editing. The same image of an actor's face was shown alternately with other images. Audiences believed that the expression of the actor changed in reaction to the shots in between. The viewers were surprised to learn that, in fact, they had projected their own responses to the images on to the blank canvas of the actor's face, which remained unchanged.

Wuxia
A popular martial arts genre whose narratives feature heroic figures from Chinese mythology. Typical dramatic devices include skillful swordsmanship, weapons infused with magical properties, elaborate lairs, and superfluous yet impressive flying sequences.

Yakuza
Term for organized crime groups in Japan—the Japanese mafia.

INDEX

PICTURE CREDITS

Many of the images that appear below are from the archives of The Kobal Collection, which seeks to collect, organize, preserve, and make available the publicity images issued by the film production and distribution companies to promote their films. Every effort has been made to credit the copyright holders of the images used in this book. We apologize in advance for any unintentional omissions or errors and will be pleased to insert the appropriate acknowledgment to any companies or individuals in any subsequent edition of the work.

8 The Kobal Collection 10 The Kobal Collection 11 Mandelbaum/Everett/Rex Features 12 The Kobal Collection 13 Getty Images 14 Fox Films 15 Getty Images 16 The Kobal Collection 16 The Kobal Collection 17 Epoch/The Kobal Collection 18 Wark Producing Company/The Kobal Collection 19 Getty Images 20 MGM/The Kobal Collection 21 Bettmann/Corbis 23 Paramount/The Kobal Collection 24 Tavin/Everett/Rex Features 24 MGM/The Kobal Collection 25 Universal/The Kobal Collection 26 The Kobal Collection 27 Roger-Viollet/Rex Features 28 Everett Collection/Rex Features 29 Snap/Rex Features 30 Ronald Grant Archive 31 Time & Life Pictures/Getty Images 32 Roger Viollet/Getty Images 33 The Kobal Collection 34 Getty Images 35 The Kobal Collection 36 Getty Images 37 Bettmann/Corbis 38 The Kobal Collection 39 The Kobal Collection 40 Fox Films/The Kobal Collection 40 The Kobal Collection 41 Everett Collection/Rex Features 42 Everett Collection/Rex Features 42 Societe Generale de Films/The Kobal Collection 43 Palladium/The Kobal Collection 44 The Kobal Collection 45 Everett Collection/Rex Features 46 Snap/Rex Features 46 Snap/Rex Features 47 Snap/Rex Features 48 Lipnitski/Roger-Viollet/Rex Features 49 Getty Images 50 Universal/The Kobal Collection 50 Universal/The Kobal Collection 51 The Kobal Collection 52 AFP/Getty Images 53 Everett Collection/Rex Features 54 John Springer Collection/Corbis 55 Nero/The Kobal Collection 55 Bettmann/Corbis 57 UFA/The Kobal Collection 58 Getty Images 59 Titanus/The Kobal Collection 60 Paramount/The Kobal Collection 60 The Kobal Collection 61 MGM/The Kobal Collection 62 John Springer Collection/Corbis 63 Bettmann/Corbis 64 Rex Features 65 Denis Cameron/Rex Features 65 Getty Images 67 Snap/Rex Features 68 Paramount/The Kobal Collection 69 The Kobal Collection 70 Itar-Tass News Agency 71 The Kobal Collection 72 Getty Images 72 Films Renoir/The Kobal Collection 73 Realisations D'Art Cinematographique/The Kobal Collection 74 Time & Life Pictures/Getty Images 75 The Kobal Collection 76 The Kobal Collection 77 The Kobal Collection 78 The Kobal Collection 78 Columbia/Hurrell, George 79 Metro-Goldwyn/The Kobal Collection 80 Source: BFI 81 Everett Collection/Rex Features 81 MGM/The Kobal Collection 83 Warner Bros/The Kobal Collection 84 The Kobal Collection 85 MGM/The Kobal Collection/Hubbell, Eddie 86 John Springer Collection/Corbis 86 United Artists/The Kobal Collection 87 RKO/The Kobal Collection 88 Warner Bros/The Kobal Collection 89 Everett Collection/Rex Features 90 Bettmann/Corbis 91 Getty Images 92 Everett Collection/Rex Features 92 MGM/The Kobal Collection 93 Universal/The Kobal Collection 94 Columbia/The Kobal Collection 94 The Kobal Collection 95 RKO/The Kobal Collection 96 Warner Bros/The Kobal Collection 97 Getty Images 98 Mosfilm/The Kobal Collection 98 The Kobal Collection/Dyar, Otto 99 Goskino/The Kobal Collection 100 The Kobal Collection 101 The Kobal Collection 102 The Kobal Collection 103 Getty Images 104 Time & Life Pictures/Getty Images 105 Time & Life Pictures/Getty Images 106 Time & Life Pictures/Getty Images 108 The Kobal Collection 109 John Springer Collection/Corbis 109 MGM/The Kobal Collection 111 Snap/Rex Features 112 Bettmann/Corbis 112 John Springer Collection/Corbis 113 Sunset Boulevard/Corbis 115 Paramount/The Kobal Collection 116 Bettmann/Corbis 116 Bunuel-Dali/The Kobal Collection 117 Paris Film/Five Film/The Kobal Collection 118 The Kobal Collection 119 Hulton-Deutsch Collection/Corbis 120 Bettmann/Corbis 121 Snap/Rex Features 122 Gaumont/The Kobal Collection 122 Tavin/Everett/Rex Features 123 Mara/Laser/Gerico/The Kobal Collection 124 Getty Images 125 The Kobal Collection 126 The Kobal Collection 127 Fox Films 128 MGM/The Kobal Collection 128 William Wyler/Columbia/The Kobal Collection 129 MGM/The Kobal Collection 130 Denis Cameron/Rex Features 131 The Kobal Collection 132 British National/The Kobal Collection 132 Anglo Amalgamated/The Kobal Collection 133 Snap/Rex Features 134 The Kobal Collection 135 Shochiku-Ofuna/New Yorker/The Kobal Collection 135 The Kobal Collection 137 Toho/The Kobal Collection 138 The Kobal Collection 139 United Artists/The Kobal Collection 140 The Kobal Collection/Bachrach, Ernest 140 Coronado Prods/The Kobal Collection/Reeks, Curtis 141 RKO/The Kobal Collection 142 Bettmann/Corbis 142 Underwood & Underwood/Corbis 143 Everett Collection/Rex Features 144 Itar-Tass News Agency 145 Fox Films 146 Fox Films 147 Universal/The Kobal Collection 148 The Kobal Collection 149 Fox Films 150 Time & Life Pictures/Getty Images 150 Excelsa/Mayer-Burstyn/The Kobal Collection 151 Ponti-De Laurentiis/The Kobal Collection 152 Getty Images 152 United Artists/The Kobal Collection 153 United Artists/The Kobal Collection 155 20th Century Fox/The Kobal Collection/Shaw, Sam 156 United Artists/The Kobal Collection 156 The Kobal Collection 157 Allied Artists/The Kobal Collection 158 Albane Navizet/Kipa/Corbis 159 The Kobal Collection/Hawkins, Bob 160 The Kobal Collection 161 Time & Life Pictures/Getty Images 162 Time & Life Pictures/Getty Images 163 20th Century Fox/The Kobal Collection 164 Crown Film Unit/The Kobal Collection 165 Fox Films 166 Sygma/Corbis 166 Filmsonor/The Kobal Collection/Limot 167 Mirkine/Sygma/Corbis 169 The Kobal Collection 170 London Weekend Television/Rex Features 171 MGM/The Kobal Collection 172 Getty Images 173 Snap/Rex Features 174 The Kobal Collection 175 London Weekend Television/Rex Features 176 20th Century Fox/The Kobal Collection 176 The Kobal Collection 177 20th Century Fox/The Kobal Collection 179 De Luca/The Kobal Collection/Limot 180 Warner Bros/The Kobal Collection 180 The Kobal Collection 181 Warner Bros/The Kobal Collection 182 Mirkine/Sygma/Corbis 183 Toho/Kurosawa/The Kobal Collection 183 Toho/The Kobal Collection 185 Toho/The Kobal Collection 186 Getty Images 188 Snap/Rex Features 189 Fox Films 190 Warner Bros/The Kobal Collection 191 Warner Bros/The Kobal Collection 192 Alain Denize/Kipa/Corbis 193 John Springer Collection/Corbis 194 R. D. Archives/Everett/Rex Features 196 John Springer Collection/Corbis 198 Sipa Press/Rex Features 199 Ealing/The Kobal Collection 200 Sergio Gaudenti/Kipa/Corbis 201 Cino Del Duca/PCE/LYRE/The Kobal Collection 201 Sipa Press/Rex Features 203 MGM/The Kobal Collection 204 Universal/The Kobal Collection 205 Time & Life Pictures/Getty Images 206 Everett Collection/Rex Features 207 Fox Films 208 Everett Collection/Rex Features 210 The Kobal Collection 211 Julio Donoso/Corbis Sygma 212 Galatea/Jolly/The Kobal Collection 212 Euro America/Tecisa/Roxy Film/The Kobal Collection 213 Snap/Rex Features 214 Mirisch-7 Arts/United Artists/The Kobal Collection 214 The Kobal Collection 215 20th C. Fox/Everett/Rex Features 216 Films De L'Astrophore/The Kobal Collection 216 RKO/The Kobal Collection/Kahle, Alex 217 Columbia/The Kobal Collection 219 RKO/The Kobal Collection 220 Pascal Baril/Kipa/Corbis 221 AFP/Getty Images 222 Everett Collection/Rex Features 223 Warner Bros/The Kobal Collection 224 Everett Collection/Rex Features 225 Arthur/Sygma/Corbis 226 Everett Collection/Rex Features 227 Everett Collection/Rex Features 228 The Kobal Collection 229 Roger Viollet/Getty Images 230 The Kobal Collection 231 Alain Potignon/Sygma/Corbis 232 Snap/Rex Features 232 Rex Features 233 Snap/Rex Features 233 Svensk Filminstitut/Gaumont/Tobis/The Kobal Collection 236 United Artists/The Kobal Collection 236 ABC/The Kobal Collection 237 MGM/The Kobal Collection 238 Jean-Paul Guilloteau/Kipa/Corbis 239 The Kobal Collection 241 Fabian Cevallos/Corbis Sygma 241 Everett Collection/Rex Features 243 Riama-Pathe/The Kobal Collection 244 JP Laffont/Sygma/Corbis 245 MGM/UA/The Kobal Collection 246 Fox Films 247 Françoise Duc Pages/Kipa/Corbis 247 Govt. Of W. Bengal/The Kobal Collection 249 Devki Chitra/The Kobal Collection 250 The Kobal Collection 251 The Kobal Collection 252 Mandelbaum/Everett/Rex Features 253 Fox Films 254 AFP/Getty Images 255 Sipa Press/Rex Features 256 The Kobal Collection 257 akg-images 258 Etienne George/Sygma/Corbis 259 Terra/Tamara/Cormoran/The Kobal Collection 260 A. Rodriguez/BEI/Rex Features 261 Etienne George/Sygma/Corbis 262 The Kobal Collection/Fefer, Stephane 263 Bassouls Sophie/Corbis Sygma 264 Newyorker/Everett/Rex Features 265 Reuters/Corbis 267 Christian Simonpietri/Sygma/Corbis 267 Geraint Lewis/Rex Features 268 AFP/Getty Images 269 Arici Graziano/Corbis Sygma 270 Allen Ginsberg/Corbis 271 Allied Film Makers/The Kobal Collection 272 Itar-Tass News Agency 274 MGM/The Kobal Collection 274 The Kobal Collection 275 MGM/The Kobal Collection 276 Fox Films 277 Getty Images 278 Dr T. Inc/Sandcastle 5 Prod/The Kobal Collection/Rosenthal, Zade 279 Spelling Films International/The Kobal Collection 281 Spellin:/Fine Line/The Kobal Collection 282 Warner 7 Arts/The Kobal Collection 282 Everett Collection/Rex Features 283 MGM/The Kobal Collection 285 Getty Images 287 Sipa Press/Rex Features 288 Orion/The Kobal Collection 289 The Kobal Collection/Fefer, Stephane 290 Time & Life Pictures/Getty Images 291 The Kobal Collection/ Fefer, Stephane 292 A.I.P./The Kobal Collection 292 The Kobal Collection/Costa, Tony 293 TM Filmgroup/The Kobal Collection 294 Douglas Kirkland/Corbis 295 Serendipity/Alliance/The Kobal Collection/Prebois, Jerome 296 The Kobal Collection 297 Julio Donoso/Corbis Sygma 298 Catherine Cabrol/Kipa/Corbis 299 Source: BFI 300 Everett Collection/Rex Features 301 Source: BFI 302 The Kobal Collection 304 Columbia/Ray Stark/The Kobal Collection 305 Everett Collection/Rex Features 306 20th Century Fox/Columbia/The Kobal Collection 307 News (UK) Ltd/Rex Features 308 Fabian Cevallos/Corbis Sygma 309 Jerome Prebois/Kipa/Corbis 310 Carole Bellaiche/Sygma/Corbis 311 Epstein S. Karin/Corbis Sygma 312 Stephane Cardinale/People Avenue/Corbis 313 Fotos International/Rex Features 314 The Kobal Collection/Fefer, Stephane 315 Corbis Sygma 315 Hawk Films Prod/Columbia/The Kobal Collection 317 Warner Bros/The Kobal Collection 318 Stills Press Agency/Rex Features 319 Everett Collection/Rex Features 320 Jerry Bergman/Rex Features 321 Hemdale/AIP/The Kobal Collection 322 Getty Images 323 Siemoneit Ronald/Corbis Sygma 324 Catherine Cabrol/Kipa/Corbis 324 Prod Eur Assoc/Gonzalez/Constantin/The Kobal

PICTURE CREDITS · ACKNOWLEDGMENTS

Collection 325 Ladd Company/Warner Bros/The Kobal Collection 326 Everett Collection/Rex Features 327 The Kobal Collection 328 AFP/Getty Images 329 Reuters/Corbis 330 Eric Fougere/VIP Images/Corbis 331 Everett Collection/Rex Features 332 Eric Preau/sygma/Corbis 333 The Kobal Collection 334 Markku Ulander/ Rex Features 335 Rufus F. Folkks/Corbis 336 Getty Images 337 Tony Korody/Sygma/Corbis 338 Christopher Farina/Corbis 338 Warner Bros/The Kobal Collection 339 Warner Bros./The Kobal Collection/Wallace, Merie W. 340 Morgan Lecomte/Systeme D/Corbis 341 Reuters/Corbis 342 Patrick Chauvel/Corbis 342 Everett Collection/Rex Features 343 Sunset Boulevard/Corbis 345 Rome-Paris/De Laurentiis/Beauregard/The Kobal Collection 346 The Kobal Collection 347 Rufus F. Folkks/Corbis 348 AFP/Getty Images 349 Getty Images 350 The Kobal Collection 351 Chip East/Reuters/Corbis 352 Christian Simonpietri/Sygma/Corbis 352 Everett Collection/Rex Features 353 Simonpietri Christian/Corbis Sygma 354 Action Press/Rex Features 355 Kairos Film/The Kobal Collection 356 Saul Zaentz Company/The Kobal Collection 356 The Kobal Collection 357 United Artists/Fantasy Films/The Kobal Collection 358 The Kobal Collection/Fefer, Stephane 359 Argos/Oshima/The Kobal Collection 360 Mosfilm/The Kobal Collection 360 The Kobal Collection 361 Mosfilm/The Kobal Collection 362 Bembaron Jeremy/Corbis Sygma 363 Sipa Press/Rex Features 364 The Kobal Collection/Fox, Ira 365 Norbert Kesten/Rex Features 366 The Kobal Collection/Fefer, Stephane 367 Sipa Press/Rex Features 368 Getty Images 369 Allen Ginsberg/Corbis 370 Getty Images 372 Axel Koester/Corbis 373 Getty Images 374 Sipa Press/Rex Features 375 Getty Images 376 Mosfilm/The Kobal Collection 376 Paramount/The Kobal Collection 377 Paramount/The Kobal Collection 378 Amet Jean Pierre/Corbis Sygma 379 Christopher Felver/Corbis 380 The Kobal Collection 381 Arici Graziano/Corbis Sygma 382 Paramount/The Kobal Collection/Hamill, Brian 383 MCA/Everett/Rex Features 384 Athanor/The Kobal Collection 385 Arici Graziano/Corbis Sygma 386 Christopher Felver/Corbis 387 AFP/Getty Images 388 Andreas Neumeier/NewSport/Corbis 389 Frank Trapper/Corbis 390 by permission of Molly Clarke 391 Source: BFI 392 Rufus F. Folkks/Corbis 392 United Artists/The Kobal Collection 393 United Artists/The Kobal Collection 395 Orion/The Kobal Collection 396 Source: BFI 397 AFP/Getty Images 398 Rufus F. Folkks/Corbis 399 Isifa/LN/Ondrej Nemec 400 David W. Cerny/Reuters/Corbis 401 Jerome Prebois/Kipa/Corbis 402 Andreea Angelescu/Corbis 403 Stephane Cardinale/People Avenue/Corbis 404 Stephane Cardinale/People Avenue/Corbis 404 Ladd Company/Warner Bros/The Kobal Collection 405 Dreamworks/Universal/The Kobal Collection/Buitendijk, Jaap 406 IFC Films/Everett/Rex Features 407 Gaspar Risko/Rex Features 408 The Kobal Collection 409 Michael White Prods/The Kobal Collection 410 Getty Images 411 New World Pictures/The Kobal Collection 412 Orion/The Kobal Collection/Epstein, S. Karin 413 Snap/Rex Features 414 Antonio La Torre/Sonia Lo Re 415 Getty Images 416 Getty Images 417 Everett Collection/ Rex Features 418 Amet Jean Pierre/Corbis Sygma 419 Malaya Films/Stephan Films/The Kobal Collection 420 Nicolas Guerin/Corbis 420 Reuters/Corbis 421 Paramount/The Kobal Collection 422 Jamie Painter Young/Corbis 423 Paramount/The Kobal Collection 424 Frank Trapper/Corbis 424 Everett Collection/Rex Features 425 Dimension Films/The Kobal Collection 426 Really Useful Films/Joel Schumacher Prods./The Kobal Collection/Bailey, Alex 427 20th Century Fox/The Kobal Collection 429 Mario Anzuoni/Reuters/Corbis 430 Rufus F. Folkks/Corbis 430 Mars/Marianne/Maran/The Kobal Collection 431 Columbia/Everett/Rex Features 432 Getty Images 433 Pacha/Corbis 434 Forestier Yves/Corbis Sygma 435 Attar Maher/Corbis Sygma 436 Getty Images 437 Diego Goldberg/Sygma/Corbis 438 Eric Robert/Corbis Sygma 439 ADC Films/The Kobal Collection 440 Frank Trapper/Corbis 440 United Artists/The Kobal Collection 441 Universal/The Kobal Collection 442 The Kobal Collection 443 Warren Toda/epa/Corbis 444 TWPhoto/Corbis 445 Krista Kennell/Corbis 446 Eric Robert/Corbis Sygma 447 Rune Hellestad/Corbis 448 Little Bear/PECF/The Kobal Collection 450 Rune Hellestad/Corbis 451 Nicolas Guerin/Corbis 452 Peter Turnley/Corbis 452 Sideral/Tor Studios/Canal +/The Kobal Collection 453 MK2/CED/CAB/The Kobal Collection 454 Robert Eric/Corbis Sygma 455 Nils Jorgensen/Rex Features 456 Sipa Press/Rex Features 457 Sipa Press/Rex Features 458 Sipa Press/Rex Features 459 Alex Oliveira/Rex Features 460 Werner Herzog Filmproduktion/The Kobal Collection 460 JC Matsuura/Vistalux/Rex Features 461 Herzog/Filmverlag Der Autoren/ZDF/The Kobal Collection 462 Nicolas Guerin/Corbis 462 Taplin-Perry-Scorsese/The Kobal Collection 463 Columbia/The Kobal Collection 464 Warner Bros./The Kobal Collection 465 AFP/Getty Images 466 Getty Images 467 Rune Hellestad/Corbis 468 Sutton-Hibbert/Rex Features 469 Camilla Morandi/Rex Features 470 Recorded Picture Co/First Independent/The Kobal Collection 470 Borislav/Rex Features 471 Columbia Tri Star/The Kobal Collection 472 Camilla Morandi/Rex Features 473 20th Century Fox/The Kobal Collection 474 Rufus F. Folkks/Corbis 475 Marcel Hartmann/Corbis 476 Morgan Lecomte/Systeme D/Corbis 477 Getty Images 478 Sam Mooy/epa/Corbis 478 Lucasfilm/Coppola Co/Universal/The Kobal Collection 479 Lucasfilm/20th Century Fox/The Kobal Collection 480 Getty Images 481 Paramount/The Kobal Collection 482 Getty Images 483 Phil McCarten/Reuters/Corbis 484 Sunset Boulevard/Corbis 484 Tangos/The Kobal Collection 485 Trios/Albatros/WDR/The Kobal Collection 486 Fabrizio Bensch/Reuters/Corbis 487 Road/Argos/Channel 4/The Kobal Collection 488 Getty Images 489 Rufus F. Folkks/Corbis 490 Freek Van Asperen/EPA/Corbis 490 Paramount/The Kobal Collection 491 Canal+/Touchstone/The Kobal Collection/Moseley, Melissa 492 Stephane Masson/Corbis 493 Grupo Novo de Cinema e TV 494 Nancy Kaszerman/Zuma/Corbis 495 Rufus F. Folkks/Corbis 496 The Kobal Collection 497 Colin McPherson/Corbis 498 Eric Catarina 499 Nicolas Guerin/Corbis 500 Rufus F. Folkks/Corbis 501 Getty Images 502 Getty Images 502 Universal/The Kobal Collection 503 Universal/The Kobal Collection 505 Amblin/Universal/The Kobal Collection 506 Nicolas Guerin/Corbis 507 Getty Images 508 AFP/Getty Images 509 Axel Koester/Corbis 510 First Run/Everett/Rex Features 511 Rex Features 512 Reents/Siemoneit/Corbis Sygma 513 Rufus F. Folkks/Corbis 514 Getty Images 515 Eddie Mulholland/Rex Features 516 Rufus F. Folkks/Corbis 517 Getty Images 518 Getty Images 519 AFP/Getty Images 520 Getty Images 521 Getty Images 522 Getty Images 523 Getty Images 524 Getty Images 524 Compania Iberoamericana De TV/The Kobal Collection 525 El Deseo S.A./The Kobal Collection 526 Nicolas Guerin/Corbis 527 Paramount/The Kobal Collection 528 J. P. Yim/Zuma/Corbis 529 Getty Images 531 Getty Images 532 Javier Echezarreta/epa/Corbis 533 AFP/Getty Images 534 Getty Images 535 Warner Bros/Channel 4/The Kobal Collection/Buitendijk, Jaap 536 Samuel Lugassy/Corbis 537 Getty Images 538 Getty Images 539 Nicolas Guerin/Corbis 540 Nicolas Guerin/Corbis 541 Fred Prouser/Reuters/Corbis 542 Rufus F. Folkks/Corbis 543 Getty Images 544 AFP/Getty Images 545 Stephane Cardinale/People Avenue/Corbis 546 Pascal Baril/Kipa/Corbis 547 Getty Images 548 Stephane Cardinale/People Avenue/Corbis 549 Kin Cheung/Reuters/Corbis 550 Larry Laszlo/Corbis 551 Paramount/Miramax/The Kobal Collection/Bray, Phil 552 The Kobal Collection 553 Getty Images 554 Süren Stache/dpa/Corbis 555 John Schults/Reuters/Corbis 556 Neal Preston/Corbis 557 Frank Trapper/Corbis 558 Richard Chung/Reuters/Corbis 559 Jean-Pierre Amet/BelOmbra/Corbis 560 Reuters/Corbis 560 Working Title/Polygram/The Kobal Collection/Tackett, Michael 561 Polygram/Working Title/The Kobal Collection 562 Su Friedrich, photo (© 2002) by Rebecca McBride 563 Stephane Masson/Corbis 564 Sipa Press/Rex Features 565 David Fisher/Rex Features 566 Getty Images 567 Theo Kingma/Rex Features 568 Getty Images 569 Colin McPherson/Corbis 570 Sipa Press/Rex Features 571 Camilla Morandi/Rex Features 572 Kim Kulish/Corbis 573 Source: BFI 574 Hubert Boesl/dpa/Corbis 574 Warner Bros/The Kobal Collection 575 40 Acres & A. Mule/HBO/The Kobal Collection 576 Stephane Reix/For Picture/Corbis 577 Reuters/Corbis 578 Reuters/Corbis 579 Getty Images 580 Getty Images 581 Scott McDermott/Corbis 582 Getty Images 583 Arici Graziano/Corbis Sygma 584 Sipa Press/Rex Features 585 Carolyn Contino/BEI/Rex Features 586 Stephane Reix/For Picture/Corbis 586 Geffen/Warner Bros/The Kobal Collection 587 20th Century Fox/The Kobal Collection 588 Itar-Tass News Agency 589 Eric Thayer/Reuters/Corbis 590 Getty Images 591 Corbis Sygma 592 Everett Kennedy Brown/epa/Corbis 593 Getty Images 594 Arici Graziano/Corbis Sygma 595 Getty Images 596 Daniel Deme/epa/Corbis 597 Getty Images 598 Guido Manuilo/EFE/Corbis 599 Nicolas Guerin/Corbis 600 Getty Images 601 New Line/Avery Pix/The Kobal Collection/Barius, Claudette 602 Siemoneit Ronald/Corbis Sygma 603 Getty Images 604 Getty Images 605 Ilpo Musto/Rex Features 606 Everett Collection/Rex Features 607 Jens Kalaene/dpa/Corbis 608 Rufus F. Folkks/Corbis 609 Getty Images 610 Lisa O'Connor/Zuma/Corbis 610 Miramax/Buena Vista/The Kobal Collection 611 A Band Apart/Miramax/The Kobal Collection/Cooper, Andrew 612 Masatoshi Okauchi/Rex Features 613 Angello Picco/Rex Features 614 Getty Images 615 Stephane Cardinale/People Avenue/Corbis 616 Sipa Press/Rex Features 617 Albert Gea/Reuters/Corbis 618 Stephane Cardinale/People Avenue/Corbis 619 Rune Hellestad/Corbis 620 Susana Vera/Reuters/Corbis 621 Rufus F. Folkks/Corbis 622 Rufus F. Folkks/Corbis 623 Getty Images 624 Getty Images 625 Hubert Boesl/dpa/Corbis 626 Matt Baron/BEI/Rex Features 627 Alex Berliner/BEI/Rex Features 628 The Kobal Collection/Birmelin, Bruce 629 Stephane Cardinale/People Avenue/Corbis 630 Touchstone/The Kobal Collection/Masi, Frank 631 Corbis Sygma 632 Rufus F. Folkks/Corbis 633 Lucas Jackson/Reuters/Corbis

ACKNOWLEDGMENTS

Quintessence would like to thank the following people and picture agencies for their help in the preparation of this book:

Sunita Sharma-Gibson for additional picture research

Ann Barrett for compiling the index

Dave Kent, Angela Levin, and Phil Moad at The Kobal Collection

Stephen Atkinson at Rex Features

Jodie Wallis at Getty Images

Duncan Crawley at Corbis

Andrey Bobrov at Itar-Tass News Agency

Nina Harding at the British Film Institute

Martin Humphries at the Ronald Grant Archive

General Editor Acknowledgments

My sincerest thanks to Jane Laing and Victoria Wiggins at Quintessence for their commitment, patience, and help every step of the way. These books are truly a team effort, and I have the luxury of working with the best publishing team imaginable. My thanks as well—and as always—to the contributors, who consistently amaze me with the insight and quality of their entries. Finally, I would like to thank my family, friends, and colleagues for their support and understanding during this entire process.

This book is dedicated to my best friend, Max Kellerman, who knows a little about movies.